Miss
Bridget
Vaughan

Bridget
Gail
Vaughan

# Isabel B. Wingate

*Professor Emeritus of Retail Management*
*Institute of Retail Management*
*New York University*

# TEXTILE FABRICS AND THEIR SELECTION

## sixth edition

PRENTICE-HALL, INC., Englewood Cliffs, N.J.

# Preface

Many technological changes have taken place since the appearance of the 5th edition of this book. Among them are the advent of durable press; the technology of soil release; the increasing use of the shuttleless loom; improved "stretch" techniques; the updating of bonding and laminating; innovation of needle-woven and sewing-knitting processes; optical finishes; improved fiber reactive dyestuffs; and the updating of the culture of cotton, linen, and newer synthetic fibers.

How often is the consumer confronted with the question: "What shall I buy? Shall I select this, or that?" She knows that if the merchandise performs satisfactorily, then the purchase will have been a wise one. Similarly, if the article provides her and her family lasting satisfaction, she will have proved herself an economically efficient individual.

Consumer buying of textile fabrics entails continual decision making. Scarcely a day goes by that some sort of decision on selection, use, and care of clothing or household textiles is not made.

All of us are either present or potential consumers. We have needs and wants, and we are motivated by emotion and reason. The consumer buying an oriental rug because she likes the one her friend has is motivated by sentiment— by emotional appeal. The consumer who buys one because she is aware of the

iii

quality, the appropriateness of the rug for a French traditional decor, and the long wear-life of an oriental rug, is motivated by a rational appeal. She has a body of knowledge about such rugs that she can use as a basis for decision making.

Merchandise knowledge can be acquired from experience in buying, using, and caring for textile articles. It can be learned from reading informative advertising and labels on merchandise, from well-informed salespeople, from knowledgeable friends and associates, and from formal classroom study.

Many years of experience in teaching textiles have proved that, of all methods, formal instruction can most quickly and accurately organize and present product information. This product information, coupled with an emphasis on the selling points of textile fabrics, will aid the retail salesman in helping the consumer make a wise selection.

But a mere presentation of facts is insufficient. The reader must assimilate the facts and apply them through study and experimentation. To assist in learning these facts, the first edition of this book was written in 1935. Subsequent revisions have attempted to keep its content up-to-date.

*The Laboratory Swatchbook for Textile Fabrics,* soon to be in its sixth edition, endeavors to give the reader an opportunity to apply the facts to actual cloths. The organization of the experiments follows exactly the Table of Contents in this book.

*Textile Fabrics and Their Selection* is divided into two parts. Part I covers the intrinsic characteristics of fabrics. This information is basic to judging the grade of a fabric, to estimating its probable performance, and to determining the care required in order to get maximum performance. Part II emphasizes the importance of the selection of appropriate fabrics for specific uses in apparel and home furnishings, and discusses the factors to be considered in examining the construction of garments or household textiles.

The plan for use of this text is flexible. It can provide for a year's course in textiles, with Part I covering the subject matter for the first semester and Part II for the second semester. The text can also be used for two separate courses in fashion fabrics: "Fashion Fabrics in Apparel" and "Home Furnishings Fabrics." For the apparel class, subject matter may include Chapters 1–8 and 15–17; for the home furnishings class, Chapters 1–2, 8, 10–14, and 18–20. It will be noted that Chapters 1 and 2 are repeated. Since one course should not be prerequisite for the other, students in both courses must familiarize themselves with the terminology from the beginning. For adult education, ten two-hour lectures the first term and eight the second term have proved effective. It should also be noted that in the *Swatchbook* yarns, weaves, and finishes are emphasized for collecting and evaluating data on domestics.

I am indebted to my students for information that they have brought to classes; to manufacturers who have arranged market trips for students for the purpose of acquainting them with the features of their lines and their methods of promotion; and to many buyers and salesmen in retail stores for their help in discussing new merchandise, styles, assortments, and prices. I am particularly obliged to the Committee on Textile Education, Council on Technology, American Association for Textile Technology for up-dating the section on textile re-

search and education; to the National Cotton Council of America for as-
sistance in the revision of the chapter on cotton; to the Belgian Linen Association
for editing and providing illustrations for the chapter on Linen; to Miss Bernice
Mohlenhoff, Education Director, Fibers Division, Eastman Chemical Products
Inc. for providing information on their fibers, and for illustrations; to the Wool
Bureau for its assistance in revising the chapter on Wool; to Mr. Robert E.
Tellis, Department of Research and Development, Dyestuffs Division, Geigy
Chemical Corporation, Ardsley, N.Y., for the section on fiber reactive dyestuffs;
to Mrs. J. Orton Buck, Interior Designer, for suggesting revisions for the chapter
on draperies and curtains and for up-dating some of the line drawings. I am also
indebted to many textile manufacturers and trade associations for their valued assistance in preparation of parts of the manuscript and for providing illustrations.

ISABEL B. WINGATE
*New York University*

# Contents

## I

## FABRIC CONSTRUCTION AND BUYING MOTIVES

# 3 Textile Yarns: Their Manufacture and Uses    59

# 4 The Basic Weaves: Plain, Twill, and Satin    85

# 5 Fancy Weaves: Pile, Jacquard, Dobby, and Leno    110

# 6 Knitting and Other Constructions    129

# 7 Finishes    153

# 8 Dyeing and Printing    191

# II

# SELECTION OF APPROPRIATE FABRICS

## 16 Apparel Fabrics for Women and Children    427

## 17 Men's and Boys' Wear 473

## 18 Household Textiles 506

## 19 Period Styles in Home Furnishings and in Rugs 548

## 20 Draperies, Curtains, and Upholstery 597

## Bibliography 618

## Appendix 627

## Index 633

# I

# FABRIC
# CONSTRUCTION
# AND
# BUYING
# MOTIVES

# 1
## Why
## Study Textiles?

"What an incredibly low price!" remarked Mrs. Vail as her eye fell on a newspaper advertisement for permanent-press men's summer shirts, 3 for $7 ($2.99 each). She would have to go to the store and see what they were like. She read the ad further. "These shirts are cool, short-sleeved, have a regular-spread continental button-down collar with perma stays in 65% polyester–35% cotton blend. Tan, beige, mint, or blue in the group. SML, XL."

Yes, her husband could use a beige and a blue button-down shirt. But permanent press? Wouldn't she really have to do a bit of touch-up ironing? And what is a polyester-cotton blend?

Fortunately for Mrs. Vail, a salesperson at the store had the necessary knowledge to answer her questions. She told Mrs. Vail that permanent press is a durable press—a term used to describe a garment that will retain its shape for its wear-life. Creases should remain sharp, seams flat and nonpuckering, and the surface texture smooth. No ironing is needed. As for the polyester-cotton blend, she explained that in a blend two different types of fibers (raw material) are mixed together. In the 65/35 blends, there is more polyester than cotton. Polyester is the family name of a man-made raw material (fiber), whereas cotton is a natural fiber obtained from a hollyhock-like plant that grows in nature. Polyesters are characterized by crease resistance, shape retention, ease of care, and non-absorptiveness. Untreated cotton has no pronounced luster, is not very strong or abrasion-resistant, but has good absorptive quality. By blending polyester and cotton, the fabric is strengthened, is more lustrous and more abrasion- and crease-resistant, and sheds water, which makes it dry faster than all-cotton. The cotton content makes the fabric more comfortable for summer because it absorbs perspiration and is soft. A permanent, or durable, press finish is applied to the fabric and set through the use of heat. (See Durable Press, Chapter 7.)

Mrs. Vail was convinced that these shirts were well worth the price, so she purchased three of them.

The saleswoman who served Mrs. Vail was a well-informed person who knew her merchandise. Often salespeople have not been trained properly to answer all the questions customers ask. Information may not be available that would enable salespeople to give intelligent answers. Some store buyers, merchandise men, and advertising men do not know all the specifications, limitations, advantages, qualities, and uses of the products that their store sells. The manufacturer may not have passed on that information to these retail executives, or, if he has done so, these retail executives may minimize the importance of such information and fail to pass it on to the customer via the salesperson.

A complexity of materials and manufacturing processes is involved in making textile products. The consumer has a right to know what she is buying and what she can expect in service for the price she has to pay. Not only the salesperson but also the copywriter should be able to give the customer informative facts about the merchandise in terms that the customer can understand.

Since approximately 75 to 80 per cent of the average total department-store sales volume is from sales of merchandise wholly or partly textile (woven, nonwoven, knitted, felted, and laminated cloths), instruction for salespeople in information about textiles is essential.

## TEACHING TEXTILES TO SALESPEOPLE

In the small dry-goods store, salespeople still acquire much textile information through experience. This method of learning is often a slow and discouraging process. A short cut to learning is the classroom instruction in textiles that training departments in retail stores may give their salespeople, supplemented by regular meetings conducted by the buyer of the department.

In a recent survey covering eight of the largest department stores and two of the largest chains in the various geographical areas of this country, the author found that the prime sources of textile information came from pamphlets, films, fact cards, and texts provided by manufacturers, vendors, and textile associations. There were no specific times for presenting this information to salespeople, but the early morning seemed preferable. When there was a felt need for textile knowledge—for example, when a new product appeared in stock, or when a reinforcement of knowledge of textiles currently in stock was required—instruction was given. A Southern department store has a semiannual Fashion and Notions Seminar for the main store and its branches. It also conducts early morning (8:15 A.M.) breakfast meetings. In a main store, it is common practice for the buyer or assistant buyer, the department manager, or the manufacturer's or vendor's representative to give the instruction on the floor (in the department). The training department may teach the subject matter (in the training department), and it is often responsible for writing informative booklets and providing the buyers with teaching materials for the main store and branches and for chain-store units. Sometimes the training department gives "reinforcement" instruction. When a new product appears in stock, the manufacturer's representative may present pertinent facts about it to salespeople. Branch stores use their sales managers or department managers (assisted by the training departments) in each branch store. Chain-store units usually receive training materials from their central training office. Department managers in the chain stores are responsible for the dissemination of information. Part-timers are given the same textile information as the regular salespeople, and by the same executives.

The main difficulty lies in training part-time salespeople and contingents who come in only for the busy season, when all the store's efforts must be concentrated on sales volume and when formal training can at best be for only one or two hours. Probably the best solution to the problem of training contingents and part-timers is a well-organized sponsor system in each department. A sponsor is a person named by the management to assist in training a new salesperson when he comes into the department. The sponsor may receive the sales of the new person for the first few days, or remuneration for each person he trains, or both.

To improve salesmanship, one store put on a "show-tell skit" for its salespeople. The purpose of this skit was to emphasize dramatically the value not only of showing the customer the merchandise but of telling her at the same time the pertinent facts about it in an accurate way. After the salespeople had seen this skit, shoppers checked on the merchandise information given customers by these salespeople.

Another store has developed the "role-playing" method. Briefly, the staff trainer selects from her group of trainees a person to represent the salesperson and another to represent the customer. The trainer tells them about the merchandise in the department (even though no physical goods may be there). Her description of merchandise location, color, and price is so vivid that the role-players can see it in their mind's eye. The person to play salesperson then is asked to leave while the trainer gives the person playing customer instructions on the type of customer he is to be. He may be told he may purchase an item only if he is really "sold." He may buy the highest priced item only if the salesperson has convinced him of its superiority. Then the demonstration sale takes place. Both salesperson and customer are left to their own devices, the customer trying to be true to her role. This method most nearly simulates an actual sales situation.

Many progressive stores encourage their sponsors and junior executives to take textile courses in high schools, colleges, museums, and other outside institutions. Stores may pay part of their employees' tuition if they pass the course. Sometimes textile experts from outside organizations give courses in the store.

## TEACHING TEXTILES IN THE HIGH SCHOOL AND COLLEGE

Most commercial high schools that offer a course in retail selling include the subject of textiles as an important part of that course. In cooperative high schools and in schools whose students spend part of their time in store service, a knowledge of textiles is invaluable, for much time is spent by students in stock rooms and in the selling of textile merchandise. Even if a store offers a course in textiles as a part of initial training, part-time employees very often miss such instruction. Frequently classes are held in the morning, and high school students cannot get to the store before noon. This fact is also true of the high school boy or girl who sells in a store on Saturdays only. Yet the store expects a high school salesperson to be at least as good as the regulars in the department. Accordingly, the courses in the school should help measurably.

Often high school students find that their store service consists of wrapping, packing, marking, and other routine work. Although this type of work is a necessary part of anyone's store training, a knowledge of textiles is a step to selling. In the average department store up to 80 per cent of the departments are devoted to the sale of all-textile or partly textile merchandise.

Commercial high schools, both day and evening, and continuation schools offer a textile course, which is frequently required for graduation from a course in retailing. Other high schools offer retailing courses under the department of business education or under the commercial or home economics department. The courses vary in length from one to three years. A great many courses in retailing are now given in high schools and department stores by teachers provided through government appropriations under the Vocational Education Act of 1963.

The college student who majors in home economics or retailing will find textiles and clothing a part of her course. Many of our women's colleges have broadened the scope of their home economics courses to include the study of textiles. Frequently, Textiles is taught as part of a general marketing course in colleges that have no special department of retailing. The School of Continuing Education at New York University includes textiles as a part of the courses in the Retail Management program. At the present time, because of the emphasis on the humanities in four-year colleges, Textiles has become increasingly important in the two-year colleges.

## A SPECIAL COURSE FOR PROFESSORS

In 1968 the National Institute of Drycleaning initiated a special pilot course on care technology for professors at the Fashion Institute of Technology. This may lead to a permanent course in this subject at F.I.T. for designers of textile apparel.

## PRACTICAL VALUE OF A TEXTILE COURSE

Although most high school courses do not attempt to turn out expert salespeople in specialized lines, they do equip the student with merchandise facts in which the customer is most interested, so that he can advise the customer intelligently.

He is taught the inherent characteristics of the raw materials and how they may affect performance and care of the finished cloth. He is taught how to judge the probable durability (wearing quality) of a fabric and how to advise the customer on the care of a fabric. He is also taught to interpret informative labels and tags.

The college graduate with a textile background will probably feel more secure in such positions as assistant buyer, fashion assistant, or copywriter. His training should be a help in moving up to the next higher position.

Graduates with a B.S. degree from a four-year college such as New York State College of Home Economics at Cornell University have taken positions as textile technician, designer of children's clothing, assistant buyer of apparel, fashion editor of a large women's magazine, fashion editor for a home economics publication, home economist with the Cooperative Extension Service, and home economics teacher in junior and senior high schools. Instruction on the graduate level emphasizes professional development. Research, especially in investigating textile end uses, is pertinent. Graduates with an M.S. degree from the aforementioned college hold positions as college teacher or university professor, apparel designer, statistician in the quality-control program of a fiber producer, statistician for a textile economics publication, museum curator, textile and clothing specialist with the Cooperative Extension Service, textile research worker in a university or commercial laboratory, textile technician, head of the Consumer Products Laboratory in the Research and Development Division of a fiber producer, supervisor of home economics in public schools, and home economist with a State welfare agency.[1]

[1] Vivian White, "Textile Education in Home Economics: A New Approach" (Proceedings of A.A.T.C.C., *American Dyestuff Reporter*, April 11, 1966).

This era of new, man-made fibers and the competition among them, plus the advent of blends (mixtures of various fibers), has caused those in the textile industry to realize the need for more and better consumer research and for improvement in textile training for the industry.

The industry is constantly trying to determine what fiber, mixture, or blend is best suited for an intended use, how the fabric can be dyed so it will serve most satisfactorily, and how the consumer should care for it. When, through research, the textile manufacturer can say, for example, "We have proved that a blend of 55 per cent wool and 45 per cent Dacron polyester is the most satisfactory blend for a man's business suit," and can give consumers logical reasons why, the consumer will have one of his most confusing problems in clothing selections solved. Only through a vast amount of research would this selection be possible. Any research necessitates trained men and women. For textile training, the industry supports education and research in numerous institutions.

## TEXTILE EDUCATION

Some schools prominent in advancing textile education:

Auburn University (formerly Alabama Polytechnic Institute, School of Textile Technology), Auburn, Ala. (B.S. degree)

Clemson University, The School of Industrial Management and Textile Science, Clemson, S.C.

Fashion Institute of Technology, New York, N.Y. (junior college)

Georgia Institute of Technology, The A. French Textile School, Atlanta, Ga. (B.S. degree, evening, extension, and graduate courses)

Institute of Textile Technology, Charlottesville, Va. (education and training in the physical sciences and textile technology leading to the M.S. degree)

Iowa State University, Ames, Ia. (Textile and Clothing Department grants B.S. and M.S. degrees)

Lowell Technological Institute, Lowell, Mass. (B.S. and M.S. degrees)

Massachusetts Institute of Technology, Cambridge, Mass. (textile technological courses leading to the B.S., M.S., D.Sc., and Ph.D.)

North Carolina State College, Raleigh, N.C. (B.S. and M.S. degrees)

Philadelphia College of Textiles and Science, Philadelphia, Pa. (B.S. and M.S. degrees)

Purdue University, School of Home Economics, Lafayette, Ind. (B.S. degree in Home Economics)

Rhode Island School of Design, Providence, R.I. (B.S. or B.F.A. degrees)

Southeastern Massachusetts Technological Institute, New Bedford, Mass., and Fall River, Mass. Formerly Bradford Durfee Institute of

Technology and New Bedford Institute of Technology. Now combined. (B.S. degree)

Textile Education Foundation, Atlanta, Ga.

Texas Technological College, Lubbock, Tex. (Bachelor of Textile Engineering [B.T.E.] and Bachelor of Textile Chemistry [B.T.C.] degrees)

Art schools with majors in textile design; textile majors in colleges in home economics departments; special textile courses in retailing departments in colleges; specialized adult courses in extension divisions of colleges

TEXTILE RESEARCH [2]

Research is being advanced in such places as the following:

American Association of Textile Chemists and Colorists, Research Triangle Park, N.C.

Callaway Institute, La Grange, Ga.

Clemson University, The School of Industrial Management and Textile Science, Clemson, S.C.

Fabric Research Laboratories, Dedham, Mass.

Institute of Textile Technology, Charlottesville, Va.

Lowell Technological Institute Foundation, Lowell, Mass.

National Bureau of Standards, Textile Division, Washington, D.C.

National Cotton Council of America, Memphis, Tenn.

New Bedford Institute of Technology, New Bedford, Mass.

North Carolina State College, School of Textiles, Raleigh, N.C.

Textile Research Institute, Princeton, N.J. (Ph.D. degree)

Research institutes or foundations that experiment with textiles:

Industrial Research Institute, University of Chattanooga, Chattanooga, Tenn.

Mellon Institute, Pittsburgh, Pa.

Research Foundation, Georgia School of Technology, Atlanta, Ga.

Southern Research Institute, Birmingham, Ala.

U.S. Department of Agriculture stations that work with textiles:

Four Regional Laboratories: New Orleans, La.; Peoria, Ill.; Philadelphia, Pa.; and Albany, Cal.

Mississippi Agricultural Experiment Station, Stoneville, Miss.

North Carolina Agricultural Experiment Station, Raleigh, N.C.

Research Station, Beltsville, Md.

U.S. Army Quartermaster Corps., Natick, Mass.

A person with textile training may enter one of two main divisions in a textile industry: production or sales. For production, the plant needs

[2] Courtesy of *American Dyestuff Reporter*.

textile engineers, research workers, specialists in fabric development (such as cloth designers), head chemist and assistants, head physicist and assistants, department directors, quality-control specialists, and analytical testers (technicians). In science and engineering, there are openings for mechanical, electrical, and industrial engineers in areas of optimum plant scheduling; time study; fiber and fabric testing, grading, and analysis; and quality control. In data processing, the field is growing and includes programming, analysis, sale and profit forecasting, estimating, sales and administrative records, and inventory control. There are also career opportunities in the manufacturing of textiles and textile products and in the administrative and secretarial supporting services.[3]

After the fabric is constructed it is called "grey goods" and must go through special processes called *finishing, dyeing,* and *printing.* These three processes are done by converters or by the finishing divisions of vertically organized textile firms. The designer who creates a printed fabric design may be employed in a converter's studio, work for an independent studio, or free-lance. The colorist paints the designer's sketches and the repeat artist plans the method of engraving the design. Frequently, the converter employs a stylist who supervises the whole design process from the forecasting and planning through the execution in the finishing plant. Actually a stylist (sometimes called designer-stylist or fashion coordinator) works with the production end of the business when she works with creative designers, and she coordinates this work with the sales division when she works with the dress designer in selling the idea of how the particular fabric design would work into the dress designer's creation.

In the sales division there are merchandising and promotion jobs as publicist or public relations manager (arranges programs and speaks to women's clubs and schools to promote good will of the firm), assistant publicist (reports on how the firm's goods are selling in the garment trade and does some writing of press releases), company representative (travels to instruct consumer groups on the product, arranges promotions for stores on the itinerary, and finds out what consumers want), copywriter, merchandiser (decides when market conditions are right to sell the product), and salesperson in the sales office or on the road. There are increasing numbers of jobs for women as fabric designers, publicists, company representatives, copywriters, and fashion coordinators.

## TEACHING TEXTILES TO CONSUMERS

Big business has brought the consumer many new lines of improved goods and new goods. The complex processes used in their production have disguised the old products completely, and many new goods are so utterly novel that the consumer does not know whether they can be

[3] "Your Career in Textiles: An Industry, a Science, an Art" (American Textile Manufacturers Institute).

washed without shrinkage and without changing color, whether the color is sunfast, of what fiber the material is made, or how to care for the cloth so it will give her her money's worth in use.

INFORMATIVE LABELS

A tag or label attached to the merchandise usually gives the consumer information about qualities inherent in the merchandise. Under the federal law, the Textile Fiber Products Identification Act,[4] the tag or label must give the name of the raw material (fiber content) of which the fabric is made. Such a label must remain affixed to the merchandise until it is sold to the ultimate consumer. This law, which was passed by the Congress of the United States in August, 1958, and became effective March 3, 1960, required that the label include not only fiber content but also percentage by weight, in order of importance of each fiber used in an article. The manufacturer's (sponsor's) name and address or his registered identification number also must be given on the label, and the country of origin must be given for imported fabrics. A list of generic or family names of fibers and their definitions compiled by the Federal Trade Commission is included in the act. Unfortunately, however, because of the technical nature of the definitions, some generic terms like "polyester" and "acrylic" cannot be understood by the consumer. These requirements are a step in the right direction to guide consumer purchases. But fiber content is not the sole criterion for judging how a fabric will perform. Of equal significance affecting use and performance are the following factors: (1) type and quality of the yarn, (2) type of cloth construction, (3) quality of the finishes including the coloring of the fabric, and (4) features of garment construction. The law does not specify that features of performance and care appear on the label.

4 "Textile Fiber Products" as defined by the T.F.P.I.A. means ". . . any fiber finished or unfinished incorporated in a household textile article and includes any yarn or fabric used in a household textile article. Such articles mean wearing apparel, costumes and accessories, draperies, floor coverings, furnishings and beddings, and other textile goods of a type customarily used in a household regardless of where used in fact."

Figure 1.1. A label (two sides) showing fiber identification, performance features, care. (Reproduced courtesy of Dan River Mills, Inc., Danville, Virginia.)

The label may be made up by the manufacturer or by the retailer. The retailer's label must subscribe to the T.F.P.I.A., and the retailer must keep a record of the data that appeared on the label together with the vendor's name. In fact, department stores, retail chain organizations, wholesalers, manufacturers, and the federal government have contributed informative labels. But it is difficult to standardize data that appear on a label. The T.F.P.I.A., in requiring fiber content and the sponsor's name, has taken a valuable step in that direction. In so doing, the government has imposed a mandatory standard. The Wool Products Labeling Act is also mandatory, since federal law requires that all products containing wool fibers, with the exception of rugs and upholstery, must be labeled. Type of wool (new wool, reprocessed wool, and reused wool) must be disclosed on these labels.[5]

Since fur fibers may be used in textile blends, the Fur Products Labeling Act of 1951, amended in 1961, should be included here. The act requires that in advertising a fur, the name of the animal from which the fur comes must be used. The use of the name of any other animal is not permissible. The name of the animal and the country of origin must appear on the label. An original pelt cannot be altered without naming the pelt that was used in the alteration. A simile to describe a fur quality, or a deceptive use of the adjectives "domestic" or "imported," is not permissible.

The Flammable Fabrics Act, which became effective July 1, 1954, is likewise mandatory. The objective in this case is to prohibit the sale of fabrics or clothing that would be so flammable as to be dangerous when worn.[6]

The Wool Products Labeling Act, the Flammable Fabrics Act, and the Textile Fiber Products Identification Act were intended to protect the consumer against deception in labeling and, with the exception of the Wool Act, against the misrepresentation of merchandise in advertising. These laws are also intended to protect the manufacturer against unfair methods of competition. The Federal Trade Commission administers these laws. A retailer who fails to follow the regulations receives complaints, cease-and-desist orders from the commission, and unpleasant publicity. The Wheeler-Lea Act of 1938 made violation of a cease-and-desist order punishable by a fine up to $5,000. Appeals for review of the case may be made to a circuit court of appeals.

On the other hand, there are voluntary standards used as a basis for labeling consumers' goods. Such standards may be set up by a manufacturer for a product he makes. The purpose is to make products which are uniform and quality controlled. Most of these voluntary standards in the textile industry are the result of the general consensus of the parties involved. For example, the USA Standard L22 is the result of a volun-

[5] See the Glossary, Chapter 12, for definitions of these terms. (Rugs and upholstery *are* required to be labeled under the T.F.P.I.A.)
[6] See Flammable Fabrics Act, Chapter 7.

tary agreement of almost thirty trade associations representing various segments of the textile industry, technical societies, and consumer groups. Minimum requirements based on features deemed essential to the satisfactory performance of various types of textile merchandise in their respective end uses are specified in L22.

For example, the proposed standard for girls' blouse or dress woven fabrics includes breaking and tearing strength; dimensional change in laundering and dry cleaning; absence of odor; colorfastness to light, perspiration, crocking, atmospheric gases, laundering, and dry cleaning; yarn shifting or slippage; retention of hand (feeling of fabrics); character and appearance; seam strength; and features of the garment other than the fabric.

These specifications serve as a guide to performance values for yarn manufacturers, mills, converters, dyers, garment manufacturers, retailers, and consumers. Since its introduction in 1960, L22 has become the accepted reference piece on textile fabrics. Textile merchandise that meets these voluntary standards is allowed to bear a tag with the L22 designation signifying the kind of performance that is guaranteed for this item.

Directions for refreshing (washing and dry cleaning) based on the USA Standard L22-1960 were originally developed for seventy-five end uses. In USA Standard L22-1968, the seventy-five end uses have been incorporated within six standards, with one new standard for men's and boys' knitted dress shirt fabrics. These instructions specify whether the merchandise is washable or dry cleanable, what the temperature of the water should be for washing, and whether a bleach can be used without damage. A letter code specifies the kind of refreshing required for the particular garment. Manufacturers of fabrics and garments who subscribe to L22 standards will use the code letters to label their products. Hence the consumer will know that there is authenticity behind such a label. The National Retail Merchants Association has requested its member stores to adopt the L22 standards and wishes them to inform their customers about the labels. (For further discussion of L22 specifications and test methods, see Chapter 8.)

## AGENCIES WORKING ON STANDARDS

The National Bureau of Standards of the U.S. Department of Commerce has worked out commercial standards for (1) testing a fabric's colorfastness to sunlight, perspiration, laundering, and crocking (rubbing off of color); (2) control of shrinkage; and (3) crease resistance. (See Chapter 8 for a discussion of standardized methods of testing and reporting.) Although manufacturers are encouraged by the National Bureau of Standards to use self-identifying quality-guaranteeing labels or tags to indicate that a set of specifications has been met or exceeded, these guarantees are not policed.

Standards and methods of testing have been established by a number

of technical societies and trade associations such as the United States of
America Standards Institute, the American Society for Testing Mate-
rials, and the American Association of Textile Chemists and Colorists.
Some of these standards have become USA standards.

When a fabric is certified by a label of the American Institute of
Laundering, it means that the goods have passed their standard laboratory test procedure for laundering. This label is therefore a reliable guide
to the consumer.

The American Home Economics Association is instrumental in protecting the consumer. Since it has membership on committees of the
USA Standards Institute, it has cooperated in the development of standards for rayon and the L22. For over fifty years, the A.H.E.A. has been
a major instrument for educating the consumer to make an intelligent
selection of apparel. All segments of the A.H.E.A. are continuing to
emphasize consumer responsibilities in their educational programs.

Laboratories may give goods that pass their tests certified seals of
approval or of quality for use in labeling and advertising. When the
consumer buys products backed by the Good Housekeeping Consumers'
Guaranty, she can be sure that the products are good. Only merchandise advertised in *Good Housekeeping* magazine bears the Consumers'
Guaranty. Specifically, "If the product or performance is defective, *Good
Housekeeping* guarantees replacement or refund to the consumer." This
guaranty assures the consumer that every product is advertised honestly
and that every product has been carefully examined by members of the
staff of Good Housekeeping Institute, who have found it to meet their
rigid requirements. Therefore, this guaranty protects readers of the
magazine and aids them in their retail purchases.

Should certain advertisers wish to extend their case of guaranty beyond
the pages of *Good Housekeeping* magazine, they may do so by incorpora-
tion of the Consumers' Guaranty Seal in their
promotional or advertising media. (See Figure
1.2.) The use of this seal is contingent upon the
advertiser's signing an agreement governing its
use. Again, endorsement of a product and the
claims made for it depend upon laboratory tests
made by the Good Housekeeping Institute.

There are also some well-known textile manufacturers' guarantee programs. A guarantee, in
strictly legal terms, means that if an article has
not lived up to its promise of performance, the
guarantor (company) will replace the item or

Figure 1.2. American Institute of Laundering Certified Laundering Seal. (*Reproduced courtesy of American Institute of Laundering.*)

return its original price to the consumer within a stated period of time. The Everfast color guarantee was the first program of this type. In 1921, Everfast Fabrics, Inc., guaranteed money back on the purchase price of the fabric plus the construction cost of the garment. In 1962, Monsanto introduced its Wear-Dated program, which guaranteed the replacement of a garment or refund of money if it failed to give normal wear for a year. The Dow Badische Company guarantees two acrylics—Zefkrome and Zefran II—money-back or replacement guarantees on apparel that does not give one year's normal wear. The Allied Chemical Corporation's program has a three-year guarantee for commercial or contract carpets. J. P. Stevens & Co., Inc., offers a ten-year guarantee for its fiber glass screening. The Collins and Aikman Corporation has a Certifab program for a garment's face fabric bonded or laminated to a Certifab tricot made of Celanese acetate. The guarantee is for one year against fabric separation in normal use when dry cleaned or laundered as specified by the garment manufacturer.[7]

The Celanese Licensed Trademark program attempts to develop the confidence of the trade and the consumer in Celanese's good fabric performance. It strives to make known that a Celanese hangtag means exactly what it says. To qualify for a licensed fiber trademark, a company's fabric must pass specific Celanese tests for specific end uses. Since the Celanese Corporation is a fiber manufacturer, it must make sure that the quality of its fiber in the tested fabric has been maintained. Only a few fiber companies have this type of program, and only a few of their brand names are included in their programs. In guiding the fiber into the appropriate end uses, the fiber company must work with the mill, converter, finisher, dyer, printer, manufacturer, and retailer. Celanese must assure the members of the textile industry and the quality-conscious consumer that the nature and quality of the product are controlled through testing for the promised performance. The company feels that this assurance is worth the price because it protects the industry's profitability and ensures the consumer against false claims.

[7] The face fabric is guaranteed not to separate from the tricot fabric.

Figure 1.3. Good Housekeeping Consumers' Guaranty Seal. (Reproduced courtesy of Good Housekeeping Consumers' Guaranty Administration.)

The Consumer Service Bureau of *Parents' Magazine* also indicates by a seal its approval of merchandise that has passed its standard laboratory tests.

Textile research laboratories are generally of two kinds: (1) public laboratories that test fabrics for anyone on a fee basis (the United States Testing Company organized in 1880 represents this type); and (2) private laboratories that test fabrics for manufacturers and retailers (in some cases the laboratory may serve as a quality control agent for certain manufacturers). Better Fabrics Testing Bureau is an example of a private organization.

In addition, large chain stores may have their own laboratories for research and quality control. Large department stores may also maintain testing bureaus for analyzing customers' complaints and for maintaining standards of quality.

When informative labeling is lacking, the consumer often consults *Consumer Reports* or the *Consumer Bulletin* for guidance about the purchase of textiles and other products. *Consumer Reports* is a monthly publication of Consumers Union of United States, Inc., a nonprofit organization established in 1936 in Mount Vernon, New York. *Consumer Bulletin* is published monthly by Consumers' Research, Inc., a nonprofit organization established in 1929 in Washington, New Jersey. These organizations are testing agencies established for the purpose of making science more effectively serve the interest of the consumer. They provide the buyer with the same type of advisory service that the technical staff provides for its own industrial establishment.

Retailers feel that the consumer is entitled to know what she is buying and how an article will perform in use. The knowledge of what a product will do should be carried from the mills on through garment manufacturing plants to the retailer and right on to the consumer. To this end, the National Retail Merchants Association and the United States of America Standards Institute developed the washing and dry cleaning instructions previously described.

In 1962 a national Consumer Advisory Council was appointed by direction of President Kennedy. It is concerned with consumer welfare and protection,

**Figure 1.4.** Seal of Quality of the Nationwide Consumer Testing Institute, Inc., a wholly owned subsidiary of the United States Testing Company, Inc. (*Reproduced courtesy of the United States Testing Company, Inc.*)

consumer education, and labeling. The Council was under the chairman-
ship of Dean Helen G. Connoyer of the College of Home Economics at
Cornell University. Subsequently, in President Johnson's Administration, this post was held by Mrs. Esther Peterson and then by Miss Betty
Furness, who was succeeded by Mrs. Virginia H. Knauer as President
Nixon's Consumer Aide. Esther Peterson was concerned with consumer
welfare and labeling. In 1966 she called a conference of executives of the
textile industry and scientists to help solve consumer complaints about
the factual content or lack of it on labels and the loss of labels either
before or after washing. The organization now called "The President's
Industry Advisory Committee on Textile Information" began its attack
on the problem by finding a common vocabulary that would cover the
confusing terms in the textile field. The result was the formulation of
the Voluntary Labeling Guide—a universal vocabulary of care instructions that lists those terms of a permanent type that continue to appear
during the wear-life of a fabric. For example, "Tumble Dry—Permanent
Press" is a term that tells the consumer to use medium to high heat on
the dryer's dial. Permanent labels that can be either sewn into the garment or printed on existing tab labels were also given consideration.
Progressive mills, chain stores, fiber manufacturers, and the federal government have pushed for promotion of the Guide and for permanent
labeling. These organizations hope to meet or to exceed the voluntary
standards before the government intervenes and makes mandatory standards for the entire textile industry. In short, there is a struggle between

Figure 1.5.  New York Testing Laboratory of Sears, Roebuck and Co.
(*Photograph courtesy of Sears, Roebuck and Co.*)

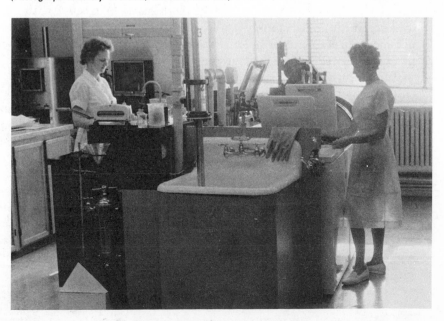

the progressives who are promoting voluntary standards and the stand-patters who prefer to dawdle, believing that the consumer has no lobby in Washington. Though "consumerism" is a current trend, no one in the trade would appear to want a Bureau of Textile Standards in Washington that would enforce everything that is done in the textile industry, including testing, checking, and enforcing standards. Many think that the textile industry can handle these matters better by itself.

### GRADE LABELING

Standards are also important in grading the quality of a textile fabric. To derive a grade, it is necessary to compare the characteristics of a cloth with one or more standards. A product that measures up to a recognized and accepted standard is a *standard grade*.

If the ultimate consumer could be assured of standardized labeling of all fabrics, her buying problem would be partially solved. But in addition to standardization, the consumer needs an explanation of terms. Suppose the customer reads an advertisement for a white *pima cotton, 2 x 2 broadcloth,*[8] *Sanforized*. What do these terms mean? Will the broadcloth be serviceable as a tailored blouse? *Pima cotton* means that the cotton fibers are extra long. Pima ranks next to Sea Island, which is the best quality. Sea Island is not grown in the U.S. but is raised in Central America and Mexico. The term *2 x 2* means that all yarns (twisted strands of fibers) are ply yarns made of two single stranded yarns twisted together. Ply yarns are stronger than single yarns of the same diameter; consequently the fabric should be more durable. Poorer grades of broadcloth are made with all single yarns or singles in at least one direction of the cloth. *Mercerized* means that the cloth has been treated with chemicals to give it added strength and luster. *Sanforized* means that there is not more than 1 per cent residual shrinkage. In other words, there should be no further shrinkage beyond one-fourth inch to a yard in length and width. Even though there was no mention in the advertisement of the closeness of the weave or the type of care required, with good quality cotton fibers, good strength of yarns, luster, and good shrinkage control, the broadcloth should be serviceable in a tailored blouse.

Would it be practical for textiles to be graded A, B, or C, as some foods are labeled? The U.S. Department of Agriculture now offers this grading service to packers and other food processors. Although the service is also offered to retailers, they seldom use it. The user of the service pays the government inspector a fee for grading the firm's entire product or sample lots. It is not customary to find U.S. Grade labels on frozen, canned, dried, or fresh fruits and vegetables or on some brands of fresh meat because processors and packers obviously want customers

[8] See Glossary at end of chapter for a definition of broadcloth.

to make identification with brand names. Foods are graded A, B, C on
the basis of degree of uniformity, tenderness, and taste rather than on nutritional value. "U.S. Grade A" or "U.S. Choice" represent more uniform, tender, and usually better tasting food items than "U.S. Grade B" or "U.S. Good." Only a few packers and food processors use this grading service, and those who do generally omit "U.S." from the grade shown on the label. To be labeled a standard grade, the particular food must measure up to that grade. Any mislabeling is subject to action by the Food and Drug Administration under the Food, Drug, and Cosmetic Act of 1938, and the processor is held liable.

However, grade labeling in the textile apparel field is uncommon. It seems impractical for the following reasons:

1. The essential characteristic of apparel is *style*, a factor that can be observed by the consumer. (There are no commercial standards for grading style.) But style merchandise can be labeled with other characteristics of the goods, such as residual shrinkage controlled to a maximum of 2 per cent and degree of colorfastness to light expressed in hours of exposure that the fabric will withstand in a standard testing device called a Fade-Ometer. Fabrics that fade in 10 to 20 hours are suitable if fastness to sunlight is not essential, that is, for evening dresses, linings, and fall and winter dresses usually worn under a coat. Fabrics that withstand a 40-hour exposure test are suitable for street or sportswear, whereas draperies and upholstery should pass an 80-hour exposure test, and Venetian-blind tapes and awnings should withstand 160 hours.

2. The cost of grading garments would be exceedingly high, because it is not possible to have one set of criteria for grading all articles of apparel. Criteria for grading the wearing quality of a cotton muslin batiste differ from criteria for a flat crepe silk dress fabric. (See Chapter 16.)

3. The consumer might have a psychological objection to grade labeling, especially if her budget required her to buy a fabric marked "C grade" when she knew that "A grade" would give more satisfactory performance.

4. The consumer satisfied with buying by brand would be likely to continue to buy by brand; she would disregard a grading system.

5. Manufacturers, too, might prefer to develop a reputation for their brand names through consumers' satisfactory experience with their products rather than to attempt to sell their product in competition with other merchandise on a grade basis.

6. Even though a manufacturers' grade label would give the consumer an indication of the quality of the fabric, she would still have to decide for herself whether the fabric was best suited to her particular needs.

The problem of grade labeling becomes even more difficult if the complexities of grading ready-to-wear garments are added to those of grading the piece goods. Part Two of this book will discuss criteria for judging the quality of items in women's, girls', men's, and boys' apparel and of articles of home furnishings.

On the other hand, the large mail-order houses give so many specific facts about the goods that a consumer can compare similar items and judge for himself which article would seem best suited to his needs at a given price. Then, too, the subscriber to Consumers Union will find in its *Consumer Reports* ratings of items that have been tested. For example, when Consumers Union judges the test samples to be of high overall quality and appreciably superior to non-check-rated items tested for the same report, they are rated by a check mark ($\sqrt{}$), meaning acceptable. A rating of one item sold under a brand name is not to be considered a rating of other items sold under the same brand name, unless so noted. "Best buy" ratings are given to products that rate high in overall quality but are also priced relatively low; they should provide more quality per dollar than acceptable items in that set of ratings.

## ADVERTISEMENTS

One of the most powerful tools for consumer education is advertising. Informative advertising goes hand in hand with informative labeling. The T.F.P.I.A. specifies that

the required information for labels be shown in the advertisement of textile fiber products *in those instances* where the advertisement uses terms which are descriptive of a method of manufacture, construction, etc., which is customarily used to indicate a textile fiber or fibers or by the use of terms which constitute or connote the name or presence of fiber or fibers. In contrast to the labeling requirement, advertising does not have to specify percentages of fiber present but simply listing fibers in order of predominance by weight. Fiber or fibers amounting to 5 per cent or less shall be listed as "other fiber" or "other fibers." This regulation applies to display signs used as advertising media but it does not apply to signs merely directing customers to location of the merchandise.

A fiber trademark may be used in an advertisement of a textile fiber product but the use of such trademark requires a statement of fiber content (including per cent by weight) in at least one instance in the advertisement. When a trademark is used, it must appear in immediate proximity and in conjunction with the generic name of the fiber. The generic name of the fiber shall appear in plain, legible type or lettering of the same size or conspicuousness as the trademark. Also, when a fiber trademark or generic name is used together with nonrequired information, it must in no way be false, deceptive or misleading, as to fiber content. Nonrequired information is permissible in conjunction with an advertisement of a textile fiber product if it is truthful, nondeceptive, not misleading or not detracting from the required information.

Swatches, samples, etc. used in display or to promote textile fiber products are not subject to labeling requirements provided:

1. Samples, swatches, etc. are less than two inches in area and the data otherwise required on the label appears in the accompanying promotional piece.
2. Samples, swatches, etc. are related to a catalogue to which reference must be made to make a sale and such catalogue non-deceptively gives information required for labels.
3. Samples, swatches, etc. are not used to make sales to the ultimate consumer and are not in the form intended for sale or delivery to the ultimate consumer.

Labeling or advertising of textile fiber products may *not* employ any names, directly or indirectly of fur animals. Names symbolizing a fur-bearing animal through custom or usage may not be employed, i.e., "mink," "mutation," "broadtail," etc. However, references may be made to furs which are not in commercial use such as "Kitten soft," "Bear Brand," etc.

Should a textile fiber product contain the hair or fiber of a fur-bearing animal in amount exceeding 5 per cent of the total weight, the name of the animal producing the fur is permissible provided the name is used in conjunction with the words "fiber," "hair," or "blend," as, for example: "80% Rabbit hair/20% Nylon."

The term "fur fiber" may be used to describe the hair or fur fiber or any mixtures of any animals other than sheep, lamb, Angora goat, Cashmere goat, camel, alpaca, llama, or vicuña where such hair or fur fiber or mixture exceeds 5 per cent of the total fiber weight of the textile fiber product, and no direct or indirect reference is made to the animals involved. For example: "60% Cotton/40% Fur fiber" or "50% Nylon/30% Mink hair/20% Fur fiber."

But mere facts used without emotional appeal are not usually so successful as a combination of the two. Newspaper advertising that is truthful and at the same time informative builds customer confidence in the store. Mail-order houses have tried to improve their catalogues through better informative descriptions of their merchandise.

The radio put consumer education on the air in the form of consumer quizzes, lectures by educational speakers, and talks by executives in merchandise and fashion divisions of stores. Now television can demonstrate merchandise in use. Fashion shows, informative interviews on how to select a given item of merchandise, and a daily television woman's magazine are a few ways television brings consumer education into the home.

Women's and men's fashion and decorating magazines and special articles and fashion columns in newspapers are read by an increasing number of consumers.

## AN INTELLIGENT SALES FORCE

Even when an adequate label is appended to the merchandise, the salesperson is the chief disseminator of merchandise information, since many customers never read the label. Suppose a customer wants a pair of boys' jeans for her seven-year-old. Before the advent of nylon or polyester blends, the customer had only a choice of all-cotton in navy blue. Nowadays, she has a choice of loden green, light blue, wheat, and other fashionable colors. They come in regular, slim, and husky cuts. About half of them are durable press. Weights range from 10–14 ounces per square yard. There is a choice of all-cotton or cotton plus an appropriate percentage of polyester or nylon. Prices range from $2.67 to $5.

The salesperson who served this customer had had instruction from her buyer and therefore could be of real assistance. She gave some practical information on all-cotton jeans: the heavier the better for tear and bursting resistance. But a lighter weight material, say an 11-ounce blend of cotton with 20 per cent nylon or 50 per cent polyester, will be about as durable as a 14-ounce all-cotton denim. As for color, yes, dark colors may darken the wash water. Durable-press blends are usually more resistant to abrasion, owing to a high percentage of synthetic fiber. The salesperson can also point out strength features, such as reinforced bar tacks at each end of the hip pockets; the stitching of the side pockets for maximum security; the reinforcement of the fly at the bottom by rivets and bar tacks; the self-locking pull tab and double-stitched zipper tape; the waistband joined to the body by multiple rows of stitching; and double or triple seams wherever there is stress and strain.

Terminology on labels that requires interpretation resolves into a training problem for the retailer. The buyer is the logical interpreter of such information because he is in a position, if he does not know all the terms himself, to get the correct meaning from (1) the manufacturer who sold him the goods, (2) the store's testing laboratory, or (3) a textile consultant outside the store. In some stores a textile expert in the training department assists the buyer in training his salespeople and helps him in other ways when necessary.

### CONSUMERS' BUYING MOTIVES

For some consumers, a brand name of merchandise may be a motivating factor in selection. For other consumers, factual information is demanded for satisfaction.

If the consumer can judge the wearing quality of a fabric, she is more likely to get her money's worth. To determine wearing quality, one must recognize the inherent characterictics of a fabric, such as the kind of raw material (fibers) used, the strength and evenness of the yarns, the construction or weave, and the permanency of the dye or the finish. Textile education attempts to teach the consumer (1) to recognize and interpret the inherent characteristics of a fabric in light of its intended use and (2) to judge the wearing quality in relation to the price.

A customer who comes to purchase a textile fabric may not ask a single question; yet the salesperson who can determine the customer's likes and dislikes through conversation and sales talk will usually make a sale. The salesperson can also determine whether the customer is trying to satisfy her physical and social needs. The customer's image of herself, or what she would like it to be, is a consideration. Perhaps she considers herself a leader. Hence she must have something new, different, high style. Perhaps she doesn't want to be out of place in her social group and therefore conforms to what they will recognize as acceptable.

The discriminating consumer has at least some of the following questions in mind when she buys a fabric:

1. What use have I for such merchandise? (*suitability*)
2. Is this suitable to my needs? (*suitability*)
3. Can it be worn for a number of different occasions or purposes? (*versatility*)
4. Will it conserve time and effort? (*convenience*)
5. Will it wear well? (*durability*)
6. Will it be warm in winter? Is the texture suitable? (*comfort*)
7. Will this material be easy to dry clean, launder, protect from moths, mildew, and so forth? (*care*)
8. Is the fabric good-looking? Will it look good on me? Will it go well with other garments or with the surroundings in which it will appear? (*becomingness*)
9. Is it in fashion? (*appearance*)
10. Does the price come within my means? Is it a "good buy"? (*price*)
11. Do I want to buy this merchandise because of its rarity? Because of associations it calls to mind? Because someone else has something like it and because I don't want to be out of style? (*sentiment*)
12. Will people be impressed with my selection? Is it in line with what my group recognizes as acceptable? (*recognition*)
13. Does this merchandise satisfy a creative urge, particularly in yard goods? (*creativity*)

In question 8, the customer is considering the "ensemble idea"—the harmonious relationship of fabrics, color, and fashion-rightness, not only among various units of apparel worn together, but also among home furnishings. She may also ask herself: Is my selection in line with my self-image?

In answer to question 9, if the fabric is in accord with prevailing tendencies and modes of expression, if it has beauty, becomingness, and fashion-rightness, it looks good in use.

In question 10, the customer is also asking, "Am I getting my money's worth?" If the customer is limited in the amount of money she can spend for an article, the price is of great importance as a buying motive.

Many people buy old tapestries, laces, and rugs, not necessarily because of durability, but for the satisfaction of acquiring collections of fabrics that few people own. Other purchasers want materials that call to mind pleasant associations. For example, to a man whose childhood was spent in Asia Minor, where beautiful rugs are woven, rugs would recall boyhood. Such a person's buying motive is based on sentiment.

Rivalry is an instinct, and the striving to equal or excel forms an appeal to the customer who buys to "keep up with the Joneses." This customer thrives on recognition.

Few consumers need to consider all these factors before making a purchase. To one consumer price is paramount; to another, style; to another, becomingness; to another, possibly comfort. Knowing the factors inherent in the merchandise, the salesperson can relate the factors to the buying motive. For the man who wants comfort, durability, and ease of care in a shirt, the salesperson can recommend Dacron polyester and cotton blend, emphasizing the strength (durability) and convenience of polyester (no starching or ironing required; quick drying) and the absorptive value of cotton (absorbs perspiration without feeling clammy).

## SUMMARY

The well-informed consumer is the one who can recognize and interpret the inherent characteristics of a textile fabric in the light of its intended use. With knowledge of facts about the goods, she can judge its probable wearing quality and can determine whether she is getting her money's worth. Consumer education in textiles may be obtained through courses in merchandise information given by high schools or colleges. The consumer is being protected and informed as a result of federal legislation. The government has also realized the value of courses in retailing which are now given in high schools and department stores with federal support under the Vocational Education Act of 1963.

Furthermore, progressive retailers have established the policy of informative newspaper, radio, and television advertising. Likewise, mail-order houses have rewritten their catalogues so that the consumer may have better informative descriptions of their merchandise.

Retailers have also realized that the consumer depends upon the salesperson for merchandise information, and therefore they have developed training programs toward that end. It is the salesperson who must determine the consumers' buying motives and, knowing the factors inherent in the merchandise, relate those factors to the buying motives.

Discriminating consumers are those who plan to get their money's worth. A person who gets value for the price paid is the one who knows the characteristics inherent in a fabric that affect the qualities of *suitability, versatility, durability, convenience, comfort, care, becomingness, appearance, price, sentiment, recognition,* and *creativity.*

## REVIEW QUESTIONS

1. With what aims are courses in textiles given to salespeople in department stores?

2. By what means may the new salesperson acquire a knowledge of the textiles that she is selling?
3. What practical value has a textile course to a high school student?
4. (*a*) Why are individual research and education important for the textile industry?
   (*b*) Name the most important textile schools.
   (*c*) Where is textile research being conducted and on what basis?
5. (*a*) How does a fashion coordinator fit into the textile industry?
   (*b*) What does she do?
6. (*a*) Why is a knowledge of textile fabrics important to the consumer?
   (*b*) How can she acquire such merchandise information?
7. (*a*) Of what value is an informative label to the consumer?
   (*b*) What limitations do informative labels have?
8. (*a*) Name four federal laws pertaining to textiles.
   (*b*) What are the objectives of each law?
   (*c*) How are these laws policed?
   (*d*) Are the provisions of the T.F.P.I.A. sufficient to give the consumer adequate information about the inherent qualities of a fabric to enable her to decide how it will perform in a given use? Why?
9. What is the responsibility of the buyer in training salespeople in the selling points of certain merchandise?
10. In what ways has the government cooperated in consumer education?
11. In what ways is the government attempting to control textile standards?
12. What is the educational value of advertising to the consumer?
13. What is meant by the phrase "getting your money's worth"?
14. (*a*) List the questions a customer may have in mind when she comes to purchase a textile fabric.
    (*b*) Which question or questions are the most important to you when you plan to buy (1) underwear, (2) hosiery, (3) a dress, (4) a suit, (5) a coat, (6) handkerchiefs, (7) curtains?
15. Explain what is meant by *sentiment* as a buying motive; by *recognition* as a buying motive.
16. Give an example, preferably from your own experience, in which the salesperson related the inherent factors in the merchandise to the buying motive.

**P R O J E C T**

1. (*a*) Clip an advertisement for a particular item of clothing, such as a dress, suit, hosiery, underwear, or hat.
   (*b*) Underline all terms descriptive of the merchandise.
   (*c*) List any terms that you believe a consumer would have difficulty in understanding.
   (*d*) What are the chief merits of the advertisement?
2. Visit the yard-goods department of a department store in your community. Observe one salesperson in the department. Notice whether she seems to give intelligent answers to the customers' inquiries about the merchandise. Notice how she displays the goods and the way in which she cuts it from the bolt. Observe the measuregraph (the device fastened

to the farther side of the counter) and the way it is used by the salesperson to measure the goods and to compute the sale.

    (*a*) When you leave the department, recall your observations and rate the salesperson as excellent, good, fair, or poor. Give 60 points if the salesperson gave the customer intelligent information about the merchandise; 10 points if the salesperson displayed the goods attractively; 20 points if she cut the goods straight and with no apparent difficulty; 10 points if she computed the sale quickly by reading the figures on the measuregraph.

    (*b*) Judging from the rating you have given the salesperson, what type of training would help her to improve her selling job?

3. Make an outline of the courses you would consider necessary for a new salesman of men's shirts. He has had no previous experience in the shirt department.

4. If you are selling in an apparel department of a retail store, examine the labels on a specific type of garment (coat, suit, dress, or accessory). Note:

    (*a*) Degree of conformity to T.F.P.I.A.

    (*b*) Kind of information given other than that required by law. Tabulate, if possible.

    (*c*) Formulate some conclusions about the value to the consumer of the information on labels that you have observed.

## GLOSSARY

**Broadcloth.** A tightly constructed cotton fabric in plain weave with a fine crosswise rib.

**Buying motives.** Reasons why consumers select a certain product for an intended use.

**Buying points.** Facts that the consumer considers important in selecting an article for a particular use.

**Cloth.** See *fabric*.

**Consumer.** The purchaser of merchandise for certain uses—that is, wearing apparel, household textiles, food, and hard lines.

**Consumer education.** The process of helping the consumer to become a more intelligent buyer of goods and services and a wiser user of what he has, a more prudent manager of his finances, and a better-informed consumer-citizen.

**Cooperative high school.** A school in which the student spends part-time in store service.

**Delamination.** The separation of the layers of fabric in bonded goods.

**Fabric (textile).** A material formed of fibers or yarns, either by the interlacing method of weaving, by the interlooping of knitting, by braiding, felting, bonding, or laminating.

**Fiber.** The basic unit used in the fabrication of textile yarns and fabrics.

**Grey goods.** Textile merchandise as it comes from the loom (after it has been constructed) before it is finished.

**Informative label.** A tag that gives a description of qualities inherent in the merchandise in order to aid the consumer in appropriate selection for her needs and to give instructions for proper care of her purchase.

**Merchandise.**  Any finished goods ready for consumer purchase.

**Merchandise information.**  Facts about goods that will aid the consumer in selecting a suitable article for her needs.

**Nylon.**  A man-made textile fiber derived from coal, air, and water.

**"Role-playing" method.**  A method of instructing trainees in selling situations in retail stores.

**Selling points.**  Facts about a product that are stressed by the salesman in selling and that help the consumer make a selection suitable to her needs.

**"Show-tell" skit.**  Method by which the salesman demonstrates *and* explains pertinent facts about the merchandise.

**Textile fabric.**  See *fabric*.

**Textiles.**  All materials that can be or have been formed into yarns or fabricated into cloth. See *fabric*.

# 2
# Fiber Content of Textile Fabrics

A customer was fingering a forest of hangtags attached to a dress she was trying on. The salesperson offered assistance, and the customer remarked, "I've found it. The dress is made of 65 per cent Dacron polyester and 35 per cent Avril rayon. Is this rayon going to stand laundering?"

"That's a good brand of rayon," replied the uninformed salesperson. Had she been instructed in facts about the merchandise, she could have told the customer that Avril is stronger than the usual type of rayon when wet and therefore can withstand repeated laundering. She could also have told her that polyester is the generic, or family, name of a class of man-made fibers characterized by strength, crease and abrasion resistance, shape retention, and ease of care. It is lightweight. Dacron is one of several brand names of polyester fibers. It is made by du Pont. An intelligent answer from an informed salesperson instills confidence in the customer, who looks to her for guidance in making a selection best suited to the customer's needs. In terms of the trade, the customer wanted to know something about the *fiber content* of the dress she was trying on.

A fiber is a hairlike unit of raw material of which cloths are made—for example, cotton, linen, rayon, silk, wool, nylon, and polyester.[1] The fiber is the basic unit of which a fabric is made. To see what a fiber looks like, unravel a thread, called a *yarn,* from a sample of sheer cotton cloth. Untwist the thread. Each of the tiny hairs that make up the yarn is a fiber. To make a yarn, several fibers are grouped (often twisted) into a strand. Cloth can be constructed from fibers or yarn in eight different ways:

1. *Weaving* is the interlacing of two sets of yarns at right angles.
   a. *Warp* (end) is yarn that runs lengthwise in a woven fabric.
   b. *Filling* (woof, weft, pick, shot) is yarn that runs crosswise in a woven fabric. These fillings are carried over and under the warp yarns.
   c. *Selvage* is the outer finished edge on both sides of the fabric. The selvage is formed by the filling yarn, which loops around the outside warp yarn to form an edge that does not ravel. Warp yarns always run parallel to the selvages. (See Figure 2.3.)

[1] The T.F.P.I.A. defines a "fiber" or "textile fiber" as "a unit of matter which is capable of being spun into yarn or made into fabric by bonding or by interlacing in a variety of methods including weaving, knitting, braiding, felting, twisting or webbing, and which is the basic structural element of textile products."

**Figure 2.1.** Fibers are shown at the loose end of a yarn that has been pulled away from the piece of cloth shown at the bottom of the picture. (*Photo by Jack Pitkin.*)

2. *Knitting* is the construction of an elastic, porous fabric by means of needles. One or more yarns form a series of connecting loops that support one another like a chain.

3. *Crocheting* is a construction made with just one hook or needle. A chain of loops is formed from a single yarn.

4. *Felting* is the process of matting fibers together by heat, steam, and pressure to form a fabric.

5. *Knotting* (*or netting*) is a process of forming an openwork fabric or net by tying yarns together where they cross one another. *Tatting* is a form of knotted lace that is made with a shuttle filled with yarn.

6. *Braiding* (*or plaiting*) is an interlacing of three or more yarns or strips of cloth over and under one another to form a narrow flat tubular fabric.

7. *Bonding* is the process of pressing fibers into thin sheets or webs that are held together by adhesive, plastic, or self-bonding. Fabrics so constructed are called *nonwoven textiles*. *Bonded cloths* are common single fabrics that are combinations of two fabrics that have joined together, back-to-back, with a binding agent.

8. *Laminating* is the joining of two or more layers of material by use of either a binding agent or heat—especially, the joining of a

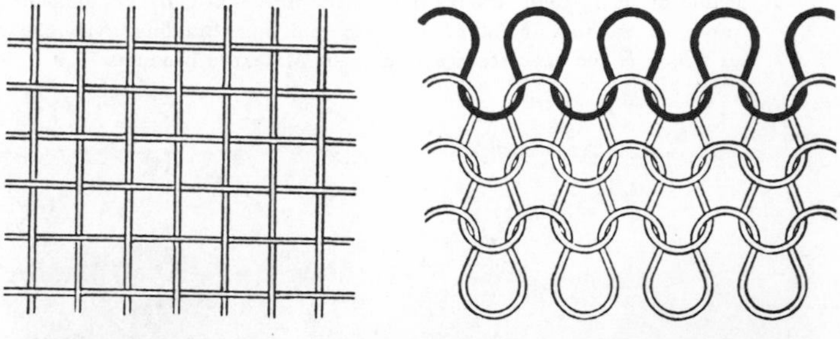

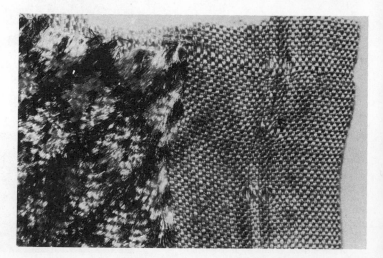

**Figure 2.2.** *Left:* Construction of a plain woven fabric. *Right:* Construction of a plain knitted fabric.

**Figure 2.3.** The selvage is the plain strip of fabric shown in the left half of the picture. (*Photo by Jack Pitkin.*)

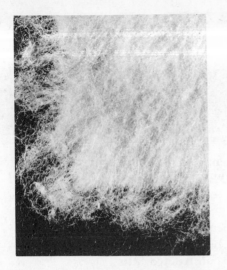

FELTED FABRIC

BONDED FABRIC

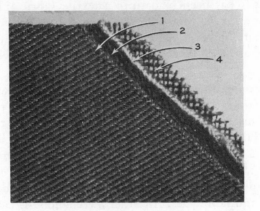

FOUR-PLY LAMINATED FABRIC

BRAID—THREE STRIPS
OF KNITTED JERSEY

KNOTTED FABRIC

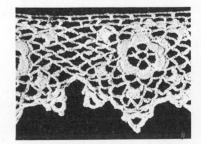

CROCHETED FABRIC

**Figure 2.4.** Types of fabrics. (*Top photos by Jack Pitkin.*)

**Figure 2.5.** A plastic supported film (a textile) and a plastic unsupported film (a nontextile).

face fabric to a foam plastic back in bonded cloths. *Laminated cloths* are fabrics composed of layers of material including foam joined together by an adhesive, a binding agent, or heat.[2]

Cloths or "fabrics" are known as "textile fabrics" when they are made from fibers by one of the aforementioned methods.[3] Leather is not a textile fabric because it is not made of fibers and is not constructed into a fabric by any of the eight methods listed here. (Sometimes, however, leather is cut into narrow strips and woven into the uppers of sport shoes. In such cases it has been made into a textile fabric.) Paper used for stationery is not a textile fabric for the previously mentioned reason. A man's panama hat, however, is a textile fabric because it is woven from straw. A disposable pillowcase is made of bonded web—a nonwoven goods (textile).

*Textiles* are fabrics or fibers from which fabrics are made. The word textile is derived from the Latin verb *texere,* meaning "to weave." Although the term originally applied only to woven fabrics, the present definition includes fabrics made by other methods of construction, such as knitting, felting, crocheting, knotting, braiding, bonding, and laminating.

Textile merchandise is woven, knitted, crocheted, felted, knotted, braided, or bonded and laminated. All other merchandise is called "nontextile merchandise." China, glassware, leather shoes and riding boots, stationery, wooden and steel furniture, jewelry, and silverware are some nontextile items.

*Classification of textile fibers.* Two main classes of textile fibers are used in consumer goods: (1) natural fibers and (2) man-made fibers.

## NATURAL TEXTILE FIBERS

These fibers that grow in nature can be divided into three groups: (1) animal, (2) vegetable, and (3) mineral. (See fiber classification, p. 39.)

[2] For a more complete description of these methods other than weaving, see Chapter 6.

[3] According to the T.F.P.I.A., "Fabric means any material woven, knitted, felted or otherwise produced from, or in combination with, any natural or manufactured fiber, yarn, or substitute therefor."

The animal fibers that are most used in consumers' goods are wool, which is the protective covering of the sheep, and silk, cultivated or wild, which is the product of the silkworm and is obtained from its cocoon.

Less important fibers include hair fibers from camels, rabbits, goats, cats, horses, and cattle. They differ microscopically from wool and, as a rule, are stiffer and more wiry than wool and do not felt well. Cashmere, a goat fiber, and camel's hair, however, are quite soft.

Cat hair and cow hair can be used as textile fibers, but they are used mostly for fur felts. Cow hair, although harsh and coarse, can be made up into blankets and carpets, but it should be mixed with other fibers. The sources and properties of hair fibers will be discussed in Chapter 14.

## VEGETABLE FIBERS

Cotton and linen [4] are the most common vegetable fibers used in consumers' goods. Cotton comes from the cotton plant, a small bush related to the hollyhock. Linen, called "flax fiber," is obtained from outside the woody core of the flax plant. Both of these fibers are vegetable because they contain a large amount of cellulose, of which the cells of plants are constructed.

*Modified cellulose fibers.* Cotton fibers can be treated with a bath of caustic soda either after they are made into yarn or after the cloth is constructed. The purpose of this treatment, called "mercerization," is (1) to give strength to the fibers, (2) to increase luster, and (3) to improve their affinity for dye. Linen is rarely mercerized because it is naturally stronger than cotton and possesses good natural luster.

The physical properties of the cotton fiber can be modified by cross linking of molecules. This technique improves a fabric's wrinkle recovery and is thus important for wash-and-wear. (See p. 180 ff. for a discussion of cross-linking.)

Minor vegetable fibers include: *Ramie or rhea*, a fiber from the nettle-like East Indian shrub. It is also produced in China, Egypt, Kenya, and the United States. *Jute* comes from fibers within a wooded stalk of a plant about twelve feet tall grown primarily in India.

*Hemp* is grown in the Philippine Islands, Yucatan, Mexico, Central America, the West Indies, and India. Italy, Poland, France, Japan, and the United States (Kentucky) also raise hemp. Ramie, jute, and hemp will be discussed more fully in Chapter 10.

*Sisal,* often called *sisal hemp,* is a hard fiber larger and stiffer than the bast fibers, flax, hemp, jute, and ramie. Sisal grows on large plantations in Java, Haiti, Kenya in East Africa, West Africa, and Central America.

---

[4] A chapter is devoted to each of the major textile fibers.

We import most of our sisal from the first three countries. Approximately 4,000 to 6,000 plants can be grown to an acre, and an interval of three years is required from the time of planting until harvesting.[5] White fibers are obtained from the leaves of the Agave plant (*Agave sisalana*) by the process of decortication (the removal of the outer woody portion to obtain the fiber). The fibers are dried and bleached in the sun and are sold in bales. These fibers are too coarse to be spun into yarn except for coarse sacking. Principal uses are for cordage, ropes, and binder twine. Sisal is weakened by salt water but not so easily by fresh water. It is adapted for use in women's straw hats.

*The uses for sisal.*[6] The main use for sisal fiber is in the manufacture of strings, twines, and ropes. Before World War II, the trade found it difficult to interest shipowners and navies in using sisal ropes, because sailors generally criticized the harshness of the ropes and also maintained that they did not "give" in the same way as Manila ropes. However, during the war, when Manila supplies were cut off, sisal ropes had to be used, and the trade has kept a considerable amount of business in peacetime. Low-grade fiber is used for sacks, but these are not very popular because of their coarseness.

In agriculture, baler and binder twines use a considerable amount of sisal fiber. A growing use of low-grade fiber is in the mat and carpet industries. Pile carpets are being manufactured successfully in Holland. And on the continent of Europe and in England sisal for matting is beginning to supersede the better-known coir matting.

Coir is a hard, reddish-brown fiber obtained from the outer shell of the cocoanut. These fibers have to be removed from the fruit, then softened in water and pounded to remove the wooded husk. Hackling, the combing of the fibers with a steel comb, is done by hand in Ceylon, where the coir fiber is prepared by hand for cordage, bristles for brushes, and coarse cloth. When coir is prepared mechanically, machines with fluted ion rollers crush the husks. Then a revolving drum studded with sharp teeth tears out the woody husks. Broken fibers that fall from this drum are dried in the sun, then cleaned and used for mattresses. The finer grades of mattress fiber can be made into rope and cocoa matting. After washing, cleaning, and hackling, the stronger, coarser fibers are made into hanks and sold for brushes, primarily to the European market. From strips of leaves of the cocoanut palm, a thread can be made that is elastic, lightweight, and waterproof.[7] It is used in mats, bags, hats, and slippers.

Paper is made mainly from linen, cotton, and hemp rags, and from

[5] J. M. Matthews, *Textile Fibers*, 6th ed., edited by H. R. Mauersberger (New York: John Wiley & Sons, Inc., 1954), p. 377. *Dictionary of Textiles*, edited by Isabel B. Wingate (New York: Fairchild Publications, Inc., 1967).

[6] Result of research written especially for *Textile Fabrics* by Tongoni Plantations, Ltd., Christo Galanos, Director, Nairobi, Kenya.

[7] Matthews, *op. cit.*, p. 417.

straw, bamboo, jute, and wood. In sheet form, paper is a nontextile, but fine strips of paper made of wood pulp can be twisted into yarn and properly treated so that they are usable in floor coverings and porch furniture. Ordinarily, paper used in the manufacture of so-called fiber rugs is weak when wet, and if thoroughly drenched will become mush.

Paper is closely allied to rayon. In one process especially, purified cellulose is rolled out into sheets of cardboard before it is treated with chemicals to form the viscous solution. (See Chapter 13.)

Although paper may be so treated as to present a good appearance as a textile fabric, it is not durable, comfortable, or serviceable as a textile yarn. Consumers should consider carefully before they purchase fabrics containing paper.

Disposable items come under the classification of *throwaway fabrics* and are really nonwoven goods made of webs of cotton, nylon, or polyester that are fused or bonded with a cementing medium such as starch, glue, casein, rubber latex, one of the cellulose derivatives, or synthetic resins.[8] So-called paper dresses are a web-type or nonwoven cloth.[9] While the early dresses were weak when wet, some current types are now colorfast, launderable, and friction- and fire-resistant. They can be of solid colors or printed. Seams can be fused or stitched. These dresses are used for daytime or evening wear.

*Kapok* is a vegetable fiber that comes from a plant or tree grown chiefly in Java, the West Indies, Central America, India, Africa, South Asia, and Brazil. Probably most of us have seen pillows in stores marked "Stuffed with kapok." It is a silky fiber, finer than cotton, but it is not adaptable to spinning; hence, it is not used in woven cloth. Mattresses and pillows are filled with kapok. It is cheaper than hair but not so durable or resilient. Kapok dries quickly and so is serviceable for bedding used at the seashore. Life preservers made of kapok are buoyant and light in weight.

*Grass, rush, and straw.* Cured prairie grass from Minnesota and Wisconsin is bound together into a rope for weaving into grass rugs for sun rooms, porches, and summer homes. Rush, generally made of reeds that grow in sluggish waters of Europe and the Far East, is similarly used in rugs.

Straw fibers are obtained from stems, stalks, leaves, and bark of natural plants. Following are names of straws, many of which are woven into hats: baku (fibers of bari palm of Ceylon and the Malabar Coast), balibuntal (from unopened palm leaf stems), leghorn (from a kind of wheat grown in Tuscany), milan (from Milan, Italy), panama (from Toquilla straw of Ecuador), toquilla (from Jippi-Jappa leaves), tuscan (from bleached wheat stalks grown in Tuscany).

---

[8] Disposable items include hospital sheets, pillowcases, diapers, curtains, wiping cloths, and paper dresses.

[9] Only paper dresses of cotton webs can be included in this class of natural vegetable fibers.

*Asbestos* is a mineral obtained from rocks, primarily in Quebec, Southern Rhodesia, South Africa, and Russia.[10] Asbestos from Canada and U.S.S.R. can be spun and woven into cloth because its fibers are over one-quarter inch long. White, soft, and silky, they resist all liquids except strong acids. Woven products of asbestos include fireproof suits, protective clothing, gloves, and safety curtains in theaters. Asbestos cloth with a metallic layer of aluminum bonded to it reflects heat.

Thin sheets of gold, silver, or aluminum foil can be cut in strips and used as yarn for luxury fabrics.

According to the T.F.P.I.A., the term *man-made fiber* "... means any fiber derived by a process of manufacture from a substance which, at any point in the manufacturing process, is not a fiber." This act lists the generic or family names and definitions for manufactured fibers established by the F.T.C. for use in labeling and advertising. No other names may be substituted for these generic names unless and until established by the F.T.C.

Rule 7 of the act lists sixteen generic names of manufactured fibers, along with their respective definitions. (See on pp. 42–50 ff.) It will be noted that the definitions of these generic names are couched in technical, chemical terminology that a salesperson or consumer would not be likely to understand. Yet these terms must be used by labelers and advertisers just as the generic names of the natural fibers—cotton, linen, silk, wool —are used. Familiarizing consumers with these terms requires considerable training of salespeople so that they can explain adequately. Simplification of these definitions should be most helpful in this training.

In order to comprehend the meanings of the generic terms, a general description of broad bases for classification of manufactured fibers should be helpful.

## MANUFACTURED OR MAN-MADE FIBERS

### FIBERS DERIVED FROM A CELLULOSIC BASE

Some fibers, such as rayon and acetate, have a base of natural plant cellulose, the same as cotton. Other fibers are based on protein found in milk, soybeans, or corn meal. Others are based on natural rubber from the rubber tree. Still others are derived from sand (silicon) made into glass marbles.

Rayon is made both from wood pulp (obtained from western hemlock and southern pine) and from cotton linters (fibers adhering to cotton seeds). The raw materials used in making rayon contain a large amount of cellulose. The manufacture of rayon is described fully in Chapter 13.

---

[10] J. Cooper, "Asbestos, The Mineral Fiber," *Fibres and Plastics*, XXII (October 1961), 289–92, 304.

Rayon, like other manufactured textile fibers, is made by converting the base raw material into a solution that can be extruded through small holes in a nozzle or jet and then hardened into fiber.

*Rayon fibers made from modified cellulose.* By treating the cellulose chemically, rayon fibers are changed (modified) in such a way as to create properties different from the usual rayons. Rayon can now be crimped so that the fiber has a kinky wool-like appearance and texture when made into cloth. This is done by "building into" the viscose rayon fiber certain properties, so that when treated with caustic soda the fiber or yarn will crimp. It first appeared in the furlike fabric called poodle cloth. (See Chapter 13 for a discussion of crimped fiber.)

Another method of modifying viscose rayon results in the so-called strong or high-tenacity rayon yarn. It is made by modifying the viscose rayon filaments chemically while they are in the plastic state. In this state, the filaments have a high stretch that can be controlled to give the desired increased tensile strength. Such fibers can be spun into yarns with strength adequate for cord tires and industrial fabrics.

Some rayon fibers are changed in molecular structure in such a way as to have properties different from the usual rayons. One of these is Zantrel, American Enka Corporation's polynosic rayon staple (short) fiber. Polynosic is the generic name of this kind of rayon fiber in several European countries. It has unique molecular structure that gives improved dimensional stability (won't stretch out of shape), a firm hand (touch), and improved wet wrinkle recovery. (See Chapter 13.)

Still another method of giving rayon fibers properties different from regular rayons is through cross-linking of molecules by chemical bonds. (See reference to cross-linking of cotton cellulose, p. 33 ff.) This cross-linking improves the wet strength and dimensional stability of rayon. A high degree of cross-linking to modify rayon's properties is needed for wash-and-wear. A trademarked fabric of the cross-linked type is Corval, by Courtaulds North America, Inc.

*Acetate* is primarily made from cotton linters. Fibers are derived from chemical compounds of cellulose (two-thirds cellulose and one-third acetyl).

Until the F.T.C. revised its ruling on rayon, which took effect February 9, 1952, acetate was called "rayon." But, because acetate fibers are not pure cellulose, as are rayons, but are cellulose plus acetyl, the fibers require different care by consumers than do the pure cellulose

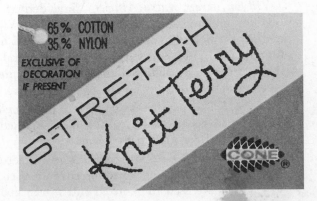

**Figure 2.6.** A label showing correct use of generic terms defined in the Textile Fiber Products Identification Act. (*Reproduced courtesy of Cone Mills, Inc.*)

fibers. Rayon is a vegetable fiber, and acetate is a vegetable and chemical fiber. Common trade names for acetate are Acele, Estron, and Celanese. (Chapter 13 has a further discussion of acetates.)

*Modified acetate fibers.* Acetate fibers may be modified by stretching the acetate yarns, generally in steam, and then treating them with an alkaline bath. Such a yarn has high tenacity, so strong that it has been used in parachute fabrics. The name Fortisan, a high-tenacity yarn developed by the Celanese Corporation, is familiar in this country. *Triacetate* is a thermoplastic material that contains three acetate components. Arnel is a trademark of the Celanese Corporation of America for triacetate fibers and yarns. These fibers are more resistant to heat than regular acetate fibers.

### FIBERS DERIVED FROM A NONCELLULOSIC BASE

*Nylon, acrylic, modacrylic.* The fibers in this classification are all "produced in a test tube." This means that the fiber-forming substances are not natural bases but complex chemical compounds. These same compounds used for extruding textile fibers may be used for plastics (nontextiles) and for finishes and coatings of textiles. There are many resins (plastics) used for textile fibers, such as polyamide resin used for making nylon fibers and acrylic resin (at least 85 per cent acrylonitrile units) used for making acrylics like Orlon and Acrilan. When acrylic fibers are modified by using 35 to 85 per cent acrylonitrile units, then resultant fibers are classified as modacrylics (modified acrylics). Trademarked fibers Dynel and Verel are modacrylics. (See Chapter 14 for a discussion of these fibers.)

*Polyester.* A fiber-forming substance made from a chemical composition of ethylene glycol and terephthalic acid is generically classified as polyester. Trademarked fibers in this category include Dacron, Kodel, Fortrel, and Vycron. (See Chapter 14.)

*Spandex.* Polyurethane plastic resin is used for spandex, of which a well-known trademarked fiber is Lycra.

*Vinyon, saran, nytril, vinal.* Vinyl derivatives of various types are used for making manufactured fibers. For example, a vinylite resin is used for the fiber vinyon, vinylidene chloride is used for saran, vinylidene dinitrile for nytril, and vinyl alcohol and acetal units for the vinal class of fibers that have achieved considerable commercial success abroad but have not appeared as yet on the American scene.

*Olefin.* The paraffin-based fibers, polyethylene and polypropylene, are classified generically as olefin. Trademarked fibers of this class include Olane, Reevon, and Royalene.

*Synthetic rubber-based fibers.* A manufactured rubber fiber is used for an elastic yarn, uncovered or covered with various textile threads. These yarns are used for knitted and woven goods.

*Metallic-based fibers.* Manufactured fibers composed of metal, metal-coated plastic, or a core completely covered by metal come under this classification of manufactured fibers. A familiar trademark of metallic yarn is Lurex.

*Glass.* Glass fibers are made from melted glass marbles. The molten glass is extruded through a nozzle with tiny holes similar to the one used in forming nylon fibers. Glass fibers are fireproof. A well-known trade-marked name is Fiberglas.

*Protein-based fibers.* These, under the T.F.P.I.A. generic classification, are named *azlon.* While United States manufacturers have made fibers of these raw materials, they are not, at the time of writing, making fibers with these bases.

The following table summarizes the broad, general classification of fibers:

## NATURAL FIBERS

|  |  |  |
|---|---|---|
| I. ANIMAL | | paper |
| silk | | kapok |
| wool | | sisal |
| hair | | coir |
| II. VEGETABLE | | grass |
| cotton | | straw |
| linen | | rush |
| ramie | III. MINERAL | |
| jute | | asbestos |
| hemp | | |

## MANUFACTURED OR MAN-MADE FIBERS

I. FIBERS DERIVED FROM A CELLULOSIC BASE
      rayon and modified fibers
      acetate and modified fibers

II. FIBERS DERIVED FROM A NONCELLULOSIC BASE (from Synthetic Polymers)

| | |
|---|---|
| nylon | vinyon, saran, nytril, vinal |
| acrylic | olefin |
| modacrylic | synthetic rubber-based fibers |
| polyester | metallic-based fibers |
| spandex | glass |
| anidex | protein-based fibers |

A general classification according to the basic raw material from which each class of fiber is derived has been presented. With this background, the generic classification of manufactured fibers established by the F.T.C. under the T.F.P.I.A. should be more meaningful. This classification follows: [11]

*Acetate.* A manufactured fiber in which the fiber-forming substance is cellulose acetate. Where not less than 92 per cent of the hydroxyl groups are acetylated, the term triacetate may be used as a generic description of the fiber.

[11] For the convenience of readers, items on this list have been alphabetized here. The T.F.P.I.A. does not list generic names in this order.

*Acrylic.* A manufactured fiber in which the fiber-forming substance is any long-chain synthetic polymer composed of at least 85 per cent by weight of acrylonitrile units.

*Anidex.* (See Glossary.)

*Azlon.* A manufactured fiber in which the fiber-forming substance is composed of any regenerated naturally occurring proteins.

*Glass.* A manufactured fiber in which the fiber-forming substance is glass.

*Metallic.* A manufactured fiber composed of metal, plastic-coated metal, metal-coated plastic, or a core completely covered by metal.

*Modacrylic.* A manufactured fiber in which the fiber-forming substance is any long-chain synthetic polymer composed of less than 85 but at least 35 per cent by weight of acrylonitrile units.

*Nylon.* A manufactured fiber in which the fiber-forming substance is any long-chain synthetic polyamide having recurring amide groups as an integral part of the polymer chain.

*Nytril.* A manufactured fiber containing at least 85 per cent of a long-chain polymer of vinylidene dinitrile where the vinylidene dinitrile content is no less than every other unit in the polymer chain.

*Olefin.* A manufactured fiber in which the fiber-forming substance is any long-chain synthetic polymer composed of at least 85 per cent by weight of ethylene, propylene, or other olefin units.

*Polyester.* A manufactured fiber in which the fiber-forming substance is any long-chain synthetic polymer composed of at least 85 per cent of an ester of a dihydric alcohol and terephthalic acid.

*Rayon.* A manufactured fiber composed of regenerated cellulose, as well as manufactured fibers composed of regenerated cellulose in which substituents have replaced not more than 15 per cent of the hydrogens of the hydroxyl groups.

*Rubber.* A manufactured fiber in which the fiber-forming substance is comprised of natural or synthetic rubber.

*Saran.* A manufactured fiber in which the fiber-forming substance is any long-chain synthetic polymer composed of at least 80 per cent by weight of vinylidene chloride units.

*Spandex.* A manufactured fiber in which the fiber-forming substance is a long-chain synthetic polymer comprised of at least 85 per cent of a segmented polyurethane.

*Vinal.* A manufactured fiber in which the fiber-forming substance is any long-chain synthetic polymer composed of at least 50 per cent by weight of vinyl alcohol units, and in which the total of the vinyl alcohol units and any one or more of the various acetal units is at least 85 per cent by weight of the fiber.

*Vinyon.* A manufactured fiber in which the fiber-forming substance is any long-chain synthetic polymer composed of at least 85 per cent by weight of vinyl chloride units.

## THE CONSUMER'S INTEREST IN FIBERS

The consumer is not usually interested in identifying fibers per se. The T.F.P.I.A. requires that all fibers used in a fabric be listed on a label in percentages by weight. This tag or label is to remain affixed to the article until it reaches the consumer. The consumer is interested in how certain fibers will perform in use in a finished cloth. She wants to know how the use of certain fibers in a cloth will affect its durability, suitability, comfort, ease in care, and attractiveness. These factors are the consumers' buying criteria.

The use of more than one fiber in a fabric might (1) give the fabric more uses than if it had one fiber, (2) give it a different feeling or "hand," (3) overcome a definite drawback of the other fiber or fibers, (4) lower the cost, or (5) give it a different appearance or style value.

There is an increasing amount of mixing of fibers. A fabric is a *mixture* if each individual yarn is composed of a particular fiber. For instance, the warp, or up-and-down yarn, might be made of acetate, and the filling, or crosswise yarn, might be of rayon. The acetate is more dimensionally stable than the rayon. The rayon filling provides the texture with surface interest of the fabric.

A fabric is a *blend* if each yarn is composed of two or more different fibers. To make a blend, different fibers are mixed together before the yarn is spun. There is an increasing amount of blending being done today, particularly where the new synthetic fibers are concerned. The technical problem lies in what percentage of a synthetic must be added to make the fabric best suited to the particular use for which it is intended. Nylon blended with wool adds strength to the wool. One technologist states that each 1 per cent of nylon increases the strength of a woolen yarn 3 per cent. But the consumer might want to know about a specific use: "Is the presence of nylon in a wool blend advantageous for use in upholstery, for example?" The answer would be affirmative, because nylon adds strength and abrasion resistance—two important factors in this end use.

The table on pp. 42–50 presents the generic names of the manufactured fibers, their chief characteristics, some typical uses, producers, representative fiber trademarks, and features.[12]

The consumer may want to know why wool yarns are used in the warp, and cotton in the filling, of a flannel shirt. The mixed fabric is less expensive than 100 per cent wool and is easier to launder (less apt to shrink). This example illustrates that more than one fiber in a fabric

[12] In general, the companies listed in the table make both fibers and yarns. The majority do not make fabrics.

## GENERIC GROUPS OF MAN-MADE FIBERS

| Generic Name | Characteristics | Some Typical Uses | Producer | Representative Fiber Trademarks | Features |
|---|---|---|---|---|---|
| Acetate | Excellent hand, good draping ability, moth and mildew resistant, cross-dyed effects with rayon, desirable hand, doesn't pill; fair wrinkle resistance, poor crease retention; must be ironed at low temperature; dimensional stability, low cost, limited strength. Triacetate: less sensitive to heat; wash-and-wear properties; resists pilling, good wrinkle resistance, pressed pleat retention, colorfastness | Apparel, home furnishings fabrics; also in blends with other man-made fibers | E. I. du Pont de Nemours & Co. | Acele | Fibers and yarns |
| | | | Celanese Fibers Co. | Arnel | Triacetate |
| | | | FMC Corporation, American Viscose Division | Avicolor | Also trademark for rayon |
| | | | | Avisco | Also trademark for rayon and vinyon |
| | | | Celanese | Celaloft | Bulked filaments |
| | | | | Celaperm | Solution-dyed (color hardened in solution before extrusion) |
| | | | Eastman Kodak Co., Tennessee Eastman Co. Division | Chromspun | Solution-dyed filaments |
| | | | | Estron | Filament yarns and cigarette filter tow |
| | | | | Loftura | Slub voluminized filament yarn |
| Acrylic | High bulk, warmth, and dimensional stability, wool-like hand, pressed crease retention; minimum care, may pill, fair strength | Furlike pile fabrics, blankets, carpets, sweaters, infants' sleepwear; also used for stuffing of pillows, comforters, etc. | Monsanto Co., Textiles Division | Acrilan | Fibers, staples, yarns, threads, and yarn and thread filaments |
| | | | American Cyanamid Co. | Creslan | Similar features to the above but slightly drier hand |
| | | | du Pont | Orlon | A broad descriptive name for a family of du Pont acrylic fibers |

| Generic Name | Characteristics | Uses | Manufacturer | Trade Name | Remarks |
|---|---|---|---|---|---|
|  |  |  | Dow Badische Co. | Zefran II (Type 200) | For carpet yarns and other end uses |
|  |  |  |  | Zefkrome | Color "built into" fiber. For double knits, carpets |
| Anidex | Elastomeric fiber. Stretches and recovers. An elastomer of an acrylic closely allied to acrylic fibers and acrylic plastics. | Foundation garments, woven and knitted clothing fabrics. | Rohm & Haas | Anim/8 | Anidex — the F.T.C.'s generic name for the newest class of non-cellulosic man-made fibers, 1969. |
| Azlon | Fibers produced from proteins found in casein, peanuts, soya beans, corn kernels |  | Not manufactured in the U.S. |  | Soft; blends well with other fibers |
| Glass | Nonflammable; wrinkle, soil, and chemical resistant; very strong; quick drying, no ironing required; poor abrasion resistance | Draperies, curtains, electrical insulators | Owens-Corning Fiberglas Corp. | Beta | Textile glass for decorative purposes |
|  |  |  |  | Fiberglas | Filament and staple fiber |
|  |  |  |  | 401 | Air-bulked yarn for decoration |
|  |  |  | Pittsburgh Plate Glass Co. | PPG | Curtains and draperies |
|  |  |  | Johns-Manville Glass Fibers Co. | Vitron | Glass fibers and yarns for industrial fabrics |
| Metallic | Metallic glitter and sheen. Stainless steel used for functional purposes | Decorative addition to fabrics, static elimination, heat resistance and conductivity | Fairtex Corp. | Fairtex | Metallic yarn laminated with Mylar, metallized Mylar; or with acetate butyrate |
|  |  |  | Metal Film Co., Inc. | Chromeflex MM | Outerwear, draperies, upholsteries |
|  |  |  |  | MF | Draperies, shoes, handbags |
|  |  |  | Standard Yarn Mills, Inc. | Lamé | Laminated foil yarns |
|  |  |  | Dow Badische | Lurex | Nontarnishing. |
|  |  |  | Malina Co., Inc. | Melora | Coated metal fiber |

# GENERIC GROUPS OF MAN-MADE FIBERS (Continued)

| Generic Name | Characteristics | Some Typical Uses | Producer | Representative Fiber Trademarks | Features |
|---|---|---|---|---|---|
| | | | Metlon Corp. | Metlon | Various types of yarn for specific purposes: polyester/aluminum foil types; polyolefin/aluminum foil type, metallized and lacquered; clear polyolefin, staple (straight or serrated cut) |
| | | | du Pont | Mylar | Polyester film for production of metallic yarns |
| Modacrylic | Chemical, fire, mildew resistant; fairly difficult to dye; resilient; strength poor; fair resistance to pilling; fair abrasion resistance; low melting point | Knitted pile fleece and furlike fabrics, carpeting, fire-resistant draperies, wigs | Eastman | Verel | Staple and tow. For pile fabrics and carpets, usually blended with acrylics. Flame-resistant draperies for public buildings |
| | | | Union Carbide Corp. | Dynel | For carpets, synthetic fur, wigs |
| Nylon | Strength and elasticity; abrasion resistance; quick drying, stability in repeated launderings, good colorfastness, fair hand (unless textured); safe ironing at 300° F.–350° F. depending upon type | Hosiery, lingerie, outer garments, carpets, upholstery; in blends for duffle bags, tents, glider ropes, threads, flak vests, tarpaulins, nets | du Pont | Antron | Filament and staple fibers with trilobal cross section |
| | | | Monsanto | AstroTurf | Man-made grass and other indoor and outdoor surface coverings |

| Trade Name | Manufacturer | Description |
|---|---|---|
| Blue "C" | | Knitted, netted, and woven textiles, for apparel and other end products. Also trademark for polyester fibers and yarns |
| Cantrece | du Pont | Bicomponent used in hosiery |
| Caprolan | Allied Chemical Corp., Fibers Division | Filament yarns; deeper dyeability and lower melting point |
| Cordura | du Pont | High-tenacity type for industrial twine and cordage |
| Crepeset | American Enka Corp. | Monofilament yarn. Crepe texture "built in" during manufacture |
| Cumuloft | Monsanto | Bulky yarns with high resiliency. For carpets and rugs |
| Enka Nylon | American Enka | Type 6 monofilament and multifilament yarns. Other trademarks for special end uses |
| Nomex | du Pont | Unusual dimensional stability, high resistance to nuclear radiation. For protective clothing, airplane lines, space age requirements |
| Nytelle | Firestone Synthetic Fibers Co. | Good hand, durable, excellent drape |
| Qiana | du Pont | Silky sheen; lightweight; filament yarns |
| Variline | American Enka | Continuous-filament yarn that produces random color variations |

# GENERIC GROUPS OF MAN-MADE FIBERS (Continued)

| Generic Name | Characteristics | Some Typical Uses | Producer | Representative Fiber Trademarks | Features |
|---|---|---|---|---|---|
| Nytril | Soft, resilient, nonpilling | | | | |
| Olefin | Lightweight, excellent chemical resistance, and good resistance to abrasion; low melting point; fair hand; polypropylene has good strength and low cost | Seat covers, outdoor furniture, marine ropes, shoe and hand-bag fabrics, indoor and outdoor carpeting, carpet backing, and commercial bagging | No domestic producers | | For furlike rugs |
| | | | Avisun Corp. | Avisun, Olane | Polypropylene |
| | | | Dawbarn Division, W. R. Grace & Co. | DLP | |
| | | | Hercules Powder Co. | Herculon | Polypropylene for carpets and other fabrics. Staple, tow, and filament |
| | | | Alamo Industries, Inc. | Marvess | Used by Phillips Fibers Corp. in the promotion of carpets and other fibers containing polypropylene fibers |
| | | | UniRoyal, Inc., Fiber and Textile Division | Polycrest | Polypropylene. Used in carpets |
| | | | National Plastics Products Co., Inc., Vectra Division | Vectra | Trademark also used in nylon or saran |
| Polyester | Great resiliency, wrinkle resistance, and pressed crease retention; quick drying; some kinds may pill; strength good; abrasion resistance good; hand fair to good depending on type; stable to repeated launderings when heat-set; automatic wash-and-wear; safe ironing at 325° F. | Minimum-care fabrics, curtains, knits; in blends for suits, slacks, and dresses; suitable for durable press garments | American Viscose | Avlin | Designated "Fiber 200" by A.V.D. Finished fabrics containing this fiber that meet performance standards to be merchandised under "Avlin" trademark |
| | | | Monsanto | Blue "C" | Trademark also applicable to nylon fibers and yarns |
| | | | du Pont | Dacron | Noted for resilience, durability, dimensional stability, wash-and-wear |

| Fiber | Properties | Uses | Manufacturer | Trademark | |
|---|---|---|---|---|---|
| | | | American Enka | Encron | Trademark applied to fabrics containing Enka's filament and staple fibers. Regular and high-tenacity continuous-filament yarns |
| | | | Celanese | Fortrel | Staple, tow, filament in various types |
| | | | Eastman | Kodel | Staple, tow. Filling for pillows. Minimum-care properties |
| | | | Phillips Fibers Corp. | Quintess | Filament and staple |
| | | | Beaunit Corp., Fibers Division | Vycron | Trademark used in the promotion of fabrics containing filament and staple polyester |
| Rayon | Versatile, very absorbent, easily dyed, good creping qualities, doesn't pill; low cost; some kinds stronger than others; fair abrasion resistance; stable to laundering if resin-treated; can be given special wash-and-wear finishes; blends well; excellent colorfastness | Women's, men's, and children's wear; carpets, upholstery, draperies, and curtains | American Viscose | Avicolor | Spun-dyed rayon staple and yarn. Trademark also used for solution-dyed acetate yarn |
| | | | | Avicron, Avifil | Novelty filament fiber. Crimps and bulks when wetted out. Pile fabrics |
| | | | | Avisco, Avril | Avisco trademark covers various types. Also applied to acetate and vinyon. Avril, called Fiber 40 (high wet strength); or Fiber 43 (bright, high tenacity). Fabrics of these fibers that meet A.V.D. standards are trademarked Avril |
| | | | | Avron | Trademark used by A.V.D. in promotion of fabrics containing Avisco XL (rayon staple fiber—bright, high tenacity) |

| Generic Name | Characteristics | Some Typical Uses | Producer | Representative Fiber Trademarks | Features |
|---|---|---|---|---|---|
| | | | Beaunit | Bemberg | Cuprammonium rayon filament and staple |
| | | | Celanese | Celanese | Filament, staple, tow |
| | | | Courtaulds North America, Inc. | Coloray | Spun-dyed rayon staple fiber |
| | | | Beaunit | Cupioni | Slubbed filament yarn |
| | | | | Cupracolor | Trademark for solution-dyed Bemberg yarns |
| | | | Industrial Rayon Corp. | Dy-Lok | Solution-dyed filament rayon yarns |
| | | | American Enka | Enka Rayon | Trademark also used for nylon |
| | | | | Enkrome | For promotion of fabrics containing acid dyeable filament and staple fiber |
| | | | | Fiber H M | Bright, high-tenacity, high wet strength staple fiber |
| | | | Courtaulds | Fibro | Staple fiber |
| | | | American Viscose | Firemaker | Fire retardant staple fiber |
| | | | Beaunit | Flaikona | Filament flake yarn for home furnishings |
| | | | Celanese | Fortisan | Strong filament yarn for draperies (saponified) modified acetate |
| | | | American Enka | Jetspun | Solution-dyed filament yarns |
| | | | American Enka | Kolorbon | Spun-dyed rayon carpet staple |

| | | Trade name | Manufacturer | Uses | Remarks |
|---|---|---|---|---|---|
| | | Lirelle | Courtaulds | | Trademark used in connection with the promotion of fabrics containing Fiber W 63, a bright high-tenacity, high wet strength staple fiber |
| | | Matesa | Beaunit | | Dull filament |
| | | Nupron | Industrial Rayon Corp. | | Used in promotion of fabrics containing Fiber 24, high wet strength staple fiber |
| | | Parfé | Beaunit | | Space-dyed (intermittently spaced color) |
| | | Zantrel | American Enka | | Polynosic—a term used along with Zantrel in the promotion of fabrics containing Fiber H M, high wet strength staple fiber |
| | | Strawn | Industrial Rayon | | Strawlike monofilament yarn for draperies, hats, and handbags |
| | | Xena | Beaunit | | For promotion of approved fabrics containing Fiber B high wet strength staple fiber |
| Rubber | Stretch and recovery | Contro | Firestone Plastics Co. | Foundation garments, swim wear, hose, webbings, surgical supports | Pure rubber fiber covered to make yarn |
| | | Lactron | UniRoyal | | Monofilament. Usually covered with textile thread and used principally in elastic garments |
| | | Lastex | | | Strictly not a fiber trademark because it is a composite product consisting of an elastic monofilament covered with various textile threads |

# GENERIC GROUPS OF MAN-MADE FIBERS (Continued)

| Generic Name | Characteristics | Some Typical Uses | Producer | Representative Fiber Trademarks | Features |
|---|---|---|---|---|---|
| Saran | Resistant to water, stains, chemicals, and weather; tough and flexible, stiff; nonflammable, resistant to sunlight; poor strength; safe ironing temperature 150° F. | Auto seat covers, insect screening, awnings, luggage, draperies, doll's hair | Southern Lus-Trus Corp. | Lus-Trus | Monofilament yarns |
| | | | Dow Badische | Rovana | Monofilament suitable for institutional draperies, bedspreads, cubicle cloths in hospitals |
| | | | National Plastics Products Co. | Vectra | Also a trademark for nylon and polyester fibers |
| Spandex | Good elasticity, good heat and abrasion resistance, impervious to body acids, lightweight. Long exposure to vegetable and mineral oils may cause slight yellowing | Foundation garments, swim wear, tops of men's socks, support hosiery, stretch yarns for apparel | Monsanto | Blue "C" | Trademark also as for nylon and polyester fibers |
| | | | du Pont | Lycra | Elastic filaments, covered or uncovered |
| | | | American Cyanamid | Numa | White multifilament yarns |
| | | | UniRoyal | Vyrene | Monofilament, covered or bare, very white |
| Vinal | Strong, abrasion resistant. Dry wrinkle resistance poor | | No domestic producers (developed by Japan) | | High strength and potentiality; inexpensive |
| Vinyon | Nonabsorptive; thermoplastic; water repellent; high strength wet and dry; excellent abrasion and fire resistance | Bonding agent for non-woven fabrics, batting, heat-sealed paper goods, industrial purposes | American Viscose | Avisco | Trademark also applied to rayon and acetate |
| | | | Vogt Plastics Division, Vogt Manufacturing Co. | Voplex | Trademark also applied to olefin |

may make the garment less expensive to care for because it can be washed at home. Since wool-and-cotton flannel is not as warm as all-wool flannel, it is more comfortable in overheated apartments. The label reveals that the fabric contains both wool and cotton, and the consumer can sense the presence of cotton by touch.

## SENSE OF TOUCH

While the sense of touch is not very reliable in helping the consumer identify textile fabrics (because of the new synthetics and blends), she can still learn much from the hand, or feeling, of a cloth. Such factors as warmth, coolness, pliability, texture, bumpiness, smoothness, or strength of a fabric can be discerned by the sense of touch.

To develop a sense of touch, grasp the edge of a cloth between the thumb and index finger, with the thumb on top. Rub the thumb and forefinger across the cloth, then lengthwise, then in a circle. Each time a fabric is felt, words that best describe the feel should be brought to mind: pliability, elasticity or "give," warmth, softness, smoothness, and so on.

When is a cloth pliable and when is it elastic or resilient? By pliability is meant the degree of flexibility or give a fabric possesses. If a fabric is gripped by the thumb and forefinger of each hand and pulled crosswise and then lengthwise, it will give; and a fabric that has give is said to be pliable. A fabric that returns to its original shape and form after stretching is said to be elastic or resilient. An all-wool jersey, to be considered satisfactory, should be resilient. A jersey dress that bulges at the elbows because it lacks resilience is unsatisfactory.

By smoothness is meant the ease with which the fabric slips if pulled between the fingers.

For the comparison of texture, the following fabrics are suitable: rayon satin and silk satin, both of which have smooth, slippery surfaces; cotton velveteen and silk chiffon velvet, which have soft surfaces; a silk flat crepe and a rayon flat crepe. Compare rayon shantung and silk shantung. Both fabrics have bumpy textures. A turkish toweling and a huck toweling, however, should not be compared, for their surfaces are entirely different and consequently would not give fair comparisons.

Fibers alone will not determine the hand of a fabric. The type of yarn used, construction, and finish will contribute to the hand of a cloth. In general, all that can be said is that fabrics made of vegetable fibers are usually cooler than animal fibers of the same weight. A 100 per cent cotton fabric is lifeless to the touch unless it is treated in the finish to give it a hand. A 100 per cent linen fabric is cool and pliable (leathery) to the touch. A fabric of 100 per cent silk is smooth, fairly slippery, and soft. A 100 per cent wool is warm and comparatively resilient. A 100 per cent rayon fabric generally is cooler to the touch than 100 per cent acetate of the same weight and texture.

Luster (or sheen), fuzziness, flatness, fineness, and coarseness of a fabric may be observed. A pure silk satin has a rich luster; a cotton flannel has a fuzzy surface; a linen table damask has a flat, smooth surface; a silk chiffon is fine and sheer; a rayon shantung looks bumpy. Texture of a fabric is easily observed.

On the basis of fiber content, sight, and touch, a consumer can decide whether the fabric has the suitability, attractiveness, ease of care, durability, and style-rightness that she requires in a given use. The informed salesperson should be able to help her make a decision.

Sometimes a manufacturer's brand name on a label may help the consumer come to a decision. The name "Botany" attached to a wool necktie is an old familiar brand name representing a wool fabric quite satisfactory for this use. Seals of approval of organizations mentioned in Chapter 1 may also help the consumer come to a decision to purchase.

## INTEREST OF THE MANUFACTURER IN FIBER IDENTIFICATION

To the manufacturers of cloth garments and household textiles the T.F.P.I.A. has made fiber identification a *must*. It is they who are responsible for seeing that fiber content is specified on labels or tags. Who knows better what fibers went into a fabric than the manufacturer of the grey goods?

## INTEREST OF THE RETAIL BUYER IN FIBER IDENTIFICATION

The retailer is legally responsible for subscribing to the T.F.P.I.A. He relies on his vendor to supply him merchandise that is labeled to conform to the act. Should the labels become detached from the merchandise or should imported merchandise be unlabeled, it becomes the retail buyer's responsibility to have labels made and affixed to the goods.

If the buyer is unable to identify fiber content himself, and most buyers do not have either the time or the equipment, then the merchandise must be sent to a testing bureau. With the advent of two or three different fibers in a blend and the variety of man-made fibers that can be blended with each other or with natural fibers, fiber identification is not easy.

## LABORATORY METHODS OF FIBER IDENTIFICATION

While no attempt will be made here to give data on scientific testing procedure, an attempt will be made to show the complexity of fiber identification under the T.F.P.I.A.

Fourteen different classes of fibers (acetate, acrylic, modacrylic, nylon, nytril, olefin, polyester, rayon, saran, spandex, cotton, flax, silk, and wool) can be identified with certain modifications by seven tests suggested by D. J. Bringardner and P. P. Pritulsky.[13] The tests and a summary of the procedures follow.

1. *Resistance to heat and flame.* A preliminary inspection is made to obtain information on the fabric's distinct characteristics. As a part of this preliminary inspection, the heat and flame test should be applied to note the effects of heat, the burning characteristics, and the burning odor of the sample. The results of this test can be used in determining what subsequent tests are to be made.

*Test Procedure:* Slowly move a specimen of the fiber to be tested toward a small flame and observe the reaction of the fiber to heat. Then push one end of the specimen directly into the flame to determine the burning characteristics of the fiber. After removal from the flame, observe the fiber's burning characteristics again and note the burning odor. (Burning odor can be compared with that of known fibers.) Then allow the specimen to cool and check the characteristics of the ash.

You can use groups of fibers, short lengths of yarn, or small pieces of fabric as test specimens, unless the product to be tested contains a combination of yarns or a blend of fibers. In such cases, select individual fibers as test specimens from the textile material with the aid of a magnifying glass.

(The behavior of fibers in the flame test appears on the next page. No changes have taken place since this table was prepared.)

2. *Microscopic examination.* (See Appendix for longitudinal and cross-sectional photomicrographs of various fibers.) It is advisable to make the first microscopic examination with low magnification (50 to 60 ×). The results of this test should verify or modify the conclusions reached in the preliminary inspection. If more microscopy is needed, groups of fibers (A.S.T.M. Test D 276-60T) from the specimen should be mounted and examined at a higher magnification (250–500 ×). The longitudinal appearance of the fibers should be compared with photomicrographs of known fibers. If further examination is needed, the cross-sectional appearance of the fibers should be studied.

3. *Solubility tests.* After completing the microscopic test, fibers are divided into groups for identification by solubility. If one already knows the identity of one or more fibers, he can verify this by testing a specimen to determine whether fibers dissolve or disintegrate in selected liquids (organic solvents as well as acids and alkalis).

4. *Stain tests.* Various manufacturers of dyes make special stains for fiber identification. The manufacturer provides test procedure and cards showing typical colors resulting from staining the principal fibers. The procedure is simple, but identification may be difficult because in an

[13] D. J. Bringardner and P. P. Pritulsky, "Latest Word on Identifying Today's Fibers," *Textile World,* III (December 1961), 47–59. Procedure for all fiber identification given in this section.

# BEHAVIOR OF FIBERS

| Fibers | Approaching Flame | In Flame | Removed from Flame | Ash Characteristics |
|---|---|---|---|---|
| Acetate | Fuses away from flame | Burns with melting | Continues to burn with melting | Leaves brittle, black, irregular-shaped bead |
| Acrylic | Fuses away from flame | Burns with melting | Continues to burn with melting | Leaves hard, brittle, black, irregular-shaped bead |
| Modacrylic | Fuses away from flame | Burns very slowly with melting | Self-extinguishing | Leaves hard, black, irregular-shaped bead |
| Nylon | Fuses and shrinks away from flame | Burns slowly with melting | Usually self-extinguishing | Leaves hard, tough, gray, round bead |
| Nytril | Fuses away from flame | Burns slowly with melting | Continues to burn with melting | Leaves hard, black, irregular-shaped bead |
| Olefin | Fuses, shrinks, and curls away from flame | Burns with melting | Continues to burn with melting | Leaves hard, tough, tan, round bead |
| Polyester | Fuses and shrinks away from flame | Burns slowly with melting | Usually self-extinguishing | Leaves hard, tough, black, round bead |
| Rayon | Does not fuse or shrink away from flame | Burns without melting | Continues to burn without melting | Does not leave a knob or bead |
| Saran | Fuses and shrinks away from flame | Burns very slowly with melting | Self-extinguishing | Leaves hard, black, irregular-shaped bead |
| Spandex | Fuses but does not shrink away from flame | Burns with melting | Continues to burn with melting | Leaves soft, fluffy, black ash |
| Cotton | Does not fuse or shrink away from flame | Burns without melting | Continues to burn without melting | Does not leave a knob or bead |
| Flax | Does not fuse or shrink away from flame | Burns without melting | Continues to burn without melting | Does not leave a knob or bead |
| Silk | Fuses and curls away from flame | Burns slowly with some melting | Burns very slowly; sometimes self-extinguishing | Leaves soft, fluffy, black ash |
| Wool | Fuses and curls away from flame | Burns slowly with some melting | Burns very slowly; sometimes self-extinguishing | Leaves soft, fluffy, black ash |

Reprinted from *Textile World*, December 1961. Copyright 1961 by McGraw-Hill Book Company.

intimate blend all fibers may be stained about the same color. In this case, a stain from another manufacturer may prove more suitable, or examination under a microscope may prove helpful.

5. *Melting-point test.* A single fiber is placed between 19-millimeter microcover glasses on a calibrated Fisher-Johns melting-point apparatus. The fiber temperature is raised to the melting point.

6. *Moisture-regain test.* In this test, the specimens are all made of one kind of fiber or of two fibers that can be easily separated from each other. A specimen of fiber is first dried, weighed, and conditioned in air at 70° F., 65 per cent relative humidity. To determine the moisture regain, record the percentage increase in weight of the fiber specimen during conditioning.

7. *Specific gravity test.* A fiber specimen is placed in a liquid of known specific gravity and is observed to determine whether it sinks or floats. This is a method of differentiating among fibers.

Other tests for identification include a refractive index test and an infrared spectrum test (an infrared spectrophotometer is used to scan the spectrum of a solvent cast or melt-pressed film or potassium bromide disk made from a specimen of the fiber). These spectra can also be used to identify fibers within a generic classification. Another test is heat discoloration. A fiber specimen is exposed for a specified time in air at 350° F. The discoloration of this specimen is to be used as a standard for comparison with discoloration of an unknown specimen. Since mechanical properties of fibers vary with different classes (such as breaking strength and breaking elongation), these properties can sometimes be used as means of fiber identification.

## SUMMARY

Although consumers are not particularly interested in the fibers themselves, they are interested in what effect the different fibers will have on the use and care of a fabric. A knowledge, then, of the classification of textile fibers is the first step in the study of textile fabrics. A knowledge of their classification will help in recognizing them in use.

Blends of various fibers will probably increase in importance because the blending of proper amounts of certain fibers will give the consumer a fabric that should serve her purpose better than one fiber alone. The new manufactured fibers, particularly, can do much for giving "plus" qualities to blends; the public is learning that these man-made fibers can give increased wearing quality, crease and wrinkle resistance, and ease in the care of fabrics in which they are used. The consumer should realize that these new synthetics are no "miracle fibers." Each fiber has certain advantages and drawbacks, and the selection of one fiber or fibers over others for an intended use is the problem of the technologist. There is no one all-purpose fiber. In later chapters the reader will discover what each fiber can do in use.

1. (*a*) What is a natural fiber?
   (*b*) What is a man-made fiber?
2. (*a*) Name the most widely used natural fibers.
   (*b*) List the man-made fibers derived from cellulose.
   (*c*) How do acetate fibers differ from rayon?
3. (*a*) What is Dynel, Orlon, Dacron?
   (*b*) What is nylon? How does it differ from rayon?
   (*c*) How does vinyon differ from nylon?
   (*d*) How does vinyon differ from saran?
4. Explain the making of metallic yarn.
5. (*a*) How are glass fibers made?
   (*b*) What are the uses of spun-glass fabrics?
6. Explain the difference between a mixture and a blend.
   (*a*) What are the advantages of the use of more than one kind of fiber in a fabric?
   (*b*) What do you think the future of blends will be?
7. (*a*) What is the importance of a knowledge of textile fibers to the consumer?
   (*b*) To the textile manufacturer?
   (*c*) To the retail buyer?
8. How may a good sense of touch be developed?
9. What adjectives best describe the feel of (*a*) pure silk, (*b*) rayon, (*c*) linen, (*d*) cotton, (*e*) wool?
10. In what way can a knowledge of manufacturers' brand names aid the consumer in identifying textile fabrics?

## PROJECT

1. For one month check the advertisements in a daily newspaper to determine the end uses for each of the classes of generic fibers. Also check the trademark of each generic fiber. Compile the data to show for what articles the manufactured fibers are being used. Analyze the data and come to some conclusions as to where the fiber and yarn companies have their markets for their various products.

## GLOSSARY

**Acetate.** A manufactured vegetable and chemical fiber derived from cellulose.

**Acrylic.** A generic name of fibers made from acrylic resin (at least 85 per cent acrylonitrile units).

**Anidex.** A manufactured fiber in which the fiber-forming substance is any long chain synthetic polymer composed of at least 50 per cent by weight of one or more esters of amonohydric alcohol and acrylic acid.

**Azlon.** A generic name for manufactured fibers with a protein base.

**Bicomponent fiber.** A continuous-filament man-made fiber composed of two related components, each having a different degree of shrinkage. Stretch results from crimping of the filament.

**Blend.**   A mixture of different fibers in the same yarn.

**Bonded-face fabric.**   The side of a bonded fabric used as the face (right side) of the cloth in a garment or other end use.

**Bonding.**   A process of pressing fibers into thin sheets or webs that are held together by adhesive, plastic, or self-bonding.

**Braiding (Plaiting).**   Forming a narrow band by intertwining several strands of cotton, silk, or other materials.

**Crimp.**   A term referring to the wavy appearance of a fiber or yarn.

**Cross-linked cellulose.**   A term referring to the way cellulose molecules are linked to produce changes in the fiber's physical properties.

**Cuprammonium process.**   One of the processes used in making rayon.

**Dimensional stability.**   Ability of a fabric to keep its shape and size.

**End use.**   Intended use by the consumer.

**Felting.**   A method of producing fabric or interlocked fibers by an appropriate combination of mechanical work, chemical action, moisture, and heat. Processes of spinning, weaving, or knitting are not employed.

**Fiber content.**   Amount of basic unit (raw material), such as cotton, rayon, wool, nylon, and so on, used in the fabrication of a textile fabric.

**Filament.**   A variety of fiber characterized by extreme length (continuous). Examples are rayon, nylon, Orlon acrylic, Dacron polyester, and other man-made fibers.

**Filling.**   Yarns that lie crosswise in a fabric from selvage to selvage, sometimes called weft or woof (in rugs).

**Finish.**   Treatment of a cloth after the grey goods come from the loom or knitting machines.

**Glass.**   A generic name for fibers made of glass.

**Hand.**   A general term referring to the feeling of a fabric or yarn obtained by touching or handling; that is, soft, smooth, pliable, springy, stiff, cool, warm, rough, hard, and limp.

**Knitting.**   The construction of an elastic porous fabric by means of needles. One or more yarns form a series of connecting loops, which support one another like a chain.

**Knotting.**   A process of forming an openwork fabric or net by tying yarns together where they cross one another.

**Laminating.**   Joining layers of material together with such substances as glue or resin to form one fabric, or bonding a foam or sheet of plastic to a cloth.

**Latex.**   Natural rubber (raw material) for fibers.

**Metallic.**   A generic name of manufactured fibers composed of metal, metal-coated plastic, or a core completely covered by metal.

**Mineral fibers.**   Textile raw material obtained from minerals in the earth, such as asbestos, silver, gold, copper, and the like.

**Mixture.**   A fabric composed of two or more kinds of yarns, each yarn made of one kind of fiber.

**Modacrylic.**   A generic name for modified acrylic fibers derived from 35 to 85 per cent of acrylonitrile units.

**Modified cellulose fibers.**   Cotton fibers treated with caustic soda to give strength, increased luster, and improved affinity for dye. Modification of a fiber changes its physical and chemical properties within the limits of a generic family.

**Natural fibers.** Textile raw material that grows in nature: cotton, linen, hemp, jute, ramie, kapok, silk, wool, and hair fibers.

**Nontextiles.** Merchandise that is not constructed by weaving, knitting, felting, knotting, or braiding. Nontextiles include such items as china, glassware, leather, cosmetics, jewelry, wooden and steel furniture, silverware, electrical goods.

**Nylon.** A generic name for manufactured fibers derived from polyamide resin.

**Nytril.** A generic name for manufactured fibers derived from vinylidene dinitrile.

**Olefin.** A generic name for manufactured fibers derived from polypropylene and polyethylene.

**Polyamide.** A resin made by condensation (a chemical rearrangement of atoms to form a molecule of greater weight).

**Polyester.** A generic name for manufactured fibers made from a chemical composition of ethylene glycol and terephthalic acid.

**Polymer.** Large molecule produced by linking together many molecules of a monomeric substance.

**Polymerization.** The way in which small molecules unite to form large molecules.

**Rayon.** A man-made textile fiber derived from cellulose. Two processes are used in this country to produce rayon: viscose process and cuprammonium process.

**Rubber.** A generic name of a manufactured fiber in which the fiber-forming substance is comprised of natural or synthetic rubber.

**Saran.** A generic term for manufactured fibers derived from vinylidene chloride.

**Selvage.** The outer finished edge on both sides of a fabric.

**Spandex.** The generic name of a manufactured fiber derived from polyurethane plastic (resin).

**Staple.** A term descriptive of the average length of any fiber.

**Synthetic fibers.** Man-made textile fibers derived from natural bases or chemical bases.

**Texture.** The appearance of the surface of the fabric.

**Thermoplastic.** A resin that, with the application of heat and pressure, can be molded and remolded.

**Tow.** A continuous loose rope of man-made filaments drawn together without twist.

**Vinal.** The generic name of a manufactured fiber derived from alcohol and acetal units.

**Vinyon.** The generic name of a manufactured fiber derived from vinylite resin.

**Viscose.** A process of making rayon.

**Warp.** The yarns running lengthwise in a woven fabric parallel with the selvage.

**Weaving.** The interlacing of two sets of yarns at right angles to form a fabric.

**Yarn.** A generic term for a group of fibers or filaments, either natural or synthetic, twisted or laid together to form a continuous strand suitable for use in weaving, knitting, or some other method of intertwining to form textile fabrics.

# 3

# Textile Yarns:
## THEIR MANUFACTURE
## AND USES

In Chapter 1 our consumer was interested in an advertisement for a white pima cotton, 2 x 2 broadcloth, Sanforized, for a tailored blouse. It was explained that 2 x 2 means that all the yarns are 2-ply (two single stranded yarns twisted together). This fact makes for strength and high quality.

A yarn is a strand of fibers or filaments, either natural or man-made, which have been grouped together or twisted for use in weaving, knitting, or other methods of constructing textile fabrics.

When fibers are selected for use in a certain type of fabric, the fibers that will perform best in that use and will satisfy customer demand at the desired price are chosen. The type of yarn to be manufactured will depend on the fibers selected, the texture, or hand, of the fabric to be made, and the qualities like warmth, resiliency, softness, and durability required in the fabric's end uses. In addition, the weave and the finish used will depend on kinds of fibers and yarns, end use of the fabric, and price.

The final fabric can be thought of as a linked chain, each link representing a process in the manufacturing of the chain. One link is fibers, another yarn, another construction, another finish. The final fabric can be of no better quality than the links of which it is composed. In the first paragraph of this chapter, 2 x 2 broadcloth was mentioned as excellent because it is 2-ply and therefore durable. If, however, the fibers, construction, and finish of the broadcloth were not of the same excellence as the yarn, then the fabric could not be excellent in quality.

## YARN MAKING

### PHYSICAL STRUCTURE

Yarn making is generally the second step in the manufacture of textile fabrics. Methods of manufacturing yarn depend on the type of fibers used and the type of yarn required. However, certain terminology is common to all yarns. For instance, a single yarn is one strand of fibers or filaments grouped or twisted together. When two or more single yarns are twisted together the final yarn is called *ply*. Two-ply yarn is composed of two singles, three-ply of three singles, and so on. A cord is the result of twisting together ply yarns in a third operation. The types of yarn just described are regular yarns. Then there are novelty yarns that may be either single or ply. When plied, there is often a core or center yarn with other yarns twisted about it to give textural effect. Frequently these yarns are bound to the core by other strands to hold all yarns together. Furthermore, there are *textured* yarns—continuous-filament synthetic yarns that have been geometrically modified or otherwise altered to change their basic characteristics.

### METHODS OF YARN MANUFACTURE

Raw fibers arrive at the yarn manufacturers in different forms. For example, cotton is in bales; wool in fleeces; cultivated raw silk in strands, waste and wild silk in bales; flax in bundles; rayon, acetate, nylon, and the other synthetics on tubes, cones, cops, spools, or skeins.

The natural fibers are restricted in length. For example, cotton staple ranges from ¾ to 1½ inches long; linen averages 18 to 20 inches long in best grades. Man-made fibers are continuous or are cut up into predetermined lengths called *staple fibers*. If a fabric is to resemble cotton, the tow (groups of continuous filaments) is cut up into staple.[1] Obviously, the basic processes for making yarn will vary. However, certain fibers are prepared for yarn by similar processes.

### CARDING AND COMBING

In general, fibers are blended or mixed before yarn manufacture actually begins. Cotton, wool, spun or waste silk, spun rayon, spun acetate, spun nylon, and many of the newer synthetics are made into

[1] See *spun rayon yarn*, Chapter 13.

yarn by carding and combing. Although the machinery and the details of these processes vary with the fibers and from mill to mill, the terms and purpose of the operations are comparable.

Carding separates the fibers and puts them in a filmy sheet called a *sliver*. In cotton, this operation removes dirt and short fibers. Wool fabrics are made of woolen yarn, which is carded only; or of worsted yarn, which is both carded and combed. For woolen yarn, three carding operations put the fibers into a thin sheet suitable for yarn.[2] Staple man-made fibers are made into yarn in the same manner as cotton or wool, depending on the intended use of the fabric.

Not all wool yarn is combed. Yarns that are carded only are called woolen yarns. These yarns are used for such fabrics as blankets, tweed coating, and suiting, wool flannel, and wool broadcloth. Worsted yarns are both carded and combed, and longer fibers are selected for worsteds than for woolens. One long combing machine, operating slowly to avoid breaking the long fibers, makes the sliver. In combing worsteds, the short fibers are removed and the fibers laid parallel. The sliver is drawn out to its desired width and thickness. Worsted yarns are used in fabrics such as tropical worsted, gabardine, whipcord, worsted flannel, and wool sharkskin.

Combing of cotton is necessary when fine, uniform yarns are needed to give sheerness, luster, smoothness, and possibly durability. All cotton yarns are carded, but not all cotton yarns are combed. Only about 8 per cent of cotton yarns are combed. For combing, longer-staple cottons are selected. Combing makes the fibers parallel in the sliver and removes the shorter fibers. The sliver is drawn out narrower and narrower, depending on the fineness of the yarn to be made. Spun silk fibers are also combed to lay fibers parallel and to remove the short ones. Man-made staple fibers intended to resemble combed cotton or worsted yarns would be combed.

## HACKLED AND WELL-HACKLED YARNS

Hackling is the process by which flax is prepared for linen yarn. The purpose of hackling is to disentangle the linen fibers and to lay them in a sliver. For fine, even yarns, the fibers must be long and parallel, hence more hackling is necessary. When yarns are well hackled, those in the trade may say the yarns are combed. At any rate, the purpose of the operation and the results are similar to combing.

## REELING AND THROWING

Raw silk is the long-fibered silk that is reeled from the cocoon and twisted into yarn. Several yarns are combined and twisted onto bobbins.

[2] See *carding of cotton*, Chapter 9; *carding of wool*, Chapter 12; *combing of cotton*, Chapter 9; *combing of worsted*, Chapter 12.

If ply yarns are required, the strands are combined and twisted together. The combining and twisting is called *throwing*. The machine that performs this operation is a *throwster*. (See p. 284.)

Rayon, acetate, nylon, glass, and other synthetic-filament ply yarns, hard-twist voile, and crepe yarns are thrown. The term "thrown," then, applies to reeled-silk ply yarn and to man-made filament ply yarns in high twist. Regular filament yarns result from grouping fibers together so they lie parallel.

## SPINNING

The spinning operation draws out the roving (very slackly twisted sliver) and puts in the required amount of twist. The purpose of twist is to bind the fibers together and to hold in the ends of fiber. Generally speaking, the tighter the twist, the stronger the yarn. This is true to a certain point; then the yarn weakens and may finally break. Long fibers like linen and long-fibered raw silk do not require so much twist to give strength as do cotton and short rayon staple fibers. A low or slack twist makes a more lustrous, softer yarn than a tight twist. Slack-twisted yarn is needed when the fabric is finished with a nap (fuzzy surface). When a yarn is twisted to the point of knotting, a crepe yarn results. Warp yarns are usually twisted tighter than filling yarns because warp yarns have to stand tension in the loom in weaving. One way to identify warp and filling yarns is to compare amounts of twist in each yarn. Warp is frequently tighter. There are exceptions, however. Warps are generally stronger and therefore harder to break. A ply yarn is stronger than the combined strength of the single yarns composing it. Similarly, a cord is stronger than a ply yarn of the same size.

Twist may be put into yarn in spinning or in subsequent plying operations. The direction of twist (right or left) and number of twists (turns) to the inch may be determined by a testing device called a twist counter. The number of turns to the inch can also be determined by very nontechnical means—a real rule-of-thumb method. Although the result may not be very accurate, the test will serve to compare amount of twist of other yarns tested by the same method. Unravel from a fabric about a two-inch length of yarn. Grasp the yarn between the thumb and index finger of each hand. Leave about

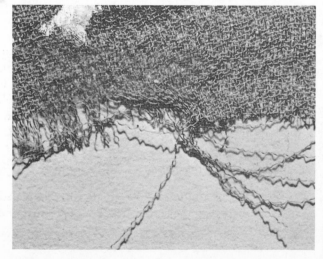

**Figure 3.1.** Chiffon, showing crepe yarns. (Photo by Jack Pitkin.)

Figure 3.2. S and Z twists.    "S" TWIST        "Z" TWIST

one inch of yarn in tension between the hands. A right-handed person should keep his left hand stationary. With the right hand, turn the yarn slightly until the direction in which the yarn untwists is evident. Then, still holding the yarn taut, roll the end between the thumb and index finger of the right hand. Each time the yarn rolls over constitutes a twist. A single yarn will pull apart when it is untwisted. When a ply yarn is untwisted, stop counting the twists when the single yarns lie parallel. The fibers will not pull apart in a ply yarn.

Single yarns are made in two directions of twist, right and left. The right twist is effected by twisting the sliver clockwise, and the left twist results from a counterclockwise motion. Right-twisted yarns are identified as Z twist, and left-twisted yarns as S twist. If a paper clip is attached to the end of a single yarn, and the end is allowed to hang free, the end will rotate. If the end rotates in a clockwise direction, the inherent twist is S; if in a counterclockwise direction, the yarn is Z twist. To make a ply yarn, the singles are usually twisted in one direction and the final ply twist in the opposite direction. For example, Z/S (Z is the direction of the twist for the singles and S is the ply twist). But a ply yarn may be S/S or Z/Z. A cable cord is S/Z/S or Z/S/Z; a hawser cord is S/S/Z or Z/Z/S. Cords, in addition to being made by twist, may be braided, woven, or knitted.

A practical illustration of how alternate direction in twist is used is in the filling yarns of rough and flat crepes. These crepes are often identified in the trade by their filling yarns as "2 x 2," which means 2S alternating with 2Z twists in the fillings of these fabrics. Two-by-two broadcloth, however, means two-ply yarn in warp and filling—not alternate direction in twist.

The word "spun" refers to a yarn that has been twisted by spinning. It also applies to a yarn made of staple fibers (man-made) that have been twisted into yarn. Hence, rayon yarn made of staple fibers is called spun rayon. "Spun dyed" has another connotation. This term is synonymous with "solution dyed," which means that the dyestuffs are put into the viscous solution (either acetate or rayon), and then the dyestuff is locked in the fiber when the fiber hardens. Rayon and acetate spun-dyed fibers are made into spun-dyed yarns.

### CARDED AND COMBED YARNS

It is important to know the fiber content of a yarn first in order to tell what has been its processing. If the fibers are cotton or wool or a blend of these fibers, carding and combing will be the processing required in manufacture. If man-made staple fibers are spun into yarn to resemble cotton or wool, these yarns will be spun on the cotton or wool systems and therefore will be carded and combed, too.

To identify a carded cotton yarn, untwist the yarn to the point where it pulls apart. Discard one piece of the yarn that has pulled apart. From the broken end of yarn, pluck out several fibers. Note whether the fibers are very short—less than one inch. Also note whether the fibers seem to branch out in all directions—are not parallel. If this is the case, the cotton yarn is probably carded only. If the yarn pulls apart and does not separate into two or three distinct yarns, then the yarn is a single. If the cotton yarn has long fibers (approximately one inch or over), all about the same length and lying parallel, the yarn is probably combed.

After identifying the yarns, the whole cloth should be studied. Notice whether the diameters of the yarns are quite even and smooth. If so, the yarns are probably combed. A very fine, even yarn, like one found in organdy, is combed.

To identify a woolen yarn used for clothing and home furnishings, excluding rugs, proceed as for cotton by untwisting it. Note whether the fibers average less than two inches, and branch out from the yarn in all directions. If so, the yarn is carded only and is a woolen.

To identify a worsted yarn, proceed as before by untwisting the yarn. Note whether the fibers average more than two inches, are all about the same length, and lie parallel. If so, the yarn is combed and is a worsted.

### REELED AND FILAMENT YARNS

The term "reeled" applies to long-fibered silk. Again, the fiber content is important to know first. If silk is reeled, the yarn is often lustrous, and there is usually less twist than for spun silk. The fibers will fan out or shred apart when the yarn is untwisted.

Filament yarns of man-made fibers have similar features. The fibers are continous, and they lie parallel and fan out when the yarn is untwisted. These yarns may be dull or lustrous, depending on their end use. Luster can be governed in the fiber stage.

### SPUN YARN (REGULAR RAYON, ACETATE, AND THE NEWER SYNTHETICS)

A nontechnical method of identifying regular spun rayon or acetate is to break a dry yarn first, then a wet one. Compare the strength of the yarn dry and wet. Since rayon and acetate are weaker wet than dry, it is easy to tell the yarn is not cotton or linen, both of which are stronger wet than dry. A flame test will reveal the presence of spun silk in a yarn. (See *heat and flame test*, p. 53 f.) A careful reading of the labels on the fabric will reveal its fiber content. Labels are particularly helpful in identifying the newer synthetics.

Spun yarns of man-made fibers have fibers of the same lengths, because the tow (a strand of continuous filaments) is cut all one length: the length of cotton, if the yarn is to resemble cotton, wool to resemble wool, and so on. The texture of the cloth and evenness of the yarn should help in determining what processes have been used to manufacture the yarn.

The yarns of spun silk are generally dull and cottony and usually have considerable twist to hold in the short ends (spun silk is made of shorter fibers than reeled silk). When the yarn is untwisted, fibers do not lie parallel and are of varied short lengths.

### LINE AND TOW LINEN YARN

Everyone is familiar with dish towels that are 100 per cent linen but are bumpy in texture. These towels are made of tow linen, which is poorly hackled yarn made of short fibers that are removed from the sliver in the hackling process. When a yarn is untwisted, short fibers of varied lengths branching out from the yarn will identify tow.

Handkerchief linen is a good example of line yarn made of long fibers that lie parallel in the sliver to make a smooth, even-diameter, fine yarn. Such yarns have been well hackled.

### SIZE OF YARNS

To distinguish differences in weight and fineness, yarns are given size numbers called counts, lea, or denier. The term "count" applies to the size of cotton, wool, and spun yarns. The term "lea" applies to linen yarn, and "denier" to reeled-silk and filament man-made yarns.

For cotton and spun yarns, the standard used is 840 yards of yarn to the pound. If 840 yards of cotton yarn weigh one pound, the count is #1. If it takes 8,400 yards to weigh a pound, the count is #10, and so on. The higher the numerical count, the finer the yarn.

There are two methods of computing sizes of woolen yarns: one method, the American run count, will be discussed here. If 1,600 yards weigh one pound, the count or size is #1, a very coarse yarn. The higher the number, the finer the yarn. The size of worsted yarns is determined by the number of hanks of 560 yards weighing one pound. If one 560-yard hank weighs one pound, the count or size is #1. If 5,600 yards weigh one pound, the count is #10, and so on. Yarns numbered 30s to 40s ("s" means single yarn) are very coarse. (See Chapter 12.) The higher the number, the finer the yarn.

Linen yarns use a lea of 300 yards as a base for figuring size. To find the size of the yarn, divide the number of yards weighing a pound by

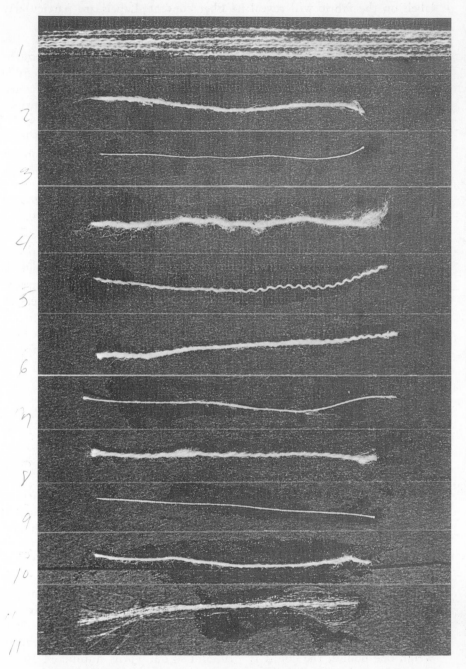

1

2

3

4

5

6

7

8

9

10

11

**Figure 3.3.** Types of yarns. *Top to bottom:* Space-dyed yarn, carded cotton, combed cotton, carded woolen, combed worsted, tow linen, line linen, spun silk, reeled silk, spun rayon, and filament rayon. (*Photo by Jack Pitkin.*)

300 yards. For example, if 3,000 yards weigh one pound, the count of the yarn is 3,000 ÷ 300, or 10. The higher the number, the finer the yarn.

The size of filament man-made yarns and reeled-silk yarns is designated in terms of denier. Denier (pronounced den'yer) is equal to the weight in grams of 9,000 meters of yarn. In yarns, 9,000 meters = 9,842.4 yards. If 9,842.4 yards of yarn weigh 150 grams, the yarn is 150 denier. If 9,842.4 yards weigh 75 grams, the denier is 75. Since the length of the yardage weighed is always the same, the yarns that weigh more must be larger in size. The lower the denier number, the finer the yarn. The number of filaments in a given filament yarn is indicated with the denier number; that is, 100–74 means 100 denier yarn composed of 74 filaments. (See Chapter 11 for the computation of International Denier in reeled silk.)

A proposed universal yarn numbering system called "Tex" expresses the weight in grams of one kilometer length of yarn. Such a system was suggested in 1873 at an international conference in Vienna. But it was not until 1956 that action was taken when ten nations attending an International Conference for Textiles unanimously voted to adopt the system. The yarn numbering called "Tex" can be applied to all fibers. It is intended to replace the many diverse yarn numbering systems.

### MONOFILAMENT AND MULTIFILAMENT YARNS

Generally speaking, the greater the number of filaments in a yarn, the stronger and more pliable and supple the yarn. Some yarns may consist of one filament, as in nylon hosiery or saran fabric for beach chairs. Such yarns are called monofilament, as opposed to the multifilament yarns.

### COLORING OF YARN

When a yarn is dyed before it is woven, it is said to be *yarn dyed*. Plaid ginghams are good examples of this method of dyeing.

Yarns can also be printed before weaving. It is common practice to print warp yarns before they are woven into cloth. By use of a white or solid-color filling with the printed warp yarns, a hazy grayed effect is produced in the design. A cloth with the warp printed before weaving is called a warp-printed fabric.

Space-dyed fabric is made of yarns that have color applied by dipping or spotting various places along the yarn. This is done to warp and/or filling yarns.

### KINDS OF NOVELTY YARNS

Fabric designers are constantly bringing out fabrics with novelty yarns to stimulate sales through a wider, more diversified variety of fabrics.

Textural effects obtained by use of novelty yarns would be impossible with any ordinary yarn.

Novelty yarns are made on a novelty yarn-twisting machine by combining different types of yarns in various ways. The weight of novelty yarns may vary from a few hundred yards per pound to as fine as 20,000 yards per pound or more.[3]

Novelty yarns are used in knitted sweaters and dresses, contemporary drapery and upholstery fabrics, and the decoration of men's and women's suiting fabrics. Such yarns are often made with blends of natural and man-made fibers. In any case, they are designed for a specific end use, and they can be varied by numerous possible combinations of fibers, twist, ply, and color.

These novelty yarns are popular today:

1. *Bouclé* is one of the most-used novelty yarns. It is characterized by tight loops that project from the body of the yarn at fairly regular intervals. It is often made of a combination of rayon and

[3] *Novelty Yarns* (a pamphlet), by Philadelphia Penn Worsted Company.

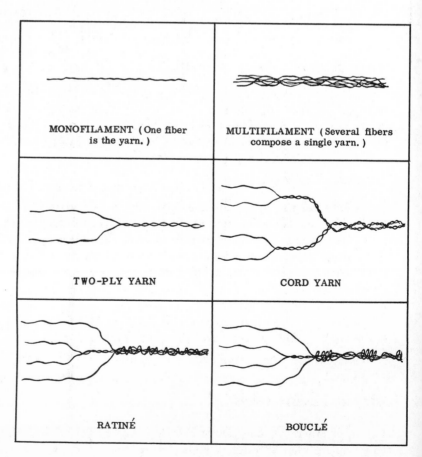

**Figure 3.4.** Drawings of yarns.

cotton or wool. Bouclé is used in knitted sweaters, both knitted and woven dresses, and upholstery fabrics. Ratiné is similar in construction to bouclé, but the loops are twisted continuously and are not spaced.

2. *Chenille* is a term derived from the French for "caterpillar." It refers to a special soft, lofty yarn with pile protruding on all sides. Wool (worsted) is generally blended with other fibers. This type of chenille yarn is used for knitted outerwear. In coarser yarns, chenille is used to obtain prominent surface effects in coats and suits. A more common type of chenille yarn, often called *chenille fur*, is used for chenille rugs. (See Chapter 19.)

3. *Metallic yarn* is metal foil of steel, aluminum, gold, or silver, coated on both sides with plain or plastic colored film, and then cut into narrow strips. Metallic yarns coated with plastic do not tarnish. Recent metallic yarns have been produced by bonding aluminum foil between two clear layers of plastic film. This is called the *foil* type of yarn. A second kind, called the *metallized* type, uses a layer of polyester film (Mylar) treated with vaporized metal that is subsequently bonded between two clear layers of film. Polypropylene, acetate, and cellophane films may also be used. For colors other than silver, color pigment can be added to the bonding adhesive. The quality of these two types of metallic yarn depends on the type of clear film used, plus the resistance it and the adhesives have to stretching and wet processing. To provide strength and to prevent stretching, these yarns are often wrapped with nylon or high-tenacity rayon (Fortisan).[4]

4. *Nub yarn* is made by twisting one end around another many times within a short space, causing enlarged places (nubs) on the surface of the yarn. Sometimes a binder is used to hold the nub in place. Nubs are generally spaced at varied intervals. Nub yarns are sometimes called knap yarns.

5. *Paper yarns*[5] are made by slitting and wet-twisting paper to form individual strands of yarn, and then are knitted or woven like other yarns. Since these yarns have strength, they are suitable for bagging, fiber rugs, automobile seat covers, hats, and handbags.[6]

6. *Plastic yarns* are coated yarns made of natural or synthetic fibers that have been dipped into a protective coating of plastic.

7. *Splash yarn* is really an elongated nub that has been tightly twisted about a base yarn. A *seed yarn* is a very small nub, often made of man-made yarns applied to a dyed or natural base yarn.

8. *Slub* is a soft, elongated nub. The yarn forming the slub may be

---

[4] "Metallic Yarns," *Textile Fibers and Their Properties* (a pamphlet), by Burlington Industries, Inc., 1968.

[5] These yarns should not be confused with nonwoven cloth. See Chapter 2, p. 32.

[6] See *fiber rugs*, Chapter 19.

**Figure 3.5.** Shantung, showing slub fillings. (*Photo by Jack Pitkin.*)

continuous or may be made of tufts of roving inserted at intervals between binder yarns.

9. *Textured yarn* is a general term applied to any filament yarn that has been geometrically modified or otherwise altered to change its basic characteristics. Texturizing is basically a simple concept. A chemical fiber, such as nylon, polyester, or acrylic, is in its molten state forced through holes in a thimble-like device (spinneret) and emerges as a long, smooth filament. Chemical fibers are thermoplastic (heat can make them malleable). Therefore these smooth, rodlike filaments can be deformed by twisting or crimping and then permanently crimped by applying heat (heat-set). As a result, these fibers have "loft," bulk, dimension, and hand—a character more nearly resembling that of the natural fibers they may simulate. Textured yarns are made by mechanical or chemical methods as follows:

### MECHANICAL METHODS

*a. Classical or three-stage method.* This is the oldest technique; it was developed by the Heberlein Company in Switzerland. There are three stages in production:

1. Twisting of the yarn
2. Heat-setting the yarn in its twisted form
3. Untwisting the yarn

Such yarns are bulky. They have loft but only a small amount of stretch (10 to 15 per cent). Familiar brands of yarn made by this method are the original Helanca and Cheveux D'Ange (Billion & Cie, France).

*b. False twist.* This process is essentially the same as the classical process but is a refinement, since it is continuous in operation. (See Figure 3.7.) Notice the false-twist spindle. This is the most-used process

"Conventional" Helanca stretch nylon yarn.

A typical "false-twist" type stretch nylon yarn.

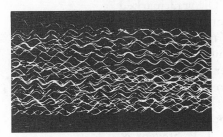
Miralon gear crimped nylon yarn.

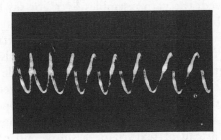
Agilon (crimped type) nylon monofil yarn.

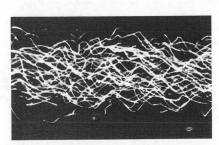
Spunize textured yarn nylon.

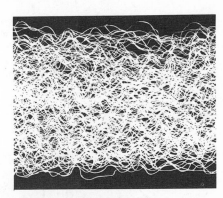
Producer textured "Blue C" nylon yarn.

Knit-de-knit textured nylon yarn.

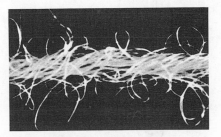
Taslan textured nylon yarn.

**Figure 3.6.** Basic methods of texturizing yarn. (*Courtesy of Monsanto Company.*)

in the world. The same basic false-twist process produces both a set and a stretch yarn. Actually, the stretch yarn is simpler to produce because it is made in three stages: twist, set, and untwist. The set yarn is made in four stages: twist, set, untwist, and heating to stabilize or destroy the twist in the yarn. Trademarked names of stretch yarn of the false-twist type are Fluflon, Superloft, and some Helanca. A similar duo-twist process, which uses no spindle, makes a yarn with a lower twist. Two yarns are then twisted together, heat-set, separated, and wound on individual cones.

*c. Crimped yarns.* In one method, yarns are made by a stuffer-box technique. Straight filaments are "stuffed" tightly into a heated box. When removed, the yarn resembles a "v" or sawtooth. The trademarked Ban-Lon fabrics are produced by this Textralizing process, which is licensed by Joseph Bancroft & Sons Co. The Textured Yarn Co. of Philadelphia produces its Tycora by this method. This is a bulky, lofted yarn —not a stretch yarn. Uses of the yarns include women's dress fabrics, sweaters, and men's knitted sport shirts. "Spunized" yarns by the Spunize Co. of America (Hartford Spinning) are crimped by the teeth of two heated gears which mesh, so that the configuration of the yarn is like the gear teeth. Instead of texturizing a single end of yarn, J. P. Stevens & Co., Inc., texturizes a multiple number of ends in warp formation. The

**Figure 3.7.** (a) This figure shows schematically how a false twister is used to produce stretch yarn. (b) Yarn is twisted above the false twister, it is heat set and relaxed while in the twisted condition, and then completely untwisted as it leaves the false twister. A continuous, delicate balance is maintained wherein downstream twist exactly cancels upstream twist. (*Courtesy of Textile World.*)

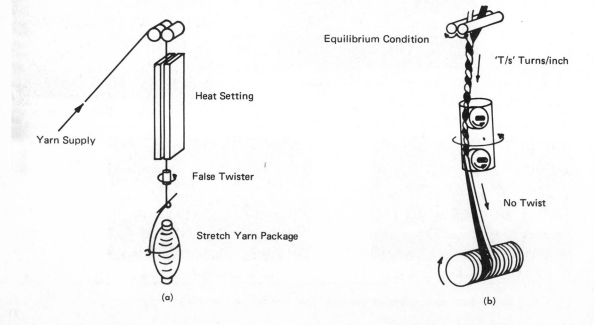

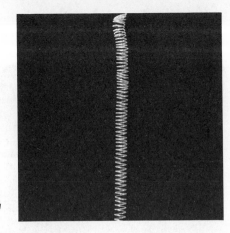

**Figure 3.8.** Monofilament Agilon yarn. *(Photograph courtesy of Deering Milliken Research Corp.)*

crimping process therefore makes the crimps uniform throughout the length of these warp yarns. Crimps per inch can be varied according to the end use. Blouse, pajama, dress, and tricot lingerie fabrics may be made with these yarns.

*d. Knit de-Knit.* Any hand knitter has had the experience of unraveling her work. The raveled yarn resembles a rounded sawtooth. The steps in the process include three stages in one continuous operation:

1. Knitting of a tubular fabric
2. Heat-setting the fabric
3. De-knitting (unraveling) the fabric

This method does not make a stretch yarn. A crepe or bouclé textured fabric results from this technique. Brand names are Bucaroni and Antron Crinkle.

*e. Curled or edge-crimped yarns.* The filament passes over a heated blade that causes alternate surfaces of the yarn to be flattened, much as one curls a ribbon by running it over the blade of a scissors. Curled yarns, which have moderate stretch, are produced chiefly under a license from Deering Milliken Research Corporation, with the trademark Agilon. They are used primarily for women's nylon hosiery.

*f. Air-bulked (air-jet) or looped yarns.* A filament yarn is subjected to an air jet that blows a number of loops per inch into the individual filaments, both on the surface and in the *yarn bundle.* Textures of smooth, silky, or worsted-like textures, as well as woolen and heavy chenille types, can be achieved. Core and effect yarns are obtainable under the registered trademark Taslan by du Pont. The yarn so formed does not have stretch properties, but it has increased bulk and texture not unlike spun yarn. Another brand name for air-jet yarns is Skyloft, by American Enka.

*g. Thick and thin yarns.* Yarns of varying diameters are produced by varying the diameters of man-made fibers. (See Chapter 12.)

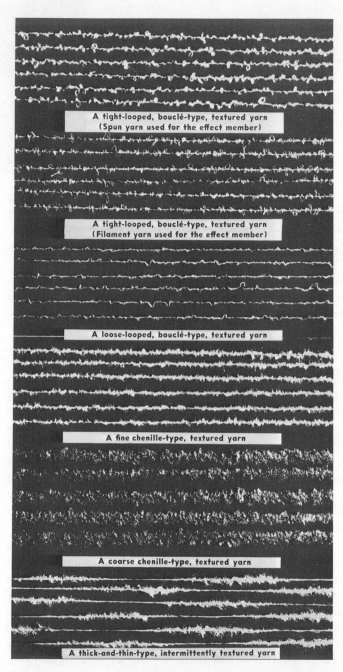

**Figure 3.9.** Examples of Taslan textured specialty yarns produced from continuous filament yarns (note exception at top) by multi-end texturing. (*Photograph courtesy of E.I. du Pont de Nemours & Company, Inc.*)

In the mechanical processes described, texturizing depended on twisting and the application of heat, the exception being the thick and thin yarns. In some instances, texturizing is chemical. Generally two polymers with different ratios of shrinkage are used. Upon the application of heat, one polymer shrinks more than the other, thus crimping the whole yarn. Since texturizing is done at the source, it is said to be "producer-textured." A yarn of this type is Cantrece, made by du Pont.

## MERITS, PROBLEMS, AND USES OF TEXTURED YARNS

Bulked-yarn fabrics are more comfortable than fabrics made from filament yarn. Bulked-nylon fabrics, for example, tend to approach the general physical characteristics of cotton and wool staple knit fabrics with respect to thickness, weight, opacity, density, packing factor, surface characteristics, and thermal conductivity. Some men may remember the coldness and clamminess of the first filament nylon shirts. Synthetic yarns now used in woven shirts are often textured.

Furthermore, in addition to improved comfort, textured yarns have a better appearance; better resistance to pilling (unless filaments break); greater durability and evenness; and improved covering power because of their bulk. Problems of fuzzing from abrasion, matting, or breaking of the filaments, which may result in pilling, have confronted the technician.

The quality of textured yarn has improved owing to the increase in production speed and the continuous and automatic processing from start to finish. These improvements are noted in the texturizing equipment of the United States, France, the United Kingdom, Germany, Italy, and Japan. Some of the most recent machines cost as much as $60,000 each.[7]

The "converter" of man-made fibers has reached a new and higher status. He is the throwster who used to be a twister of silk. Now he twists continuous-filament man-made fibers. Originally he performed only a commission service, but now he is responsible for custom designing of yarns for specific markets. His goal is variety and flexibility of the products. A quick glance at the list on p. 76 will indicate the increasing use of textured yarns and a reason why the U.S. throwster's volume has grown from $10 million to some $500 million in 1967–68, and why there are a dozen customers for every pound of textured yarn produced.[8]

A bright future seems indicated for textured yarns. There are new markets in men's knitted suits, children's wear, outer wear, and textured tricot and full-fashioned knits. Textured polyesters, so important in

[7] *American Fabrics*, summer 1968, p. 72.
[8] *Ibid.*, pp. 74–75.

| 1953–54 | men's hosiery |
| 1956–57 | women's swim wear |
| 1957–58 | women's tights |
| 1959 | Crimplene launched in England |
| 1960 | Pucci stretch pants |
| 1961 | textured acetate knit dresses |
| 1962 | stretch denims as staples |
| 1965 | advent of pantyhose |
| 1966 | printed nylon tricot dresses, textured stockings |
| 1967–68 | boom in set polyester double knits |

England, and "set" yarns have potential. The problem lies in meeting the demand for textured yarns.

## STRETCH YARNS IN FABRICS

Stretch yarns have the ability to extend and recover rather than remain rigid. Stretch garments are akin to skin. Just as our skin moves freely as we bend or twist, so do stretch garments move with the body. Nonstretch garments may be so rigid as to be uncomfortable because they constrict bodily movements.

Fabrics, then, are made to stretch for three reasons: comfort, control, and fashion. Freedom of movement is desirable in active sportswear, in suit jackets, and in straight skirts. For foundation garments, ski pants, and swimsuits, body control or support is needed. For a trim, slim, sleek look in ski pants, jumpsuits, and slacks, fashion plays an important role.

Stretch yarn can be used in warp, in filling, or in both directions. The warp stretch yarns give in the vertical direction; the filling in the horizontal; warp and filling in both directions (two-way).

Stretch woven fabrics, which originated in Europe in the early 1950's, were used principally for ski pants. Originally they were made of Helanca yarn with stretch nylon warp and acrylic filling. In 1960, Pucci, the Italian designer, introduced sportswear made of a fabric with stretch nylon warp and silk Dupioni filling. The stretch concept grew in importance. But with the advent of durable press, stretch was eclipsed for a time. However, durable press has helped to bring back stretch. Pants manufacturers added stretch to their durable press offerings. A men's shirt manufacturer employed stretch as a durable press principle in his use of stretch batistes for shirts. Another manufacturer added all-rayon stretch dresses to his line. With the increased use of textured yarns, many of which are of the stretch type, an upward trend in stretch fabrics is evidenced.

Why do fabrics stretch? A yarn made in loop formation, as in knitting, makes a stretchy fabric. Stretch may be imparted to woven fabrics at the fiber, yarn, or fabric stages.

*a. Fiber stage.* Elastomeric fibers such as rubber or spandex are fibers that stretch. Natural rubber was one of the first materials used to give stretch in clothing. The familiar trade name Lastex is still in use. Other trade names include Buthane, Contro, Darleen, Filatex, Hi-Flex, Lactron,

Laton, and Revere. Rubber deteriorates from exposure to oxygen in the air, continuous flexing, chlorine, salt water, sunlight, contact with bodily oil, perspiration, cosmetics, and repeated laundering. Rubber's usage includes surgical supports, tops of men's socks, support hosiery, bindings, foundation garments, swimsuits, trimmings, and sewing thread.

Spandex, a man-made polyurethane fiber, has supplanted rubber for many uses. Its stretchability is comparable to rubber. It is one-third lighter in weight than rubber, and twice as strong. Hence it can be made much finer—a reason why fabrics of spandex are lighter and more sheer with the same control features and stretch properties as fabrics made with rubber. Furthermore, Spandex is unaffected by sunlight, water, most oils and oil-based cosmetics, salt water, and dry cleaning agents. However, white spandex may yellow in usage, and chlorine bleach may degrade and yellow the fiber quickly and severely. Trade names of spandex fibers include Blue "C," Lycra, Numa, and Vyrene.

Spandex and rubber, covered or uncovered, may be woven or knitted into fabrics. Uncovered yarns give good elasticity but an undesirable rubbery feel to the fabric. When spandex is used as the core of a yarn, with other fibers wrapped spirally around it, the yarn has considerable stretch, a bulkier hand, and a more pleasant feel than uncovered yarns. Core spun yarn, as these covered yarns are called, are used in such fabrics as batiste, flannel, gabardine, lace, poplin, seersucker, taffeta, and twills. Yarns stretch about 25 to 40 per cent on the average in these fabrics.

The T.F.P.I.A. has been amended to allow "the disclosure of any fiber present in a textile product which has clearly established definite functional significance." Prior to the amendment, the act required that all fibers constituting over 5 per cent of a fabric be listed on the label or hangtag according to the generic name. Frequently a small percentage of spandex in a yarn was unidentified. Since as little as 1 per cent spandex in a yarn gives stretch, it is highly desirable to have the generic name specified.

*b. Yarn stage.* It has been noted that some of the classical or three-stage textured yarns may stretch; that the false-twist method is the dominant stretch-yarn process in use today; and that the curled or edge-crimped technique develops a certain degree of stretch in the yarn. Uses for heat-set stretch yarn include infants' wear, ski wear, lingerie, sportswear, and swimsuits.

*c. Fabric stage.* The simplest and least expensive method for imparting stretch in woven fabrics

**Figure 3.10.** Test for woven stretch fabrics. After working stretch level is determined, fabrics are tensioned at proper level for two hours on the Extension Tester. (*Courtesy of American Institute of Laundering.*)

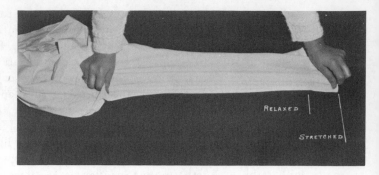

**Figure 3.11.** Sleeve of shirt manufactured of stretch fabric containing Polyester, cotton and spandex. (*Courtesy of American Institute of Laundering.*)

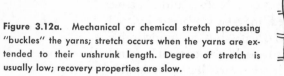

**Figure 3.12a.** Mechanical or chemical stretch processing "buckles" the yarns; stretch occurs when the yarns are extended to their unshrunk length. Degree of stretch is usually low; recovery properties are slow.

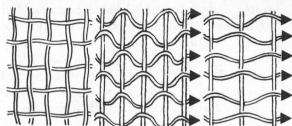

**Figure 3.12b.** Twist texturing induces a coil or crimp in filament yarns. Yarns then provide stretch characteristics to the woven or knit fabric. Degree of stretch is both high and long-lasting.

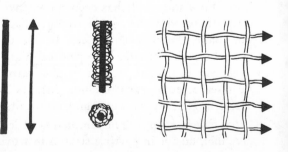

**Figure 3.12c.** Core-spun yarns incorporate the stretch of a core of Lycra spandex inside a bundle of staple fibers. Performance and esthetics are those of the covering yarn; the stretch is high, recovery properties are strong and permanent. (*Photographs courtesy of E.I. du Pont de Nemours & Company, Inc.*)

is called "slack mercerization." In Chapter 2, mercerization was described as a treatment of cotton yarns or fabrics under tension in a bath of caustic soda. When only warp yarns are held in tension in a bath of caustic soda, the loosely held filling yarns shrink. This shrinkage is permanently set by a chemical treatment that provides stretch and recovery properties ranging from 13 to 22 per cent beyond its finished width. To be sure, this range is lower than stretch from elastomeric fibers and heat-set yarns. Also, recovery is said to diminish with wear and repeated laundering. Stretch levels for different end uses will be discussed in Chapter 16. The care of stretch fabrics will be considered in Chapter 15.

For wool, one process employs special spinning, weaving, and finishing techniques and the use of chemicals to increase the wool fiber's natural crimp—a method similar to permanent waving.[9] It has been found that two-ply stretch worsted yarns having 92 to 105 per cent stretch were produced by the twist, set, and untwist method with setting done in the wet state at a temperature of 212° F. or higher. A resin application on the yarn prior to untwisting in order to make the yarn shrink-resistant results in a significant increase in the amount of stretch obtained in a laboratory test.[10]

## CLASSIFICATION OF YARNS ACCORDING TO USE

Yarns may be divided into two classifications according to their use: weaving yarns and knitting yarns.

### WEAVING YARNS

Yarns to be used for warp, the lengthwise direction of a cloth, are generally stronger, tighter twist, smoother, and more even than filling yarns (crosswise yarns in a cloth).

### KNITTING YARNS

These may be divided into yarns for hand knitting and yarns for machine knitting. Knitting yarns are more slackly twisted than yarns for weaving. Hand-knitting yarns are generally ply, whereas those for machine knitting can be either single or ply. The following are some of the yarns that are used for hand knitting:

1. *Baby yarns.* Yarns of 100 per cent wool or wool and rayon in light or medium weight for infants' garments.
2. *Dress yarns.* Plain or novelty yarns in all-wool, blends, or mixtures with cottons and rayons.
3. *Fingering yarns.* Two- or three-ply, light and medium weight, smooth, even diameter for children's and other apparel.
4. *Germantown.* Soft wool, medium weight for women's and children's sweaters and blankets.

---

[9] Plus X is a process that uses chemicals to increase wool fiber's natural crimp.
[10] *American Dyestuff Reporter*, December 18, 1967.

5. *Shetland floss.* Soft, lightweight, fluffy yarn for infants' and children's sweaters.
6. *Sock yarns.* Especially spun wool or nylon yarn for knitting socks.
7. *Worsted* (knitting). Soft, well-twisted, heavy wool yarn for sweaters; very strong and durable.
8. *Zephyr yarns.* Very fine, soft, 100 per cent new wool yarns for lightweight garments.

Special yarns are also sold for hand embroidery. Embroidery floss is a slack or medium-twisted ply or cord-type yarn. For darning, softly spun yarn is wound on spools, balls, or cards.

## WHAT IS THREAD?

The chief difference between yarn and thread lies in the method of twisting strands together. If a six-cord cotton thread is to be made, six strands of yarn are twisted together. Each strand is balanced in twist and the finished thread approximates a perfect circle in cross section. Like yarn, thread is inspected and reeled into hanks.

In hank form, thread can be mercerized, bleached, or dyed. It is then wound on spools, inspected, and boxed.

A good thread must be (1) even in diameter, to move under tension easily and quickly through the eye of the needle; (2) smooth, to resist friction caused by sewing; (3) strong enough to hold seams firmly in laundering and in use; and (4) elastic enough to make stitches that will not break or pucker.

Sewing threads are made of cotton, linen, silk, rayon, nylon, and polyester. The size of cotton and linen thread is indicated on the end of the spool. As we have already mentioned, the higher the number, the finer the thread. For special uses such as luggage, shoes, carpets, bookbinding, gloves, umbrellas, upholstery, and awnings, special sewing threads are made. Special thread called *buttonhole twist* is made for buttonholes. Just a few yards of thread are wound on a spool for this purpose. Special thread in gold is made for crocheting and tatting.

Research has revealed that apparel made from water-repellent fabrics gives the wearer better protection when the seams are sewed with a thread that has been made water repellent.

Nylon thread is recommended for nylon fabrics, but other threads may be used. A nylon thread is difficult to break and should be cut with scissors. A cut thread is easier to put through the eye of a needle and will avoid pulled seams. It should be remembered that fewer stitches to the inch can be made when sewing nylon. On tightly woven fabrics as few as seven stitches to the inch may be used. Nylon's strength makes a long stitch possible.

The type of yarns used has an effect on the fabric's texture, hand, warmth, weight, resiliency, durability, and luster.

Specifications for a particular yarn are determined by the fabric's end use. Ply yarns, for instance, are desirable in men's broadcloth shirts, in tropical worsted suitings, and in women's cotton voile dresses. In the first two uses, ply yarns give strength to the fabrics; in the third use, ply yarns in tight voile twist give the characteristic thready feel of voile and also give strength.

Yarns differ in weight and fineness, and in sheerness, smoothness, fuzziness, nubbiness, and elasticity—all varied to create qualities required in the final fabric.

Yarns may be classified according to their structure (single or ply, direction of twist, size or count), or according to how they are used (as warp, filling, or other purposes). The present text has considered two classifications: (1) ordinary yarns; and (2) novelty yarns (including textured and stretch yarns).

There have been innumerable pluses built into stretch fabrics. Therefore stretch should be a plus factor and not a sole selling point. Stretch fabrics should be used only where its properties are genuinely useful and beneficial to the consumer. The degree of stretch must be adequate to the function.

## REVIEW QUESTIONS

1. (*a*) Define: core yarn, textured yarn, solution-dyed yarn, Germantown yarn, bouclé yarn.
   (*b*) Describe the methods of making textured yarn. Give a trade name of each type.
2. (*a*) What yarns are carded?
   (*b*) What yarns are combed?
   (*c*) Give the advantages of combed cotton yarns.
   (*d*) What are the differences between woolen and worsted yarns?
3. (*a*) To what types of yarn is the word "spun" applicable?
   (*b*) For what purposes are spun nylon yarns used?
   (*c*) What are some advantages and drawbacks of stretch yarns in woven fabrics?
4. (*a*) In what ways does twist affect the yarn?
   (*b*) Of what value is it to know the number of turns to the inch?
   (*c*) What is meant by an S twist? a Z twist?
   (*d*) Of what value is it to know direction of twist?
5. Explain the terms:
   (*a*) Count of yarn
   (*b*) Denier
   (*c*) Monofilament yarn
   (*d*) Multifilament yarn

6. Which is finer yarn, 30 denier or 15 denier? Explain your answer.
7. Which is finer, 100s cotton yarn or 150s cotton yarn? Why?
8. (*a*) What are novelty yarns?
   (*b*) What effect have they on the finished cloth?
9. (*a*) How are metallic yarns made?
   (*b*) What is the purpose of metallic yarn?
10. (*a*) How are yarns used?
    (*b*) What are the differences between thread and yarn?

## EXPERIMENT

1. Using the technique for identification of yarns given in this chapter, take yarns from the following fabrics:

   (*a*) Dress satin
   (*b*) Brocade
   (*c*) Shantung
   (*d*) Donegal tweed
   (*e*) Tropical worsted
   (*f*) Stretch corduroy or stretch denim
   (*g*) Silk organza
   (*h*) Fiberglas marquisette
   (*i*) Sailcloth
   (*j*) Linen crash

   Answer the following for each yarn:
   (*a*) Regular or novelty yarn?
   (*b*) If regular, indicate:
      1. Single or ply
      2. Carded or combed, hackled
      3. Spun or filament, reeled
   (*c*) If novelty, indicate:
      1. Name of yarn
      2. How made

## GLOSSARY

**Air-bulked yarn.**  A textured yarn that is made by subjecting the filaments to air jets, which blow loops both on the surface of the yarn and in the *yarn bundle*.

**Blended yarn.**  A strand of fibers produced from two or more constituent fibers that have been thoroughly mixed (blended) before spinning.

**Bouclé yarn.**  A novelty yarn characterized by tight loops projecting from the body of the yarn at fairly regular intervals.

**Bulky yarn.**  A yarn that has been textured to give it bulk without increasing weight.

**Cable cord.**  The result of twisting singles together in various directions of twist, such as S/Z/S or Z/S/Z. See S *twist* and Z *twist*.

**Carding.**  An operation in yarn-making that separates the fibers and puts them in a filmy sheet called a sliver.

**Chenille yarn.**  A soft, lofty yarn, somewhat rough in texture. See *Chenille fur,* Chapter 19.

**Combination yarn.**  A ply yarn composed of two or more single yarns of the same or different fibers or twists.

**Combing.**  An operation in yarn making that makes the fibers parallel in the sliver and removes the shorter fibers.

**Construction.**  The way a cloth is fabricated. Construction includes weaving, knitting, felting, knotting, bonding, braiding, laminating, and so on.

**Continuous filament.**  See *Filament yarns*.

**Cord.**  The result of twisting together ply yarns in a third twisting operation.

**Count of yarn.**  Size of yarn as distinguished by its weight and fineness. This term is applied to cotton, wool, and spun yarns.

**Crimped yarn.**  A textured yarn made from man-made fibers that have been crimped to resemble wool.

**Curled yarn.**  A textured yarn made by a heated blade that "curls" the filaments.

**Denier.**  Size of silk and filament man-made yarns. See *Count*.

**Double and twist yarn.**  A two-ply yarn made from single yarns of different colors. A mottled effect is produced.

**Durable press.**  A measure of garment performance. Features include (1) shape retention; (2) durable pleats and pressed creases; (3) durably smooth seams; (4) machine washability and dryability; (5) wrinkle resistance; (6) fresh appearance without ironing.

**Filament yarns.**  Made of long continuous man-made fibers.

**Fingering yarns.**  Light, medium weight, two- or three-ply yarns for hand knitting.

**Frill or spiral yarns.**  A corkscrew effect produced by twisting together a fine and a coarse yarn.

**Hackling.**  The process by which flax is prepared for yarn.

**Hand.**  The feel of a fabric. See *Texture*.

**Hawser cord.**  The result of twisting together singles with various directions of twists.

**Lea.**  Size of linen yarn. See *Count of yarn* and *Denier*.

**Line yarn.**  Well-hackled, even linen yarn made of long fibers.

**Loop yarn.**  The slack-twisted strand is twisted to form loops or curls. This strand is held in place by one or two binder yarns.

**Metallic yarn.**  Metal foil either wrapped around natural or synthetic yarn or coated on both sides with plain or plastic-covered film cut into strips.

**Monofilament yarn.**  A yarn made of one filament (as in nylon hosiery).

**Multifilament yarn.**  A yarn consisting of a number of filaments.

**Novelty yarns.**  Yarns made on a special twisting machine by combining various types of yarns in various ways.

**Nub yarn.**  Enlarged places (nubs) on the surface of a yarn caused by twisting one end of yarn around another many times within a short space.

**Paper yarn.**  A strand made of paper that is slit and twisted in web form.

**Permanent press.**  See *Durable press*.

**Plastic-coated yarns.**  Made of natural or synthetic fibers that have been dipped into a coating of plastic.

**Ply yarn.**  Composed of two or more single yarns twisted together.

**Raw Silk.**  Reeled silk wound directly from several cocoons with only a slight twist.

**Reeling.**  Winding of silk filaments directly from cocoons.

**S twist.**  A left-hand twisted yarn.

**Seed yarn.** A very small nub often made of dyed man-made fibers applied to a dyed or natural-base yarn.

**Sheath-core yarn.** A very bulky yarn of synthetic fibers consisting of a core of fine denier fibers with considerable shrinkage and a cover or wrapping of coarse denier relaxed fibers.

**Single yarn.** One strand of fibers or filaments grouped or twisted together.

**Sliver.** A filmy sheet of fibers resulting from carding. See *Carding*.

**Slub.** An elongated nub. Slub yarn is identified by its elongated nubs.

**Solution dye.** Dyestuffs are put into the viscous solution before fibers are hardened.

**Space-dyed yarns.** Those yarns that have been dipped in dye or spotted in various places along the yarn.

**Spinning.** The process of drawing and twisting fibers together into yarns or thread.

**Spiral.** See *Frill yarns*.

**Splash yarn.** An elongated nub yarn that has been tightly twisted about a base yarn.

**Spun yarn.** A yarn twisted by spinning; also yarn composed of man-made staple fibers.

**Stretch yarn.** A textured yarn that has good stretch and recovery. It may also refer to yarns made of fibers that have elastic properties or to those yarns whose elastic properties are obtained by alterations of the basic fiber.

**Texture.** The surface effect of a fabric; that is, stiffness, roughness, smoothness, softness, fineness, dullness, and luster. See *Hand*.

**Textured yarn.** Any filament yarn that has been geometrically modified or otherwise altered to change its basic characteristics.

**Thick and thin yarn.** Produced by varying the diameters of man-made fibers.

**Thread.** A special type of tightly twisted ply yarn used for sewing.

**Throwing.** The combining and twisting of strands of reeled silk into tightly twisted yarn.

**Tow.** Poorly hackled, uneven linen yarn made of short fibers. It may also refer to strands of continuous filaments to be cut in lengths for spun yarn.

**Turns.** See *Twist*.

**Twist.** The number of times (turns) one inch of yarn is twisted.

**Woolen yarn.** A carded yarn made of relatively short fibers of varying lengths.

**Worsted yarn.** A combed yarn made of long-staple wool fibers.

**Yarn dyed.** Yarn that is colored (dyed) before it is woven into cloth.

**Z twist.** A right-hand twisted yarn.

**Zephyr yarn.** Very fine, soft, 100 per cent new wool hand-knitting yarns.

# 4

# The Basic Weaves:

## PLAIN, TWILL,
## AND SATIN

When a customer sends a garment with a hole burned in it to be re-woven, she is often astounded by the price she must pay. She does not realize that the reweaver must match the yarns exactly and must make an entirely new cloth in the same woven-in pattern as the original. The reweaver must do a very high-quality darning job. First, he puts in the up-and-down yarns (warps or ends) spaced the same distance apart as the fabric's warps, then he works in the crosswise yarn (filling) over and under the exact number of warp yarns required to match the pattern.

Like the reweaving of a small hole, whole cloth (fabric by the yard) is woven with two sets of yarns (warps and fillings) interlacing at right angles. *Weaving*, then, is the process of interlacing two sets of yarns at right angles. This operation is done either on a hand or a power loom. If one set of yarns forms loops—one loop caught into another and one row of loops hanging on the one below—the cloth is made by *knitting*.

Weaving and knitting are two processes of making cloth. Weaving is the most common method, although recently knitting has become more important because new and improved knitting machines make cloth more quickly, more satisfactorily, and with more attractive patterns.

The principles of weaving were known to primitive man. He knew how to make baskets and mats by interlacing twigs, reeds, and grasses. But these fibers were long and required no spinning into yarn. Man learned later how to twist together short fibers, such as wool and cotton, to form yarn; and woven cloths for clothing and home use were made on a *loom*.

The first hand loom was crude. It is chronicled that *warp* yarns—the lengthwise yarns in a fabric—were suspended from a limb of a tree and held in tension by stone weights at the ends near the ground. The loom of the American Navajo Indian shows warp yarns tied between two sticks. In less primitive looms a wooden frame was made to hold the warps; when strung parallel in this frame, they resembled the slats of a bed.

In early looms the crosswise yarns, or *fillings*, were carried over and under each of the warp yarns (as is done in darning). A sharpened stick was used for this purpose. Greater speed in weaving was attained when the *harness* (composed of *heddles*) was developed. It was found that the filling yarn could be interlaced with the warps much more quickly if each warp yarn could be separated automatically so that the fillings could be shot through. This separation is done by the harness, and the operation is called *shedding*.

The hand loom in Figure 4.1, equipped with four harnesses, is designed to weave a variety of articles, such as neckties, collars, cuffs, belts, garters, table mats, and shopping bags. It has an extremely simple mechanism and can be operated by an amateur.

This loom is constructed like an inverted letter "T." The *bottom frame*

Figure 4.1. Four-harness loom. (Photograph courtesy of Structo Manufacturing Company.)

corresponds to the crossing of the "T." The *main upright frame* is placed at the middle of the bottom frame and perpendicular to it. There are four harnesses (four frames suspended from the main upright frame). These frames hold a series of wires called heddles, each of which has an eye like that of a needle.

The cylindrical spool, called a *warp beam*, at the back of the loom holds warp yarns. To prepare the loom for weaving, the warp yarns are passed (1) up over the *breast beam* (the bar just above the spool of warp); (2) through the eyes of the heddles; (3) through the *reed* or swinging frame in front of the heddles; (4) over a breast beam in front of the loom; and (5) around a cylinder, called *a cloth beam* or *merchandise beam*, to which they are attached. When a portion of material has been woven, it is wound on the cloth beam. If a cloth is several yards long, the entire yardage of warp yarns cannot be in tension on the loom at once; accordingly the rest of the warp is wound on the warp beam, which unwinds at the speed the cloth is woven.

Just below the nameplate in Figure 4.1 are four hooks, each suspended from an arm of a lever at the upper right of the main upright frame. Each hook is attached to the upper bar of one of the heddle frames or harnesses. Each heddle, or flattened wire, suspended between the upper and lower bars of the harness, controls the warp yarn that is threaded through its eye. The purpose of the harness is to raise groups of warps to form a shed so that the shuttle can be passed through the separate warps. Figure 4.1 also shows the *shed*.

To make the plain weave, a two-harness loom is sufficient. The weaving method, if a two-harness loom is used, is as follows: warps 1, 3, 5, 7, 9, and so on are threaded through the heddles of one harness, and warps 2, 4, 6, 8, 10, and so on are threaded through the heddles of the other harness.

The reed frame located directly in front of the harnesses swings forward to beat the last filling inserted against the previous fillings in order to make a compact construction.

A two-harness loom can make only a plain weave or its variations. Looms with more heddle frames are necessary for more elaborate weaves in which more than two combinations of warp yarns must be raised. A simple twill weave may be made with a four-harness loom. Some looms have as many as twelve harnesses.

All woven cloth is made on some kind of loom. Power looms have supplanted the hand looms and have taken weaving from the home into the factory. Intricate designs, once considered masterpieces of the hand loom, can now be duplicated quickly and inexpensively by machinery.

## THE SHUTTLELESS LOOM

A recent development is the shuttleless loom, which carries the filling yarns through the shed by the use of rapiers, grippers, air jets, or water jets. The rapier and the gripper shuttle systems were established some time ago; they are broad looms that carry filling yarn from outside the loom, as opposed to the conventional shuttle looms that contain their own supply of filling within themselves. Some would argue that a loom with a carrier or projecting part extending through the warp shed is not a shuttleless loom. The present text will include these two systems as well as the newer jet looms. One machine, manufactured in Spain by Maquinaria Textil del Norte de España, South America, is now available in the United States from the American Iwer Corporation. This machine weaves with any kind of yarn. It produces upholstery, worsted and curtain fabrics, burlap, blankets, shirtings and linings, dress goods, automotive materials, decorative fabrics, and domestics (common cotton cloth, such as sheeting). It can weave up to eight different yarns and colors. No separate bobbin winding machinery is required. French shuttleless looms (MAV weaving machines—Société Alsacienne de Constructions Mécaniques) combines some of the best technology of two continents in specialty weaving.[1]

[1] *Textile World,* June 1968, p. 51.

**Figure 4.2.** A Model 1500 Iwer shuttleless loom weaving two fabrics at once. The fabrics in this particular illustration are jute. (*Photograph courtesy of American Iwer Corporation.*)

A Pennsylvania weaver has installed twenty-four French-built shuttle-less looms, 71 inches wide. They are said to be far less noisy than the conventional loom and speedier (210 picks per minute compared with 110 p.p.m. on conventional shuttle looms). Each loom equipped with two Jacquards produces weave patterns twice as long as one conventional Jacquard, without repeats. The card pattern for the machine is smaller, and it is easier to cut and store than the conventional Jacquard.[2] These looms, 54 and 71 inches wide, are used for dress goods; men's dinner jackets, cummerbunds, and neckties; and ultramodern draperies. However, at the terrific speed that the filling streaks through the tension devices, heat and friction occur. A replacement of the rapier-like needle ends that hold the end of the filling is required at times.

In addition to Spain and France, the following countries have shuttle-less looms in operation: West Germany, Switzerland, Japan, Czecho-slovakia, Italy, England, Belgium, Ireland, Sweden, Canada, and the United States.

In 1967 the Draper Corporation had some 6,000 shuttleless looms in mills in the United States. These looms make six loom widths: 40, 44, 50, 64, 82, and 90 inches.[3]

The textile industry's progress in the newer shuttleless looms will come gradually as new looms are installed and improvements in loom motions and parts are made. An important advantage of these new looms is their speed, which increases production and hence profits. Greater profits, in turn, mean higher wages. Also, women prefer to work in the quieter weave rooms.

[2] See Chapter 5, p. 117.
[3] *Textile World*, August 1966.

**Figure 4.3.** A Model 1800 Iwer shuttleless loom utilizing a Jacquard head to weave a blanket material in eight colors. (*Photograph courtesy of American Iwer Corporation.*)

The steps in weaving may be summarized as follows:

1. After the warp threads (called *ends*) have been strung into the frame of the loom, the warp yarns are separated. This is the first operation; it is called *shedding*.
2. The filling is carried through the shed. This operation is called *picking*. The term probably originated before the invention of the shuttle and the heddles, when every other warp had to be picked up, as in darning, so that the filling could be passed over and under the warps. Each time the filling is carried across the cloth, one pick is made. A *pick* is synonymous with a *filling*; an *end* is synonymous with a *warp*.
3. Each filling or pick is pushed up against the previous filling. This process is called *battening*.
4. The warp is released from the *warp beam*, and the finished cloth is taken up on the *merchandise beam*. This operation is called *letting off and taking up*.

These operations are repeated over and over again until the cloth is the desired length.

### THE SELVAGES

In yard goods the outer edges are finished so they will not ravel. These finished edges are called the selvages (self-edges) and are often made with heavier and more closely spaced warp yarns than are used in the rest of the fabric. Tape selvages are firmer and wider than plain selvages. For towels, sheets, and drapery and curtain fabrics, tape selvages give added strength to the edges. Selvages vary in width from one-quarter to three-eighths inch. The warp yarns always run parallel to the selvages.

### COUNT OF CLOTH

The yarns used for warp and those used for filling are frequently not of the same diameter; and those used for one dimension may be closer together than those used for the other. Usually there are more warp yarns than filling yarns to the inch, because the strain on a fabric that is being used comes primarily on the warp. Some cloths, like ginghams, are closely woven; others, like voile, are loosely woven. If the cloth is held to the light, the porosity of the fabric or the closeness of the weave can be discerned. Ordinarily, a closely woven fabric keeps its shape better, shrinks less, slips less at seams, and wears longer than a loosely woven cloth of similar texture and weight.

The closeness or looseness of the weave is measured by the count of the cloth. This is determined by the number of picks and ends (warps and fillings) to the square inch. A small pocket magnifying glass, called a *pick glass* or *linen tester*, is used for this purpose. Several warp yarns and several fillings are removed from the cloth. If the fabric is light in color, a piece of black material is put under it, or vice versa. The linen tester is then set against the raveled edge. Since the usual opening in the tester is ¼-inch square, the yarns are counted in this space (first the number of warps, then of fillings). Then the number of the yarns that run each way is multiplied by four to give the count per inch. A pin sometimes helps in separating yarns for counting.

The textile weaving mill does its count of cloth at the loom. An electric-impulse mechanism counts the picks for each of ten looms on each of three shifts of personnel, plus the total picks per loom. Counters (actual counting mechanisms) remote from the loom are now set in a panel with a glass door. These count data are easy to read, encourage competition between shifts, and keep production high.

If the count of the cloth is 80 warps and 80 fillings to the inch, the count is expressed as 80 x 80, or 80 square. If there are 60 warps and 50 fillings to the inch, the count is expressed as 60 x 50. This count is found in a plain gingham of medium quality. The count of surgical gauze is approximately 28 x 24. In a comparison of the two counts, a 96 x 88 cloth is considered the higher-count cloth because it has more picks and ends (warps and fillings) to the square inch than has surgical gauze. There are, then, high-count and low-count cloths.

Since the yarns are closer together in high-count cloths than they are in low-count cloths, there is less danger of the yarns slipping out of place and causing a shreddy effect. Low-count cloths may be woven with only a few yarns to the inch, either to make the fabric lightweight and porous or to cheapen it.

The consumer can test the strength of a weave by gripping two edges of the cloth and, with thumbs close together, pressing the thumbs downward on the cloth as hard as possible, and turning the cloth over as pressure continues. If the fabric gives way when hard pressure is exerted, the cloth will not be durable. Any slipping of yarns will also show weakness in the construction of the fabric, and will make an unsightly, weak seam.

## BALANCE OF CLOTH

The proportion of warp yarns to filling yarns is called the *balance* of a cloth. If the number of warps and the number of fillings to the inch are nearly the same (not more than ten yarns difference), a cloth is said to have good balance. The gingham whose count is 60 x 50 would be considered a fair-balanced cloth. Gauze with a count of 28 x 24 also has a good balance. A sheeting with 61 warp ends and 40 picks (61 x 40) has poor balance because there are too many warps and two few picks. Even though the sheeting is woven in the plain weave, ordinarily a strong construction, there are so few fillings that the warps will slip over them very easily, causing a shredded effect. If this cloth were held to the light, the yarns would seem to run all one way—lengthwise. The cloth count is substandard for a sheeting and is not durable.

Good balance is very important in cloths that have to stand hard wear and many washings. Sheets, pillow slips, and towels for glasses and dishes, for instance, should have good balance. A cloth is not always durable, however, just because it has a balanced count. The count of a cloth may be 58 x 50, which looks like a splendid balance, but the cloth may not prove durable if the warps are only half as coarse and half as strong as the fillings. On the other hand, a cotton broadcloth may have an off-balance count, say 144 x 76 (about twice as many warps as fillings). In this fabric, the fillings are larger than the warps to give a crosswise ridged effect; hence there are fewer fillings than warps to the inch. Better grades of broadcloth have ply warps and single fillings (2 x 1) to make up in tensile strength for the fine warp yarns used. Best grades have both warps and fillings plied (2 x 2). A buyer, then, must consider both the comparative sizes and the tensile strengths of warp and filling yarns. The warp should be the stronger and usually the more tightly twisted.

The count of cloth and the count of yarn should not be confused. The former denotes the number of picks and ends to the square inch; the latter indicates the weight and fineness of the yarn.

## CLASSIFICATION OF WEAVES

The ways in which the filling yarns are interlaced with the warps change the appearance of the fabric and produce many intricate designs that are woven into the cloth. Weaves are named according to the system or design followed in interlacing warp and filling yarns.

The different weaves are named as follows (each weave will be discussed in the order given):

1. plain
2. twill
3. satin
4. pile
5. Jacquard
6. dobby
7. leno or gauze
8. swivel
9. lappet          } ornamental
10. clipped spot   } embroidered
11. schiffli embroidery } effects

## PLAIN WEAVE

In this, the simplest weave, the filling is passed over one warp yarn and under the next, alternating in this manner once across the cloth. The second time across, the filling passes over the warp yarns it went under,

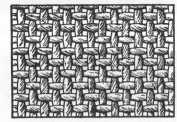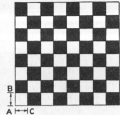

**Figure 4.4.** *Left:* Plain weave, showing interlacement of warp and filling yarns. *Right:* Point paper design for the same construction.

and under the warps it went over on the previous row. The third time across is a repetition of the first; the fourth repeats the second; and so on. (See Figure 4.4.)

### POINT-PAPER DESIGN

Each weave can be presented in a squared paper design. For intricate woven-in patterns, designers use the point-paper pattern. Those who do not know how to use it often find their designs impractical from the weaver's standpoint. Figure 4.4 illustrates the pattern for plain weave. The blackened squares represent the warp on the face of the fabric and the filling at the back. The warp runs lengthwise of the paper, and the fillings run crosswise. The diameter of filling yarn is represented by AB; AC represents the diameter of a warp yarn.

### CLOTHS MADE IN THE PLAIN WEAVE

The plain weave is sometimes called cotton, taffeta, or tabby weave. Some of the most durable fabrics are made in this construction. The weaving process is comparatively inexpensive because the design is so simple. Plain-weave cloths can be cleaned easily, and when firm and closely woven, they wear well.

A partial list of plain-weave fabrics follows:

1. *Cottons.* Gingham, percale, voile, plissé crepe, batiste, nainsook, calico, chambray, cheesecloth, chintz, crash, cretonne, muslin sheeting, cambric, lawn, organdy, shantung, unbleached muslin, scrim, crinoline, bunting, buckram, canvas, flannelette

2. *Linens.* Handkerchief linen, art linen, crash toweling, cambric, dress linen

3. *Nylons and other synthetics.* Organdy, lingerie crepe, shantung, taffeta, shirting (many of these constructions are also made in blends with natural yarns and with other synthetic yarns)

**Figure 4.5.** Plain weave. (*Photo by Jack Pitkin.*)

4. *Rayons and/or acetates.* Taffeta, georgette, flat crepe, seersucker, ninon, organdy, voile, rough crepe, chiffon, challis

5. *Silks.* Taffeta, organza, voile, Canton crepe, crepe de Chine, flat crepe, chiffon, pongee, shantung, silk shirting, broadcloth, habutai, China silk

6. *Wools.* Homespun, challis, crepe, batiste, some tweeds, voile

7. *Blends and mixtures of the various fibers*

## VARIATIONS IN PLAIN WEAVE THAT PRODUCE DIFFERENT EFFECTS

*Rib variation.* The plain weave without any variation, as is found in sheeting and unbleached muslin, does not make a particularly interesting fabric. Several methods can be used to make a plain-weave fabric more attractive. The first is to produce a ribbed or corded effect by using fillings much heavier than warps, as in poplin, or by using warps much heavier than fillings, as in dimity. The former method is the most common. Bengaline and faille have regular fillingwise ribs; cotton broadcloth has a fine, irregular, broken fillingwise rib.

Figure 4.6.   Point paper design for striped dimity.

Figure 4.7.   Rib weave (striped dimity).

A striped effect is produced by alternation of fine and heavy warps at regular intervals, as in striped dimity or corded madras shirting. In addition, fine and heavy fillings may be alternated to produce a crossbar effect. Examples of this are crossbar dimity and tissue gingham.

The durability of fabrics in the rib variation of the plain weave may be questionable if the rib yarns are so heavy that they slip over or cut adjacent finer yarns. Such might be the case in striped dimity. The rib must be completely covered by many finer yarns, and the difference in weight between the rib yarn and other yarns should not be too great if wearing quality is to be assured. In heavily corded fabrics, like ottoman and bengaline, good coverage of the ribs is vital because abrasive wear occurs first on top of the ribs.

*Basket variation.* The basket variation of the plain weave is interesting from the design point of view, but it is not so durable as the average rib variation. One or more filling yarns are passed alternately over and under two or more warp yarns. If one filling yarn passes alternately over and under two warp yarns, the weave is called 2 x 1 basket. This weave is common in oxford shirting. The fabric is sometimes made in 3 x 2 (two fillings pass over and under three warps). A 3 x 2 oxford makes an interesting woman's blouse when made of colored warp yarns and white fillings.

In Figure 4.8 the 2 x 1 basket weave shows one large filling yarn used for every two warp yarns. If a filling is exactly twice the size of a warp, the interlacing of one filling and two warps forms a design of a perfect square; if either set of yarns is not in this proportion, the interlacing of one filling and two warps makes a design in the form of an oblong.

In Figure 4.9 two fillings pass alternately over two warps. Warps and filling yarns are the same size. A 4 x 4 or 8 x 8 basket weave is found in monk's cloth.

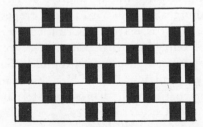

**Figure 4.8.** 2 x 1 basket weave.

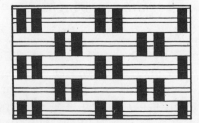

**Figure 4.9.** 2 x 2 basket weave.

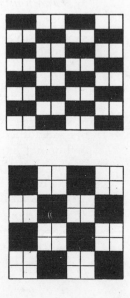

The basket weave is a decorative weave, but it is loose; therefore it permits slippage of yarns and stretches, and it may shrink easily in washing. Monk's cloth frays badly unless it is bound on the cut edges.

## VISUAL DESIGN OR EFFECT

In both the rib and basket variations of the plain weave, there are structural changes in the point-paper designs. (See Figures 4.7 through 4.9.) But the following ways of varying the plain weave may be employed, without structural changes, to give a visual effect (design) that is quite different from the usual appearance of the plain weave. Textural and new color effects can be produced by—

1. *Varying the size of yarns.* When uneven yarns are used at irregular intervals (hit or miss), a roughened, bumpy texture is the result. Crash, shantung, and pongee illustrate this use of different sizes of yarns at irregular intervals. Modern drapery fabrics employ such visual effects. (See Chapter 20.)

   Another rough texture can be produced with different sizes of ply yarn, as in ratiné and bouclé. Each ply yarn may be made up of different sizes of single yarns with varying amounts of twist.

2. *Varying the number of warp and filling yarns.* The count of cloth is dependent on the number of warps and fillings to the inch; the more yarns to the inch, the closer the weave and the higher the count, and vice versa. The fewer the warp and filling yarns to the inch, the more porous and open the cloth, provided the yarns are fine. Cheesecloth, gauze, voile, and theatrical gauze are low-count cloths. Batiste, lawn, organdy, and cotton broadcloth are considered high-count cloths.

3. *Variations made by use of different degrees of twist in yarns.* If the warp or the filling is spun so hard that it crepes or crinkles, the appearance of the cloth is textured. Crinkled bedspreads of seersucker are made from yarns with different degrees of twist and tension in the loom. Creping, such as is found in flat crepe, Canton crepe, rough crepe, and crepe de Chine, is made with tightly twisted fillings, alternating right-hand and left-hand twisted yarns (S and Z twists). (See Chapter 3, p. 62.)

   Another variation is made with one set of yarns twisted tightly, but not enough to crepe or crinkle, and fillings twisted so loosely that a nap can be raised in the finishing process. Flannelette is an example.

4. *Combinations of different textile raw materials.* Some cloths are made more attractive by the use of yarns of different textiles or blends of different raw materials. A novel visual effect is produced by the use of a black cotton warp and orange jute filling. A metallic yarn put in here and there in a wool crepe is very attractive because the metallic yarn is so much more lustrous than wool

that it shows up to advantage. Alpaca and romain crepes are made of acetate and viscose yarns plied together to form an abraded yarn. The shiny viscose ply and the dull acetate ply give varied luster and sparkle. Metallic yarns may be introduced in any weave for effect. (See Chapter 3, p. 69.)

5. *Variations made by use of fibers or yarns dyed in different colors.* A cloth with a colored warp and a white filling gives a grayed effect. Cotton chambray has this appearance. End-to-end madras, a men's shirting, is quite similar to chambray, the greatest difference being that in the former dyed and white yarns alternate in the warp. This cloth has less depth of color than chambray because there are more white yarns in it. Yarn-dyed stripes are common in madras shirting.

Plaid gingham is made with a series of colored yarns and a series of white yarns used alternately in both warp and filling. This alternation makes the plaid effect. Linen crash may be made with the insertion of large, irregular fillings dyed a different color from the rest of the yarns. Wool tweeds and homespuns use yarns of different colors. Fibers dyed different colors when in raw stock produce cloth with a mottled effect. Gray flannel with a mottled appearance is made in this way.

6. *Variations in dyeing and finishing.* Printing, piece dyeing, and various finishes will vary the appearance not only of plain-weave fabrics but also of all other weaves. Variations due to different fiber combinations, kinds of yarn, and methods of dyeing, printing, and finishing vary the appearance of the cloth but do *not* affect the *structural* design (the weave).

## TWILL WEAVE

Twill is the most durable of all weaves. In this weave the filling yarns are interlaced with the warps in such a way as to form diagonal ridges across the fabric. These diagonals, called *wales,* may run from upper left to lower right [Figure 4.10 (a) ], from upper right to lower left [Figure 4.10 (b) ], or both ways in the same cloth [Figure 4.10 (c) ]. If the wales run from upper right to lower left, the weave is called a *right-hand* twill; if the wales run from upper left to lower right, the weave is called a *left-hand twill*; if the wales run both ways, the weave is a *herringbone.*

The twill weave may also be called the serge or diagonal weave. In a piece of coarse serge the filling yarn passes over two and under two warp yarns, alternating across the cloth. This is the first pick. For the second pick, or second time across, the filling passes over two and under two warps, but it laps back on the ground on the previous row, thus forming a stair pattern. In serge the twill runs in the same direction as the twist in the yarns. Point-paper designs for two types of twills appear in Figures 4.10 (b) and (c).

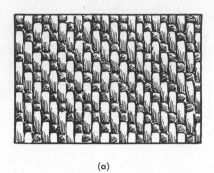

1 2 3 4 5 6 7 8 9 10 11

(a)                                    (b)

1 2 3 4 5 6 7 8 9 10 11

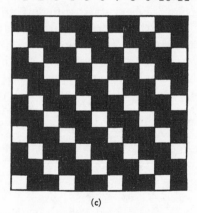

**Figure 4.10.** (a) Interlacement of yarns in uneven twill weave. Wales run from upper left to lower right in this illustration. (b) Even twill weave. Wales run from upper right to lower left in this illustration. (c) Uneven twill weave. Wales run in the same direction as in (a).

(c)

In the even twill [Figure 4.10 (b)], the filling passes over the same number of warps as it passes under. The wale on the right side of the cloth is represented by the black squares. In this weave the wales and the valleys between them are the same width. On the wrong side of the cloth the wales run from upper left to lower right.

The uneven twill [Figure 4.10 (c)] shows diagonals in black squares on the right side of the cloth. The filling passes under more yarns than it passes over (under 2 and over 1). A twill pattern might also require the filling to pass over 1 and under 3, 4, 5, 6, or over 2 and under 1, 3, 4. To recognize even and uneven twills, compare the width of a wale with the width of a valley between two wales. If the wales and the valley are the same widths, the twill is even; if they are of unequal widths, the twill is uneven. If the valleys are narrower than the wales, the wales stand out predominantly.

**Figure 4.11.** Even twill cloth. *(Photo by Jack Pitkin.)*

Below is an outline of the shedding that forms the even twill in Figure 4.10(*b*). Beginning at the right, the warps are lifted in the following combinations to allow the shuttle to pass under:

First row (top) ..........................warps 1, 4, 5, 8, 9, etc.
Second row .............................warps 11, 8, 7, 4, 3, etc.
Third row ..............................warps 2, 3, 6, 7, 10, 11, etc.
Fourth row ............................warps 10, 9, 6, 5, 2, 1, etc.
Fifth row ..............................repeat first row

In Figure 4.10(*b*) it takes 4 picks (rows) to complete a design; 4 series of warps must be lifted and 4 harnesses must be used. This twill construction is called a *4-shaft* twill. A quick method to determine the number of shafts required is to add together the number of warp yarns the filling goes over and under. In this case, over 2 under 2. Therefore, $2 + 2 = 4$ shafts.

The outline of shedding for the construction in Figure 4.10(*c*) is as follows (the method is the same as already mentioned):

First row (top) ..........................warps 1, 2, 4, 5, 7, 8, 10, 11, etc.
Second row .............................warps 11, 9, 8, 6, 5, 3, 2, etc.
Third row ..............................warps 1, 3, 4, 6, 7, 9, 10, etc.
Fourth row ............................repeat first row

Since it takes 3 picks or rows to complete a design and 3 series of warps must be lifted, this weave is called a *3-shaft* twill. Using the quick method: the filling goes under 2 and over 1 ($2 + 1 = 3$ shafts required).

## VARIATIONS OF THE TWILL WEAVE

The most common variation of the twill weave is the *herringbone*. In this weave the diagonal runs in one direction for a few rows and then reverses and runs in the opposite direction. The effect resembles the backbone of a herring, as the name implies. Figure 4.12 shows a point-paper design of a herringbone weave. Either the even or the uneven

**Figure 4.12.** Herringbone weave. *Left:* Point paper design. *Right:* Cloth. (*Photo by Jack Pitkin.*)

twills can make a herringbone, but, in either case, there must be a variation in the weave at the apex of the ∧ in order to reverse the wales.

Other variations of the twill may be made to form diamond patterns, as demonstrated by some worsted cheviots. Passing the filling over a large number of warps at a time produces a heavy, corded wale, common in whipcord. The wales may be broken at intervals or may curve or wave for a more unusual effect. If the twist of the yarns runs opposite to the pattern, a rough twill is made.

Variations in the use of fiber blends and yarns of different sizes, qualities, colors, and finishes make possible many visual effects in the twill weave, as in the case of plain weaves.

### ADVANTAGES AND DISADVANTAGES OF TWILL WEAVES

Twill weaves usually make fabrics closer in texture, heavier, and stronger than do plain weaves. This is why twills are so suitable for men's clothing fabrics. Also, it is possible to produce more fancy designs in twills than in plain weaves. As has been seen in the illustrations, more elaborate shedding is needed for the twill than for the plain weave. Therefore twill cloths may cost more. Twills do not show dirt so quickly as plain weaves, but once they are dirty, they are harder to clean.

### CLOTHS IN TWILL WEAVE

Cloths made in twill weave may be classified as follows (it will be noticed that the twill is frequently used for cottons and wools):

1. *Cottons.* Jean, ticking, drill, Canton flannel, denim, gabardine, covert cloth, khaki, serge
2. *Linens.* Ticking and table and towel drills
3. *Silks.* Twill foulard, serge, surah

4. *Wools.* Serge, worsted cheviot, gabardine, covert, flannel (twill or plain), tweed (twill or plain), unfinished worsted, broadcloth, sharkskin
5. *Rayons, acetates, and blends.* Gabardine, surah, foulard, flannel

## SATIN AND SATEEN WEAVES

Why do satins have sheen? In what way are they different from the dull-finished silks?

Any consumer may have asked these questions. The answer to both questions is that the type of cloth construction called the *satin weave* gives great sheen to a fabric and reflects the light better than dull-finished fabrics in plain or twill weave do.

The consumer should notice that whenever she feels a silk or rayon dress satin, the hand slips more easily lengthwise than crosswise of the fabric (the right or shiny side should be felt). The reason is that more warps than fillings are exposed on the right side. If the fabric is turned over, more fillings than warps are visible. The sheen of the fabric runs warpwise on the right side. Dressmakers must be sure that dresses are cut so that the sheen runs lengthwise of the dress.

In sateen (or satine), a cotton fabric, the principle just mentioned is reversed. On the right side more fillings than warps are visible, and the sheen is crosswise of the fabric. When there is more warp than filling on the right side of a fabric, the weave is called *satin*. If more filling than warp shows on the right side, the weave is called *sateen*. These exposed fillings or warps are called *floats*. The floats in sateen are generally shorter than those in satin. The sateen weave is not used for silk or rayons, except in combination with other weaves. Cotton, if highly mercerized, may be woven in the satin weave, as in cotton satin for linings; but ordinarily the fuzz on cotton yarns makes long floating warps undesirable.

Both satin and sateen weaves use the principle of the twill. In fact, some authorities call these weaves *rearranged* or *skipping* twills. In this discussion, however, the twill and the satin are considered separately. In satin and sateen weaves there is a semblance of a broken diagonal, but the interlacings of the warp and filling are placed as far apart as possible to avoid the forming of a wale. In the satin construction the warp may not interlace with the filling for 4 to 12 yarns. Thus, varying lengths of warp are left exposed on the surface of the cloth. When a warp skips 7 fillings before it interlaces, the weave is called a *7-float warp* satin; if the warp skips 5 yarns, the weave is a *5-float warp* satin, and so on. If the filling skips 4 yarns before interlacing with a warp, the weave is a *4-float filling* sateen weave, and so on. Point-paper designs of the satin and sateen weaves appear in Figures 4.13 and 4.14.

Figure 4.13 (*b*) illustrates a long-float satin weave. The warp floats

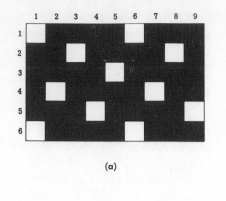

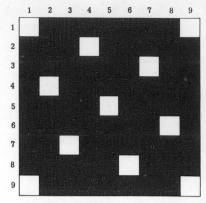

**Figure 4.13.** (a) Four-float satin weave. (b) Seven-float satin weave.

(a)

(b)

**Figure 4.14.** Short-float sateen weave.

over 11 filling yarns. The blackened portion represents warp yarns brought to the face of the fabric. A predominance of blackened squares denotes a predominance of floating warps. Figure 4.14 illustrates a short-float filling sateen weave.

## ADVANTAGES AND DISADVANTAGES OF SATIN AND SATEEN WEAVES

These constructions produce smooth, lustrous, rich-looking fabrics that give reasonably good service if they are not subjected to excessive hard wear. Short-float fabrics are more durable than long-float fabrics, for the former have less exposed yarn to catch on rough objects; long-floats, although they increase the sheen of a fabric, snag and pull if there are any protrusions or splinters on furniture.

When style calls for luxurious fabrics for formal wear, satin is often chosen. It is an especially suitable fabric for coat linings because its smooth surface allows coats to be slipped on and off very easily. In general, it sheds dirt well, but a bright rayon in a long-float satin weave will often have a metallic sheen that may appear greasy after continuous wear.

The satin weave usually requires more shafts in the weaving than do the plain or twill weaves, thereby increasing the cost of production. For instance, in the design in Figure 4.14, the filling passes over 1 and under 4 warps, so 5 shafts are required (4 + 1 = 5). When the filling passes over four or more warp yarns, the weave is *sateen*.

To lay out a regular satin weave in a point-paper design, it is necessary to find the counter or base. For example, in a 4-float satin, 5 harnesses are needed. Therefore, the regular progression in which the warp interlaces with the filling is determined by taking the required number of harnesses and dividing them into 2 parts or counters. The rule is that these parts must not be equal (2 and 3 are not equal); these parts cannot be divided by the same number ($3 \div 2 = 1\frac{1}{2}$, *not* 5); these parts cannot be multiples of each other ($2 \times 3 = 6$ and *not* 5). The sequence or regular progression of interlacement of yarns is 1, 3, 5, 2, 4. The repeat will come after 5 picks in this 5-harness weave. (See Figure 4.13.) This is the sequence for a regular satin. Other regular satin weaves are 7-harnesses with interlacements at 1, 3, 5, 7, 2, 4, 6, and 8-harnesses with interlacements at 1, 4, 7, 2, 5, 8, 3, 6.

For an irregular satin weave, 4 and 6 harnesses are used. Four is divisible into 2 equal parts or counters; and for 6 harnesses, counters are 3 and 3. Two can be divided only by 2, 4 can be divided by 2, and 3 by 3. In a 4-harness weave, the interlacements are at 1, 3, 2, 4, and in a 6-harness, at 1, 3, 5, 2, 6, 4.

## VARIATIONS IN THE SATIN AND SATEEN WEAVES

Warp yarns may be twisted loosely, and long floats may be used to produce a high sheen. When a softer, lower luster is desired, warp yarns may be twisted more tightly and the floats may be shortened.

By the use of creped yarns of reeled or spun silk for filling and very loosely twisted reeled silk for floating warps, a warp satin face with a creped back can be made; the lustrous, smooth reeled-silk warps are thrown to the face of the fabric in warp floats, while the tightly twisted, dull, creped filling yarns are kept on the back. The fabric is reversible and is called satin crepe. Likewise, cotton or spun-silk yarns may be used for the filling. Since the warp made of lustrous reeled silk covers the face of the fabric, the cotton or spun silk can be carefully concealed. Since rayons, acetates, and nylons are woven in the same satin construction as are silks, their appearance can be changed in a similar manner.

The finishing processes and the amount of twist in the yarn affect the feel of the fabric. For example, a cloth may feel soft after the weaving; but, if stiffened in finishing, the fabric will feel more crisp, less soft, and less elastic.

The sateen as well as the satin weave may be varied. If highly mercerized cotton yarns are used, the sheen of sateen will be increased. The sateen weave can be used in combination with the satin weave in making elaborate figured designs. (See Chapter 5.)

### CLOTHS MADE IN SATIN AND SATEEN WEAVES

The materials that are made with the satin weave are antique satin, bridal satin, cotton satin, dress satin, satin bengaline, satin crepe, satin faille, slipper satin, and Venetian satin. Sateen is made in the sateen weave.

### IDENTIFICATION OF WARP AND FILLING

The plain, twill, and satin weaves are the three fundamental weaves. Before studying more complicated ones, the reader should learn how to distinguish warp from filling in these weaves and how to choose between them for various uses.

In a large piece of yard goods it is easy to tell warp from filling, for the selvages, or finished edges, run parallel to the warp. But if there are no selvages and the consumer has only a sample of cloth of mail-order size, other methods to distinguish warp for filling must be used.

### IN PLAIN WEAVE

The count in plain-weave cloths is usually the determining factor. There are generally more warps than fillings to the inch. In a square count cloth, 80 x 80, the way to identify warp is first to break a yarn in each direction to compare breaking strengths. The greater breaking strength is usually the warp because the warps are generally twisted more tightly—with the exception of the creped cloths like flat crepe and satin crepe, in which the filling is the more tightly twisted yarn. In rib variations of the plain weave, the ribs of cotton broadcloth, cotton poplin, bengaline, grosgrain, and faille run fillingwise, but the rib in Bedford cord runs warpwise. In 2 x 2 and 4 x 4 basket weaves the warps can be recognized by their twist or by their greater strength. In 2 x 1 basket weave there is usually one large filling to two close, parallel warps. The uneven bumpy yarns in pongee and shantung run fillingwise.

### RIGHT AND WRONG SIDES OF A FABRIC

To tell the right side from the wrong side of a plain weave cloth is often difficult unless it is on a bolt, in which case the cloth may be folded with the right side inside to keep it clean. If one side of a fabric is more lustrous than the other side, the shinier side is the right side. A printed fabric design usually shows more clearly on the right side. In ribbed fabrics, the rib is often more distinct on the right side. Slub-yarn fabrics often show the slub more predominantly on the right side. Napped cloths are softer and fuzzier on the right side.

### IN TWILL WEAVE

The side on which the wale shows up more clearly is the right side—unless the fabric is napped, in which case the side with more napping is the right side.

With the right side to the observer, the fabrics should be turned until the wales run from the upper right corner to the lower left corner, or vice versa. When the sample is held in this position, the warp should run up and down, and the filling crosswise. Warps are usually stronger and more tightly twisted than fillings. Sometimes warp yarns can be distinguished from filling yarns by the amount of wave or kink in them. Fillings are likely to be more wavy, because they are not held in tension in the loom as they go over and under the warps.

### IN SATIN OR SATEEN WEAVE

If the fabric is extremely lustrous and smooth, the consumer may suspect it is a satin construction. First the finger should be run over the cloth to determine in which way the floats lie. The way the finger slips more easily is the way the floats run. If the fabric is silk, rayon, acetate, or a synthetic mixture, or a blend of these fibers, the warp floats, and the weave is satin. Silk and cotton mixtures, rayon and cotton, and acetate and cotton also have warp floats. If the fabric is all-cotton, the float is usually fillingwise. But the cotton satin that is used for coat linings—called farmer's satin—has a warp float.

## GUIDES TO CONSUMERS IN CHOOSING WEAVES

The consumer should know first the factors that enable one to choose suitable fabrics from the standpoint of type of fibers and yarn and should consider second the fabrics from the standpoint of construction or weave. In this chapter the three basic weaves—plain, twill, and satin—have been discussed.

If suitability is a factor of major consideration, the consumer should carefully consider the purpose for which the fabric is to be used. The plain weave is probably the most serviceable of all weaves. It is easy to dry-clean and to launder, wears well, is becoming to the majority of people, is comfortable, is usually in style in one cloth or another, and is comparatively inexpensive. However, loose weaves (the basket in particular) are more likely to shrink than are close weaves. The more the yarns slip or give, the more danger there is of their shrinking. A twill in wool keeps its press and shape well when used for suitings. For daily business wear, a plain-weave wool or silk crepe requires little pressing and is always becoming. For infants' wear, plain or twill cloths are best. Twill weaves do not show dirt so quickly as plain weaves, but more effort is required to clean them. For boys' wear, the twilled worsted is a durable suiting. For girls, a plain weave or a twill are both good. Many mothers prefer plain weaves for fabrics requiring frequent laundering and twills for wool goods.

Satins are impractical for active sports and for hard daily wear. There is the danger not only that they will snag, but also that in time they will look greasy. If style calls for a lustrous sheen for evening, the consumer should choose satin—provided she is not too stout—for satins tend to make a large woman look larger. Style and becomingness go hand in hand. If wearing quality is a factor in selecting satin, a short float should be chosen. Beauty, appearance, and style usually govern the choice of satin. Since the satin weave requires more complicated machinery than do the plain or twill weaves, it is more expensive.

## SUMMARY

Plain, twill, and satin weaves with their variations are considered the three basic weaves in the construction of textile fabrics. The weaves are arranged according to the simplicity of their manufacture (with the plain weave as the simplest) and according to the frequency of use.

The plain weave is made from all types of textile yarns, but it is most common in cottons. Twill, the strongest weave, is used mainly when durability is the prime requisite. The satin and sateen weaves are beautiful but may not be durable. The satin weave is most common in silks, rayons, acetates, and synthetics, where beauty depends upon richness of sheen. The sateen weave is found in a few mercerized cotton fabrics, and it appears in combination with the satin weave in elaborate woven-in patterns. Fancy weaves are discussed in the next chapter.

## REVIEW QUESTIONS

1. (*a*) What is weaving?
   (*b*) What is a loom?
   (*c*) How is the loom prepared for weaving?
   (*d*) Describe the action of the loom.
   (*e*) Can weaving be done without a shuttle? How?
2. (*a*) How is the plain weave made?
   (*b*) Draw a point-paper design to illustrate the plain weave.
3. In what ways may the plain weave be varied—
   (*a*) In actual construction?
   (*b*) In visual design or effect?

4. (*a*) What are the advantages of the plain weave?
   (*b*) What are its disadvantages?

5. Draw a point-paper design to illustrate (*a*) a rib weave; (*b*) a 2 x 2 basket weave; (*c*) a 2 x 1 basket weave.

6. (*a*) What is meant by the count of cloth?
   (*b*) How does count of cloth differ from count of yarn?
   (*c*) Why is the count of cloth important to a buyer of cottons or linens?

7. (*a*) Explain the construction of a twill weave.
   (*b*) Draw a point-paper design to illustrate a 4-shaft twill, a 3-shaft twill.

8. (*a*) What are the advantages of a cloth made in twill weave?
   (*b*) What are its disadvantages?

9. (*a*) In what respect does the satin weave differ from the twill weave?
   (*b*) Explain the construction of the sateen weave.
   (*c*) Draw a point-paper design illustrating a 5-shaft warp satin weave.
   (*d*) Draw a point-paper design illustrating a 5-shaft filling sateen weave.

10. Which of the three standard weaves is—
    (*a*) The most durable? Why?
    (*b*) The most beautiful? Why?
    (*c*) The most serviceable? Why?

11. List ten fabrics made in (*a*) plain weave, (*b*) twill weave, (*c*) satin or sateen weaves.

12. Define: float, 4-shaft twill, point-paper design, warp, heddle, pick, shuttle, end, selvage, filling, balance of a cloth, letting out and taking up, breast beam, merchandise beam, wale, herringbone, shedding, high-count cloth, crepe, pick glass.


# EXPERIMENTS

1. *Identification of warp and filling.* Examine a number of swatches. Be sure you have the right side, the more lustrous side, toward you. Note whether or not there is a selvage to indicate which dimension is the warp. If there is no selvage, unravel a yarn either way. Which yarn is stronger? Which yarn has the tighter twist? Which yarn was in tension on the loom? Which yarn has the more kink in it? Which yarn, then, is the warp?

2. *Identification of weave.* Mount each sample on a sheet of paper with the warp running lengthwise of the paper. With the aid of a pin or a pick glass, look at the filling and count the number of warps it goes over and under. Write down the system of shedding used for each row. When does the design repeat? Are there wales in the fabric? Are there floats? Are there ribs? Is the design like the plaiting of a splint basket? What is the name of the weave? Draw a point-paper design to illustrate the weave.

3. *Count of cloth.* Unravel a number of yarns both ways to make wide, frayed edges. If the fabric is of a light color, put it against something black, and vice versa. With the aid of a magnifying glass, or better, a pick glass, count the number of yarns to the ¼-inch, first one way of the cloth and then the other way. Express the count of the cloth by giv-

ing the number of picks and ends to the inch. Does the cloth have good balance? Why? Will the cloth wear well? Why?

4. *Test for durability of the weave.* Grip opposite edges of the cloth tightly. Put your thumbs together and press down hard on the fabric. Does the cloth tear? Does the weave become badly distorted? Is the weave durable?

## PROJECTS

1. Construct a cigar-box loom, using the illustration on page 86 as a guide. Use knitting yarns or pieces of string and construct one or more of the three basic weaves.
2. Use strips of paper about one-quarter inch wide. Two colors are preferable—one for warp and one for filling. Interlace these strips of paper to form a paper mat of plain weave. Then make the twill and satin weaves. These mats should be kept in the textile notebook or manual.

## GLOSSARY

**Balance of cloth.**  Proportion of warp yarns to filling yarns.

**Balance of count.**  Number of warps and fillings to the inch are nearly the same.

**Basket weave.**  Variation of the plain weave in which two or more filling yarns are passed alternately over and under two or more warp yarns.

**Battening.**  Pushing each filling (or pick) against the previous filling. See *Reed*.

**Cloth beam.**  See *Merchandise beam*.

**Count of cloth.**  Number of picks and ends to the square inch.

**Drill.**  A strong cotton fabric in an uneven twill weave.

**Even twill.**  Filling passes over the same number of warps it passes under.

**Filling.**  Crosswise yarn in woven cloth.

**Float.**  In a satin weave, the number of fillings a warp skips over before interlacement. In a sateen weave, the number of warps a filling skips over before interlacement.

**Frame.**  See *Harness*.

**Harness.**  The frame holding warp yarns, which are threaded through the eyes of its heddles. See *Heddles*.

**Heddles.**  Series of wires held by the frame or harness. Each wire has an eye like that of a needle through which a warp yarn is threaded. Heddles are raised to form the *shed*. See *Shedding*.

**Herringbone weave.**  Variation of the twill in which the wale runs in one direction for a few rows and then reverses.

**Letting off.**  Releasing warp yarns from the warp beam as the weaving operation proceeds.

**Linen tester.**  See *Pick glass*.

**Loom.**  A machine for weaving cloth. It is operated either by hand or by machine.

**Merchandise beam.**  Cylinder in the loom on which finished cloth is wound (taken up). It is synonymous with *cloth beam*.

**Pick.** See *Filling*.

**Pick glass.** A magnifying glass for counting cloth, also called a *pick counter*.

**Picking.** Carrying the filling through the shed.

**Plain weave.** Each filling yarn passes successively over and under each warp yarn, alternating each row. A synonym is *tabby weave*.

**Point-paper design.** Squared paper pattern to represent a certain weave.

**Reed.** This frame, located directly in front of the harnesses, swings forward to batten the last filling inserted against previous fillings. See *Battening*.

**Rib weave.** A variation of the plain weave made by using fillings heavier than the warps or vice versa.

**Sateen weave.** Characterized by floats running fillingwise. See *Float*.

**Satin weave.** Characterized by a smooth surface caused by floats running warpwise.

**Selvage.** See Glossary, Chapter 2.

**Shedding.** The separation or opening between warp yarns made by the harness (composed of heddles) for the passage of the shuttle carrying filling yarn.

**Shuttleless loom.** A machine that carries the filling yarns through the shed by the use of air or water jets and grippers.

**Structural design.** A woven-in design, as opposed to one printed on a fabric.

**Tabby weave.** See *Plain weave*.

**Taking up.** Winding up finished cloth on the merchandise beam as weaving proceeds.

**Twill weave.** Filling yarns are interlaced with the warps in such a way that diagonal ridges are formed in the fabric.

**Uneven twill weave.** The filling passes under more yarns than it passes over.

**Wales.** Diagonal ridges characteristic of the twill weave.

**Warp beam.** Cylindrical spool at the back of the loom on which warp yarns are wound.

**Weaving.** A process of making cloth by interlacing two sets of yarns at right angles.

**Weft.** See *Filling*.

# 5

# Fancy Weaves:

## PILE, JACQUARD, DOBBY, AND LENO

Luxurious velvets with downlike textures, elaborate brocades with intricate woven-in designs, small geometrical patterns, and cobwebby lace effects are quite impossible to make on the plain harness loom described in Chapter 4. These fancy effects call for either special looms or attachments for the regular harness loom; the actual weaving is usually slower than standard weaving; and the price of these elaborate effects is higher than that of the plain weaves. Nevertheless, these fabrics are in demand; they are attractive and often high style.

### PILE WEAVE

Cloths with soft, downy textures are velvets, velours, and plushes. All three of these fabrics are made in pile weave. The right side of these cloths consists of soft, clipped yarns, called *pile*. The wrong side of the fabric is smooth, with no pile and with the weave showing distinctly.

Pile weave is not an entirely new construction, for it uses the plain or twill weave as its base. The back of the fabric indicates the basic weave. But the soft pile made from extra yarns is the novelty. There are five methods of making pile. These are discussed in the following pages.

**Figure 5.1.** A carpet in a pile weave by the wire method (uncut pile).

## THE WIRE METHOD

Good-quality velvets, plushes, and Wilton and Axminster rugs are made with extra warp to form the pile. One set of warps interlaces with the filling to form the plain- or twill-weave ground of the fabric; the other set of warps forms the pile. When a row of pile is made, the warp yarns to form the pile are first raised by the harness to form the shed. Then a wire is inserted through the shed, much as filling yarn is shot through. The size of this wire is determined by the size of the pile to be made. When the set of warps to form the pile is lowered, it loops over the wire and is held in place by the next filling. The wire is then withdrawn. As this is done, a small, sharp knife attached to the end of the wire cuts the pile warp loops. The ground is then woven for a certain number of picks; then the wire is again inserted to form the pile. If the pile has not been cut evenly by the wires, the fabric is sheared again with a device like a lawnmower.

Sometimes the pile is left uncut: a wire with no knife is used, or a number of filling threads are substituted for the wire and are then withdrawn. Friezé used for upholstery is usually made with uncut loops.

## THE TERRY-WEAVE METHOD

A less expensive method of pile weaving omits the wires. Groups of warps are held in tension for the groundwork of the fabric. The warps

Figure 5.2. The three-thread system in a Martex terry towel. (*Photograph courtesy of Wellington Sears Co., Inc.*)

that form the pile have their tension released at intervals and are thus shoved forward. The tension is restored, and the battening up of the filling causes these warps to appear in loops. The easiest way to make this construction is to use four harnesses, two for the slack pile warps and two for the tight ground warps. On the first shed, pile warps are raised; two fillings are shot through this shed, but are not battened by the reed. The pile warps are lowered, and a third filling is shot through to interlace with the ground warps. Then all three fillings are battened back. Because the tension on the pile warps is loose when the fillings are battened, the pile warps appear in loops. This is known as a three-pick terry cloth because two picks go under the looped pile and one pick goes between two rows of pile. Figure 5.2 shows the ground of terry with pile removed. The ground weave of the fabric is a variation of either plain or twill. The pile is usually on both sides of the fabric (pile yarns alternate in forming loops on the face and the back of the cloth). However, the pile may be made to form stripes or designs. Turkish towels are woven in this manner. Instead of "pile weave," use the name "*terry* weave" when referring to turkish toweling. Terry cloth used for bathrobes is made in this construction. Loops are uncut in terry cloth and in turkish toweling. The loops make the surface absorbent. Terry facecloths, beach robes, and bath mats are also made in this manner.

### THE FILLING PILE METHOD

In both the wire and terry methods of making pile, extra warp yarns form the pile. To make corduroy, velveteen, and some plushes, extra fillings are floated over four or five warps. (See Figure 5.3.) The floats are cut after weaving, and then the cut ends are brushed up to form the pile. These floats require precision cutting in the center of the float by a special device equipped with knives. In corduroy, characterized by a pile stripe or wale alternating with a plain wale (no pile), a separate cutting

**Figure 5.3.** *Left:* Grey goods with wire inserted. *Right:* Finished corduroy. (*Courtesy of Crompton-Richmond Company. Photos by Jack Pitkin.*)

knife is necessary for cutting the floats of each wale. If there are 5 wales to the inch in a wide-wale corduroy 40 inches wide, then 20 cutting knives would be required. A wide-wale cloth can have all the wales cut in one operation. Very narrow wale, called *pinwale*, would have 16 to 23 wales to the inch. Pinwales are fed through the cutting machine twice. Velveteen and filling plush have an all-over pile construction. The grounds of all these fabrics are either plain or twill weaves—the twill is the stronger. Hence a twill-back velveteen is more durable than a plain back. Another point in durability is the way the pile is held to the ground. If a pile loop is pulled from the fabric, its shape will be a V or a W. A V reveals that the pile filling has interlaced with only one warp yarn, whereas a W reveals an interlacement with three warps. W is more durable because it is held to the ground by three warps instead of one.

### THE DOUBLE-WEAVE AND BACKED-CLOTH METHOD

Many average-grade millinery and transparent velvets are woven double; that is, two cloths are woven at the same time, face to face. Two sets of warps and two sets of fillings are used, and an extra set of warps binds the two cloths together. Either the plain, rib, twill, or satin weave may be used as the ground. The effect is not unlike a sandwich, with the extra set of binding warps corresponding to the jam inside. When the cloth is woven, a knife in the loom cuts the binding yarns, making two separate fabrics with sheared pile surfaces. (See Figure 5.4.)

Reversible coating may be woven double but is not cut apart like velvet. This double weave makes a thicker, warmer cloth that can be worn with either side out. Matelassé crepe for women's dresses is also

Figure 5.4. Double cloth.

woven double. The tight plain-weave back keeps the heavy blistered crepe on the right side from stretching out of shape.

Similar to the double cloth is the backed cloth. Whereas a true double cloth has two sets of warps and two sets of fillings, a backed cloth has two sets of fillings and one set of warps or two sets of warps and one set of fillings. Beacon robing (a cotton bathrobing in double-weave construction) and some blankets use two sets of fillings and one set of warps, and heavy satin reversible ribbons in two colors often use two sets of warps and one set of fillings. Backed cloths cannot be cut apart.

### THE RUG METHOD

Hooking, tufting, tying, chenille, and buried pile are ways of making pile for rugs and carpets. These methods will be discussed in Chapter 19.

### PILE FABRICS OF FUR FIBERS AND SYNTHETICS

Real fur, fur blended with rayon or cotton, nylon acrylic, or mod-acrylic imitation fur may be used as pile. The back may be the same fiber content as the pile or a different fiber content. According to the T.F.P.I.A., the fiber content of pile fabrics, excluding rugs, must be labeled in percentages of fibers as they appear in the product by weight. Or, if desired, pile may be stated separately, and the ratio between the pile and the back or base must be stated. (See Chapter 1 for the identification of fur fibers under the T.F.P.I.A.) Some pile fabrics are woven as double cloth and are cut apart like velvet; others are made by the filling pile or terry methods, and still others are knitted. (See Chapter 19 for the labeling of pile rugs and carpets.) In the finishing process the pile can be printed to resemble leopard, for instance; or it can be processed to look like broadtail or ermine; or it can be sheared to resemble other furs. Sometimes the pile is curled to resemble Persian lamb. But the T.F.P.I.A. has specified that textile fiber products may not employ any name directly or indirectly of fur-bearing animals, such as mink, mutation, and broadtail. (See Chapter 1 for other points on labeling of fabrics made of fur fibers.)

In the pile construction, extra sets of warps or fillings make the pile. Velvets made of silk or synthetic fibers have extra warps forming the pile. To identify warp and filling, fold the fabrics first one way and then the other. The direction that shows distinct rows of pile is the filling direction. To check for accuracy, a yarn can be unraveled in each direction. One yarn looks like a caterpillar because the pile is clinging to it. Since extra warps make the pile in the fabrics mentioned, the *filling* yarn holds the pile and resembles the caterpillar. The pile does not adhere to the warp yarns. In cotton velvet, velveteen, and in some plushes, extra fillings make the pile. When yarns are unraveled both ways, one yarn holds the pile; this caterpillar-like yarn is the *warp*. The filling yarn will be smooth. Folding the fabrics shows distinct rows of pile lengthwise because extra fillings form the pile. No folding is required to identify the warp of corduroy. The wales run warpwise.

In terry weave with uncut pile, the best way to identify the warp is to pull a loop. Notice the direction from which it pulls. Since extra warps form the loop pile, the direction from which the loop pulls is the warp. A selvage always eliminates any complicated methods of identifying warp and filling.

## GUIDES TO THE BUYER OF PILE FABRICS

*how do you get loops in pile weaves*

If pile construction is used for silk, synthetic fibers, or fur, these textiles are presented to the consumer in their richest, most luxurious textures. Pile fabrics feel soft and downy. Silk pile takes a rich, deep color, especially when one looks directly into the pile. If the pile is pressed down, the fabric takes on a silvery, satin cast.

Pile fabrics are warm and hence are best used for fall and winter wear. Transparent velvet with a long rayon pile and a loosely woven rayon back is not so warm as a fabric with a short pile and a tightly woven back. An all-silk velvet is warmer than a silk with a cotton back or rayon pile.

Pile fabrics are becoming to young and old. A downy pile texture softens the face. Some women think they cannot wear velvets because the pile makes them look stout, but if a fabric is made correctly so that the pile creates shadows of depth, the silhouette becomes indistinct, and the illusion of slenderness is achieved. Very short pile makes a woman look more slender than does long pile. Seams in the garment are made inconspicuous by the pile covering.

For velvet dresses, dressmakers usually cut the fabric so that the pile runs up. The wearer then can appreciate the richness of the fabric by looking into the pile. Another reason for having the pile run up is that the pile is less likely to mat from friction. Velvet is suitable for afternoon and evening wear. It drapes well, especially when it is all silk, and looks effective in both tailored and feminine lines. Cotton velvet is stiffer and seems more bulky when made into dresses. Velvets and corduroys can be made spot-resistant and of durable press. Corduroys are frequently made water-repellent for raincoats. And there are now some washable velvets.

In upholstery, pile fabrics look soft, cushiony, and inviting. Pile upholstery is warm-looking in summer, and so may be covered with lighter fabric covers.

### THE CARE OF PILE FABRICS

Upholstery pile fabrics should be brushed frequently. If the pile is made of wool or mohair, a brushing first against the pile and then with the pile will usually remove matted spots.

It is best to steam velvets and velveteens to remove creases and matted spots. A good way is to hang the fabric near the shower bath. Very hot water, hot enough to make steam, should be run from the shower for about ten minutes, but at no time should the fabric be allowed to get wet. When it is removed from the steam, it should be shaken gently and hung over a line (with the pile out) or on a hanger to dry. A garment should not be worn until the pile is thoroughly dry. Water spots can usually be removed by steaming, but other stains can best be removed by a reliable dry cleaner. Transparent velvet has rayon pile, and although it can be steamed in the same way as silk velvet, care should be taken not to shake it while it is wet.

Velvets and velveteens may be steamed by still another method. Stand a hot iron upright on the ironing stand; place a damp cotton cloth over the iron to generate steam; pass the velvet slowly over the damp cloth, with the pile away from the cloth. Velvets should never be ironed flat.

The terry weave generally appears in towels, bath mats, and bathrobes. The fibers are usually cotton. Since the pile is uncut cotton yarn, the fabric washes well. The more loops on the surface of the fabric, the more absorbent the cloth. Bath mats may have rayon pile and cotton groundwork. While these fabrics are most attractive, their laundering quality and durability are questionable.

Friezé, a popular upholstery and drapery fabric, is made in wool, in mohair, and in cotton. It is a very durable, uncut-pile fabric that dry-cleans satisfactorily, but, since the dirt settles between rows of pile, frequent brushings are essential.

### FACTORS DETERMINING THE WEARING QUALITY OF PILE FABRICS

The lashing of the pile to the back of velvets, fabrics of fur fibers, and plushes is an important factor in determining wearing quality. As has been stated, some pile yarns are passed around only one background yarn before showing a cut end again on the surface. One interlacing of the pile is not secure; the V-shaped pile pulls out easily. If the pile yarns are woven over and under three yarns before they reappear on the surface, the resulting W-shaped pile will not pull out so easily. When pile pulls out, bare spots appear on the fabric. No one wants a bald velvet. If the fabric is a tight weave and the pile is close, the cloth is likely to wear better than a loosely constructed one.

Several factors must be considered in judging the wearing quality of a terry cloth: (1) Are the loops firmly held so that they will not pull out in laundering? (2) Will the ground warp yarns stand the strain of hard wear? (3) Will the selvage pull out? The first factor depends on the number of fillings used to interlace with the warp for every horizontal row of loops. If only one filling yarn interlaces with the warp for every horizontal row of looped pile, the cloth is termed *1-pick*. The construction is not durable, because one filling or pick is not enough to keep the pile warps from pulling out. A 3-pick cloth is an average quality. Better grades may be 4-, 5-, or 6-pick.

The weakness in ground warp is overcome if ply yarns or more ground warps and fewer pile warps are used. Although the resultant fabrics may have decreased absorptive qualities, their durability is increased.

Selvages often fray because the fillings or binding threads are loosely twisted and weak, or because only a few of the fillings come all the way to the edge and bind the outer warps. In some inexpensive towels fake selvages may be found; two towels are woven together (side by side on a loom) and then cut apart. The cut edge, which is not bound, frays at the first use.

## CLOTHS MADE IN PILE WEAVES

The most important pile fabrics are the following:

| COTTON | RAYON | SILK | WOOL | BLENDS OR MIXTURES OF SYNTHETICS OR NATURAL AND SYNTHETIC FIBERS |
|---|---|---|---|---|
| velveteen | transparent | plush | velour | friezé |
| velour | velvet | velvet | friezé | plush |
| terry cloth | chenille | velour | corduroy | velvet |
| friezé | Lyons-type | chenille | plush | chenille |
| corduroy | velvet | | Wilton rugs | velour |
| chenille | | | Axminster rugs | rugs |
| plush | | | oriental rugs | |
| rugs | | | | |

## JACQUARD WEAVE

Up to this point no explanation has been made of how beautiful floral designs or elaborate figures are woven into a cloth. How are shamrocks woven into linen tablecloths? What makes the basket of flowers in the silk upholstery damask? How is the wide border with the sailboat made in the turkish towel? There are two methods of making all-over figured weaves: the *Jacquard* and the *dobby*.

**Figure 5.5.** *Top:* A Jacquard loom. *Left:* Punching the cards for a Jacquard pattern. (*Photographs courtesy of Bigelow-Sanford Carpet Co., Inc.*)

The most elaborate designs are woven on an intricately constructed loom called the Jacquard loom, and the weave of these fabrics is called the Jacquard weave. (See Figure 5.5.) The loom was invented by a Frenchman, Joseph Marie Jacquard, in 1801. Elaborate designs could not be made on the regular harness loom that makes the plain, satin, and twill weaves, because intricate designs require many variations in shedding. So it was necessary to find a means of controlling not a series of warps but individual warps. The Jacquard loom supplied the need.

This loom is very expensive and requires a room with a fairly high ceiling to house it. Several weeks to three months are needed to prepare the loom for making a new complicated pattern, and the weaving operation is comparatively slow. Many, however, consider Jacquard-woven cloths the most beautiful and most interesting of all. The price is correspondingly high. Since the Jacquard loom is extremely complicated, and a detailed explanation would be too lengthy, only an outline of its workings will be given.

The design for the cloth is worked out in point-paper pattern first. Instead of harnesses, a series of oblong punched cards not unlike a large punched I.B.M. card controls the raising of the warps. As many cards are made as there are picks in the design. In other words, if there are 4,000 picks or fillings to be shot across before the same design is repeated, 4,000 cards must be made, which involves much labor and expense.[1] The cards are laced together in proper order and are rotated over an oblong cylinder on the upper part of the loom. From a frame hang long cords that hold fine steel wires, each with an eye through which a warp yarn is threaded. If the cloth is to have 4,500 warps, there will be 4,500

[1] Compare with Jacquard-weave patterns for shuttleless looms, p. 89.

Figure 5.6.   Pattern for a Jacquard weave.

of these wires, one to control or lift each warp. It is quite evident that a great deal of effort and work are required to thread 4,500 warps through the eyes.

At the top of the loom each of these many cords is attached to a horizontal wire called a needle. These needles press forward against a card. The needles that go through the punched holes in the card pull on the cords that raise the warps to form the shed. The shuttle shoots through. The card just used is automatically passed on by a partial turn of the oblong cylinder, and the next card is raised into position for contact with the needles. Again and again the principle of shedding is carried out until all the cards have been used once. The pattern is then repeated.

In view of the skill required to make the cards, the labor and time required to set up the loom, and the slow action of the loom, it is small wonder that Jacquard weaves are expensive. Even though the use of the same cards again and again helps to decrease the price, the weaving is accomplished very slowly. To save expense, when one cloth is completed, new warps are tied to the old ones and pulled through the loom, and another cloth is begun. Jacquard attachments are used on many types of looms and knitting machines.

The Jacquard weave is really a combination weave; two or more of the basic weaves are combined in the same cloth. For example, in table damask the design may be a sateen weave with filling floats, and the background may be a satin weave with warp floats. (For the difference between single and double damask see Chapter 18, p. 514.) The sheen in the design runs in the opposite direction from that in the background, with the result that the design stands out clearly. Different colored yarns for warp and fillings make an even sharper contrast.

In a brocade the background may be a warp satin and the design may be a fine twill or plain rib. Rayon and cotton damask draperies are made with mercerized cotton in the design and rayon in the background. In borders of turkish towels the design may be in pile weave and the background in plain or basket weave.

### IDENTIFICATION OF WARP AND FILLING IN JACQUARD WEAVE

If a combination of satin and sateen weaves is used, the warp usually floats in the background and the filling floats in the design when observed from the right side of the cloth.

Figure 5.7. A traditional damask in Jacquard weave with 100 per cent Enka nylon warp. (*Photograph courtesy of American Enka Corporation.*)

In fact, the warp is most easily distinguished if the background is observed first. If the background is plain or twill weave, the principles of identifying warp and filling in these constructions should be applied. (See Chapter 4.)

## FACTORS GOVERNING THE DESIRABILITY OF JACQUARD WEAVE

As the satin construction appears frequently in either the background or the design of a Jacquard weave, the length of the float affects the wearing quality of the fabric. This principle is especially true in table damasks, which have to stand much friction and laundering. If long floats are used, the fabric shows a higher sheen, but durability is decreased. Cotton used in long floats is apt to lint as a result of friction. A loose weave in Jacquard construction is a great deal weaker than a tight, close weave. In selecting a cloth with a Jacquard weave, the purpose for which the fabric is intended and the kind of wear expected should be carefully considered.

## CLOTHS MADE IN JACQUARD WEAVE

The more important Jacquard cloths are listed below. (These cloths may be made in mixtures of natural and/or synthetic fibers.)

| COTTON | LINEN | RAYON | SILK | WOOL |
|---|---|---|---|---|
| damask | damask | damask | damask | damask |
| terry cloth | borders | brocade | brocade | brocatelle |
| (with Jacquard | of huck | brocatelle | brocatelle | tapestry |
| designs or | towels | lamé | tapestry | |
| borders) | | | lamé | |
| tapestry | | | | |

## DOBBY WEAVE

Small designs can be made inexpensively by the *dobby* attachment that is put on the plain harness loom. The dobby is an English invention. A chain of narrow strips of wood with pegs inserted in each indicates the pattern. These strips take the place of the cards of the Jacquard loom. Each strip of wood represents a pick in the design. The pegs raise the harness to form a shed. A second chain controls the shuttle. The dobby attachment may control as many as thirty-two harnesses, whereas the plain harness loom can control only two to eight harnesses.

An American invention called the *head-motion attachment*, which is also connected to the plain harness loom, performs an operation similar to that performed by the dobby.

Simple, small geometrical figures in which the repeat in design appears often (every 16 rows, possibly) can be satisfactorily made by these two devices. Since a woven-in design of this character was originally made

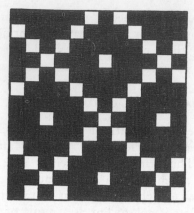

Figure 5.8. Point paper pattern for a dobby weave.

Figure 5.9 Huck toweling, a dobby fabric weave. (Photo by Jack Pitkin.)

only by the dobby attachment, the construction of these designs is still called dobby weave, even when the head-motion attachment rather than the dobby is used. Figure 5.8 shows a point-paper design for the dobby weave.

*Bird's-eye,* used for diapers, is made in dobby weave, and is characterized by small diamond-shaped figures with dots in the center. Small figures in the stripe of men's woven madras shirting are usually of dobby weave, as are also small, woven-in patterns in men's ties. Nail-head or bird's-eye sharkskin men's suiting is made in dobby weave.

*Huckaback,* or *huck toweling,* is made of slack-twisted cotton or linen yarns (dobby weave) in small geometrical designs. (See Figure 5.9.) This absorbent, slightly rough cloth is used mostly for face towels, although bird's-eye piqué and waffle cloth are made in a similar manner. The durability of huckaback depends on the balance of the count and the tensile strength of warp and filling; the closer the weave, the more durable the fabric. The dobby-weave design, when used for huckaback toweling, is sometimes called the honeycomb weave.

## LENO WEAVE

Lacelike effects, such as are found in marquisette and madras curtains, dishcloths, and old-fashioned grenadine, are made by a *leno* attachment; consequently, the weave is called the *leno weave.* Leno weave comes in both curtain-weight and dress-weight fabrics, many of which are lacelike and diaphanous. In weaving, adjacent warp yarns are twisted around each other, usually in pairs. Both warps may be twisted like a figure eight, or one may be held in tension and the other twisted about it. The filling passes through the twisted warps. If one warp is in tension, and one warp twists, the weave may be called gauze. Surgical gauze is plain weave, however.

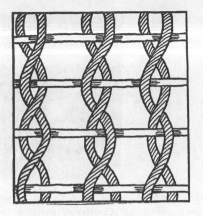

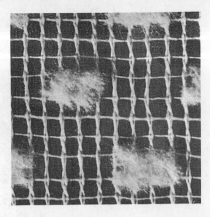

Figure 5.10.  Leno weave.

Figure 5.11.  Figured marquisette, a fabric in leno weave.

Sometimes the leno weave is combined with the plain or basket weaves to produce a lacy mesh called lace cloth. Again, a fabric of plain weave may have stripes of leno weave.

Mosquito netting uses the leno construction. The fabric is made of loosely twisted yarns, and the weave is coarse compared with marquisette. After the fabric is woven, it is heavily starched to prevent dirt from sticking to it. Heavy warps and heavy fillings may be inserted at intervals to add strength.

Considering their open construction, cloths of leno weave are durable. The figure-eight twist of the warp not only adds strength to that set of yarns, but also prevents the filling from slipping. This weave is found in cotton or in rayon and cotton mixtures in which cotton is used for the warp and rayon for the filling. Leno is also used in nylon, Orlon acrylic, Dacron polyester, or glass-fibered curtain marquisette. Silk or one of the synthetic fibers can be used to make marquisette for dresses. This weave is not an expensive one.

## ORNAMENTAL EMBROIDERED EFFECTS

Patterns similar to embroidery can be woven into cloth at the time the groundwork is woven. The difference between these patterns and Jacquard or dobby patterns is that embroidered effects can be pulled out by hand without injury to the rest of the cloth. Dobby or Jacquard patterns are such an integral part of the whole fabric that they cannot be removed. There are four types of these embroidery-like patterns.

### CLIPPED-SPOT DESIGN

This is an ornamental woven effect most commonly used on cotton fabrics. An extra filling yarn generally of different size or color from

123

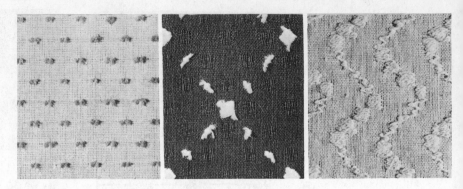

Figure 5.12. *Left:* Clip spot (wrong side). *Center:* Swivel (wrong side). *Right:* Lappet (right side). (*Courtesy of Stoffel & Co. Photos by Jack Pitkin.*)

the regular fillings is shot through at regular intervals in the weaving of the cloth. This extra filling is floated at points between the designs. After the cloth is woven, the floated yarns are raised so that the shearing knives may be run over these floats to cut them. The cutting is similar to that in corduroy. A single design consists of several parallel filling yarns. Swivel and clipped spot give the same effect. (See Figure 5.12.)

### SWIVEL DESIGN

Extra bobbins called "swivels" carry extra filling yarns several times around a group of warp yarns to give an effect of being tied. The yarn is clipped at the end of a figure. The design, therefore, consists of one thread only. Imported dotted swiss made in Switzerland may be made in this manner. (See Figure 5.12.) Most swivel patterns are woven into cotton fabrics. In this country the clipped-spot and flock-dotted designs have almost replaced swivel.[2] Rayon yarns can be used for swivel designs, but rayon is too slippery to stay in well. To ascertain the wearing quality of a swivel design, pull out a cut end. If the yarn pulls out very easily, the design is not likely to be durable.

### LAPPET DESIGN

Still another pattern resembling embroidery is made by the lappet attachment. Needles threaded with yarns for the design are set upright in front of the reed, but the design yarns threaded through them do not pass through the reed. By moving the needles sideways, simple designs are woven over the regular filling yarns. A true lappet design thread is often carried in a zigzag line and is woven without being clipped. (See Figure 5.12.)

The essential difference between a lappet design and a swivel is that

[2] See the Glossary.

in the swivel the design is done with extra *filling* yarns, which are cut off short at the end of each design. The lappet pattern appears only on the right side of the fabric, since the floats forming the pattern are fastened to the ground fabric only at their extremities. Lappet designs are made of one continuous yarn and are not clipped.

Lappet, swivel, and clipped spot are all woven fabrics; none is embroidered, although the effect is that of machine embroidery.

### SCHIFFLI EMBROIDERY

Intricate machine embroidery on fabrics like batiste, lawn, organdy, and piqué is generally done by the Swiss patented Schiffli machine. The embroidery yarn may run in any direction, not just fillingwise as in clipped spot or zigzag as in lappet. Eyelets may be embroidered by the Schiffli machine. (See Chapter 16.)

### GUIDES TO PROPER SELECTION OF WEAVES

A consumer should have a few general principles in mind when selecting a woven fabric. The purpose for which the fabric is to be used is very important. Some weaves are made for strength and durability; others are made for beauty, richness of texture, and design. In the former category are the plain and twill weaves; in the latter, satin, Jacquard, dobby, pile, and leno. To be sure, there are gradations of strength and durability in each classification. For example, a poorly balanced count in plain weave will not wear so well as a good balance. A rib weave may have ribs that are so large as to be out of proportion to other yarns in the fabric and consequently may cut the finer yarns. In pile weave, if the pile is lashed under only one background yarn, it will pull out more easily than pile woven over and under three background yarns. If a fabric is suited to the purpose for which it is intended, it will give good service.

The consumer should determine the durability of the weave. Several factors influencing durability must be considered. First, the warp and filling yarns should be spaced evenly. Second, the weave should be straight, to ensure both strength and good appearance. Third, there should be no broken yarns or other defects in the weave. Fourth, the weave should be close, both to produce strength and to

Figure 5.13. Schiffli embroidery.

minimize shrinkage. Fifth and last, the selvages should be strong.

Do the style, novelty, beauty, and appearance of the fabric govern the price? Does the intricacy or elaborateness of the construction of the cloth govern the price? Are age and hand workmanship the chief factors? Do the raw materials and the weaving justify the price asked? The consumer should answer these questions for herself and then come to a decision.

## SUMMARY

Elaborate weaves, such as pile, Jacquard, dobby, and leno, should be purchased not so much for their wearing quality as for their beauty and appearance. The pile weave in velvets and in fabrics made to resemble fur has a richness of texture and a depth of coloring not found in other constructions. Terry weaves in turkish towels have soft, absorbent surfaces and may have beautiful Jacquard borders. Leno weaves are purchased for their lacy, porous effects. In dress fabrics this weave is sheer and dainty. Jacquards are characterized by elaborate and intricate designs of remarkable beauty. Their price is correspondingly high. Dobby weaving makes simple geometric figures inexpensively. Embroidered effects produced by the lappet, clipped spot, and schiffli methods add to cloths interesting designs that are not integral parts of their construction.

## REVIEW QUESTIONS

1. (a) Outline four methods of making pile weave.
   (b) Name a cloth that is woven by each method.
2. How is the durability of pile weave determined (a) in silk velvet?
   (b) in terry cloth?
3. (a) How may matted pile in a velvet dress be restored to its original condition?
   (b) What instructions should the salesperson give a customer for cleaning and caring for pile fabrics used as upholstery?
4. (a) By what methods can fabrics be made to resemble fur?
   (b) Explain briefly the law for labeling and advertising such fabrics.
5. Explain the action of the Jacquard loom.
6. How can the consumer tell whether the fabric is made on a Jacquard or a dobby loom?
7. What advantages has dobby weaving over Jacquard weaving? Explain fully.
8. What factors determine the wearing quality of a Jacquard weave?
9. (a) Explain the construction of the weave found in marquisette.
   (b) What are the purposes of this weave?
   (c) Is this weave usually durable? Why?
   (d) For what fabrics is this construction used?
10. (a) Describe a method of weaving the dots in dotted swiss.

(*b*) How can the durability of these dots be determined?
11. (*a*) What is the difference between swivel and clipped-spot designs?
   (*b*) Which weave is the more economical in the use of embroidery yarn?
   (*c*) How can one tell the difference between swivel, lappet, schiffli, Jacquard, and dobby patterns?
12. What factors determine the durability of any weave?
13. Define three-pick terry weave, ground warp, fake selvage, double-cloth weave, pile, velveteen, Jacquard cards, long float, huckaback, pile warp.

## EXPERIMENTS

1. *Identifying fancy weaves.* Feel each fabric and look at it closely. Does the fabric have pile? Does it have a woven-in design? If so, is it small, or large and intricate? Is the design an integral part of the cloth or can it be pulled out without injury to the fabric? Is the construction open and lacelike?
   (*a*) What is the name of each weave?
   (*b*) Which yarns are warp?
2. *Determining the wearing quality of fancy weaves.*
   *Tearing test.* Tear a sample of material. If the fabric tears easily, the cloth will not wear well.
   *Seam test.* Make a seam by pinning two edges of material together. Grip the fabric on either side of the seam. Pull the fabric. Does it show elasticity or does it split immediately? If the fabric splits easily, it will not wear well.
   *Pulling test.* Grip the fabric at opposite edges; then pull slowly and evenly. Note how much strength it takes to split the fabric. Then pull the cloth with quick jerks. The fabric that will best stand quick, jerky pulling is the strongest.

## GLOSSARY

**Backed cloth.** A variety of double cloth that has two sets of fillings and one set of warps or two sets of warps and one set of fillings. See *Double weave.*

**Clipped-spot design.** Ornamental woven effect in which extra filling yarn is shot through at regular intervals in weaving of a cloth. The extra filling yarns are floated and later cut between designs. One design consists of several clipped parallel filling yarns.

**Corduroy.** A pile fabric identified by warpwise pile wales alternating with plain wales. See *Filling pile method.*

**Dobby weave.** A type of construction in which small geometrical figures are woven into the cloth.

**Double weave.** Two cloths are woven at the same time, face to face. Two sets of warps and two sets of fillings are used. One set of warps binds the two cloths together. The two cloths may or may not be cut apart. See *Backed cloth.*

**Filling pile method.** Extra fillings are floated over four or five warps. The floats are cut after weaving and then the cut ends are brushed up to form the pile. See *Corduroy*.

**Flock-dotted.** Designs of short fibrous materials printed in or onto the fabric with the aid of an adhesive. Electrostatic and lacquered applications of designs are two methods used. The former is durable in washing and drycleaning; the latter may be nondurable.

**Fur-fiber fabrics.** Cloths woven of hair or fur fiber intended to resemble fur. In order for a manufacturer to use this term, the T.F.P.I.A. states that the fiber content of a fabric must be hair, fur fibers, or any mixtures of animals (other than wool-producing animals) in excess of 5 per cent of the total fiber weight of the textile fiber product. No direct or indirect reference to the animals' names is permitted.

**Jacquard cards.** Oblong punched cards used to control the raising of warp yarns in a Jacquard loom.

**Jacquard weave.** A construction characterized by very intricate woven-in designs. A special Jacquard loom makes these designs by controlling each warp yarn.

**Lappet.** An ornamental embroidery effect woven into a cloth by a series of needles. The design, often in zigzag effect, is not clipped.

**Leno weave.** A lacelike construction made by twisting adjacent warps around each other like a figure eight. The filling passes through the twisted warps.

**Pile.** The cut or uncut loops composing the surface of a pile fabric.

**Pile weave.** A construction characterized by soft, looped yarns called *pile*. Pile may be on one or both sides and may be cut or uncut.

**Pinwale.** Pertaining to a cotton corduroy with very narrow wales (sixteen to twenty-three wales to the inch). See *Wale*.

**Schiffli.** Machine embroidery. The embroidery yarn is carried by a boat-shaped shuttle that can move in all directions to make intricate designs.

**Swivel.** Ornamental design woven in by extra filling yarns. Each design consists of one thread only, covering only the distance of one figure.

**Terry cloth.** Absorbent fabric made with uncut pile loops. See *terry-weave method* in the text.

**Three-pick terry cloth.** Two picks (fillings) go under the looped pile and one pick goes between two rows of pile.

**Velvet.** Pile fabrics made of silk or synthetic fibers in which extra warps usually form the pile by the wire method. The double-weave method may be used for average-grade transparent velvet.

**Velveteen.** A cotton pile fabric usually made by the filling pile method and characterized by a plain weave or twill back.

**Wale.** Alternating stripes of pile and plain cloth, found in corduroy.

**Wide-wale.** Pertaining to a cotton corduroy with about five wales to the inch.

**Wire method.** Extra warp yarns form the pile. These yarns are raised to form the shed and then a wire is inserted through the shed. When the extra warp yarns are lowered, they loop over the wire and are held in place by the next filling. A sharp knife attached to the end of the wire cuts the pile when the wire is withdrawn.

# 6

# Knitting
## and Other
## Constructions

"That which is or may be woven" is a definition of the noun *textile* found in one standard dictionary. This definition is correct as far as it goes, but who would say that the fabrics used in the making of a knitted sweater, a nylon net, a felt hat, or a braided rug are not textile products? Yet none of these articles are woven; instead, they are made into cloth by other methods, which include knitting, lace-making, felting, and braiding. Bonding and laminating should also be included.

Although weaving is the most usual method of constructing cloth, knitting is the second most common method. Knitted fabrics have invaded the woven market owing to the increase in bonding and laminating processes, the need for a diversity of constructions, and the variety of fibers and finishes available. Realizing the potential for knitted goods, a number of weavers have embarked on the manufacturing and distribution of knitted fabrics.

How are knitted cloths made? For knitted fabrics a continuous yarn or set of yarns is used to form loops. For woven fabrics two sets of yarns are necessary. The knitted cloth is composed of rows of loops, each row caught into the previous row and depending for its support on both the row below and the row above.

## HISTORY OF KNITTING

The knitting operation was supposedly invented in Scotland in the fifteenth century. The first stocking firms appeared in Nottinghamshire, England, in 1589. In 1758 the ribbing apparatus was invented by Jedediah Strutt. But it was not until the middle of the nineteenth century that circular machinery was used to produce tubular fabrics. Now the improved circular knitting machines are most common. Some types of hosiery, underwear, and jersey are made in tubular form.

## TYPES OF YARN NEEDED

Since the object of knitting is to construct an elastic, porous fabric, the yarns are more loosely twisted than they are for weaving; and since some knitted fabrics (eiderdown, for example) must have napped surfaces, slackly twisted yarn is preferable. Yarn types include filament, spun, blended, and textured for man-made fibers.

In knitted cottons, mercerized or lisle yarns (see p. 456) may be used when extra strength or luster, or a rich, fast color is required. Lisle yarns are usually ply-made of long, carefully combed staple cotton. Only when high luster is desired are lisle yarns mercerized.

In knitted wool fabrics any fiber, short or long, may be found. Whereas long fibers make a stronger, more even and durable yarn, short fibers are used for napped materials, such as those from which overcoats and sweaters are made. Therefore both woolen and worsted yarns are used. Worsteds are used for better-grade knitted dress fabrics and suits.

Linen is seldom knitted. It makes very comfortable underwear when it is treated in this way, but is too expensive for the average consumer.

Nylon is commonly used in women's regular hosiery and in stretch seamless and mesh knits. Women's sport socks can be made of almost any of the fibers or blends. For sportswear, spun yarn is more popular than filament yarn because the spun yarn has a warmer, more absorbent, softer texture. For women's knitted underwear, filament rayon, acetate, and nylon yarn are used in tricot slips and panties. Spun yarns are used when the surface is to be finished like suede.

With the advent of the mini skirt, pantyhose became popular. Commonly made of stretch nylon and spandex, the legs are net, fishnet, or flowery net, on a flat-knit panty.

For men's socks, cotton, nylon, and blends of these fibers, polyester, textralized nylon, and spandex tops are used. Crew-type socks are made of high-bulk acrylic or stretch nylon. Nylon is often plated (*plated*, not plaited) with wool at the heel and toe to reinforce these points of wear. In men's hosiery for cold weather, wool may be used on the inside and nylon on the outside of the sock. Many men still prefer cotton for knitted underwear, although man-made fibers and yarn are on the market. For support hosiery, textured stretch yarns or elastic yarns are used.

Girls may wear stretch socks of cotton or cotton and nylon blends; Orlon acrylic and cotton; or spun nylon outside for strength and pima cotton inside for comfort, with stretch nylon in between for greater elasticity. Leotards and tights are commonly made of stretch nylon.

Boys' socks of the crew type may be bulky knit of a blend of 65 per cent cotton, 33 per cent Marvess olefin, and 2 per cent spandex; or acrylic and stretch nylon; or mercerized supima cotton and stretch nylon. Long socks are made of cotton, Lycra spandex, or nylon crochet knit.

Knitted dress and blouse fabrics are very popular. Double-knit, jersey, and tricot are names of fabrics commonly used for dresses and blouses. Jerseys can be made of any of the fibers or blends. A fancy sweater made of Orlon acrylic spun yarn has the feel of cashmere and launders easily, with quick drying and no shrinkage. It may be ornamented with beads or a mink collar. When wool is blended with staple fibers of Orlon acrylic, Dacron polyester, or nylon, it is stabilized (shrinkage is minimized) and strengthened. Textured yarns of the high-bulk variety are used for bulky knit sweaters. (See Chapter 3 for bulky yarns.)

For swimwear and for foundation garments, spandex yarn has become popular. (See *spandex*, Chapter 2.) In surgical bandages, corsets, and the heavier foundation garments and in some swimwear styles, elastic rubber yarns may be used.


## TYPES OF KNITTING

There are two methods of constructing knitted cloth. One method forms loops running crosswise on the fabric and links each loop into the one on the preceding row. Hand knitting is done in this way. The technical name for this type of knitting is *weft* knitting. *Weft* is synonymous with *filling* in weaving and so denotes crosswise loopings in knitting.

The second type is called *warp* knitting. It cannot be done by hand. The machine for this operation is called a *chain loom*; it produces mostly flat fabrics, but some warp-knitting looms can make tubular cloths. For warp knitting, parallel yarns must first be arranged in two tiers on the loom, with a needle for each warp yarn. Each needle makes a separate chain stitch, and the chains are tied together by the zigzag of the yarns from one needle to the other. The resultant fabric, which has a cobwebby mesh, will not drop stitches or "ladder," because loops interlock with one another both ways in the fabric. Warp-knitted fabrics are stronger and generally of closer construction than weft-knitted fabrics, for the former have about four times as many stitches to the inch. Fabric gloves, tricot, and underwear and some mesh fabrics are made by the warp-knitting method. Owing to the popularity of warp-knitted fabrics, mills are designing new constructions to increase the versatility of their products. Warp-knitted fabrics appear in dresswear, outerwear, men's shirts, and women's blouses.

## STITCHES IN KNITTING

### BASIC STITCHES IN WEFT KNITTING

The stitches in knitting correspond to the different kinds of weaving. In knitted goods three major stitches are used.

Purl

Stitch

or

Plain

Knitting

Flat

Knit

or

Stockinette

Stitch

Rib

Stitch

**Figure 6.1.** Hand knitting (right side).

*Purl stitch.* Hand knitters call this stitch *plain knitting*. Rows of stitches, or components of the loops, run crosswise of the fabric on both sides. The first row of loops is connected on the right side of the fabric; the second row is connected on the back; the third row is connected on the right side; and so on. These horizontal ridges are called *courses*. So, in the purl stitch, courses appear on both sides of the fabric. The purl stitch stretches more lengthwise than crosswise. Consequently it is not suitable for garments such as sweaters, hosiery, and underwear, in which the greater strength must be crosswise. Baby carriage covers, stoles, pot

Purl

Stitch

or

Plain

Knitting

Flat

Knit

or

Stockinette

Stitch

Rib

Stitch

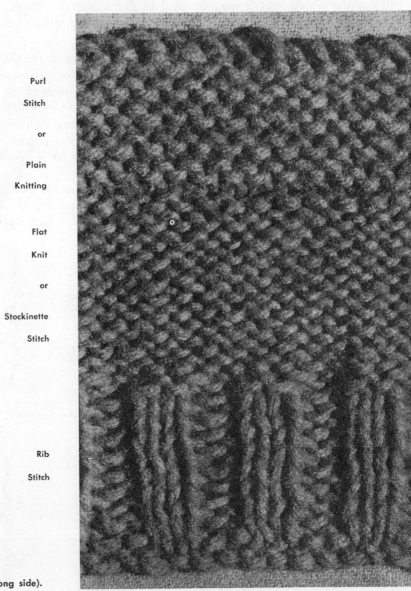

**Figure 6.2.** Hand knitting (wrong side).

holders, and dishcloths can be made with this stitch. (See Figures 6.1 and 6.2.)

*Stockinette stitch.* In hand flat-knitting, utilizing the stockinette stitch, instructions call for plain knitting on one row and purling on the next, the steps alternating in this order until the fabric is finished. The stockinette stitch is identified by vertical ridges on the face and horizontal courses on the back. (See Figures 6.1 and 6.2.) Since the stockinette stitch stretches more in width than in length, it is particularly suitable for hosiery, dress fabrics, underwear, sweaters, bathing suits, coats, gloves, caps, and mittens. The stockinette stitch is generally found in tubular goods, but it may be used in flat materials. Where a flat-surfaced fabric with a crosswise stretch is needed, the stockinette stitch is most common. Jersey is a fabric made in this stitch.

*Rib stitch.* This is a stitch used often for boys' hosiery, for the ribbed cuffs on sleeves and legs of knitted union suits, and for garter welts on socks. Lengthwise wales appear on the right and wrong sides of the fabric. (See Figures 6.1 and 6.2.) The hand-knit stitch is made by knitting two and purling two across the first row and then purling two above the two plain-knitted stitches and knitting above the two purled stitches on the second row. The result is called 2 x 2 rib. Each rib is two stitches wide, and each valley is two stitches wide.

Although this stitch is slower to make by machinery and requires more yarn than the plain stitch, it has an advantage in that it stretches in the width and generally returns to normal width after stretching.

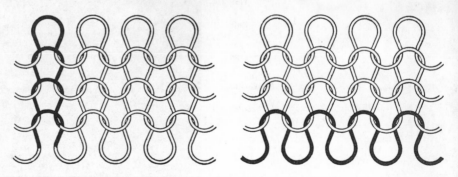

**Figure 6.3.** *Left:* A wale in a plain circular knit fabric. *Right:* A course in a plain circular knit fabric.

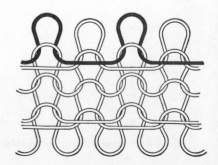

**Figure 6.4.** Run-resistant circular knit fabric.

Fabrics made with this stitch are heavier and warmer than those made with other stitches.

The rib stitch can be varied somewhat by making the ribs wider or narrower and by plating—that is, throwing one color yarn to the right side for the wales and the other yarn to the right side for the valleys between the wales. The colors are reversed on the back. Different fibers may be mixed in plated goods.

Interlock knitting is often mistaken for rib knitting (1 x 1 rib) because it has the same stitch appearance on both sides of a fabric. But interlock knitting makes a compound fabric composed of two separate 1 x 1 rib fabrics interknitted with each other to form one cloth. This type of knitted construction is made on an interlock knitting machine, which knits circularly.

An interlock fabric is run-resistant and has a similar stitch appearance front and back. It is smooth in texture and has considerable elasticity, so it is suitable for most underwear and sleeping garments. It will not curl badly at the edges, because there is equal tension on both surfaces.

## DOUBLE-KNIT AND KNITTED PILE CONSTRUCTIONS

When two cloths are knitted double and are held together with an occasional binding stitch like a woven double cloth, such fabrics are called *double knit*. The term "double knit" refers not to a single fabric but to a family of knitted fabrics. The characteristics of this family are a fine rib structure and full body. A wide variety of machines produce this construction by utilizing a double-needle mechanism that gives the back and the face of the fabric a similar appearance so it can be used reversibly. Double knits have good draping quality and dimensional stability (more like woven fabrics), are comfortable, and can be easily packed for traveling.

Cotton, acrylic, nylon, or blends of polyester and wool may be used for double-knit fabrics. Double piqué, a blend of 60/40 Kodel polyester and wool, can be permanently pleated and can be machine-washed and -dried.

Knitted pile fabrics are made by introducing extra yarn that is drawn out in long loops to form the pile. These loops may be left uncut as in knitted terry cloth or certain pile fabrics made to resemble velour. Fur-like fabrics employ a plain jersey foundation with pile built up by supplying laps of fibrous material to the knitting needles. (See *pile fabrics of fur fibers and synthetics,* p. 114.)

## VARIATIONS OF THE BASIC STITCHES

Like the plain, twill, and satin constructions in weaving, the purl, plain, and rib are the fundamental stitches in knitting. But there are a number of variations.

1. *Openwork stitch.* Openwork sweaters, sacques, hosiery, mitts, bonnets, facecloths, and mesh underwear may be weft-knitted according to this principle. In hand knitting, the open space or hole is made as the yarn is thrown over the needle, and the next two stitches are knitted as one. This stitch is repeated at regular intervals across the cloth. On the following row the yarn looped around the needle is knitted individually as though there were no openwork on the row below. Knitted laces are made in this manner.

2. *Tuck stitch.* When a knobby, bumpy knitted texture is desired, the tuck stitch is used. In this stitch certain loops are slipped from one needle to the other without being knitted. This system is followed across one row at desired intervals. On the following row the unknitted loops are knitted as regular stitches. The unknitted stitches gather or bunch between the knitted ones, thus forming an uneven surface.

By using the tuck stitch in combination with the rib stitch, a thicker, heavier fabric, warm enough for an outer garment, can be made. The rib-and-tuck stitch is often used for winter-weight knee-length knitted underwear. Several yarns can be knitted as one to make a hard-wearing, heavy fabric suitable for boys' sweaters and cardigan jackets (Figure 6.5.)

3. *Jacquard patterns.* Fancy patterns knitted into sweaters, golf socks, and neckties have to be made by a special attachment of the knitting machine. Like the Jacquard loom for woven materials, this Jacquard attachment regulates each needle to be used for each course. Paper rolls, perforated metal cards, or perforated metal bands regulate each needle. A Jacquard knitted fabric is one produced on either a rib or a purl machine in which the knit-in colored pattern is produced by knitting and welting (miss-knitting) stitches on selected needles.

Rib Jacquards may have (1) striped backs, usually in two colors; or (2) bird's-eye or twill backs, mostly in three colors or possibly in two. The latter type is reversible, with the pattern in color on both sides. Bird's-eye is preferable to striped because loops do not show through on the face and because it is more resilient, lighter in weight, and more supple. The reversible type usually has a superior design. A second type of Jacquard, called the "Jersey Jacquard," uses knit-and-tuck, knit-and-welt, or knit-tuck-and-welt stitches. The operation is slow and more expensive than regular knitting.

The term "Jacquard pattern" may apply to patterns woven by the Jacquard loom or made by the Jacquard knitting attachment. Small Dobby designs are often sold as Jacquards.

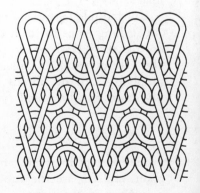

**Figure 6.5.** Double knit entails the use of two sets of needles which cast off stitches in opposite directions. The basic structure is 1 x 1 rib, a loop drawing of which appears above. (*Reprinted, courtesy of Knitted Outerwear Times, official publication, National Knitted Outerwear Association.*)

The consumer should distinguish between real Jacquard loomed designs and dobby designs. Jacquard designs in knitted goods should be called Jacquard knitted patterns to distinguish them from woven Jacquard designs.

STITCHES IN WARP KNITTING

In warp knitting there are three basic stitches: the single-bar tricot; the two-, three-, and four-bar tricot; and mesh.

1. *Single-bar or one-bar tricot* [1] (*single-warp tricot knit*). In Figure 6.6 the heavy black line indicates a yarn that is knitted in one direction and then is knitted in the reverse direction. Other yarns follow a similar course. Hence, one set of yarns is needed. A ribbed effect is produced. To make the rib wider, the thread is knitted farther across the fabric before it is reversed. A broken thread may cause a run down the fabric. Since each loop consists of one thread, a weak, unstable construction results. Although the single-bar tricot is economical to produce, the stitch is not knitted in any great volume.

2. *Two-bar tricot* (*double-warp tricot knit*). In Figure 6.7 the heavy black lines indicate two yarns, one knitted in one direction and the other in the opposite direction. Hence, two sets of yarns are needed for this fabric—one set to be knitted in one direction and another in the opposite direction. A ribbed surface results. Broken yarns do not cause runs.

Colors appear prominently on both surfaces. The two-bar tricot is wispy and airy. Its uses include shirts, blouses, and lingerie.

In the three-bar tricot, fabrics are used for dresses, shirts, and gloves. The design scope is greater than in the two-bar tricot. Warp-knitted fabrics are also made in four-bar constructions. "Angel laces"—narrow edgings and trimmings—are made on tricot machines.

[1] Tricot, pronounced "tree-co," comes from the French verb *tricoter,* meaning *to knit.*

**Figure 6.6.** Single-warp (one-bar) tricot fabric.

**Figure 6.7.** Double-warp (two-bar) tricot fabric.

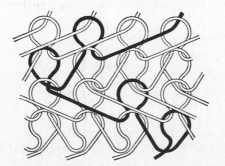
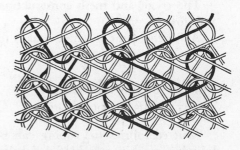

**Figure 6.8.** Three-bar tricot of Arnel/nylon.

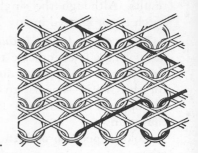

**Figure 6.9.** Mesh construction (milanese).

3. *Mesh.* In Figure 6.8 two black lines show that each yarn is knitted in one direction—one toward the right and one toward the left. Hence, two sets of yarns are needed. There is no reversal of direction as in the two-bar tricot. The crossings of the yarns make diamond effects. This construction may be called milanese.

There are a number of fancy stitches, including stripes of all kinds, lace-like patterns, and fancy knits that resemble woven cloth. Many of these fancy stitches are found in rayon or nylon underwear.

The tricot and mesh constructions are widely used for slips, panties, and gowns.

A Raschel knit machine makes fishnet and bobbinet.

## SHAPING OF KNITTED FABRICS

### FLAT VERSUS CIRCULAR KNITTING

Knitted fabrics for tubing can be made flat or circular. Most warp-knitting machines make flat fabrics, but it is possible to knit circular ones. On the other hand, weft knitting is done mostly in tubular form.

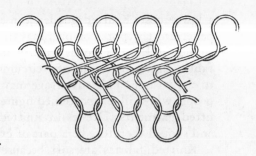

**Figure 6.10.** Fashion marks in full-fashioned stockings.

For a tubular or circular knit, the needles are arranged in a circle on the machine. They automatically form loops that run around and around the fabric, row on row. In a flat knit the looping is done across the fabric; each row is made by loops that are forced back and forth in flat form.

In flat weft knitting it is possible to shape the fabric during the process. Adding stitches at the end of certain rows makes the fabric wider; knitting two or more stitches as one makes the fabric narrower. This shaping process is called *fashioning;* it is used in making full-fashioned hosiery. In woven goods, the fabric must be cut to a shape after weaving. Fashioning, then, gives a distinct advantage to flat-knitted fabrics, because they fit and hold their shape better than the tubular-knitted cloths. In tubular knitting the shaping is done by changes in the tension of the needles: a tightening of tension makes a fabric narrower. This method is used in knitting semifashioned hosiery. (See Figure 6.10.) Tubular goods can be shaped after they are knitted if they are put on forms and steamed to the size required. The shape, however, is not permanent.

One of the ways to stabilize knitted constructions and to give them warmth is by bonding and laminating (see p. 145).

## WHY BUY KNITTED GOODS?

Even though there are more woven than knitted goods on the market, knitted fabrics have achieved an increasing importance in fashion apparel. For garments that must cling to the body and still give as the body moves, knitted goods are more suitable than woven goods. Infants' sacques, sweaters, many bathing suits, hosiery, certain types of underwear, and some dresses and blouses are knitted. Cut and tailored knitted fabrics are now made to look like woven fabrics. They can be made in plaids, checks, and solid colors. Skirts, dresses, and jackets for girls and women of all ages have increased the demand for knitted cloth.

Knitted fabrics are practical and serviceable, and they are no more expensive than woven materials. Moreover, greater speed in knitting due to improved machines requiring less knitter-labor, plus automation in inspection and hosiery-size identification, means more knitted goods at a lower cost. Knitted goods cleanse easily because the suds can quickly penetrate the pores or openings in the knitted construction. The loops found in knitted goods greatly increase the elasticity of the knitted fabric, and under ordinary circumstances the garment will shape itself to the wearer. This advantage may become a disadvantage, however, to people whose ill-proportioned figures are revealed when they wear snugly fitted garments. Dresses of knitted construction do not wrinkle easily and should therefore be a part of every woman's wardrobe for traveling.

Knitted fabrics are soft because the yarns are loosely spun and the pores between the yarns hold air enmeshed in the fabric. They are comfortable because of their elasticity and the ventilation provided for the skin. Very sheer knitted garments are cool in summer, for the open mesh allows the air to reach the skin. Heavily constructed fabrics hold in air that has been warmed by the body. The cold air is warmed before it can penetrate to the skin. Only a stiff breeze will disturb the enmeshed warm air. Knitted garments that are napped or brushed in the finishing process are warmer than smooth-surfaced garments because they retain more still air. Fleece or brushed fabrics in double knits of cotton, nylon, or acrylics are used for sweater shirts, jacket and coat linings, underwear, and outerwear.

Knitted fabrics do not stick to the skin when they are damp. Woven cottons stick badly when filled with perspiration. A knitted fabric made of loops and loosely twisted yarns absorbs more moisture than a woven material of comparable weight. Therefore knitted bathing suits are popular. There is less danger of catching cold from damp knitted garments, because the yarn itself absorbs more moisture than does the yarn in woven garments.

Knitted fabrics can be adapted to style changes, as has been evidenced by the increasing number of designs in warp knitting and the improvements in double-knit fabrics. Variations in knitting construction can be

**Figure 6.11.** Power net of Lycra spandex and nylon knitting yarns shown being stretched in both directions. It is used largely for underwear.

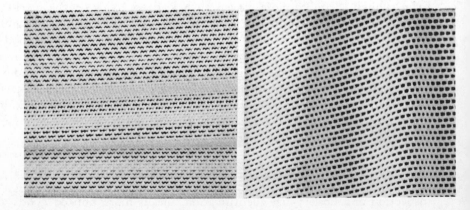

made by changes in the action of the needles. Colors can be printed on a garment after the knitting is completed, provided the pattern is such that it will not be too distorted by stretching. Numerous Jacquard pattern variations are used. Mixtures of fibers of different textiles and textured yarns and the use of plaiting also produce interesting effects.

Knitted fabrics are durable. Their construction gives them pliability and stretch, and if properly laundered they usually come back to their original size. Certain precautions must be taken in laundering and wear to ensure long service.

A tricot fabric laminated to the back of a knitted cloth is a popular construction. This technique not only stabilizes the knitted goods but also adds warmth. A looser knitted construction is possible when a backing is applied.

## CARE OF KNITTED GARMENTS

Every woman knows how provoking it is to notice a dropped stitch or a runner in one of her stockings. As each loop in knitting depends on other loops for its strength, a break in one loop affects all the loops below. Runners develop only in weft knitting. Hosiery can be made by regular warp knitting, but it is usually too heavy for the average consumer. If a consumer must have runproof underwear, she should buy a mesh. These fabrics have runs limited to only one direction. Runless, seamless nylon hosiery in a lock-stitch mesh is popular.

To avoid runs in weft-knitted dress goods and underwear, it is advisable not to use pins, for they break the loops and start runs. Always fasten garters in the garter welt at the top of the stocking or sock. This welt is of stronger construction than the boot or body of the stocking, and if a run should develop in the garter welt, it will not run below the run stop. All runs should be mended as soon as they are discovered to prevent them from running farther. Often the application of a little water, run-stop fluid, or nail polish to the ends of the run will stop it temporarily.

The consumer should know a few points about the hand laundering of knitted goods. Because of their great elasticity and open construction, they may shrink or lose shape when they are washed. "Care" labels will specify hand laundering if required.

1. To remove dirt, use a neutral soap and the same cupping motion of the hands as is used for fine fabrics. (See Chapter 15.)
2. After rinsing, wrap cloth in a towel and squeeze out as much water as possible.
3. Knitted fabrics should not be hung up to dry. They should be dried flat, for the weight of water will pull a fabric out of shape and may break a loop and so cause a hole or a runner. If knitted fabrics must be hung, however, it is better to throw them over a

line than to attach them with clothespins (attach clothespins only to the reinforced portion of the toe or to the garter welt). Wool hosiery is best dried on a frame or form that is the same size as the foot. Wool sweaters and blouses should be measured and their dimensions recorded before the washing process. An easier method is to lay the garment on a piece of paper and draw around it before washing. Then, when the garment is still wet, it can be pulled gently to its original dimensions. Knitted wool dresses should be dry-cleaned. Laminated fabrics should be dry-cleaned only.

## OTHER METHODS OF CONSTRUCTION

### NET AND LACE-MAKING

Net is a geometrically shaped figured mesh fabric made of silk, cotton, nylon, rayon, or other synthetic fiber. It comes in different sizes of mesh and in various weights. On the one hand, machine-made net is closely related to warp knitting because it is constructed on either a tricot or a Raschel warp-knitting machine; on the other hand, net is related to lace because many of the machine-made laces have geometrically shaped nets as their grounds. Bobbinet made in a hexagonal-shaped mesh of rayon, nylon, silk, or cotton is a popular fabric for evening dresses, veils, curtains, and trimmings. Like most nets and laces, bobbinet was originally made by hand on a pillow of the same width as the lace to be made. Small pegs or pins were stuck into the design. Thread was thrown around the pegs marking the design. When the lace was completed, the pillow was removed. (See *bobbin lace,* Chapter 18.) A closely constructed, very fine silk or nylon net is called *tulle.* The first nets to be made by machine were the warp-knitted tricots that appeared about the middle of the eighteenth century. At the beginning of the nineteenth century, a bobbinet machine that could handle yarns in three directions was invented and patented by John Heathcote. Shortly after that, a patterned lace loom was devised.

Another type of net is the knotted-square mesh type with knots in four corners to form the mesh. Originally made by hand and used by fishermen, it is now made by machine. These modern fishnets of linen or cotton are used for glass curtaining in contemporary living rooms, sun porches, and dens. (See pp. 603 ff.)

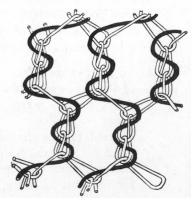

Figure 6.12. The structure of tulle fabric, the characteristic of which is the hexagonal shaped holes. Two guide bars are required, both fully threaded; the front guide bar knitting and the back guide bar laying-in. This net forms the basis of many patterned Raschel lace fabrics. (Reprinted, courtesy of Knitted Outerwear Times, official publication, National Knitted Outerwear Association.)

A lace is an openwork fabric made of threads usually formed into designs. (See the description of various laces, Chapter 16.) By hand, lace can be made with needles, bobbins, shuttle, or hooks. Handmade lace is called real lace. When needles are used, the lace is called *needle-point;* when bobbins are used the lace is called *bobbin* or *pillow;* when knotted with a shuttle, the lace is *tatting;* when made with a hook, it is called *crocheted.* Laces can also be made by hand with knitting or crochet needles.

Real lace was the only lace known until the invention of the lace machine in the early 1800's. This machine was later modified by several inventors, among them John Levers, whose name has come down to us via the Levers machine we use today.[2] Patterns of real laces can be reproduced on the modern lace looms, so we can now have their designs in quantity at a fraction of the cost of the handmade. Sometimes designs from various real laces will be combined in a single lace, which can be designated as *novelty lace.*

## BRAIDING (OR PLAITING)

This is a method of interlacing (plaiting) three or more yarns or bias-cut strips of cloth over and under one another to form a flat or tubular fabric. These braided textile bands, which are relatively narrow, can be used as belts, pull-cords for lights, trimming for uniforms and dresses, tapes for pajamas, and some shoe laces. Several widths of plastic or straw braiding can be sewn together to make hat shapes. Similarly, braids of fabrics or yarns may be sewn together to make braided rugs.

## FELTING

It is said that early peoples discovered what we know to be the felting process. By wearing the fur side of animal skins next to the body, these people discovered that the fur matted from the body's heat and perspiration and the pressure of the skin against the body. In our modern felting process, wool or fur fibers tend to mat or interlock when they are subjected to heat, moisture, and pressure. Hair of cows as well as hair of rabbits is used for woven felts and hair felts. Coarse hair of domestic cattle is used for inexpensive felted goods like insoles and underlays for rugs.[3] Fur felt hats are made from Australian, French, English, and Belgian rabbit fur.

Wool is probably most ideal for felting because the fibers swell in moisture, interlock, and remain in that condition when pressed and shrunk. When the fibers have been selected and, if necessary, blended with cotton or synthetic fibers, they are carded into a flat sheet or bat. Bats are placed first one way and then the other in layers until the

2 "Lace," *Fairchild's Dictionary of Textiles* (1967), p. 325.
3 "What Is Felt?" *Ciba Review,* XI, 29 (November 1958), 2–3.

desired thickness is reached. Allowance has to be made for shrinkage, because steam and the pressure of heavy presses in the process of felting may increase the bats as much as 20 per cent in thickness. To make the felt fabric stronger and more compact, the fabric is placed in warm soapy water, where it is pounded and twisted. For heavy felt, a weak acid is used instead of warm soapy water. (See *felting*, Chapter 12.) The cloth is then ready for finishing processes consisting of scouring, dyeing, possibly pressing or shearing, and treatment with special functional finishes to make it water-repellent, mothproof, and shrink-, crease-, and fire-resistant. Felt is made for men's and women's hats, women's skirts, vests, and slippers; also for table covers, padding, and linings. Woven felts have their place primarily in the industrial field.

### BONDING

Felting is a much older process than bonding, but the two processes are closely allied. In felting, heat and pressure of the fibers in the presence of moisture cause fibers to adhere; in the bonding process, the fibers are pressed into thin sheets or webs that are held together (bonded) by a plastic adhesive. Rayon, cotton, or polyester are frequently selected for bonding. Long fibers are preferable to give strength to the web. The fibers are first carded to lay them in a web (called a *card lap*). Methods of binding are as follows:

1. A web is made by blending fibers that melt or fuse (nylon, acetate, vinyon) with fibers (cotton and rayon) that do not melt when heated. As heat is applied to the web, the nylon, acetate, or vinyon fuse just enough to hold the cotton or rayon permanently together.
2. Instead of heat, a solvent may be used to soften the acetate or plastic fibers.
3. The web is sprayed or treated with a plastic binder to make the fibers adhere. Color can be added to the binder.

*Bonded* or *nonwoven* fabrics are becoming more popular every day. With crease-resistant and fire-resistant finishes, embossing, soft or crisp hand, increased flexibility, porosity, and printed designs, varied uses are made possible. A few important ones include draperies, towels, tablecloths, coat interlinings,[4] interfacings,[5] window shades, noncracking wall-paper, disposable tissues, diapers, bibs, and shoulder pads. Since bonded fabrics are inexpensive to produce, they are cheaper than woven or knitted constructions.

[4] Pellon is a popular brand name of a fiber fleece made from 60 per cent wool and 10 per cent camel's hair and other fibers. Pellon interfacing is predominantly nylon with some acetate and cotton. Fibers are bonded chemothermically.

[5] Keybak is a trademarked name of a nonwoven interfacing made of rayon and du Pont virgin nylon. It is suitable for collars, cuffs, sleeves, waistbands, bodice fronts, jacket fronts and hemlines, and coat and skirt hemlines.

In Chapter 2, bonding was described as a process of pressing fibers into thin sheets or webs (nonwoven goods). Laminating is joining together two or more layers of fabric, back to back, or fabric and foam, with a binding agent. By this definition, then, "layered goods" are laminated fabrics, while fabrics made of webs are bonded goods.

There is no standard definition for either of these terms. In 1966 and 1967 these terms were being used interchangeably; but at present the term "laminated" is commonly limited to the joining of fabric to foam. The term "bonded" seems to be doing triple duty to cover (1) two fabrics stuck together by adhesive; (2) a fabric stuck to a sheet of urethane foam; and (3) nonwoven goods made of webs of fibers. So if one wants to be properly understood, one can use the term "bonded" for all the foregoing techniques. Perhaps one should mention what the layers consist of and which is intended to be the face. An acetate or a nylon tricot-backed wool knit would describe a common "bonded" fabric.[6]

## METHODS OF PRODUCING LAYERED FABRICS AND NONWOVEN GOODS

### a. THE FABRIC-TO-FABRIC METHOD

Two layers of fabric are joined together by use of an adhesive, a binding agent, or heat. An example of layered fabric is a pair of girls' denim dungarees that have been lined at the cuffs with plain flannelette. The flannelette has actually been stuck (laminated) to the wrong side of the denim so that when the pants are rolled up the plaid shows. Another example is men's permanently stiffened collars, in which a layer of plastic binder is placed between two layers of fabric. In the process of shirt manufacture, the operator stitches along one edge of the collar through the two layers of fabrics with plastic between. Then heat and pressure are applied to fuse the two fabrics. Stitching the rest of the collar completes the laminating operation. Many homemakers have occasion to use this same principle to mend or reinforce clothing, sheets, or tablecloths with tape or patches by ironing the tape or patch with the binder side against the cloth. If the proper amount of heat and pressure is applied, the patch will adhere satisfactorily.[7]

### b. FABRIC-TO-FOAM METHODS

There are two possible ways to laminate foam to fabric:

1. *Wet adhesive.* A water-based acrylic compound is applied to the fabric, followed by curing by heat, which creates a permanent bond

[6] Research done by the author for an article in *Textile Service Management* (a periodical for cleaning and laundry management), June 1967.

[7] Brand names of mending tape are Bondex and Irontex.

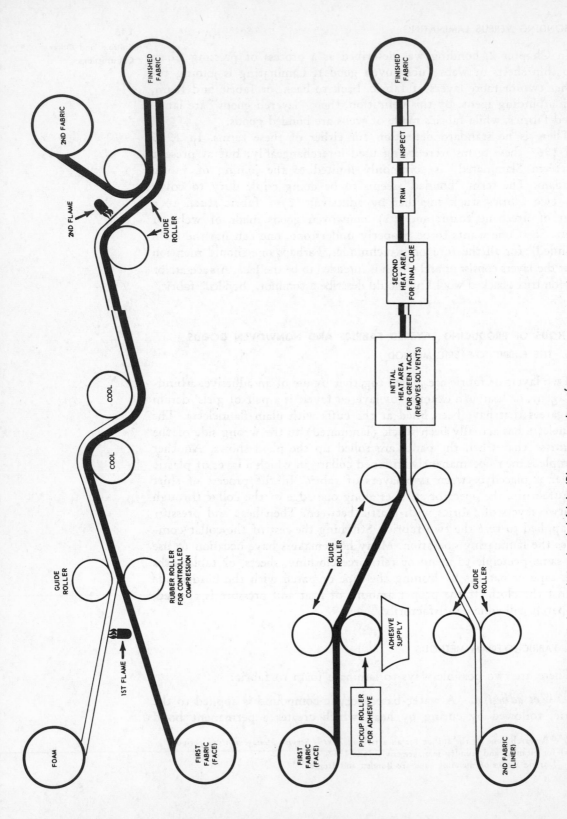

**Figure 6.13.** The two basic methods for producing bonded fabric. (*Diagrams courtesy of American Fabrics Magazine.*)

without affecting the draping qualities of the face fabric or the softness of hand.

2. *Foam flame.* The foam is made sticky with a gas flame. A small fraction of the foam's thickness is burned off. The foam in this case takes the place of an adhesive or binding agent.

### c. WEBBED FABRICS (nonwovens)

Webs, or mats of fibers, are held together (bonded) in the following three ways:

1. *Plastic or other adhesives.* Examples are Pellon and Keybak.

2. *Spun-bonding.* A bonded-fibered fabric is produced directly from the spinneret by electrically charging the extruded fibers and rubbing them over a suitable guide, releasing the tension, and moving filaments forward by air jet to a receiving surface. The electrical charge causes filaments to separate, loop, and crimp. The fiber web is bonded. In a dry-spun method, a solvent under pressure is kept above its normal boiling point. The frothing of the solution causes filaments to join at random points.

3. *The Rasmussen process.* In this spot-welding technique, a sheet of polyethylene or polypropylene is stretched lengthwise to orient the fibers' molecular chains. The disintegration into fibrous form results in a network of fine fibers that are relatively parallel to each other. Two or three layers of fibers can be spot-welded together.

### PROBLEMS OF SERVICEABILITY OF LAMINATED AND BONDED FABRICS

Layered fabrics may come apart (be delaminated) by abrasion, because the adhesive cracks and the face fabric separates from the backing. In drycleaning, the fabric layers may pull apart if the solvent solubilizes the adhesive. Designs formed by spot-welding are likely to discolor or disappear—a common occurrence in simulated quilted fabrics. Mechanical action in drycleaning may cause separation of the fabric and obliteration of the design. However, decided improvement in resistance to delamination has been noted. Urethane backing may attract loose soil or dye particles during drycleaning or use. This often occurs with foam-backed place mats. The foam may turn yellow or darken owing to exposure to heat and atmospheric conditions. The outer layer of a garment may change color. Ripples and puckers may be caused by a shrinkage of one of the layers of the cloth. The spun-bonded fabrics may have finishes that are not colorfast to light, washing, and perspiration.

### NEEDLE-WOVEN PROCESS

This process involves a so-called "needle loom"—a device that punches through a thick web of fibers, forcing the fibers from layer to layer until they gradually become entangled. An example of the use of this process is the Lantor blanket of lofty Acrilan acrylic web. A synonymous term is "needle punch," which is used in the carpet industry.

Needling as done by the Arachne machine feeds a web (cross-laid) into the back of a warp-knitting machine. Uses of the finished cloth include upholstery, windbreakers, and coats. The fabric is too stiff for dresses.

### SEWING-KNITTING PROCESS

A recent development in the textile industry is the sewing-knitting process, which utilizes three types of equipment: the Malimo, Malipol, and Maliwatt machines. These machines produce a different type of fabric by a combination thread-laying and sewing-and-knitting technique. The process completely omits certain production steps. The machines were developed in East Germany in 1956.

The Malimo makes fabric-like woven goods, including warp and filling. Warp yarns are laid on top of the filling yarns; both warp and filling are connected with a third yarn system composed of a sewing thread. It is also possible to have a two-yarn system in which only filling and knitting thread are used. In this case, filling layers are arranged at slight angles to each other. Layers of fibers may also be used in a three-yarn system. Malimo stitch-knitted goods made of three layers with carded yarns in a three-yarn system are distinguishable from traditional fabrics of the same mixture by a considerably superior crease recovery.[8]

The Malipol machine makes a one-sided pile fabric using a backing cloth of either a woven or a Malimo construction. In Malimo terry cloths the back shows chain stitches or interlaced wales. Since the pile yarns are knitted into the back, pile fabrics will not pull or shed. Products of the Malipol machine include coat fabrics, blankets, and carpets.

The Maliwatt machine makes fabrics more closely resembling nonwoven goods.[9] In this process a web of fibers is presented to the machine, which uses a sewing thread to interlace the carded web into a nonwoven fabric. The stitch is the lock-chain or conventional type, which is done lengthwise (7.2 mm. apart). The effect is a series of parallel seams. The chief advantages of this technique are (1) the preservation of the fabric's fluffiness, and (2) the ease of further processing, such as laminating, coating, applying latex for use as a stiffener, and napping and dyeing.

The styling possibilities of stitch-knitted goods seem to be unlimited, and developers of the process are working on technological improve-

[8] "New Styling Developments in Malimo" (an excerpt from the Annual Report of the Malimo World Trade Mark Association, 1967–68).

[9] *Watt* is a German word meaning a bat of fibers.

ments. Novelty textures and space-dyed yarns provide interesting design possibilities.[10]

## SUMMARY

Knitted goods are especially suitable for garments requiring a snug fit and elasticity. They are warm without feeling heavy, have good absorptive quality, and are hygienic. There are two methods of constructing knitted goods: weft and warp knitting. Although weft knitting has good elasticity, stitches may be dropped. On the other hand, warp knitting is a stronger, closer construction than weft knitting. Stitches are not dropped, but garments do not conform to the contour of the body as well as those constructed by weft knitting.

Net-making is closely allied to knitting because machine-made net can be made on a warp-knitting machine. Many laces have net grounds and all have patterns.

To braid, three or more yarns are interlaced over and under to form a fabric. Braids are narrow goods, and several widths must be sewn together for shaped articles such as hats or rugs.

Felting and bonding are nonwoven constructions, although there is a woven felt. In felting, heat, pressure, and moisture cause the fibers to adhere. For bonding, a web of fibers is made and the fibers are held together by a binding agent.

Laminating is a process of holding together two or more layers of material by a process similar to the construction of plywood in the non-textile field. Foam may be laminated to a knitted or woven fabric.

## REVIEW QUESTIONS

1. In what respects does the knitted construction differ from the woven? Consider the yarns and the knitting operation.
2. What are the three principal stitches in weft knitting? For what purposes is each used?
3. What advantages has the plain stitch over the ribbed or the purl stitch?
4. Name three fancy stitches. For what purpose is each used?
5. (a) Describe warp knitting.
   (b) What advantages has warp knitting over weft knitting?
   (c) What fabrics are made by warp knitting?
6. (a) How do fabrics knitted flat differ from circular or tubular knitted goods ?
   (b) What are the advantages and the disadvantages of goods knitted by each method?
7. What instructions should salespeople give to customers on the care and laundering of knitted fabrics?

[10] Malimo World Trade Mark Association, *op. cit.*

8. Explain the following constructions:
   (a) Bobbinet
   (b) Tatting
   (c) Fishnet

9. What braided articles are used in apparel? In home furnishings?
10. Explain how a gray wool felt skirting fabric is constructed.
11. (a) Differentiate between bonding and laminating.
    (b) For what purposes are nonwoven fabrics used?
    (c) For what purposes are layered (laminated) fabrics used?
    (d) By what methods are fabrics laminated to foam?
    (e) Explain the merits and drawbacks of each method.

## PROJECT

Visit the yard goods and lace departments of your local store. List in
separate columns all fabrics that are (a) woven, (b) knitted, (c) net or
lace, (d) felted, (e) bonded, (f) braided, (g) laminated. What percentage of the fabrics listed comes in each category? What conclusions
can you draw?

## EXPERIMENTS

1. *Determining the stitch used in knitting.* Unravel a yarn from a sample.
   Does it unravel back and forth from the fabric? If so, is it weft or warp
   knitting? Look at the right and wrong sides of the fabric and answer
   the following questions:
   (a) Are there courses on both sides?
   (b) Are there wales on one side and courses on the other?
   (c) Are there wales on both sides?
   (d) Does the fabric have an openwork or mesh design?
   (e) Is the surface roughened or puckered in the knitting operation?
   (f) Has a pattern been knitted into the fabric?
   (g) What stitch or combination of stitches is used in this fabric?
2. *Determining the durability of the fabric.* Hold the fabric to the light.
   Answer the following questions:
   (a) Do you see thick and thin places in the yarn?
   (b) Is the knitting regular?
   (c) Is it a close construction?
   (d) Does the fabric spring back to its original shape after stretching?
   (e) Will the fabric be durable? Why?
   (f) Will a garment made from this cloth keep its shape? Why?

## GLOSSARY

**Bobbinet.** See *Net*.
**Bonding.** See Glossary, Chapter 2.
**Braiding.** See Glossary, Chapter 2.

**Circular knit.** Knitting in tubular form. Shaping is done by tightening or stretching stitches.

**Courses.** Horizontal ridges (components of the loops) in weft knitting.

**Curing.** The application of heat to a fabric or garment to impart properties such as dimensional stability, crease resistance, water repellency, and durable press.

**Cut.** Number of needles per inch on the circular bed of a knitting machine.

**Double knit.** Two cloths knitted double and held together with an occasional binding stitch—like a woven double cloth.

**Drop-stitch knit.** Open design made by removing certain needles at intervals.

**Fashioning.** A shaping process in making flat knitted fabrics by adding stitches or by knitting two or more stitches as one to narrow the fabric.

**Felting.** See Glossary, Chapter 2.

**Flat knit.** Knitting done in flat form, as opposed to *circular knit*.

**Foam laminate.** A construction made by laminating a synthetic foam to a woven or knitted fabric.

**Full-fashioned.** See *Fashioning*. A term applied to sweaters and hosiery shaped by fashioning.

**Gauge.** See *Cut*.

**Interlock knitting.** A process of making a compound fabric composed of two separate 1 x 1 rib fabrics interknitted to form one cloth—made on an interlock knitting machine.

**Jacquard patterns.** Fancy patterns knitted in articles made by a special attachment of the knitting machine.

**Jersey.** A knitted fabric of cotton, wool, nylon, acetate, rayon, or blends with the newer synthetics. It is usually made in stockinette stitch or two-bar tricot.

**Knitted pile fabrics.** Extra yarn introduced and drawn out in loops to form the pile that may or may not be cut.

**Knitting.** The process of constructing a cloth by interlocking a series of loops of one or more yarns. It may be done by hand or by machine.

**Lace.** An openwork fabric made of threads usually formed into designs. It is made by hand or by machine.

**Laminating.** The holding of two or more layers of material together with a plastic binder or the bonding of a fabric to a synthetic foam.

**Lisle yarn.** Made of long-staple cotton of defined length in two or more ply and with a minimum twist for a given count specified by the F.T.C. rules for hosiery.

**Mesh.** A knitted or woven fabric with an open texture. It can be made of any fiber, mixture, or blend.

**Milanese.** A kind of warp knitting with several sets of yarns. Crossings of the yarns make diamond effects.

**Net.** A geometrically-shaped, figured mesh fabric made in nylon, rayon, silk, or cotton. It has no pattern and is usually made on a warp-knitting machine.

**Nonwoven fabrics.** Webs of fibers held or bonded together with plastic, heat, pressure, or solvent.

**Openwork stitch.** A construction of open spaces purposely made at regular intervals across the knitted cloth. It is a variation of a basic stitch.

**Plain stitch.** A synonym for *flat knit* or *stockinette stitch*. It is identified by vertical wales on the face and horizontal courses on the back of a fabric.

**Plated goods.** Knitted fabrics that have one kind of yarn on the right side of the fabric and another kind on the back.

**Purl stitch.** Rows of stitches run crosswise of the fabric on both sides. Horizontal ridges are called *courses*.

**Real lace.** Handmade lace. See *Lace*.

**Rib stitch.** A weft knit identified by vertical ribs on both sides of the fabric—a very resilient stitch. When combined with tuck stitch, it is called rib-and-tuck stitch.

**Runless.** A type of seamless nylon hosiery in a lock-stitch mesh.

**Run-resistant.** Knitted fabric constructed to make runs difficult. See *Interlock knitting*.

**Single-bar (one-bar) tricot.** A warp knit using one set of yarns. A yarn is knitted in one direction and then reversed, producing a striped effect.

**Stockinette stitch.** Weft knitting characterized by vertical wales on the face and horizontal courses on the back of the fabric. See *Plain stitch*.

**Tricot.** From the French *tricoter*, meaning to knit—a fabric made by a warp-knitting (tricot) machine. See *Two-bar* and *Single-bar tricot*.

**Tubular knit.** See *Circular knit*.

**Tuck stitch.** A variation of a basic stitch in weft knitting to make a knobby, bumpy, knitted texture. Unknitted loops are slipped from one needle to another. On the following row, the unknitted loops are knitted as regular stitches.

**Two-bar (double-bar) tricot.** A warp knit in which two sets of yarns are required, one knitted in one direction and the other in the opposite direction. A ribbed surface results. It is synonymous with double-warp tricot knit.

**Warp knitting.** A process that makes a closer, flatter, less elastic fabric than weft knitting. It is frequently run-resistant. Examples are tricot and mesh.

**Weft knitting.** A process in which the thread runs back and forth crosswise in a fabric. See *Warp knitting*.

# 7

# Finishes

"Is there such a thing as heavy cotton slacks that I won't have to iron?" asks the customer. "Yes," replies the salesgirl, "we have corduroy slacks that you can wash in your automatic washer, then tumble-dry or drip-day them, and they will need no ironing. They are durable press, which means that they stay smooth after washing and drying." Two weeks later the customer returned to buy a second pair, in a different color. She had washed the slacks, and to her surprise they didn't need ironing and were softer after washing.

In this instance the chief selling point, the minimum-care finish, is a treatment applied to the fabric *after* weaving. The treatment given a cloth after it is constructed is called *finishing*.

## WHY FABRICS ARE FINISHED

The stiffness of organdy, the smooth, silky feeling of batiste, the colored print on cretonne, the watered or moiré effect on silk, and the whiteness of table damask are all the result of finishing treatments to which the fabrics are subjected after they are made. A whole industry, called the *converting* industry, devotes itself to this finishing of cloth. The converter takes the fabrics from the mills and either treats them himself or has them treated to make them more attractive, more serviceable, and hence more salable. Before goods are finished they are said to be *in the grey* (or *greige*)—which does not necessarily mean gray in color.

There are the regular or basic finishes, such as napping, brushing, shearing, calendering, and the like, without which a fabric would not be suitable to sell. Basic finishes, in some form, have been applied to textile fabrics for centuries. Then there are the functional or special finishes that contribute a special feature to the merchandise. Permanent starchless, crease-resistant, and water-repellent are a few of the functional finishes. Finishing processes can be considered *mechanical* if they are done by copper plates, roller brushes, perforated cylinders, tenter frames, or any type of mechanical equipment. If fabrics are treated with alkalies, acids, bleaches, starch, resins, and the like, they are considered to have been subjected to *chemical* finishing processes. It is in the field of chemical finishes that the greatest developments are being made.

## PERMANENT AND NONPERMANENT FINISHES

### PERMANENT FINISHES

Some fabrics must be so finished that friction will not harm the surface; others must be crease-resistant; and some must be unaffected by light, perspiration, washing, or water spotting. Fortunately for the manufacturer, fabrics do not have to be finished to withstand every hazard equally well; if they did, the finish would of course be considered permanent. But permanency of finish is not usually determined in this way. If a cloth has a finish that will withstand whatever affects it in its particular use, the finish is considered permanent. For example, an evening dress does not have to be fast to light or to friction. A man's wool suit must be particularly fast to light and should be fast to friction, but it need not be fast to washing.

It is not wise to say that all types of any finish are permanent. For example, bleached silks may turn yellow sooner than bleached linens. One mercerized cotton broadcloth may lose its sheen in laundering sooner than another broadcloth. The mercerizing of the first piece may have treated only the surface of the fiber, whereas the mercerizing in the second piece may have penetrated to the core of the fiber. Permanency of finish is, of course, only a relative term.

Wash-and-wear finishes for cotton, first used in the late 1950's, have been improved considerably since then. Consumers found that early wash-and-wear cottons did not all perform as the term indicated. Most of them required ironing to make them look fresh and smooth. The resin in the finishing caused the cottons to have a heavy, somewhat stiff hand. Many of the first wash-and-wear cottons turned yellow if a chlorine bleach was used on them.

Now most of these finishes do not turn yellow. In fact, standards of quality have been set to ensure good performance of wash-and-wear finishes. Quality manufacturers asked the Sanforized Division of Cluett, Peabody & Company, Inc., to establish a standard, whereupon they invented an electronic instrument (the Electronic Smoothness Evaluator), which has an electric eye that sees—and counts—every crease and wrinkle. A fabric after washing must dry without too many wrinkles to measure up to this standard. It must resist wrinkling, not shrink out of fit, have good tensile strength, and have good tear strength.[1] Wash-and-wear cottons that come up to all five of the Sanforized Division's specifications bear the label "Sanforized-Plus." Merchandise so labeled gives the consumer insurance of satisfactory wash-and-wear performance. Such a finish would be considered permanent.

The term "permanent press" indicates a long life in durability. Hence the term *durable press* is being used in this text. "A permanent or durable press garment, or any other end use textile product such as sheets or drapery, does not require ironing for the use life of the product under normal usage conditions." [2] It should be noted that from a consumer's point of view the degree of seam puckering that is acceptable in a woman's printed blouse would not be acceptable in the collar or front seam of a man's dress shirt. To be sure, manufacturers' quality-control standards call for a certain level of performance in use.[3] But again, a wash-wear rating of a sheet emerged from a tumble drier should be higher than durable press pajamas or dresses. What the industry needs, then, is level of performance standards.

Some processes producing finishes that can be made to withstand a reasonable amount of wear without injury and that are therefore called permanent finishes include:

| COTTON | LINEN | RAYON | SILK | WOOL |
|---|---|---|---|---|
| Bleaching | Bleaching | Printing | Bleaching | Printing |
| Glazing | Beetling | Dyeing | Dyeing | Dyeing |
| Dyeing | Dyeing | Moiréing (if | Printing | Napping |
| Printing | Printing | resin-treated | | Moth-repellent |
| Mercerizing | Shrinkage control | and heat-set) | | Shrinkage control |
| Shrinkage control | Starchless | Shrinkage control | | Wash-and-wear |
| Trubenizing | Crease-resistant | Starchless | | Durable press |
| Starchless | | Crease-resistant | | |
| Crease-resistant | | Water-repellent | | |
| Wash-and-wear | | Durable press | | |
| Durable press | | (modified | | |
| (cross-linked | | rayons) | | |
| cotton) | | | | |
| Cotton/polyester | | | | |
| blends | | | | |

[1] "What Every Shopper Should Know about Wash-and-Wear," a pamphlet by the Sanforized Division, Cluett, Peabody & Company, Inc.

[2] Definition given at the Sixth Annual Conference of the American Association of Textile Technology (AATT), 1966.

[3] Fabrics that have passed the test for performance standards of the Sanforized Division of Cluett, Peabody & Co. are labeled Sanforized-Plus-2.

| NYLON | POLYESTER | ACRYLICS | GLASS FIBERS |
|---|---|---|---|
| Stiffening (resin) | Wrinkle-resistant | Crease-resistant | Crimp setting |
| Nonslip | Shape retention | Permanent pleating | Wrinkle-resistant |
| Embossing (heat-set) | Heat-set | Water-repellent | |
| Moiréing | Moiréing | Heat-set | |
| Durable press (cotton/ nylon blends) | Durable press | Moiréing | |
| Durable press (100% nylon) | | Durable press | |

Piece-dyed and printed fabrics may be fast to light, friction, and washing if their fibers have an affinity for the dyestuffs.

Beetling produces a comparatively permanent finish because the process flattens out the fibers themselves. Pressing tends to keep the fibers flat.

Nap wears off with friction but, if well made, does not wash off and is not affected by light. It is therefore generally considered a permanent finish.

Many fabrics are now finished with resin finishes. The resin is fixed in the fiber so that it becomes a part of it and cannot be felt or seen even under a microscope. The resin doesn't change the surface of the fabric, but it adds resilience and hence muss resistance and reduces shrinkage in sponging and pressing. Flannels, light worsteds, and blankets so treated have better resistance to shrinkage. Oil-modified resins protect glass fibers. Cottons are often heat-set by applying resin first and then embossing. Wrinkle resistance and wash-and-wear properties are given to cotton dress goods by using thermosetting resins, by using a catalyst, by curing at a high temperature, and preferably by washing afterward.

Glazed chintz and tarlatan may be treated with starch, glue, paraffin, or shellac and run through hot friction rollers to give the fabrics a high polish. These finishing materials are not permanent. However, synthetic resins can be baked into the fabric to produce a permanent, washable finish. Everglaze is a trade name of such a finish.

Permanent or durable press is a finish obtained through chemical treatment applied to either a fabric or a garment for the purpose of creating permanent shape, permanent pleats, permanent pressed creases, durable smooth seams, wrinkle resistance, machine washability and dryability, and a fresh-pressed look without ironing. If care instructions are followed, durable press finishes eliminate the need for ironing after laundering. To be effective, many fabrics must be tumble-dried. Trade names include Koratron, Dan Press, Super Crease, Coneprest, and many more. Durable press can also be added to stretch fabrics. The technology of durable press will be discussed under "functional or special finishes."

## NONPERMANENT FINISHES

Surfaces that rub off when a cloth is brushed briskly are not permanent. Also, if the fabric loses its surface attractiveness or a good deal of its weight from cleaning or laundering, the finish is not permanent.

Sizing is a dressing that generally rubs off and washes out. With one or two exceptions, sizing is not permanent. Cotton organdy, which is heavily sized, can be given a starchless finish that will come back when the fabric is ironed. Glazed chintz, which is sized first and then calendered, can be so treated that the cloth may be wiped with a damp rag in the same way as oilcloth.

Weighting is applied to both silk and wool and is not a permanent finish. If the finish washes out, the fabric becomes flimsy and shows its defects. Weighted silks water-spot easily. As the chief constituents of loading in wool are a chemical and moisture, this finish is also easily removed. Flocking, which can be removed by brushing, is not a permanent finish. A table damask may be recognized as cotton if fuzz or lint appears after the cloth is washed. Cotton towels that are carefully singed to imitate linen also become fuzzy after washing. Cottons singed preparatory to mercerization do not develop lint so quickly.

Creping put in as a finishing process is not considered permanent unless heat-set. The roller type of creping comes out with the first washing, but the type put in by the caustic soda method is likely to be more permanent.

Embossing done by steam and rollers washes out and is not permanent. Heat-set treatment is permanent when done properly.

Moiréing can be made a permanent finish. The finishing of acetate cloth to produce moiréed effects that will withstand washings has been important for the moiré industry.

Tentering is a process of stretching a fabric to make it even. (See p. 161.) If a cloth is stretched excessively to make it even in width, the fabric will return to its original size after laundering (it shrinks). Therefore a preshrunk fabric evenly tentered is important to the cutter of the garment. Later, when the consumer launders the garment, it is not likely to shrink to a narrower width.

Calendering is only pressing and is removed by washing and wear. This finish can be replaced by the consumer.

Some of the finishing processes that have been discussed in detail are mechanical in nature, including those that employ rollers, steam, and pressure. The rest of the finishing processes are chemical in nature and include weighting, mothproofing, and fireproofing; crease-resistant, wash-and-wear, and water-repellent finishes; and bleaching, dyeing, and printing. (Dyeing and printing will be discussed in Chapter 8.)

The great improvements in finishing equipment and continuous finishing and dyeing operations have been primarily responsible for increased production of finished goods. With increased production of finished goods, consumers will have greatly improved assortments in almost unlimited quantities.

The consumer should be advised to consider, before a purchase is made, the purpose for which a fabric is to be used. Some finishes withstand laundering, sunlight, perspiration, and friction; others do not. The experiments at the close of this chapter should aid the consumer in making a decision.

## PREPARATORY TREATMENTS

Before the basic or functional finishes can be applied, cloths usually are given some preparatory processing. For example, if a linen fabric not already bleached in the yarn is to be white or is to be dyed or printed, it is pretreated by being bleached.

### BLEACHING [4]

The object, of course, is to whiten the cloth, which comes from the loom grayish brown in color. Inexpensive cottons are often merely washed and pressed after coming from the looms and are sold as unbleached goods. The natural tan color of flax makes bleaching one of the most important processes in finishing linen. Wild silks are usually bleached before they are dyed. If a silk cloth is to be a light color or pure white, it must be bleached. Wool is frequently bleached in the yarn, but may be bleached after weaving or scouring.

### SCOURING

When scouring is done as a finish, it is called *piece scouring*. The purpose of the process is to remove any sizing, dirt, oils, or other substances that may have adhered to the fibers in the processing of the yarns or in the construction of the cloth. To avoid the formation of an insoluble soap film on the fabric, soft water is used for scouring.

### DEGUMMING

Before a silk fabric can be dyed or other finishes applied, it must be degummed, unless the yarns were degummed before weaving. Boiling silk fabrics in a mild soap solution followed by rinsing and drying will accomplish this purpose. As a result, the fabric will have a beautiful sheen and will have a soft hand.

### IMMUNIZING OF COTTON FABRICS—A CHEMICAL MODIFICATION OF THE FIBERS [5]

Cellulose fibers, like viscose and cuprammonium rayons, take regular cotton dyestuffs; acetate fibers do not. (See Chapter 13, p. 349.) There-

[4] *Bleaching of cotton,* Chapter 9; *bleaching of linen,* Chapter 10; *silk,* Chapter 11; *wool,* Chapter 12; *rayon and acetate,* Chapter 13.
[5] *Fairchild's Dictionary of Textiles* (1967), p. 292.

fore, if cotton is treated with an agent such as acetic anhydride to change it from pure cellulose to an ester of cellulose (having the same chemical composition as acetate fiber) the cotton will be made immune to regular cotton dyestuffs and will take the same dyes as the acetates. The result is a paler stain on the cotton than on the acetate, but a wider range of colors is possible. Cross-dyed effects may be obtained by weaving immunized cotton with regular cotton. (See *cross dyeing*, Chapter 8.)

## MERCERIZATION OF COTTON

Although this process can be done in the skein of yarn, frequently mercerization is done after weaving. Any type of cotton can be mercerized, but best results are obtained on long-staple cottons. (New rayon and cotton blends are now also being mercerized.) The process consists of holding the fabric in tension while treating it with a strong solution of sodium hydroxide at a uniform temperature of 70° to 80° F. Mercerization can be done before or after bleaching and occasionally after dyeing. In the last two instances, mercerization may be considered a basic finish. The purposes of mercerization are threefold: (1) to increase the fabric's luster; (2) to improve its strength; (3) to give it greater affinity for dye.[6]

## BASIC FINISHES

Finishes that enhance the beauty and attractiveness of a cloth and cover defects appeal to the eye. Finishes that add weight, body, or warmth to a cloth appeal to the sense of touch.

### FINISHES THAT APPEAL TO THE EYE

An unbleached cotton muslin is not considered a beautiful fabric, yet when the same fabric is bleached, brushed, singed, starched, printed, and calendered, it is attractive.

Unbleached muslin is commonly sold for household purposes, whereas a finished muslin print can be used for children's dresses, sportswear, and housedresses. Finishes that add attractiveness to a cloth will be described.

*Shearing.* After a nap has been raised on a cloth, it is sheared to make the surface smooth and uniform. Shearing is also done to even the pile. To make carved effects, designs and ground can be cut in different lengths. In the case of hard-surfaced fabrics such as gabardine, shearing removes all surface fibers. The process also serves to cut off knots, ends, or other defects. The shearing device has revolving blades similar to a

[6] *Ibid.*, p. 364.

lawn mower. Shearing can be applied to any of the textile fibers or blends.

*Singeing.* Smooth-surfaced cloths are passed over either heated plates or gas flames to remove projecting fibers. The fabric must be passed rapidly over the gas flame so only these fibers are burned.

*Brushing.*[7] For smooth-surfaced fabrics, such as cotton dress percale, brushing with rollers covered with bristles removes short ends of fibers. In the case of wool fabrics, brushing frequently follows shearing, because in the shearing process cut fibers fall into the nap and must be removed. Two brush cylinders lay the nap in one direction and steam sets it. Brushing may be applied to any fabric.

*Beetling.* Linen damask has a glossy, hard, leathery feeling. To give this feeling, linen fabrics and cotton fabrics made to resemble linen are pounded (beetled) with little hammers. (See Chapter 10.)

*Mercerization.*[8] When mercerization is applied after bleaching or after dyeing, the process may be considered a basic finish.

*Decating.* Decating is a mechanical finish involving heat and pressure. It is applied to silk, rayon, and blends to set the luster and in wool especially to develop a permanent luster. It softens the hand, reduces shine, helps even the set and grain of the cloth, and delays the appearance of breaks and cracks. (See Chapter 12 on dry and wet decating of wool.)[9]

[7] See "Brushed Fabrics," *Fairchild's Dictionary of Textiles*, p. 84.
[8] See mercerizing, Chapter 9.
[9] For finishes for wools, see *fulling, gigging, napping,* and *steaming,* Chapter 12.

**Figure 7.1.** The tenter frame. After dyeing, the linen is dried to a uniform width. This picture shows the linen passing over hot air vents. (*Photograph courtesy of the Irish Linen Guild.*)

*Tentering.* To even fabrics in the width and to dry them, a tenter frame is employed. Pins or clips grip the fabric automatically by both selvages as the cloth is fed to the tenter frame. The distances between the two sides of the frame can be adjusted to the appropriate width of the fabric. Creases and wrinkles are pulled out and the weave is made straight as the fabric is moved along the frame. The drying is done by machines, which either radiate heat from steam pipes or blow hot air through the fabric.

*Calendering.* After all chemical and mechanical finishes have been applied, the cloth is pressed, or calendered, by passing it between hollow heated rollers. If the fabric is to receive a high polish, the cloth is usually stiffened with sizing before it is calendered. The more heat and pressure applied, the greater the luster produced. Calendering, then, not only smooths out wrinkles but also adds sheen to the fabric. All cloths having a smooth, flat surface have been calendered.

When the consumer irons a fabric, she is really calendering it. In the making of velveteen, where flatness of surface is not desirable, the cloth is merely steamed while in tension; but it is not pressed. Calendering is an important finish for most cottons. It is used also for linen, silk, filament and spun rayons, and other synthetics when a smooth, flat surface is needed.

Variations of calendering operations include those producing moiréed, embossed, and glazed finishes.

*Moiréing.* One of the most interesting surfaces is the moiré finish. A cloth with a fillingwise rib weave is run between rollers engraved with many lines, and is thus given a watered effect. On acetate cloths, this finish will remain in good condition after the fabrics are laundered. Rayons may be given resin treatment to set the design.

*Pressing.* Pressing accomplishes the same result for wool as calendering does for other fibers. Calendering is really a pressing process, but the term is not applied to wool.

To press wool, the fabric is placed between heavy, electrically heated metal plates that steam and press the fabric. Sometimes the cloth is

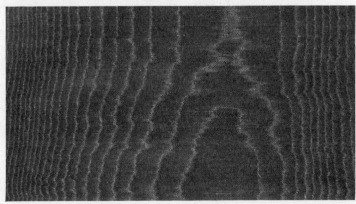

**Figure 7.2.** A moiréed fabric. (*Photo by Jack Pitkin.*)

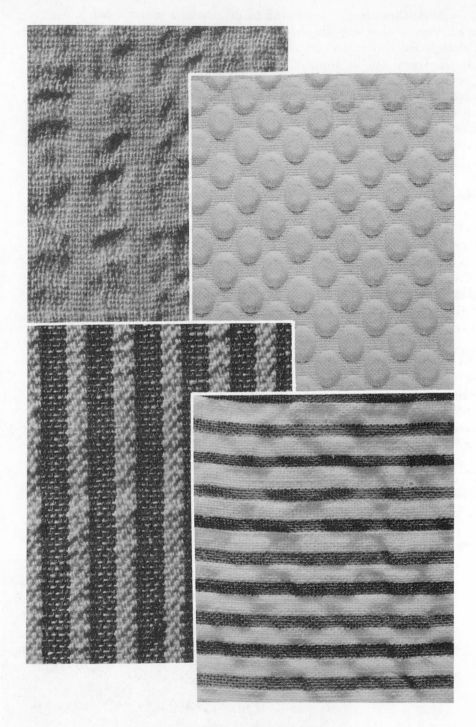

**Figure 7.3.** *Top left:* Crepes made by embossing. *Top right:* Crepes made by steam rolling. *Bottom left:* Crepes made by tension. *Bottom right:* Crepes made by caustic soda printing. (*Photos by Jack Pitkin.*)

wound round a cylindrical unit that dampens the fabric and then presses it. This method can be used not only for woolens and worsteds, but also for rayons and silks.

*Embossing.* So that a design may be made to stand out from the background, the fabric is passed between steaming rollers that imprint or emboss the design on the fabric. This design is less expensive than a woven-in design. Rayon pillows are embossed in this manner.

Very poor cotton tablecloths may be made to look like Jacquard linens by an *embossing* process. This finish is not a satisfactory one because it will not stay in after laundering unless it is heat-set.

*Creping.* As a finishing process, creping may be accomplished by passing the cloth between hot rollers in the presence of steam. These rollers are filled with indentations, the counterparts of the waved and puckered areas to be produced. This method is inexpensive, but the crepe will iron out and wash out unless a heat-setting treatment is used.

A more permanent creping is done by the caustic soda method. Caustic soda paste is rolled onto the cloth in stripes or figures. The fabric is washed, and the parts to which the paste was applied shrink. The rest of the cloth does not shrink but appears puckered or creped. Sometimes a paste that resists the effect of caustic soda is put on the cloth in spots where the fabric is not to shrink. The whole cloth is then immersed in caustic soda; the untreated spots shrink and the rest puckers or crepes. Crinkled bedspreads are made in this manner. This method results in a more permanent crepe than does the first method.

*Glazing.* After fabrics are bleached, dyed, or printed, they may be given a stiff, polished, or glazed surface. Starch, glue, mucilage, shellac, or resin may be used to stiffen the fabric. Then smooth, hot rollers that generate friction are used. Chintz for upholstery and curtains is generally glazed.

Since the advent of resins in the finishing field, permanent-finish glaze can be applied to chintz and other muslins. The melamine formaldehyde or urea formaldehyde resins are used to give a smooth surface that resists oil. They produce a permanent finish.

*Polishing.* Polished cotton may be mercerized first and then friction calendered. These fabrics, which look shiny and shed dirt very well, are softer than glazed chintz. Cottons that are commonly polished are nainsook and sateen.

## FINISHES THAT APPEAL TO TOUCH

Some finishes improve the softness of a fabric. For example, softeners and hand builders must be used on nearly all durable press fabrics. Since 1964, polyethylene emulsions have been found to improve abrasion resistance, sewability, and fabric hand. These emulsions have increased in use as softeners since the advent of durable press.[10]

[10] *American Dyestuff Reporter* (November 20, 1967).

Other finishes give weight and body; others give crispness; others make the cloth warmer.

*Napping.* The warmth and softness of a wool flannel or a brushed wool sweater is partly due to the fuzzy soft surface called *nap*. Napping, then, is a process of raising short fibers of a cloth to the surface by means of revolving cylinders with metallic points. Cottons and synthetic fabrics of spun yarns may be napped to resemble wool in texture. (For the processes of napping woolens, see Chapter 12.)

*Weighting.* Weighting in silk is intended to replace boiled-off gum. If weighting is excessive, it can be employed to add body to an otherwise flimsy structure. The poor wearing quality of heavily weighted silks has been discovered by most consumers. Weighting is also accomplished in the finishing process when the weighting substance is put in the dye. (The practice of weighting fabrics will be discussed more fully in Chapter 11.)

To make a firmer, more compact wool cloth, manufacturers steam fibers (obtained by shearing a cloth or reused wool) into the back of a fabric. This is *flocking*. Its presence can be detected by brushing the back of the cloth with a stiff brush to see whether short fibers come out.

*Sizing or dressing.* To increase weight, body crispness, and luster, cottons are often stiffened. Substances like glue, wax, casein, or clay are used. Sizing is not a permanent finish. (See Chapter 9 for a more thorough discussion of sizing of cotton.) Very soft, limp rayons and linens are often improved by some dressing. Permanent finishes to give stiffness, called *permanent starchless finish,* will be discussed under "functional finishes."

*Starching.* (See *sizing.*)

*Inspection and repair.* After the fabric is finished, visual examination to detect imperfection is a must. The process might consist of throwing the fabric over a horizontal bar [11] for examination under a powerful lamp. Visual examination is a final step for the finisher. The cloth must then have nubs, burrs, hair, slubs, and straw removed. Any knots must be opened and loose ends pushed through to the wrong side. If there are any exceptionally irregular yarns, they are pulled out and replaced. If any yarns are missing, they must be run in by hand.

### SHRINKAGE

Nothing can prove more distressing to a customer than to find the garment that fitted her perfectly before laundering shrunk to a size smaller afterward. The worst fabric offenders are cotton, linen, wool, and filament rayon. Acetate, silk, nylon, and the other synthetics are not subject to shrinkage, although the type of yarn used, the count of the cloth, and the type of finish are factors affecting this property of a

---

[11] See *perching, burling,* and *mending,* Chapter 12.

fabric. For example, creped yarns and loosely constructed fabrics frequently shrink. Also, wool knitted fabrics, unless laundered properly, are likely to shrink.

## PRESHRINKING (F.T.C. RULINGS ON SHRINKAGE)

Prior to June 30, 1938, when the F.T.C. issued its shrinkage rules, which are applicable to all woven cotton goods whether finished or not, the word "preshrunk" was misleading to the consumer. Many consumers were led to believe that if a fabric was labeled preshrunk, it would shrink no more. When the consumer washed the fabric, she often found it did shrink. In short, this fabric, after preshrinkage, had a capacity to shrink more. This capacity to shrink further is termed *residual shrinkage.*

According to the F.T.C. ruling,[12] if the words "preshrunk" or "shrunk" are used on a cotton-goods label, the manufacturer must guarantee the maximum shrinkage. For example, "These goods have been shrunk (or preshrunk) to the extent that residual shrinkage will not exceed —per cent when tested in accordance with the recognized and approved standards or tests." A test devised by the American Standards Association known as Commercial Standard CS 59-44 has been recognized as a standard test by the F.T.C. Another suggested form of label may read: "Preshrunk—residual shrinkage 1 per cent, or 2 per cent." Terms such as "full shrunk," "shrinkproof," "nonshrinkable" are banned by this ruling if the goods so labeled have any further capacity to shrink at all.

In brief, if a manufacturer labels his goods as "preshrunk" or "shrunk" he must adhere to the F.T.C. rules, but if he does not label his goods as "shrunk" or "preshrunk," then he need not indicate the percentage of residual shrinkage.

According to the Good Housekeeping Institute, 5 per cent fabric shrinkage changes a size dress 16 to a size 14 in bust, waist, and hip and to a size 12 in length. Even a 3 per cent fabric shrinkage is undesirable. Should the collar of a man's shirt shrink 3 per cent, a size 15 collar is reduced to 14½, and the sleeve shrinks ½ inch.

Cotton fabric shrinks because its yarns have been stretched during weaving and finishing. When the fabric is being laundered, the yarns relax and return to their normal position, thus causing shrinkage. Not all cottons shrink alike. They vary according to type and construction. Percales shrink 3 to 8 per cent. Flannelettes may shrink 10 per cent or more.

## SHRINKAGE CONTROLS

Almost everyone is familiar with the Sanforized label. Sanforized is a trademark owned by Cluett, Peabody & Company, Inc., which permits

[12] The ruling applies legally to goods sold in interstate commerce.

its use only on fabrics that meet this company's rigid shrinkage requirements. Fabrics bearing the trademark Sanforized will not shrink more than 1 per cent by the government's standard wash test. Sanforized is not the name of a shrinkage process; it does not denote a method of shrinking; it *does* denote a checked standard of shrinkage performance.[13] Hence, when a consumer sees this Sanforized trademark on a crisp blouse in white broadcloth, she knows that the fabric shrinkage will not exceed 1 per cent despite repeated laundering. When she sees the trademark Sanforized-Plus by the same company, she knows the fabric has passed standard tests for proper performance in use of a wash-and-wear fabric. Similarly, Sanforized-Plus-2 refers to a fabric that has passed performance tests for durable press.

When a compressive shrinkage process is used on a fabric to eliminate customers' complaints of shrinkage, fabrics so treated gain in durability, because shrinkage increases the number of warp and filling yarns to the square inch (raises the count of cloth). The finish of the cloth is also improved, because the yarns are crinkled and drawn closer, and the fabric is dried against a polished cylinder. These processes give smoothness, soft luster, and improved draping possibilities. The compressive shrinkage process adds a few cents a yarn to the price the customer must pay, but this increase is not exorbitant, since untreated cloth may shrink as much as 10 per cent. Practically every cotton can be so treated—even mixed fabrics made of cotton, silk, and wool.

*For rayon.* Rayon fabrics and blends of these fibers may be stabilized (so they will not shrink or stretch more than 2 per cent) by resin impregnation. This treatment forms resin within the fiber rather than on the surface. Even though this treatment may change the hand, the advantage of shrinkage control outweighs the disadvantages. Rayon shrinkage can also be prevented by chemical reaction (cross-linking) with acetals. Special additives are required to prevent excessive weakening of the fabric and to retain a pleasing hand and appearance. Another method utilizes a combination of dialdehyde, glyoxal, and urea formaldehyde resin. Fabrics so treated are said to be resistant to any temperature wash water and repeated launderings.

*For the newer synthetics.* The man-made thermoplastic fibers such as the polyesters and the nylons are heat-sensitive. They are usually heat-set during finishing to make them stable.

*For wool.* The four commonest methods of controlling the shrinkage of wool are (1) the chlorinating process; (2) the resin treatment; (3) treatment with enzymes that attack the fiber scales; and (4) microscopic coating of a polymer. (See Chapter 12.)

[13] "How to Use the 'Sanforized' Trademark," a leaflet by the Sanforized Division, Cluett, Peabody & Company, Inc.

Finishes that are applied to fabrics to make them better suited for specific uses come in this category. In general, these finishes are newer than the basic finishes, many of them having been perfected during World War II.

### ABRASION RESISTANCE

Abrasion resistance is a matter of the degree to which a fabric can withstand the friction of rubbing or chafing. The newer man-made fibers, such as nylon, acrylics, and polyesters, have good abrasion resistance, but the natural fibers do not have this property. To overcome this problem, fibers with high-potential abrasion resistance can be blended with fibers of low abrasion resistance (not a finish). The application of certain thermoplastic resins (particularly acrylic) may be used. The chief objection to the use of resins lies in the fact that these finishes may increase wet-soiling of the fabrics.

In durable press cottons, abrasion resistance is reduced to a third or less of untreated fiber. In the original concept of durable press cotton, either the molecules were loaded with resin or the fiber structure was immobilized with cross-links. This reaction made the fiber brittle as well as resilient. No amount of softeners would overcome this fault while retaining the resilient property. Considerable research has been done along these lines. By 1967 the Southern Regional Research Laboratory (New Orleans, La.) reported that cotton fabrics and garments made of blends of cotton fibers—part of which have been impregnated with certain thermosetting and/or thermoplastic resins and untreated cottons—show excellent ability to resist damage by abrasion during laundering.[14] A number of treatments have aimed to keep the cotton fiber slightly swollen while it is being cross-linked. Then there are possible improvements made in

50% FORTREL* POLYESTER • 50% COTTON

CELANESE FORTREL*

SOIL RELEASE AND PERMANENT PRESS

*Registered trademark of Fiber Industries, Inc.

---

50% FORTREL* POLYESTER
50% COTTON
EXCLUSIVE OF DECORATION

This is the official Fortrel tag. It gives you added assurance of satisfaction for it is only awarded to fabric styles meeting the performance requirements of the Celanese Fortrel Trademark Licensing Agreement.

With SOIL RELEASE stains float away during washing.

This PERMANENT PRESS fabric NEEDS NO IRONING for the normal use-life of the garment.

CARE INSTRUCTIONS

• MACHINE WASH—use warm water

• MACHINE DRY—use wash/wear setting—remove as soon as dry

• If line or drip dried—requires little or no ironing

F02   1

[14] *American Dyestuff Reporter* (February 1967), p. 23.

**Figure 7.4.** Label for Fortrel polyester fabric. (*Courtesy of Celanese Fibers Marketing Company.*)

cross-linking agents. Finally, polyester blended with cotton compensates for loss of abrasion resistance and strength.

## ABSORBENT FINISHES

For such articles as towels, bed linens, diapers, and underwear, the absorption of moisture is important. A treatment with ammonium compounds causes cottons, linens, and rayons to absorb water more readily.

A chemical finish has been found that corrects the hardness and lack of water absorbency of nylon. The use of this finish has improved the appearance, comfort, and salability of finished nylon hosiery and piece goods.[15]

## AIR CONDITIONING

Short, fuzzy fibers are sealed into the yarn by a chemical process. The fabric is thereby made more porous to permit circulation of air.

## ANTIBACTERIAL FINISHES

In a study of perspiration made by the Chief Bacteriologist of the U.S. Testing Company, it was found that sterile perspiration, which is odorless, has no effect on fabrics and fabric finishes. The finish, if soluble, may be dissolved by perspiration just as by any other liquid, but sterile perspiration does not alter the chemical composition of the finish. Neither are the fibers weakened in tensile strength.

However, perspiration does not remain sterile. When perspiration is produced, it is immediately contaminated with various types of bacteria on the skin. Bacterial decomposition begins. It is this bacterial action that causes the odor of perspiration and has a deteriorating effect on the fabric.

Antiperspirants, applied under the arms, are commonly used to check perspiration, but they sometimes irritate the skin. To prevent the odor of perspiration, bacterial decomposition must be prevented. Germicides can be applied on the skin or on the fabrics. If the latter is the case, the germicide has to be carefully chosen. It must be colorless, in order not to stain the fabric, and odorless; it should not affect the dyes or finishes of the fabric, should not irritate the skin, and should not be removed by the first few washings. A few compounds have been found to possess these qualities. Fabrics treated with these germicides-fungicides have been found to be semipermanent (do not wash out in as many as forty washings) and to pass the sterility test of the U.S. Pharmacopeia. Fabrics treated with these compounds also sufficiently protect the wearer against the fungi that cause athlete's foot. This fabric treatment will prove effective for as many as twenty-five launderings.

[15] Nylonex by W. F. Fancourt Company, Greensboro, N.C.

Antibacterial finishes prevent bacteria-caused odors in textiles and/or the reduction of the chances of bacterial infections resulting from contact with contaminated textiles. Sanitized is a trademarked finish that protects fabrics from deterioration and odor-causing effects of bacteria, mildew, and mold.

### ANTISLIP FINISHES

Seam fraying and yarns shifting (slipping) in the fabrics are common annoyances to the consumer. Finishing agents such as rosins—hard, waxy substances remaining after distillation of volatile turpentine—have been used but are not generally durable to washing. Other chemical treatments reduce surface slickness but are not durable. Urea and melamine formaldehyde resins are the most durable of the finishing agents used to reduce yarn slippage.

### ANTISTATIC FINISH

A chemical treatment applied to noncellulosic synthetic fibers in order to eliminate static electricity is a boon to the consumer. An annoyance to the wearer is a nylon slip that clings to the body or to an outer garment; or a crackling sound as a coat is taken off; or acrylic slacks that cling to the legs on a cold, windy day. Static charge or static electricity is controlled in natural fibers and in rayon by the introduction of humidity into the air and by employing some weaving lubricants in the processing of the fibers. The newer synthetics, like nylon, polyesters, and acrylics, are more difficult to process. Humidity is not the sole answer. Some type of coating must be used to carry away electrostatic charges built up on the fiber. The homemaker can partially control static by the use of softeners such as Nusoft, Sta Puf, Downy, and Negastat. Permanent antistatic agents have been developed by the finishing industry.

### CREASE-RESISTANT FINISHES

A crease is a fold or deformation of a fabric intentionally formed by pressing, while a wrinkle is unintentionally formed by washing and wearing. A wrinkle can usually be removed by pressing, but a crease is usually not removable. A durable press article should not have wrinkles.

Synthetic resins (melamine, epoxy, urea formaldehyde or vinyl) can be used to give resiliency. In one process, cloth is immersed in a resin solution that has a molecule small enough to permeate the cotton fibers. The fabric is then pressed between rollers to squeeze out the excess fluid. The impregnated cloth is heated until the molecules swell inside the fibers so that the resin cannot be removed by normal use, dry cleaning, or washing. A resin may be applied during the dyeing process or immediately after the dyeing when dyes have dried. Cottons so treated resist crushing, wrinkling, and creasing.

The Southern Regional Research Laboratory, Agricultural Research Service. U.S. Department of Agriculture, New Orleans, Louisiana, has developed several types of new wrinkle-resistant finishes that cost only a few cents per square yard and can be easily applied in the usual equipment for resin finishing.[16]

Other strides have been made in crease-resistance experimentation. Modified starches called *oxidized starches* give crease-resistant finishes. Chemists also have discovered a compound that produces crease resistance as well as resistance to damage from chlorine after repeated washings.[17] The Electronic Smoothness Evaluator by Cluett, Peabody & Company, Inc. has already been described as the standard device for appraising the ability of a crease-resistant, wash-and-wear fabric to dry with a minimum of wrinkles after laundering. "Crease resistant" does not mean that cotton so treated will not crease, crush, or wrinkle; it means that if and when wrinkles do appear they can be shaken out and hung out in the air.

The crease-resistant finish has been a great boon to velvets and to linens, in which crushing and wrinkling are highly undesirable.

Wash-and-wear finish ensures minimum care of fabrics treated. (See wash-and-wear, p. 154.) The wash-and-wear concept was built on the idea that such a finish would prevent both the removal of permanent-

[16] Crease-resistant finishes developed at the Southern Regional Research Laboratory include formic acid colloid of methylolmelamine resin and formaldhyde finish.

[17] This is an almost unpronounceable compound: 1, 3 Dimethyl—4, 5 dihydroxy—2—imidazolidinone. *American Dyestuff Reporter* (July 24, 1961), 27–30.

Figure 7.5. *Left:* Untreated fabric, knotted, and fabric treated (Unidure-processed) for wrinkle resistance, knotted. *Right:* Same fabrics after unknotting. Note the difference in wrinkle recovery after one-half hour. (*Photographs courtesy of the United Piece Dye Works.*)

press creases and the formation of wrinkles during wearing and washing. But durable press does more. It locks in the shape and locks out wrinkles for the life of a garment. Seams stay flat; no ironing. (See *durable press*, p. 180.)

In October 1947, Monsanto Chemical Company introduced a testing device to measure wrinkle recovery. Prior to Monsanto's method of testing, a sample of fabric was creased under a one-pound weight and suspended by the fold for several minutes over a thin wire. The spread between the dangling ends was measured to determine the amount of recovery. The reading might vary with changes in temperature, "curving" of the sample, gravitational effects, and human error in measuring the gap between the ends.

The wrinkle-measuring device by Monsanto resembles a clock face on which a cam holds a pendulum for the cloth in place and on which degrees of a half-circle have been marked. A direct reading of the angle of recovery from 0 to 180 degrees can be made. This method is designed to eliminate the variables of the standard procedure.

### FLAMMABILITY OF TEXTILE FABRICS

The problem of flammability in textile fabrics came to the fore when some toddlers dressed in cowboy suits were fatally burned when they came too near a campfire. In another case, a woman wearing a sequin-trimmed gown accidentally came in contact with a lighted cigarette of a passer-by. Suddenly her gown became a flaming torch. Disasters like the Cocoanut Grove and the Ringling Brothers Circus fires have shown us the dangers of using flammable fabrics.

California was the first state to make rules and regulations relating to the sale of flammable merchandise. The fire marshal was designated as the person to decide on the flammability of an article. For aid in this extremely difficult task he consulted with textile experts in laboratory testing. The problem of fire hazard in wearing apparel was nationwide; it was present in every community. There was also the hazard of flammable wearing apparel that is shipped in interstate commerce. A problem of such import required federal legislation.

How was an average retailer to know whether merchandise was flammable? Through the endeavors of the National Retail Merchants Association and the research efforts of the American Association of Textile Chemists and Colorists, a testing device was built to determine the rate of burning of a fabric by measuring the speed with which a flame travels over the surface of a six-inch sample. The fabric to be tested was hung on a rack at a 45-degree angle. There have been other such machines invented, but the A.A.T.C.C. tester was accepted by the California fire marshal and also by the National Bureau of Standards. This device is standardized for testing fabrics under the Flammable Fabrics Act.

The difficulty in setting up a performance standard is the fact that

testing standards do not and cannot duplicate or even wholly represent
actual service or use conditions. But the A.A.T.C.C. worked for six years with various standard and technical committees under the Department of Commerce's commercial standard on flammability and with the National Fire Protection Association. A most difficult problem to overcome was the public's possible misconception that a fabric once termed "safe" or "dangerous," based entirely on an arbitrary burning limit, was therefore inherently and necessarily safe or dangerous. The committee dealt with these and other problems.

At any rate, in 1953 the A.A.T.C.C.'s committee recognized that the standard was sufficiently improved to warrant its use as a voluntary commercial standard of the U.S. Department of Commerce and as a basis for a federal law. The committee realized, however, that the method was not perfect.

The Flammable Fabrics Act (Public Law 88) was approved by the Congress in 1953. It was amended in 1954 and further amended and revised in 1967. This act prohibits the introduction [18] or movement in interstate commerce of articles of wearing apparel and fabrics that are so highly inflammable as to be dangerous when worn by individuals or used for other purposes. The term *fabrics* includes woven, knitted, and felted materials produced from natural and synthetic fibers—materials that are ready for retail sale for use in either wearing apparel or interior furnishings. The act does not apply to fabrics or products for export or those imported solely for finishing and processing prior to export. Also excluded are fabrics intended or sold for processing into interlinings or other covered parts of articles of wearing apparel and fabrics intended or sold for use in most hats, gloves, and footwear that are not attached to other garments. However, marketers must keep records of such intended use and designate such use in selling and shipping documents. Hosiery is subject to the act; also handkerchiefs affixed to other articles of wearing apparel. But handkerchiefs that do not exceed a finished size of 576 square inches are excluded. The raised-fiber surface of sweat shirts and similar articles are covered by the act because the shirt may be worn with the raised fibers exposed.

Current regulations of the Federal Trade Commission, the agency that administers the Flammable Fabrics Act, provide the following standards based on the application of a flame the size of a match for one second to a 2 x 6 inch swatch:

Textile fabrics that do not burn or fuse or where the burning time for the sample is less than 3.5 seconds are not deemed dangerous. But for fabrics with normal flammability (3.5 seconds or more), successive tests are required of additional samples during the production process.

Raised-fiber-surface fabrics, such as velvets, velours, and corduroys, that do not produce a surface flash or do not ignite or fuse are con-

---

[18] Manufacture, sale, offering for sale, or importation.

sidered safe; also fabrics of this type where the flame spread is 4 seconds or more. In the case of fabrics with looped yarn, the spread of the flame must be in excess of 12 seconds to be deemed safe. Where there is any surface flash fusing or burning, repeated tests are required for goods of the same composition in production.

The act authorizes the seizure and confiscation of fabrics or articles that are found to be dangerously inflammable as indicated above. They may, by order of the court, be destroyed. Or they may be released to the owner only after his posting a bond guaranteeing that the seized articles will not be used for wearing apparel or other prohibited use, or that they will be adequately treated. Willful violation of the act is a misdemeanor that upon conviction permits a fine of up to $5,000 or a prison sentence of not more than one year or both.

A person is not subject to prosecution if he establishes a guarantee received in good faith from the manufacturer or his supplier to the effect that the material has been tested and found not so highly inflammable as to be dangerous. The issuance of a false guarantee is deemed an unfair method of competition, subject to penalties.

### FLAMEPROOF AND FIREPROOF, FLAME-RESISTANT OR FLAME-RETARDANT FINISHES

A case history described by the U.S. Public Health Service illustrates the problem of danger of clothing being set on fire. A two-year-old girl was trying to reach her pet bird, which was perched on top of a refrigerator. She used an opened door of a gas stove to climb up on top of the stove to reach the bird. In so doing she is believed to have hit the burner knob of the gas stove. Flames from the gas burner ignited her cotton quilted housecoat and flannel pajamas. Over half her body was burned. Her mother, who was outdoors at the time, blamed herself for the accident and developed an emotional nervous condition. The child was hospitalized ninety-seven days. The $12,460 cost of her treatment was partially covered by insurance but was primarily paid by the County Crippled Children's Commission.[19]

The problem is serious, since an estimated 150,000 persons in this country are burned each year in accidents in which clothing is set on fire. Thousands are burned from bedding and home furnishings fires.[20]

There is a slight technical difference between flameproofing and fireproofing. One authority defines a "flameproof" material as one "showing no afterflame or afterglow." "Fireproof" as applied to a material denotes ability to "withstand exposure to flame or high temperature and still perform the function for which originally intended."

There are several processes of rendering fabrics flameproof. One of

[19] Conference on Burns and Flame-Retardant Fabrics, New York Academy of Medicine (December 2–3, 1966).
[20] *Ibid.*

the early processes involved an oil-in-water technique. A new process
involves coating nylon or Dacron polyester fabrics with a new plastisol
plus an adhesive bonding agent that will not drop off in molten drops
when flame is applied to them. Three coats are given to each side of the
fabric. The result is that there is no dripping under a gas flame and that
burning stops when the flame is removed.

There is also a flameproof finish for acetate, nylon, and acrylic fibers,
but the process cannot be used on cotton or rayon. This flameproofer
is an emulsified clear liquid applied by specific methods in the dyebath.[21]

[21] This product is made by the Apex Chemical Company, Inc.

**Figure 7.6.** Flame from automatic, high-pressure burners is applied equally to two
pieces of fabric. As indicated on the cards attached to each piece of fabric, the exhibit on the left is a piece of untreated cotton flannel, which immediately ignites and
completely disintegrates. The cotton flannel exhibited on the right is treated with a
flame retardant fabric finish called "Firegard." The fabric will char, but will not
support combustion once it is away from a flame. (*Courtesy of M. Lowenstein & Sons,
Inc.*)

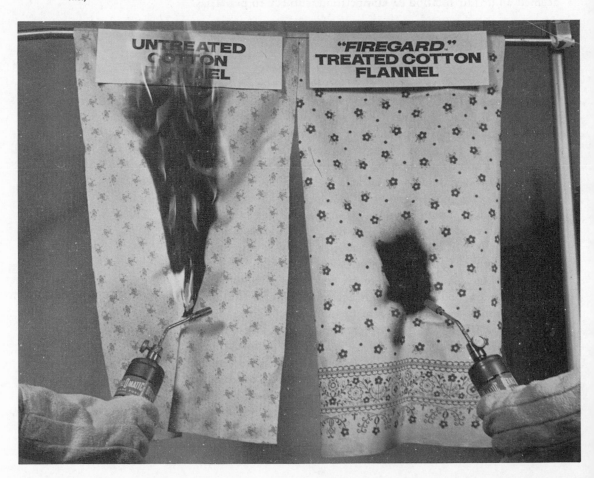

The chief difficulty in flameproofing seems to be that if, in overcoming combustibility, a large amount of material has to be applied to the cloth, it gives the fabric a different feeling.

One principle of fireproofing is to create a finish that smothers a flame as fire extinguishers do. Carbon tetrachloride or carbon dioxide has this effect. They cut off the supply of oxygen necessary to make a fire burn and fill the air about the flame with gases that do not induce burning.

Another principle is to treat the fabric with chemicals that, when heat comes in contact with the fabric, melt and cover the fabric with non-flammable film. Simultaneously, these chemicals give off a steam that, along with the film, gives the fireproof effect. Treatment with various carbonates and ammonium salts results in the creation of noncombustible vapors.

Flame-retardant fabric exhibits appreciable resistance to afterflaming (the continuation of flaming after the source of ignition has been removed). It is an untreated fabric that shows high resistance to afterflaming or a treated fabric that, after treatment, shows greater resistance to afterflaming than the untreated material.

A new "Firegard" finish suitable for styled fabrics was announced in December 1968 by M. Lowenstein & Sons, Inc., who claim that it is nontoxic; that it does not support combustion once it is away from flame; that it lasts through fifty washings; and that it does not affect the natural softness of cotton flannel.

A fabric can be made mildly fire-retardant at home by dipping the cloth in a solution of 30 per cent boric acid and 70 per cent borax. It is advisable to dip dry fabrics into this solution rather than wet ones, because dry materials absorb the solution in greater quantity, thus becoming more fire-resistant. For fabrics that cannot be saturated with the solution, such as water-repellent or heavily sized fabrics, soap should be added to the solution. Soap causes the solution to spread and to wet the surface evenly. Draperies and bulky fabrics can be sprayed with an ordinary garden spray, but this method is not always so effective as saturation of the fabric. Fire-resistant fabrics should be ironed with a warm iron, not a hot one.

How can flame-retardant finishes ensure protection? For a slightly extra cost (minimal in the case of small items) a treated flame-retardant fabric can save life or prevent severe burns.

What fibers are comparatively flame-resistant? Wool will ignite but will burn very slowly and go out by itself. Man-made textile fibers (modacrylic) are inherently flame-retardant. They do not support combustion when exposed to flame or heat. A high-temperature-resistant type of nylon does not support combustion, as evidenced by the fact that astronauts' outer suits on the Gemini spacecraft twins were made of this type of nylon.

Glass fibers are flame-retardant for their entire wear-life.

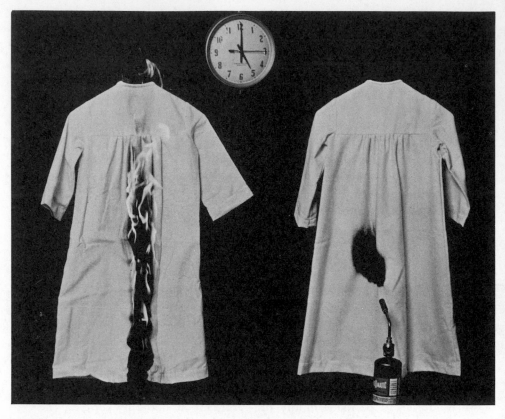

**Figure 7.7.** Self-extinguishing cotton flannel nightgown at right, treated with PYROVATEX CP, a flame retardant compound developed by CIBA Chemical & Dye Company, chars but puts itself out when exposed to flame from a Bunsen burner. However, the untreated flannel gown at the left, which was exposed to a lighted match at the same time, became engulfed in flame in 15 seconds. (*Courtesy of CIBA Chemical & Dye Company.*)

Cotton and rayon burn rather quickly but can, with the exception of very sheer garments, be treated with chemicals to make them flame-retardant.

Chemicals that can impart flame resistance to polyester fibers are available. An agent used is tris (2-,3-dibromopropyl) phosphate. It is not suitable for cotton.

### METALLIZED TREATMENTS

Woven fabrics may be coated with synthetic resin containing a good percentage of finely ground aluminum bronze. Such fabrics have increased insulation and are therefore claimed to be warm. Another method is to vaporize a variety of metals onto fabrics in a high vacuum to produce a metal coating less than 1/1000 millimeter thick. Still another method impregnates the textile material or fabric with aluminum. This finish, which may be added to one or both sides of the fabric, makes the fabric heat-resistant to 2500° F. It is claimed by the United States Testing Company that the aluminum coating prevents 96 per cent of the heat from penetrating the material. The coating has many consumer and industrial uses, among them barbecue mitts and curtains for industrial furnaces.

Draperies with metallized linings reflect sunlight, hence keep out heat. When the room is being heated, this finish holds the heat in. Satins and taffetas respond well to metallized treatments. Trademarked names for these treatments include Milium, Temp-Resisto, and Therm-O-Ray.


### MILDEW- AND ROT-REPELLENT FINISHES

Mildew is a parasitic fungus that grows rapidly in warm, humid weather. Fabrics of cotton, linen, rayon, and wool are particularly vulnerable to this fungus. Microorganisms present in the air and soil can grow on wet fibers. Consequently, if clothing is not completely dry before it is put away, it can mildew. If clothing is improperly rinsed, soap or oils adhere to the fibers and provide a field for the growth of mildew.

Prevention of mildew is possible by treating the fabrics with nontoxic odorless germicides. Certain metallic salts have this effect. For cotton, one method is to modify the cotton fiber so its surface is cellulose acetate, which is resistant to mildew. A resin impregnation of the cotton fiber, which prevents contact of the microorganism with the fiber, can be used.

Permanent rotproofing of cotton is possible through a treatment with a condensation resin. A new technique overcomes the drawback of loss of strength of the cotton fiber that resulted from conventional methods of applying condensation resins. If a suitable organic mercury compound is added to the rotproofing finish, then it is possible to protect cotton against surface mildew growth.[22]

The burying of treated and untreated specimens in soil rich in rot-producing fungi for a definite time is the procedure of the test for resistance of textiles to mildew and rot. When the specimens are removed from the earth, they are tested for breaking strength against controls.[23]


### MOTH-REPELLENT TREATMENTS

To mothproof a fabric in the finishing process, colorless chemicals similar to dyestuffs are added to the dye bath. This treatment makes the fabric permanently moth repellent. Although this method is effective,

[22] Process by Ciba, Ltd., Basel, Switzerland, as reported in *American Dyestuff Reporter* (October 2, 1961), 21.

[23] American Association of Textile Chemists and Colorists (A.A.T.C.C.) Standard Test Method 34-1952.

some blanket manufacturers have discontinued its use because of the high cost of the chemicals required. Another way is to atomize the finished fabric with the mothproofing chemical, which is colorless, odorless, and harmless to humans. Fabrics so mothproofed are delivered to the garment manufacturer. The compound used in processing the fabric either poisons the moth or kills it upon contact.

Consumers and dry cleaners often make a fabric moth repellent by spraying it thoroughly with Larvex or a similar solution. This treatment is not a finishing process (see p. 611 for methods of mothproofing upholstery). Paradichlorobenzene crystals or naphthalene mothballs are recommended for the closet where wool garments are stored. A clean fabric does not attract moths so quickly as a soiled fabric.

Wool or silk fabrics may be made moth repellent. Cotton, linen, and the synthetics do not attract moths.

To test for insect resistance, a specified number of insects (black carpet beetles, furniture carpet beetles, webbing clothes moths, or other species of insect pests) are allowed to feed on a fabric for fourteen days under controlled conditions of temperature and humidity. Below a set tolerance limit, textiles are considered satisfactorily insect resistant, and above this limit they are considered to be inadequately protected (A.A.T.C.C. Standard Test Method 24-1952).

### OPTICAL FINISHES

*a. Luster.* Mercerization has been described as a finish that increases a fabric's luster. Glazing and calendering also produce luster. The way in which a light is reflected from a fiber's surface owing to its transparency or shape produces luster. Silk has a natural sheen, and some man-made fibers may have considerable luster.

*b. Delustering treatments.* In finishing, fabrics can be delustered by special heat treatments that change light reflection by softening the yarn and surface of the cloth. Coating the surface of the fabric has a delustering effect.

*c. Optical brighteners.* Consumers may find that many fabrics lose their whiteness, brightness, and clearness during the wear-life. To prevent this, optical brighteners have been employed. They are used as finishes and may be added to many home laundering agents. These brighteners become affixed to the fabric so that they appear to create whiteness and brightness the way they reflect light. Some optical brighteners (bleaches) are built into the product to ensure continued whiteness. The fluorescent material of the agent changes ultraviolet light wavelengths into visual wavelengths and remits them as such, to give fluorescent effect. Loss of energy of this fluorescent material through usage fails gradually to transform these light waves. A change of shade occurs slowly. Possibly the natural yellow cast of fabric that has been masked by the fluorescent material may show. Brighteners can be replaced by fresh opticals. Some progressive laundries are spending time and money to obtain the best optical whiteners. At present, whiteness and changes in color may be considered to be under control but not completely solved.[24]

## PLASTIC COATING

Actually coated fabrics are not new. What boy can't remember his black rubber-coated raincoat? Who of us hasn't smelled a handbag to determine if it was real or artificial leather? Remember the oiled silk raincoats and the pyroxylin-coated "oilcloth"? We still have these coated fabrics, but in the past sixteen years plastics have gained popularity because they have a soft pliable hand and do not stiffen with age like rubber and pyroxylin; they resist staining, have a high degree of waterproofness, and can be wiped off with a damp cloth.

Plastic-coated fabrics differ from plastic sheets or films in that the former have a woven or knitted cloth to support them (supported films). Therefore, plastic-coated fabrics are textiles. Those plastic sheets with no fabric for support (unsupported films) are nontextiles. A raincoat, then, may be either a textile or a nontextile, based on the foregoing definition.

The word "plastic" refers to something that can be shaped or molded. Clay has this property when moistened. Nowadays we apply the term to a specific group of man-made substances. Rayon is derived from the natural source cellulose, whereas nylon is a chemically based fiber.

Fabrics may be supported:

1. By applying the solution of plastic substance to the cloth, passing the fabric under a knife to scrape off excess coating, baking it in a hot oven, and passing it through an ironing machine (calender) to press the coating into the cloth and to smooth it out and give it sheen.
2. By dipping fabrics into plastic materials.
3. By pressing a sheet of plastic against a cloth.
4. By melting or fusing the plastic with heat so the plastic and cloth adhere permanently, which is termed *laminating*. (See Chapter 6.)

Plastic-coated fabrics such as chintz aprons, baby pants, and bibs are often produced by the first method. Shower curtains, play-pen covers, mattress covers, children's rainwear, closet accessories, raincoat materials, and artificial leather are often produced by the second method. Plastic coating is classed as a functional finish because the coated fabric is suitable for uses other than those of the original fabric.

[24] Research by the author for an article in *Textile Service Management* magazine, June, 1968.

To obviate the use of starch for a crisp finish that can be durable for repeated washings, cottons are treated with an acid or a resin. This starchless finish is permanent and does not dissolve in laundering. The fabric can be washed, and, when ironed, presents its original crisp appearance.

The permanent starchless finish is used on organdy, lawn, voile, and other sheer cottons. Fibers are sealed down by the starchless finish, so that cotton fabrics stay clean longer. Bellmanizing is one of the patented processes that prevents cottons from appearing wilted after being worn. Heberlein is the original Swiss process for permanent crisp-finish organdy. In this process chemicals fuse the cotton fibers, making the fabric smooth and lintless.

The Heberlein process is also used on curtains, draperies, bedspreads, and sheer cottons for apparel. Embossed or frosty-etched white patterns, formerly put in cloth by weaving, can now be applied in the finishing process at moderate cost. When applied to plissé crepe, greater permanency of crinkle is obtained.

Starchless finish can be used on cotton, linen, silk, and rayon fabrics to ensure permanent crispness without starch.

## WASH-AND-WEAR, DURABLE PRESS, SOIL RELEASE

At the time of writing the fifth edition of this book (1964), durable press was a technical curiosity. In 1968, durable press became part of our household language.

*a. Wash-and-wear.* Prior to the development of durable press, certain cross-linking chemicals had been applied to cotton and rayon yard goods in the dyeing and finishing processes for the purpose of improving wrinkle resistance and reducing shrinkage. Garments made of these chemically treated and cured (baked) fabrics were known as wash-and-wear. However, these garments often required touch-up ironing, and few garments retained their creases or pleats after repeated wearings and launderings.

*b. Durable press* (*permanent press*). In short, these wash-and-wear fabrics were precured at the mill before the garment was constructed.

By adding two to three times as much resin as before to 100 per cent cotton slacks and by precuring, excellent wrinkle resistance, crease retention, and dimensional stability were made possible. But reduced tensile strength and reduced edge abrasion became very noticeable. So the 100 per cent cotton content of slacks was replaced by polyester/cotton and polyester/nylon blends. The cotton content gave required wrinkle resistance and the man-made fibers provided improved edge and flat abrasion resistance.[25] However, the precuring as a flat fabric presented a

[25] Special Edition of *Modern Textiles Magazine* (Sixth Annual Conference of the AATT, 1966), pp. 6–16.

problem in some garments because when the garment was constructed the fabric had a "memory" for its flat state and tended to return to that condition. Particularly was this a problem in retention of sharp creases in slacks, pleats in dresses, and nonpuckering seams. Where the shape of a garment and its pleats and creases were factors, methods had to be found to give "memory" to the shape of the completed garment. The answer was to postcure the garment (after garment construction). Nowadays, polyester/cotton fabric is chemically treated at the mill or finishing plant, but it is not cured. The chemical component (a thermosetting resin) reacts with the cellulose fiber and is cured only when subjected to certain degrees of heat (300° to 340° F.) This is called post-, or deferred, curing because heat is applied for from 14 to 18 minutes after the garment has been constructed and pressed. Postcuring sets the pleats and the garment's shape permanently. The cotton content in the blend may lose strength and abrasion resistance in curing, but the polyester compensates for the cotton's loss in strength.[26] It should be remembered that 100 per cent thermoplastic fibers in a fabric give durable press results; also that medium-to-heavy weight slacks, sportswear, rainwear, and sheeting fabrics are predominantly 50/50 polyester/cotton. A 50/50 polyester/acrylic can be thermally shaped into a garment that, if properly constructed, has good wrinkle resistance. Research and development have made great improvements in 100 per cent durable press cottons.

At the time of writing, there are no national commercial standards for durable press. Manufacturers have been trying to avoid offering too much in their promotions. The Koratron process for durable press has minimum requirements for licensees of the process. Various manufacturers have their own quality controls and test procedures. Among these tests is a visual comparison scale. (See Figure 7.8.) Trademarked names for precured processes include Never-Press, Primatized, Coneprest I, II,

26 "An Up-to-Date Guide to Permanent Press," a report by the editors of *American Fabrics* Magazine in conjunction with the staff of Celanese Fibers Marketing Company, (1968).

Figure 7.8. Flow diagrams of the post-cured process and the precured process. (*Courtesy of Celanese Fibers Marketing Company.*)

THE POST-CURED PROCESS

IMPREGNATE + DRY → CUT + SEW + PRESS + CURE

THE PRE-CURED PROCESS

IMPREGNATE + DRY + CURE + WASH → CUT + SEW + PRESS

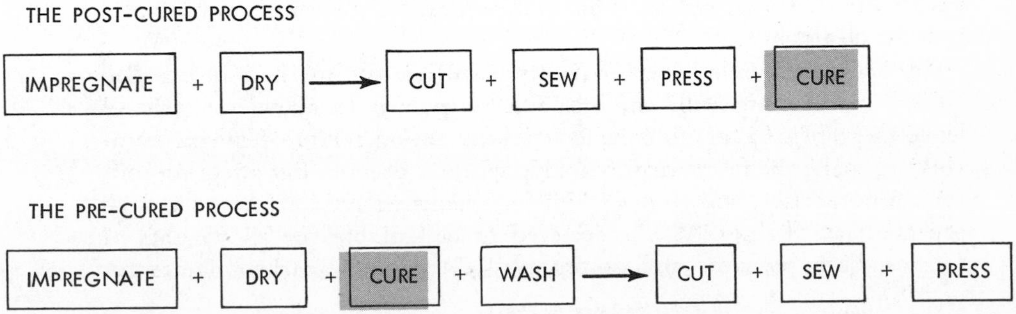

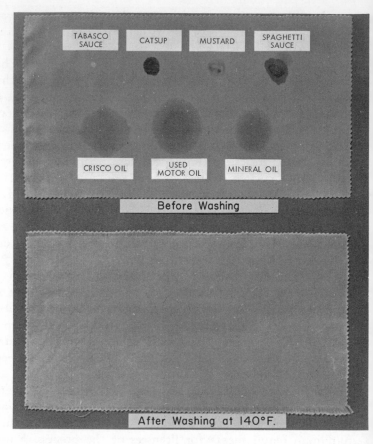

Figure 7.9. Acrylic Polymer Soil Release Finishes are neither hydrophobic nor oleophobic, but holds stains off the fiber. This soil release product is based on new fluorochemical technology developed by 3M. (*Courtesy of Textile World.*)

and Reeve-Set. Names for postcured processes include Coneprest III, Koratron, Dan-Press (postcure, partial cure), Reeve-Set, and Grid Press.

*c. Soil release.* How many consumers have experienced the black soil line inside the collar and cuffs of a polyester/cotton blend shirt or blouse? When the fabric is treated for durable press, soil becomes extremely obstinate to cleaning. Polyester fibers have static attraction for soil, and their water resistance makes these soil lines hard to clean with detergents.

Scotchgard is a soil and stain repellent. Fabrics so treated have resistance to both water and oil stains when they are new and even after a few drycleanings.

In 1966 a soil-release technique appeared on the market. It is called "Visa" by Deering Milliken, Inc. The purpose is to allow the stain to leave the fabric faster; to enhance wicking action for greater wear comfort; to make the fabric dry-cleanable without appreciably affecting soil-release properties; and to maintain the brightness of the fabric through repeated launderings. Visa is declared to be suitable for all weights of fabrics, both precured and postcured.[27] Other trademarked names for

[27] *American Dyestuff Reporter* (May 6, 1968).

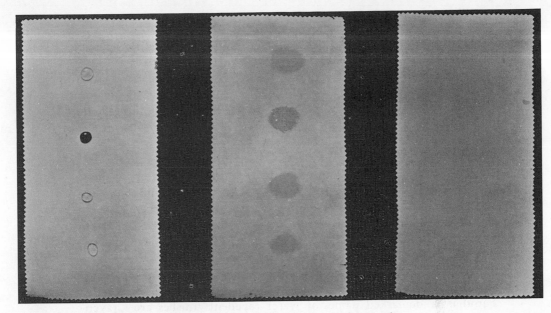

**Figure 7.10.** This Soil Release Finish is resistant to either oil- or water-borne stains, which were applied, rubbed in and removed in one home laundering. The finish is chemical, using a modified fluorocarbon resin. (*Courtesy of Textile World.*)

soil-release finishes are Burlington Industries' Come Clean; McCampbell Graniteville's X-it; Lowenstein's Soilex; and Dan River's Dan Clean. Many soil-release finishes are available through commission dyehouses.

## WATERPROOFING

The use for which a fabric is intended determines whether it should be waterproof, water-repellent, or spot-resistant. For umbrellas, galoshes, and raincoats, the fabrics should be waterproof. Waterproofing, done by several patented processes, closes the pores of the fabric. The most common processes consist of treatment with:

1. Insoluble metallic compounds such as aluminum soap, basic acetate of aluminum, mineral khaki, cuprammonium.
2. Paraffin or mixed waxes.
3. Bituminous materials, such as asphaltum or tar.
4. Linseed oil or other drying oils.
5. Combinations of methods 1, 2, 3, and 4.

Treatment 1 (cuprammonium) is often used to make cotton mildew-resistant. But this treatment cannot be applied at home. Formulas for waterproofing and mildewproofing are given in the *Farmer's Bulletin* No. 1454.[28]

28 House and Garden Bulletin No. 62, Consumer Service of U.S.D.A., Supt. of Documents, U.S. Government Printing Office, Washington, D.C., 20402.

Water-repellent finishes do not close the pores of the fabric against air as does waterproofing. Hence, water-repellent fabrics are not so warm to wear as waterproofed fabrics; they can "breathe." The fabrics are treated to reduce their affinity for water. The degree of resistance varies from a spot-proof or stain-resistant fabric to a shower-proof cloth. To be showerproof, a cloth must resist penetration of water under considerable pressure.

Water repellents are surface finishes. Therefore, sizing, dirt, fats, and other foreign matter should be removed before finishing. Water-repellent fabrics are treated with wax and resin mixtures, aluminum salts, silicones, aluminum compounds, or other chemicals. Fluorochemicals are the most recent and most promising agents for this purpose. Water-repellent finishes for polyester fabrics can be based on silicones or fluorochemicals. With proper preparation of polyester/cotton fabrics, water-repellent finishes can be applied in combination with cross-linking agents to give durable press rainwear.[29]

Familiar trademarked names of water-repellent finishes are Cravenette, Unisec, Syl-mer, Wat-a-set, Zepel (spot- and stain-repellent), and Impregnole.

The general tendency on wool fabrics is to use the durable repellents of the fluorocarbon types, such as Scotchgard and Zepel because of the resistance of these agents to oil as well as water.

Tests for water repellency can be made by the spray tester (A.A.T.C.C. Standard Test Method 22-1952; A.S.T.M. D583-54) and the hydrostatic measuring machine—neither of which is an accurate method of measuring water repellency. (Also, there is no correlation of measuring with actual rain conditions.) The du Pont research laboratory has developed a machine called the Raintester, which gives accurate readings equivalent to the force of rain when applied to a fabric. Garments made of specimens of cloth tested on the Raintester were worn in the rain room of the Philadelphia Quartermaster Depot, and the length of time required for water to

[29] *American Dyestuff Reporter* (April 8, 1968).

**Figure 7.11.** Unisec-processed fabric, which retains water repellence and stain resistance even after dry cleaning. Note the droplets on the surface of the jacket; they do not penetrate the fabric. (*Photograph courtesy of the United Piece Dye Works.*)

penetrate the fabrics was correlated with results of laboratory tests.

The A.A.T.C.C. devised a method for predicting, by means of an air-porosity test before a fabric is treated, whether it is suitably constructed for a water-repellent finish, and also the degree of protection that may be expected from this fabric when it has been treated.

The problem of water-repellent finishing is a difficult one because the fabric, to be comfortable, must be porous to allow circulation of air, and at the same time it must prevent water from leaking through. Consequently the fibers and yarns must be water resistant, and the construction must be well balanced and sufficiently close. In one test, two fabrics weighed the same number of ounces per square yard, the count of cloth was similar, the balance of the cloth was good, and it was adequate for the water-resistant finish; but the yarns in one sample were finer than the other, and the fabric with finer yarn showed leakage.

According to the results of this research, fabrics suitable for water-resistant finishing should have a combination of the following: (1) proper construction; (2) suitable permeability to air; (3) satisfactory water resistance of fibers and yarns.

Generally the label indicates whether the water-repellent finish can be dry-cleaned or laundered. Instructions on the label should be followed to ensure the maximum service from such finishes.

## SUMMARY

Fabric finishes vary in their effectiveness and durability. Sometimes a finish that gives a fabric a desirable characteristic creates an undesirable characteristic at the same time. For example, a fabric with a wash-and-wear finish may retain chlorine in laundering and hence become yellowed. The wise consumer can avoid this possibility, however, by using a non-chlorine bleach.

Some of the finishing processes that have been discussed are mechanical in nature; this group includes those that employ rollers, steam, and pressure. The rest of the finishing processes are chemical in nature; they include weighted, mothproof, fire-resistant, crease-resistant, water-repellent, and mildew-resistant finishes; wash-and-wear; durable press; and bleaching, dyeing, and printing. These last two processes will be discussed in the next chapter.

## REVIEW QUESTIONS

1. Why is a fabric not ready for sale to the consumer as soon as it is woven?
2. What is the purpose of finishing processes?
3. List and describe the finishing processes generally used for cotton broadcloth shirting.

4. (*a*) What finishes give luster to a fabric?
   (*b*) Describe each finish.
5. (*a*) What is sizing?
   (*b*) Why is sizing used to finish cotton fabrics? linen fabrics? silk fabrics?
6. (*a*) How may permanent creped effects be produced?
   (*b*) How is permanent embossing possible?
7. (*a*) What is calendering?
   (*b*) What textile fabrics are calendered?
8. When is it necessary to bleach a fabric?
9. (*a*) How is silk weighted?
   (*b*) What is the purpose of weighting?
10. (*a*) What is flocking?
    (*b*) When would it be used?
11. Give the provisions of the F.T.C. ruling for shrinkage.
12. Give the provisions of the Flammable Fabrics Act.
13. Compare durable press and wash-and-wear.
    (*a*) Give the methods of producing each.
    (*b*) What are the merits and drawbacks of each?
14. Define the following terms: moiré, crease-resistant, beetling, mercerizing, permanent finish, glazing, singeing, tentering, Sanforized, heat setting, embossing, sizing, rubberizing, piece dyeing, flame-resistant, water-repellent, waterproofing, mothproofing, preshrinkage, antistatic finish, antibacterial finish, abrasion-resistant, optical brighteners.

# EXPERIMENTS

1. *Determining the permanency of finishing processes.* Before making any experiment, read the label or determine by any test previously outlined the kinds of fibers in the warp and filling of each sample:
A. If the fabric is cotton:
   1. Rub your thumbnail over the cloth. Note whether little particles flake off the cloth. If so, the cloth is sized.
   2. If the fabric is colored, rub a white handkerchief briskly against it. Note whether some color is transferred to the handkerchief. If so, the cloth is heavily sized.
   3. Divide your sample in half. Take one half and tear it quickly. Note whether particles fly as the cloth is torn. If so, the cloth is sized.
   4. Wash a portion of the sample with warm water and soap. Dry and iron the sample and compare the washed and unwashed portions as to weight of fabric and crispness of finish.
   *Questions:* (*a*) For each sample, indicate which test or tests removed the sizing or finishing.
   (*b*) Were any finishes so tested permanent? How do you know?
B. If the fabric is linen:
   1. Tear the fabric and notice whether particles fly as it is torn.
   2. Wash and iron part of the sample. Compare the laundered and unlaundered portions as to weight and luster.

*Questions:* (*a*) Was the linen sized? If so, what do you deduce?

(*b*) What finish or finishes were used? Were any of them permanent?

C. If the fabric is rayon:

Wash part of the fabric in warm water and soap flakes. Dry it and compare with the unwashed sample.

*Questions:* (*a*) Was any of the luster or design removed by the washing?

(*b*) Is the finish fast to washing?

D. If the fabric is silk:

1. Burn a corner of the sample. Note the rapidity with which the cloth burns and examine the residue.

2. Wash and dry a portion of the sample. Compare the washed with the unwashed portion as to weight, depth of color, and design.

3. Drop some water on an unwashed portion. Dry the cloth and note whether the fabric spots.

*Questions:* (*a*) Was the sample weighted? How was it done?

(*b*) Is weighting a permanent finish for silk? Why?

(*c*) Does weighted silk water-spot?

(*d*) Does weighted silk lose weight when washed?

E. If the fabric is wool:

1. Brush the back of the cloth with a stiff brush. Note whether short fibers come out.

2. Rub two pieces of the cloth briskly together. Note whether the surface shines more after friction is applied. Was any nap removed?

3. Cut the sample in half. Wash one half with warm water and soap. Dry and iron it; then compare the washed with the unwashed portion as to size, color, and softness.

*Questions:* (*a*) Was the sample flocked? If so, did flocking affect the durability, weight, or warmth of the cloth?

(*b*) Was the cloth tested fast to friction? Why?

(*c*) Was the cloth fast to laundering? Why?

(*d*) Would you consider the finish of a wool fabric permanent if it were fast to friction and to laundering? Explain.

F. If the fabric is labeled wash-and-wear or durable press:

Cleanse one half of the sample, following instructions for laundering or cleansing on the label. Note the appearance, smoothness, and hand after cleansing, and compare with an unwashed sample.

*Question:* Does the sample require ironing? If yes, is the sample durable press?

# GLOSSARY

**Absorbent finish.** Chemical treatment of fabrics to improve their absorptive qualities.

**Antibacterial finishes.** See *Germ resistant.*

**Basic finishes.** Regular processes (mechanical or chemical) applied in some form to a fabric after it has been constructed.

**Beetling.** A process of pounding linen or cotton to give a flat effect. Beetling gives a linen-like appearance to cotton.

**Bleaching.** A basic finishing process to whiten fabrics. Different chemicals are used for different fabrics. Sun, air, and moisture are good bleaches for some materials, though bleaching by this method is slower.

**Brushing.** Removing short, loose fibers from a cloth by means of cylinder rolls covered with bristles.

**Burling.** Removing of irregularities, such as knots or slubs, with a small pick.

**Calendering.** A finishing process for fabrics that produces a shiny, smooth surface by passing the cloth through hollow, heated cylinder rolls or by running the cloth through a friction or glazing calender, as for chintz.

**Carbonizing.** A chemical treatment of wool to burn out vegetable matter.

**Chemical finishing processes.** Treatments with alkalies, acids, bleaches, starch, resins, and the like.

**Crabbing.** See Glossary, Chapter 12.

**Crease resistant.** A chemical finishing process to enable a fabric to resist and recover from wrinkling.

**Creping.** A chemical or embossing process that, when applied as a finish, gives a cloth a crinkled surface.

**Decating.** A process for setting the luster on wool, silk, spun silk, and rayons.

**Degumming.** A process for removing natural gum from silk by boiling it in a soap solution.

**Dressing.** See *Sizing*.

**Drip dry.** To hang up without wringing and let the article drip and dry. Wash-and-wear garments drip dry.

**Durable press.** See Glossary, Chapter 3.

**Embossing.** A finish produced by pressing a raised design into a fabric by passing the fabric through hot engraved rollers. Permanent when heat-set.

**Finishes.** Those basic or functional processes applied to a cloth after it has been constructed.

**Fireproof.** A fabric that is not affected by fire.

**Fire resistant.** A fabric treated to prevent the spread of flame.

**Flammable Fabrics Act.** A law passed by the Eighty-third Congress and signed by President Eisenhower on June 30, 1953, prohibiting the introduction or movement in interstate commerce of clothing fabrics that are flammable enough to be dangerous when worn.

**Flocking.** A finish to add weight to woolens by steaming fibers into the back of a fabric. It is also the sticking of short fibers to a fabric base. Flocking is done with an adhesive or by electrolysis.

**Fulling.** A shrinking process to make wool fabrics more compact and thicker. See *Felting*, Glossary, Chapter 2.

**Functional finishes.** Special finishes that contribute a specific attribute to the merchandise; for example, permanent starchless, crease resistant, and water repellent.

**Germ resistant.** Fabrics treated with compounds to protect the wearer against fungi and germs.

**Gigging.** A process of raising fibers on the surface of a fabric to make it softer and to increase its warmth. It is done by teasels. See *Napping*.

**Glazing.** A finishing process consisting of treating the fabric with glue, starch, paraffin, or shellac and then moving it through hot friction rollers to polish it. Permanent washable glazes are achieved by treating the cloth with synthetic resin and then baking it in at high temperature.

**Grey goods.** See Glossary, Chapter 1.

**Mechanical finishes.** Those finishing processes done by copper plates, roller brushes, perforated cylinders, tenter frames, or any type of mechanical equipment.

**Mercerization.** A treatment of cotton with caustic soda to make it stronger, more lustrous, and more absorbent and to increase its affinity for dye.

**Mildew resistant.** Fabrics treated with metallic compounds and certain organic compounds. Waterproofed fabrics will also resist mildew.

**Milling.** See *Fulling*.

**Moiréing.** A finishing process producing a waved or watered effect on a textile fabric. Made by engraved cylinders that press the design into the material. When heat-set, the design is permanent.

**Moth repellent.** Fabrics treated with colorless chemicals, similar to dyestuffs, added to the dye bath. Another method atomizes the fabric with mothproofing chemicals.

**Napping.** The process of raising short fibers of a cloth to the surface by means of revolving cylinders with wire brushes.

**Nonpermanent finish.** A finish that is removed when subjected to such agents as friction, laundering, light, and heat.

**Permanent finish.** One that will withstand whatever affects it in its particular use.

**Permanent starchless.** A process that impregnates a cloth with compounds that are not dissolved in laundering. When ironed, the cloth returns to its original crispness.

**Plastic-coated fabric.** A plastic film having a woven or knitted cloth to support it.

**Preshrunk.** Fabrics that have been given a shrinking process before being put on the market. The percentage of residual shrinkage must be declared.

**Residual shrinkage.** The percentage of possible shrinkage remaining in a fabric after it has been preshrunk.

**Scouring.** A finishing process for removing oil, sizing, and dirt from various fabrics.

**Shearing.** Cutting off excess surface fibers from a cloth.

**Singeing.** Removing surface fibers and lint from a cloth with hot copper plates or gas flames.

**Sizing.** A finishing process in which a substance such as glue, wax, casein, or clay is added to the cloth to give it additional strength, smoothness, or weight.

**Soil release.** The ability of a fabric to permit the removal of water-borne or oil stains by the usual laundering methods. There may be a special finish.

**Special finishes.** See *Functional finishes*.

**Spot resistant.** See *Water repellent*.

**Stabilizing.** Treating a fabric so that it will not shrink or stretch more than a certain percentage, perhaps 2 per cent.

**Starching.** See *Sizing*.

**Tentering.**   A basic finishing process done by a frame that makes the fabric even in width.

**Wash-and-wear.**   A finish for cottons and linens that is wrinkle resistant both dry and wet, will not shrink out of fit, and has good tensile and tear strength. See Chapter 12 for wash-and-wear finishes on wool.

**Waterproofing.**   Treatment of fabrics to close the pores of the cloth.

**Water repellent.**   A chemical treatment of a fabric to reduce its affinity for water. Pores of the fabric are not closed, and the degree of repellency varies from spot-resistant to showerproof cloth.

**Weighting.**   Finishing materials applied to a fabric to give increased weight. For example, metallic salts that are applied to silk increase weight and tend to make the cloth look more expensive. Overweighting causes deterioration of the fabric.

# 8

# Dyeing
# and Printing

Mrs. Ferris purchases a pair of Bermuda shorts at her favorite sportswear department. When she reaches home and removes the label, she notices that it reads: "This fabric is colorfast." "That's good," she thinks, and promptly throws away the label. A few days later when the shorts need laundering, she wonders: "Should I send them to the commercial laundry or do them in my washer? Should I use hot or warm water? Can I use the setting for regular garments, or must I set the machine for modern or fine fabrics?" All these questions and more might have been answered on the label had Mrs. Ferris saved it.[1]

## COLORFASTNESS

### SUITABILITY OF DYESTUFF

Perhaps if Mrs. Ferris had read the label on her shorts, she would have found not only instructions for laundering but also the information that the color was fast to sunlight—a characteristic so important in

[1] See L22 Standard, Chapter 1.

sportswear. The wise consumer considers, in addition to the qualities of the fibers, yarns, weaves, and finishing processes, the element of color—the suitability of dye to various uses. The buyer nowadays has a right to expect dyed fabrics to withstand the deteriorating elements or influences to which the finished cloth will be subjected—sunlight, perspiration, washing, and friction. Although most fabrics are not equally fast to all these destructive agents, they must be fast to those with which they will come in contact in their particular uses. For example, upholstery fabrics should withstand sunlight, but it is not so important that they withstand washing or perspiration. Summer furniture covers, on the other hand, must be fast to sunlight and to laundering. An evening dress should be fast to perspiration and to dry cleaning, but it does not have to be fast to sunlight. Fabrics for sportswear should be fast to sunlight, to washing, and generally to perspiration. Dyes that are fast for the purpose for which the fabric is intended are termed *fast dyes*.

### FASTNESS TO SUNLIGHT

The National Bureau of Standards of the U.S. Department of Commerce standardized methods of testing and reporting colorfastness to light in 1944 (CS 59-44). Now this standard is being withdrawn. Commercial testing agencies frequently use the A.A.T.C.C. standard tests for lightfastness. The United States of America Standards Institute subscribes to this test. A specially designed powerful carbon-arc lamp has the same effect as strong sunlight. Samples to be tested revolve around this lamp for a definite period of exposure.[2]

Because consumers do not have access to standard laboratory equipment, some simple home tests are suggested in the following text. For comparison, commercial tests are briefly outlined. The commercial test for lightfastness is done by a standard device called the Fade-Ometer. (See "Commercial Test B.")

*Home test.* Exposure to outdoor light: a 3-inch square of colored fabric is cut in half. One half is placed under a glass outdoors in a spot where it will get the maximum of hours of sunlight. After one week's exposure, the exposed half is compared with the other half which has been kept in a box. Any change of color is noted. The same fabric can be exposed similarly for two weeks, and then for three weeks. Any change of color can be noted each time. If there is an appreciable change of color, the color is not fast to sunlight.

*Commercial tests.*[3]   A. Sunlight method: Specimens are exposed against standards, on sunny days only, between the hours of 9 A.M. and 3 P.M.

B. Carbon-arc method: Colorfastness is rated in terms of number of

---

[2] A water-cooled xenon-arc lamp may be used as the source of radiation.

[3] Based an AATCC Standard Test Method 18A-1963.

"standard fading hours required to produce just appreciable fading" (change of color of any kind).

C. Daylight test: Specimens are allowed to remain in a test cabinet for 24 hours a day. Specimens are also exposed to low intensity radiation (before 9 A.M. and after 3 P.M.), and on cloudy days, during which time the specimen temperature may be low and the moisture content high. Since the three tests may produce varying results, laboratories test a specimen under a variety of conditions simulating the performance from the fabric.

## FASTNESS TO PERSPIRATION

Light-colored silks, especially those used for evening wear, should be fast to perspiration. Most consumers rely on the salesperson's advice concerning the fastness of a fabric to perspiration. In fact, some large department stores have their own merchandise testing laboratories, to which buyers may send new materials for testing fastness before instructions are given to the salespeople. Reliable manufacturers often provide the buyers with the same information. In buying yard goods, however, the consumer can usually obtain a sample of material, take it home, and test it before buying enough for her needs.

*Home test.* It is best to subject the fabric to actual wear. A small piece of material may be worn in the sole of the shoe for a day. A quicker test is to sew a swatch of material to a white cloth of the same general texture, then immerse both for a moment in vinegar (not cider but synthetic vinegar), and let it dry. If stained, the sample is not fast to perspiration. Synthetic vinegar is used because it comes closest to perspiration; both contain acetic acid.

*Commercial test (AATCC 15–1962).*[4] AATCC perspiration tester: Separate specimens are wetted out in alkaline and acid perspiration solutions. Fabrics are inserted in the perspiration tester; are subjected to a fixed mechanical pressure; and are allowed to dry slowly in an oven $10 \pm 2°$ F. for at least six hours. Bleeding, migration of color, or changes of dyed material are evaluated.

## FASTNESS TO LAUNDERING

The best way to determine fastness to laundering is actually to launder a fabric. Ideally, the consumer should launder a small piece of material as many times as the fabric would be expected to resist laundering in actual use. Of course, this is too much to ask of the average consumer. Many testing laboratories do this very thing for the manufacturers and retail stores. For example, suppose that the specifications for a certain brand of sheet require that "the sheet must be fast to 20 washings in a reliable laundry and after these washings shall lose not

---

[4] USASI Standard L 14.56-1963.

more than 8 per cent of its tensile-strength testing to make sure it is up to specifications."

At home, the testing of a fabric for fastness to washing may be speeded up by the use of a soap stronger than that normally used. One or two washings with strong soap generally give the same result as many washings with a mild soap.

*Home tests.* A. Hand laundering: A six-inch square of colored fabric should be cut into three equal parts. One of the parts is sewn to a 2-inch swatch of white cotton cloth of about the same weight and texture as the test cloth. It should be washed with warm water and yellow soap, rinsed in clear water, and then dried. It should be ironed if necessary to make it smooth. The color of the washed and unwashed samples is compared, and the white fabric is examined for any discoloration.

B. Automatic washing: A 2-inch white swatch is basted to a colored fabric. These fabrics are subjected to a normal washing cycle in an automatic washer with usual soap solution and water temperature. No chlorine is used. Washing of the test samples can be done with a regular load of colored clothes. If there is a change of color of the washed fabric or discoloration of the white fabric, the color is not fast to the test method used.

*Commercial tests (AATCC 61–1965).*[5] A 45-minute accelerated test: Specimens are placed in stainless steel tubes or glass jars that revolve at a standard speed in a water bath that is thermostatically controlled. Metal balls are added to each tube to simulate washing action.

**TESTING METHODS**

| Test Number | Temperature | Soap (per cent) | Sodium Carbonate (per cent) | Available Chlorine (per cent) | Time (minutes) |
|---|---|---|---|---|---|
| 1. | 105° | 40 | 0.5 | None | 30 |
| 2. | 120° | 49 | 0.5 | None | 30 |
| 3. | 160° | 71 | 0.5 | 0.2 | 45 |
| 4. | 182° | 83 | 0.5 | 0.2 | 45 |

Tested specimens are evaluated for alteration in color by comparing them with the international Geometric Scale. Color staining is evaluated by comparison with the AATCC chart for measuring transference of color or the Geometric Staining Scale.

### FASTNESS TO CLEANING, DRY AND WET

*Home tests.* A. Dry cleaning: The procedure for dry cleaning should be followed explicitly as given in the directions on any standard brand of dry cleaning fluid.

[5] USASI Standard L 14.81-1963.

B. Wet cleaning: To wet-clean a fabric, the dry cleaned swatch should be wetted with distilled water (90–100° F.) containing one gram of neutral soap per liter. The fabric is rinsed in distilled water of the same temperature as the previous solution. The fabric is removed from the water without squeezing and is laid on a flat surface to dry at room temperature. Fabrics that do not show appreciable color change are considered fast to wet cleaning.

*Commercial tests* (*AATCC 85–1963*).[6]   A. Dry cleaning: A specimen is agitated 30 minutes in a chlorinated hydrocarbon solvent at 115° F. in the Launder-Ometer. The specimen is pressed with a hand iron or pressing machine until it is smooth. The tested specimen is compared for color with the International Geometric Gray Scale.

B. Wet cleaning: The fabric is rinsed in distilled water of the same temperature as the previous solution. The fabric is laid on a flat surface to dry at room temperature. Fabrics that show no change of color are fast to wet cleaning.

### FASTNESS TO PRESSING, WET AND DRY

*Home tests.*   To test fastness to pressing of cotton and linen fabrics, two samples, each 2 x 4 inches, are used. One sample is covered with a wet piece of bleached, unsized cloth.

The sample is ironed for ten seconds at 350° F. The tested sample is placed in a dark room for about an hour to regain its natural moisture. The other test sample is ironed dry for five seconds at 425° F. and is then placed in a dark room. Cotton and linen fabrics pressed wet that show no appreciable change in color and no appreciable staining of the white fabric are considered colorfast to wet pressing. Similarly, cotton and linen fabrics that show no change in color after dry pressing are colorfast to dry pressing.

For testing fabrics other than cotton and linen and other than woolens and worsteds, pieces of white wool, silk, desized cotton, rayon, and acetate cloths are sewn to one test sample. For wet pressing, the test sample is wetted, the surplus water is shaken off, and the sample is placed face down on the dry-test sample. Then the fabric is allowed to rest for one hour. Another sample is tested for ten seconds with a flat iron between 275° and 300° F. Fabrics that pass both tests are color fast to wet and dry pressing.

*Commercial test* (*AATCC 117–1966*).   A piece of colored fabric is placed between two pieces of uncolored cloth (composite specimen). The fabrics are placed in a heating device or Scotch tester, German Precision Heating Press, or Molten Metal Bath for 30 seconds at one of the following test temperatures:

$$300° \pm 5° \text{ F.}$$
$$325° \pm 5° \text{ F.}$$

[6] USASI Standard L 14.120-1961.

$$350° \pm 5° \text{ F.}$$
$$375° \pm 5° \text{ F.}$$
$$400° \pm 5° \text{ F.}$$

The composite specimen is removed from the heating device and evaluated for each component by comparing with the Gray Scale for Color Change and the Gray Staining Scale.

### FASTNESS TO CROCKING

Fabrics used for street and business dresses must withstand a great deal of friction, that is, the color should not rub off, or crock, even though the fabric is not intended to be washable. Dyestuffs that crock are very likely to bleed or run. In washable fabrics crocking may be an indication that the colors are not fast to laundering. Furthermore, if a dye crocks badly, it may discolor fabrics rubbed against it.

*Home tests.* A. Dry crocking: A two-inch square of colored fabric is rubbed against a piece of white sheeting. Any discoloration of the white cloth should be noted. If there is any discoloration of the fabric itself, the color is not fast to dry crocking.

B. Wet crocking: A piece of white sheeting should be dampened and rubbed against a piece of the untested colored fabric. Any discoloration of the white cloth should be noted. If this occurs, the color is not fast to crocking.

*Commercial tests (AATCC 8–1961).*[7] A. Dry crocking: A test specimen is fastened to the base of the Crockmeter. A standard crock cloth is attached to the rubbing finger. The finger is lowered onto the test specimen, and by turning the crank the finger is caused to slide back and forth 20 times.

B. Wet crocking: Wet out squares in distilled water and squeeze between filter papers or a hand wringer. Evaluate the transfer of color (both wet and dry) by comparing with the AATCC Chart for Measuring Transference of Color or the Geometric Staining Scale.

## DYEING CLOTH

### THE DYESTUFF

Fabrics in colors such as blue, yellow, red, green, and their combinations are made by impregnation of the cloth with certain color substances called *dyestuffs.* The fastness of these colors depends on the chemical content of the dyestuff, the affinity of the dyestuff for the fabric, and the method of dyeing the cloth. If a color has a greater

[7] USASI Standard L 14.71-1963.

affinity for the fabric than it has for sunlight, perspiration, washing, or friction, the color will be fast to these influences.

## SELECTION OF THE PROPER DYESTUFF

Until 1856 all dyestuffs were natural dyestuffs; that is, they were obtained from plants, shellfish, insects, and woods. Some of the most common natural dyestuffs are cochineal—made from the dried bodies of female insects found in Central America and Mexico—used to dye scarlet; logwood, taken from the brownish heart of a tree found in Central America; quercitron, which comes from the yellow inner bark of a large oak tree growing in the eastern part of this country; fustic, a light yellow dye coming from a tree growing in Mexico and the West Indies; and indigo, a blue dyestuff derived originally (by the Indians) from plants but now made artificially also.

History relates that natural dyes were used in the early days of the Roman Empire—when the so-called Tyrian purple was used for the ruling family. The substance that first produced the color purple was derived from a kind of snail. Pliny tells us that the art of dyeing yellow, green, and black was brought from India to Greece by Alexander the Great. In the Middle Ages, northern Italy was most skilled in the art of dyeing. The early explorers who came to America brought back many dyestuffs. Certainly dyeing is one of the oldest of the arts.

In oriental rugmaking a century ago, the modern commercial dyestuffs were unknown. Each family was skilled in making certain colors that would be fast to washing and sunlight. The secret formula for making a certain color from natural dyestuffs was handed down from one generation to another.

Obtaining natural dyestuffs and mixing them to obtain the desired color is a slow process compared with our present methods of commercial dyeing, in which all the dyes are synthetic or chemical. They are man-made by the mixing of certain chemicals whose bases are either salts or acids. At the present time synthetic dyes have practically replaced natural dyes.

The first dyestuff from chemical sources was discovered by William Henry Perkin in 1856. He was experimenting with aniline, whose base is principally coal tar (a substance produced in the process of making coke). The color substance he discovered was mauve. Later other coal-tar colors followed. But the great development in chemical dyestuffs in this country has come since World War I. During the war years 1914–1918, the fabrics dyed in the United States were poor and were not fast. The United States had to do much experimenting before it knew the secret of making fast synthetic dyes. Before and during the war Germany held that secret.

Dyestuffs may be classified according to their method of application to a cloth. The principal synthetic dyestuffs are (1) acid dyes; (2)

mordant dyes; (3) basic colors, comprising most of the older aniline dyes; (4) direct dyes; (5) developed colors; (6) disperse dyes; (7) naphthol or azoic dyes; (8) pigment dyes; (9) vat dyes; (10) fiber-reactive dyes.

## ACID DYES

Acid dyes are essentially organic acids that are obtained by the dyer in the form of salts. They are applied to the fiber directly from solutions containing an acid, such as sulphuric, acetic, or formic acids. Acid dyes can be used on wool, acrylic, nylon and certain modified polyester fibers, and spandex and certain selected polypropylene olefin fibers.

Fibers sensitive to weak acid solutions and cellulosic fibers cannot be dyed with acid dyes. To dye vegetable fibers, a mordant is necessary. A mordant is a chemical that has an affinity for both the dyestuff and the fabric and acts as a bridging agent.

When wet-treated, bright acid colors may not be colorfast. Acid colors are only fairly to poorly fast to washing; they vary in degree of colorfastness to perspiration; but they give good colorfastness to dry cleaning and to light.

Acid dyes are water-soluble and can be applied to silk, wool, casein, and nylon without a *mordant*. Acid colors can be applied to Orlon 42 and acetate fiber at high temperatures by a special method. At present, it is possible to obtain a larger range of dyes and better wet-fastness than previously. Dynel modacrylic and the older Acrilan acrylic fibers can also be colored by acid dyes.

## MORDANT OR CHROME DYES

So-called chrome colors are made by mordant dyes in which chromium is used as the mordant to fix the dye on the cloth. Other metallic salts, such as iron, aluminum, or tin, may be used. These dyes are much more satisfactory on wool and silk than on cotton or linen. On cotton, these dyes usually fade when laundered; but on men's wool clothing, which is dry-cleaned rather than laundered, chrome colors are often used. Nylon colored with these dyestuffs gives good colorfastness.

In an experiment to determine the behavior of textiles under fluorescent light, a mercury lamp fitted with a filter furnished ultraviolet light. It was found that dyed materials show varying degrees of fluorescence; that it, each dyed fabric emits light to a certain extent. Therefore it is possible to say whether patterns of the same shade (if they are not too dark) have been dyed with the same dyestuff. This fact is important in matching colors; if one lot of fabric is dyed with one kind of dyestuff, and a second lot is dyed with another dyestuff that produces apparently the same hue, the fluorescence test will reveal that the two dyestuffs were not the same chemically. Hence the second dyestuff may not be fabrics might not give the same degree of service.

Mordant or chrome dyes have properties in common with acid dyes. They are used to dye the same fibers. But the major difference lies in the fact that metal is added to the dye molecule. The metallic compound combines with the fiber and the organic dye and forms an insoluble color compound in the fiber.

### BASIC OR CATIONIC DYES

These colors were the first synthetic dyestuffs to be discovered. Basic dyes are salts of colored organic bases. They may be called cationic because the colored portion of the dye molecule is positively charged (cationic).

At present organic basic dyes are called aniline colors because the first few colors were made from aniline. Basic dyes can be applied to cotton, linen, rayon, silk, and wool for excellent color value and penetration. Medium and full shades of Acrilan 16 can be produced with basic dyes. When used on the older Acrilan, basic dyes are fast but are limited to pale and medium shades. Selected basic dyes may be used on the acrylic Orlon 81. To be used successfully on cotton or rayon they must be applied with an acid mordant; but wool and silk can be dyed directly. This class of dyes is chiefly used on cotton to brighten other, duller, colors (these are "topped" with basic dyes). Basic dyes are seldom used on wool, because acid colors are generally more fast. For dyeing silk, basic dyes give brilliancy and depth of color. These colors are satisfactory for silks weighted with tin. Basic dyes are not fast to light or washing, and the method of dyeing is slow. For these reasons, basic dyes are not included in Figure 8.1.

### DIRECT OR SUBSTANTIVE DYES

These dyestuffs, like acid dyes, are salts of color acids. They are applied directly to cotton, linen, and rayon, requiring no mordant. Shades so produced are duller than those colored by basic dyes, but they can be topped with basic dyes to brighten them. Direct dyes may be used for dyeing wool yarns used for knitting and weaving, for reused wool, and for casein fibers. These colors are generally not fast to washing. They are more fast to light when applied to wool than when used on cotton.

Direct colors may also be applied to silk, and shades so obtained are faster than they are on cotton. But these colors have normally been regarded as cotton dyes and have therefore not been used so frequently on silk and wool. When direct colors are used to dye nylon, the dye is usually applied from a bath set with either acetic or formic acid.

Direct dyes may be developed after application to the fabric. Naphtholic compounds are used as developers. A radical in the dye

DEGREE OF FASTNESS TO---

| | | Home Washing (AATCC #2) | Laundry (AATCC #3) | Light | Slasher Sizing | Chlorine | Cross Dyeing | Mercerizing |
|---|---|---|---|---|---|---|---|---|
| 1. | VAT | Excellent | Excellent | Excellent | Excellent | Excellent | Excellent | Excellent |
| 2. | NAPTHOL | Excellent | Excellent | Excellent | Excellent | Excellent to good | Excellent | Excellent |
| 3. | BONDED (Fiber-reactive) | Excellent | Very good | Fair to good | Excellent | Most dyes poor | Good | Excellent |
| 4. | DEVELOPED | Good | Fair | Fair to poor | Excellent | Poor | Good | Good |
| 5. | SULPHUR | Very good | Good | Good to fair | Excellent | Most dyes poor | Excellent | Excellent |
| 6. | DIRECT | Good in light shades of selected dyes | Fair in light shades | Excellent in selected dyes. Others fair to poor | Good in light shades | Poor | Poor | Some good |

NOTE: This table is only a generalization. It refers to the relative fastness of the different dyeing methods as a class. It should be borne in mind, however, that there are exceptions within each class.
The numbers on the left indicate the price class, No. 1 being the highest priced, No. 2 next, and so on.

**Figure 8.1. Fastness of dyes.** (Reprinted courtesy of the Franklin Process Company, a division of Indian Head Yarn Company.)

molecule reacts with the developer. Developed direct dyes may have excellent fastness to washing but a decreased lightfastness. (See *developed colors*.)

Bright shades are obtained from both direct and developed direct dyes.

## DEVELOPED COLORS

These are dyestuffs that may be applied directly to the cloth and may change to a new color on the fabric when treated with nitrous acid and certain chemicals called *developers*. The intensity of the color and the fastness of the dyestuff may be changed by this treatment. A dye that is navy blue when applied directly to a cloth may become a fast black when developed. Cotton dyed with developed colors may be washed satisfactorily at home but should not be sent to a commercial laundry.

Developed dyes may also be used on rayon and other man-made fibers when developed from disperse-dye bases. (See *disperse dyes*.) Developed color are sometimes used for discharge printing. (See p. 210.)

## DISPERSE DYES

These dyes were formerly called acetate dyes because they were originally used to dye acetate fibers. They are now used for coloring acetate, polyester, acrylic, and nylon fibers. The molecules of these dyes are small, and the dye is slightly soluble in water but is easily *dispersed* throughout a solution. The dye sites are made more accessible by swelling the fiber with wetting agents, heat, etc. The small particles are "inserted," and the water medium is evaporated by heat. This seals in the dye molecule. One theory is that dye particles attach themselves to the surface of the acetate fiber and then dissolve when exposed to nitrogen in the air (fume fade). When used on nylon and polyester this fume fading is not serious. Ratings for colorfastness to light, washing, and dry cleaning vary depending on the fiber used.

## NAPHTHOL OR AZOIC DYES

Naphthol dyes are commonly applied to cotton piece goods and are used extensively in cotton printing. The cotton is first impregnated with beta-naphthol that has been dissolved in caustic soda; then it is immersed in basic dye. Naphthol colors are fast to washing and to soaping when properly applied. The application of this type of dye requires a good knowledge of organic chemistry, and failure to follow directions for its application may result in poor colorfastness to crocking and washing. Fast bright scarlets and reds can be obtained at a fairly low cost. A naphthol dye can produce a green or blue-green shade on polyester fibers.

For the dyeing of acetate, certain of the insoluble compounds of azoic dyes are used. These compounds are treated with sulfonated oil or soap. By this treatment, a stable suspension for dyeing acetate is possible.

Azoic dyes can be applied to nylon by methods similar to those used for acetate; however, the colors are not as brilliant as on cottons. By first impregnating nylon with Naphthanil, then immersing in a second bath containing hydrochloric acid, and finally developing in a sodium-nitrite-acid liquor, strong, bright, well-penetrating colors with fastness to crocking are possible. Azoic dyes may be applied to the older Acrilan acrylic fiber by the use of a modified technique. Insoluble azoics dye polyester fibers well.

### PIGMENT DYES

This type of coloring of textiles has been a comparatively recent discovery, because it utilizes the synthetic resins in the preparation of the dye emulsion. A common method of preparing the dye is to use fine synthetic pigment in a solution of synthetic resins in an organic solvent. Water is stirred in with a high-speed mixer. Since the pigment itself has poor affinity for the fibers, the resin serves to bind the pigment to the fibers. Usually the dye so prepared is padded or printed onto the cloth. (See *pad dyeing*, p. 207.)

Pigment colors are used mostly on cotton, acetate, rayon, cellulose/polyester blends, and glass. Almost all types of fibers and blends can be colored by pigment dyeing or printing.

When properly applied, pigment prints excel in lightfastness. With the proper binder and application, such prints have acceptable washability. Abrasion may remove color as surface fixing agents wear away, making the color vulnerable to crocking.

### VAT DYES

The name originated in the making of the old indigo dyes, when the dyestuff had to steep for some days before it could be used. There are three classes of vat dyes: (1) indigo, indigoids, indigosols, and algosols; (2) anthraquinoids; (3) sulfur.

Modern indigo is perhaps the most famous vat dye, because of its fastness to light and washing. Increasingly important in this group are the indigosols (colorless dyestuffs), which are being used for dyeing wool. The wool or silk is saturated with dye, and color is later developed. The indigoids are a group of vat dyes that have pigment-bearing sacs similar to indigo.

The anthraquinoids are the fastest of the vat dyes. They are especially suitable for cotton and can be applied to acetate. In this category are the indanthrene dyes, which are extremely fast.

Sulfur colors are used on cottons and vegetable fibers. Although the colors are dull, they have good fastness to light, washing, and crocking, and are relatively inexpensive. Sometimes sulfur black dye attacks and weakens the fiber, because the oxidation of the sulfur gradually develops sulfuric acid.

Probably the reason for the increased importance of the vat dye is that it possesses a higher degree of fastness to washing, light, bleaching, cross-dyeing, and mercerizing than do the other dyes. (See Figure 8.1.) As a class, then, vat dyestuffs are particularly fast when applied to cotton. They are used to produce fast colors in cotton dress fabrics and in shirtings. Vat dyes can also be used for dyeing silk, linen, rayon, and wool. They can be used for acetate, but many dyers consider them unsuitable for silk. The dye bath must be strongly alkaline, and so must be weakened to prevent the alkali from attacking the silk fiber. Vat colors on nylon possess all the characteristics of these dyes on other fibers with the exception of fastness to light. For improved color value and penetration, vat dyes can be applied at high temperatures to Orlon 81 and to Acrilan. When similarly applied to Orlon 42, bright shades of excellent fastness are possible. This high-temperature dyeing technique has been successfully adapted for the processing of cotton sliver containing an appreciable amount of dead fibers.

Probably the most interesting and technical part of dyeing with vat colors is the dyeing of one shade to match another. The difficulty of matching colors lies in guessing what the final color will be after the fabric is dried, because the action of air on the newly dyed cloth changes the hue. (See "Computer processes in shade matching," p. 216.)

### FIBER-REACTIVE DYESTUFFS

In general, all classes of dyestuffs are fixed to the fabric by means of physical absorption or mechanical retention of an insoluble pigment by the fiber. In both cases, the color appears to be a part of the fiber.

Fiber-reactive dyestuffs, however, couple the color to the fabric by a reaction with the hydroxide (OH) group of the cellulose molecule. In this reaction the dye molecule becomes an integral part of the cellulose. It is because of this chemical integrity that reactive dyes possess excellent wash-fastness and dry-cleaning properties.

Most reactive dyes are fixed to the fabric by a system that employs an alkali as a catalyst. This alkali promotes the transfer of electrons, which causes the color to be integrated with the cellulose. Of the many alkalies (electrolytes) used, the most common are sodium carbonate, sodium bicarbonate, and caustic soda.

In practice, the fabric would first be padded with the dye, then dried. The fabric would then undergo a second padding containing the alkali. Once this is completed, the fabric would be exposed to extreme heat, steam, or air.

Fabrics such as wool or silk can be dyed in this fashion. However, the best results are obtained on cotton. This system has obvious labor- and time-saving advantages. These are brought to light in a consideration of the time it takes to fix a dye in a system that fixes only when an exchange between dye and fabric comes to an equilibrium. An example of this is exhaustion dyeing. The time element here may be from ten minutes to hours. Today, some reactive dyes can be fixed in thirty seconds.

### DYEING OF BLENDS

The problem of dyeing textiles has never been an easy one if the selection of the dyestuff and its application is adequate to give the performance in use expected by the consumer. With the advent of the newer synthetics, and now with the increasing use of blends, the problem has become even more complex. To cite one example, consider the dyeing of a blend of Dynel modacrylic (not less than 25 per cent and not more than 30 per cent) and rayon. Dynel is described in Chapter 14 as a partially acrylic fiber that is sensitive to heat at the normal textile dyeing temperatures of 240° to 250° F.; unless the fabric is put in tension, it will shrink enough to make the cloth feel firm. However, the problem is being surmounted by heat treatment before dyeing in order to shrink the fiber and to reduce the tendency to feel firm after dyeing. Selected dyestuffs for acetate and regular rayon dyestuffs can be used, but, again, application of heat over 250° F. is necessary. Consequently, neutral, premetallized dyestuffs are used to give lightfastness superior to acetate dyestuffs.[2]

Ciba Ltd., Basel, Switzerland, has developed a one-bath process to dye 50 per cent wool/50 per cent cotton blends. The process begins with an acid dyebath to which a wool-immunizing agent is added to keep direct color off the wool. Another ingredient is added to alkalinize the dyebath as the dyeing progresses. The fabrics are brought to a boil in thirty minutes and boil for one hour. A typical dyebath would consist of 100 units of fabric; 4,000 units of water; 6 units of 40 per cent acetic acid; and 40 units Glauber's salt; and 13 units immunizing agent. Color shades are made in the usual way, and excellent cross-dyes are possible.

These are only two of the many possible blends that a dyer may encounter. Percentages of each fiber as well as the kind of fibers and the number of different ones included in a blend are considerations in the proper selection and application of a dyestuff for a blend.

### METHODS OF DYEING FABRICS

When the proper type of dyestuff has been selected, the textile can be dyed by one of the following methods:

[2] Premetallized dyestuffs are those that are chemically coupled with nickel, copper, and cobalt salts to make the dye on the fiber.

1. *Dyeing the raw stock.* This method is very common in dyeing wool. "Dyed in the wool" is a familiar expression; it means that the wool fibers were dyed before they were carded or spun. This method enables the dyestuff to penetrate the fibers thoroughly, so that the color is likely to be fast. Interesting mixtures can be made by mixing two or more colors of raw stock. This method is more costly than other methods of dyeing textile fabrics. The favorite mottled gray flannel suiting is

**Figure 8.2.** Methods of dyeing. The cross-dyed sample at lower right consists of acetate, viscose rayon, and cotton. Some of the acetate yarns have been dissolved by acetone in a laboratory test. (*Photos by Jack Pitkin.*)

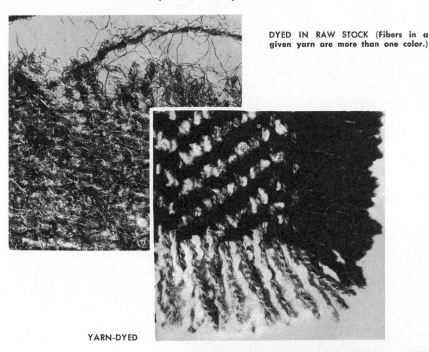

DYED IN RAW STOCK (Fibers in a given yarn are more than one color.)

YARN-DYED

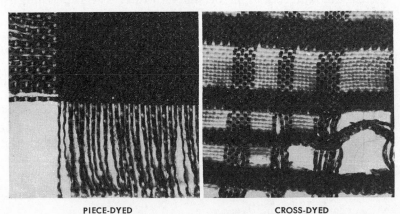

PIECE-DYED          CROSS-DYED

dyed in raw stock. Solution-dyed fibers also come in this category. Rayon, acetate, and Dynel may be solution-dyed.

2. *Dyeing the slub.* When the fibers have been carded and combed preparatory to spinning, they lie in the shape of a smooth slub, sliver, or rope. This sliver can be printed with dye at the desired intervals. By drawing and spinning the yarn, interesting mixtures may be obtained. This method is also common for wool mixtures. The dyestuff penetrates the fibers easily, thus ensuring permanency of color.

3. *Dyeing the yarn.* One of the best selling points a salesman has for textile fabrics is the term *yarn dyed*. This means that the yarns were dyed before the fabric was woven. (See *space-dyed yarns*.) Because the dyestuff penetrates the yarns to the core, a yarn-dyed fabric is faster than a piece-dyed fabric; and a yarn-dyed fabric usually has a deeper, richer, and more lustrous appearance. In speaking of hosiery, the term *ingrain* is synonymous with *yarn dyed;* the term *dip dyed* has the same meaning as *piece dyed*. Plaid ginghams, shepherd checks, and denims are yarn-dyed fabrics. An important method of dyeing yarn is called *package dyeing*. Yarn is wound around a cylinder known as a *package*. It is approximately six inches long by five and one-half inches in diameter. Dye packages are placed in the dyeing machine—a stainless steel cylinder (like a pressure cooker) with vertical spindles fastened to the bottom or to a removable carrier. The packages are placed on the spindles and the lid is closed. The dye is pumped through the packages from the inside out.

4. *Dyeing in the piece.* Although it is possible to make fast colors by piece-dyeing, the dyer must make sure that the cloth is covered evenly and that the dye has penetrated the fibers thoroughly. Piece-dyeing is done a great deal, for it is economical for the manufacturer—especially in fabrics such as hosiery, whose style in colors changes rapidly. Another advantage is that any shade can be dyed on short notice. The knitting mills can make up a huge stock of undyed hosiery and wait until the demand comes for a definite amount in a certain color, dye that amount, and wait for another order. The same thing is done with other woven fabrics.

Since not all dyestuffs have an equal affinity for both vegetable and animal fibers, very interesting mixtures and frosted effects are produced by *cross dyeing*. For example, when a cloth contains both vegetable and animal fibers, a dyestuff may be used that colors the animal but not the vegetable fibers.

Rayon and acetate mixtures can be dyed with a dyestuff that takes on the rayon but is resisted by the acetate. Blue wool suiting with a white cotton hairline stripe can be made by cross-dyeing. The dyestuff colors the wool blue but does not color the cotton stripe. Similarly, the acrylics Acrilan and Acrilan 16 can be cross-dyed. If basic dyes are applied under strong acid conditions, Acrilan 16 is dyed, whereas the older Acrilan resists the dye.

Acrylic blend of Acrilan and Orlon 42 is also being cross-dyed. Acid dyestuffs applied to the blend leave Orlon relatively undyed and Acrilan in color. A two-tone effect can be obtained by first dyeing the cloth with basic dyestuffs to get the required shade on the Orlon and then dyeing the blend with acid dyestuffs in the same bath to get the Acrilan component in the desired shade.

Another type of piece-dyeing is called *pad dyeing*. This cloth is passed through a trough containing the dyebath. It is then squeezed between heavy rolls to remove excess dye. This is a very quick method of applying the dye, but unless there is some aftertreatment the colors are not usually so fast as in other methods of dyeing. Pad dyeing is frequently chosen to produce lighter shades.

Still another method of piece-dyeing is called *jig dyeing,* because the cloth is passed through a jig-dyeing machine that consists of a large tub holding dye and rollers that guide the cloth through the dyebath. A great number of yards of cloth can be dyed at once by this method. Jig dyeing is used particularly for dark, direct dyes.

A reel-dyeing machine, consisting of a dye tub with a reel that lifts the fabric into the dyebath, is used for lightweight fabrics that cannot stand tension in dyeing. Heavy crepes are dyed in this way, because this method does not flatten the creped surface.

When great quantities of one fabric have to be dyed, the continuous dyeing process is a definite timesaver. Previous to this discovery, dyeing was all done on comparatively small batches of cloth. The dyeing operation had to be stopped after each operation to transfer the cloth from one machine to another machine that might be in a different location. Now, all dyeing and subsequent operations can be done in one continuous process. Disadvantages of this method lie in the fact that it does not, without difficulty, dye cloth in deep shades, and it is not economical for dyeing short lengths of cloth. Du Pont has overcome these disadvantages with a process called the Pad-Steam Continuous Dyeing Process. By this process coat dyes can be applied to a cloth in about one-tenth the time required for the old type of dyeing in batches. Another du Pont invention, called the Multi-lap Continuous Processing Machine, enables dyeing of lightly constructed fabrics by continuous processing without stretching or distorting them.

The process of dyeing blends in one dyebath is both time-and labor-saving. Alexis Massainoff, of Lake Arrowhead, California, has patented a multiple-color process for any type of fabric. Only one dipping of the fabric is required.

5. *Printing.* Fabrics with colored figures stamped on them are known as printed cloths. The design in this case is not woven into the cloth but is printed on after the cloth has been woven. If the background of the fabric is to be white, the cloth is usually bleached before it is printed.

The printing of fabrics represents an important part of the textile industry. (See *dyeing of wool and cotton blends,* p. 204.) It is interesting to note that printed goods are often bought on impulse by the con-

sumer because a particular pattern, design, or color combination in a
dress, sport shirt, or blouse appeals to her. To retain this market, the
print industry and those involved in the textile business face a major
problem of meeting competition and maintaining price levels in the face
of increasing raw material and labor costs. To alleviate this problem,
chemists have developed new methods. One that seems to give promise
is an emulsion (oil in water or water in oil) print paste that can be used
on any regular printing machine with conventional engraved rollers.
Color effects unobtainable with old paste methods are possible with emulsion printing. Also, procedures may be simplified and cost of printing
cut.

*Steps in printing.*   First, artists submit their designs to manufacturers.
Out of an assortment of designs submitted, a great number are rejected.
The few accepted ones are then printed on samples of fabrics. Some of
these may be scrapped. The design is next enlarged so that flaws may be
detected and corrected. On this large scale, the design is carved on a zinc
plate. Each color in the design appears clearly on this plate. A *pantograph*
transfers the design from the zinc plate to the copper rollers (a different
roller for each color) and at the same time reduces the design to its
original proportions. Thus we see that when a particular design contains
red, yellow, green, and black, four distinct rollers must be used—one
for each color and all of the same size. The design scratched on the
copper rollers is then treated with nitric acid, which eats out the design
as it would an etching. The etching of fine parallel lines inside the design
proper serves to hold enough of the dyestuffs to penetrate the cloth as
it is printed. Rollers may also be engraved by hand or by a photochemical process that reproduces the shading and detail of a photograph.
The actual printing is done as the cloth passes over a series of rollers
that revolve in a vat of dye. Each roller retains its particular color in the
etched design and prints it on the fabric.

Dyestuffs used for printing are the same as those used for piece-dyeing
or yarn-dyeing, except that dyestuffs may be thickened with starch,
gum, or resin to prevent a color from bleeding or running outside the
outline before it is dry. When they are dried, printed cloths are passed
over hot rollers and then steamed so that the colors are set. Any excess
dye is removed by a washing after the steaming. Colors carefully printed
can be fast to both light and washing. It has been found that mercerization of the grey goods before printing results in a brighter, stronger
colored print.

## KINDS OF PRINTING

There are many different ways of printing fabrics. The chief ones are
as follows:

1. *Direct or roller printing.*   This is the simplest method and prob-

**Figure 8.3.** Fabric being roller (direct) printed. *(Photograph courtesy of Cranston Print Works Company.)*

ably the most used. The cloth is passed over a series of rollers (as already described), the number of rollers depending on the number of colors in the design. As many as sixteen colors can be printed at the rate of up to 200 yards a minute. Almost any textile fabric can be printed in this manner. Printed percale, printed dress linen, printed rayon and silk crepes, and printed wool challis are generally printed by this method.

A design may be printed on the warp yarns before the cloth is woven. When so printed, the fabric is called *warp printed*. The designs may appear grayed and their outlines may be hazy. This is because the filling yarns are usually a neutral shade—often white. *Vigoureux printing* is a variation of warp printing that is used on wool. Before the yarn is spun, color is applied to the wool tops or slubbing in the rope form. A variation of the roller method applies the colors in horizontal or cross-striped designs. When the wool is spun into yarn and woven into cloth, the stripes are broken into colored flecks. This type of printing is also called *mélange*.

2. *Discharge printing or dyeing.* When the design is to contain not more than two colors, the method called *discharge* is often used. The whole cloth is dyed a solid color first; then the design on the roller is covered with a chemical, which, when it is applied to the cloth, discharges (removes) the color from it in those portions that correspond to the design on the roller. The background is left colored and the design is white. The same depth of color appears on both sides, because the colored portion was piece-dyed first. Likewise, the color in the background can be discharged if the background is printed with chemical so that the design is left colored. Usually, however, the background is darker than the design. Polka dots and the figures in foulards are often printed in this manner.

3. *Resist printing or dyeing.* In this method the design is printed first with a chemical paste so constituted that when the cloth is dyed the parts covered by the paste resist the dye and retain their original color. Batik work is an excellent example of one type of resist dyeing. The portions of the fabric that are to resist the dye are covered with paraffin. The whole cloth is then dyed and, when dried, the paraffin is removed. At times the paraffin cracks during the dyeing, so that little runs of color appear in the resisted portions. Often the resisted portions are painted by hand in different colors.

Sometimes certain yarns are chemically treated to resist dye before they are woven. When the cloth is piece-dyed, the yarns so treated do not take the dye. Accordingly, stripes and checks appear in piece-dyed goods.

Another type of resist dyeing is called *tie dyeing.* In certain seasons tie-dyed scarfs and other accessories are very stylish. Pieces of string are tied around bunches of cloth where the dye is to be resisted. The fabric is left tied in many little bunches while immersed in the dyestuffs. When the fabric is dry, the strings are removed, and very interesting sunburst designs appear. Parts of the fabric may be tied in different proportions and dipped in more than one color. It is possible to produce a varicolored design in this way. Still more complicated designs can be made by stitching the design areas rather than by tying.

Another type of resist dyeing is *stencil printing,* which is done by hand. Paper or metal is cut in the desired pattern and is placed over the fabric where the pattern is to be resisted. The parts that are covered do not take the dye.

4. *Hand block printing.* Before the method of direct roller printing was discovered, fabrics were printed by hand. The method is very similar to rubber stamping. A wooden block with a portion of the design carved on it is inked with dyestuff and stamped on the cloth by hand. The number of blocks used corresponds to the number of colors in the design. Great skill is required to stamp each portion of the design accurately so that all designs will be clear in outline and proportionate without a change in depth of color. Hand blocking gives a greater variety

ROLLER (DIRECT)                               DISCHARGE

*(Right sides are shown at the top; wrong sides in the turned-up portions at the bottom.)*

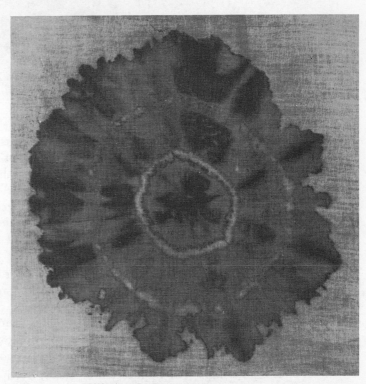

RESIST (DONE BY TIE-DYEING)

**Figure 8.4.** Methods of printing. (*Photos by Jack Pitkin.*)

of designs and color effects, for the regular repetition of a pattern that is necessary in the roller method is not necessary in hand blocking.

Linen is used quite extensively for hand blocking because it has the proper texture and quality. As hand-blocked fabrics are generally expensive, it does not pay to do such handwork on a poor grade of cloth. Real India prints are produced by hand block printing.

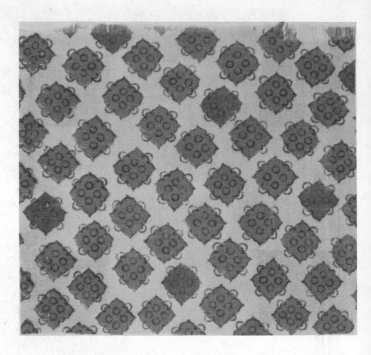

**Figure 8.5.** Hand-blocked wool challis.

One way to detect hand blocking is to look along the selvage for the regularity of the repetition of the design. In roller printing, the design must be repeated at regular intervals. Not so with hand blocking. Another way to detect hand blocking is to look at the edges of the designs. Almost invariably one color runs into another in at least a few places. Also, the quality of workmanship may be determined by the clearness of each color, the sharpness of outline, and the regularity of the design.

5. *Duplex printing.* When a fabric is intended to be reversible, it is printed on one side, turned over, and then printed again on the other side so that the outlines of the designs on each side coincide. There is a special machine called a *duplex printing machine* that prints both sides of a fabric simultaneously. This method is called duplex printing. If it is done well, it gives the impression that the design is woven in.

6. *Flock printing.* The application of short, dyed cotton, rayon, or wool fibers to fabric or to paper is called flock printing. There are two methods of application: (1) The flock fibers are pressed into the resin substance, which has already been printed on the fabric. (2) The flock is applied to the resin-printed fabric by electrolysis. The second method produces a velvety surface.

7. *Painted design.* Hand painting is most effective on silks. The design is outlined on the fabric with wax and is filled in later by hand brushwork. Usually the wax is mixed with dye so that the outline appears a different color and so stands out from the background. The

21

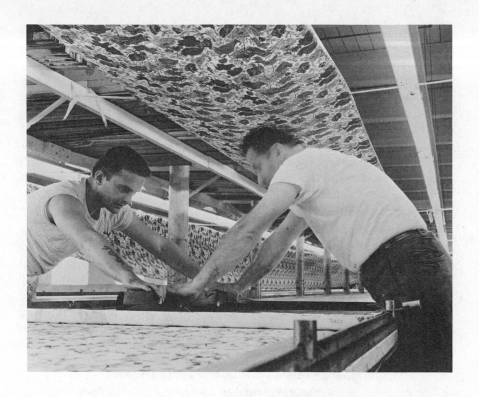

**Figure 8.6.** *Top:* Hand screen printing. *Bottom:* Automatic screen printing. (*Photographs courtesy of Cranston Print Works Company.*)

dyes may be thickened, as is done for roller or block printing, or real
oil paint may be used for the design. Most hand-painted fabrics are expensive because of the great amount of artistic labor involved.

Another method is painting the fabric with mordants rather than with color. When the dyebath is applied, each mordant reacts differently to the same dyebath. For more complicated designs, mordant printing can be combined with the wax-resist process. A modern version of mordant printing is called *madder* printing, so called because a dye prepared from the madder plant was formerly used for painting fabrics. This natural dyestuff has now been replaced by a synthetic dyestuff. Mordants are printed on the fabric first, and different colors are developed from a single dyebath.

8. *Screen printing.* When a design calls for delicate shading, the process originally employed to produce the pattern was similar to that used for reproducing photographs in newspapers. Today a photochemical process reproduces the design exactly as it was painted. Elaborately shaded effects can be printed exactly like the original and reproduced many times. The fabric is first stretched on a padded table. A printing screen, made of silk, nylon, or metal stretched on a frame, is placed over the fabric. The parts of the pattern on the screen that are not to take

**Figure 8.7.** Screen-printed fabric. (*Photo by Jack Pitkin.*)

the print are covered with enamel or certain paints to resist the printing paste. The printing paste is poured on the screen and pushed through the pattern portion with a wooden or rubber paddle called a *squeegee*. When one section of a pattern has been finished, the frame is moved to the next section, and so on until the entire length has been completed.

For screen printing, a continuous operation has now been mechanized, so that several yards can be printed every minute. The fabric moves along a table, and the automatic application of the screens is electrically controlled. An automatic squeegee operates electronically. Mechanized printing reduces costs appreciably for large batches. Whenever high-quality-fashion prints on exclusive dress goods or intricate patterns and big repeats are requisites, screen printing is an important process.

Fabrics with large designs in limited quantities are frequently screen-printed by hand. Rayon jerseys, crepes, and other dress fabrics, luncheon cloths, bedspreads, draperies, and shower curtains are often screen-printed. Although screen printing is a slower and more expensive process than roller printing, the pattern repeats can be large—up to eighty inches. Pigment colors are sometimes put on in layers to give a look of handcraftsmanship.

9. *Photographic printing.* A design is photographed and the negative is covered with a screen plate to break up the solid areas of the design. A light is then projected through the screen plate onto another film to make a contact print. This film is placed on a copper roller treated with sensitizing solution. A powerful arc light focused on the film affects the sensitized roller by baking the coating where the light passes through. The roller is then washed to take away the solution from sections that the light did not reach. These portions of the roller are etched away to form the pattern. The roller is then treated to remove the baked coating, and printing is done from the roller. This method provides fine designs for dress goods.

10. *Airbrushing.* Another method of producing shaded effects on fabrics employs a mechanized airbrush to blow color into the fabric. The hand guides the brush. This method is most effective on silk brocades and fabrics that are made in Jacquard or dobby designs.

## DISTINGUISHING DYEING AND PRINTING PROCESSES
### YARN-DYED AND PIECE-DYED FABRICS

Although raw stock and yarn dyeing usually produces the best color-fastness, depth of color, and luster, many piece-dyed fabrics are color-fast and equally attractive. Colorfastness depends on the degree to which the fibers have been penetrated by the dye. Since fibers and yarns are more easily penetrated before they are woven, a yarn-dyed cloth is more likely to be colorfast than is a piece-dyed cloth.

Of course, microscopic examination will reveal the degree of penetration of the fibers by dye, but the consumer does not usually have access to a microscope. A simple though not infallible test is to unravel yarns and untwist them. In piece-dyed cloths the core of the yarn may be white or a lighter color than the outer surface. This is especially true in piece-dyed linens and in cottons finished to resemble linens.

## PRINTED AND WOVEN DESIGNS

Many consumers confuse a small, geometrical printed pattern with a dobby weave. But if the cloth is unraveled enough to include a portion of the design, an examination of the yarns may reveal a printed pattern. In a design printed on the cloth, the individual yarns will be in two or more colors where the design is present. For example, one yarn may contain white, yellow, and blue, and another yarn white and blue. Such a cloth is printed. In a woven-in pattern, individual yarns are the same color throughout their length. One yarn may be blue and another white, but from selvage to selvage a yarn is either all blue or all white.

## COMPUTER PROCESSES IN SHADE MATCHING

In the dyeing industry, as in nearly every industry, there is an effort to computerize those processes that lend themselves to repetitive actions and inventory controls.

In short, what the computer does is to recreate a certain color by analyzing the information stored in the computer. The information is derived from machines that can break down the color constituents of a sample of fabric or liquid. This information is then put into terms of concentration of color, which colors are to be used, and the desired shade. In turn, all these earmarks of the specific color are translated into computer language to be stored and cross-referenced for later usage.

The most common devices used to find the fingerprints of a color are the spectrophotometer and the colorimeter. The spectrophotometer measures the amount of light reflected by a sample of colored material. The measurement derived is in the form of a graph that shows at what parts of the spectrum the sample reflects light, hence its color to the eye, and the intensity of this reflectance. Once it is known what colors the sample reflects—what it is made up of—then it is known what it takes to make the color.

In a somewhat similar way the COMIC (acronym for colorant mixture computer) is a device for shade matching. The colorimeter, of which there are only one hundred in the United States, takes the information derived from a spectrophotometer and establishes 16 points on the spectrum that, if matched, will yield the desired color. After the 16 spectral points have been fed into the colorimeter, the 16 points on the spectrum are established for the undyed substrate. At this point the dyer will select various "plug-in" boxes, each representing a certain dye that he feels will be useful in the match. By varying concentration dials for each of the dyestuffs selected to match the shade, the operator can line up the 16 points of the spectrum on an oscilloscope and obtain a prediction of how much of each dye should be used to match the standard.

In these systems a digital computer has a great advantage in speed. Once the colorist decides on the dyes he feels will make the shade, the 16 points for each individual dye used in the match, as well as for the unknown, are fed into the computer, which in turn prints out the formula for the match. The computer's large storage capacity and rapid calculating speed allow the computer to make formula selections. In this case, the colorist selects a range of colors—10, 15, or 20—which he feels will be suitable for matching all shades. For example: A colorist finds he needs 12 different dispersed dyes to make all the shades he comes in contact with on polyester fabric. The 16 points for the 12 dyestuffs have already been programmed into the computer at three or four different concentrations. When the complementary 16 points of the unknown are fed into the computer, it will search through all possible combinations and print out the right formulas of up to five dye combinations along with their costs and change in shade from one source of light to another.

In general, it seems unlikely that the industry can ever be computerized in the same sense as those giant plants that need but a handful of men to run their computers. Indeed, the computer is a tool that narrows the field of dyestuff selection, checks over results, eliminates some of the trial-and-error methods, and keeps stock of what has been done. However, the matches the computer makes can never really be perfect. Variables such as substrate, dyeing procedure, auxiliaries, and even the devices used to check the result must all be constant in order to ensure a precise match. In fact, the identical temperature and humidity on a particular day would help toward better results.

The experience of the dyer and colorist are still essential. Although it is possible to quantify many of these variables, experience is still the greatest asset. The substrate's preparation for dyeing, the action of the dyes themselves and their interaction, the differences in machinery, and the end use of the fabric, all must be considered in making a match. A computer can probably store the information if the Herculean task of programming it were ever undertaken. Yet, some of the factors that influence the dye match cannot be measured by machines. However, when two dyers get together they know exactly what they are talking about.

## SUMMARY

The average consumer is becoming more conscious of the color of fabrics. Through the educational aid of intelligent salespeople and national advertising, the consumer is learning what colors and their combinations best suit certain types and is becoming more particular in selecting colors for the home. Furthermore, the consumer wants fabrics to perform satisfactorily in their intended use. She has learned how to care for fine fabrics to preserve their original beauty. For these reasons manufacturers must produce a variety of beautiful and at the same time fast dyes.

Prints have become classic with Americans and are here to stay. To be sure, some years are more definitely print years than others. But most women like the gaiety of at least one printed dress a year.

In conclusion, a fabric made from good raw stock, beautifully and strongly woven, can be enhanced manyfold by the application of the proper coloring. The reverse is also true—that good fibers and yarns, even if durably woven, can be ruined by the use of fugitive dyestuffs crudely applied.

## REVIEW QUESTIONS

1. When is a dye considered fast? Explain fully.
2. Is there such a thing as an absolutely fast dye? Why?
3. Outline a method for testing the fastness of a color to light; perspiration; washing; friction; wash-and-wear.
4. When is a color considered absolutely fast to light? Moderately fast? Fugitive?
5. (a) What is meant by bleeding of colors?
   (b) What test can be used to determine whether or not colors will bleed?
6. (a) What is crocking?
   (b) What is a good test for crocking?
7. (a) Explain the difference between natural and synthetic dyestuffs.
   (b) Name some of the most important dyestuffs of each classification.
8. What are the advantages of synthetic dyestuffs over natural dyestuffs?
9. (a) What are basic dyes?
   (b) What are acid dyes?
   (c) To which fibers are basic dyes applied directly without prior chemical treatment?
10. (a) What is a mordant?
    (b) When is a mordant necessary?
11. (a) What are vat dyes?
    (b) Describe their method in application and use.
    (c) What are pigment dyes?
    (d) When are they used?
    (e) What are some of the most recent developments in the dye industry? Explain.
12. (a) Explain fiber-reactive dyes.
    (b) How are they used?
13. (a) List the methods of dyeing cloth.
    (b) Explain each method.

14. (*a*) What kinds of cloth are made from dyed raw stock?
    (*b*) Name two fabrics that are usually yarn-dyed.
    (*c*) When is cross-dyeing advantageous?
    (*d*) List the different methods of printing cloth.
    (*e*) Explain each method.
15. Describe the procedure in transferring the design from the original to the copper roller.
16. (*a*) How does resist printing differ from discharge printing?
    (*b*) How is batik made?
17. (*a*) What are the selling points of a hand-blocked linen drapery?
    (*b*) How can hand block printing be distinguished from roller printing?
    (*c*) How can a duplex-printed fabric be distinguished from a woven cloth?
18. What test is helpful in distinguishing yarn-dyed from piece-dyed fabrics?

## EXPERIMENTS

1. *Determining the permanency of dye.* Samples of five different materials should be tested for both permanency of dye and method of dyeing.
A. Fastness to light:
   Follow the instructions for *Home test*, p. 192.
   *Questions:* (*a*) When did the fabric fade slightly?
   (*b*) When did it fade appreciably?
   (*c*) Is the dye fast? moderately fast? fugitive?
B. Fastness to perspiration:
   Follow the instructions for *Home test*, p. 193.
   *Question:* Is the dye fast to perspiration? Why?
C. Fastness to laundering:
   Follow the instructions for *Home test*, p. 194.
   *Question:* Is the dye fast to washing? Why?
   1. Baste half of the fabric to a piece of white silk. Wash and dry.
   2. Compare the washed colored fabric with the unwashed piece. Note especially, after the two washed fabrics are separated, whether the white silk has been discolored.
   *Questions:* (*a*) Did the colors bleed?
   (*b*) Are the colors fast?
D. Fastness to crocking:
   Follow the instructions for *Home test*, p. 196.
   *Question:* Is the dye fast to friction? Why?
2. *Determining the method of dyeing.*
A. If the fabric is solid colored:
   1. Untwist several yarns in both warp and filling.
   2. Note the evenness or unevenness of color penetration.
   *Question:* Is the cloth piece-dyed or yarn-dyed? Why?
B. If the cloth is figured:
   1. Unravel yarns in both warp and filling.
   2. Note the color of individual yarns.
   *Questions:* (*a*) Are individual yarns the same color throughout their length or are they of more than one color?
   (*b*) Is the design printed or woven in?

C. If the cloth is printed:
  1. Count the colors in the design.
  2. Note the shape, regularity, and order of the patterns.
  *Questions:* (*a*) Are there more than two colors in the design?
         (*b*) Are the designs small and geometrical?
         (*c*) Are the designs placed at regular intervals with regular repetition of the patterns?
         (*d*) Are the outlines clear?
         (*e*) Does one color overlap another?
         (*f*) By what method is the cloth printed?
         (*g*) Is the printing done well?

## GLOSSARY

**Acetate dye.**   See *Disperse dyes.*

**Acid dye.**   A type of dye used on wool and other animal fibers. When used on cotton or linen, a mordant is required. It has poor color resistance to washing. A special method of application is required for acrylic fibers of Orlon 42. Dynel modacrylic fibers may be colored in light shades.

**Airbrushing.**   Blowing color on a fabric with a mechanized airbrush.

**Alizarin dye.**   A vegetable dye originally obtained from the madder root, now produced synthetically. It is best used on wool but can be used on cotton, particularly in madder prints.

**Aniline dye.**   A term generally applied to any synthetic, organic dye. Any dye that is derived from aniline.

**Azoic dye.**   See *Naphthol dye.*

**Basic dye.**   A type of dye that will dye wool and silk directly without a mordant. It can be used on cotton with a mordant.

**Batik.**   A kind of resist dyeing in which parts of a fabric are coated with wax to resist the dye. It is usually done by hand but can be imitated by machine.

**Chrome dye.**   See *Mordant.*

**Crocking.**   Rubbing off of a fabric's color.

**Crock meter.**   A standard device for testing a fabric's fastness to crocking.

**Developed dye.**   A type of dye in which one color may be changed by use of a developer. The intensity of the color and the fastness of the dyestuff may be changed by this treatment.

**Dip dyeing.**   A process of piece dyeing hosiery or other knitted goods after construction.

**Direct dye.**   A type of dye with an affinity for most fibers. It has poor resistance to washing.

**Direct printing.**   Application of color by passing the cloth over a series of rollers engraved with the designs. Developed direct dyes have good resistance to washing.

**Discharge printing.**   A method by which the cloth is piece-dyed first and then the color is discharged or bleached in spots, leaving white designs.

**Disperse dyes.**   Dispersions of colors or pigments in water. They were originally known as acetate dyes. At present these dyes are also used to color the new synthetic fibers.

**Dope dyed.**   See *Solution-dyed.*

**Duplex print.** Method of printing a fabric on the face and then on the back.

**Dyed in raw stock.** See *Raw-stock dyeing.*

**Dyeing.** A process of coloring fibers, yarns, or fabrics with either natural or synthetic dyes.

**Fade-Ometer.** A standard laboratory device for testing a fabric's fastness to sunlight.

**Fast dyes.** Those dyes that are fast for the purpose for which the fabric is intended.

**Fiber dye.** See *Raw-stock dyeing.*

**Fugitive dye.** Those colors that are not fast to such elements as light, washing, perspiration, and crocking.

**Hand-blocked print.** Fabrics printed by hand with blocks made of wood or linoleum.

**Indigo.** A type of dyestuff originally obtained from the indigo plant, now produced synthetically. Blues are brilliant. It has good colorfastness to washing and to light.

**Ingrain.** A knitted or woven fabric made of yarns dyed before knitting or weaving.

**Jig dyeing.** Passing the cloth through a jig-dyeing machine (a large tub holding dye). It is used particularly for dark, direct dyes.

**Launder-Ometer.** A standard laboratory device for testing a fabric's fastness to washing.

**Madder.** See *Alizarin dye.*

**Mordant.** A substance that acts as a binder for the dye. A mordant has an affinity for both the dyestuff and the fabric.

**Naphthol dye.** Insoluble azoic dyes formed on the fiber by impregnation of the cotton fabric with beta-naphthol that has been dissolved in caustic soda and then immersed in a basic dye. It is used primarily on cotton and gives brilliant scarlet and red at relatively low cost.

**Pad dyeing.** A process of first passing the cloth through a trough containing dye, then squeezing it between heavy rolls to remove excess dye.

**Photographic printing.** Application of a photographic image to a fabric.

**Piece-dyeing.** A fabric dyed after weaving, knitting, or other method of construction.

**Pigment dyes.** Dye emulsion made with certain kinds of fine synthetic pigment in a solution of synthetic resins in an organic solvent; water is stirred in with a high-speed mixer. Often applied by pad dyeing. Good colorfastness to light, washing, acids, and alkalies. When resin binder is ineffective, dye may crock or have poor resistance to washing.

**Printing.** Methods of stamping colored figures on cloth.

**Raw-stock dyeing.** Dyeing of fibers before spinning into yarn. It is synonymous with *fiber-dyed.*

**Resist printing.** Application of substances to a cloth to resist dyeing; the cloth is immersed in dye, the "resist" is then removed. See *Batik.*

**Roller printing.** See *Direct printing.*

**Screen printing.** Background of design painted on screen first. Dye is printed on exposed portions of fabric.

**Slub-dyed.** Sliver-dyed or printed.

**Solution-dyed.** Man-made fibers dyed in the spinning solution.

**Space-dyed yarns.** Those yarns that have been dipped in dye or spotted in various places along the yarn.

**Spun-dyed.** See *Solution-dyed*.

**Stencil printing.** A type of resist printing where portions of the design are covered with metal or wood so the covered parts do not take dye.

**Sulfur dye.** A dye derived from chemicals containing sulfur. It is used mostly for vegetable fibers. It has fair resistance to washing; poor resistance to sunlight.

**Tie dyeing.** A type of resist printing in which pieces of string are tied around bunches of cloth, or the fabric is stitched where dye is to be resisted.

**Vat dyed.** This process uses an insoluble dye made soluble in its application. It is then put on the fiber and is oxidized to its original insoluble form. Excellent colorfastness to washing and sunlight.

**Warp printing.** Printing of warp yarns with the design before weaving. A hazy grayed effect is produced.

**Yarn-dyed.** Yarns are dyed before the fabric is constructed.

# 9

# Cotton
# and the Consumer

Which should she choose for her husband? A white durable press broadcloth dress shirt at $5.95 or one with the same style collar and cuffs, also durable press, at $4.70? The less expensive shirt did not mention the feature of a soil-release finish. While ironing would be unnecessary with either shirt, she had read that soil-release-treated fabrics do seem to be effective against stains. Oily stains are usually removed in a single home laundering. Mustard can usually be removed in two or three home washings, but not always. The customer decided to buy the $5.95 shirt.

In short, this customer was considering the buying point *ease of care*.

The factors or *buying points* important to the customer in selection are the same factors or *selling points* that a salesperson emphasizes in selling. The salesperson should have a knowledge of the qualities of each of the textile raw materials: the kind of fiber used, the type and quality of yarn, the construction and finish. Such knowledge helps the salesperson assist a consumer in making a proper selection of fabrics for different uses.

From a knowledge of the qualities of the different textile raw materials, the salesperson should develop selling points. In the foregoing illustration, ease of care was, for this customer, who has an automatic washer and dryer, the chief selling point.

This chapter will consider the physical and chemical characteristics of cotton fibers and how these factors contribute to buying points. The type of yarn, construction, finishes, and coloring of cotton and their specific contributions to buying points will be discussed.

## CULTURE OF COTTON

Cotton is a white or yellow-white vegetable fiber grown in greatest amounts in the United States, the U.S.S.R., China, and India. Ranked in descending order of importance in cotton production are Brazil, Mexico, Egypt, Pakistan, Turkey, and Sudan. Over fifty-five other countries produce lesser amounts. In this group, the major producers are Syria, Peru, Iran, Nicaragua, and Argentina.[1]

Cotton fibers come from a plant, related to the hollyhock, that ranges in height from 2 to 20 feet, depending upon the variety. The plant requires a warm climate with about six months of summer weather for full development. It blossoms and produces bolls, or pods, of cotton fibers. (See Figure 9.1.)

In the United States, cotton is grown in what we call the Cotton Belt, which covers roughly the southern and western states from the Carolinas to California.

Production methods differ in various parts of the Cotton Belt, according to the National Cotton Council of America. Such factors as types of soil, climate, moisture, growing conditions, and physical features of a locality determine the varieties of cotton to be planted, crop income, size of farms, and yield per acre.

[1] All countries mentioned have produced a total of one million or more bales per year. The ranking was prepared with the assistance of the National Cotton Council of America.

**Figure 9.1.** Cotton bolls.

The chief steps in cotton production are as follows: [2]

## PREPARATION OF THE SOIL

Production of next year's crop generally starts right after the completion of harvesting in the fall. Old stalks are chopped and shredded by machine. The residue is plowed under, and the field is generally left rough until spring tillage.

Before planting, the soil is tilled to a depth of several inches. Smoothing and laying off in rows follows.

## PLANTING

This is done by machine planters. Cotton may be planted in hills or in continuous drills. In the former case, plants must be thinned to two or three per hill every nine to fourteen inches. Workers usually do the thinning with hoes.

## CULTIVATING

A cotton grower has a wide choice of fertilizer material and equipment. Application of fertilizer may be made prior to, during, or after planting.

Pre-emergence weed control is carried out by applying a chemical herbicide to a ten- to fourteen-inch band over the drill area at the time of, or just after, planting. For a few weeks, this band is not disturbed. The chemical does not harm cotton seedlings, but it does kill germinating weed and grass seeds.

Postemergence weed control consists in spraying an area six to eight inches wide on both sides of the plant. Weed and grass seedlings are killed without injury to the young cotton. Care must be taken not to kill the cotton by spraying chemicals on leaves or branches.

Improved cultivators and rotary hoe attachments for cultivators also help keep weeds and grass under control. High-speed rotary hoes travel through the field at rates up to seven and a half miles per hour.

Another weed control is the flame cultivator. Four to eight nozzles, two to a row, mounted near the ground, emit a gas flame in two jets of fire straddling the cotton row. The tough cotton stalks are unharmed by the fire, but weeds and grass die.

## INSECT CONTROL

Losses due to insects amount on the average to about one bale out of every eight bales. It is estimated that the boll weevil accounts for

[2] Condensed from *Cotton from Field to Fabric* (New York: National Cotton Council, 1968), pp. 3–6, by permission of the Council.

about 90 per cent of this damage. Insecticides are applied at various intervals during heavy infestation—either by airplanes, which can cover up to 1,500 acres a day, or by tractor-mounted ground rigs, which can spray several rows of cotton at one time.

*Maturation of the cotton boll.* The cotton plant first buds, and, about twenty-one days thereafter, creamy white to yellow flowers appear. These later turn deep red, and, after about three days, wither and drop from the plant, leaving the ovary on the plant. When the ovary ripens, a large pod, known as the cotton boll, is formed. Moist fibers growing inside the boll expand it until it is about 1½ inches long and 1 inch in diameter. The boll opens approximately 1½ to 2 months after the flowering stage.

### HARVESTING

So that the bolls will open quickly and uniformly, before the fall rains damage fibers and seed, cotton plants are treated chemically to make them shed their leaves. This process, called *defoliation*, is important if cotton is to be picked mechanically. Furthermore, it is a method of insect control. Cotton is then ready for picking.

### PICKING

Before the advent of the mechanical picker, cotton was picked by hand. The great labor shortage in the south was a major reason why

**Figure 9.2.** Mechanical cotton picker. (*Photograph courtesy of the National Cotton Council of America.*)

mechanical pickers became so important. Now that smaller farms are being consolidated into larger farms and mechanical pickers can be leased for harvesting periods, mechanical picking is increasing. In the United States machine harvesting has jumped from 32 per cent in 1957 to approximately 94 per cent in 1961.[3]

To accompany this accelerated shift to mechanical harvesting, changes in ginning processes have taken place. An increasing number of gins are now using multiple lint cleaners, and there is a marked increase in the use of stick- and green-leaf removing machines. Two types of machines harvest the cotton: the *picker* and the *stripper*. The picker has vertical drums equipped with spindles (barbed or smooth) that pull the cotton from the boll. This machine can harvest 5 to 15 acres a day depending on whether the machine does 1 or 2 rows at a time.[4] The stripper pulls the bolls off when they enter the rollers of the machine. Some strippers have mechanical fingers to do the job. This type of tractor-mounted machine can harvest 2 rows at once and 10 to 15 acres a day. To compare hand and machine picking: a single stripper can harvest as much cotton as twenty-six laborers hand-snapping the bolls.

## PROCESSING OF COTTON

### GINNING

After the cotton has been picked, the fibers are separated from the seeds by a process called *ginning*. The ginning is done by circular saws revolving on one shaft. The planter normally takes the cotton to the gin and pays for ginning. After the ginning, the cotton is packaged in bales of about 500 pounds each. At this point, the seeds and the fibers go separate ways.

### PROCESSING THE SEEDS

Seeds go to the crushing mill, where they are *delinted* (fuzz is removed mechanically). The short fuzzy fibers so removed, called *linters*, are used in mattresses and other cushioning and in the making of plastics, fine paper, etc.

Hulls are next removed from the delinted seed. The hulls serve as cattle fodder or as the source of a chemical used in making synthetic rubber or nylon. Inside the seed is oil that has been pressed out in the crushing mill or by solvent extraction. This cottonseed oil is valuable in making cooking oil, shortening, salad dressings, and margarine. The meat of the cottonseed serves as feed for cattle.

[3] U.S. Department of Agriculture, "Charges for Ginning Cotton, Costs of Selected Services Incident to Marketing, and Related Information."
[4] National Cotton Council, *op. cit.*, p. 6.

Cotton is baled after ginning, and then it is classified by (*a*) staple length (fiber length), (*b*) grade, and (*c*) fiber character. Fiber properties measured are fineness, color, length, and uniformity.

A practical but unofficial basis of classifying by staple length is as follows: [5]

1. *Extra-short-staple cotton* (not over ¾ inch). This length is not very suitable for spinning and is best used in batting and wadding.
2. *Short-staple cotton* (¾ inch to 1 inch). This type is spinnable and is used for coarser, inexpensive goods.
3. *Medium-staple cotton* (1 inch to 1⅛ inches). The United States produces the bulk of this variety for its own use and for export.
4. *Long-staple cotton* (1⅛ but less than 1⅜ inches). The United States produces the bulk of its own requirements. Imports are relatively small.
5. *Extra-long-staple cotton* (1⅜ inches and longer). United States production is limited; we import from Egypt, Sudan, and Peru.

Long staples account for 4 per cent of the domestic crop. Group 3 accounts for 84 per cent, and group 2 accounts for 5 per cent.

*Classification by grade.* In the trade, American cotton is classified not only according to length of fiber, but also according to the condition of the cotton, on a basis called *middling.* Middling cotton is creamy white, with no evidence of dirt or gin cuts (fibers matted and cut) and with only a few pieces of leaf and immature seeds. The following grades and half grades are recognized:

1. Good middling
2. Strict middling
   Middling plus
3. Middling
   Strict low middling plus
4. Strict low middling
   Low middling plus
5. Low middling
   Strict good ordinary plus
6. Strict good ordinary
   Good ordinary plus
7. Good ordinary

Good middling, the best, has lustrous, silky, clean fibers, whereas good ordinary contains leaf particles, sticks, hulls, dirt, sand, gin cuts, and spots. To indicate the degree of whiteness of the cotton, five distinct color groups are used: white, spotted, tinged, yellow-stained, and gray. Practically all the United States cotton falls below good middling.

[5] *Ibid.,* p. 7.

Classification of American cotton according to length of staple is probably more logical than a geographical classification, because the length of staple and fineness of fiber are criteria in judging the quality of cotton.

### PIMA

That the importance of fine long-staple cotton is realized by American cotton growers can be seen from the fact that an American-Egyptian type is being grown here, chiefly in the irrigated lands of Arizona, New Mexico, and around El Paso. This pima has an extra-long (1⅜ to 1⅝ inches) staple. Of the American cottons, pima ranks next to sea island in order of quality. It is used in sheer woven goods and in fine knitted fabrics.

Cotton farmers and the U.S. Department of Agriculture, in cross-breeding seeds of all kinds, were responsible for the producing of the silky, long-staple, lustrous, and strong *pima cotton*. They cooperated in development work and produced a superlative cotton fiber. Marketed under the trademark Supima, it is used in promoting garments and fabrics made from the pima variety. It is grown in Arizona, New Mexico, Texas, and California, where climate and soil are right for its growth. The staple is longer, finer, stronger than any other, takes colors well, and has a smooth silky hand. It can be woven from a sheer chiffon weight to a heavy broadcloth.

### UPLAND (*Gossypium hirsutum*)

The term " upland" originally denoted cotton raised away from the sea coast on higher land, as distinguished from cotton grown on the lowlands along the Mississippi Delta. Now upland denotes a staple length of about ¾ to 1½ inches. It is produced on lands of all altitudes, from the foothills of the Ozark and Blue Ridge Mountains to the Mississippi Delta. Sheetings, carded broadcloths, twills, drills, print cloths, and carded yarns for knitting are commonly produced from fibers of this class. Upland cotton constitutes over 99 per cent of United States production.

### DELTAPINE

A new variety of cotton, called Deltapine, has spread from its original locale in the Mississippi Delta to the Far West, particularly to the Imperial Valley of California and to the Salt River Valley of Arizona. This variety owes its increased use to a high yield per acre, the ease with which it cleans at the gins, and its comparative strength. In fact, many

cotton varieties are shifting geographically across the country because
cotton breeders are trying to meet the demands of increased mechanical
harvesting and modern ginning practices. There are new varieties also
with improved fiber properties that make mechanical harvesting and
modern ginning practices less harmful. Deltapine 16, Rex, and Dixie
King are new cotton varieties developed since 1957. The last two types
are gaining in acreage in the Southeast.

## SPECIES OF FOREIGN COTTON

### EGYPTIAN (Gossypium barbadense)

Egyptian cotton, next to sea island cotton, has the longest fiber. It
can be made to look almost like silk by mercerizing. This type of cotton
is grown along the Nile Delta. It is a light tan or brown in color and
therefore must usually be bleached. Hoisery, knit goods, underwear, and
cords for automobile tires are often made of Egyptian cotton. It is only
slightly shorter in length than the sea island variety, the former averaging mostly 1½ inches or less. Other African production (except Egyptian) is now in medium- and long-staple groups.

### TANGUIS (Gossypium barbadense)

Tanguis cotton has fibers averaging 1¼ inches in length. It comes
from Peru. Most Tanguis cotton fibers have a rough, harsh, wiry, woolly
feel and a slight crimp. For this reason they are often mixed with short-
staple wool. Such cotton-and-wool mixtures may be used for underwear, if knitted so that the cotton will be next to the skin and the
harsher wool will be on the outside. Hosiery may be similarly made of
this cotton.

### INDIAN (Gossypium arboreum and Gossypium herbacium)
### AND OTHER VARIETIES

India and Pakistan also grow the American upland type of cotton.
The fiber length averages from 1 to 1 1⁄32 inches. China also grows
cotton, but it has a yellowish-brown fiber and is not often exported.
Israel is now growing the American-type Acala and fine pima cotton
and has one of the highest average yields per acre of cotton fiber in the
world.

## CHARACTERISTICS OF THE COTTON FIBER

### MICROSCOPIC APPEARANCE

When seen under the microscope, unmercerized cotton fibers resemble
flat twisted ribbons. The unripe cotton fiber is a tubelike structure or

canal (lumen). Within this tube is a cell protoplasm that either dries as the cotton ripens or shrinks back to the stalk of the plant. The disappearance of this substance causes the fiber to flatten and twist, so that under the microscope it appears like a twisted ribbon. The canal can be seen. (See the Appendix.) When cotton is mercerized by treatment with caustic soda, the twist comes out to some extent, depending on the degree of mercerization.

### LENGTH OF FIBER

Cotton ranges in length of staple from ¾ to 1½ inches. Since the very short lengths are difficult to spin, they are not considered in the figures given here. Yarns made of shorter staple are more apt to be linty and fuzzy than those of longer staple. For combed yarn, a long staple is advisable.

### DIAMETER OF FIBER

The diameter of the cotton fiber ranges from .0005 to .0009 inch. The U.S. Department of Agriculture *Bulletin No. 33* places the range from .00064 (sea island) to .00844 (Indian) inch. Pima and Egyptian fibers have the smallest diameters and so can be spun into the finest yarns.

### LUSTER

Untreated cotton has no pronounced luster. Therefore cotton fabrics that need to be lustrous to imitate silk must be mercerized to produce the desired result.

### STRENGTH

Tensile strength is obtained on a small bundle of fibers. (A.S.T.M. [American Society for Testing Materials] method D-1445.) A single cotton fiber will sustain a dead weight of two to eight grams. Such a fiber is not very strong, but the finished cotton cloth can be made very strong if tightly twisted, mercerized yarns are used in it. Mercerization adds both strength and luster. Through scientific breeding, cotton farmers are growing a better product—longer, finer, more lustrous, and stronger. With further developments in scientific breeding there are even greater possibilities of improving the value of cotton for the end uses the consumer wants.

### ELASTICITY

In a study of the feeling of different textile fibers, it was found that cottons have more elasticity than linens but not so much as the animal fibers. The natural twist in cotton increases the elasticity and makes it easier to spin the fiber into yarn.

### HYGROSCOPIC MOISTURE

Hygroscopic moisture is not the water content of the raw material, but the moisture (water) held in the pores of the fiber and on its surface. It is not a part of the chemical constituents. Some scientists give raw cotton 5 to 8 per cent of hygroscopic moisture, whereas others rate it as high as 7 to 10 per cent. If the moisture in the air is great, the moisture content in the fabric is increased.

### COMPOSITION OF FIBER

The chief constituent of cotton is cellulose (87 to 90 per cent). Cellulose is a solid, inert substance that is a part of plants. The fact that it is the chief component of cotton fibers and is an inert substance explains cotton's lifeless feel. Water (5 to 8 per cent) and natural impurities (4 to 6 per cent) are the other components of a cotton fiber. The cellulose can be modified by cross-linking to give cotton the properties of wash-and-wear. (See Chapters 2 and 7.)

### HYGIENIC QUALITY AND LAUNDERABILITY

Cotton is the whitest and cleanest natural fiber. It can be laundered easily, for it withstands high temperatures well (boiling water does not hurt the fiber), and it can be ironed with a hot iron because it does not scorch easily. A new chemical process, called partial acetylation, gives cotton fabrics additional heat resistance. Cottons so treated make excellent ironing-board covers. Weak alkalies, such as ammonia, borax, and silicate of soda, and cold dilute bleaching agents, such as hypochlorites or chlorine bleach, are not detrimental to the fiber. Bleaching agents must be used only under controlled conditions, since too high temperatures and concentrations destroy the fiber. Treatment of cotton fabrics with resins improves crease resistance and crease recovery after washing.

### ACTION OF STRONG ACIDS

Concentrated acids, such as sulfuric, hydrochloric, hydrofluoric, and nitric, destroy cotton fibers, if the latter are cooked in these acids for a few minutes. Dilute solutions of the acids may weaken a cotton fabric and may destroy it if it is allowed to dry without being rinsed.

### ACTION OF LIGHT

If cotton is continuously exposed to sunlight, it loses strength. This fact is particularly true of curtains, which may appear in perfect condition when hanging at the windows but when taken down may fall apart in spots where sunlight has reached them.

## AFFINITY FOR DYESTUFFS

Cotton takes dyes that are fast to washing and to sunlight. For a vegetable fiber, cotton has a fair affinity for dye. Vat dyes as a class are the fastest to all the elements listed below. Vegetable fibers do not take dye as readily as do animal fibers. The table gives information about the quality of particular dyes.

FASTNESS OF DYES OF DIFFERENT CLASSES ON COTTON GOODS

| Price class: | 1 | 2 | 3 | 4 | 5 | 6 |
|---|---|---|---|---|---|---|
| Color type: | Vat | Naphthol | Developed | Sulphur | Basic | Direct |
| HOME WASHING | Exc. | Exc. | Good | Good | Poor | Good (light shades) Poor (heavy shades) |
| LAUNDRY | Exc. | Exc. | Fair-poor | Fair-poor | Very poor | Poor |
| LIGHT | Exc. | Very good | Poor | Good | Very poor | Some poor, Some very good |
| BLEACHING (Chlorine) | Exc. | Exc. | Bad | Bad | Bad | Bad |
| CROSS DYEING | Exc. | Exc. | Good | Good | Bad | Bad |

NOTE: There are some exceptions to these general rules in each class.

Reprinted from *American Fabrics*, 52 (Spring, 1961), 74. (*Reprinted courtesy of the Franklin Process Company, a division of Indian Head Mills.*)

## MILDEW

Cotton is subject to rotting caused by mildew, which is caused by fungi. Heat and dampness further the growth of mildew. Considerable research has revealed that a chemical compound produced by the fungi has the power of changing cellulose in the cotton to sugar. The fungi feed on the sugar. It was found that there is less rotting if the cotton is treated to make it fire-resistant and water-repellent. (See Chapter 14.) Hence, mildew can be prevented. Former attempts to protect cotton against mildew by treating it with fungicides proved ineffective under climatic conditions favorable to the growth of fungi. Cotton can be treated with a chemical called acrylonitrile. (See Chapter 14.) Such

(1) Cotton from several bales is blended together in opening room.

(2) Cleaning and separation of individual fibers takes place in carding machine. Thin web of fibers is formed into rope-like strand or "sliver."

**Figure 9.3.** Steps in the manufacture of cotton textiles (*Courtesy of the National Cotton Council of America.*)

(3) Lap composed of slivers is passed through comb which combs out short fibers. Output of comb is formed again into sliver.

(4) In drawing, several slivers are combined into strand and reduced to about same diameter as original sliver. Drawing blends fibers and arranges them in parallel order.

**Figure 9.3.** (Cont.)

(5) Slivers are fed into roving frame where cotton is twisted slightly and drawn into a smaller strand.

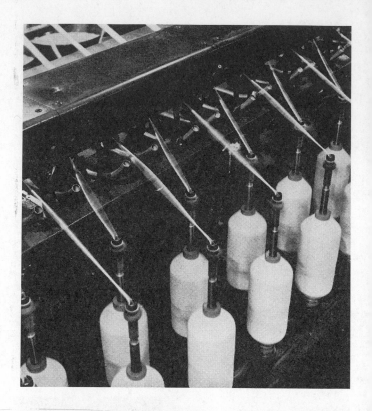

(6) Roving is fed to spinning frame where it is drawn out to final size, twisted into yarn, and wound on bobbins.

**Figure 9.3.** (Cont.)

(7) Several hundred warp yarns are rewound from cones or cheeses into large section beams.

(8) In slashing, threads are unwound from assembly of warper beams, immersed in sizing mixture, dried, and rewound on loom beams.

**Figure 9.3.** *(Cont.)*

(9) Weaving room.

(10) Inspecting cloth.

**Figure 9.3.** (Cont.)

treatment makes cotton not only permanently resistant to mildew but also more resistant to wet and dry heat and gives it greater affinity for dyes.

## COTTON YARNS

### PREPARING THE COTTON

At the mill, cotton is unbaled and then pulled out in small tufts and beaten to remove impurities. The tufts are compressed into a sheet called a *lap*. Several laps may be combined into one.

### CARDING

Cotton is not thoroughly clean until particles of leaf are removed. A machine called a *card* separates the matted fibers and removes leafy matter. Carding used to be done by hand with a pair of *cards*—rectangular pieces of wood with wire teeth on one side of each card and with wooden handles. The teeth were placed together, and the cotton was pulled and straightened between the teeth. Now this process is done by machinery. The carded cotton in lap form is drawn through an aperture and comes out in rope form called a *card sliver*. The short fibers that fall to the floor or cling to the machinery during the carding are never wasted, but are often used to make fabrics in which evenness and strength of yarn are not requisites.

### DRAWING

If the yarn is to be fine enough for use in clothing, the diameter of the yarn must be reduced to a size appropriate to the particular fabric. Several card slivers may be fed between two pairs of rollers, the second of which revolves faster than the first. This operation draws out or stretches the sliver, thus decreasing its diameter. The sliver may be drawn three times and may be reduced further in size and given a slight twist by a process called *roving*. In this process, the sliver is passed through rollers and wound onto bobbins set in spindles. Improved carding devices, together with new and faster machinery for drawing, and new roving frames have increased production and decreased labor costs.

### COMBING

This process is really a continuation and refinement of the carding process. Short fibers are eliminated from the sliver; fibers are laid more nearly parallel; and the filmy sheet of fibers is further attenuated. Cotton yarns for fabrics are carded, but not all are combed. On the other hand, some fabrics are made of yarns that have been combed several times. Combed yarns are even and free from extraneous material. Yarns that

**Figure 9.4.** *Left:* Carded cotton cloth. *Right:* Combed cotton cloth. (*Photo by Jack Pitkin.*)

are merely carded are not so clean or so even as those that are given further treatment. Yarns can be made finer by combing; those used for fine-quality French voiles and batistes receive a good deal of combing. Yarns for coarse, unbleached muslins and unbleached duck are usually only carded. Even many good-quality fabrics are only carded.

### SPINNING

The spinning process puts in the twist. Some yarns are loosely or slackly twisted, whereas others are tightly twisted. The more twists or turns to the inch, the stronger the cotton yarn.

### WINDING

Yarns are wound on spools, on paper tubes, on double-headed bobbins, in skeins or hanks, in ball form, or on warp beams, ready for the weavers.

### SINGLE AND PLY COTTON YARNS

Cotton yarns are made in singles or in plies. A tightly twisted cotton yarn may have a rayon yarn twisted loosely with it to form a two-ply yarn.

Ply yarns are ordinarily stronger than singles of the same diameter. Unique effects are produced in ply yarns by the use of singles with different degrees of twist. A ratiné or bouclé has a rough turkish-towel effect made by ply yarns in different tension. Slack-twisted yarns make

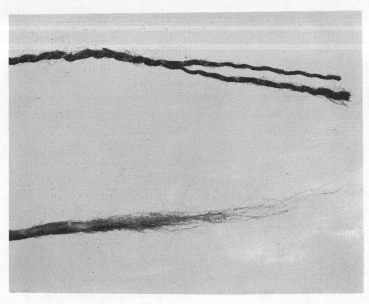

**Figure 9.5.** *Top: Two-ply yarn. Bottom: Single yarn. (Photo by Jack Pitkin.)*

soft fabrics that drape gracefully. Tightly twisted yarns make strong, hard-feeling fabrics.

The finer the yarn count, the higher the price. Also, two-ply yarns cost more than single yarns; combed yarns cost more than carded yarns; and yarns ready for use as warp cost more than yarns in skeins (used for filling).

### SIZES OF COTTON YARNS

Most sewing cotton is marked 60 or 80. These numbers, as we have already mentioned, denote the fineness of the thread—80 being finer than 60. Accordingly, yarns used in fabrics are given numbers or counts to denote their weight and fineness. In size 10 yarn there are 10 x 840, or 8,400 yards to the pound. Size 10 in this case is the count of the yarn. A small "s" after the number means the yarn is single; that is, 10s, 20s, 30s. The notation 10/2 means that size or count 10 yarn is two-ply. Yarn spun in this country reaches as high as 160s; a medium count is 30s; Egyptian is 100; Brazilian, 40; Surat from India, 30; Peruvian, 30.

### COTTON THREAD

American women have had cotton sewing thread for only 130 years. This thread was first produced in 1812 in Paisley, Scotland (the small town where Paisley shawls were made) by James and Patrick Clark, who were searching for a new material for making the heddle eyes of the loom. The heddle eyes have to be smooth, for it is through these eyes that warp yarns are threaded into the loom. The Clark brothers perfected a cotton yarn smooth and strong enough to replace silk for this purpose. By chance, the yarn was found to be suitable for sewing. At first this yarn, called *thread*, was sold in hanks, but it was later wound on spools as it is today.

James Coats, who had also been associated with the manufacture of Paisley shawls, employed his knowledge of yarn making and weaving when he built a factory to make high-grade cotton thread. His factory, later owned by his sons James and Peter (J. & P. Coats), competed with the Clarks.

In 1840 Andrew Coats, a brother of James and Peter, came to America as a selling agent for J. & P. Coats of Scotland. A factory was built in Pawtucket, Rhode Island, and, in 1841, George and William Clark, sons of the third generation, came to the United States. Mills for making thread were built in Newark, New Jersey.

The O.N.T. so commonly seen on Clark's spool cotton stands for "Our New Thread." This softer, stronger thread was composed of six strands of cotton twisted together, instead of the usual three.

Cotton thread comes in sizes ranging from coarse to fine: 8, 10, 12, 16, 20, 24, 30, 36, 40, 50, 60, 70, 80, 90, 100. (See Chapter 3 for the differences between thread and yarn.)

## WOVEN COTTON FABRICS

### PLAIN WEAVES

Cotton can be made in all weaves and variations. The cotton fabric called *muslin* traces its name to the French *mousseline*, which in turn derived its name from the town of Mosul in Mesopotamia. Muslin is the generic name of cotton fabrics in plain weave ranging from the sheerest batiste to the coarsest sheeting. The lower counts, 48 square to 80 square (finished), are called *print cloths*, the higher counts in sheer fabrics are *lawns*, and the higher counts in sheetings are *percales*.[6]

Cottons in the basket weaves include oxford 2 x 1, 2 x 2, 3 x 2, and monks cloth 4 x 4 and 8 x 8.

In rib variations of the plain weave, there is the poplin or *popeline*, first woven at Avignon, France, as a compliment to the reigning pope. Ribs are closely spaced next to each other fillingwise. Broadcloth is similar to poplin, with finer, closer ribs. Dimity is also a ribbed fabric, but the ribs are spaced at regular intervals either in warpwise stripes or in crossbars. Numerous fabrics in plain weave will be described in Part II.

### TWILL WEAVES

*Denim* (de Nîmes), first woven in Nîmes, France, and *jean*, first made in Italy, are typical twill weave fabrics. Another, called *tackle*

[6] See Glossary at end of the chapter. See also Chapter 16.

*twill,* is a closely woven, wind-resistant cotton and rayon twill used in ski suits, parkas, football and basketball uniforms, and rainwear. It is lustrous and durable.

### SATIN OR SATEEN WEAVES

When the warp floats in cotton, the fabric is called *warp satin.* When the filling floats, which is more common, the fabric is called *sateen,* the suffix "een" meaning cotton. Cotton satin is often found in linings of men's clothing. Cotton sateen is frequently used for lining draperies.

### FANCY WEAVES

Damasks for both dresses and tablecloths are illustrations of cotton *Jacquards. Dobby* appears in bird's-eye diaper fabrics and in huck toweling. White-on-white broadcloth or madras shirtings are Jacquard or dobby.

Terry cloth and turkish toweling is uncut looped pile. Velveteen is also *pile weave.* Beacon robing is double cloth.

Marquisette for curtains is made in *leno.* It may have embroidered effects. In fact, any cotton fabric may be embroidered or given an embroidered effect.

### LACES

Cotton is currently used more than any other textile for laces. (See Chapter 18 for kinds of laces.)

### NONWOVEN COTTON FABRICS

A web of fibers held or bonded by an adhesive is called a nonwoven fabric. (See Chapter 6 for methods of bonding.) Articles such as disposable napkins, wallpaper backing, bandages, polishing cloths, tea bags, dish and guest towels, and tablecloths can be nonwoven fabrics. Perhaps the greatest potential for the nonwoven goods industry is in hospital and medical supplies.

### KNITTED COTTON FABRICS

A common weft-knitted cloth in stockinette stitch is cotton jersey, used in T-shirts and basque shirts. The tops of men's socks and the wrists of sweat shirts are commonly rib-knit. The purl stitch called *plain knitting* by hand knitters, is used for scarfs, baby carriage covers, and pot holders.

The warp-knitted cotton fabrics in tricot and milanese are frequently used in fabric gloves. A modified tricot knit of fine cotton yarns sueded on one side, called *atlas cloth*, is manufactured into gloves and sports jackets.

## FINISHES FOR COTTON FABRICS

Improved finishes for cotton have been responsible in a large measure for cotton's current popularity. Among them are the resin and nonresin finishes that give cottons the same easy- or minimum-care features that synthetics possess. Advances in antibacterial, mildew-resistant, and flame-resistant treatments have improved the effectiveness of the performance of cotton in various end uses. Since the regular and special finishes have been described in Chapter 7, only those finishes applied to cotton will be considered here.

## REGULAR FINISHES

### PRELIMINARY TREATMENT

This includes singeing or gassing to remove lint and loose yarn, which is followed by a chemical bath to desize the fabric. Kier boiling further removes foreign material, waxes, and sizings. (See p. 267 for a detailed explanation of this process.) Bleaching is then done if the fabric is to be white or if it is to have some further surface interest. Bleaching and kier boiling are now combined.

If a cloth is to resemble linen, it is beetled; if it is to be used for warmth, it is often napped. When surface irregularities appear, the fabric must be sheared by rotating spiral blades at various stages in finishing. Then the cloth must be dried.

### MERCERIZATION

If a cotton fabric is to have a glossy surface, it is mercerized after it has been bleached. Sometimes the mercerizing is done in the yarn stage or possibly in the fiber stage, in which case the operation is not repeated in the finishing of the cloth.

The process of mercerizing was discovered by John Mercer about the middle of the nineteenth century. He happened upon it quite accidentally when he found he had left some cotton in a caustic soda solution and feared the treatment had been too long. Upon microscopic examination, he found the fibers had lost their natural twist, appeared structureless like silk, were shiny, and had increased in tensile strength. For about thirty years the discovery was practically forgotten, because the process was too expensive to be used commercially. Then, in 1890, Lowe of England patented a process by which the cotton fiber was made lustrous if held in tension in caustics. Improvements have been made in the combined methods of Mercer and Lowe, and now mercerization is used on a large scale.

Formerly, few mercerized cotton fabrics were available. Now we have many, including sateen, batiste, cotton satin, better grade of cotton broadcloth, cotton poplin, and knitted underwear.

For mercerizing, cotton of long staple (long fiber) gives best results. The fibers are carefully combed, and the cloth is singed and bleached before it is mercerized. Since most cloths are mercerized in the piece, this process is generally considered a method of finishing.

Mercerization gives cotton fabrics definite advantages. It makes them stronger, more elastic and pliable, more lustrous, and more absorbent, and it gives them a greater affinity for dyestuffs.

## SIZING OR DRESSING

Mucilage, China clay, starch, flour, casein, or wax may be used. Sometimes oily or greasy substances, such as oil, tallow, or glycerin, are applied after the stiffening substance to soften the texture of the cloth. Because sizing makes a cotton more susceptible to mildew, antiseptics such as zinc chloride or formaldehyde are added to the sizing to prevent this growth. In sizing, the cloth is passed between two rollers, one roller dipping into the vat of sizing. The sizing process follows the singeing, bleaching, and dyeing, because subjecting cloth to liquids after it is sized removes the stiffening.

If a cotton is sized too heavily, the substance may crack and rub off with friction; a thumbnail, if rubbed over the cloth, causes little particles to flake off. Also, if the cloth is heavily sized, particles fly off the cloth as it is being torn. If a colored fabric that has been sized is rubbed briskly against a white handkerchief, the sizing may rub off onto the handkerchief. Washing generally removes sizing, and then any defects in the yarn or weave become noticeable.

Sized cotton cloths include organdy, costume cambric, sheeting, and mosquito netting. Other cloths, such as lawn, marquisette, nainsook, and dimity may contain small amounts of sizing to give them a fresh, crisp appearance. (See *glazing*, p. 163.)

## STARCHING

(See *sizing.*)

## DYEING AND PRINTING

Cotton may be dyed in raw stock, yarn, or piece. It may be printed by roller, discharge, resist, screen, hand-block, duplex, or photographic methods.

### CONDITIONING

After the fabric has been colored (dyed or printed), it is starched (sized) as a basic finish to give a hand to the cloth.

### TENTERING

This process evens the fabric in the width.

### CALENDERING

This process smooths the cloth by a series of rollers. Sometimes the rollers are engraved to give an embossing like the watered design of moiré or a crepey texture.

## SPECIAL FINISHES

Probably more special or functional finishes are applied to cotton than to any other fibers. These finishes include crease, perspiration, mildew, flame, and stain resistance; also waterproofing and water repellency, shrinkage control, permanent glazing, heat setting, permanent starchless, absorbency, germ resistance, wash-and-wear, and durable press. (See Chapter 7.)

## WHY CONSUMERS BUY COTTON FABRICS

### CONSUMER DEMAND FOR COTTON

Cotton is plentiful and economical to produce, and it has the inherent characteristic of easy care that consumers want.

According to the *Textile Organon*, the world output of basic textile fibers (cotton, wool, and man-made fibers) was 39.5 billion pounds in 1967. Of the total output, cotton accounted for 57 per cent; wool for 9 per cent; and man-made fibers for 34 per cent. Silk was a nominal percentage of the total.[7]

To be sure, cotton continues to feel the competition of the man-made fibers that began to invade the market during the 1930's. Man-made fibers still present cotton and the other natural fibers with a challenge.

Man-made fiber and yarn companies have spent huge sums of money on basic research, development, and promotion of their products. In fact, man-made fiber producers in the United States invest in advertising more than thirteen times the sum used to advertise natural fibers. Yet these producers sell less than one half of the total poundage of fiber consumed.[8] This expenditure has paid off to the extent that in the United

---

[7] *Textile Organon*, XXXIX, 6 (June 1968), 89.
[8] U.S. Department of Agriculture, "The Cotton Situation," March 1968.

States, in 1966, man-made fibers were used for approximately 37 per cent of all apparel uses; about 46 per cent of all home furnishings; and approximately 59 per cent of industrial fiber products. Obviously, man-made fiber producers have succeeded in capturing an increasing share of the natural-fiber market.

The cotton industry is making every effort to meet this challenge through improvement of processing machinery, reduction of labor costs, and the development and promotion of resins for cotton fabrics to make them wash-and-wear.

What will happen? Eventually, there will probably be a balance between the use of natural and man-made fibers. Blends will maximize the advantages and minimize the disadvantages of each. Each fiber must continue to improve its quality, beauty, and suitability. None can remain static.

The basic properties of cotton (versatility, durability, comfort, fashion rightness, ease of care, and economy) cause consumers to buy cotton fabrics. Let us consider these buying points.

### VERSATILITY

Cotton can serve for food (cottonseed products), for clothing, and for shelter. Cotton clothing can be worn around the clock. A single cotton fabric, piqué, can be used for a house dress, a sports dress, a summer business dress, a bathing suit, or a beach bag. It is particularly adapted to children's dresses. Cotton, then, is appropriate for wearing apparel, home furnishings, industrial uses, and military supplies.

### DURABILITY

Durability refers to the length of time that a fabric will wear. Workmanship indicates the skill and care that is given to a fabric when it is manufactured. Cotton fibers are comparatively short; therefore one would expect them to produce a yarn that is fairly weak in tensile strength. However, a cotton fiber, because of its natural twist, spins so well that it can be twisted very tightly; hence, since tightly twisted yarns are more durable than those that are slackly twisted, cotton yarns are strong and fabrics made from them are durable. Cotton fabrics have been proved by the U.S. Army to be especially suited for uniforms because of their superior abrasion resistance.

Two-ply yarns are more durable than single yarns of the same diameter; so a turkish towel made of two-ply yarn will be stronger and more absorbent than one constructed from a single yarn. It is also important to remember that yarns of even and regular texture are usually stronger than irregular yarns of the same average diameter. Also, since cottons are temporarily stronger when wet than when dry, there is no need to worry about their breaking when they are in the wash.

Cotton yarns, then, can be given considerable tensile strength, and the cloth made from these yarns can be durable. It is the quality of the yarn (in addition, of course, to weave and finish) that primarily determines the durability of the cloth.

There is little need for the consumer to fear that a guaranteed colorfast cotton fabric will fade if hung as a window drapery. It is not likely that the hand laundry or the household automatic washer will remove color from table damasks, dresses, or colored domestic cotton. There is still some danger that an unreliable commercial laundry will use bleaches under poorly controlled conditions and consequently cause fading of color. Any good laundry soap may be used, since cottons resist the alkali of which some soaps are made.

Cotton can be pressed with a hot iron; its scorching point is high. Since cotton fiber is fairly inelastic, most cotton fabrics wrinkle easily, and hence, unless they are finished for crease resistance, need frequent pressing. But cottons require no particular care in pressing. Unless they are treated for mildew resistance, they should not be folded and kept on shelves where there is dampness. Moths, however, will not attack cottons.

### COMFORT

Cotton conducts moisture away from the body and allows the cooler temperatures outside to reach the body, so it is a cool material for summer or tropical wear. But, since short cotton fibers nap easily, cotton fabrics can also be made warm when necessary. Knitted cotton underwear absorbs perspiration and keeps the wearer comfortable.

### FASHION RIGHTNESS

The couturiers of New York and Paris have considered cottons glamorous enough for inclusion in their collections. Probably the special finishes have been largely responsible for the fashion rightness of cotton today. Then too, the textured effects obtained by blending cotton with other fibers in nubby, bouclé, and novelty yarns have glamorized cotton. New fabrics, such as cotton brocades, tweeds, shantungs, and suitings, have appeared. Staple fabrics, such as chambray, denim, corduroy, and jersey, have been restyled for the casual mode.

The National Cotton Council of America, which is a central organization representing all branches of the cotton industry in both research and promotion, has been instrumental not only in bringing to consumers improved cotton products but also in presenting distinct fashion and practical advantages to the consumer's attention.

### EASE OF CARE

The factors of light, laundering, ironing, and perspiration are the common consideration in colorfastness of cottons. Possibly dry cleaning should be added, but inasmuch as cotton per se is considered washable, it would be assumed that it is dry cleanable if colorfast. Some consumers will not purchase a cotton fabric if the label reads "Dry clean only."

In the discussion of physical characteristics of cotton it was stated that cotton takes dyes that are fast to washing and to sunlight. Standard Fade-Ometer tests appropriate to the fabric's end use can be made to determine the degree of colorfastness.

In resistance to fading by perspiration, cotton is considered good.

### RESISTANCE TO SHRINKAGE

One of the chief objections to cotton was its danger of shrinkage. A generation ago, consumers allowed a whole size for shrinkage of a shirt after laundering. Shrinkage-control treatments can now be applied to cottons so that not more than 1 per cent residual shrinkage remains to be taken into account.

### IMPROVEMENTS IN FINISHES

The recent improvements in finishes have given new and improved uses to cotton. Other than the basic finishes, there are treatments for resistance to stains, water, flame, mildew, and germs; also functional finishes for permanent stiffness, crease resistance, crease retention, wash-and-wear, durable press, and embossed or heat-set patterns. (See Chapter 7 for a discussion of each process.)

### ECONOMY OR PRICE

The fact that cotton is plentiful in this country and, with increased mechanization of the industry, can be produced economically means that it can compete favorably with other textiles. The waste can be utilized for by-products. Cotton fabrics are made to fit all income levels, from the fashion-conscious consumer in the higher income group to the budget-minded and fashion-conscious consumer in the lower income group. By and large, cotton is relatively inexpensive; so price may be appropriately considered a consumer's buying motive.

In considering the price of cotton garments, the following factors are involved: (1) classification of fibers, (2) quality of yarn, (3) construction, (4) finishes, (5) style, and (6) workmanship.

## SUMMARY

Mistakes are frequently made by both the consumer and the salesperson because each fails to appreciate the inherent qualities of a fabric. The consumer will make a better buyer if she knows the *characteristics* of cotton and their *effect* on the finished fabric. Salespeople will improve their selling efficiency if they increase their technical knowledge of how cotton will best serve the customer; and they will be better equipped to answer customers' questions, such as, Will the fabric wash well? Will the material be suitable for an evening dress?

Satisfied customers are those who buy the fabrics best suited to their needs. These customers are assets to any store.

## REVIEW QUESTIONS

1. (*a*) Of what value to the salesperson is a knowledge of the qualities of cotton?
   (*b*) Of what value is such knowledge to the consumer?
2. (*a*) In what countries is cotton raised?
   (*b*) Which species of cotton has the longest fibers? Which cottons have the finest fibers?
   (*c*) Which kind of cotton is best for use in hosiery and knit goods? Which for mixing with wool?
3. (*a*) What advantages has the mechanical cotton picker?
   (*b*) What are its disadvantages?
4. Explain the classification of upland cotton.
5. What effect have the fineness of the fiber and the length of the fiber on the finished cotton fabric?
6. Define: tensile strength, mercerization, hygroscopic moisture, cellulose, carding, count of yarn, ply yarn, combing, spinning.
7. (*a*) What effect on cotton have weak alkalies, such as borax, ammonia, phosphate of soda, and soap?
   (*b*) How will this knowledge help the consumer in laundering cottons?
   (*c*) What is the effect on cotton of strong, concentrated mineral acids such as sulfuric acid, nitric acid, and hydrochloric acid?
8. (*a*) Under what conditions does cotton mildew?
   (*b*) How may mildew be prevented?
9. Describe the process of making cotton yarn.
10. Describe the effect of the following types of yarn on the finished cloth:
   (*a*) slack-twisted yarns     (*f*) coarse yarns
   (*b*) tight-twisted yarns     (*g*) fine yarns
   (*c*) irregular yarns        (*h*) carded yarns
   (*d*) even yarns           (*i*) combed yarns
   (*e*) ply yarns            (*j*) low-count yarns
11. (*a*) In what woven constructions are cotton fabrics made? Give fabric illustrations in each construction.
   (*b*) In what knitted constructions? Give fabric illustrations in each knitted stitch.
12. In what ways have finishes improved cotton fabrics?
13. What is meant by *versatility*? Illustrate the versatility of cotton.
14. (*a*) What qualities in the cotton fibers and yarns make cotton fabrics durable?
   (*b*) Why does cotton launder easily?

15. What factors make for style in cotton fabrics?

16. Forecast the use of cotton in consumer goods.

## EXPERIMENTS

*(Tests to determine the effect of chemicals on cotton.)*

1. *The alkali test.* Ordinary lye, which can be bought in the grocery store, may be used for this experiment. Boil several pieces of cotton cloth for 5 minutes in a 5 per cent solution of lye. Remove from the fire and place what remains on a blotting paper. Describe the residue left after boiling. What was the effect of the lye on the cotton yarns? Boiling the test fabrics for 5 minutes in a 10 per cent solution of sodium hydroxide is equally effective.

2. *The acid test.* An ounce of concentrated sulfuric acid will suffice for this experiment. Place the liquid in a beaker or a heavy, shallow, glass dish. Drop several cotton yarns into the acid, but do not boil them. Let the yarns remain in the acid for 5 or 10 minutes. Note any changes that take place during that time. Remove any residue and describe the result of this test. A 25 per cent solution of aluminum chloride may be used instead of concentrated sulfuric acid. In this case, saturate the fabric thoroughly, then press the cloth with a very hot iron. Vegetable fibers scorch and pulverize when abraded between the fingers.

3. *The microscopic test.* This test is the most accurate of all for distinguishing one textile fiber from another. Consumers will have difficulty in obtaining a microscope, but college students can arrange to use the biology laboratory if they have no microscope in the textile laboratory.

   Unravel a cotton yarn and pull out one or two of the fibers. Put a small drop of water or glycerin on the glass slide. Place one or two fibers in the drop of water and cover all with a cover glass. Use the low power first and note the general appearance of the fiber. Then, without moving the slide, switch to the high power. In your textile notebook draw the cotton fiber as seen through the microscope.

## GLOSSARY

**Acrylonitrile.** A chemical used for treating cotton to make it permanently resisant to mildew and to give it greater affinity for dyes.

**Apparel fabrics (cotton).** See listings in Glossary, Chapter 16.

**Atlas cloth.** A modified tricot knit of fine cotton yarns with cloth sueded on one side. Used in gloves and sports jackets.

**Beacon robing.** A cotton bathrobing in double-cloth construction.

**Bird's-eye.** A woven-in dobby design used in cotton diapers, piqué, and wool sharkskin.

**Carded yarn.** See *Carding,* Glossary, Chapter 3.

**Chambray.** A cotton muslin made of yarn-dyed yarns. Staple chambray has colored warps and white fillings.

**Classed.** Classification of cotton by staple length, grade, and character.

**Combed yarn.** See *Combing,* Glossary, Chapter 3.

**Conditioning.** A finishing process of sizing a fabric after dyeing to give it a hand.

**Cotton.** A white or yellowish white vegetable fiber coming from a plant related to the hollyhock, grown in the U.S., the U.S.S.R., Egypt, Peru, India, and other countries.

**Cultivating.** In the common sense, controlling weeds in cotton fields by mechanical means.

**Defoliation.** Chemical treatment of cotton plants to make them shed their leaves.

**Delinting.** Mechanically removing short fuzzy fibers from cotton seeds.

**Dimity.** A cotton ribbed fabric with ribs spaced at regular intervals either in crosswise stripes or in crossbars.

**Durable press.** See Glossary, Chapter 3.

**Egyptian cotton.** A species grown along the Nile Delta. It averages less than $1\frac{1}{2}$ inches in length.

**Extra-long-staple cotton.** Fibers $1\frac{3}{8}$ inches and longer.

**Ginning.** A process of separating fibers from the seeds.

**Good middling.** The best grade of cotton—lustrous, silky, clean fibers.

**Good ordinary.** The poorest grade of cotton. Contains leaf particles, sticks, hulls, dirt, sand, and the like.

**Hill dropping.** A method of planting cotton seeds by dropping them in hills.

**Home furnishings fabrics (cotton).** See Glossaries, Chapters 19 and 20.

**Linters.** Short fuzzy fibers removed from the cotton seeds.

**Lumen.** The open structure or canal from which the protoplasm has disappeared.

**Marquisette.** A cotton, silk, rayon, or other synthetic fabric in leno weave. May have clip-spot design.

**Mechanical picker.** See *Picker* and *Stripper.*

**Medium-staple cotton.** Fibers 1 to $1\frac{1}{8}$ inches long.

**Mercerization.** See Glossary, Chapter 7.

**Muslin.** Generic name of cotton fabrics in plain weave, ranging from the sheerest batiste to the coarsest sheeting.

**Nonwoven cotton fabrics.** See *Bonding*, Glossary, Chapter 2.

**Oxford.** A cotton fabric or blend with a synthetic, in basket weave 4 x 4 and 8 x 8.

**Picker.** A mechanical device with vertical drums equipped with spindles that remove the cotton from the boll.

**Pima.** American cotton grown chiefly in the irrigated lands of Arizona, New Mexico, and El Paso. Extra-long staple averaging $1\frac{3}{8}$ to $1\frac{5}{8}$ inches.

**Poplin.** A cotton, acetate, rayon, wool, or silk fabric in the rib variation of the plain weave. Ribs are closely spaced fillingwise. Broadcloth has finer ribs.

**Print cloths.** Cotton muslin fabrics ranging in counts from 48 square to 80 square (finished).

**Rugs.** See *Cotton rugs*, Chapter 19.

**Sanforized.** Trade name of a process for shrinkage control. Residual shrinkage of not over 1 per cent guaranteed.

**Sateen.** Mercerized cotton fabric in (filling float) sateen weave.

**Sea island cotton.** A species of American cotton once produced off the coast of the Carolinas. Has the longest staple, averaging about 2 inches. Now produced on the Lesser Antilles—Montserrat, St. Kitts, Nevis, and St. Vincent.

**Short-staple cotton.** Fibers $\frac{1}{4}$ to $1\frac{5}{16}$ inch long.

**Stripper.** A mechanical device that pulls the bolls off when they enter the rollers of the machine.

**Tackle twill.** A very durable rayon and cotton twill suitable for athletic uniforms and rainwear.

**Tanguis.** A species of cotton averaging $1\frac{1}{4}$ inches in length. Grown in Peru, which also grows other types of cotton, including pima and Egyptian.

**Terry cloth.** A cotton fabric with uncut looped pile, used in turkish toweling.

**Thread.** See Glossary, Chapter 3.

**Upland.** Cottons of the species *Gossypium hirsutum*. They usually produce staples from $\frac{3}{4}$ to $1\frac{1}{2}$ inches.

**Velveteen.** A cotton pile-weave fabric in filling pile construction, with either a twill or a plain weave back.

**Wash-and-wear.** See Glossary, Chapter 7.

# 10

# Linen
# and the Consumer

The use of linen, or _flaxen cloth_, dates back to the European Neolithic people who lived before the appearance of metals—probably about 10,000 years ago. These people dressed in skins, but they made coarse cloth and fishnets from flax. Fragments of the cloth and nets have been discovered in parts of Switzerland, the home of the Neolithic Lake Dwellers.[1]

Fine linens have been the burial shrouds of the Egyptian Pharaohs, the textile of Bible times, a fashionable and regal fabric of the Middle Ages, and the pride of the modern hostess.

Linen, then, has served man as a textile for thousands of years, and it has been more important in the past than it is today. Flax lost much of its importance when the cotton gin was developed, and it declined in consumption to a great extent for many years. Recently the emphasis on quality, high-fashion linen fabrics and blends for apparel and for the home has revived somewhat. But even so, world production of flax fiber is only 1 per cent of all fibers produced.

[1] H. G. Wells, _The Outline of History_ (New York: The Macmillan Company, 1921).

## FLAX FOR FIBER

Flax is a vegetable fiber plant. Flax fibers are obtained from the outside of the woody core of the plant.

Belgium, France, Holland, and the Soviet Union and its satellites are the principal producers (Ireland, England, Germany, Sweden, and Italy discontinued production after World War II). Belgium produces the best grade of flax. In Ireland, the best linens are made at Belfast and other parts of Ulster. The United States raises flax, but mostly for seed; its grade is inferior to the Belgian variety.[2] The Oregon flax industry partially attributes its growth to new and better methods of harvesting and spinning strong yarns (the wet spinning method used in Belgium, France, Ireland and most of the other European countries spinning line yarns).[3] This method allows moisture to soften the pectic gum so that the fibers adhere together and less breakage occurs. The cost of labor for cultivating, harvesting, and preparation of the fiber, and the lack of suitable climatic conditions have caused flax fiber production to fail to become important in the United States.

## FLAX FOR SEED

Flax for seed is raised in Michigan, Minnesota, and the Dakotas. Flax plants raised for seed do not produce good fibers. The seed is sold to manufacturers of linseed oil for paints and varnishes, and the woody stalks of the plant (the straw) are used as fodder for cattle. The best portion of the flax may be used for fibers, for twine, and for rope.

[2] The yield per acre is lower in the eastern countries. See Food and Agriculture Organization of the United Nations Monthly Bulletin of Agricultural Economics Statistics, Vol. 16, No. 5, May, 1967.

[3] Long-fibered even yarns.

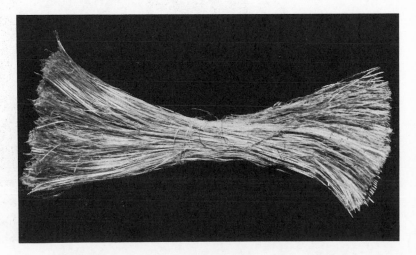

**Figure 10.1. Flax.**

Quality tow and line fibers are used to back upholstery and rugs, depending on the weave.[4] Linen fibers used as backings include those used for damasks, velvet, satin, twill and plain weaves, and pile or woven rugs.

Argentina ranks first in flaxseed production in the southern hemisphere. India, Canada, Morocco, Lithuania, and Latvia produce flaxseed and hempseed.

### FLAX CULTURE

A consistently moist but mild climate is necessary for the growing of flax for fiber. The fiber requires more care than cotton before it can be made into cloth, and a considerable amount of the labor in foreign countries is performed by hand—selecting, sorting, grading etc. If climatic conditions are right, large quantities of flax for fiber can be produced. Harvesting machines pull up the flax by the roots and bundle it. There are also machines for removing seeds from the flax. Progress has been made in the last twenty years to mechanize the flax industry. Specially designed machines have replaced many of the laborious hand operations. In northern countries flax is sown in the spring, like wheat

[4] Short flax fibers.

Figure 10.2. Early in Spring flax seed is planted and grows to maturity about three feet high. Large machines harvest the plants by pulling. They are never cut. The stalks are bundled and threshing machines remove the seeds used for linseed oil. (*Courtesy of the Belgian Linen Association.*)

**Figure 10.3.** Here men are loading the bundles of flax into retting tanks filled with heated water from the River Lys. The soaking action loosens the outside flax fibers from the woody center stalk. (*Courtesy of the Belgian Linen Association.*)

**Figure 10.4.** The retting process finished, bundles of flax are stood upright in the fields and dried again. Then they are retied and taken to be scutched, where rollers crush the straw, separating the soft flax fibers from the hard straw. (*Courtesy of the Belgian Linen Association.*)

**Figure 10.5.** Emerging from the combing process, these long wisps of fiber have passed over the series of graduated metal pins of the combing machine. A man gathers the glossy flax which now resembles switches of human hair. (*Courtesy of the Belgian Linen Association.*)

**Figure 10.6.** In large mills spinning methods vary according to the type of yarn desired. Here fine linen threads are being spun for the weaving of sheer linens. (*Courtesy of the Belgian Linen Association.*)

and rye. The flax plant has an erect stem about three feet in height, toward the top of which are branches that carry the blue flowers and bolls containing the linseed. The flax fibers surround the pithy center and the skin of the stem. Flax is therefore a bast fiber, because the fiber is found within the woody stalk or stem. Little care is needed until harvesting time, which comes in late July or August. Flax plants are pulled up by the roots when the stalks begin to turn yellow at the base and when the seeds are turning green to pale brown. Pulling up by the roots ensures long, unbroken fibers that can be spun into yarn easily. Bundles of flax are laid together to resemble wigwams. In this way the flax is dried and seasoned.

## DRESSING THE FLAX

### RIPPLING

Rippling is a process of removing the seeds. Today it is done by threshing machines that strip the seeds before tank-retting is undertaken.

### RETTING

The object of this process is to loosen the flax fiber from the outside woody stalk. Retting, or soaking, is done by the following methods:

1. *Pool retting.* The flax is put into stagnant pools of water to loosen the fibers from the stalks. Today this work is done by pulling and binding machines, so the pool-retting method is seldom used.

2. *Dew retting.* The object of this process is to let the dew loosen the fiber from the stalk. If the flax is dew-retted, the harvesting machine lays out small bundles of uprooted plants in orderly rows. The seeds are extracted by a special machine (rippling process). The bundles of flax are turned by a mechanical tedder to ensure retting of the upper and lower layers. A great deal of flax seed is often wasted. Although dependent upon the weather, dew-retting is the most common method in use today and the most economical process. However it is difficult to control the quality uniformly. This process is used extensively in France, Belgium, and the U.S.S.R.

3. *Tank retting.* This is a method of loosening the flax fibers from the stalks by immersion in tanks of water. The best grades of Belgian flax are retted in water from the River Lys. Bundles of flax are placed in huge concrete tanks with river water which is heated to 75° F. and gradually increased to 90° F. This process requires four to five days and produces strong, lustrous, highest quality flax.

4. *Chemical retting*. Many processes have been tested but this method is limited mainly to experiments.[5]

## SCUTCHING

After the flax has been thoroughly dried, it is run through a machine that breaks the wooden stalk by crumbling or crushing it. The flax is now ready for *scutching*—the removal of the fibers from the woody stalks. A machine with a series of fluted rollers beats the fibers free.

## HACKLING

This process, sometimes called *combing*, corresponds to the carding and combing of cottons. The object is to prepare the fibers for spinning by laying them parallel with one another. When this process is done by hand, a series of combs with iron teeth ranging from very coarse to very fine are used. The scutched fibers are pulled through each comb, beginning with the coarsest one. Some short fibers adhere to the teeth of the comb, become entangled, or drop to the floor. These short fibers, called *tow*, are used in irregular or uneven yarns found in table linens and dish towels. Such fabrics are called *tow linens*. The long, regular, even fibers, laid parallel in the hackling, are called *line*; they are used in fine table damasks, handkerchiefs, and sheer dress fabrics. Machines equipped with steel bars comb the flax. The flax is held in the machine so that the root ends are combed first; then the top ends are put through the machine and combed. Tow is separated from line. Even yarns are spun from line, and coarse, irregular yarns from tow. Cotton and/or rayon may be blended with tow linen for glass or hand toweling.

In recent years, technological advances in spinning tow yarns have

[5] *Ciba Review*, Ciba Corporation discusses methods. Vol. 1965/2 pp. 18–23.

**Figure 10.5.** *Left:* Tow linen. *Middle:* Line linen. *Right:* A poorly hackled tow linen. **(Photos by Jack Pitkin.)**

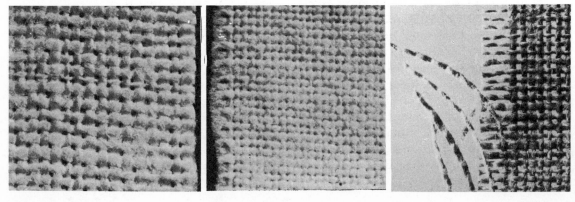

broadened their use. These yarns are often preferred to achieve artistic effects in creating novelty casements, textures, and homespun weaves of high quality (often quite expensive, too).

## CHARACTERISTICS OF THE LINEN FIBER
### MICROSCOPIC APPEARANCE

Linen fibers are round, transparent, and at intervals have cross-markings (nodes or joints) that give the fibers the appearance of bamboo poles. There is evidence of a central canal, but it is not continuous like that of cotton. The nodes keep the fiber from collapsing. These round, jointed structures make linen harder to spin than cotton, but the length of the fiber makes up for this.

### LENGTH OF FIBER

Linen fibers are longer than cotton fibers. In fact, linen fibers used in fine yarns average eighteen to twenty inches in length. Consequently it is not so necessary to spin linen fibers tightly to hold the ends in as it is with cotton.

### DIAMETER OF FIBER

Linen fibers range from .0047 to .0098 inch in diameter—the average breadth being greater than that of cotton. All cotton fibers are finer than the finest flax fibers.

### COLOR OF FIBER

The average linen is yellowish buff to gray in color. The best flax is pale yellowish white. Flax retted by dew is steel gray; Egyptian varieties are pearl gray.

### LUSTER

Linen fibers have a characteristic silky luster, much more pronounced than that of untreated cottons. Linens are rarely mercerized, but natural luster can be increased if the linen is beaten or pounded after it has been woven.

### STRENGTH

Linen is stronger than cotton, and its tensile strength increases when the fiber is wet. Overretting weakens the fiber appreciably. If linen becomes bone dry, it is difficult to spin; that is why linens are often spun in damp cellars. A great deal of bleaching causes linen to lose strength and tends to decrease its weight.

## ELASTICITY

In comparing cotton and linen by feeling, linen is found to be less elastic than cotton. This is why linen fabrics feel hard and smooth and why they wrinkle and crease easily. Chemical treatments are applied to linen for the purpose of increasing its elasticity. Crease-resistant dress linen is treated in this way.

## HEAT CONDUCTIVITY

Linen is better than cotton as a conductor of heat. It carries heat away from the body faster. Hence, garments made of linen feel cooler than those of comparable weight in cotton.

## HYGROSCOPIC MOISTURE

Flax fibers have about the same amount of hygroscopic moisture as cotton—between 6 and 8 per cent. Linen fabrics, unless beetle-finished, absorb moisture quickly and dry faster than cotton. Linen dish towels will dry more dishes than cotton before feeling damp. Linens dry faster than cottons.

## COMPOSITION OF FIBER

Like cotton, linen is composed chiefly of cellulose, but it has 15 to 30 per cent more natural impurities. The chemical constituents are pure cellulose (65–70 per cent); pectic substances—plant cells (20–25 per cent); woody and cuticular tissue (4–5 per cent); and ash (1 per cent).

When linen is bleached, it requires more care than cotton because more of the natural impurities must be removed to obtain a clear white.

## HYGIENIC QUALITY AND LAUNDERABILITY

Linen fiber is smooth; dirt and germs do not collect on it easily. This quality makes it especially hygienic and adaptable to sanitary use.

Linen launders easily, but not so easily as cotton. The linen fiber is attacked more readily by alkalies and, like cotton, is destroyed by concentrated mineral acids. Bleaching agents, such as chlorine bleach and hypochlorites, have about the same effect on linen as on cotton. Possibly linen is slightly more sensitive to hypochlorites. It is more difficult to bleach than is cotton because of the natural impurities in its fiber. Weak alkalies, such as borax, ammonia, phosphate of soda, and laundry soap, do not injure linen.

Linens, like cottons, are vegetable fibers; hence acids have the same effect on linens as on cottons. Concentrated mineral acids, such as sulfuric, hydrochloric, hydrofluoric, and nitric acids, destroy linen fibers that are soaked in them for a few minutes. Dilute acids also affect linen and cotton similarly; They tend to weaken the fabric, but do not destroy it if it is not allowed to dry.

## ACTION OF LIGHT

Ultraviolet rays of the sun attack linen, but not so quickly as they attack cotton.

## AFFINITY FOR DYESTUFFS

Linen has a very poor affinity for dye because of the hardness and lack of penetrability of the fiber. Its cells are held together with tissue that is broken down only under a severe bleaching process. In a piece of colored dress linen of moderate price, all yarns will probably not have the same depth of color; or, if a yarn is untwisted, the core will probably be a lighter shade than the outside of the yarn. This shows that the dyestuff has not penetrated evenly.

## MILDEW

Linen is quite resistant to attack by bacteria and mildew.

# MAKING LINEN YARN
## PREPARATION

After the flax fibers have been sufficiently hackled or combed for the intended use, the fibers go to the *preparing room*. The first machine, called the *spread board*, lays wisps of flax fibers parallel on traveling bands in continuous lines, with the ends of the wisps overlapping. These lines of fiber are then passed through sets of rollers that draw one fiber away from the other to produce a thick ribbon of fibers (sliver). Ribbons of sliver are drawn out longer and thinner until the last machine, the *roving frame*, puts in a loose twist. The roving is then wound on large wooden bobbins that are mounted on the top of the spinning frame.

## WET SPINNING

The roving on the bobbins is first passed through a trough of hot water and through another set of rollers to further draw out the sliver before it reaches the rapidly revolving spindles (2,000 to 3,000 revolu-

**Figure 10.6.** A vast amount of research has gone into the production of fast dyes. This picture shows the Moygashel fabrics going through the machine in the warm, damp atmosphere of the dyehouse. (*Photograph courtesy of the Irish Linen Guild.*)

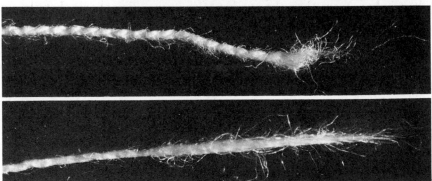

**Figure 10.7.** The breaking test, showing broken ends of two yarns. Cotton (*top*) is brushlike; linen (*bottom*) is pointed. This is a non-technical test that may be made by removing a yarn from a fabric and pulling it until it breaks. An all-linen yarn is more difficult to break than an all-cotton yarn. (*Photo by Jack Pitkin.*)

tions per minute) that put in the twist. The twist or spin of the spindles is the operation of spinning the flax fibers into linen yarn.

*Twist.* It is not necessary to twist linen yarns as tightly as cotton yarns because the flax fiber is much longer and smoother, so that the ends are less likely to stick out. Cotton yarn is fuzzy in appearance unless it is twisted very tightly, but loose-twisted linen yarn remains smooth and lustrous indefinitely.

*Ply.* Ply yarns do not ordinarily appear in linen fabrics—probably

because the tensile strength of linen is so much greater than that of
cotton as to make the use of ply yarns for added strength unnecessary.
Furthermore, ply yarns would be quite round and hard, and the usual
desired surface of linen is flat and smooth. However, bouclé yarns are
made of linen plied with some other fibers, such as wool, when textural
interest is important.

*Count.*   To find the size or count of the yarn, divide the number of
yards weighing one pound by 300 yards, the unit or lea.

*Mixtures of different yarns.*   Cotton yarns are often used in the same
cloth with linen yarns. The linen yarns may be used lengthwise and the
cotton yarns crosswise. The price of such material is less than that of an
all-linen fabric.

## WEAVING

Usually linen is supplied to the weaver in hank form. Essentially the
preparation and weaving of linen is not very different from that of wool,
cotton, silk, and other textile yarns.

From hanks the manufacturer winds the yarn onto spools, then onto
the warp beam; several of these beams then go to the weaver's beam.
Yarn can be sized as it goes from the warper's to the weaver's beam. The
warps are set up in the loom, the filling shuttles are prepared with yarn,
and weaving begins.

### PLAIN WEAVE

In the apparel field, linen crash in plain weave is used for dresses,
and in heavier weights for suiting. In the home, similar fabric in various
weights and colorings can be used for draperies and dish and glass
towels. Embroidered, printed, or plain luncheon sets and cloths are often
made of crash. Sheetings and embroidery linens are in this weave.

A sheer linen in plain weave, called linen lawn or handkerchief linen,
is commonly used in handkerchiefs, blouses, and summer dresses. Plain
weave linens may be attractively embellished by schiffli embroidery.

### TWILL WEAVE

Linen fabrics are far more numerous in plain weave than in twill.
However, linen suiting in twill or herringbone is on the market.

Twill weaves are used to a greater extent for drapery and upholstery
linens than for suiting. Fine twills are used for crewel work, which has
revived in popularity in recent years.

### JACQUARD AND DOBBY WEAVES

Linen is at its best in beauty when woven in Jacquard as a table
damask. On the right side, the warp floats in a satin-weave ground and

the filling floats in the design to give a three-dimensional effect. Linen damask in color is frequently used for furniture covers. It is particularly suited for institutional use where durability is required.

The small honeycombed dobby of the linen face towel called *huck* (a short term for huckaback) is durable, soft, attractive, and absorbent.

Many interesting casement designs are dobby weaves, which are more economical than Jacquard weaves. Many techniques have been developed to create the novelty casements that are an important part of the drapery linen market.

### PILE WEAVE

The terry cloth we call *friction towel* is correctly named when made with linen pile. It is often unbleached and may be made up as a mitt for ease in household uses such as dusting and washing.

The linen-faced velvets are an important item made of a pile construction. They include not only plain and antique velvets, but also crushed, embossed, and printed designs. They are in great demand. Currently Belgium is the main producer for the U.S. market.

Linen yarns are often used as backing for wool-pile rugs or for silk or cotton velour upholstery fabrics. Linen makes a strong groundwork for the pile.

## FINISHING LINEN FABRICS

### SCOURING

To prepare for the application of finishes, linen fabrics are scoured. (See Chapter 7.)

### BLEACHING

In the past the snowy whiteness of linen was obtained by the centuries-old practice of *grass bleaching*. Grass bleaching produces beautiful color and does not injure the strength of the fiber. But since this process requires weeks or even months, much capital and land are necessary.

In today's modern bleaching processes, chemicals are used under carefully controlled conditions. The principal steps follow:

1. Impurities such as wax and gums are boiled out in a lime solution (8–10 hours) under pressure.
2. The fabric is rinsed and treated with dilute hydrochloric acid.
3. The fabric is washed and boiled in caustic soda.
4. The fabric is then bleached with one of several bleaching agents, neutralized, and washed.

**Figure 10.8.** Grass bleaching flax in Ireland. (*Photograph courtesy of the Irish Linen Guild.*)

5. Before framing the fabric to its desired width, it passes through a solution containing an optical whitening agent to give it a level full white color.

The first three steps in the process merely clean the fiber of impurities; the fourth step does the whitening. The first three steps are called *kier boiling.* This process is accomplished in large tanks called *kiers,* which hold approximately two to five tons of water. The fabric is fed into the *kiers* automatically in rope form and only opened to full width after the cloth is fully bleached.

## REGULAR FINISHES

Regular finishes for linens may include shearing, beetling, sizing, shrinkage control, tentering, and calendering. These finishing processes have been discussed in Chapter 7.

## SPECIAL OR FUNCTIONAL FINISHES

There has been much discussion about flameproofing linens for contract use, about durable finishes, and about effects on the fiber after a period of time. A number of processes now used are successfully applied to linens.

Brand names of durable flameproof processes include Pyroset by American Cyanamid, Flametrol "69" by the Perma-Dry Division of Kiesling-Hess and x-12 by du Pont. It should be noted that there are two distinct groups of flameproof finishes: those that will withstand dry cleaning without losing their flameproof features, and those that will not and therefore require re-flameproofing. Flameproofing has the following additional features: (1) It may shrink fabric to the same degree as plain water. (2) It does not accelerate fading. (3) Water-repellent fabrics may be flameproofed with the durable types of flameproofing.[6]

Many cities and states have their own flameproofing regulations for fabrics used in public buildings—regulations that surpass the federal regulations.

Among the most recent functional finishes are permanent-press soil-release finishes for table linens. (See table linens, Chapter 18.)

## FIBER IDENTIFICATION OF LINEN

Linen is a generic fiber name recognized by the F.T.C. under the Textile Fiber Products Identification Act. Consequently, fabrics made of linen must be labeled with this generic fiber name and with percentages (over 5 per cent) in order of predominance by weight of the constituent fibers in the textile fiber product, exclusive of ornamentation.[7] For example: 60 per cent linen/40 per cent cotton. The act states that "Fiber or fibers in an amount of 5 per cent or less must appear last and be designated as 'other fiber' or 'other fibers,' as the case may be." A label might read, for example, 60 per cent linen/36 per cent cotton/4 per cent other fibers.

If the article is all linen, it may be identified by those words or by "100 per cent linen."

In advertising, the percentages of the fiber need not be stated but simply listed in order of predominance by weight. The rule for fibers in an amount of 5 per cent or less is the same as for labeling.[8]

Under the T.F.P.I.A., a retailer who imports linen products directly must assume full responsibility for the correct labeling of his product. Should he purchase an imported linen article from any person residing in the United States, he should obtain a guarantee issued in good faith by such a person. This rule applies to all imported textile fiber products.

## SOURCES OF OUR LINEN FABRICS

Great Britain (especially Northern Ireland) and Belgium are the principal exporters of linen to the United States. Smaller amounts are imported from other European countries.

[6] "A Guide to Fabric Finishing, Flameproofing, and Service" (Perma-Dry Division, Kiesling-Hess Finishing Co., Inc., New York, Philadelphia, and Los Angeles).
[7] "Ornamentation" is defined as "any fibers or yarns imparting a visibly discernible pattern or design to a yarn or fabric."
[8] See Chapter 1 for a discussion of the T.F.P.I.A.

The difference between the linen produced in Northern Ireland and Belgium is mostly a matter of specialization. Both produce the weaves they are most skilled at manufacturing, and each produces some of the same items as the other country—for example, oyster and plain linens used for table linen—in comparable quality. However, sheer handkerchief weaves, hemstitched linen, and damasks are mainly Irish, whereas the novelty weaves—textured and drapery weaves—are mainly Belgian.

Damask is produced by Belgium chiefly for the European market. There has been a decline in sales of Belgian and Irish damask to the United States, owing to competition from Japan's rayon/cotton damask.

In the table linen area, Ireland produces more finished goods, while the greater part of Belgian linen enters the United States as grey goods, which is dyed, printed, trimmed, and finished here. Both Ireland and Belgium ship large quantities to Portugal and the Azores for hand-embroidered cloths.

Ireland continues to purchase large quantities of flax from Belgium.

In 1955 a New York center for the Belgian Linen Association was opened. Its activities include publicity, sales promotion, public relations, and educational aspects.

The Linen Trade Association was organized by linen (flax) importers. Today it includes all table linen and domestics (sheets, towels) manufacturers, importers, and fiber producers.

## TRADE NAMES OF LINENS

Over the years, even for several generations, certain names on labels have spelled quality of linen fabrics to consumers. One such name is *Moygashel*, which refers to an old Gaelic castle of the same name in Dungannon, Ireland. It is in the plain near this castle that Moygashel flax grows. The making of linen fabrics at Moygashel goes back 1500 years.

The people of Dungannon are no longer flax growers. Today they are spinners, weavers, and finishers of linen fabrics. In 1953 Moygashel Ltd. was formed and became a public corporation, incorporating the interests of Stevenson & Sons, Ltd., and twenty-two other firms. In the spring of 1969, Moygashel Ltd. became a subsidiary of Courtaulds, Ltd.

Many of the old Irish firms have gone out of business. The York Street Flax Spinning Company is a name retained in New York by selling agents and importers. The names of other old table linen firms have been retained by importers and agents, but most of them have not developed advertising trade names that would be easily recognizable to consumers. Perhaps the better-known trademarks are the Irish Linen Guild's logo and the Belgian Linen Association's shield. Both organizations have labeling programs for table linens, apparel, drapery, and upholstery linens.

## ATTRACTIVE APPEARANCE

Linen can be bleached snowy white and still keep its natural silky luster. A good-quality linen improves with use. It becomes whiter and more smooth and shiny. Since natural linen is not pure white, bleaching is necessary; but, once bleached, linen never becomes gray-looking or fuzzy like cotton. Linen has a flat, smooth, shiny surface and a strong, leathery feeling that are particularly attractive to the purchaser who wants good-looking and durable fabrics.

A word of warning should be given: The whitest linens are not always the strongest. Often the strength of a fabric has been lessened by numerous bleaching processes. Customers should decide whether they prefer beautiful whiteness to durability.

Linens can be dyed or printed, but often dyes are merely surface colors, because of the impenetrability of the linen fiber. The consumer can buy fast-dyed linen, but she should first examine the yarns thoroughly to see whether the fabric has taken the dye evenly.

If fine, evenly spun yarns are used, fabrics as fine as the sheerest cottons can be produced from linen. Linen fabrics made of long fibers are lintless. This factor is appreciated in drying glasses or dishes. Also, a smooth surface is characteristic of a beautiful linen cloth. The average or poor grades of linen are more likely to be made of irregularly spun yarns than are the comparable grades of cotton. Coarse, uneven yarns make linen fabrics hard, rough, and heavy. Finishing processes, including beetling and calendering, increase the luster and smoothness.

Linen drapery and upholstery fabrics may have attractive textured surfaces and textured weaves, contemporary or classical screen prints, or embroidered effects. The fabrics may be applied to plain and crushed velvets, and they are suitable for plaids, checks, solid colors, textured and patterned casement cloths, damask, and quilted effects.

## DURABILITY AND WORKMANSHIP

The durability of the cloth depends on the fibers and yarns of which it is made. Care in growth, harvesting, and dressing of flax affects the quality of the fiber. If flax is allowed to overripen, the fiber becomes too brittle to make good cloth. If fibers are overretted, they become too tender. If care is not taken in scutching and hackling, good-quality fibers may be broken or wasted. Consequently, the durability of linen cloth depends upon the degree of skilled workmanship. Since the linen fiber is longer and stronger than cotton of the same diameter, linen should be more durable than cotton, considering fibers alone. Linens and cottons are stronger when wet than when dry, so that washing should not weaken them.

The strength of linen yarn does not increase with the number, of twists or turns to the inch, as does the strength of cotton. The linen fibers are sufficiently long and strong to require little twisting. Linen is more durable when unbleached, as was explained under the discussion of appearance.

The durability of a good quality of linen may make the fabric cost less in the long run, even though the initial investment may seem high. An Irish linen damask, for instance, bought for a bride's trousseau, may still be in use on her golden wedding anniversary. Linen laces of exquisite fineness and workmanship, dating back to the sixteenth century, can be seen today in the Metropolitan Museum of Art.

## ABSORBENCY

In glass, dish, and hand towels, and in dresses and suits, absorbency is important. Linen is absorbent because the flax fiber is hollow through the center, like bamboo. Since linen dish towels will dry more dishes than cotton before feeling damp, fewer dish towels are required to dry a day's dishes; hence, fewer towels have to be laundered each week. The consumer may not appreciate the absorbency of linen until after it has been laundered, for frequently linen's leathery beetle finish restricts absorbency when the towel is first used.

Since linen absorbs moisture readily, dries quickly, does not "perspire" nor mold, it is well suited for drapery use in humid climates. Also, the absorptive nature of linen yarns contributes to sound deadening. For this reason, linen wall coverings are often selected—as in the Ford Foundation Building in New York City.

## EASE IN CARE

Because linen fiber is inelastic, linen fabrics require frequent pressing to remove wrinkles, unless the fabric has been treated for crease resistance. It is best to sprinkle the fabric and to iron it while damp.

Linen does not get soiled so quickly as cotton because the fibers are longer, harder, and smoother. Hot water and soap will not injure the fiber, but care should be taken not to starch linens heavily (especially damasks), for there is a danger of breaking the fibers under a heavy iron.

Washability of linen is a strong buying motive for any consumer. Household linen, handkerchiefs, and linen apparel (but be sure to check the label, since many articles require dry cleaning), all wash easily week after week, year after year. Linen is a clean, sanitary textile. White linens should be dried in the sun if they are to keep their whiteness. (For care of specific articles, the storing of linens, and stain removal, see Chapter 15.)

Generally speaking, dry cleaning is the recommended method for drapery and upholstery linens. Decorative linens should not be washed, unless labeled washable and preshrunk. Since linen does not have static properties, dust particles are not attracted and do not cling to the fabric, and therefore it may require less cleaning.

The permanent-press soil-release finish for table linens has been a boon to the consumer. The finish is applied in Belgium, Ireland, and in the United States. See *soil-release finish for table linens*, Chapter 18.

## COMFORT

Since linen is a better conductor of heat than cotton, fabrics made of linen are cooler. Linen is therefore appropriate for a summer wardrobe. Some customers argue that a linen dress is warmer than a cotton one; probably they are comparing a heavy dress linen with a cotton voile or lawn. Linen is also practical for summer athletic underwear, because it is cooler than cotton. The chief objection, however, is that it may be clammy when wet with perspiration.

So linen is not a warm fabric even though it may be comparatively heavy. It is used chiefly for comfort in summer apparel, sheets, and summer coverings for wool upholstery. Linen sheets, although expensive, are much cooler than cotton ones for use in the summer.

## SENTIMENT

Probably more fine linens than cottons are bought for sentiment. No trousseau would be complete without a formal linen tablecloth and a set of dinner napkins. Linen hand towels and linen glass towels are usually included. Fine linens, like beautiful china and furniture, are the hallmark of homes in which fine things are appreciated. The bride-to-be takes pleasure in knowing that she has fine linens and takes joy in handling them.

Some people buy linens because of their rarity. They collect rare, old linen laces just as others collect antique rugs, furniture, or china. Still others may spend money lavishly for an exquisitely hand-embroidered, fifteen-hundred-dollar linen tablecloth—not because it will outwear a more inexpensive fabric but because it is a lifetime investment and work of art. A customer appreciative of the beauty or artistic value of such a cloth might purchase it for pride in ownership.

## MINOR NATURAL FIBERS

### RAMIE

Ramie, or rhea, is a bast fiber that has often been sold as a substitute for flax. The fiber comes from within the upright five- to six-foot stems of a nettle-like East Indian shrub. It is also produced in Europe, China and Egypt.

The first ramie plants were brought to the United States in 1855. Ramie grows best in a semitropical climate with abundant rainfall. The stems must be cut at maturity, because immature plants yield coarse, brittle fibers. The plants send up a new growth after each cutting. Hence three to five crops a year are possible.

Research on ramie by the U.S. Department of Agriculture has led to the growth of ramie in Florida. E. B. Elliot, president of his own out-door advertising firm, is credited, on the basis of his personally financed research, with finding a method of recovering and refining ramie fibers on a large commercial scale. Experimental plantings of ramie in Savannah and New Brunswick, Georgia, southern Mississippi, Louisiana, Alabama, and Texas augured success. But it has not been possible for promoters to develop a process commercially.

The fiber ranges from $2\frac{1}{2}$ to 18 inches in length, and from .002 to .003 inch in diameter (finer than flax); and it is very strong. One authority states that ramie is seven times stronger than wool and twice as strong as flax. Ramie is claimed to be stronger than flax when wet. Its smooth, lustrous appearance seems to improve with washing. Ramie fabrics keep their shape and do not shrink. They resist mildew, absorb more moisture than linen, and dry quickly. They dye easily, but fibers are brittle and have low twisting and bending strength. In the United States, processors experienced difficulty in spinning methods. Ramie is spun here on the worsted system; but to do so, fibers must be cut into staple lengths. The shortened fibers produce coarser fabrics. Finer fabrics would require the use of the full, lengthy ramie fibers. The countries of Europe find it practical to spin ramie on the silk system. By so doing, the whole length of fiber can be used.

Our present use of ramie is for shirts, suitings, automobile seat covers, and industrial fabrics. It is also blended with wool and rayon in carpets.

## JUTE

Jute is a bast fiber that comes chiefly from India, because the plant grows well in rich land, especially along tidal basins. India, through improved methods, financial aid, and greater acreage, has increased its production. There has been some attempt to raise jute along the Gulf of Mexico, but the cost of labor has been too high to warrant its cultivation.

The jute plant grows to a height of about twelve feet. It is cut off close to the ground when it is in flower. Like flax, it is stripped of its branches and leaves and put through a retting process to loosen the fibers from the stalk. After they are separated from the outer bark, the fibers are dried and cleaned.

Jute fibers are weaker than those of linen. The fibers are very short, but lustrous and smooth. Because jute is affected by chemical bleaches, it can never be made pure white. It is not very durable and is very much weakened by dampness. Like cotton, it is attacked by sunlight. Since alkalies used in the laundry weaken jute, neutral soaps containing no free alkali should be used. Jute can be distinguished from linen or cotton if the fibers are stained with iodine and then concentrated sulfuric acid and glycerin are applied. Jute fibers remain yellow; cotton and linen turn blue.

Jute is used chiefly for gunny sacks, burlap bags, cordage, and binding and backing threads for rugs and carpets. One company [9] finishes burlap with a flame-resistant finish for uses on walls of bowling alleys and night clubs with modern décor. The company also makes a rotproof finish that permits nurserymen to bury shrubs wrapped in burlap in the soil.

## HEMP

It was explained in Chapter 2 that hemp is grown in the Philippines, Mexico, Central America, the West Indies, and India. The Manila variety is white; the outer fiber is used for cordage and the inner fibers can be woven into webbing and gauzes. The Central American variety is not so strong as Manila hemp and is used mainly in cordage. The Indian product is not so strong as the Central American and Manila varieties, but it can be used in cables and canvas. Hemp is stronger than flax, jute, or cotton. It is dark brown in color and cannot be bleached without an appreciable loss of strength. It is less elastic and harsher than linen, and so cannot be used extensively in woven cloth.

Hemp fiber has the microscopic nodes and joints of linen, but the central canal is wider. If the same test (sulfuric acid, iodine, glycerin) is applied to hemp, jute, linen, and cotton, hemp turns bluish green, jute yellow, and cotton and linen blue.

## SUMMARY

Linen is a competitor of cotton for household use and apparel. But although it may be suited to almost as many uses as cotton, the cost of producing and manufacturing linen keeps the price of good, durable qualities higher than that of comparable qualities of cotton. Now that a chemical treatment has been found to increase the elasticity of linen, the consumer is more likely to use linen for dresses and outer garments.

It is highly improbable that the United States will ever be able to compete with Ireland in the production of fine linen fabrics. Since we have to import most of our linen, the cost will doubtless exceed cotton. Although the initial investment in a linen article is high, its beauty and durability make the purchase less costly in the long run.

[9] Jonell Corporation, Bridgeton, R.I.

Other minor vegetable fibers similar to flax are ramie, jute, hemp, and sisal.

## REVIEW QUESTIONS

1. What are the chief physical and chemical characteristics of linen fibers?
2. Compare each of the above characteristics with the corresponding characteristic of cotton.
3. Describe flax production and culture.
4. (*a*) What are the different methods of retting flax?
   (*b*) Give the advantages of each method.
5. (*a*) How are linen yarns made?
   (*b*) How does this method differ from that for making cotton yarns?
6. (*a*) What care must be taken in laundering linen?
   (*b*) Why does linen require more care in bleaching than cotton?
7. Why does sentiment seem to be an important reason for buying linen?
8. What is the law on labeling textile fiber products made of linen?
9. Write a label for a fabric that contains 20 per cent cotton, 15 per cent rayon, 65 per cent linen.
10. Does linen mildew?
11. (*a*) Why is linen suitable for glass and dish towels?
    (*b*) Why is linen suitable for table coverings?
12. From your knowledge of production and manufacturing of ramie, what would you consider to be the future of ramie in the United States?
13. (*a*) For what purpose is jute used?
    (*b*) What are the advantages of hemp for use in cordage?

## EXPERIMENTS

1. *Alkali test.* Use the procedure outlined for cotton, Chapter 9.
2. *Acid test.* Use the procedure outlined for cotton, Chapter 9.
3. *Microscopic test.*
   (*a*) Unravel linen fibers and look at them through the microscope. Draw and describe their microscopic appearance.
   (*b*) Perform the same experiment on jute, hemp, and ramie. Describe the results of your tests.
4. *Test to determine the durability of yarns.*
   (*a*) Use yarns from three linen and two cotton fabrics.
   (*b*) Untwist each yarn and note:
      (1) Whether yarn is linen or cotton.
      (2) Amount of twist.
      (3) Evenness of yarn.
      (4) Construction (single or ply).
      (5) Amount of hackling or of combing.
      (6) Length of fibers.
   (*c*) Judging from the above factors, is the yarn durable?
5. Determine the construction and count of the fabric.
6. List the finishes applied to the fabric.

**Art linen.**   An ecru, white, or unbleached linen fabric in plain weave. It is used for embroidery, dresses, uniforms, and table linens.

**Bast fiber.**   Fibers between the pithy center of the stem and the skin. Flax, jute, hemp, and ramie are bast fibers.

**Beetle finish.**   See *Beetling*, Glossary, Chapter 7.

**Bouclé yarn.**   Linen yarn often plied with yarns of other fibers for textural interest. See Glossary, Chapter 3.

**Butcher linen.**   A variety of plain woven crash originally used for butchers' aprons. All-rayon or rayon and acetate blend in crash is often erroneously called butcher linen.

**Crash.**   A coarse linen fabric made of thick, uneven yarns and having a rough, irregular surface. It may also be cotton, spun rayon, or blends. It is used for dresses, draperies, and table linens.

**Damask.**   A glossy linen, cotton, rayon, silk, or mixed fabric. Patterns are flat and reversible. Linen and cotton damask are used for table coverings.

**Dress linen.**   See *Crash*.

**Embroidery linen.**   See *Art linen*.

**Flax.**   Fibers of the flax plant, which are spun into linen yarns and woven into linen cloth.

**Friction towel.**   A terry cloth made with linen pile. It may be made into a mitt used to develop friction after bathing.

**Grass bleaching.**   Whitening fabrics by laying them on the grass in the sun.

**Hackling.**   A process that prepares the flax fibers for spinning by laying them parallel. It may be done by hand or by machine and corresponds to the carding and combing of cottons.

**Handkerchief linen.**   A well-hackled sheer linen fabric in plain weave that is used for handkerchiefs, blouses, summer dresses. It is synonymous with *lawn*.

**Hemp.**   A plant grown in the Philippines, Mexico, Central America, the West Indies, and India. Outer fibers are used for cordage, inner fibers for cables and canvas.

**Huck or huckaback.**   A honeycombed dobby face towel. It may be linen or cotton or mixtures with rayon.

**Irish linen.**   Linen products that come from Ireland, mainly Belfast in Northern Ireland.

**Jute.**   A bast fiber, chiefly from India, used mostly for gunny sacks, bags, cordage, and binding threads of rugs and carpets.

**Lawn.**   A light, well-hackled linen fabric first made in Laon, France. Linen lawn is synonymous with handkerchief linen. Cotton lawn is a similar type of fabric. It can be white, solid colored, or printed.

**Line.**   Longest flax fibers, used for fine, even linen yarns. Shortest flax fibers are called *tow*.

**Linen.**   A vegetable fiber obtained from the inside of the woody stalk of the flax plant.

**Moygashel.**   A trade name representing excellent quality in imported Irish linen.

**Ramie or rhea.**   A bast fiber from a nettle-like East Indian shrub, also produced in China, Egypt, and the United States. It is used for shirts, suitings, automobile seat covers, table covers, and, in blends with wool, for carpets.

**Retting.** A process for loosening the flax fiber from the outside woody stalk. This may be done by several methods: pool, dew, tank, and chemical.

**Rippling.** Threshing of flax to strip the seeds or bolls from the plant. This process may be done by hand or by machine.

**Roving frame.** A machine that puts a loose twist in the drawn-out sliver.

**Scutching.** Removing the flax fibers from the woody stalk by a series of fluted rollers.

**Sisal.** A variety of hemp grown chiefly in Kenya, East Africa. It is used primarily for cordage but may also be used for millinery.

**Spinning.** The operation of putting the twist into linen yarn.

**Spread board.** A machine that lays wisps of flax fibers parallel on traveling bands in continuous lines, with the ends of the wisps overlapping.

**Spun linen.** Finest hand-woven linen fabric, used for handkerchiefs, women's collars, and so on.

**Suiting.** A heavy, fairly coarse linen fabric in plain, twill, or herringbone weaves, used for women's and men's suitings. It is also made in cotton, spun rayon, or acetate.

**Tow.** Short flax fibers, separated by hackling (combing) from the longer fibers.

**Tow linen.** Fabric made of uneven, irregular yarns composed of the very short fibers.

# 11

# Silk
# and the Consumer

"I read in Chapter 9 that silk is only a nominal percentage of the world's total fiber production. Will silk ever again be as important to the consumer as it was before World War II?" asks a college student in a class in textiles. To be sure, because of the war, silk production fell 75 per cent during the years 1939–1946. While silk was off the market, rayon and nylon took its place for many uses, notably nylon for hosiery and rayon for apparel.

The answer to the student's question is a qualified yes. The customer demand for silk has increased and is increasing, but price and its natural limitations will prevent silk from becoming a major natural fiber in terms of volume. Consumers like it because it is beautiful, warm, and lightweight. It is absorbent and has excellent affinity for dyes. In the consumer's mind it is a textile fiber for fabrics of high quality. Whereas silk dries rapidly, it requires a washable and stain-resistant finish to compete with the wash-and-wear fabrics. These finishes are being developed. Basic research and aggressive sales promotion programs (to compete with the man-made fibers) are needed to bring the favorable qualities of silk to the attention of the public. Then, if consumers are looking for fabrics with esthetic and luxurious qualities, silk's market may increase appreciably.

Silk was used by the ancients. History records the Chinese as the first people who knew how to raise and manufacture it. About 1725 B.C. silk culture, sponsored by the wife of the Emperor, was begun in China. Until the time of the Chinese People's Republic of 1958, the Chinese Empress paid homage to the "Goddess of the Silkworms" on a special day each year by feeding the insects.

About 1765 B.C. the mulberry tree was cultivated to provide food for the silkworm. The secret of the cultivation of these worms and of the manufacture of their fibers into cloth was carefully guarded for about 3,000 years. Eventually, according to one story, two monks sent to China by the Byzantine Emperor Justinian stole mulberry seeds and silkworms' eggs. At the risk of their lives, they brought them back to Byzantium in their walking staffs. From these monks, Justinian learned of the Chinese sericulture. From this knowledge a large silk industry grew up in the Byzantine Empire. Rich fabrics woven of silk on imperial looms are still in existence there.

With the rise and spread of Islam, silk culture spread to Sicily and Spain with the Moslem conquests. After the Moslems withdrew from conquered soil, the art of silk weaving remained.

By the twelfth and thirteenth centuries A.D., Italy had become the silk center of the West. The art of weaving ecclesiastical and ducal silk fabrics was unexcelled. For over 500 years Italy was the leader in silk production. But by the seventeenth century, the French city of Lyons was vying with Italy for excellence and beauty in weaving silk.[1]

Parts of Japan had been raising silkworms as early as A.D. 300, when the Japanese had learned the secret of sericulture from four Chinese girls they had kidnapped. Still later, India learned this secret when a Chinese princess came to India to marry an Indian prince.[2]

England began to manufacture silk in the sixteenth century, when Flemish weavers fled to England from the Low Countries. In the seventeenth century Huguenot weavers settled in the vicinity of Spitalfields. The English climate was not suitable for sericulture, but silk weaving was extensive.

England showed interest in the silk industry and sponsored its introduction to the American Colonies about 1732. The Colonial government allotted grants to Georgian settlers on condition that they plant one hundred mulberry trees on every ten acres. Carolina also raised silk. In the eighteenth century Connecticut became the most important silk-raising section. The first silk mill in America was built in 1810 at Mans-

---

[1] *Silk,* a pamphlet of the International Silk Association (U.S.A.).

[2] *The History of Silk and Sericulture,* a pamphlet by John Kent Tilton, formerly Director, The Scalamandré Museum of Textiles, p. 4.

field, Connecticut. Pennsylvania followed, and in 1838 New Jersey set up a silk mill in Paterson.

The cost of the labor needed for silk cultivation has done much to exclude the United States from importance as a *silk-raising* country. While the United States is not important in silk production, it is the largest importer of raw silk. Today some of the most beautiful silk fabrics in the world are woven on American looms.

## LIFE OF THE SILKWORM

Silk is an animal fiber. It is the product of the silkworm, of which there are two varieties: the wild and the cultivated. The fibers of the wild silkworm are yellowish brown, instead of yellow to gray, and have a coarse, hard texture. This worm feeds on the scrub oak instead of the mulberry leaf. It grows in India, China, and Japan.

The cultivated silkworm requires a great deal of care. Quiet and sanitation are necessary. A whole scientific industry, that of raising mulberry trees for food for the worms, has grown up. The best mulberry leaves seem to come from plants that are the result of a combination of the tall mulberry tree and the dwarf or shrub mulberry tree.

Silkworms live a very short time—only about two months. During that period they pass through four stages of development: (1) egg, (2) worm, (3) chrysalis (pupa) or cocoon, and (4) moth. (See Figure 11.3.)

**Figure 11.1.** When the silkworms are ready to spin their cocoons, the farmers put them in a "mabushi," or bed of straw. In three days the worms will have spun their cocoons, which are then ready to be treated in the next stage of silk-making. The beds shown here are old-fashioned, but they are used by 20 per cent of the Japanese silkworm-farming households. (*Photograph courtesy of the International Silk Association, U.S.A., Inc.*)

Figure 11.2. An up-to-date "apartment house" for cocoons. Separate living quarters ensure a finer gloss and more uniformity in the finished silk. (*Photographs courtesy of the International Silk Association, U.S.A., Inc.*)

Eggs that have been kept in cold storage for approximately six weeks after they were laid are bathed in warm water and dried in the air. Then they are placed in incubators, where they remain until all are hatched (about thirty days).

A tiny white worm about one-quarter inch long is hatched from each egg. These worms are very delicate and require the utmost care. They are placed on bamboo trays covered with straw mats on which selected mulberry leaves are laid. The worms are very greedy; it is estimated that each worm eats about 30,000 times its initial weight. During this stage the silkworm molts (sheds its skin) four times. At the end of about thirty days the worm ceases to eat, attaches itself to a piece of straw, and begins to spin its cocoon.

Two filaments are ejected from the mouth—one an almost invisible silk filament and the other a glutinous substance. The filaments merge and harden when exposed to the air. The worm covers itself with these filaments, completing the cocoon in about three days. The worm is then transformed into moth in about eight days. One manufacturer estimates that 2,500 to 3,000 cocoons are necessary to make one yard of silk fabric. The color of the cocoon is either white or yellow, depending on the species. The color is not dependent on its feeding, and there is no difference in the quality of silk produced. However, the white cocoon silk does not have to be bleached.

If the moth is permitted to emerge from the cocoon, the silk filament is broken into many short pieces. Therefore the chrysalis (unless it is selected for breeding) is steamed or subjected to hot air to kill the larvae inside the cocoon. Long thin fibers can be reeled from the unpierced cocoons.

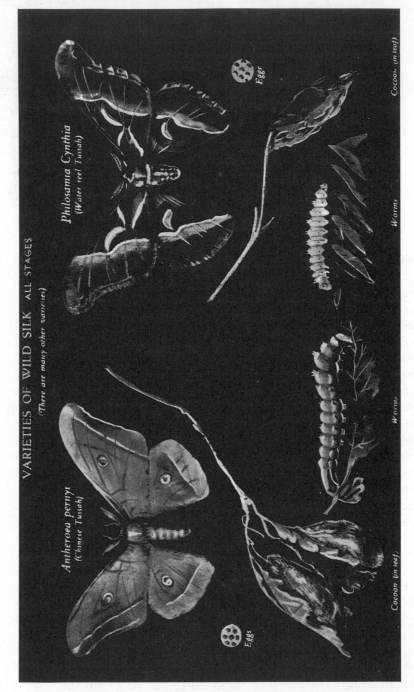

VARIETIES OF WILD SILK ALL STAGES
(There are many other varieties)

Philosamia Cynthia
(Water reel Tussah)

Eggs

Cocoon (in leaf)

Worms

Worms

Antheroea pernyi
(Chinese Tussah)

Eggs

Cocoon (in leaf)

**Figure 11.3.** Varieties of wild and cultivated silks. (Reproduced courtesy of Cheyney Brothers, Inc.)

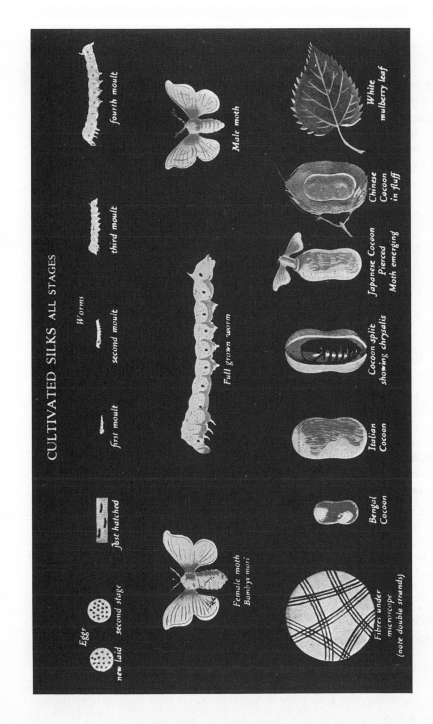

CULTIVATED SILKS ALL STAGES

Eggs
new laid    second stage

Just hatched

Worms
first moult    second moult    third moult    fourth moult

Full grown worm

Female moth
Bombyx mori

Male moth

White mulberry leaf

Bengal Cocoon

Italian Cocoon

Cocoon split showing chrysalis

Japanese Cocoon Pierced Moth emerging

Chinese Cocoon in fluff

Fibres under microscope (note double strands)

**Figure 11.3.** (Cont.)

283

The moths that are reserved for breeding purposes emerge from cocoons creamy white. Three days after they have hatched, they mate, lay eggs, and die. Their cycle of life is complete.

### SORTING

Cocoons most suitable for propagation of the species are separated from those to be used for weaving. For propagation, it has been found that cocoons with a "waist" are preferable. Elliptical or nearly round cocoons are used for reeling into yarn. The former type is sorted by sex. Cocoons pass along a belt that allows the heavier ones (males) to drop down into a container and the lighter cocoons (females) to continue on the belt.

### REELING

The unpierced cocoons, whose larvae have been killed, are used for reeling. Cocoons are aired to dry the dead chrysalis. Then they are put in basins of hot water, to melt the gum, or sericin. Dexterous fingers must find the end of the silk filament that will unwind (reel). Filaments from five or six cocoons are reeled and twisted together into a strand finer than a human hair. Next, six to eight of these strands are attached to revolving reels that twist them into a stronger yarn. The resultant yarn is the product of thirty to forty-eight cocoons. This yarn is now ready for winding into skeins and packing into bales. In this condition the thread is too thin and weak to be used without further twisting (*throwing*) and doubling into strands of varying thicknesses. Throwing increases the strength of a yarn. However, a silk thread need not necessarily be thrown to make a yarn for weaving, thus differing from wool and cotton, which must be spun and twisted.[3]

Yarns made of reeled-silk threads twisted together are called *thrown silk*. These yarns are wound on spools or in skeins, ready for the weavers. To facilitate handling, oils may be added to the gum weight by the throwster. Up to this point, silk is lusterless and harsh to the touch. This is because the gum is still in it. Silk in the gum is called *raw silk*. To make it soft and lustrous, it is boiled in soap and water until the gum is removed.

### CHARACTERISTICS OF THE SILK FIBER
#### MICROSCOPIC APPEARANCE

Under the microscope, cultivated silk fibers in the gum appear rough, like sticks of wood. Sometimes two fibers are held together by silk gum. After degumming, the fibers are structureless, transparent, and rodlike.

[3] *What Is Silk?*, a pamphlet of the International Silk Association.

The unevenness in diameter of the fibers distinguishes them from rayon. (See the Appendix.) Wild-silk fibers are very irregular and resemble flattened, wavy ribbons with fine lines running lengthwise.

## LENGTH

The silk fiber ranges from 800 to 1,300 yards in length. This characteristic—great length—aids the manufacturer because he can easily combine a number of the filaments, which require little twist to give them strength. Also, long fibers make more lustrous yarns than do short fibers.

## DIAMETER

It is estimated that the diameter of silk fibers ranges from .00059 to .00118 inch. Longer fibers can be spun into finer yarns, and the resultant fabrics are sheer. Furthermore, many fibers can be combined in a fine yarn. The silkworm's fiber varies in diameter throughout its length, but the combination of several fibers to form a yarn equalizes the natural unevenness of the individual fibers.

## COLOR OF FIBER

Cultivated silks are yellow to grayish white in color. The color of the wild-silk fiber is usually yellowish brown. The brown color is in the fiber itself, but the color of cultivated varieties is in the gum and so can be removed by washing.

## LUSTER

Silk in the gum does not possess high luster, but after the gum has been removed silk has a soft, fine luster. This fact is important in the manufacture of satins, the beauty of which lies in unbroken sheen. Yarns of long reeled-silk fibers lie flat, lengthwise on the right side of the cloth, with only occasional interlacing with the filling or crosswise yarns.

## STRENGTH

Silk is one of the strongest of the textile fibers—that is, of fibers of the same diameter. Silk is often compared with iron wire of the same diameter. Although it has only about one third the strength of good-quality iron wire, these fine fibers are very strong. Silk is weaker when wet than when dry, but, like rayon, its original strength returns when it dries.

A silk fiber can sustain a dead weight of five to twenty-eight grams before breaking. One silk filament is so strong that it will support the weight of a cocoon. However, hosiery made of silk snags if it is given a sudden, sharp pull. But silk will withstand even pulling better than it will a sudden, severe strain.

### ELASTICITY

Silk is very elastic—more so than linen, rayon, or cotton. In fact, silk will stretch one-seventh to one-fifth of its length before breaking. Rayon and others of the synthetics will elongate, but they may not return to their original length. Therefore silk weavers prefer all-silk warp yarn to a synthetic warp in Jacquard weaving (see pp. 117 ff.), for in this weave warp yarns are subjected to stretching due to the pull exerted on the yarn. Silk, then, is resilient (elastic); synthetics elongate. Silk's elasticity means that no loose threads will be evident on the finished fabric. One of the first questions a silk weaver asks the synthetic yarn manufacturer is, "How much will the synthetic yarn elongate?" On the basis of elongation a silk weaver can determine whether he can use the synthetic for warps. Garments made of silk keep their shape and do not wrinkle badly.

### HYGROSCOPIC MOISTURE

Silk absorbs about 10 per cent of moisture. It has a higher average for absorptive quality than cotton, linen, or rayon. The strange and important fact is that silk can absorb a great deal of moisture and still feel comparatively dry. Silk absorbs perspiration and oil from the skin, but it sheds dirt easily.

### COMPOSITION

The chief constituents of silk are fibroin, the silk fiber, and sericin, the silk gum. Cultivated silk also contains small percentages of fats, waxes or resins, and mineral matter. The chemical constituents of fibroin are carbon (48.3 per cent), hydrogen (6.5 per cent), nitrogen (19.2 per cent, and oxygen (26.0 per cent).[4]

### EFFECT OF LIGHT

Laboratory tests show that silk is not so resistant as cotton to strong light. And yet, when damask draperies made of a combination of silk and cotton were removed from the White House in 1953, the silk was in about the same stage of deterioration as the cottons. In this instance, silk and cotton had about the same degree of resistance to light. Heavily weighted silks are less resistant to light than pure silks.

[4] George H. Johnson, *Textile Fabrics* (New York: Harper and Row, 1927), p. 64.

Mildew is seldom found on silk. It is relatively resistant to other bacteria and fungi. Rot-producing conditions will decompose silk.

### EFFECT OF HEAT

White silks turn yellow after fifteen minutes in an oven at 231° F. Cottons would not be affected at this temperature. Silk fabrics may turn yellow with the use of too hot an iron. Silk scorches if heat exceeds 300° F. This factor is important to the tailor who uses a steam press.

### EFFECT OF ACIDS

Acids, such as sulfuric, hydrochloric, and nitric, do not injure silks if they are dilute. Silk is more resistant to acids than are the vegetable fibers, but concentrated acids destroy silk if it is soaked in them or if the acids are allowed to remain on the silk any length of time.

Formic acid and acetic acid (found in vinegar) have no injurious effect on silks. Oxalic, tartaric, and citric acids are not injurious if they are removed promptly.

### EFFECT OF ALKALIES

Concentrated solutions of alkali, such as caustic soda or caustic potash, dissolve silks if the solutions are hot.

Weak alkalies, such as ammonia, phosphate of soda, borax, and soap, attack silk more quickly than they attack cotton or linen. It is therefore advisable to use a neutral soap with no free alkalies for washing fine silk fabrics.

### ACTION OF BLEACHES

Chlorine or hypochlorites are not used on silk, because of their deteriorating effect. Hydrogen peroxide and perborate bleaches are used when silk requires bleaching. Care should be taken to control bleaching conditions. Many popular-priced printed silks develop holes because acid bleaches are too strong.

### AFFINITY FOR METALLIC SALTS

As previously stated, silk has a great affinity for metallic salts; this characteristic is utilized in weighting silks. Silks are weighted either in the yarn or in the piece—that is, after the fabric has been woven. There is more danger to the wearing qualities of the fabric if it is weighted in the piece, for the following reason: The usual specifications for the weighting of yarn require sixteen ounces of weighting for warp (enough to replace the gum lost), and twenty-two ounces for filling ($37\frac{1}{2}$ per cent of the weight of the raw silk in addition to the weight required to replace the gum). There can be no such discrimination in weighting if the whole fabric is immersed. If the whole fabric is weighted equally, the warp and filling carry equal loading; and if the amount of weighting is correct for the filling, it is too great for a durable warp. (For a discussion of silk weighting, see p. 290.)

At the present time, weighting appears in some men's silk neckties and in some silk taffetas. Some of our weighted silk is imported from Europe.

## AFFINITY FOR DYESTUFFS

Silk has a natural affinity for dye. Probably the chief reason is that silk fiber has good penetrability. Basic, acid, and direct dyestuffs are all used on silks. (For a description of these dyestuffs, see Chapter 8.) Cotton and linen do not have so good an affinity for dye as silk. Rayon has a good affinity for dye. Acetate requires the use of special dyestuffs.

## KINDS OF SILK YARNS

### REELED SILK

*Thrown silk* is a single yarn made of several strands of reeled silk twisted together.

*Organzine* is a ply yarn of the type that must be made if yarns are to be used for warp where strength is required, as in upholstery, drapery fabric, or sheeting. The twist of the ply is in the reverse direction to that of the singles, in order to give additional strength and hold in the twist. Organzine is the center section of the yardage reeled from the cocoon (500 to 1,000 yards).

*Tram* is also made for fabrics requiring tensile strength. It, too, is a ply yarn, but the twist of the singles and the final twist are in the same direction. This yarn has a higher luster because it has a slacker final twist than the organzine (about two and one-half turns to the inch for tram and four and one-half turns for organzine). Generally, tram is used for filling yarns and organzine for warp, although this is not always the case.

*Douppion* is derived from the Italian word *doppione,* meaning double. Two silkworms (regardless of sex) have an affinity for each other and want to stay together, so together they spin one cocoon. It is difficult to reel filaments evenly from these cocoons, so that a knotted yarn results. This textured yarn is particularly suited to fabrics such as shantung and some of the contemporary draperies and upholsteries. Douppion can also be made into spun-silk yarns.

*Tussah* is wild silk reeled from cocoons of uncultivated worms that have fed on oak leaves. These rough, yellowish brown fibers are made in tussah silk yarns.

## SPUN SILK

Before silk can be reeled from the cocoon, long, tangled ends must be removed so that an end can be found with which to start the reeling process. The tangled ends, called *floss,* are put aside because they cannot be reeled. Likewise, when most of the fiber has been reeled from a cocoon, there may be short lengths. Only about half of the silk of a cocoon is fit to be reeled, but the rest cannot be wasted; it is made into spun silk. All floss and silk from pierced and defective cocoons appear in spun-silk yarns. Spun silk requires more twisting than reeled silk, to hold in all the short fibers. Twisting decreases luster, so that spun silk appears less lustrous than reeled silk. It also has less tensile strength, less elasticity, and a rather linty, cottony feeling.

Spun silk is less expensive than reeled silk and is suitable for the cross-wise or filling threads in a cloth. These threads do not have to be so strong as warp yarns. Plush, velvet, satin, lace, flat crepe, and silk broadcloth may have spun-silk yarns. Upholstery materials, knitted ties, sweaters, outerwear, scarfs, underwear, and hosiery use mixtures of spun silk and other fibers.

The silk to be used for this purpose is scoured, the gum is boiled off, and the fibers are dried. Then the fibers are combed in order to separate and straighten them and make them lie parallel. The filmy sheets of fibers are then drawn out between rollers, several times. A slight twist is put in—called *roving.* A spinning frame, which winds and rewinds the yarn on spindles, puts in the twist. A tighter twist than that used for thrown silk is necessary.

## NOIL SILK

In the processing of spun-silk yarn, there is a certain amount of waste called *silk noil.* According to the F.T.C. Trade Practice Rules for the Silk Industry, such waste shall be labeled "silk noil," "noil silk," "silk waste," or "waste silk." Silk noil is used extensively for powder bags in artillery units. It can also be used in modern textured draperies and upholstery. Noil silk is dull, rough, and lifeless.

## IDENTIFICATION OF SPUN, REELED, AND NOIL SILK

Long fibers of reeled silk lie parallel and are only slackly twisted together. The yarns are lustrous, and the fibers shred apart. If the fibers are short and of uneven length, generally in dull yarns, the yarns are spun silk. If the yarns are coarse and very dull, and if the fibers are very short and very uneven, the yarns are noil silk.

Chiffon crepes look dull and sometimes cottony, but that does not necessarily mean that the yarns are of spun silk; rather, the tightness of the twist—made tight to produce fine crepe—has decreased the luster.

### SILK WEIGHTING

When yarns are prepared for weaving, the skeins of yarn are boiled in a soap solution to remove the natural silk gum, or sericin. The silk may lose 20 to 30 per cent of its original weight as a result of boiling. Since silk has a great affinity for metallic salts such as those of tin and iron, the lost weight is replaced through the absorption of metals. Tannin may also be used as weighting material.

Thus a heavier fabric can be made. Heavily weighted silk may not wear as long as pure unweighted silk, because sunlight and perspiration weaken or destroy the fibers. Furthermore, heavy weighting causes silk to crack. The long treatment of silk in the weighting process may also have a weakening effect on the fibers. Silks can be weighted only about 1 per cent in each application of weighting, which makes the process costly. There is very little weighting done in the United States.

The burning test may be used to identify pure and weighted silk. If the yarns char but do not burn, they are weighted; if they burn slowly and leave a residue in the form of a gummy ball, they are pure silk.

According to the F.T.C. rules, a weighted silk must be marked "weighted," with the amount of weighting indicated. A variation of five points from the stated percentage is tolerated to allow for unavoidable variations in processing, but not to allow for a lack of "reasonable effort to state the percentage or proportion accurately." For example, a weighted silk label may appear as "Silk, weighted 5 per cent" or "Silk (weighted 25 per cent) and rayon."

The percentage of weighting may be disclosed as not over a certain percentage or as ranging from a certain minimum to a maximum figure.

### PURE SILK

Silk containing no metallic weighting may be called "pure silk," according to the F.T.C. rules. The terms "all silk" or "pure dye silk" may also be used for fabrics whose fiber content is silk exclusively, with no metallic weighting. The rules for labeling and advertising as specified under the Textile Fiber Products Identification Act are required for silk textile fiber products. (See Chapters 2 and 10.) The F.T.C. rules allow the finisher or the dyer to use special finishing materials, other than metallic weighting, that will make the fabric more useful—water-repellent finishes, for instance. The maximum percentage of the finishes present must be disclosed if such special finishing materials exceed 10 per cent on colored fabrics and 15 per cent on blacks.

Sizes or counts of reeled-silk yarns, like rayon counts, are expressed in terms of denier (den'yer).[5] There are several methods of computing denier, all differing slightly from that used for rayon. The International Denier method uses 500 meters of silk yarn, weighed with a .05 gram weight. If 500 meters weigh .05 gram, the yarn is #1 denier. If 500 meters weigh 1 gram, the denier is $1 \div .05$, or #20. The size of thrown silk yarn is also expressed as the weight (in drams) of a skein of 1,000 yards. The dram weight times 33.36 equals the size in deniers.[6]

Spun-silk sizes are computed in two ways: by the English and French systems. The English system sets 840 yards as equal to 1 pound (the same as with cotton). The yarns are designated as 20/1 or 20/2, meaning 20 single or 20 two-ply. In a pound size of 20/2 there are 840 yards times 20, or 16,800 yards. The French system uses as its base the number of 1,000-meter skeins weighing a kilogram.

## WEAVING AND KNITTING SILK FABRICS

### PLAIN WEAVE

No matter in what construction silk is used, the fabric appears attractive. In plain weave, silk apparel dress fabrics include habutai, shantung, flat crepe, crepe de Chine, taffeta, pongee, ninon, organza, chiffon, and broadcloth. For men's wear there are silk broadcloth and habutai (shirtings). In ribbed variations there are several favorites for both men and women: faille, moiré faille, grosgrain, bengaline, rep, poplin, and ottoman. (See Glossary, Chapter 16.) For home furnishings there are taffeta (pillow covers, bedspreads, and curtains), voile and ninon (glass curtains), China silk, flat crepe, and pongee (lampshades).

### TWILL WEAVE

There are not as many silk twills as there are satins or plain weaves, but the following twills are most common: silk serge, piqué, foulard, and surah. These fabrics can be used in dresses and men's ties.

### SATIN WEAVE

Probably this is the most beautiful of the basic weaves to which silk is adapted. All varieties of satin, including dress, slipper, bridal, and upholstery satins, are made in this construction. Slipper and upholstery satins may have cotton backs. Antique satin has become very popular for

---

[5] Legal denier: When the weight of 450 meters is 0.5 gram, the denier is #1.
[6] See "Tex" system, Chapter 3. Also E. R. Kaswell, *Handbook of Industrial Textiles* (New York: Wellington Sears, 1964).

draperies and upholsteries. Although this fabric is not always made of silk, some of the most beautiful and high-priced draperies are silk.

## FANCY WEAVES

Silk, because of its natural beauty, is particularly suited to the fancy constructions. Jacquards, such as brocades, damasks, and brocatelles, make luxurious draperies for formal traditional living rooms. (See Chapter 20.) Lamé and brocade make exquisite evening gowns. Small dobby designs are found in silk scarfs, linings, and men's tie fabrics. In pile construction, silk velvet, velour, and brocaded velvet are always considered luxury fabrics. Silk pile rugs are museum pieces.

In leno weave, silk marquisette is suitable for evening dresses and glass curtains.

## KNITTED CONSTRUCTION

Silk knitted jersey and bouclé are excellent fabrics for traveling because they are attractive and do not wrinkle when worn.

## FINISHES OF SILK FABRICS

Some of the regular finishes applied to silk include the usual tentering and calendering (particularly for polished surfaces), dry decating to permanently set the luster, napping of spun silk to raise the fibers, shearing when needed to cut the surface fibers, steaming to shrink and condition certain spun silks, and weighting to give body. (See pp. 159 ff., and 164).

Silk fabrics may be treated for fire resistance to comply with the Flammable Fabrics Act. They may also be given germ-resistant, moth-resistant, permanent starchless, and water-repellent finishes.

## WHY CONSUMERS BUY SILK FABRICS

### BEAUTY

No fabric is so luxurious in appearance as silk. It has a natural, deep luster that makes it an aristocrat among textiles. Compare a Louis Quinze chair covered in silk damask (woven in floral design) with a similar chair covered with wool damask in the same design. The silk covering has a regal look; wool has a utility look.

A silk dress, whether it is a shantung for sport or an organza for evening, looks dressy. Similarly, silk draperies are more luxurious than the average cotton, linen, or wool. Cotton draperies are particularly suited to informal rooms, whereas silks in varied textures are appropriate in any room except possibly the kitchen and the bathroom.

Since silk fiber has a good affinity for dye, the colors found in silks are innumerable.

Fabrics of wild silk and douppion silk appear rougher, often gummier, and less lustrous than the cultivated or mulberry silks. Crepes made with tight-twisted yarns are less lustrous than satins made with loose-twisted yarns. Spun silks are soft, but less lustrous than thrown silks.

### DURABILITY

Silk fiber is the strongest natural fiber. Consequently, silk fabrics can be made durable. If silks are pure and unweighted, they will last for years, as is evidenced by the perfect preservation of many silks worn generations ago. Overweighting weakens the tensile strength, decreases elasticity, and encourages quick deterioration from sunlight and perspiration. Weighted silks may shrink badly, lose shape, or crack in washing or cleaning; they cannot be called durable. At present, weighted dress silks are seldom found in retailers' stocks. Spun silk has a lower tensile strength and lacks the elasticity of reeled silk. It has short fibers, which, though twisted tightly, may work themselves loose and make a fuzzy, rough, uneven surface. Noil silk is inferior to reeled or spun silk, but it has textural interest when used for draperies.

### COMFORT

Silk, like other animal fibers, is warmer than rayon, cotton, or linen of comparable weights. Because silk is very absorptive, silk fabrics, when they become drenched with perspiration, do not feel so damp and clammy as do fabrics made entirely of hydrophobic fibers. Hence, underwear and blouses are appropriately made of silk.

Silks can be woven of very fine yarns in open weaves, a fact that makes silk fabrics feel cool in summer. Organza, georgette, net, and chiffon are illustrations of sheer silk fabrics. Silk is lightweight, a factor in traveling comfort.

Because of its elasticity, silk can be made up into accordion pleats that hold creases. One designer of exclusive misses' dresses who has used a pleated skirt successfully finds that by starting the skirt's fullness below the hips, by pressing each pleat individually, and by stitching the pleats properly, the creases will stay. This same designer prefers silk and natural fibers for her line because they hold their shape better. Pure silk ties also retain their shape better than rayon or acetate ties. Silk dresses are very serviceable for traveling: They can be packed in a small space; in dark colors they do not show dirt; and wrinkles in silk crepes will hang out especially well.

Silk mixes easily with rayon, adding the elasticity that rayon lacks. It also mixes with nylon and with Orlon acrylic in shantung.

## SUITABILITY

The purposes for which silks are intended determine in a large measure the methods used in their manufacture. For example, long, reeled-silk fibers are used in fine silk yard goods, such as satins, crepe satin, and ribbons. Fine sewing thread is also made of reeled silk.

Silk thread comes in more than 300 colors, so that fabrics can be matched easily. For sewing lustrous fabrics, silk thread should be chosen to match the luster of the fabric. All-silk or all-wool materials should be sewn with silk thread because silk and wool are animal fibers and so react similarly to laundering or dry cleaning. Silk threads makes smooth, flat seams. Spun silk is suitable for knit goods, such as sweaters, hosiery, and underwear; for embroidery silk, braids, bindings, laces, crochet silk, and crepes; and for the pile of plushes, velvets, and velours.

Some yarns are twisted more tightly than others, according to the type of fabric in which they are to be used. Creped yarns used crosswise of the fabric are twisted forty to eighty turns to the inch. Silk creped fabrics include, among others, flat crepe, satin crepe, chiffon, and crepe faille.

Warp yarns—those running lengthwise—should have a very slack twist, so that fibers lie on the surface of the fabric and do not break the sheen. Dress satin, satin crepe, and satin linings are made this way.

Fabrics that have rather rough, bumpy surfaces, dull luster, and a gummy feeling may be made of wild silk. Shantung and pongee are examples.

Since wild silk cannot be made a snowy white and since it is rougher than cultivated varieties, its uses are limited more to sports fabrics, underwear, and draperies. For the latter use, it is desirable to line silk with silk or cotton material, because a lined drapery hangs better. The lining should be placed next to the glass.

Pongee and shantung may also be made of douppion silk, which results when two or more worms cooperate in making a single cocoon. The fibers are very irregular and cannot be reeled in long, even filaments, but the irregularities of the fiber and resultant yarn make an interesting fabric quite suitable for modern textured draperies and for shantung. Douppion can be reeled or spun yarn.

Silk fabrics lend themselves to any style changes that may occur. At one time the mode for evening dresses may demand a firm fabric that can be tailored easily. In another season, evening dresses may have to be fluffy, ruffly creations. Silk faille, broadcloth, and shantung will suit the tailored mode, for these fabrics are dull, strongly constructed materials of plain weave. (See Chapter 4, pp. 93, 94.) Chiffon and marquisette give the soft, fluffy, feminine effect. Organza gives a bouffant effect.

Since silk fits into the mode for both tailored garments and the more feminine frills, the consumer should select the silk fabric with the purpose for which she wishes it clearly in mind. She should always consult fashion publications and advertisements of leading stores to be sure that she selects a fabric then in style.

Silk has a wide variety of uses, especially in the apparel, drapery, and upholstery fields. There is not an hour of the day when a silk dress is not appropriate. House dresses, however, are more often made of cotton, synthetics, or blends.

## SENTIMENT

Silk, like linen, is sometimes purchased for reasons of sentiment. An old silk prayer rug may be bought because of associations it brings to mind or because of its rarity. Old silk damask hangings or silk laces may be bought for similar reasons. Works of art made of silk are bought by museums, collectors, and those who appreciate rare things. A living room may be furnished chiefly in silk damasks, satins, and brocades because its owner likes the elegance and luxury that silk reflects.

## PRICE

If raw silk is selling at 6 dollars a pound and rayon yarn at 82 cents, the price—by the time the silk is processed into ply yarn, with labor costs included—may well be at least 9 dollars a pound. Such a yarn made into silk drapery damask may retail for 16 dollars a yard, whereas the 82-cent rayon yarn may make up into a fabric to sell at 9 dollars a yard—over half the price of silk. In this instance, silk damask is less than twice as expensive as the price of a pound of yarn.

Ordinarily, silks are more expensive than cottons or most rayons. But silks are less expensive if—

1. Spun silk can be used one way of the fabric; reeled silk the other way.
2. Spun silk can be used entirely, instead of thrown silk.
3. Wild silk can be used instead of mulberry silk.
4. Rayon may be used one way of the fabric and silk the other.
5. Mercerized cotton can be used one way of the fabric and silk the other.
6. Spun douppion silk may be used one or both ways of the fabric.

## S U M M A R Y

Silk, an animal fiber, is the product of two distinct varieties of silkworms: wild and cultivated. Wild silks, often called tussah silks, are gummy in feeling, dull in luster, and have rough, uneven yarns. From the cultivated silkworm's cocoon a fine, even, long fiber can be reeled.

There are several terms applying to raw or reeled silk that should be borne in mind. Raw silk is the fiber reeled in the gum from the unpierced cocoon.

Several strands of reeled silk are twisted together into a yarn called thrown silk. Two kinds of ply are made from the same yarn: a yarn for warps called organzine and a yarn for fillings called tram. Douppion silk comes from one cocoon spun by two silkworms. Yarns of douppion silk can be reeled or spun.

Spun-silk yarns are made from silk waste—the tangled fibers removed from the outside of the cocoon before the reeling; the short lengths of fibers from the inside of the cocoon; and the short fibers from the pierced cocoon. These fibers are usually twisted into yarn. They are duller in luster than reeled silk and weaker in tensile strength. Noil silk is the waste from spun-silk yarn manufacturing.

## REVIEW QUESTIONS

1. What is the effect of the degumming process on the silk yarn?
2. (a) Explain the meanings of pure silk and weighted silk.
    (b) What effect has weighting on durability, versatility, launderability, comfort, and price?
    (c) What is the F.T.C. ruling on weighted silk?
    (d) According to the T.F.P.I.A., how should an all-silk with no weighting be labeled?
3. Describe the life cycle of the cultivated silkworm.
4. What are the chief advantages of spun silk? The chief disadvantages? Its principal uses?
5. In what ways do the length and the fineness of silk fiber affect the appearance of the finished fabric?
6. (a) What are the chief characteristics of wild silk?
    (b) What are the uses of wild silk?
7. In what way does the elasticity of silk fiber affect the finished cloth?
8. (a) What is the T.F.P.I.A. regulation on labeling silk mixtures and blends?
    (b) What is the F.T.C. ruling on special finishing materials?
9. Outline instructions for laundering a pure-silk flat crepe.
10. (a) What texture in silk fabrics may become the matron with a mature figure?
    (b) What texture in silks may the young high school girl with a slender figure wear?
11. (a) What factors should be considered in determining whether or not silk yarn is durable?
    (b) How are sizes of silk yarns computed?
12. By what methods can the cost of a silk fabric be lowered?
13. Define the following: reeled silk, thrown silk, spun silk, wild silk, douppion silk, mulberry silk, weighted silk, tussah, chrysalis, noil silk, resilient silk, degummed silk, organzine, tram, raw silk.

1. Unravel silk yarns from each of five samples of silk material and place a few fibers of each under the microscope. Draw the fibers as you see them. Are the fibers mulberry silk or wild silk, silk in the gum or degummed silk? Give reasons for your answer.

2. Burn yarns from each sample. Note the speed with which each yarn burns and describe the residue. Are the yarns weighted or pure silk? Give reasons for your answer.

3. Unravel yarns from each sample. Do the fibers seem about the same length? Are they long and parallel, or are they of different lengths and not parallel? Are the yarns reeled or spun silk? Why?

4. *Alkali test.* Prepare an alkaline solution of 10 per cent sodium hydroxide. Boil a small piece of silk in this solution for five minutes. Note the results of strong alkali on silk.

5. *Acid test.* Dip a few yarns or a piece of silk in concentrated sulfuric acid for one or two minutes. Wash the residue with water and dry it on a clean blotter. Note the results of concentrated acid on silk. What is the effect of acid on an animal fiber? What is the effect of acid on a vegetable fiber?

## GLOSSARY

**Antique satin.** See Glossary, Chapter 20.

**Antique taffeta.** A taffeta often woven of douppion silk (see *Shantung*) to resemble beautiful fabrics of the eighteenth century. It may be yarn-dyed with two colors to make an iridescent effect.

**Brocatelle.** See Glossary, Chapter 20.

**Canton crepe.** A fabric heavier than crepe de Chine with a slightly ribbed crepe filling. It was originally made of silk in Canton, China. It is also made in synthetics.

**Chiffon.** An extremely sheer, airy, soft silk fabric with a soft plain or rippled finish that is used for evening dresses and scarfs. It is made also in rayon and other synthetic fibers.

**Chiffon velvet.** A lightweight, soft, usually silk fabric with a dense pile.

**Chrysalis.** The dormant silk larva within the cocoon.

**Cocoon.** A covering of silk filaments extruded by the silkworm.

**Crepe de Chine.** A very light, sheer flat crepe as now made. It was originally a pebbly, washable silk fabric, degummed after weaving.

**Cultivated silk.** Fibers from a silkworm that has had scientific care.

**Damask.** See Glossary, Chapter 10.

**Douppion.** Silk from two silkworms that have spun one cocoon together.

**Faille.** A soft, finely ribbed, glossy silk fabric. It may also be made in cotton or synthetics.

**Flat crepe.** A firm silk crepe with a soft, almost imperceptible crinkle. See *Crepe de Chine*. It may also be made of synthetic fibers.

**Floss silk.** Tangled silk waste. Floss is also a twisted silk yarn used in art needlework.

**Foulard.** A fine, soft twill-weave silk fabric, often printed—used for neckties and dresses. It may be made in mercerized cotton, rayon, acetate, or thin worsted.

**Gauze.**  A thin, sheer fabric in plain weave silk, rayon, or other synthetic. It is used for curtains and trimmings of dresses. In cotton, gauze is used for surgical dressings.

**Georgette.**  A soft, sheer, dull-textured silk fabric with a crepy surface, obtained by alternating right-hand and left-hand twisted yarns.

**Grenadine.**  A tightly twisted ply yarn composed of two or three singles. The final ply twist is in the opposite direction to the singles.

**Honan.**  The best grade of Chinese silk; a finer weave but similar to pongee.

**Lyons velvet.**  A stiff, thick pile velvet; may be silk pile and cotton or rayon back. Lyons-type velvet may be 100 per cent of synthetic fibers.

**Mousseline de soie** (*silk organdy*).  A very sheer, crisp silk fabric.

**Noil silk.**  Short fibers of waste silk produced in the manufacture of spun silk.

**Peau de soie** (*skin of silk*).  A reversible silk fabric in a variation of the satin weave with riblike fillings.

**Piqué.**  A silk, rayon, or cotton fabric with raised cords or wales. In true piqué the cords run crosswise, but most of the piqués are now made like Bedford cord with warpwise wales.

**Pongee.**  A light or medium-weight Chinese silk fabric made from wild silk.  See *Tussah.*

**Pupa.**  See *Chrysalis.*

**Pure silk.**  Silk containing no metallic weighting. It is synonymous with pure-dye silk. See *Weighted silk.*

**Raw silk.**  Reeled silk wound directly from several cocoons with only a slight twist.

**Reeling.**  The process of unwinding silk from the cocoon onto silk reels.

**Satin.**  A shiny, smooth fabric in warp satin weave. It may be made of acetate, rayon, or synthetic blends or mixtures.

**Satin brocade.**  A satin with a raised woven-in design. It resembles a fine embroidered pattern.

**Scroop.**  The rustle of crisp silk. See *Taffeta.*

**Serge.**  Twilled silk or rayon commonly used for linings. It is also made of worsted.

**Sericin.**  Silk gum extruded by the silkworm; it holds fibers together.

**Sericulture.**  See *Silk culture.*

**Shantung.**  A silk fabric with a nubby surface similar to but heavier than pongee. It was originally woven of wild silk in Shantung, China. Now made of almost any fiber, blend, or mixture.

**Silk.**  The natural fiber that a silkworm spins for its cocoon.

**Silk broadcloth.**  A soft spun-silk fabric in plain weave, used for shirts, blouses, and sports dresses.

**Silk culture.**  The care of the worm that produces silk fiber, from the egg to the moth.

**Silk illusion.**  A net similar to tulle but even finer in mesh, used primarily for bridal veils.

**Spun silk.**  Either yarn or fabric made from short silk fibers that cannot be reeled.

**Surah.**  A soft fabric, usually in a variation of a twill with a flat top wale (sometimes described as a satin-faced twill). It is used for neckties, mufflers, dresses, and blouses, is made in plaids, stripes, or prints, and is also made in synthetic fibers.

**Taffeta.**   A fine yarn-dyed, plain weave fabric (closely woven) with a crisp feel. The rustle of silk taffeta is called *scroop*. It is also made in rayon and other synthetics.

**Throwing.**   See Glossary, Chapter 3.

**Tissue taffeta.**   A crisp, lightweight taffeta.

**Tulle.**   A very soft, fine, transparent silk net used for evening dresses and veiling. It may also be made of nylon or rayon.

**Tussah silk.**   Fibers from the wild silkworm. Tussah is strong but coarse and uneven. Its tan color is difficult to bleach. Used in shantung and pongee.

**Weighted silk.**   Fabric in which metallic salts have been added in the dyeing and finishing to increase its weight and to give a heavier hand. F.T.C. ruling requires weighted silk to be marked and the amount of weighting indicated.

**Wild silk.**   See *Tussah silk.*

# 12
# Wool
# and the Consumer

## HISTORY OF WOVEN CLOTH

The herding of flocks of sheep was one of the earliest stages of man's cultural development between barbarism and civilization. In the Old Testament of the Bible, we read of sheep wandering "through all the mountains and upon every high hill." History records that in the fourth century B.C., when Alexander the Great conducted an expedition to India, he found that natives were wearing wool cloth. In A.D. 50, an Italian took sheep from Italy to Spain to be crossbred with the Spanish variety—the *merino*. In the thirteenth century, Spain was producing fine wool cloth. Later, France, Saxony, Germany, England, Austria, South America, South Africa, and New Zealand imported the Spanish merino for breeding. Beginning in 1810, Australia showed the best results in raising this variety of sheep. England was the only country that was unsuccessful; English sheep were primarily raised for mutton, and crossbreeding for the fleece-wool variety was not satisfactory. The United States imported Spanish sheep about 1810. They were first raised along the Atlantic seaboard. Later, sheep raising spread westward. In the Ohio Valley the merinos were crossbred with native sheep, with good results.

The wool produced is called Ohio Delaine, and the fibers are the best quality of merino wools produced in this country.

## KINDS OF WOOL

There are three main classes of wools in the United States, depending on the region from which they come: (1) *domestic* wools, from the Eastern and Middle Western states; (2) *territory* wools, from the Rocky Mountain Plateau states; (3) *southwestern* wools, from Texas, New Mexico, Arizona, and Southern California.

The domestic wools are softer and finer than the territory wools. The southwestern states mentioned are great sheep-raising states but, since they usually shear their sheep twice a year, their wools are not classified as domestic or territory wools, which are usually clipped once a year. Texas wools have become finer and are more nearly like the merino.

Merino wools come from Australia, South Africa, and South America. The best come from Australia (the world's largest wool producer), because better care is given the sheep there than in other places. The Australians use what is known as the *paddock system*, where the sheep are allowed to graze in large enclosed areas called paddocks.

## CONCENTRATION OF WORLD WOOL PRODUCTION, 1967 *

| Country | Estimated Number of Head (in millions) | Percentage of Total Production |
|---|---|---|
| BRITISH COMMONWEALTH | | 32.7 |
| Australia | 164.4 | |
| New Zealand | 60.0 | |
| United Kingdom | 29.0 | |
| Others | 55.6 | |
| Total | 309.0 | |
| SINO-SOVIET BLOC | | 25.6 |
| Soviet Union | 135.5 | |
| China | 58.0 | |
| Others | 48.5 | |
| Total | 242.0 | |
| OTHER COUNTRIES | | 41.7 |
| Argentina | 48.7 | |
| South Africa | 36.8 | |
| Turkey | 34.7 | |
| Asia (excluding those countries separately listed) | 31.6 | |
| United States | 23.9 | |
| Iran | 22.4 | |
| Fifteen other countries | 195.9 | |
| Total | 394.0 | |
| Grand Total | 945.0 | |

* It will be noted that the British Commonwealth produces about one third of the world's wool, and that Australia leads all countries, with the Soviet Union second and New Zealand third. Data are from the *World Wool Digest*, Vol. XIX, No. 13 (June 20, 1968).

Merino wool has shorter fibers than wool from native English sheep.
Lincolnshire and Leicestershire raised the longest wool fiber. Carpet or
braid wools are very coarse; they come from Turkey and Argentina.

After having remained virtually static for five consecutive seasons,
world sheep numbers advanced 2 per cent, or some 14 million head,
during 1966/67, to about 945 million head.

Of all countries, the United States is the third largest consumer of
wool.

## ESTIMATED WORLD CONSUMPTION OF VIRGIN WOOL, 1967
(Million lb. clean basis)

| COUNTRY | MILLION LB. |
|---|---|
| United Kingdom | 359.9 |
| Japan | 354.0 |
| United States | 303.3 |
| Italy | 218.3 |
| France | 216.6 |
| West Germany | 122.5 |
| Belgium | 80.7 |
| Australia | 75.7 |
| Sino-Soviet Bloc * | 834.0 |
| Other Countries * | 1,960.6 |
| Total | 3,225.6 |

* Estimated. All the other figures are based on complete consumption data. (From *World
Wool Digest,* June 20, 1968.)

Boston is the largest wool port in this country, and, along with Philadelphia and New York, is a big wool marketing center. Since we cannot
supply enough wool to meet domestic demands, we must import large
quantities from abroad. In fact, all our carpet wool is imported.

### SHEEPSHEARING

Most sheep are shorn in the spring in the northern hemisphere, and
in our fall in the southern hemisphere. Formerly wool was clipped from
the sheep's body by hand, but now as many as two hundred sheep can
be clipped in one day by machinery. In the United States, the fleeces
clipped from sheep are usually all one piece. In Australia, separate fleeces
are taken from the same animal—that is, fleece from the belly is kept
separate from fleece from the sides. The Australian method is the better,
because different grades of wool come from the same sheep. The fleece
of the head, belly, and breech is inferior to fleece from the shoulders and
sides of the sheep.

### FLEECE WOOL VERSUS PULLED WOOL

The wool shorn from the live sheep is termed *fleece wool*. Some sheep
die from disease or are slaughtered. Their skins are wetted, treated with

lime paste, and then "sweated." The fibers can then be pulled easily from the skin. This class of wool is called *pulled wool*. It is not so good a grade as fleece wool, but pulled wool can be blended with noils (short fibers separated from the long by combing) and with reprocessed and reused wool in very inexpensive suitings and blankets.

## SORTING AND GRADING

Wool is graded by men who have developed an extremely keen sense of touch; they grade wool according to the fineness of the individual fibers. Each fleece is graded according to what the grader believes the majority of the fibers to be. The sorter shakes out each fleece and separates fibers from different parts of the body. The wool is then ready for the worsted or woolen goods manufacturer.

Australian wool is delivered to manufacturers sorted and graded. Actually, Australia uses some 5,000 classifications for grading. This practice lowers conversion costs.

The U.S. Department of Agriculture, in cooperation with experimental stations, is promoting the sorting and grading of our domestic wool before it is delivered to the manufacturer. It is felt that this will help the wool grower to get a better price for his product. The Department has set up standards for grading wool by fineness of diameters of wool fiber and "wool tops" (long combed slivers). The method followed is that prescribed by the American Society for Testing Materials (A.S.T.M. Designation D472-50T, issued 1947, revised 1950). Effort is being made to grade wool in the grease (before it is scoured) by this method.

## INTERPRETATION OF THE
## WOOL PRODUCTS LABELING ACT

The Wool Products Labeling Act requires that all wool products that move in "commerce"[1] be labeled.[2] Prior to the Textile Fiber Products Identification Act, carpets and rugs containing wool were exempt. Labels shall indicate the percentage of total fiber weight, exclusive of ornamentation that does not exceed 5 per cent of the total fiber weight, of each fiber amounting to 5 per cent or more of the total.

The labeling law defines wool as new fibers (unused before in a fabric) from sheep, goats, and certain specialty fibers, such as camel's hair, alpaca, llama, and vicuña.

The labeling law sets forth three kinds of wool, depending upon the extent of its previous use in consumer goods:

[1] The general meaning is interstate commerce.

[2] The T.F.P.I.A. specifies that any product composed in whole or in part of wool or furs must be labeled by reference to the respective regulations on wool and furs issued under the Wool Products Labeling Act or the Fur Products Labeling Act, respectively.

1. *Wool*—refers to fleece wool being *used for the first time in the complete manufacture of a wool product*. The term "wool" may also include (*a*) new fleece wool that has previously been processed up to, but not including, weaving or felting, and (*b*) clips of knitted fabric made of new wool and not used or worn in any way. A fabric labeled "wool" may therefore contain certain wastes, resulting from carding, combing, and spinning, which have been recovered and processed again without being previously used.

2. *Reprocessed wool*—includes scraps and clips of woven and felted fabrics made of previously unused wool. These scraps or clips, never having been used by a consumer, are *garnetted* (shredded into fibrous state), and remanufactured into woolen fabrics. For example, cuttings from workrooms of garment manufacturers are a source of this class of wool.

3. *Reused wool*—old wool that has been woven, knitted, or felted into a wool product and, after having been used by the ultimate consumer, has been cleaned, returned to a fibrous state, then blended to make yarns for fabrics. Reused wool is also called *shoddy*.

If an article contains any fiber other than new wool, it must be labeled to show the percentage by weight of new wool, reprocessed wool, and reused wool. This provision has caused the retailer no end of problems. From the standpoint of accurate fiber identification, no one but the yarn manufacturer knows what percentage of fibers by weight goes into a certain yarn. When a wool fabric is old stock, it is very difficult to make this identification accurately. But law allows a product to be designated as reused wool if amounts of wool or reprocessed wool cannot be accurately determined. Some yarn manufacturers have pointed out that when they indicate the percentage of reused or reprocessed wool on the label, the figure may not be accurate when the cloth is finished, as some of the fibers fall out in the finishing process.

Certain specialty names for fibers falling within the definition of wool may be used on a label instead of the term "wool." If desired, the terms "mohair," "cashmere," "camel hair," "alpaca," and so on, may be used instead of "wool." If the word "cashmere" or "mohair" is used in lieu of the term "wool," the percentage of each fiber must

**Figure 12.1.** Two descriptive labels. (*Reproduced courtesy of J. P. Stevens & Co., Inc.*)

be designated. If these specialty fibers are reprocessed or reused, that fact
also must be indicated.

If nonwoolen fibers amount to less than 5 per cent each, they may be
labeled as "other fibers"; for example, a fabric consisting of 55 per
cent wool, 30 per cent reprocessed wool, 4 per cent rayon, 4 per cent
linen, 4 per cent silk, and 3 per cent cotton, may be labeled for fiber
content as follows: "55 per cent wool/30 per cent reprocessed wool/15
per cent other fibers."

Preferably, fibers should be listed in order of predominance by weight.

If a fabric has fiber ornamentation (a stripe or woven figure, for
instance) not exceeding 5 per cent of the total fiber weight of the
product, a phrase such as "exclusive of ornamentation" must follow the
statement of other fiber content. Should the fiber ornamentation exceed
5 per cent, the percentage must be included in the percentage statement
of fiber content. A label might read: "50 per cent wool/25 per cent
rayon/25 per cent cotton (exclusive of ornamentation)."

All wool products imported into the United States, except those made
more than twenty years before importation, are subject to the provisions
of the act.

The retailer can secure a guarantee from a manufacturer that a specific
wool product is not misbranded under the provisions of the act, or the
retailer may secure a continuing guarantee filed with the Federal Trade
Commission that will be applicable to all wool products handled by a
guarantor. These guarantees must conform to the rules and regulations
of the Commission. Such guarantees between manufacturer and retailer
must be made in good faith.

Since the wool labeling law pertains to sales of wool products in interstate commerce, every retailer must actively and intelligently comply
with its requirements.[3] Manufacturers, wholesalers, retailers, and consumers have a common interest in maintaining truthful merchandising
practices.

The consumer is probably familiar with the term "virgin wool." The
Wool Products Labeling Act does not define "virgin wool," but the
F.T.C. has defined it. The term is applicable to fabrics or products that
do not contain within them any wastes from preliminary processing of
new wool. It should be remembered that wool wastes and reprocessed and
reused wool can be used only in fabrics of woolen (as opposed to
worsted) type. (See pp. 314 ff. for a description of processing woolen
yarn.) Thus, the reliable manufacturers of woolens are proud to identify
their fabrics with their own brand names if their fabrics are made of
100 per cent virgin wool. The improper use of the term "virgin wool"
on tags or labels and in advertising of fabrics represents a deception of

[3] The retailer may also substitute his own label—revealing, instead of the manufacturer's name, the name under which he does business. He may employ a word trademark or housemark for this purpose if it has been registered with the U.S. Patent Office
and if, prior to use, the F.T.C. is furnished a copy of the registration.

**Figure 12.2.** The woolmark label is your assurance of quality-tested products made of the world's best . . . Pure Wool. *(Reproduced courtesy of The Wool Bureau, Inc.)*

**PURE WOOL**

the consumer and therefore, under provisions of the Wool Products Labeling Act, constitutes an offense subject to corrective measures.

The consumer should bear in mind that this act is intended to inform him of the exact fiber content of a fabric containing wool from which garments are made. The consumer must also realize that the presence of reprocessed and reused wools does not necessarily make a fabric inferior in quality. The grade of the fabric depends upon the *quality* of the reprocessed or reused wool. Sometimes a mixture of new wool with reprocessed and reused wool is like a metal alloy—particularly strong and durable for the purpose for which it was made. In other cases, the use of reprocessed or reused wool does not have the effect of a strengthening agent, but makes it possible for a manufacturer to sell a garment at a price that would be impossible if first-grade new wool were used.

A manufacturer who has always made it his practice to use good-grade new wool in his fabrics will not suddenly change to using reprocessed or reused wool. Similarly, a manufacturer who has been making popular-priced clothing containing reprocessed or reused wool is going to keep on making that clothing. What the act has done is to make all manufacturers label their product as to fiber content. The fact that a garment is labeled "reused wool" doesn't mean that the consumer is not getting service commensurate with what he pays for the garment. Labels, then, are merely a guarantee as to the content of the fabric.

## CHARACTERISTICS OF THE WOOL FIBER

### MICROSCOPIC APPEARANCE

Under the microscope, a wool fiber resembles a worm with horny scales. Wool fiber consists of three parts: (1) the medullary, (2) the cortex, and (3) the outside scales. The medullary is a honeycombed cellular section found in medium and coarse wools. Not all wool fibers have a medulla, and it is not necessary to the growth of the fiber. Its chief function seems to be "to increase the protective properties of the fiber by adding internal air spaces."[4] The cortex consists of cortical cells that are really bundles of fibrils.[5] The outside scales have a protecting membrane called the *cuticle*. The scales overlap, and their free ends point toward the tip of the fiber. Hence the scales are partially responsible for the wool fiber's slipping and sliding more easily toward the root of the fiber. On the other hand, materials coming in contact with the fiber slip more easily toward the tip of the fiber. This difference in friction on a sheep's back causes burrs and dust particles to work their way out of the wool. This same frictional difference is a factor in giving wool its felting quality. When wool is wet, the fibers move and entangle as the wet cloth is manipulated chemically. Excessive shrinkage occurs when felting is not controlled. (See *shrinkage control of wool*, p. 321.)

### LENGTH OF FIBER

Wool fibers range from 1 to 14 inches in length, depending on the kind of sheep and the part of the sheep from which the wool is taken. Wool is a comparatively short natural fiber and is surpassed in length by silk and linen. The shorter fibers are used chiefly in woolens, and the longer ones are used primarily in worsteds. Fibers used for worsteds average 3 to 8 inches in length, whereas those used for woolens are 1 to 3 inches (usually 2 inches or less).

### DIAMETER

The average wool fiber is coarser than rayon, silk, linen, or cotton fibers. The approximate diameter of wool fiber is .0005 to .0015 inch. Therefore, wool yarns are ordinarily not so fine as other textiles.

### COLOR OF FIBER

Wool fibers range from whitish to gray, brown, and sometimes black. The color pigment is distributed through cells in the cortex and medulla. As in

[4] Werner Von Bergen and Herbert Mauersberger, *American Wool Handbook*, 2nd ed. (New York: Textile Book Publishers, Inc., 1948), pp. 133–34.

[5] The nucleus at the center of each cortical cell is a granular strucure. The electron microscope reveals still finer filaments than fibrils, called microfibrils. *Ibid.*, p. 130.

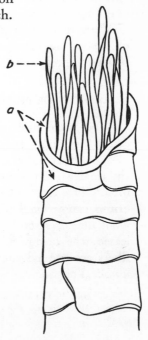

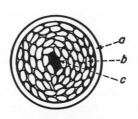

a – cuticle
b – corticle cells
c – medulla

**Figure 12.3.** Elements of the wool fiber. (*Reproduced courtesy of The Wool Bureau, Inc.*)

the case of human hair, it is easy to dye the scales and the cortex, but the dye rarely penetrates the medulla. Bleaching has a similar effect, although for all practical purposes bleaching with peroxide is permanent. Black sheep's wool cannot be bleached white.

### LUSTER

Luster of wool will vary according to the origin and breed of the sheep and with climate. The luster is higher in poor-quality wools than in good grades. A poor-grade serge suit is more shiny when purchased and will show a greasy shine more quickly than a better-grade serge. Although luster is temporarily removed by a sponging with an ammonia solution, the shine will return. Dull wools are better buys in the long run with one exception—broadcloth, which is purposely steam-lustered in the finishing process to increase the luster and lay the nap.

### STRENGTH

A single wool fiber can sustain a dead weight of fifteen to thirty grams. A silk fiber will break at five to twenty-eight grams. But although wool fiber seems stronger than silk according to these figures, the diameters of the two fibers are usually quite different. Wool fiber is coarser than silk, so it is logical to expect greater tensile strength from wool; but if the five major fibers of equal diameter are compared, nylon ranks first, silk second, wool third, and then come rayon and cotton. There are so many different grades of each fiber that it is difficult to generalize.

Wool is stronger dry than wet. Vegetable fibers, with the exception of rayon, are stronger when wet. Rayon's wet strength has been improved appreciably.

### ELASTICITY OR RESILIENCE

Wool is the most elastic of the major fibers. It stretches 25 to 35 per cent of its length before breaking.

Wool fiber possesses crimp or wave, the amount of crimp varying with the fineness of the fibers from almost no crimp to 22 to 30 crimps per inch.[6] The finer fibers have a pronounced crimp. This characteristic crimp causes wool fibers to repel each other when in fabrics. When a wool fiber is stretched, the crimp comes out, but when the fiber is released, the crimp returns—the fiber springs back. If masses of wool fibers are pressed together, they spring apart as soon as pressure is released. This quality is called resilience or elasticity. It is very important

[6] Giles E. Hopkins, *Wool as an Apparel Fiber* (New York: Holt, Rinehart and Winston, 1953), p. 9.

in wrinkle resistance and insulation of wool. Resilience is also a factor in tailoring. Wool tailors easily because it is a "live" fiber. Furthermore, it is easily shaped and steamed while parts of the garment are being put together.

## INSULATION VALUE

Heat conductivity and insulation are not the same, although the terms are related. The insulation value of a fabric depends on the amount of air enmeshed within the fabric and on its surface. In this, the actual heat conductivity of the enmeshed or trapped air is important, rather than that of the fibers themselves. Trapped air is a nonconductor of heat. In wool fabrics, because of their porosity and the fact that by nature wool fibers stay apart (repel each other), about 80 per cent of the entire fabric volume is air.[7] The air held closely against the fiber surfaces prevents heat loss by the body, thus keeping the body warm. Even when the wool is wet, its resilience remains, so its insulating trapped air remains. Hence, the wearer of wet wool garments does not chill suddenly.

Furthermore, a loosely twisted woolen yarn with varied lengths of nonparallel fibers can enmesh more still air than a worsted yarn with its long parallel fibers held in the yarn by twist. A porous plain weave would also serve to create air pockets. Woolen yarns, with their resilient fibers of varied lengths, lend themselves to napping, and napped fibers of varied lengths create more air pockets. Not only the repellence of fiber to fiber and resilience of the fiber, but also the type of yarn, weave, and finish are factors in heat conductivity.

## HYGROSCOPIC MOISTURE

Wool has a high absorptive quality, but it absorbs moisture in the form of water vapor very slowly. Observation of liquid spilled on wool garments shows that if the surface is slanted, the liquid runs off, but if horizontal, the liquid is absorbed very slowly. Wool is naturally water-repellent, because the membrane protecting the scales is nonprotein, so that liquid water is not attracted to the fiber's surface. However, water vapor can penetrate the fiber's interior, which has a strong affinity for moisture. This quality of wool explains why wool garments can absorb body moisture in the form of water vapor without feeling damp. This moisture from the body is then released to the atmosphere slowly, so that the body is not chilled.

Although wool can absorb a great deal of moisture, it does so slowly, and it dries more slowly than silk or linen. Wool can absorb much moisture before it feels damp; this is the reason for making bathing suits of wool.

[7] *Ibid.*, p. 67.

Wool is the only fiber containing sulfur. Its chemical composition is carbon, hydrogen, nitrogen, oxygen, and sulfur. The wool fiber is composed of animal tissues, which are classed as a protein called *keratin*.

### EFFECT OF LIGHT

Some scientists believe that the ultraviolet rays of the sun are the direct cause of deterioration of textile fibers. Others believe that ozone is developed, which, in combination with moisture, affects fibers. At any rate, it is agreed that the sun's rays cause vegetable fibers to lose strength. Laboratory tests show that raw wool is about as resistant to light as cotton or jute. Dyed wool, used in woolen suits and hats, does not seem to lose so much strength in the same test.

### MILDEW

Wool is attacked by mildew only if the fabric has remained damp for some time. Mildew-resistant processes may be applied in finishing wool goods.

### EFFECT OF ACIDS

Dilute acids, even if boiling, do not injure wool. Concentrated acids, such as sulfuric, hydrochloric, and nitric, will destroy wool if the fabric is soaked in them for more than a few minutes or if the acid is allowed to dry in the fabric. Often raw wool is treated with dilute sulfuric acid to remove any vegetable matter, such as burrs, from the fibers. Formic and acetic acids are not detrimental to wool. Oxalic, tartaric, and citric acids are not injurious if the acid is removed from the cloth. In fact, formic, acetic, oxalic, tartaric, and citric acids are less injurious than dilute sulfuric, hydrochloric, or nitric acids.

### EFFECT OF ALKALIES

Weak alkalies such as ammonia, borax, phosphate of soda, and soap are not injurious to wool if care is taken to keep the temperature below 68° F. But boiling in a 5 per cent solution of caustic soda (lye) for five minutes will completely disintegrate wool. Wool is sensitive to alkalies; therefore the use of neutral soaps with no free alkali is advised.

### EFFECT OF BLEACHES

Chlorine bleach is ordinarily harmful to wool. The use, in the past, of a form of chlorine to shrink wool was very unsatisfactory, because it made wool lose strength and elasticity. Furthermore, fabrics so treated would still shrink, and they did not have the durability of untreated wool. Now, however, the use of a chlorinating agent can be satisfactorily controlled so that shrinkage is prevented. (For a discussion of shrinkage control, see p. 321.)

Potassium permanganate, sodium peroxide, and hydrogen peroxide are used for bleaching and removing some kinds of stains.

### AFFINITY FOR DYESTUFFS

Wool has a good affinity for dyestuffs. Its chemical structure enables the fiber to unite chemically with a wide variety of dyestuffs. Acid or basic dyes, chromes, indigo, and even vat types can be used for wool. Selected basic dyes can be used for dyeing wool and acrylic fiber blends and mixtures, but the cationic dyes, developed especially for acrylics, are better.[8] Deep rich colors and pale pastels are possible because of the wool fiber's affinity for dye.

### MANUFACTURE OF WORSTED YARNS

Wool fibers can be manufactured into two kinds of cloth: worsteds and woolens. Worsteds are characterized by smooth surfaces, and they are harder to the touch than woolens. The weave or pattern is clearly visible in worsteds, and for this reason they are described as *clear finished*.

Worsteds are made from long wool fibers, usually two to eight inches in length. The English wools are often imported for worsted manufacture.

#### SORTING

When wool reaches the mill it is sorted; this process has been described earlier in the chapter.

#### OPENING

After sorting, the wool is put through a machine, called an *opener* or *breaker*, containing a tooth cylinder, the purpose of which is to remove all loose dirt and sand and to separate the whole fleece into small sections.

#### SCOURING

Since wool contains grease, dirt, and other substances, the fibers must be washed or scoured. An alkaline solution of soap or soda ash is the most usual method of removing grease and swint (perspiration). Other methods include *swint washing* (wool is steeped in water, and the swint

[8] *Textile World*, CXII, 4 (April 4, 1962), 82.

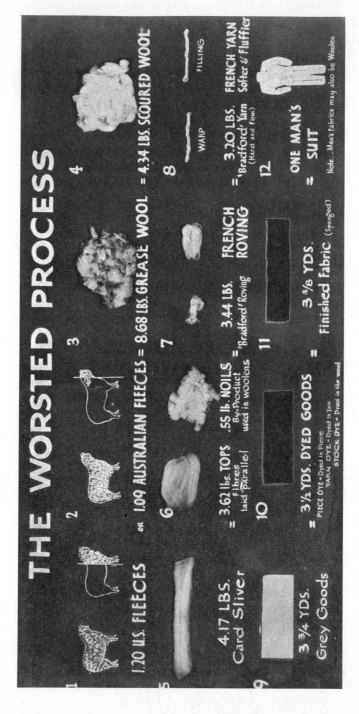

**Figure 12.4.** The worsted process. (*Reproduced courtesy of Industrial By-Products & Research Corp.*)

liquor, after removal of sand and dirt, is used for scouring); solvent scouring (with white spirit and chlorinated hydrocarbons) followed by water; refrigeration processing (wool grease is frozen and removed as powder by treatment in a dusting machine); and scouring by using soda ash to remove free fatty acid oils and an emulsifier and synthetic detergent to remove mineral oils.

## WOOL DRYING

The wet scoured wool is dried in a machine that provides a gentle flow of air and heat.

## CARDING

The carding of wool is similar to the carding of cotton. Large revolving cylinders with wire teeth all running at different speeds lay the fibers in a filmy sheet, or sliver. Carding partially straightens the wool fibers and lays them in one direction. The carded wool sliver is then made even.

## COMBING

Worsted cloths show the woven pattern clearly, so that any unevenness in the yarn is noticeable in the finished cloth. The carded slivers are run through a combing operation to (1) remove the short fibers from the sliver; (2) straighten the remaining fibers and make them parallel; (3) remove any foreign matter, such as straw, burrs, or dirt.

The short fibers are called *noils*—corresponding with *tow* in linen. The long fibers lying parallel in the sliver are called *tops*. (See specifications and methods of test for determining fineness of wool tops, p. 303.)

Slivers of tops are combed and drawn out. This drawing process is called *drafting*. Slivers are drawn out narrower and narrower until the desired thickness is reached. A sufficient twist is put in to prevent further drafting (*drawing*). The combed top can now be dyed, because the color can penetrate through the fibers at this point in the process better than it can after the cloth is woven.

## SPINNING

Spinning puts in the required twist. Spools holding slivers are arranged horizontally to revolve on a frame. From these spools the slivers are carried to another series of spools, arranged vertically on another frame. The speed and tension of winding are so regulated as to twist the yarn as it is wound from one spool to the other. Worsted yarns are usually more tightly twisted than woolen yarns. (See Figure 12.6.) The yarns are sold to the weavers on these spools, or in skeins or hanks.

## TWISTING

Twisting is spinning two, three, or four yarns together (plies). Two-ply yarns are generally used for weaving and machine knitting, and three- and four-ply are sold for hand knitting.

## REELING

Worsted yarns are then reeled into skeins.

## INSPECTION

Inspecting the skeins and putting them into bundles of about 40 pounds each completes worsted yarn manufacture.

## SIZES OR COUNT OF WORSTED YARNS

The size of worsted yarns is determined by the number of hanks of 560 yards weighing one pound. If one 560-yard hank weighs one pound, the count or size is #1. If 5,600 yards weigh one pound, the count is #10, and so on. Yarns numbered 5s to 10s are very coarse and used for heavy sweaters; 10s to 30s are medium; 40s to 60s are fine. Worsted yarns are two-ply, three-ply, and four-ply, as well as single. (See Tex System, Chapter 3.)

## QUALITY OF WORSTED YARN

The quality of worsted yarn depends on the grade of the fibers used, the amount of carding and combing, the skill applied to these operations, and the regularity of the spinning.

Fabrics made of worsted yarn include tropical worsted, unfinished worsted, worsted flannel, worsted cheviot, worsted covert, sharkskin, and gabardine.

## MANUFACTURE OF WOOLEN YARNS

### SELECTING THE FIBER

Fibers averaging less than two inches in length are customarily selected for woolen yarns. Short-fiber merino wool is especially good. Since the beauty of a woolen lies in its softness and warmth, this type of cloth lends itself more to adulteration than does worsted. The woven pattern is usually indistinct and often obliterated. The felting, or shrinking, of wool goods after they are woven makes it possible to conceal many varieties of fibers.

For woolen yarns, then, short fibers of new or virgin wool can be used, as well as reprocessed or reused wool. If any reprocessed or reused

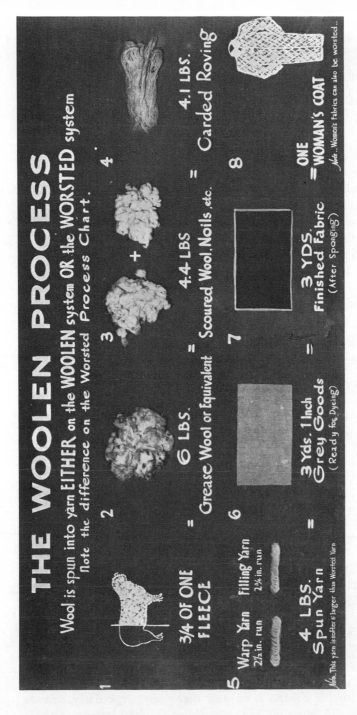

**Figure 12.5.** The woolen process. (Reproduced courtesy of Industrial By-Products & Research Corp.)

wool is used, the percentage of each by weight must appear on the label. Blends of wool with other natural or synthetic fibers are becoming more prevalent.

Wool and the Consumer

## PROCESSES PRELIMINARY TO CARDING

The processes of preparing wool for carding are similar to those used in preparing wool for making worsted yarn.

## CARDING

The purpose of carding woolen yarn is to make it fuzzy enough to allow a nap to be raised later. The process is more violent than that used for worsteds; rollers with wire teeth revolve in opposite directions, whereas for worsteds they revolve in the same direction. Woolen yarn may be carded several times, but it is not combed. Short fibers are not taken out of the sliver as they are for worsted yarn. Like worsted yarn, it is drawn out and twisted. Woolen yarn has a slacker twist than worsted yarn. (See Figure 12.6.) It is then wound on bobbins and rewound on spools or made into skeins. Woolen yarn may be dyed before it is woven, and when that is done the cloth is said to be yarn-dyed.

## SIZE OR COUNT OF WOOLEN YARNS

There are two methods of computing sizes of woolen yarn: one method, the American *run count*, will be discussed here. If 1,600 yards weigh one pound, the count or size is #1. This yarn is very coarse and is used for overcoats and blankets; #3 and #4 yarns are medium; and #6½ to #10 yarns are fine. (See Tex System, Chapter 3.)

Fabrics made of woolen yarn include homespun, tweed, wool flannel, wool cheviot, wool covert, wool shetland, and wool broadcloth.

## WEAVING AND KNITTING WOOL FABRICS
### PLAIN WEAVE

Although more men's suitings are made in twill than in plain weave, the plain weave is popular where porosity, softness, and sponginess (in women's wear) are factors. Men's and women's suitings and coatings in this construction include homespun, donegal tweed, and tropical worsted. Women's dress fabrics include wool crepe, batiste, nun's veiling, poplin, faille, and some flannels and tweeds.

### TWILL WEAVE

The twill is a durable construction and therefore particularly suited to men's suitings and coatings. Kersey (heavy felted overcoating), cheviots, coverts, tweed, broadcloth, cassimere, flannel, whipcord, and

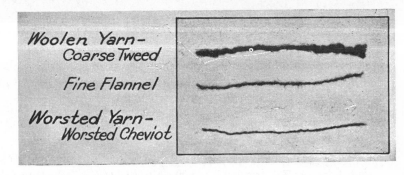

**Figure 12.6.** Woolen and worsted yarns.

serge are made in twill for men's wear. Women wear most of the fabrics listed, but the weight is lighter and the finish usually softer for women's wear.

### PILE WEAVE

Many fabrics are made in pile construction to imitate fur. Some fleeces, double-cloth coatings, velours, velvets, friezés, and plushes are made in this manner. Velour, velvet, and plush are upholstery fabrics in pile weave. Rugs with wool pile include Wilton, Axminster, tufted, and velvet. (See Chapter 19 for construction of rugs.)

The very durable elastique and cavalry twill, originally for uniforms for the armed forces, is dobby weave and is particularly appropriate in civilian jackets and trousers when durability is a major factor.

### KNITTED CONSTRUCTION

Jersey blouses, wool basque shirts, some fleeces, and bouclé dresses, are knitted. The familiar sweater and wool sock are of this construction. Wool's resilience and ease in handling make it most appropriate in knitted goods.

### FINISHES FOR WOOL FABRICS

Worsteds look more ready for sale than woolens when they come from the loom, because their attractiveness depends on their even yarns and structural design, whereas much of the attractiveness, softness, and often the warmth of the woolen depends on its finish. Usually woolens are more heavily felted than worsteds. Woolen and worsted fabrics are given one of two finishes: (1) clear or hard finish; (2) face finish.

The clear-finished fabric, which includes most of the worsteds, has a smooth, even surface with the weave clearly visible. For clear finishes very little, if any, fulling is done. (See p. 320.) A slight fulling of a worsted would produce a good, firm hand.

The face finish has either a pile or a nap on the surface, which almost, if not entirely, obliterates the weave. Considerable fulling is done, and a nap is raised. The nap may be pressed in one direction, as in broadcloth. Sometimes the finisher produces a fuzz or nap on a worsted, called *unfinished worsted*. Then again he may make one side of the fabric *clear finished* and the back *face finished* with a nap.

### PERCHING OR INSPECTING

All fabrics must be subjected to this visual examination. (See *inspection*, Chapter 7). Inspection is done both before and after finishes have been applied.

### BURLING [9]

For inspection the cloth is laid over a smooth, sloping table. The inspector or burler first examines the back of the cloth to detect and remove snarls, slubs, and straws. All thick warp and filling yarns are opened with a pick called a *burling iron*. The burler next examines the face of the cloth for irregularities. All imperfections are pushed through to the back of the cloth so that the right side of the fabric will be smooth.

### MENDING

This is a finishing process in which weaving imperfections, broken yarns, tears, etc., are repaired before further finishing.

### BLEACHING

Wool is frequently bleached in the yarn, but it can also be bleached after weaving and scouring.

Natural wool fibers are slightly yellowish, black, or brown. The yellowish color predominates. As the amount of deeply colored wool is small, these wools are rarely bleached. The yellowish tinted wool can be whitened by (1) tinting, (2) sulfur dioxide, or (3) hydrogen peroxide.[10]

Tinting is not a bleach but a dyeing of the wool with violet or blue to neutralize the cast of the natural pigment and change the tint to gray. There is no destruction of the natural pigment, and the gray tint is so slight that the eye perceives the wool as white.

In point of time, the sulfur dioxide bleach is an older method of bleaching, but it is less permanent than the hydrogen peroxide bleach. In the sulfur dioxide method the cloth is subjected either to a sulfur dioxide gas or to an acidified solution of bisulphite.

[9] Von Bergen and Mauersberger, *op. cit.*, pp. 809–10.
[10] *Ibid.*, pp. 791–94.

In the third method of bleaching, the well-scoured fabric is saturated and steeped for about twelve hours in a bath of hydrogen peroxide made slightly alkaline with sodium silicate or ammonia. A thorough rinsing in dilute acetic acid removes bleaching chemicals. To cheapen the bleaching process and to provide a milder bleach, stabilized hydrosulfite compounds are used. Frequently this method is combined with the peroxide method.

### SCOURING AND CARBONIZING

Both of these processes are preliminary cleaning processes. Scouring removes oil, dirt, and sizing from wool, cotton, linen, and rayon fabrics. Carbonizing frees wool of burrs and vegetable matter by the use of an acid solution and heat. A rinse is an alkali that neutralizes the acid. When the wool is dry, the carbonized matter "dusts off." [11] This process can be done in the fiber stage, but the purpose is the same when done as a finishing process.

### BRUSHING AND SINGEING

These processes, described in Chapter 7, remove short, loose fibers and lint from wool.

### SHEARING

To cut off excess surface fibers and to even the pile in length, wool may be sheared.

### CRABBING [12]

This operation is a permanent setting of the weave in order to prevent uneven shrinkage, which may develop in crimps, creases, or cockles when the fabric is fulled. The process consists in passing the fabric in full width around a series of rollers and immersing the cloth in a number of tanks. Each tank is equipped with steam pipes and cross sprays. At the end of the machine there are two rollers that squeeze water from the fabric. This equipment is used not only for worsteds but also for wool and rayon blends.

### DECATING (DRY AND WET)

Wool is dry-decated to set the luster and wet-decated to add luster.

1. *Dry decating* (often called semidecating).[13] The operation consists of applying hot steam to a dry cloth wound under tension on a

---

[11] *Dan River's Dictionary of Textile Terms*, Dan River Mills, Inc., p. 17, 10th edition.
[12] Von Bergen and Mauersberger, *op. cit.*, pp, 813–14.
[13] *Ibid.*, pp. 860–61.

perforated roller. The roller is not really sealed, but merely contains the steam and allows the steam to escape through the perforations and hence through the fabric.

Then the process is reversed by forcing steam through the cloth from the outside to the inside. The cloth is then removed from the tank and is cooled by air.

2. *Wet decating.*[14]   If the finished wool fabric must have luster and a more permanent setting of the fibers, the fabric is wet decated. For this process, heat, moisture, and tension are needed. The cloth is wound in tension around a perforated metal cylinder that is placed in a trough of water 140° to 212° F. The five- to ten-minute treatment consists in circulating the water from the tank through the fabric into the cylinder, and vice versa. Hot water plus steam will make the process more effective. The fabric is then cooled with cold water or cold air.

### FULLING

If wool is to be made more compact and thicker, the fabric is placed in warm soapy water or a weak acid solution, where it is pounded and twisted until it has shrunk a desired amount—10 to 25 per cent. This process may last two to eighteen hours and is called *fulling, felting,* or *milling.* The secret of fulling lies in the structure of the wool fiber. The scales of the fiber swell in the warm water, and the pounding and twisting cause them to entangle or interlock with one another. When the fabric is dried, the fibers stay massed together—they are felted. Worsteds are fulled to close the weave and to soften the cloth. Slight fulling of a woolen will give it compactness and softness.

### GIGGING

The raising of a nap on a wool fabric may be done with teasels—burr-like plants one and one-half to two inches in length.[15] The teasels are set in rows in frames mounted on revolving drums. As the cloth comes in contact with the teasels, the fibers are untangled and lifted. It is wise to use worn teasels first, so that fibers will not be torn out. New teasels are sharper and are best introduced gradually until the desired nap is raised. Gigging is also used for spun silk and spun rayon.

### NAPPING

Those woolen fabrics that are to have a fuzzy surface are fulled a great deal more than others, because the more the short fibers of wool are massed together the thicker will be the nap. After they are fulled, woolens are washed, dried, and tentered (evened in their width). The

[14] *Ibid.,* pp. 837–38.
[15] *Ibid.,* p. 839.

cloth is then passed over cylinders whose surfaces are covered with wire bristles. When teasels are used, the process is called gigging. The teasels make a more natural nap and are not so rough on the cloth as the wire bristles. But where fibers have formed a felted surface, napping is necessary to untangle them. The nap is then sheared to a certain length.

### STEAMING [16]

This operation, when applied after drying, partially shrinks and conditions the fabric. After the cloth has been decated, steaming takes off unsightly glaze. The fabric is run over a steam box with a perforated copper cover, and the steam is passed through it. While this process is not essentially for shrinkage, it does have that effect. Silk and spun rayons may also be steamed.

### WEIGHTING OF WOOLENS

To make a firmer, more compact cloth, manufacturers steam fibers (obtained by shearing a cloth) into the back of a fabric. Reused wool may also be used for this purpose. Probably most men have discovered little rolls of wool in the pockets of their overcoats. This is *flocking*. Its presence can be detected if the back of the cloth is brushed with a stiff brush to see whether short fibers come out. If the manufacturer uses a good quality of wool fiber for flocking and does not use it merely to cover defects in weaving, the practice is considered legitimate.

Unscrupulous manufacturers may take advantage of the absorptive qualities of wool and treat fabrics with magnesium chloride so that the cloth may absorb more moisture than it naturally would. This practice is called *loading*. It gives the buyer a good percentage of water with his purchase.

### SHRINKAGE CONTROL

Great strides have been made in overcoming objectionable shrinkage of wools. Although such finishes as steaming, fulling, and decating help to lessen wool shrinkage, these finishes do not ensure fabrics against excessive shrinkage in washing.

It is estimated that there are hundreds of shrinkage-control processes for wool. Three of the methods in current use in this country are (1) chlorination (either dry or in neutral or acid solutions); (2) resin treatment; and (3) combination of alkaline hypochlorite and permanganate.

These chemical methods cause the wool to resist felting and hence to resist shrinkage. Chlorination consists in subjecting wool tops, yard goods, or garments to a chlorine agent. The chlorination process modifies the fiber structure of wool. Under the microscope the scales of treated fibers

[16] *Ibid.*, p. 870.

may appear less clear or may disappear substantially. Since the treatment prevents felting shrinkage, directional frictional effect (discussed earlier as fiber slippage from tip to root and root to tip) is diminished, and that reduces resilience. It has been found that chlorination may reduce wash-fastness of the dyes.

Application of melamine formaldehyde resin masks the scale structure but does not modify that structure. Essentially the process deposits resin on the surface of the fabric. One scientist compares resin's action to spot welding of the fibers—an action preventing movement of the scales and hence preventing felting. This method, although it is effective in preventing shrinkage, causes fabrics to lose wool-like hand because of fiber-bonding and increase in fabric weight.

Acrylic resins stabilize wool and avoid the undesirable effects on secondary fabric properties from which other commercial treatments suffer.[17]

The third method has enjoyed considerable commercial success. When applied to grey goods, decreased affinity for dyes and uneven dyeing have been drawbacks. Also there have been few dyes that maintain their shade and fastness if applied before this treatment.[18]

Present industrial shrink-resistance treatments are capable of preventing any wool fabric from felting in any washing machine. However, there may be disadvantageous side effects, such as loss of strength and woollike hand, change in appearance, and possible stretching of the treated fabric when given a mild laundering. (For brand names of finishes for shrinkage control, see Chapter 7.)

WASH-AND-WEAR

In the previous discussions of wash-and-wear, particular emphasis has been placed on the cellulosic fibers, cotton and linen. After laundering, such characteristics as smoothness of the surface of the fabric, wrinkle resistance dry and wet, and shrinkage control were considered. Wool, by nature, is elastic and therefore wrinkle resistant, and wrinkles tend to hang out. Therefore the major problem in making wool fabrics wash-and-wear are those of shrinkage, felting, and fuzzing in laundering. The shrink-resistant finishes are being improved to the point where wash-and-wear wools may become commonplace.

Heat-set treatments have become a boon to the synthetics and to cottons in permanent pleating of fabrics. Now a process for improving the permanence of pleating in wools has been developed by Unilever, Ltd., of Great Britain. In this pretreatment process, the salt linkages in the keratin are partly broken, after which the fabric is steam-pressed.

[17] Fred H. Steiger, "Reducing the Felting Shrinkage of Wool," *American Dyestuff Reporter* (February 6, 1961), 37–44.
[18] *Ibid.*, 40.

Evening a fabric in its width is important. (For a description of the tentering process, see p. 161.)

## PRESSING

Pressing accomplishes the same result for wool that calendering does for other fibers. Calendering is really a pressing process, but the term is not applied to wool.

To press wool, the fabric is placed between heavy, electrically heated metal plates that steam and press the fabric. Another method is to wind the fabric around a cylindrical unit that dampens the fabric and then presses it. The latter method can be used not only for woolens and worsteds but also for spun rayons and silks.

## FIRE-RESISTANT FINISH

Some fire insurance companies recommend wool blankets for smothering fires. Why? Laboratories have found that wool absorbs about twice as much moisture as cotton and that moisture absorption is a factor in reducing flammability. Another factor involved in flammability is the construction of a cloth. A flame must have sufficient heat concentration and new fibers to consume, plus enough oxygen to keep burning. If a flame is applied to an all-wool fabric, it is slow in ignition, and, if the material is dense enough, the fire will often go out when the flame is removed. It may be deduced that flammability is not a problem in 100 per cent wool fabrics. However, blends, depending on the nature and percentage of other fabrics, may create a flammability problem. Also, if flammable finishing materials are used in sufficient amounts, flammability must be reckoned with under the Flammable Fabrics Act.

## OTHER FUNCTIONAL FINISHES FOR WOOL

Wool is not subject to mildew unless it is allowed to remain damp for some time; however, wool may be given a mildew-resistant finish. (See Chapter 7.)

The attack on wool by moths is always a worry to a consumer. Again a proper moth-repellent finish done by the finisher or by the consumer can be adequate to prevent eating by moths. (See p. 177 for chemicals used in this finish and common trade names for this type of finish.)

Wool fabrics for rainwear are treated for water repellency. The degree of repellency and the length of time the treatment will last after dry or wet cleaning depends on the nature of the finish. Trade names of water-repellent finishes for wool include Cravenette, Wat-a-set, Neva-Wet, Rainfoe, Zelan, and Zepel (spot- and stain-repellent).

### APPEARANCE

The attractive appearance of a wool fabric lies partly in its natural low luster for good-grade wools; or in its steam-lustered finish for fabrics like wool broadcloth. But the rich coloring of wool fabrics is probably more important to the fashion-minded consumer. Colors can be soft and muted or high in intensity, with depth and permanence. The depth and softness of a woolen pile, the nap of a woolen, and the intricacies of weave in a worsted have an eye appeal. A fabric that drapes and fits well always presents a good appearance.

### EASE IN CARE

Wool's elasticity is responsible for its wrinkle-resistant quality, a particularly important factor in suits and coats that have almost daily wear. The ability of worsteds to take and hold a crease is also important, particularly in men's slacks. Wools are slow to show soil because of the fiber's resilience. Since moisture is absorbed slowly, many liquids can be sponged from the fabric before it dries, thereby taking the soil particles with the liquid. It has been explained that the covering of the scales makes the fiber naturally water repellent; hence, liquid will run off the fabric if it is slanted. Wool's low static quality is also a factor in resisting soil. Once soil becomes embedded in the fabric, it can generally be removed by washing or dry cleaning. Improvements in shrinkage control and resistance to felting will make laundering of wool easier. (See Chapter 15 for simple rules to follow in the care of wool.)

The Wool Bureau, Inc., has been instrumental in perfecting and introducing to the trade a permanent creasing (and pleating) process for all-wool garments. Known as the WB-4 process, it is a chemical add-on which imparts a "memory" to the wool fiber helping it to keep its crease throughout the life of the garment.

### HAND

The soft, springy, warm feel (hand) of wool is pleasing to the buyer of wool fabrics. To be sure, the softness or stiffness of a fabric is controlled not only by the choice of fibers but also by the kind of manufacturing processing they receive. In general, large-diameter fibers produce a stiffer hand than fine fibers. Large slub or nubbed yarns present a more bumpy surface texture than smooth, even yarns. A woolen usually has a more hairy surface than a worsted, which has had the short fibers removed from the yarn. Therefore, woolen feels warmer, generally softer, less firm, and less smooth than a worsted. The amount of other fibers mixed or blended with wool may affect the hand.

Why wool is warm and therefore comfortable, particularly in cold weather, has been explained. The same principle of trapped air is applicable to napped wool blankets And yet wool fabrics can be woven or knitted so that they are so loose and porous that air transmission is good. The wearer is protected from sudden chill by the wool fabric's natural water repellency and slow absorptive quality. The fact that wool is slow to ignite protects the user of wool pile rugs and wool blankets.

## SUITABILITY

Wool fabrics are made in many weights, from the filmiest sheer veiling to the heaviest overcoating.

Sheer fabrics, such as wool georgette, voile, featherweight tweeds, lightweight crepes, and some sheer wool meshes, can be worn by the woman with a full figure. The stout woman may feel that wool jersey is too stretchy. She may have had jerseys that bulged at the elbows and knees. But this objection can be overcome by lining a knitted garment, as is now done by manufacturers of better-quality women's apparel. Double knits are stabilized by linings.

Certain fabrics, such as checked or plain tweeds, are adapted to sports clothes, depending on the climate. Smooth, luxurious flannels and broadcloths are suitable for dress wear for men, again depending on the style and the time of year and climate. Women can look as trim and tailored as men, because men's suitings (some in lighter weight) are being used extensively for women's suits. Nearly every man, woman, and child owns a sweater of all wool or a blend.

The hard-finished worsteds are good for the tailored woman, because these fabrics tailor easily, hold their shape, and press better than woolens. A woolen in men's suiting requires frequent pressing, since creases do not stay long in the cloth. As a class, worsteds are more durable than woolens, and they are generally more expensive. (For a more complete discussion of men's suitings, see Chapter 17.)

## MINOR HAIR (SPECIALTY) FIBERS

Hair fibers classed with wool as specialty fibers by the F.T.C. include various breeds of goats and camels. In addition, less-used hairs from the cow and horse, fur from rabbits, and feathers from the duck, goose, and ostrich are not to be overlooked. (See the requirements of the Wool Products Labeling Act, pp. 303 ff.)

Microscopically, the medullas show in hair fibers and differ from wool. (See the Appendix.) In some, hair scales are faintly visible; in others they are not.

A list of hair fibers and their most common uses follows:

| Fiber | Animal | Major Source | Uses (alone and in blends) |
|---|---|---|---|
| Mohair | Angora goat | Asia Minor (Turkey) and the Cape Colony, Texas | Upholsteries, draperies, spreads, linings, braids, men's suits, riding habits, brushed-wool sweaters, gloves, mittens, socks, imitation astrakhan, plush |
| Alpaca | Camel-like ruminants | South America (Peru) | Men's coat linings, women's furlike fabrics, dress goods, linings |
| Llama | `` | South America | Dress goods, sweaters |
| Vicuña | `` | South America | Sweaters, fleece fabrics, coats (very rare) |
| Cashmere | Cashmere goat | Himalaya Mountains, Tibet, Kashmir | Shawls, sweaters, coats |
| Camel's hair | Camel | Asia, Africa, China, Russia | Oriental rugs, sweaters, blankets, coats, gloves, piece goods |
| Horsehair | Horse | South America | Braid, upholsteries, fur |
| Rabbit hair | Angora rabbit | Turkey | Felt, knitted garments |

## MOHAIR

Mohair is obtained from the Angora goat, which is raised in the southwestern United States, South Africa, and Turkey. The United States is producing good grades domestically.

Mohair comes in different grades. Adult and kid hairs are the broad classifications. Kid hair, clipped twice a year, is the finest grade; adult hair, very strong and resilient, is the lowest grade.

The fiber, which ranges from six to twelve inches for a full year's growth, is smooth and lustrous, because the scales scarcely overlap.[19] Since mohair has fewer surface scales and less crimp than sheep's wool, it is more lustrous, smooth, and dust-resistant. The bundles of fibrils in the cortex are similar to wool, and the cells in the medulla are few in a good grade fiber. Chemical properties are similar to those of wool.

Mohair can be used alone or blended with wool and other fibers. It is desirable for men's suitings, women's dresses, coats, and sweaters, net and braid trimmings, the pile of rugs, automobile and furniture upholstery, draperies, lap robes, and stuffing around the springs in furniture.[20]

## CASHMERE

Those who have worn cashmere sweaters or coats appreciate its warmth and lightness. The fleece is grown on a small, short-legged animal of Central Asia. Fibers from Tibet, Mongolia, and China are the

[19] Von Bergen and Mauersberger, *op. cit.*, p. 221.
[20] *Mohair, Distinguished Fiber of Unlimited Uses,* a pamphlet by the American Wool Council, Inc.

finest, while those from India, Iran, and Iraq are coarser. This goat produces the finest fleece when it lives at great altitudes.

We read of Kashmir shawls prized by the Roman Caesars, woven of cashmere from the Vale of Kashmir. Actually, very little cashmere now comes from the state of Kashmir, India.

Cashmere is naturally gray, brown, or white (white is very rare). Fleece of the animal is never shorn but is plucked or combed out by hand. When the animal molts, it rubs itself against the shrubs to relieve itself of itching. The fibers adhering to shrubs are picked off and used.[21] In handpicking, much long hair from the animal's outer coat is mixed with the soft inner fibers. These coarse outer fibers can be removed by special machinery.

Fibers range from one and one-quarter to three and one-half inches long. The scales are hardly visible under the microscope. The diagonal edges of the scales are more or less sharply bent. The cortical layer is striated and filled with color pigment. Some medullas are continuous. Chemical properties of cashmere are similar to those of wool.

The amount of fibers from a single animal is very small: A male produces about four ounces and a female about two ounces per year. It is estimated that fleece of from four to six animals would be needed for a sweater.[22] Small wonder then, that articles of 100 per cent cashmere must be high priced.

### CAMEL'S HAIR

There are two types of camels: the dromedary, which is not heavy enough to produce usable fiber for cloth manufacture, and the Bactrian, the heavier, two-humped, pack-carrying species whose hair is suitable for cloth. This animal lives in all parts of Asia, from the Arabian Sea to Siberia, Turkestan, Tibet, Mongolia, Manchuria, and to all parts of China.[23]

The camel has a fleece with an outer layer of coarse hair and an inner layer of finer hair like a cashmere goat. The inner fibers, called *down*, run one to five inches, whereas the outer fibers range up to fifteen inches. Down is used for clothing. The camel is never sheared or clipped like sheep. At certain seasons, when the warmth of the body expands the skin, the animal sheds his hair. The hair is gathered from the ground. Only when soft under-fibers or down is desired must the camel be plucked.[24] A combing process separates the down from the hair. Wool is often added to camel's hair to give it strength in spinning into yarn. However, the more wool added, the coarser the fabric becomes. Polo cloth, by the Worumbo Manufacturing Company, is an illustration of a

[21] *Cashmere* (New York: Bernhard Ulmann Co.).
[22] *Ibid.*
[23] *The Story of Camel Hair* (New York: S. Stroock & Co., Inc.), p. 3.
[24] *Ibid.*, p. 11.

fine camel's hair and wool blend. Also, the camel's natural pale tan hair is sometimes blended with clear white cashmere, llama, or some of the fine, rare wools for the purpose of obtaining light-colored fabrics. Camel's hair can also be blended with cheaper grades of fibers to bring down the cost. One of the most common uses of camel's hair is in men's and women's coats, because it has a high insulation quality and wears satisfactorily. It may also be found in oriental rugs, blankets, and sweaters.

## THE LLAMA FAMILY

This family is large and may be called "the camel of South America." A few members of this family: the alpaca (the closest relative to the llama), the huarizo and misti (hybrids of the llama and alpaca), and the guanaco and vicuña. The family inhabits the heights of the Andes Mountains. These animals have some of the characteristics of the camel, yet there is no real proof that the camel and llama have the same origin.

The llama and the alpaca are domesticated members of the family, and the guanaco and vicuña are the wild members. Most scientists believe the llama and alpaca to be direct descendants of the guanaco, and the vicuña to be a distinct species.[25] Until shearing time, alpacas roam the range during the day and return to primitive corrals at night. November and December, the spring in llamaland, is shearing time. This is done by hand, half a fleece at a time. Sorting and baling follow. Fleeces of llamas are fine and lustrous but not curly, and the fiber is strong in relation to its diameter. Scales of the fiber are only partly visible and, like the camel's hair, the fiber has a medulla down the center.

The alpaca fibers are white to black in color, and eight, twelve, sixteen, or even thirty inches in length. Llama fibers are black to brown, the guanaco is reddish brown, and the vicuña cinnamon brown (generally used in natural color because of its resistance to dye). Since the vicuña has only recently been domesticated, in small numbers and under government control, production of the fiber is limited. These animals live at great heights, and are found in Peru, Chile, and Bolivia.[26] The vicuña, which produces the world's most valuable specialty fiber known, is protected by law. Only the most opulent consumer can buy a coat of vicuña. Knitting yarns and knit goods are possible uses.

Llama fabrics include women's coats, suits, and dresses; men's summer suits, topcoats, and overcoats.

## MUSK OX

The Federal government is protecting a herd of musk ox, similar to the bison, which is being raised in Alaska. One domesticated breed, the white-faced, has soft, fine, grayish colored fleece similar to cashmere.

[25] *Llamas and Llamaland* (New York: S. Stroock & Co., Inc.).
[26] *Vicuña, The World Finest Fabric* (New York: S. Stroock & Co., Inc., 1946).

*Cow hair*, obtained from our own slaughtered animals and from Japan, England, Canada, and Spain, is used for rug cushions, felts, and coarse rugs.

We import *horsehair* from Argentina and Canada. Horsehair is used principally in interlining for men's suits and coats, and as a stuffing for upholstered furniture.

The *Angora rabbit's fur* has proved very popular for knitting. It can also be blended with wool for filling yarn of a fabric. Such a cloth will feel soft and luxurious. The United States, England, the Netherlands, and Belgium raise the Angora rabbit.

*Common rabbit's hair* is used for our felt hats. The most desirable is the white-faced rabbit, found on this continent and in Europe, parts of China, and Japan. The cheaper gray, wild rabbit's fur, from New Zealand, Australia, and Great Britain, is also used.

## FEATHERS AND DOWN

Goose and duck feathers and down have always had considerable use for stuffing pillows, comforters, and upholstery. Sometimes down in blended with wool to produce a luxurious effect in fabrics.

## SUMMARY

The consumer who selects a wool fabric should be willing to pay for wearing quality, if that is the major factor governing the decision. A good-quality wool is not cheap. A good grade of reprocessed or reused wool, however, is sometimes superior to a poor grade of new wool. Blends of wool with the synthetics and with the natural fibers are growing in importance. The consumer should read the percentages of each fiber and any selling points on the label. Her own judgment and that of the salesperson will help her decide whether the particular blend will satisfy her needs.

## REVIEW QUESTIONS

1. (*a*) What is the definition of wool as given in the Wool Products Labeling Act?
   (*b*) What are "specialty fibers"?
2. (*a*) What is the difference between *domestic* wool and *territory* wool?
   (*b*) In what respects is Australian wool superior to wool grown in the United States?
   (*c*) What is the difference between Australian merino wool and English Lincolnshire or Leicestershire wool? For what purposes is each used?

3. (*a*) Tell the differences between new wool and reused wool.
   (*b*) Define reprocessed wool.
   (*c*) How does reprocessed wool differ from new wool? From reused wool?
4. What factors determine the grade or quality of wool fiber?
5. (*a*) How do worsteds differ from woolens in manufacture?
   (*b*) What are the chief characteristics of worsteds?
   (*c*) What are the chief characteristics of woolens?
6. (*a*) Name five fabrics made of woolen yarn.
   (*b*) Name five fabrics made of worsted yarn.
7. In what ways do the length, diameter, and strength of the wool fiber affect the final cloth?
8. What part do the scales on the fiber play in the manufacture of wool goods?
9. Which would you advise a young lawyer to buy for office wear, a worsted or a woolen fabric? Why?
10. What factors should be considered in judging the durability of wool yarn?
11. (*a*) For what purpose is reused wool important?
    (*b*) If a label reads "all wool," what should the consumer infer?
    (*c*) Write a label for a fabric whose fiber content is 35 per cent reprocessed wool, 4 per cent rayon, 4 per cent linen, 3 per cent silk, 4 per cent cotton, and 50 per cent wool.
12. Why are wool fabrics comfortable?
13. What laundering instructions should a salesperson be able to give a purchaser of a wool fabric?
14. Define mohair, alpaca, cashmere, fleece wool, pulled wool, merino wool, noils, scouring, tops, yarn dye.
15. Write a label for a fabric whose fiber content is 45 per cent rayon, 50 per cent cotton, and 5 per cent wool.
16. (*a*) What characteristic must a wool fabric possess to be considered wash-and-wear?
    (*b*) What is the biggest problem in making wool fabrics wash-and-wear? Discuss fully.

## PROJECT

Make a tabular presentation comparing the physical and chemical properties of the four major natural textile fibers. Use the following form:

| Physical Characteristics | Cotton | Linen | Silk | Wool |
| --- | --- | --- | --- | --- |
| Microscopic appearance | | | | |
| Length of fiber | | | | |
| Diameter | | | | |
| Color | | | | |
| Luster | | | | |
| Strength | | | | |
| Elasticity | | | | |
| Heat conductivity | | | | |
| Hygroscopic moisture | | | | |

| Chemical Characteristics | Cotton | Linen | Silk | Wool |
|---|---|---|---|---|
| Composition of fiber | | | | |
| Effect of light | | | | |
| Effect of mildew | | | | |
| Effect of acids | | | | |
| Effect of alkalies | | | | |
| Effect of bleaches | | | | |
| Affinity of dyestuffs | | | | |

## EXPERIMENTS

1. Examine a wool fiber under the microscope. Draw the fiber as you see it.
2. Boil several wool yarns or a sample of wool fabric in a 10 per cent solution of sodium hydroxide for five minutes. Describe the result.
3. Boil a wool-and-cotton fabric for five minutes in a 10 per cent solution of sodium hydroxide. Describe the result.
4. Place several wool yarns in concentrated sulfuric acid for five minutes. Note the result.
5. Unravel yarns both ways from the fabric. Untwist the yarn. Is it loosely or tightly twisted? Are the fibers parallel, or do they run in every direction? Are the fibers less than two inches or more than two inches in length? Are the fibers all about the same length? Is the yarn a worsted or a woolen?

## GLOSSARY

**Alpaca.** Domesticated member of the llama family, species of "South American camel."

**Breaker.** A machine containing a tooth cylinder used to remove all loose dirt, sand, and the like, and to separate the whole fleece into small sections.

**Camel's hair.** Fibers from the Bactrian, two-humped, pack-carrying species.

**Carding.** A process of opening and cleaning the fibers and putting them in a sliver or web preparatory to spinning.

**Carpet or braid wool.** Very coarse wool from Turkey, Siberia, China, and South America, primarily used in carpets; not suited for clothing.

**Cashmere.** Fleece from the cashmere goat of Tibet, Mongolia, China, Iran, India, and Iraq.

**Cassimere.** See Glossary, Chapter 17.

**Cheviot.** A woolen or worsted fabric in twill weave originally made of wool from sheep of the Cheviot Hills along the English-Scottish border. It has a slightly rough, napped surface and is used for men's and women's coats and suits.

**Chlorinated wool.** Woolens chemically treated to decrease shrinkage and to increase affinity for dyes.

**Clips of knitted fabric.** New wool—never used or worn in any way.

**Combing.** Removing short wool fibers from the sliver and making the fibers parallel.

**Cortex.** Cortical cells in the wool fiber consisting of bundles of fibrils.

**Covert.** A woolen or worsted coating or suiting in twill weave made with two-ply yarns. One of the yarns in the ply may be white and the other colored. This gives a flecked appearance. Covert has recently been made in solid color. It is very durable and is also made in cotton fabrics for work clothes.

**Crimp.** Natural wave of a wool fiber.

**Domestic wools.** From the eastern and middle-western states.

**Donegal tweed.** Originally a thick woolen homespun tweed woven by hand by Irish peasants. Now it refers to a tweed in plain weave characterized by colorful slubs woven into the fabric.

**Drawing.** Attenuating a sliver till it becomes narrower and narrower. Drawing is synonymous with *drafting*.

**Dry decating.** A process of setting the luster of a wool fabric.

**Finished worsted.** Fabric with a softened finish. It is synonymous with *semifinished*.

**Finishes for wool fabrics.** See Glossary, Chapter 7.

**Flannel.** An all-wool fabric of woolen or of worsted yarns, finished with a soft snap that practically obliterates the weave. It is also made in cotton.

**Fleece wool.** Wool shorn from the live sheep. It is superior to *pulled wool*.

**Gabardine.** A tightly woven twilled worsted with a raised diagonal wale on the right side. It can also be cotton, rayon, and blends or mixtures.

**Garnetting.** Shredding wool fabrics into fibrous state, prior to remanufacture into woolen yarn.

**Gigging.** Raising nap by means of teasels.

**Grading.** Determining by touch the fineness of the diameters of individual fibers. *Wool tops* are graded in this fashion. Efforts are now being made to grade wool in the grease by this method.

**Grease.** Natural grease adhering to the wool fiber, which must be removed by scouring.

**Guanaco.** A wild animal of the llama family. See *Llama family*.

**Hard-finished.** A term applied to woolen, worsted, and cotton fabrics that are finished without a nap. Synonym: clear-finished.

**Homespun.** A coarse, nubby woolen in plain weave.

**Horsehair.** Fibers for the most part from Canadian and Argentine horses.

**Jersey.** A wool fabric, usually in stockinette stitch, used for blouses, dresses, and basque shirts. See Glossary, Chapter 6.

**Kemp.** Short-fibered, harsh wool, used principally in carpets.

**Keratin.** A protein substance that is the chief constituent of the wool fiber.

**Lamb's wool.** Soft, resilient wool from lambs seven to eight months old. It is used in fine-grade woolen fabrics.

**Llama family.** A large family of "South American camels." It includes the llama, alpaca, huarizo and misti, guanaco, and vicuña.

**Medulla.** Honeycombed cellular section found in medium and coarse wools.

**Merino wools.** From merino sheep of Australia, South Africa, and South America.

**Mohair.** Hair fibers from the Angora goat.

**Napping.** Raising nap by means of wire bristles.

**New wool.** Wool not previously woven, knitted, or felted into a wool product.

**Noils.** Short wool fibers separated from the long fibers by combing.

**Opener.** See *Breaker*.

**Paddock.** A large enclosed area for sheep grazing. The paddock system is common in Australia.

**Perching.** Visual inspection of wool fabrics.

**Polo cloth.** Trade name for a fine camel's hair and wool blend by the Worumbo Manufacturing Company.

**Pulled wool.** Wool taken from pelts of dead animals by means of chemicals.

**Rabbit hair.** Fur from the angora rabbit.

**Reprocessed wool.** Includes scraps and clips of woven and felted fabrics made of previously unused wool. It must be labeled "Reprocessed wool."

**Reused wool.** Old wool that has been made into a wool product and used by consumers, then cleaned, garnetted, and remade into merchandise. It must be labeled "Reused wool."

**Scales.** Protective covering of the wool fiber.

**Scouring.** The process of freeing wool from dirt, grease, and swint.

**Serge.** Worsted fabric in even twill with the wale showing on both sides. It is piece-dyed a solid color. It may be cotton, rayon, or silk.

**Sharkskin.** A wool fabric in twill weave, originally made of yarns of two colors; it is so-called because of its resemblance to sharkskin leather. Used for men's and women's suitings and slacks, it comes in a clear or semi-finished worsted. Patterns include plaids, stripes, nailheads, and bird's-eye. It is made also in synthetics and blends.

**Sheared wool.** See *Fleece wool*.

**Shoddy.** See *Reused wool*.

**Sorting.** Separating wool fibers by touch according to fineness of fibers.

**Southwestern wools.** From Texas, New Mexico, Arizona, and southern California.

**Specialty fibers.** Hair fibers from various breeds of goats and camels. Also included are cow- and horsehair, fur from rabbits, and feathers of the duck, goose, and ostrich.

**Swint.** Perspiration on the wool fiber.

**Territory wools.** From the Rocky Mountains plateau states.

**Tops.** Long wool fibers in the combed sliver.

**Tropical worsted.** A lightweight, plain weave suiting for men's and women's summer wear. To be labeled "tropical worsted," it must be all-wool worsted. It is made in a variety of fiber blends and mixtures.

**Unfinished worsted.** A worsted fabric finished with a nap.

**Vicuña.** Wild member of the llama family. It produces the world's most valuable specialty fiber.

**Virgin wool.** A term applicable to fabrics or products that have not used any wastes from preliminary processing of new wool.

**Wash-and-wear.** A wool fabric that is shrink-resistant, will not felt or fuzz in washing, has good wrinkle resistance and recovery, and has good tensile strength. See *wash-and-wear*, Chapter 7.

**Wet decating.** A finishing process to add luster to wool fabrics.

**Whipcord.** A twill-weave worsted fabric with a pronounced diagonal wale on the right side, more pronounced than in gabardine. It may also be made in cotton. It is used for riding habits and outdoor wear.

**Wool.**  Fibers from lambs, sheep, and other animals that are used for clothing. It is unlike carpet wool, which is much coarser and unsuitable for clothing. "Wool" refers to fleece wool used for the first time in the complete manufacture of a wool product.

**Wool Products Labeling Act.**  A law requiring that all wool products moving in "commerce" shall be labeled. Carpets, rugs, and upholstery fabrics containing wool come under the T.F.P.I.A.

**Wool rugs.**  A wool floor covering made of carded yarn.

**Woolen.**  A class of wool fabrics made of short fibers of varied lengths and carded yarns.

**Worsted.**  A wool fabric made of long-staple combed yarn.

# 13

# Rayon
# and Acetate
# and the Consumer

In paging through the advertisements of the Sunday newspaper, Mrs. Gallagher notices a particularly attractive fall dress in acetate and rayon crepe satin. She likes the style, and the size and the price are right for her.

But some questions enter her mind: First, Will the crepe shrink in dry cleaning? (Crepes often do.) Secondly, Will the material hang in graceful folds? Thirdly, Will it wear well? (Satins aren't naturally durable, but how about acetate and rayon?)

The answer to the first question is No, if she has a reliable dry cleaner. The acetate in a satin is generally in the warp to help the dimensional stability of the fabric—in short, to keep the shape, size, and fit of the garment. The answer to the second question is Yes. The acetate falls in graceful folds and in soft lines. As for the third question, satin is a beautiful fabric, but its construction (warp floats) does not make it a durable cloth. However, the rayon crepe filling yarns, kept mostly on the back, add strength to the fabric. Rayon crepes excellently.

"Rayon" is a name coined to describe man-made textile fibers derived from cellulose. This textile was first made in the latter part of the nineteenth century. The present name was not applied to this fiber until 1924. Prior to that year it had been sold under the names "artificial silk," "fiber silk," and "gloss."

Count Hilaire de Chardonnet is considered the father of the rayon industry. He was a pupil of Pasteur, who, in 1878, was studying the silkworm diseases that threatened silk production in Europe. Chardonnet studied the silkworm and its product carefully in the hope that he might make silk through some chemical means. In 1884 he did make a fiber by dissolving nitrocellulose in alcohol and ether. In Paris, in 1889, he exhibited his fabrics made of this fiber. Chardonnet admitted that he had not produced silk—his fiber was of cellulose, a vegetable matter, whereas silk is an animal product. He had made an artificial textile fiber *resembling* silk. Logically, then, this man-made fiber was called "artificial silk" for many years.

In 1924 there were three other methods of making this product besides the one discovered by Chardonnet. The industry had flourished appreciably, and there was need of a better generic name to cover all synthetic fibers. In 1924 the National Retail Dry Goods Association was the first to select and sponsor the term "rayon" as a generic name for all textile fabrics formerly known as "artificial silk." Rayon was then more lustrous than it is today, and the name was considered descriptive of the textile; that is, reflecting the rays of the sun.

At the time this name was selected, the National Retail Merchants Association (formerly the National Retail Dry Goods Association) intended that "rayon" should apply to all synthetic fibers, regardless of the manufacturer or the process used in making the fibers. After much discussion, the name "rayon" was adopted generally by the trade. The National Bureau of Standards of the U.S. Department of Commerce defined the term as follows: "Rayon—the generic name of filaments made from solutions of modified cellulose by pressing or drawing the cellulose solution through an orifice and solidifying it in the form of a filament or filaments, by means of some precipitating medium." The Better Business Bureau of New York, the Committee of Textiles of the American Society for Testing Materials, and the Federal Trade Commission adopted this name.

At the time this name was coined, most rayon was made by what was called the *viscose process*. (See p. 339.) The rayons then were exceedingly metallic in luster and not so durable as they are today. The public had bought rayon, which was commonly associated with bargain basements, and many were dissatisfied. Consumers did not know how to care for this new textile, and they expected too much from it. In short, rayon sales dropped, and there was doubt whether rayon could hold its place in competition with the other textiles. Other processes of making synthetic fibers were perfected, and better-quality cloths appeared on the market. Manufacturers who were making good-quality fabrics by methods other than the viscose process refused to have their products shelved because of the customer's sales resistance to the viscose type. So these manufacturers, notably the Celanese Corporation and the American Bemberg Corporation (now Beaunit), named their yarns Celanese and Bemberg, respectively. Through advertising and educational campaigns, these brand names were presented to the public not as rayon yarns but as Celanese or Bemberg yarns.

The branding of synthetic fibers was extremely confusing to both the salesperson and the customer. These brands were sold as "all silk," as "something like silk," as "something brand new," and as "a mixture of silk and something else." To overcome misrepresentation of their products, the manufacturers organized educational bureaus whose representatives traveled about the country lecturing and giving style shows for salespeople in stores, for schools, and for women's clubs. With all the contradictory statements, such as "This is rayon," and "This is not rayon, but a synthetic fiber," the customer had been decidedly confused.

Under the impetus of the consumer movement, the term "rayon" was again clarified in 1937, this time by the F.T.C., as follows: "rayon" is "the generic term for manufactured textile fiber or yarn produced chemically from cellulose or with a cellulose base and for thread, strands of fabric made therefrom, regardless of whether such fiber or yarn be made under the viscose, acetate, cuprammonium, nitrocellulose, or other process." According to this ruling, the consumer thought of rayon as a man-made textile fiber made from cellulose.

The F.T.C. ruling made it an unfair trade practice for a store to sell a fabric made of rayon or having a rayon content (1) as not being rayon, (2) as being something other than rayon, or (3) without disclosing the fact that the product or such material composing it was rayon. Furthermore, if an article was composed of rayon and fibers other than rayon, the predominant fiber by weight was to be mentioned first. Then the other fibers were to be listed in order of their predominance. If a label on a blanket read "Wool, rayon, and cotton," the consumer might assume that wool was the predominant fiber, with rayon in greater amount by weight than cotton. Some manufacturers gave the percentages of fiber content on the label. At the time this ruling was written, certain fabric names connoted the use of a particular fiber. For example, "chiffon" meant silk; "gabardine" meant wool. Therefore, such staple names were not to be applied to articles made of rayon unless the fiber content was named; that is, "rayon chiffon" and "rayon gabardine." Furthermore, when manufacturers used trade names to identify their products, the term rayon had to be used as a part of the name; for example, Bemberg rayon, Celanese rayon, du Pont rayon.

When the Textile Fiber Products Identification Act became effective, on March 3, 1960, all "textile fiber products" were required to be identified. (See Chapter 2.) The terms rayon, acetate, acrylic, etc., were defined by the F.T.C. as generic names of man-made textile fibers. There has been agitation on the part of manufacturers of modified cellulosic fibers to identify them by a generic term other than rayon. At the time of this writing the F.T.C. has not done so.

## PROCESSES FOR MAKING RAYON AND ACETATE

Rayon is made from cellulose treated with chemicals so that it forms a viscous solution. Cellulose was obtained at first from cotton linters (short hairs covering the cotton seeds). Now the cellulose used in the production of cellulosic fibers is the high-alpha cellulose derived from spruce and other soft woods.[1]

New sources have been found for improved cellulose. It can be extracted from vegetable matter such as deciduous instead of coniferous trees. By modified extraction techniques, cellulose similar to that which is made from cotton fiber can be produced; in some cases it may even be better than cellulose from cotton fiber. The solution is forced through almost microscopic holes in a jet or *spinneret*. The solution emerges from the spinneret in the form of a fiber and is hardened either by the evaporation of the chemicals as they come in contact with the air or by coagulation resulting from a bath in chemicals.

Rayon processes were put into commercial use in the following order: (1) the *nitrocellulose* (Chardonnet) method (not used in the United States and Canada); (2) the *cuprammonium* method; and (3) the *viscose* method.

### NITROCELLULOSE PROCESS

The process discovered by Chardonnet in 1884 produced a very inflammable, explosive fiber. Many improvements had to be made. Since nitrocellulose rayon is not being made in the United States, the steps in the process will not be given.

### CUPRAMMONIUM PROCESS

Louis Henri Despaisses developed this process in France in 1890, one year after Chardonnet's exhibition. The process was later improved. The following steps are necessary:

1. Cotton linters are boiled with caustic soda and soda ash and are then bleached with chlorine.

[1] *Man-Made Fiber Fact Book*, Man-Made Fiber Producers Association, Inc. (October, 1968), p. 9.

2. They are washed, dried, and then dissolved in copper oxide and ammonia.
3. The dark blue solution is forced through spinnerets having rather large holes.
4. Filaments are stretched and finally hardened in mild sulfuric acid.

Cuprammonium rayon is sold under the trademark "Bemberg."

## VISCOSE PROCESS

Three English chemists, Cross, Bevan, and Beadle, discovered the process in 1892, but commercial production of viscose rayon did not begin until after the turn of the century. The steps in the process follow. (See Figure 13.1).

1. Bleached sulfite wood pulp is cut into sheets.

**Figure 13.1.** The viscose process for making rayon. (*Reproduced courtesy of FMC Corporation.*)

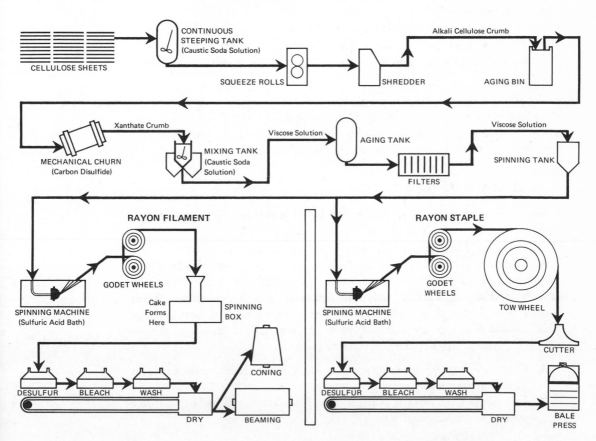

RAYON YARN MANUFACTURING PROCESS

**Figure 13.2.** Extrusion of viscose fibers into a hardening bath. *(Photograph courtesy of FMC Corporation.)*

2. The sheets are steeped in caustic soda; the product (alkali cellulose) is aged.
3. It is treated with carbon bisulfide (cellulose xanthate).
4. It is treated with a weak solution of caustic soda.
5. The honey-colored solution is forced through spinnerets into sulfuric acid, which regenerates the cellulose as a continuous filament.

Cuprammonium and viscose are regenerated rayons because they begin with cellulose and the final product is regenerated cellulose. Other forms of regenerated cellulose fibers that are classified by the F.T.C. as rayon without separate, distinctive names include fibers of cuprammonium, high wet modulus rayon, cross-linked rayon, and saponified rayon.

### CELLULOSE-ACETATE PROCESS

The acetate solution was discovered by Maudin and Schutzenburger in 1869, but it was not used for spinning commercial fibers until after World War I. The British Cellulose & Chemical Manufacturing Company had utilized this method to make dope for airplane wings. Dope prevented the fabric from deteriorating in the ultraviolet rays of the sun. A coating of varnish was the necessary weatherproofing. After World War I, the factories that had made this material would have closed had it not been for the discovery of a method of making yarn by a similar process. Briefly, the steps are as follows:

1. Cotton linters are treated with a solution of acetic anhydride in glacial acetic acid.
2. The ripened product is plunged into cold water, where the cellulose acetate separates into white flakes.

**340**

FLOW DIAGRAM

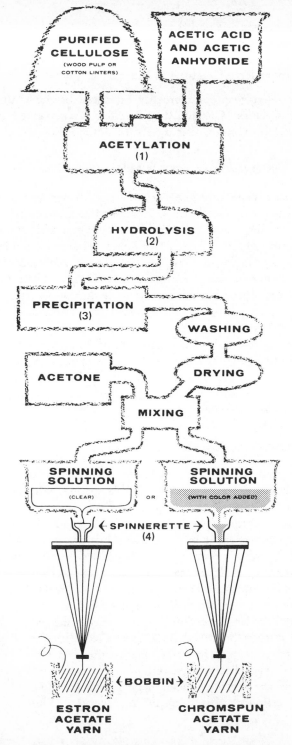

**Figure 13.3.** The cellulose acetate process. (*Reproduced courtesy of the Tennessee Eastman Company, Division of Eastman Kodak Company.*)

3. The flakes are washed and dried.
4. They are dissolved in acetone and filtered.
5. The syrupy, colorless solution is forced through jets and hardened by the evaporation of acetone in the air.

Acetate fibers were first commercially produced in the United States in 1924 by the Celanese Corporation. Familiar trademarked names of acetate fibers are Chromspun, Estron, Acele, Avisco Acetate.

### SIMILARITY OF THE RAYON AND ACETATE PROCESSES

All three processes use cellulose derived from either spruce wood or cotton linters. The purified cellulose is treated with chemicals (the choice of chemicals depending upon the process) to convert the treated cellulose into a solution, which is forced through a spinneret (a nozzle with tiny holes). The tiny holes in the spinneret govern the diameter of the filaments. The filaments are then hardened. During each process in manufacturing, the fibers are controlled in length, size, strength, and luster. Fibers are spun into yarn and woven or knitted into cloth.

Each process derives its name from an important step in the process. The word *cuprammonium* is descriptive of the copper and ammonia solution used to dissolve cotton linters. The name viscose is derived from the viscous or sticky, thick, honey-like solution that is forced through the spinneret in the viscose process. The treatment of cellulose with acetic acid gives the cellulose-acetate process its name.

### DIFFERENCES BETWEEN RAYON AND ACETATE

The burning test (explained in Chapter 2) revealed the fact that acetate fiber burns and leaves a brittle, black residue, whereas cuprammonium and viscose rayon burn like paper and leave no appreciable residue. The reason acetate fiber burns differently from the other two is that the acetate fibers are not pure cellulose, but are cellulose combined with acetic acid. In other words, acetate fiber is a vegetable *and* chemical fiber. Cuprammonium and viscose rayons are pure cellulose, and these two vegetable fibers burn like cotton, which is also vegetable.

Viscose and cuprammonium rayons are classified as "regenerated rayons," because the cellulose, a solid, is changed to a liquid and is then hardened back into a solid in the form of filaments (fibers). In brief, the viscose and cuprammonium processes begin with cellulose and end with cellulose, whereas the acetate process begins with cellulose and ends with cellulose plus a chemical (acetyl). This

**Figure 13.4. Spinneret.** (*Photograph courtesy of FMC Corporation.*)

chemical element gives acetate fibers physical and chemical characteristics that the rayon fibers do not have. Those qualities will be discussed later in the chapter.

## MODIFIED RAYONS

Basic technical developments in the field of cellulosic fibers have caused rayon to achieve renewed importance to the consumer. These developments include high-tenacity rayon, especially for cord tires; the improved wet strength of rayon, which has increased its durability in apparel; rayon fibers with permanent crimp, which are adaptable to fabrics of a bulky texture; polynosic fibers (cellulosic-based fibers with a basic inner structure similar to the natural cellulosic fibers), which result in a fiber that has an extremely high tensile and wet strength.

### HIGH-TENACITY RAYON

Viscose rayon filaments can be "modified" by chemical treatment while they are in a plastic state to give them high tenacity. (See Chapter 2.) Brand names of high-tenacity modified rayons are Cordura and Tenasco.

The cross-linking method, also described in Chapter 2, produces another high-tenacity rayon, which, although it has dimensional stability, has a tenacity that is not so high as the high-wet-strength type discussed later. This product, Corval, is made by Courtaulds North America, Inc. This type of rayon shows greater dimensional stability in washing than regular rayon. The cross-linking method is used in the production of Corval.

### CRIMPED-FIBERED RAYON

Crimped (viscose process) rayon is achieved by several different processes, each of which modifies the internal structure of the fiber. In one method the crimp is due to an asymmetry in the molecular structure of the fiber. The crimp is permanent because it is an integral part of the fiber itself. Crimped Fibro by Courtaulds, Ltd., is produced by this method. Crimped fibers when used in dress goods are warm and soft, and may be solid-colored or printed.

### HIGH-WET-STRENGTH RAYON

This type of modified rayon has been commercially available only since 1961. In a scientific study of the natural cellulosic fibers, it was found that these fibers are characterized by a very fine fibril structure and that the molecular orientation is very regular. Scientists know that natural cellulosic fibers like cotton have increased tensile strength when wet, a low swelling factor, and good dimensional stability. So scientists have directed their efforts to develop man-made cellulosic fibers whose structure would be similar to the natural cellulosics. On the other hand, a study of the properties of man-made cellulosic fibers has contributed to the improvement of the natural cellulosic types.

This type of fiber—referred to as high wet modulus rayon—is sold under the trade names Avril, Lirelle, Nupron, Xena, and Zantrel.

"Polynosic" is the anglicized spelling of the name used in France and Belgium as the generic classification for regenerated cellulosic fibers with high wet strength. Some authorities claim that the polynosic fibers have lower absorptive qualities than regular rayon.

A 50/50 blend of high-wet-strength rayon and carded cotton produces a fabric with the esthetic quality the hand and appearance of 100 per cent combed cotton at a lower price. Hence, style can be added to a cotton fabric, and at the same time carded cotton can be upgraded to the combed category. Furthermore, to enhance their beauty, these fabrics can be mercerized, because they are more resistant to caustic soda than regular rayon. Fabrics can be stabilized by compressive shrinkage (as is the case with cotton) and treated with resins for wash-and-wear properties. Creslan and wool, in a 50/50 blend, make a lightweight fleecy fabric for coatings.

### SAPONIFIED RAYON

Saponified rayon is made by converting cellulose to cellulose acetate, which is dissolved in an organic solvent for extruding. The extruded filaments of cellulose acetate are reconverted to cellulose. This chemical regeneration process is called *saponification*. Saponified rayon has exceptionally high strength, good shape retention, fine textures in lightweight fabrics, and good dimensional stability.[2] Fortisan rayon, by the Celanese Corporation, is such a high-tenacity filament yarn. Its fibers when treated are known as *regenerated cellulose*, yet its yarn can be finer than silk. It does not shrink or stretch, it is easier to dye because the fiber is saponified, and it resists sunlight and chemicals. Since it feels a bit clammy, it is not used for apparel. It is frequently made in blends for curtains and draperies. Fortisan may be machine-laundered or dry-cleaned.

### MODIFIED ACETATES

Acetate fibers can be modified. We have seen how cellulose acetate can be saponified to become high-tenacity rayon.

[2] *Man-Made Fiber Fact Book*, p. 10.

Since acetate fibers fuse with heat, a mechanical crimp is possible. A treatment of acetate to give permanent crimp apparently originated in Germany. Crimped acetate is inexpensive and seems to have possibilities for use in blends with wool in cotton skirts, dresses, and shirtings.

## TRIACETATE

One of the consumer's objections to acetate is that it fuses when ironed with a hot iron. Arnel is an answer to this objection. As was stated in Chapter 2, it is a thermoplastic material that contains three acetate components. In short, triacetate fibers contain a higher ratio of acetate to cellulose than do acetate fibers.

We are all familiar with 100 per cent Arnel jersey—its wash-and-wear properties; its minimum-care characteristics when blended with cotton for blouses, dresses, and skirts; its good colorfastness to light and washing; its basic stability in washing; its relatively low cost; its ability to be pressed at a much higher temperature than regular acetate; its permanency in holding pleats. Yet even Arnel is not perfect in all respects. It has relatively limited abrasion resistance and tensile strength.[3] But it is the modified rayons and acetates that have helped rayon and acetate to compete successfully with other man-made and natural fibers.

## CHARACTERISTICS OF RAYON AND ACETATE FIBERS

### MICROSCOPIC APPEARANCE

Under the microscope, viscose rayon has even, rodlike fibers. Small, lengthwise striations, like shadows, are distinguishing features of bright or lustrous viscose. In viscose rayon that is made dull, the fibers become specked as with pepper.

Under the microscope, acetate fibers also appear even and rodlike. In cross section the fiber is similar to the clover leaf. The lustrous type does not seem so glossy as the regenerated rayons. There are heavy grooves or line marks running the length of the fiber. (See the Appendix.) Arnel's lengthwise microscopic view is much like regular acetate, but its cross-sectional view has less distinct clover-leaf configurations.

Cuprammonium rayon fibers are even in diameter and rodlike, but with no lengthwise markings. When delustered, the surface of the fiber is covered with fine pigment. Under the microscope the fiber looks peppered. (See the Appendix.)

The modified rayons Avril and Zantrel are cylindrical in cross section. Due to saponification, Fortisan rayon's appearance becomes more like

---

[3] *Textile Fibers and Their Properties*, a pamphlet by Burlington Industries, Inc. (1968).

that of regenerated rayon. The groove markings of the original acetate fiber are less distinct and the cross section is more irregular.

## PHYSICAL CHARACTERISTICS OF RAYON AND ACETATE FIBERS
### LENGTH OF FIBER

There are two types of rayon and acetate fibers as determined by length:

(1) Filament type is called *continuous* because it can be made any desired length as long as the viscous solution continues to be forced through the spinnerets. Prior to 1934, this was the only kind of rayon and acetate yarn made. The continuous filaments of rayon and acetate fibers are made into *continuous filament yarns*. This type of yarn is very important in fabrics such as satin, the lustrous surface of which depends to a great extent upon even, unbroken fibers.

(2) Rayon or acetate staple is a fiber made in controlled lengths. To make these staples, the filaments from several spinnerets are gathered into a rope called *tow*. The tow is cut into the length appropriate for the intended use of the staple. For example, if the yarn is to have a woolly texture, the staple will approximate the length of a wool fiber. If the yarn is to resemble the short, fuzzy cotton yarn, the staple is cut the length of a cotton fiber. Staple has to be bleached, rinsed, and dried before yarn can be spun. These processes may precede or follow cutting of the tow. Staple is made into *spun yarns*. Rayon or acetate staple can be mixed with other short fibers, such as cotton, short-fiber silk, and wool, to make spun yarns called *blends*. Staple may be made to resemble wool by crimping it mechanically or by modifying the molecular structure of the fiber. Crimped fibers are more resilient and hence more crease-resistant than untreated fibers. (See p. 37.)

Viscose rayon staple can be made into bonded-fiber webs. (Methods for constructing these webs were discussed in Chapter 6.)

Bonded-fiber webs are used in industry for filters, tapes, ribbons, wrappers, tags, insulation covering, bags, and lens-wiping tissues. Household uses include curtains, draperies, napkins, tablecloths, towels, and wiping cloths.

### DIAMETER OF FIBERS

The diameter of the staple fiber depends partly upon the size of the openings in the spinneret. If a smooth, even texture is desired, the diameter of the fiber can be kept the same throughout its length. The diameter of single filaments may be varied by adjusting the pressure of the viscous solution as it passes through the spinneret. Fibers with varying diameters are called *thick and thin* and are made into yarns with varying diameters called thick-and-thin yarns.

Since natural fibers are uneven in diameter, staple fibers can simulate the texture of natural fibers.

To appreciate the fineness of individual filaments, one should realize that there are sometimes over two hundred filaments in a single yarn (depending upon its size or denier).

## COLOR OF FIBER

When the fiber is spun, the color of viscose is yellow, acetate is colorless, and cuprammonium is white.

Rayon and acetate yarns for weaving are white or colored. If bleaching is required, it can be done after the filament is hardened or after the yarn is spun and before or after it is made into skeins. If the yarn is to be colored, the dye may be applied to the yarns, as in the dyeing of cotton, linen, silk, or wool; or dyestuffs may be added to the spinning solution. The filaments, when hardened, are colored; hence yarns made from these fibers are called *spun dyed, solution dyed,* or *dope dyed,* all of which mean dyed in the spinning solution. The coloring of the fibers by this method has a double advantage: It produces durable colors and it saves the time and expense involved in dyeing large quantities of yarn one color—black, for instance. This spun-dyed method is now available for both acetate and rayon.

Trade names of acetate solution-dyed yarns include the Tennessee Eastman Company's Chromspun and Celanese's Celaperm. In rayon, there is American Enka Corporation's filament rayon solution-dyed Jet-spun, Courtaulds' rayon staple called Coloray, and Beaunit's Cupra Color. The solution-dyed fibers have improved colorfastness, particularly to light and to laundering. For acetate, this method of dyeing has overcome the gas-fading problem.

## LUSTER

When a rayon manufacturer follows the steps in the processes of making rayon outlined on page 338 ff., he makes high-luster rayon fibers, which would be made into what are called *bright yarns.*

For dull fabrics, such as crepe and wool-like, linen-like, and cottony textures, bright rayon has to be dulled. A permanent delustering process is achieved by incorporating mineral oil or insoluble white pigments (microscopical solids) in the spinning solution before the viscous solution passes through the spinneret. Mineral oil in the spinning solution forms microscopic bubbles that deflect light. The fine pepper-like particles of pigments also break up the clear, glassy appearance of rayon fibers. (See the Appendix.)

Rayons and acetate can be made in three degrees of luster: bright, semidull, and dull.

Conventional rayon is stronger dry than wet, whereas cotton and linen are stronger wet than dry. Rayon, wet or dry, is not so strong as nylon. Acetate is slightly stronger than rayon when wet. Rayon's breaking tenacity (grams per denier) wet is 0.8 to 1.2; acetate is 0.7 to 1.8.[4]

Although conventional rayon is weaker when wet than when dry, its original strength returns after drying.

Modified rayon fibers now produced are of three types: (1) high strength or high tenacity, (2) high wet-strength, and (3) cross-linked. (For a discussion of the advantages and drawbacks of each type, see p. 343.)

Triacetate has become a wash-and-wear fabric of the generic class of acetate fibers. Its performance has already been discussed.

## ELASTICITY

Rayon is more elastic than linen, and it may be as elastic as the average cotton, but it is not so elastic as the higher-priced, good-quality pure silk. The greater proportion of cuprammonium rayon is made by a stretch spinning process that increases normal elasticity and makes the yarn more usable for such garments as hosiery and underwear. The viscous solution is forced through a hole in the spinneret larger in diameter than the final fiber is to be; as the fibers emerge from the coagulating process, they are pulled or stretched and then twisted to form yarn.

Probably many customer complaints about rayon garments that split at the seams are caused by the customer's purchasing a tight-fitting garment. Rayon thread and yarn are not so resilient as good-grade pure silk, and often the purchaser is unaware of the danger that a garment may split at points of strain. However, finishing treatments for crease resistance improve resiliency in rayon fabrics. (See pp. 169 ff.)

## HYGROSCOPIC MOISTURE

Acetate absorbs about the same amount of moisture as cotton (6.5 per cent); cuprammonium and viscose absorb a little more than silk (11 per cent).

## EFFECT OF LIGHT

Rayon has about the same resistance to sunlight as cotton. Acetate is more resistant to sunlight than cotton and viscose rayon.

[4] *Man-Made Fiber Fact Book,* p. 30.

Acetates are more resistant to mildew than viscose or cuprammonium rayons.

## HEAT

Viscose decomposes at 350° to 400° F. Cuprammonium decomposes at 300° F. Acetate shines at 275° F. and sticks to the iron at 350° to 375° F. A safe ironing temperature for Arnel triacetate is 350° F. Zantrel and Corval rayons may be ironed safely at 375° F. Rayon is therefore more resistant to heat than acetate. A hot iron should not be used on acetate.

## ACIDS

Oxalic, tartaric, and citric acids weaken rayons slightly if the fibers are allowed to remain in the acids any length of time or if heat is used. Formic and acetic acid injure the acetate fiber if used in strong solutions. The rayons are not harmed. Concentrated strong acids, such as sulfuric, hydrochloric, and nitric acids, destroy rayon fibers. Cold, dilute mineral acids must be washed out at once or be neutralized. The effect is the same as on cotton and linen.

## ALKALIES

Ammonia, borax, soap, and phosphate of soda may deaden the luster of acetate fibers unless care is taken. Other types are not harmed. Potassium permanganate bleach weakens rayon and so should not be used. Cuprammonium is attacked by strong oxidizing agents. Chlorines and hydrochlorites are used to bleach these fibers in the same way as for cotton and linen. A treatment with alkali will convert acetate fiber into regenerated cellulose. A partial modification raises the fusing point and changes the affinity for dyes. (See p. 38.) Modified rayons are more resistant to caustic soda than the regular type.

## AFFINITY FOR DYESTUFFS

Viscose and cuprammonium rayons have good affinity for the same dyestuffs that are used on cottons and linens. Acetate fiber, unless partially modified, does not have affinity for the same dyestuffs as viscose and cupra rayon, so special dyes or treatment must be used for acetates.[5] Therefore, acetates in combination with rayons or with other fibers produce unusual color effects by virtue of cross-dyeing. (See *methods of dyeing*, Chapter 8.)

[5] See disperse dyes, Chapter 8.

A new way to give rayon fibers an affinity for acid wool dyes has been produced by Courtaulds, Ltd., of Great Britain. A mixture of aminoethyl cellulose and diethylaminoethyl cellulose ethers in the form of their sodium xanthate salts is incorporated in the viscose spinning solution. An alternate method is to add these chemicals to the alkali cellulose prior to its conversion to a viscose solution.

With the appropriate dyestuffs, most rayons have good color and can be dyed so as to be colorfast to light and to laundering, if the fabric is well finished and correctly dyed. Acetate has fair sunlight resistance. Solution-dyed acetate does not gas-fade.

## RAYON AND ACETATE YARN

### METHODS OF SPINNING

It is necessary to go back to the step in making rayon where the solution is in a viscous state and ready to be forced through the jets or spinnerets.

The filaments are twisted into yarns by (1) the continuous spinning method or (2) the box method.

Briefly, in the continuous spinning method the viscous solution passes through the spinnerets and is coagulated into yarn. Several filaments are grouped together, the number depending on the size of the yarn required. The grouped filaments are wound on spools. They are then rewound on other spools, being twisted at the same time. The yarns are then wound from spools onto bobbins.

In the box method the box or container revolves, and the centrifugal force of the revolutions throws the grouped filaments to the side of the box, putting in the twist at the same time. The yarns emerge from the box in hollow form, resembling an angel cake. The yarns are reeled into skeins, washed, bleached, and dried.

The cellulose-acetate and cuprammonium processes use the continuous spinning method of spinning. The cuprammonium process uses the stretching device previously explained. Some viscose yarn is also made by this method, but the bulk of it is made by box spinning.

### KINDS OF RAYON AND ACETATE YARNS

1. *Filament rayon* and *acetate yarns* are made of continuous filaments grouped together so that they lie parallel. Because they are all long, only a very slight twist is needed to hold the fibers together.

   *Thick and thin* and slub yarns vary in diameter because they are made of continuous filaments that vary in diameter.[6] Such

   ---

   [6] Spun yarns may also be made *thick and thin* and slubbed.

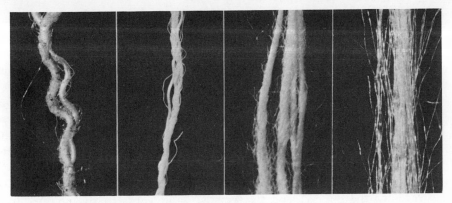

**Figure 13.5.** Types of rayon yarns. *Left to right:* Combination, abraded, spun, and filament. (*Photo by Jack Pitkin.*)

yarns are novelty yarns. Another type of novelty yarn is made by flattening the yarn so that it has the gleam of crystal. These yarns are sold under the trade-name Crystal Yarns by the Tennessee Eastman Company. Other novelty yarns include du Pont's textured and spiral yarns.

2. *Filament high-strength yarn* is made of continuous filaments chemically or mechanically while in the plastic state. These yarns may be used in hosiery, sports clothes, shirtings, towelings, sailcloth, draperies, filter cloths, football uniforms, belts, tire-cord fabrics, and coverings for elastic yarns. (See p. 343.) The high-wet-strength modified rayons are good blenders (with cotton in particular). Minimum-care finishes employ resins in these rayons much the same as in all-cotton.

3. *Spun yarn* is spun from staple fibers. Staple fibers are sometimes combined with one or more of the natural or newer synthetic fibers. This mass of short fibers gathered together has to be straightened before being twisted into yarn. Spun yarns are tightly twisted to hold the short fibers together. The ends of the fibers project from the yarn to make a fabric with a fuzzy surface.

4. *Combination yarns* can be made (1) with rayon and acetate yarns combined in ply form (often in different degrees of twist), or (2) with rayon yarns combined with yarns of another fiber. It should be remembered that filament or spun yarns can be composed of fiber blends.

5. *Textured and novelty rayon yarns* can be made. The bulky types are used in pile fabrics particularly. Novelty types include yarns with small random nubs, Ondelette filament rayon by du Pont; Strawn, a high-luster monofilament ribbon cross-section filament yarn that is like straw, by Industrial Corporation; and Glitter, a cuprammonium sparkling yarn, by Beaunit.

**351**

The size of filament rayon and acetate yarn is computed on the denier basis. (See p. 67.) Rayon yarns average between 100 and 200 denier, with 150 the most usual. The coarsest yarn is 2,200 denier. Fifteen denier would be considered a fine yarn. There are 1-, 1¼-, and 1½-denier Avril rayon staples made by the American Viscose Division of the FMC Corporation, which makes possible finer, softer spun-rayon fabrics. These fine rayon fibers can also be used in blends with pima and Egyptian cotton, fine wools, and silks. Acetate yarns have similar deniers.

The sizes of spun-rayon yarns may be computed on the same basis as cotton (840 yards to the pound for count #1), but the woolen (1,600 yards to the pound) and the worsted (560 yards to the pound) bases are also used, depending on the spinning system employed. Single rayon yarns range approximately from a coarse yarn of #10 to a fine yarn of #80, with an average of #30 on the cotton system of spinning.

### COMPANIES MANUFACTURING RAYON AND ACETATE YARN

Now that rayon fabrics have to be labeled, the consumer is becoming more familiar with brand names and their fiber content.

It is important to note that some manufacturers use fibers made by both the viscose and the acetate processes. Also, the growth in popularity of acetate yarn has caused many companies that formerly manufactured only viscose to launch upon the production of acetate. Companies that make rayon yarns do not, as a rule, make cloth. A list of leading manufacturers of rayon and acetate fibers in the United States, together with their trademark names, was given in Chapter 2. Since it is customary for fiber producers also to make yarn, a list of yarn producers will not be given.

### RAYON AND ACETATE PRODUCTION

Of the total world production of man-made textile fibers (nearly 13½ billion pounds), slightly over one-half is rayon and acetate, and a little less than half is noncellulosic fibers. In the United States, the noncellulosic fibers production is ahead of rayon and acetate.[7]

### CONSTRUCTION OF RAYON AND ACETATE FABRICS

Since rayon and acetate can be made to resemble cotton, linen, silk, or wool textures, the choice of fiber (staple or filament), type of yarn (filament, spun, combination, or novelty), construction, and finish will

[7] *Man-Made Fiber Fact Book,* p. 35.

be determined by the appearance and the use desired of the resultant fabric.

### IN PLAIN WEAVE OR ITS VARIATIONS

In the cotton-like textures, rayon and/or acetate may be made in gingham, seersucker, poplin, and sharkskin (for blouses). A 50/50 cotton and modified rayon blend is used in broadcloth. One of the most popular textures, made to resemble linen, is rayon and/or acetate butcher. To resemble wool, there are challis, some flannels, some bouclés, and crepe. Rayon or acetate shantung, moiré, voile, ninon, taffeta, faille, bengaline, georgette, chiffon, and flat crepe are but a few of the silk-like textures in plain weave.

### IN TWILL WEAVE OR ITS VARIATIONS

A good many rayon or acetate suitings for men and women are made in twill. For this use, a wool-like texture is required. Many tweeds, most flannels and gabardine, and many sharkskins (suiting) are twills. In silk-like textures, there are foulard and surah.

### IN SATIN WEAVE

Satin in dress, bridal, slipper, or drapery weights is frequently made of these fibers and resembles silk in construction.

### IN JACQUARD AND DOBBY

There are many rayon and/or acetate necktie fabrics in Jacquard or dobby that are silk-like in texture. Brocades, damasks, brocatelles, and tapestries for draperies and upholsteries may be made in part or entirely of rayon or acetate. Lamé for women's formal wear is also Jacquard.

### IN PILE WEAVE

Probably the best-known pile fabric in these fibers is transparent velvet. Brocaded velvets frequently are made with the pile designs of rayon. Furlike fabrics made to simulate broadtail, beaver, mink, and Persian lamb may be partially of rayon. There are a few novelty terry cloths made with rayon pile.

### IN LENO WEAVE

Marquisette for glass curtains and dress fabrics is always made in leno weave, no matter what fiber is used.

Two-bar tricot construction is used for slips, gowns, and blouses. Single-bar tricot is used primarily in lingerie, whereas weft knitting frequently appears in rayon jersey and hosiery. Development of a knitting yarn of 50/50 blend of cotton and modified rayon gives an improved appearance. Since lace is closely allied to knitting, chantilly, and bobbinet, which are often made of rayon, should also be mentioned.

## RAYON AND ACETATE FABRICS: REGULAR FINISHES

### BLEACHING

Although rayon is usually bleached in the yarn or skein, the finisher may bleach rayon fabrics. To do so, he uses sodium hydroxide, sodium perborate, and hydrogen peroxide. Sodium hypochlorite is used for acetate cloth. A wool-and-acetate blend is generally bleached with hydrogen peroxide.

### BRUSHING

To remove short, loose fibers, brushing is important.

### DRY DECATING

When a rayon is made to resemble wool or when rayon is blended or mixed with wool, dry decating is done to set the luster permanently (see p. 319).

### NAPPING

Again, when a fabric is to resemble wool, it is napped. (See *gigging* and *napping*, pp. 320 f.)

### SINGEING AND SHEARING

Both processes are needed to remove surface fibers and lint. Even though a fabric has been singed, fibers may become raised as the cloth passes through various finishing processes and may have to be sheared. Pile is shortened by shearing.

### SCOURING

This process is applied to most fabrics to remove oil, sizing, and dirt.

### SIZING

Sizing increases weight and crispness of a fabric.

Shrinkage of rayon in width and in length can now be controlled (stabilized to repeated launderings). (See Chapter 7 for shrinkage control finishes.) When the fabric is resin-treated, the stability is good. The new modified rayons have greatly improved stability over the regular type. Cotton and rayon blends are stabilized with mechanical compressive shrinkage procedures similar to those used on all-cotton fabrics. There is less loss of strength in the new modified rayon than in the cotton component. Acetates normally have good dimensional stability; and have fair stability after repeated launderings.

### INSPECTING, TENTERING, AND CALENDERING

All fabrics must be visually inspected and then tentered in order to even them in the width. The calendering finish smooths, glazes, moirés, or embosses. On acetate, a slight fusion by heat embosses or moirés a fabric permanently.

## RAYON AND ACETATE FABRICS: FUNCTIONAL FINISHES

### ABSORBENT

Since foundation garments and underwear are required to absorb moisture, an absorbent finish is used for these fabrics.

### CREASE-RESISTANT

Synthetic resins give additional resiliency to these fibers. Tebelized is a trademark of the T. B. Lee Company indicating a fabric's ability to hold a press. Prestwick, by Courtaulds North America, Inc., is a familiar crease-resistant finish. (See Chapter 7.)

### FIRE-RESISTANT

Vegetable fibers, such as cotton and rayon, burn much more rapidly than wool. The speed of burning depends not only on the fibers but also on the twist of yarn, construction, and finish. Napped or so-called brushed rayon is highly flammable unless treated for fire resistance. (See pp. 172 ff. for Flammable Fabrics Act.) Trademark finishes in this field include Pyroset, by American Cyanamid Company, and Flamefoil, by Philadelphia Textile Finishers, Inc.

### GERM-RESISTANT

Fabrics to be made germ-resistant, such as linings in slippers, are treated with germicides-fungicides.

STARCHLESS

Bobbinets, glass curtainings, and organdies are fabrics in which stiffness and crispness are characteristics. Wat-A-Set is a durable, washable finish that may be applied in manufacture. It is used particularly for curtains, to keep them crisp. This is a trademark of the Mount Hope Finishing Company.

WASH-AND-WEAR

Since modified rayons can be treated for crease resistance, can be shrinkage controlled, and have good tensile strength when wet, these rayons are used particularly in blends with cottons, polyesters, and acrylics.

WATER REPELLENT

(For the method of treatment for water repellency, see pp. 184 ff.) Most consumers, and servicemen in particular, are familiar with the permanent Zepel finish by du Pont for rayon, acetate, cotton, and blends. The Cravenette Company has several water-repellent finishes: (1) a non-durable wax finish, (2) a semidurable wax finish called Long Life, and (3) a durable Super Silicone finish. These finishes are used on apparel, slipcovers, draperies, and curtains. Impregnole, by Warwick Chemical Company, Inc., is made in both nondurable and semidurable types. Laundries and cleaners use another nondurable type to reapply to cleaned articles. Permel Plus, manufactured by American Cyanamid, is a durable water-repellent finish. Hydro-pruf, by the Arkansas Company, is a durable silicone finish for water repellency.

## WHY CONSUMERS BUY RAYON AND ACETATE FABRICS

### ECONOMY

Rayon and acetate by themselves or in blends are economical. They are sold in a wide range of prices and can be found at a price to fit any pocketbook. When blended with wool or with the newer synthetics, rayon and acetate help keep the prices down.

### ATTRACTIVENESS

Rayons can be made as sheer as the most cobwebby silk crepe or voile and as heavy as any silk satin. The luster of rayon is permanent. It can be bright, semidull, or dull. One method of making triple-sheer dull crepe is by the use of extremely fine, multifilament yarn. These very fine filaments are twisted together very tightly for crepes but little or not at all for sheer fabrics, where softness and drapability are important.

Fine denier rayon staple has made possible unusually strong, beautiful, and soft fabrics. Novelty fabrics with a new glint are being created by the use of nubbed textures and sparkling yarns.

All rayon or blends with other fibers can be made to be aristocratic-looking fabrics as well as dull, practical-looking material for hard wear. From among fabrics made in all weights, in all weaves, and in all colors and prints, the college girl, debutante, matron, mother, homemaker, businesswoman, or well-dressed man should be able to find a fabric becoming to his or her type and appropriate to the surroundings in which the fabric is to be used. New textures and blends also provide new designs and patterns for contemporary décor in carpets, rugs, and draperies.

### VERSATILITY

There are good, medium, and poor qualities of rayon and acetate, just as there are of cottons, linens, silks, and wools. The blending of rayon with other fibers definitely increases its uses. Also, the various types of yarns have contributed to the versatility of rayon.

Rayons can be worn at all hours of the day: for sleeping, sports, business, street, afternoon tea, cocktails, dinner, and evening wear. They are important in home furnishings, too.

### COMFORT

Filament rayon yarns make a very cool fabric, because they are cellulosic. A fabric made of filament acetate yarns feels warmer than a fabric of filament rayon. Filament yarns are smooth and therefore feel cooler than spun yarns, which have fuzzier and more wool-like textures. Spun yarns are frequently napped, a treatment that makes for warmth. When rayon is mixed with silk or wool, the resultant fabric is warmer than all-rayon. The modified high-wet-strength rayons have a comfortable feeling when worn next to the skin because they absorb moisture and allow air to pass through the woven cloth.

Spun rayons and acetates have a soft, relatively warm feel and are frequently used in suits and dresses of wool-like texture. Acetate has a stabilizing influence when used with rayon—a factor that helps garments like skirts and bathing suits keep their shape, size, and fit.

Absorption of moisture and perspiration is important to comfort. Rayon absorbs a little more than silk (11 per cent) and acetate about as much as cotton (6½ per cent).

### DURABILITY

Rayon yarns are stronger than they once were, both wet and dry. The advent of high-tenacity yarns has greatly increased industrial, army, and civilian uses, where strength and durability are highly important. The improved wet strength of the modified rayons has been discussed.

The length of wear that may be expected from rayon depends upon the grade of rayon, the quality of yarn, the quality of the weave, the excellence of the finish, and the kind of care the consumer gives the fabric in use. Since rayon lacks the natural elasticity of silk, rayon clothes, unless treated for crease resistance, may lose their trim appearance after continued wear and washing. Novelty weaves, unless bonded to a tricot fabric, frequently fail to hold their shape. If a good grade of fiber is used and if good quality spinning is combined with good fabric construction and stabilization, stretching or shrinking will be minimized.

Although most rayon fabrics today are durable, they sometimes fail to give satisfaction when made up into clothing. Dress customers may complain of slippage at the seams. Rayon does require greater allowance for seams than does silk, and it is very important to have the tension and length of stitch properly regulated. A reinforced seam also helps prevent slippage.

## THE FUTURE OF RAYON AND ACETATE

Early in this chapter it was explained why rayon went under a cloud at the time its name was coined and how, in the late 1930's, rayon staged a comeback when it was restyled. Then came nylon to challenge rayon and acetate, and more recently the acrylics and polyesters, spandex, and others have arrived.

Cotton was still king in 1967 with 57 per cent of the total output of basic textile fibers. Wool was 9 per cent; the man-made fibers were 34 per cent; and silk was a nominal percentage of the total. The largest increase in U.S. production of man-made fibers during the past seventeen years has been in the noncellulosic fibers. In 1967, the production of noncellulosic fibers had increased 13 per cent over 1966 production. In 1965 the noncellulosic fibers for the first time exceeded the rayon and acetate production in the United States,[8] and there seems to be an upward trend in this direction. By 1967 rayon and acetate represented three-eighths, and noncellulosic fibers five-eighths of U.S. production of man-made fibers.

In 1967 the U.S. mills, in an all-time record, consumed almost four billion pounds of man-made fibers or a 132.2 per cent increase in ten years, and over two-fifths of all fibers consumed in the U.S., including cotton, wool, and silk. The consumption in 1967 of man-made fibers averaged almost twenty pounds for every man, woman, and child in the United States. This represented an increase of 111 per cent per capita consumption over the previous ten years.

The increased use of acetate in tricot fabrics for bonding, the in-

[8] *Man-Made Fiber Fact Book*, p. 35.

creasing use of blends in which acetate and rayon are components, and the improvements in modified rayon and acetate should have a bearing on the continued importance of rayon and acetate to the consumer.

Quality-control programs of the manufacturers of the new modified rayons and tested performance standards like the L22 will insure the public of fabrics that perform satisfactorily. New blends of modified rayons and triacetates with natural and the noncellulosic synthetic fibers lend themselves to new styling and to new end uses.

These improvements in the cellulosic-based man-made fibers may continue to emphasize the importance of rayon and acetate in consumer goods.

### SUMMARY

Of all the synthetic fibers, rayon is the oldest. Although its original creators were trying to make silk artificially, they actually discovered a new and distinct fiber more versatile than any natural one. Rayon can be made to imitate cotton, wool, silk, and even linen, and it can produce effects not possible with these fabrics. The availability of the raw materials from which rayon is made and the cheapness of its production process have assured the consumer of an ample supply at moderate prices. Acetate, another of the oldest man-made fibers, has properties different from rayon. These properties must be considered in the end uses for acetate and in its care. (For the care of rayon and acetate, see Chapter 15.)

However, the pre-eminence of rayon and acetate has been challenged by nylon and the other newer synthetics. Each of these fibers has properties peculiar to itself and all possess certain properties in common. There is a place for all these fibers in consumer goods. The problem lies in the proper selection of fibers to give the best service in end uses.

### REVIEW QUESTIONS

1. (a) Who was the father of the rayon industry?
   (b) What method did he use to make artificial textile fibers? What was its chief disadvantage?
   (c) Is that method used today?
2. (a) When was the name rayon coined?
   (b) Trace chronologically the F.T.C. rulings on rayon.
3. (a) What is the present federal law on labeling and advertising of rayon and acetate fibers?
   (b) How does this law protect the consumer?
   (c) Is the present T.F.P.I.A. adequate? Explain.
4. (a) Outline briefly the most important steps in the making of rayon by the viscose and cuprammonium processes.
   (b) Explain the differences between rayon and acetate fibers.

5. (*a*) How are dull rayon yarns made?

(*b*) How would you identify filament rayon yarn, spun-rayon yarn, and combination yarn?

(*c*) Give some uses of each type of yarn.

(*d*) How is high-strength rayon yarn made? Give its uses.

(*e*) How does high-tenacity rayon yarn differ from high-wet-strength yarn? Give the selling points of the latter.

6. (*a*) Which type of acetate fiber has the strongest tensile strength?

(*b*) Which is the strongest when wet: cotton, regular rayon, regular acetate, or linen?

7. By what process or processes do the following companies manufacture rayon or acetate? (See Chapter 2.)

(*a*) E. I. du Pont de Nemours & Company

(*b*) Celanese Fibers Company

(*c*) American Viscose Division, FMC Corporation

(*d*) Beaunit Corporation, Fibers Division

(*e*) Courtald North America, Inc.

(*f*) Eastman Chemical Products, Inc.

8. In what ways do the following characteristics of rayon and acetate affect consumer demand?

(*a*) Length of fiber

(*b*) Microscopic appearance

(*c*) Strength of fiber

(*d*) Elasticity

(*e*) Hygroscopic moisture

(*f*) Effect of light

(*g*) Composition of fiber

(*h*) Heat

(*i*) Effect of acid and alkali

(*j*) Affinity for dyestuffs

9. Describe briefly the differences between the direct method and the box method of spinning rayon yarn.

10. (*a*) How are the sizes of rayon and acetate filament yarns computed?

(*b*) What is the range of denier in rayon yarn?

(*c*) Give the denier number of a coarse yarn; of a fine yarn. What is the average denier?

(*d*) What is the "Tex" system of numbering yarn? (See Chapter 3.)

11. (*a*) List the uses for rayon.

(*b*) List the uses for acetate.

(*c*) In what textures are rayons and acetates made? Name a fabric to illustrate each texture.

12. (*a*) List the finishes that would be applied to a rayon blanket.

(*b*) When would a water-repellent finish be considered durable? Give two trade names of durable water-repellent finishes.

(*c*) What is the chief advantage of moiréing an acetate fabric?

# EXPERIMENTS

1. *Alkali test.* (*a*) Boil some rayon yarns for about five minutes in a concentrated solution of caustic soda (lye). Describe the effect of strong alkali on rayon. (*b*) Make the same test with acetate yarns. Describe the effect of strong alkali on acetate.

2. *Acid test.* (*a*) Place a few rayon yarns in concentrated sulfuric acid for five or ten minutes. Describe the effect of strong acid on rayon.

(*b*) Make the same test on acetate yarns. Describe the effect of strong acid on acetate.

3. *Microscopic test*. Examine a rayon fiber under the microscope. Draw the fiber as you see it. How does its appearance differ from that of cotton and linen? Draw an acetate fiber.

## GLOSSARY

**Abraded yarn.**   A two-ply combination yarn, of which one ply is abraded and the other is filament viscose rayon.

**Acetate.**   Man-made fibers or yarns formed by a compound of cellulose and acetic acid that has been extruded and hardened.

**Acetate process.**   Method of making man-made fibers derived from cellulose. See *Acetate*.

**Arnel.**   See *Triacetate*.

**Bright yarns.**   Made with rayon or acetate fibers of high luster.

**Brushed rayon.**   A rayon fabric that has been heavily napped. This type of fabric is highly flammable and must be treated for fire resistance.

**Chardonnet, Count Hilaire de.**   Made the first synthetic fiber by dissolving nitrocellulose in alcohol and ether.

**Combination yarn.**   A ply yarn in which each ply is composed of a different fiber; for example, one-ply acetate, one-ply rayon.

**Cuprammonium.**   Fibers or yarns made by dissolving cellulose in ammoniacal copper oxide, extruding the solution, and hardening.

**Delustered fibers.**   Those permanently dulled by incorporating mineral oil or microscopic solids in the spinning solution. When delustered, fibers are said to be pigmented; for example, pigment taffeta.

**Dimensional stability.**   Ability of a fabric to keep its shape and size.

**Dope-dyed.**   See *Solution-dyed*.

**Filament.**   A fiber of indefinite length (continuous). This term is applied to the continuous synthetic fibers.

**Filament yarn.**   Yarns made of continuous filaments.

**Gas fading.**   Change of color of some acetates when exposed to nitrogen in the air.

**Groove markings.**   Rather heavy line markings running lengthwise of the acetate fiber; a mark of identification.

**High tenacity.**   See *Modified rayon* and *Modified acetate fibers*.

**Jersey.**   Weft-knitted rayon, acetate, or two-bar tricot-knitted rayon or acetate used for slips, gowns, and blouses. Jersey is also made of wool, cotton, silk, nylon, or blends with the newer synthetics.

**Linters.**   Very short fibers that cover the cotton seeds after the long fibers have been removed by ginning. Linters are a source of cellulose for rayon and acetate.

**Marquisette.**   A sheer fabric in leno weave used for glass curtains. It is made of cotton, rayon, acetate, nylon, polyester, acrylic, glass, silk, or mixtures.

**Modified acetate fibers.**   Stretching the fibers and then treating them with alkali. See Chapter 2.

**Modified rayon fibers.**   Chemical treatment while fibers are in the plastic state to give them high tenacity (high strength). Changes in the molecular structure of the fiber have been made.

**Nitrocellulose rayon.** The first type of synthetic fiber discovered—no longer made in the United States. This type of rayon is made of a solution of nitrated cellulose solidified into filaments.

**Pigmented fibers.** White or colored pigments added to a fiber-forming substance before spinning.

**Rayon.** See Glossary, Chapter 2.

**Solution-dyed.** Dyestuff is put into the spinning solution, and the color is "locked in" as the fiber is coagulated. Synonymous with *spun-dyed* and *dope-dyed*.

**Spinneret.** A jet or nozzle containing very fine holes through which the spinning solution is forced (extruded).

**Spinning solution.** Chemically treated cellulose in viscous solution preparatory to extrusion through the spinneret.

**Spun-dyed.** See *Solution-dyed*.

**Spun yarn.** Yarn made of staple.

**Staple.** Discontinuous lengths of fibers that have been cut or broken from large bundles of continuous monofilaments called "tow."

**Striations.** The many fine microscopic lines extending lengthwise on the viscose rayon fiber; a mark of identification.

**Thick-and-thin yarns.** Yarns made of fibers with varying diameters.

**Tow.** See *Staple*.

**Trade names of rayon and acetate fibers.** See Table, Chapter 2.

**Transparent velvet.** A sheer cut-pile velvet usually all-rayon or with rayon pile, suitable for evening dresses, wraps, and millinery.

**Triacetate.** A thermoplastic fiber classified under the generic name of *acetate*. It does not dissolve in acetone, and it can be ironed with the heat set for linen.

**Viscose process.** A method of making rayon fibers from purified cellulose.

**Wash-and-wear.** See Glossary, Chapter 7.

# 14

# The Newer
# Man-Made Fibers
# and the Consumer

The consumer may be satisfied that she is acquainted with rayon, acetate, and nylon. She may think she knows how they will perform and how to care for them. But does she? As was stated in the previous chapter, improvements in rayon and acetate may change the consumer's image of these fibers if she purchases a newly manufactured rayon or acetate article. The noncellulosic fibers nylon, acrylic, polyester, glass, and the others to be discussed in this chapter are also undergoing improvements to meet the needs of consumers. Nothing is static in the textile fiber field.

The Federal Trade Commission's Rules and Regulations under the Textile Fiber Products Identification Act, defines seventeen generic names of man-made fibers:

| | |
|---|---|
| acetate | olefin |
| acrylic | polyester |
| anidex | rayon |
| azlon * | rubber (includes lastrile) |
| glass | saran |
| metallic | spandex |
| modacrylic | vinal * |
| nylon | vinyon |
| nytril * | |

(The fibers marked with an asterisk are currently not produced in the United States.) In addition, there are many registered trade names of fiber and yarn manufacturers who produce fibers. The average consumer, not familiar with the chemistry of the fibers and deriving very little clarification from the F.T.C.'s definitions of generic classes, must rely on labels that give information on performance and care. As we have seen, research shows that labels leave much doubt in the consumer's mind. We have also seen that ideally the salesperson could be an excellent source of merchandise information. But she, too, requires knowledge about performance of the various classes of fibers, to enable her to answer her customer's questions intelligently. Fiber and yarn manufacturers are good sources of information of this type. But in their zeal for promotion of their own brands, they may give all the advantages of their products and overlook their limitations.

In this chapter, brand names will be de-emphasized, and the advantages and drawbacks in performance of the various generic fiber classifications will be discussed. Within a classification, of course, there may be certain brands of fibers and yarns that vary slightly in their plus or minus qualities from characteristics of the generic classifications. But discussion will necessarily be limited to the general classification.

Rayon and acetate were the first man-made fibers to be produced. These fibers are based on cellulose. (See *classification of man-made fibers,* Chapter 2.) Certain others are based on protein found in zein, cornmeal, soybeans, and skim milk (not currently produced in the U.S.). Others are derived from rubber and glass; still others are entirely compounded from chemicals. Fibers wholly compounded from chemicals are generally classified as noncellulosic fibers.

## NYLON FIBERS

"Nylon" is spelled with a small "n" because it is a generic term. There are several types of nylon that differ in their basic chemistry, but all are made by condensation, and all are polyamide fibers. We consumers glibly say that nylon is made from coal, air, and water. Although this is true, coal, air, and water cannot simply be mixed to produce nylon. Carbon is derived from coal; nitrogen and oxygen are derived from the air; and hydrogen is derived from water to form intermediate chemicals of adipic acid and hexamethylene-diamine, the *polyamide* resin used for nylon. Another type of nylon is made into a polyamide resin from caprolactam, which is heated in the presence of a catalyst.

Nylon was the original brand name coined by the du Pont Company for a fiber born as the result of a research study begun by du Pont in 1928 on *polymerization* (the way in which small molecules unite to form large molecules). These large molecules so formed are called *polymers* and can be likened to growing plant tissue. The du Pont research chemists found that certain chemicals would combine to form long-chain polymers, some of which could be drawn out or extruded into filaments (fibers). Experiments were then made to find the chemicals best suited for making these filaments. The basic elements derived from coal, air, and water were found to combine satisfactorily for this purpose, and nylon was the result. Nylon fiber was announced to the consumer on October 30, 1938, but it was not available to the public until a year later, and then only in limited quantities in Wilmington, Delaware. In the spring of 1940, nylon reached retailers in New York City and throughout the country in limited amounts. By the end of 1939, nylon was being manufactured commercially in a plant at Seaford, Delaware, not only as a textile fiber but also as bristles, sheets, and other forms that are characterized by extreme toughness, elasticity, and strength. By 1942, the War Production Board allocated the total production of nylon to the armed forces. It was used in parachutes, uniforms, tires, and many other articles. It was not until after World War II that civilians could again purchase nylon.

In 1952 Chemstrand Corporation, now the Textiles Division of Monsanto Company, was licensed in this country to produce nylon. More recently, American Enka, Allied Chemical Company, Inc., and others have been producing nylon variants referred to by type and number. Each type of nylon possesses certain advantages and is engineered for specified end uses. Type 6 is produced by several companies, among them Enka and Allied. Monsanto and du Pont both make Type 66 (a nylon that dyes lighter and melts at a higher temperature than Type 6). Du Pont makes many additional types—90, 100, 300, 680, and 700, to mention only a few. Besides du Pont there are eleven companies that make nylon in one form or another in America. Toyo of Japan makes nylon under the name of Amilan; the Netherlands under the name of Bifil; and Germany under the name of Perlon. Type 11 has the trade name Rilsan in Italy, Brazil, and France. In Mexico nylon is Nyfil; in Argentina it is Perfilon; in Venezuela it is Sudalon, and so on. How naïvely the so-called informed consumer accepts the fact that nylon is made from coal, air, and water. She is right, of course, but *how* is it made?

Hydrocarbon is obtained from coal; nitrogen and oxygen are obtained from the air; and hydrogen is obtained from water. These are the basic raw materials for nylon. Now the chemists have extended that basic list to include natural gas, petroleum, and certain agricultural by-products, such as corncobs and the hulls of cottonseed, rice, and oats.

Under high pressure, hydrocarbon and other intermediates are formed into so-called *adipic acid* and *hexamethylene diamine*. Specific amounts of the acid and diamine solutions are combined with water to form a solution of a salt called *hexamethylene-diammonium-adipate*.[1] Then

[1] *Fibers by du Pont,* a pamphlet by the Product Information Section, Textile Fibers Department, E. I. du Pont de Nemours & Company, Inc., Wilmington, Delaware.

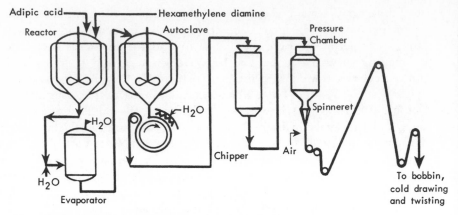

Adipic acid

Hexamethylene diamine

Reactor

Autoclave

Pressure Chamber

H₂O

H₂O

Spinneret

Chipper

Air

H₂O

Evaporator

To bobbin, cold drawing and twisting

**Figure 14.1.** Method of manufacturing nylon. (*Reproduced courtesy of E.I. du Pont de Nemours & Company, Inc.*)

comes polymerization, or the linking of small molecules into large molecules. To do this, the nylon salt solution is run through an *autoclave* (a vessel like a pressure cooker), where the solution is heated under pressure. As the heat is applied a diamine molecule hooks up with a dibasic acid molecule to form a larger new molecule. These new molecules hook up with others similarly formed to compose a molecular chain or polymer. The polymer in viscous state leaves the autoclave through a slot in the bottom and is poured over a rotating wheel, where water hardens it into a translucent, ivory-colored, solid ribbon. A rotary cutter processes the solid into chips or flakes.

The flakes are then melted and extruded into nylon filament (fiber). This method is called *melt spinning*. The extruded strands of nylon can be stretched like warm taffy. When cooled, they can be stretched again to three or four times their original length. This stretching improves strength and elasticity. Nylon is made both in filament and in staple fibers. Single filaments (monofilaments) are made into such items as sheer hosiery, blouses, gowns, and veils.

PHYSICAL PROPERTIES OF NYLON

Under the microscope, bright nylon filaments closely resemble the filaments of cuprammonium rayon. Their diameters are even and the surfaces smooth and structureless, like glass rods. There are no crenulations such as there are in most rayons. (See the Appendix.) One of du Pont's fibers, trilobal in cross section, makes a bright, textured yarn, designed for use in upholstery. Under the trade name Antron, it is now a delustered yarn used for women's jersey blouses.

The dull filaments show pigmentation of titanium oxide, similar to that of medium-dull rayon, but the pigmentation of nylon is more sparse and looks more like pockmarks than specks.

Nylon's dry strength is tremendous, and its wet strength is only 15 per cent lower. Those who have knitted with nylon yarn realize how difficult it is to break it. Nylon fiber is also light in weight, a factor important in sheer, lightweight materials. Laboratory tests have revealed that nylon's abrasion resistance is as much as three times that of wool. Tests have also shown nylon to be very elastic. When a filament is stretched 20 per cent, the recovery (springback) after the first stretch is 95 per cent; thereafter, 93 per cent. Nylon will also return to its original form after compression. Since nylon filaments are smooth and non-porous, they do not soil easily. Fibers of nylon can be made fine or coarse, according to the type of yarn required in the end use. The denier of the fiber ranges from #1 to any desired size. Nylon does not absorb perspiration, because it is hydrophobic—hence the clammy feel of nylon clothing (made of filament yarn) in the hot summer months. Since nylon is nonabsorbent, it dries quickly.

Like the other true synthetics, nylon has dimensional stability if heat setting (which is responsible for this characteristic, for wrinkle recovery, and for softness of hand) is properly done. Nylon also has excellent stability to repeated launderings. One technique used to maintain this stability is to introduce small amounts of stabilizers to the nylon polymer before spinning.

Nylon staple fibers have the ability to take a crimp, a factor that is very important in good spinning in the wool, worsted, and cotton systems. Such fibers can be used for sweaters, socks, flannels, rugs, and blankets. These nylon staples blend well with wool, as the nylon contributes strength, abrasion resistance, and dimensional stability in washing.

## CHEMICAL PROPERTIES OF NYLON

Nylon is a chemical compound that reacts to sulfuric acid by melting. An example of this occurred when several women shoppers suddenly discovered that holes were forming in their nylon stockings. It was found that when sulfur-dioxide and sulfur-trioxide gases, produced by combustion of low-grade industrial fuels in factories, meet moist dust and dirt particles in the air, sulfuric acid is formed on the particles. Since nylon stockings are in tension on the leg, these tiny specks are sufficient to start runs.

In a test to separate nylon from wool and vegetable fibers, these fibers were immersed in No. 101 cresylic acid, pale 99/100 per cent solution, for sixty minutes at room temperature. The nylon was separated from the other fibers in a jelly-like form.

On the other hand, nylon has excellent resistance to alkalies. In a 10 per cent caustic soda solution, nylon filaments are unaffected. Unlike rayons, they swell minimally in water. (Natural fibers swell from 7 to 17 per cent.) Nylon is to all purposes insoluble except in the case of a few solutions that are not generally encountered, such as phenol, m-cresol, xyenol, and formic acid (all at 25° C.). Since nylon dissolves in phenol and hot glacial acetic acid, these acids are frequently used in fiber identification. A special bleach for nylon fabrics is being sold in department stores. However, if the user follows directions on the bottle, Clorox may be used.

Suitable pigments may be added to the polymer before it is spun to control the luster. Nylon can also be dyed in the yarn or in the piece. Nylon yarns and fabrics take a variety of dyes. The dyestuffs developed for acetate give filament nylon a uniform dye (see p. 196 ff.) but are not so lightfast as acid dyestuffs. Metal-complex dyes are also used. More research has to be done on the dyeing of blends, particularly blends of nylon with rayon, cotton, or acetate. (Some of the problems of dyeing of blends are discussed in Chapter 8.)

Strong sunlight or long exposure to ordinary light injures ordinary nylon. Bright nylon is about as resistant to sunlight as linen. Dull nylon's strength is seriously impaired by sunlight. Certain types of nylon yarns are engineered for light resistance. However, a yarn with exceptional light resistance should not be chosen if this is of secondary importance to the consumer, since certain other undesirable properties usually accompany the desirable feature of light resistance.

Nylon fibers are not attacked by those fungi that are responsible for mildew, nor are they vulnerable to moths or silverfish.

Since regular nylon may soften at 365° F., nylon fabrics should be ironed at low temperatures. Nylon has a very low resistance to flames both before and after dyeing and finishing. Nylon will melt at about 480° F., if a flame is applied. But improvements in the properties of nylon now feature a type with high heat resistance.

## YARN MAKING

After the fibers have been extruded from the spinneret, they are hardened, grouped together in a strand, and wound into a "cake" or spinning bobbin preparatory to stretching. A series of rollers revolving at different speeds stretches the fibers. The operation arranges the molecules in an orderly fashion, parallel to the axis of the filaments. Polymerization merely links the molecules together at random. The stretching adds both strength and elasticity to the yarn.

Nylon is made in both multifilament (yarn) and monofilaments (single filaments). (See Chapter 3.) Throwsters twist the multifilament yarn to give it tensile strength, snag resistance, and durability; and spinners spin or twist nylon staple into yarn, much as cotton and wool are spun. Most nylon yarns are made in the multifilament type and are used in dresses, hosiery, blouses, lingerie, shirts, and upholstery. Monofilaments are used in such items as sheer hosiery, veils, gowns, and blouses.[2]

Spun yarn is made of either 100 per cent nylon or blends of staples. Nylon staple is cut in different lengths, one and one-half to five inches, depending upon the spinning system being used—cotton, woolen, worsted, silk, or other. Spun yarn is light, soft, and springy and is very popular in wool-like textures and blends, especially in socks and sweaters.

The making of bulky yarns was described in Chapter 3. By combining different deniers and plies of looped, curled, and crimped varieties of yarn, it is possible to obtain a great many new textures from continuous-filament nylon. Stretch yarns were also discussed in Chapter 3. Improvements in the luster of yarn have occurred, as evidence by du Pont's Sparkling Nylon in 1959 and a nylon jersey of Antron trilobal multi-filament yarn with a certain type of delusterant chemical (1960). A silklike nylon has been created in the laboratory by bombarding nylon with ultrasonic sound waves.

Texturizing nylon and changing the luster of the yarn have expanded the market and fashion end uses for nylon. Now we have a whole family of nylons, each engineered for a particular end use.

### SIZES OF NYLON YARNS

The sizes of filament nylon yarns are figured on the denier basis, similar to rayon. Spun nylon yarns are on a count basis, like spun rayon.

### KNITTING AND WEAVING OF NYLON

The early type 66 nylon was essentially concentrated on fashion uses in intimate apparel. Continuous monofilament nylon was important for basic knit construction in foundation garments, lingerie, and women's and men's hosiery. In 1957 du Pont introduced Tissue Tricot, and in 1960 Tricot Satinette. These constructions of warp knitting were achieved through the trilobal modification of the fiber's cross section by combining special yarn denier and fabric finishing. (See *warp knitting*, Chapter 6.) Stretch fabrics can be both knitted and woven. Bulky-knit sweaters, either hand- or machine-made, are popular for sports and casual wear.

A recent development in lingerie is the molded nylon seamless brassiere produced by Liberty Fabrics of New York, Inc.[3] The Monsanto Company produces a nylon with a special molecular construction that is knit on special Raschel lace machines. The fabric undergoes a chemical process that further modifies the structure for permanent molding. The

---

[2] *Fibers by du Pont*, p. 5.
[3] The trade name is Libform.

molded bra is comfortable because it has no seams; it keeps its size and shape permanently after machine washing and drying; it is durable; and it has an esthetic appeal.[4]

A nylon monofilament straw, made by a process developed in Switzerland and marketed by Scheuer Associates of New York, is sold under the name of Yuva. It can be woven or knitted into shoes, belts, hats, handbags, lamp shades, curtaining, and automobile fabrics.

Any type of weave—plain, twill, satin, or fancy—can be made in 100 per cent nylon or in blends or mixtures. The principal constructions are hosiery, tricot slips, gowns, shirts, and blouses. Nylon fleeces, furlike pile fabrics, and rugs are popular, as well as laces and nets.

## FINISHES FOR NYLON FABRICS

Nylon fabrics can be safely bleached with sodium chlorite without risk of tendering. All nylon fabrics are subjected to heat-setting conditions, which must be carefully controlled. All parts of the fabric must be subjected to setting, and excessive time at high temperatures must be avoided. Setting is a matter of degree, but an unset finished cloth would not be stabilized; it would not be smooth; and it would wrinkle easily.

To make a durable stiff finish, a melamine resin is used that cannot penetrate but polymerizes on the surface. Nylon taffeta petticoats are finished in this fashion. Thiourea-formaldehyde resin flameproofs nylon nets and laces. Nonslip finishes do not penetrate the fabric either, but they bond the warp and filling yarns to make a firm hand. A resin polyethylene oxide finish is claimed to eliminate fiber static. Some fabrics are calendered. (See Chapter 7.) Piece dyeing and printing are methods of coloring nylon after construction. (See Chapter 8 and page 368 for dyeing of nylon.)

## WHY CUSTOMERS BUY NYLON FABRICS

### DURABILITY

The wearing quality of a nylon fabric depends on the tensile strength of its fibers and yarns. This exceptional strength, coupled with lightness in weight, makes very desirable sheer fabrics. Nylon also resists abrasion, another factor in durability.

### SUITABILITY

The engineering of various types of nylon for specific end uses has widened the market for the product. The resilience and strength of nylon make it suitable for hosiery and underwear. Stockings do not

---

[4] *America's Textile Reporter*, 50 (December 14, 1961), 23, 25, 26.

become baggy at the knees, because nylon's resilience brings the stocking back to shape. In pile velvets of nylon, the pile is not deformed when crushed. Nylon fabrics are nonflammable when finished with dyes and finishes that are nonflammable. But new nylon materials and sheer ones should be tested for flammability. It will be remembered that the Flammable Fabrics Act (see Chapter 7) governs all fabrics that are worn as clothing but does not govern the fibers before they are made into fabrics.

## EASE IN CARE

Heat setting makes embossing of fabrics permanent and sets permanent pleats. Heat setting also keeps a fabric from shrinking or sagging noticeably. Nylon fabrics are easy to wash, many of them can be hung to drip dry, and many need no ironing. Nylon dries very quickly, and filament nylon dries faster than spun nylon.

The consumer will never need to mothproof 100 per cent nylon fabrics. Nylon is not adversely affected by water, perspiration, or dry-cleaning agents. However, mildew might discolor nylon.

## VERSATILITY

The versatility of nylon seems limitless, particularly in blends with other fibers. When nylon and rayon are blended, nylon adds strength, abrasion resistance, and stability in washing and wearing. A nylon-rayon blend makes a fine-count, strong yarn for lightweight washable fabrics. When nylon and cotton are blended, nylon again contributes its strength, abrasion resistance, and dimensional stability, as well as better resistance to perspiration, a softer hand, better elasticity, and quick-drying qualities. Nylon combined with acetate adds strength and wearing quality.

**Figure 14.2.** *Left:* Garment woven of spun yarn does not dry rapidly because each of the air spaces fills with water. *Right:* Garment woven of continuous filament nylon has practically no air spaces to trap moisture. (*Reproduced courtesy of E.I. du Pont de Nemours & Company, Inc.*)

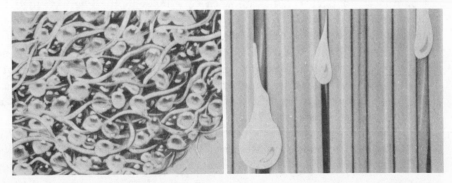

Nylon staple is particularly suitable for socks, anklets, sweaters, swimsuits, undershirts, dress flannels, upholstery, tufted rug, industrial fabrics, sewing and darning threads, work clothes, uniforms, and summer suiting. A small percentage of nylon in an overcoat will improve its wearing quality at points of friction, such as the cuffs, lapels, and front closing. Nylon is also used for nontextiles such as bristles and films, which are characterized by toughness, elasticity, and strength.

With the development of textured yarns, it is possible to produce nylon fabrics that are more comfortable because of their stretch properties. (See *textured yarns,* Chapter 3.)

## LIMITATIONS OF NYLON

Research has been responsible for the great strides made by nylon. Consumer objections to faults such as pilling (the forming of little balls on the surface of the fabric), development of static electricity, graying of white nylon, and clamminess of 100 per cent filament nylon may eventually be overcome by further research.

Some fabrics may always retain one or more objectionable features. There is no one perfect fiber for all purposes. If the fiber possesses all the minimum requirements needed to perform satisfactorily in a given end use, then there should be no customer objections. However, in order to meet price competition, certain treatments necessary for satisfactory performance may be omitted by the manufacturer. As a result, the consumer may have legitimate grounds for dissatisfaction with a fiber.

## ACRYLIC FIBERS

Acrylic fibers are made from a chemical compound called *acrylo*nitrile (the italicized letters of the compound indicate the derivation of *acrylic* fiber). The raw materials involved in the production of this fiber are coal, air, petroleum, limestone, and natural gases. After a series of complicated chemical reactions, the solution formed is extruded through a spinneret—a perforated plate with tiny holes in it. The extruded filaments are dried and stretched to improve the strength and elasticity of the fiber. Acrylic fibers are used either in continuous-filament or in staple-fiber form. Continuous monofilaments can be crimped by heat setting and then chopped into any desired length for use in spun yarns. Multifilament yarns are popular in women's dresses and blouses, men's shirts, and curtains. Spun yarns are very frequently used in sweaters and skirts and in blends with wool and silk for suits and coats.

The first major acrylic fiber was Orlon. Preliminary work on Orlon started in the Pioneering Research Division of du Pont's Textile Fibers Department as early as 1940, but the fiber was not available commercially until 1948. Filament Orlon yarn was first produced commercially in a plant in Camden, South Carolina. Staple yarn was developed as filament yarn went into production. Now there are several acrylic fibers used in textile fabrics—among them are Acrilan produced by the Monsanto Company, Creslan by American Cyanamid Company, and a nitrile alloy named Zefran by Dow Chemical Company.

The principal properties of these four acrylic fibers are the following:

| PROPERTIES OF FIBERS | RATINGS [5] |
|---|---|
| Strength | Fair |
| Abrasion resistance | Fair |
| Wrinkle resistance | Good |
| Sunlight resistance | Good |
| Pressed-crease retention | Excellent |
| Hand (soft and wool-like) | Good to excellent |
| Stability to repeated laundering | Good |
| Colorfastness | Good |
| Affinity for dye | Acrilan 16 (not regular Acrilan), Creslan 61, and Orlon can be dyed bright colors. Zefran can be vat-dyed with cotton |
| Wash-and-wear | Good |
| Resistance to pilling | Fair |
| Resistance to moths or microorganisms | Excellent |

The acrylics are soft, since the majority are made in staple form, and though they are bulky, they are light in weight. Acrylics are not as strong or as resistant to abrasion as nylon. Excellent resistance to sunlight, to pressed-crease retention, and to moths is important to the consumer. Finishing acrylics presents no particular problem. Acrylics have only fair resistance to pilling; and they have the problem of static electricity. (See *antistatic finish*.)

A great deal of experimentation has been necessary on dyestuffs for acrylics. The yarns and fabrics of staple fibers have been easier to dye than the yarns and fabrics of continuous filaments. Vat dyes applied at high temperatures have proved successful in dyeing Orlon 81, and bright, fast colors can be obtained with the dyestuffs on Orlon 42. Orlon, like many of the synthetics with chemical bases, is somewhat expensive to dye.

In 1960 du Pont announced Orlon type 72, which was designed to be cool in summer and warm in winter. It is cool in summer because it is made of 1.5 denier-per-filament fiber; it is warm in winter because of its bulk and insulating properties. Orlon type 72 is suitable for T-shirts, shorts, pajamas, sport shirts, and underwear for men and children.

Orlon bicomponent acrylic (formerly called Orlon Sayelle) is a permanent-crimped fiber. The shape of the crimp is comparable to the spiral of a reversible corkscrew. The fiber is not a conventional type but is made of two components, each of which differs from the other in

[5] Compiled from ratings given in *Textile Fibers and Their Properties,* a manual prepared by Burlington Industries, Inc. (1961).

**Figure 14.3.** A typical use of Orlon acrylic fibers in Nordic sweater and scarf. (*Courtesy of E.I. du Pont de Nemours & Company, Inc.*)

molecular structure. Because of this unique structure, the fiber reacts to temperature changes and heat treatment differently from conventional Orlon. It develops a three-dimensional spiral crimp when the fabric is wet-treated and dried in a relaxed state. This fiber has been responsible for new style developments in knitwear because of its esthetic appearance and wool-like resilience. Special dyes have been developed for it. Now it is a luxury or prestige fiber for styled fabrics.[6]

Acrylics have served well in 100 per cent acrylic-fibered sweaters and blankets and in blends of 50/50 per cent acrylic-cotton (or acrylic-rayon) for men's hosiery. Raschel-knit fabrics in 50/50 per cent blends of acrylic-cotton improve resilience and reduce the shrinkage of cotton. Acrylic-nylon blends are found in fancy yarns (slub and textured) for knitwear that is washable and lightweight. Commercial acrylic blends are used for men's suitings, woven dress fabrics, slacks, sportswear, and carpeting.

[6] "New Fibers from du Pont," *American Dyestuff Reporter* (May 1, 1961), 45–47.

Because acrylics can be produced on the cotton, worsted, or woolen system, textures and uses can be diversified.

Consumers buy 100 per cent acrylic fabrics and blends for a variety of reasons: acrylic holds its shape well; it resists abrasion; it washes easily, dries quickly, and needs little or no ironing. Sweaters of spun acrylic have softness comparable to cashmere.

## MODACRYLIC FIBERS

When man-made fibers are composed of less than 85 per cent but at least 35 per cent by weight of acrylonitrile units, the generic name of such fibers is modacrylic (modified acrylic).

Dynel is a modacrylic fiber produced by the Union Carbide Corporation. This fiber, made from a combination of vinyl chloride and acrylonitrile, is resistant to flame, water, microorganisms, and insects. Because

Figure 14.4. Coat, showing typical use of Verel modacrylic fibers. (*Photograph courtesy of Eastman Chemical Products, Inc., a subsidiary of Eastman Kodak Company.*)

of its good flame and sunlight resistance, the fiber is appropriate for draperies and upholstery; and because of its resistance to nearly all chemicals but acetone, it is suitable for industrial filter cloths. It is somewhat sensitive to alkalies. Its resilience makes the fibers particularly well adapted for use in the stuffing of pillows, comforters, and linings. Dynel has good colorfastness, wash-and-wear properties, and wrinkle resistance. It can be made in pile construction to resemble fur and has found use in carpeting. Because it retains a crease well, the fiber can be appropriately used in fabrics for men's and boys' slacks. Thirty per cent blends of Dynel with rayon, cotton, or wool have proved satisfactory, and there are some three-way blends in rayon-acetate-Dynel and rayon-nylon-Dynel.

One recently found use for dynel is in the making of wigs. Dynel can be safely ironed at 225° F.; its tensile strength is poor; its stability to repeated launderings is fair; its resistance to pilling is fair; and its abrasion resistance is fair.

Another modacrylic is Verel, produced by Eastman Chemical Products, Inc. Like Dynel, it is resistant to chemicals, resilient, and nonflammable. It has better abrasion resistance than Dynel but not quite as good crease retention. Like Dynel it has a low melting point and is somewhat difficult to dye. Other properties are similar to Dynel. It is primarily used for furlike fabrics and carpets. Both of these modacrylic fibers come only in staple form and have limited use at present.

Verel can be dyed in a variety of shades and cross-dye effects. The neutral-dyeing premetallized dyes are usually best for fastness to light and washing. For most purposes Verel does not require bleaching, because it is unusually white. Should bleaching be desired, sodium chlorite and formic acid are used.

## POLYESTER FIBERS

The process of producing polyester fibers is an intricate one. Basically, this fiber is derived from coal, air, water, and petroleum. The chemicals dimethyl terephthalate and ethylene glycol are "cooked" in a vacuum at very high temperatures until they form a solid, hard, porcelain-like substance that can be melted (melt-spun) into a honey-like liquid and then extruded through a spinneret. Filaments are cooled and solidified. The drawing or stretching of these filaments many times their original length gives strength and elasticity to each filament.

Polyester fibers are made in filament and staple fiber forms for yarns that can be woven or knitted. The long continuous filaments that are twisted together form filament yarns. The number of filaments and the amount of twist determine the size and texture of the yarn. Fibers made from short-cut staples are processed into spun yarns.

Smooth-filament yarns are used in taffetas, glass curtaining, satin, and lightweight apparel fabrics. Spun yarns are used in fabrics whose textures are cotton or wool-like, since they produce softer, bulkier yarns. These yarns are especially appropriate for blends. A polyester-cotton blend 65/35 per cent (65 per cent polyester and 35 per cent cotton) has become popular in minimum-care men's shirtings, women's blouses, dresses, slacks, knitted T-shirts, uniforms, and sportswear. A polyester-acrylic blend (50/50 per cent) was introduced in 1960 for men's summer suitings; it is also used in slacks, sportswear, and dresses. A blend of polyester and worsted (55/45 per cent) has become popular for men's regular suiting. Men like this fabric because it holds its press and resists wrinkles, and because wrinkles tend to hang out. It is lighter in weight than 100 per cent worsted and tailors beautifully. Another blend is polyester and rayon 65/35 per cent to 50/50 per cent for dresses. Among United States trademarks of polyester are the following:

| TRADEMARK | MANUFACTURER | MISCELLANEOUS DATA |
|---|---|---|
| Dacron | du Pont | Pronounced Day'cron |
| Fortrel | Fiber Industries, Inc. | Fiber Industries is owned jointly by Celanese Corporation and Imperial Chemical Industries Ltd. of Great Britain |
| Kodel | Eastman | |
| Vycron | Beaunit | |

The following table gives comparative ratings of the properties of four polyester fibers: [7]

| | DACRON | FORTREL | KODEL | VYCRON |
|---|---|---|---|---|
| Automatic wash-and-wear | Excellent | Excellent | Excellent | Excellent |
| Resistance to pilling | Poor on regular Dacron. Good on types 64 and 35. | Poor | Excellent | Fair |
| Permanent pleating | Excellent | Good | Good | Good |
| Abrasion resistance | Good | Good | Fair | Good |
| Hand | Fair on regular Dacron. Good on types 64 and 35. | Fair | Fair (softer than Dacron) | Fair |
| Pressed-crease retention | Good | Good | Good (elevated temperature for pressing) | Good |
| Safe ironing temperature | 325° F. | 325° F. | 400° F. | 300° F. |
| Stability after repeated launderings | Excellent when properly heat-set | Excellent (must be heat-set) | Excellent | Excellent |

[7] Compiled from data found in *Textile Fibers and Their Properties*, pp. 13, 21, 23, 36.

| | Dacron | Fortrel | Kodel | Vycron |
|---|---|---|---|---|
| Strength | Good | Good | Fair | Excellent |
| Sunlight resistance | Good | Good | Good | Good |
| Colorfastness | Good | Good | Good | Good |
| Wrinkle resistance | Excellent | Excellent | Excellent | Excellent |

The ratings reveal that polyester fibers are truly easy-care fibers. They possess excellent wrinkle resistance, have outstanding stability after repeated launderings, can be heat-set to control shrinkage and sagging of the fabric, and can be made permanently pleated. Polyesters are not damaged by sunlight and weather and are not attacked by moths or mildew. When dyes and finishes are properly selected and applied, fabrics possess a low degree of flammability.

Polyester-cotton blends are finished differently from 100 per cent cotton. The cloth is singed before scouring and heat-set after finishing. To obtain dimensional stability, these blends must be given a compressive shrinkage treatment. Polyester-rayon blends are treated with resins for shrinkage control. However, the polyester-modified-rayon blends do not require resin treatment.

British chemists first developed the polyester fiber that was known as Terylene. In 1946 du Pont secured the exclusive right to produce this fiber in the United States. After several years of intensive experimentation and development, it was put on the market as fiber V. In 1951 du Pont named this fiber Dacron. Consumers like Dacron polyester because they find that it washes and dries with little or no ironing. Since its resiliency and strength are good, a necktie can be tied many times without showing objectionable wrinkles. It has become an all-purpose fiber because it blends so well with worsted for suits of all weights.

There are many types of Dacron polyester, each particularly outstanding in certain properties. As in nylon, selectivity of the appropriate type for an intended use is important. Microorganisms do not attack Dacron. Ordinary, dry-cleaning solvents, hot dilute mineral acids, and bleaches do not affect standard Dacron adversely. The original standard Dacron is dyed with acetate dyes at high temperatures. It is costly to dye. The newer type can be dyed with basic and also disperse dyes. (See Glossary, Chapter 8.)

Fortrel, Kodel, and Vycron are similar in many respects to Dacron 54 (a regular polyester made in staple and tow form that is semidull and of normal tenacity).

Since polyester can be made in both multifilament and spun yarn, many uses are possible, such as men's shirts, suits, women's dresses, blouses, lingerie, and curtaining. Polyester stuffing for pillows, comforters, sleeping bags, furniture, mattresses, and auto cushions does not mat, is lightweight, and is comfortable and nonallergenic. Polyester is also used for boat sails.

Du Pont produces a polyester film called Mylar that is used for lamination in making metallic yarn.

Fortrel polyester is similar to Dacron 54. Kodel polyester is somewhat weaker, softer, and less resistant to abrasion than Dacron. Because it is less subject to pilling than the other polyesters, it is suited to napped fabrics like flannel and also to summer suitings. Vycron, though slightly more sensitive to heat, is stronger and somewhat more resistant to pilling than Dacron 54. They are similar in easy-care performance.

Static has been a problem and with fibers made from synthetic polymers, but antistatic finishes may now be applied to overcome this objection. Laundering with synthetic detergents also causes an antistatic effect. Antistatic agents such as Glim, Negastat, and Nul will reduce lint pick-up. One tablespoon is used to each gallon of water in the final rinse.

## SARAN FIBERS

Saran is the generic name for vinylidene chloride and vinyl chloride copolymer resin and yarns extruded from it.[8] It was first introduced as a fiber in 1939 by the Dow Chemical Company, but now a number of yarn manufacturers extrude saran fiber.

Like nylon, polyester, and other fibers made from synthetic polymers, saran is thermoplastic. Its basic raw materials are petroleum and salt. Ethylene is made from the petroleum, and chlorine from the salt. These two chemicals combine to form another chemical, which is converted into vinylidene chloride. The chemical is easily polymerized. Resin is supplied to the manufacturer in powdered form. The powder is first heated to form a fluid, which is forced through a spinneret. The filaments are hardened in water, stretched, and wound on spools.

A large proportion of the yarn is monofilament, although a limited amount of staple is produced. Because it is a stiff, plastic-type yarn, resistant to sunlight and weathering, it is particularly suitable for screening and outdoor furniture. It has good resistance to chemicals and is nonflammable. Colorfastness of saran is excellent; stability to repeated launderings is good; and abrasion resistance is good. However, it has low tensile strength; the hand is stiff and plastic; and safe ironing temperature is low—150° F. It is more expensive than olefin fibers.

[8] Defined by the F.T.C. under the T.F.P.I.A.

**Figure 14.5. Outdoor chair, showing typical use of saran. (Photograph courtesy of Firestone Tire & Rubber Company, former manufacturers of saran.)**

Saran is used for trolling lines, fishing leaders, tennis racquet strings, laundry nets, and suspenders. Originally made in monofilament yarn for outdoor furniture, seat covers of automobiles and buses, and upholstery, its more recent uses include drapery fabrics, sheer curtaining, rugs, and doll's hair. Saran is appropriately used where colorfastness (color is "built in"), easy cleaning, quick drying, and resistance to mildew, moths, soil, grease, chemicals, and abrasion are requisites.

## OLEFIN FIBERS

The generic name *olefin* denotes fibers with paraffin bases, of which there are two: polyethylene and polypropylene.

Polyethylene is a resin that is formed as a result of polymerization of ethylene under heat and pressure. This resin is melted, extruded, and cooled in continuous monofilament form. The polyolefin fibers so formed still have a waxy hand, low heat resistance, a fair-to-good average strength (depending on the type), fair abrasion resistance, and floating ability. Such characteristics appear to render these fibers unsuitable for use in apparel. But because of their good resistance to sunlight, they have found uses in drapery and upholstery fabrics. Since these fibers have excellent resistance to chemicals, they can be used in fiber cloths, braids, cords, ropes, and webbings. These fibers are less costly than saran fibers; they can be produced in numerous pigmented colors but are non-dyeable as yet. (See *pigment dyes*, Chapter 8.) Considerable research and development may soon bring new uses for these fibers. Manufacturers include Dawbarn Brothers, Inc., producing DLP; and Reeves Brothers, Inc., producing Reevon. Du Pont's product, Vexar, is a polyethylene netting made by extruding the polymer directly into net form. Diameter, size, design, and color of each filament can be controlled. Vexar has the usual properties of polyethylene resins: flexibility and resistance to moisture, chemicals, rot, and mildew.

Polypropylene, based on propylene gas, was first produced for textiles in Italy by Montecatini in 1951. It was named Meraklon. Like polyethylene, it is a paraffin-based fiber and therefore is classed under the generic name of olefin. Polypropylene's advantages over polyethylene are that it is lighter, stronger, and less sensitive to heat, and it does not have the undesirable waxy hand. It is also quite inexpensive and has excellent resistance to chemicals, excellent strength, good resistance to sun-

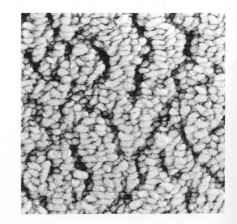

Figure 14.6. Rug, showing typical use of polypropylene olefin fibers. (*Photograph courtesy of Alexander Smith, a division of Mohasco Industries, Inc.*)

light and very good abrasion resistance. Its chief drawbacks have been its low melting point (326° to 333° F.). Montecatini has developed the first commercial polypropylene fiber that is dyeable. It is a chemically modified type that can be dyed in raw stock, yarn, or piece, alone or in blends. Acid, premetallized, chrome, vat, and reactive dyestuffs may be used. (For a description of these dyestuffs see Chapter 7.) A range of colors from soft pastels to deep, rich hues is possible. However, the cost is approximately 10 per cent higher than standard Meraklon.[9]

Significant developments in dyeability of fibers, which previously resisted available dyes, are accelerating the use of olefin in apparel and home fashions. Both solution-dyed and dyeable forms of bulked continuous filament yarns are available for carpet use.

The largest single application of polypropylene is in carpeting. Carpets made from this olefin have received acceptance throughout the home and in nonresidential installations (hotels, schools, offices, and stores). In addition to conventional carpet pile, polypropylene olefin is being used in nonwoven felts for outdoor use and in carpet backing. The durability of polypropylene olefin has made it a dominant fiber for indoor-outdoor carpeting, where weather resistance, good cleanability, strength, and resistance to moisture, mildew, and rot are important factors.

One hundred per cent polypropylene olefin and polypropylene olefin in combination with other fibers, are used in hosiery, ties, sport shirts, undergarments, sweaters, pile fabrics, and sportswear. Olefin contributes comfort, shape retention, long wear, and easy maintenance to apparel. In household furnishings, olefin is finding wider use in upholstery fabrics, slipcovers, and carpets because of its long wear, stain resistance, and easy care.

Olefin fibers, both the woven and nonwoven forms, are receiving extensive use in industrial application. These include filter fabrics, industrial felts, laundry bags and dye nets, rope and cordage, sewing thread, and sandbags.

Wool and polypropylene (30/70 per cent and 35/65 per cent) have been blended, as well as cotton (35/65 per cent). Accordingly, polypropylene has possibilities for an increasing market in a number of fields.

Important producers of polypropylene fibers in the United States are the Dawbarn Division, W. R. Grace Co.; Enjay Fibers and Laminates Company; Hercules Incorporated; and Phillips Fiber Corporation.


**VINYON**

The basis for the generic class of fibers called *vinyon* is polyvinyl chloride whose basic materials are found in salt water and petroleum. In order to be generically classified as vinyon, the F.T.C. has specified that the fiber be composed of not less than 85 per cent of polyvinyl chloride.

9 "Fiber Modified," *Textile World* (March 1962), 117.

Vinyon was first commercially produced in the United States in 1939 by the American Viscose Corporation.

Vinyon, although it has poor tensile strength, shrinks at 150° F., and melts at 260° F., but has good resistance to chemicals, bacteria, and moths and can be dyed with (dispersed) acetate dyes. It is used for mixing with other fibers for the purpose of heat bonding, for fishing lines and nets, and for industrial purposes.

### VINAL

Vinal is the generic name for fibers of polyvinyl alcohol derived by complex chemical processes from limestone and coke. This class of fibers was developed in Japan.

Vinal is claimed to have very good strength and abrasion resistance but does not match nylon in these qualities. Vinal has good chemical resistance, the moisture capacity and softness necessary for comfort in apparel, and a high dry melting point (410° to 450° F.). Excellent colorfastness can be achieved in vinal with vat dyes. For apparel uses, its poor dry-wrinkle resistance is a drawback. It is made in filament, staple, and water-soluble forms. There are two types of vinal: one type is made by a system that approximates rayon technology in its sequential stages of coagulation, drawing, heat treatment, and formalization to develop and harden the fiber structure.[10] With certain modifications, this fiber has been the chief commercial type. Its high-strength and its abrasion and weather resistance have made it useful in products in which cotton is traditionally used. The second type of vinal, used for tire cord, is a highly crystalline form of pure polyvinyl alcohol.

### NYTRIL

Nytril is a man-made fiber composed largely of a complex chemical substance known as vinylidene dinitrile (where the vinylidene dinitrile content is no less than every other unit in the polymer chain),[11] derived from ammonia and natural gas.

Until 1962, this fiber, under the trade name Darvan, was made in this country by Celanese Fibers Company, a division of Celanese Corporation. Early in 1962, however, Celanese reached an agreement with Farbwerke Hoechst of Germany to build a jointly owned plant in Europe for the production and marketing of Darvan. (In Europe the fiber is known as Travis, and in this country it retains the name Darvan.) Its uses include sweaters, suits, and coats.

Darvan nytril's properties resemble those of the acrylic fibers, al-

[10] *American Dyestuff Reporter* (July 24, 1961), 54.
[11] See F.T.C. definition of this generic fiber, Chapter 2.

though it is weaker, harder to dye, and slightly more sensitive to heat than either the Orlon or Acrilan acrylics. Its wash-and wear performance can be rated somewhere between the acrylics and the polyesters. Darvan nytril can be permanently pleated and has an excellent soft, woolly hand. It has good colorfastness, excellent sunlight resistance, good stability after repeated launderings, fair tensile strength, and fair resistance to pilling. Its safe ironing temperature is 325° F.[12]

Available in staple form, its uses are sweaters, suits, coats, and a variety of other products.

## SPANDEX

Spandex is the generic name of synthetic fibers derived from a chemical substance known as segmented polyurethane. Plastic foams of this kind suitable for lamination were discussed in Chapter 6. Spandex fibers are known for their excellent elongation and nearly instantaneous recovery. They are *not* rubber and are superior to it in their resistance to oils and oxidation. Garments of spandex fit, control, and wear well. However, they do discolor, and the spandex industry is trying to correct this fault. One of the best-known trade names is Lycra, by du Pont, which has been most succesfully used for foundation garments, support hosiery, the tops of socks, and elastic tapes. Lycra threads may be covered or uncovered. Uncovered Lycra has the outward appearance of an unsupported, white rubber yarn. Uncovered Lycra yarns are more sheer, thinner, and lighter than covered yarns. Warner Brothers Company, makers of foundation garments, claims that covered spandex adds weight and opacity to an article but it does not add control power. In 1961 Warner's Lycra garments were made of more than 80 per cent uncovered Lycra yarn. Some garments contain spandex as well as nonspandex elastic in waistbands, closures, and panels. This factor may affect both the fit and wearing qualities of the garment.

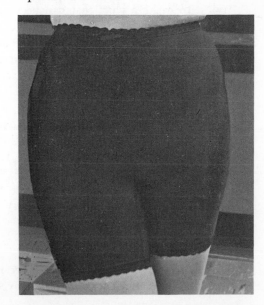

Other United States trademarks for spandex fibers are Vyrene by UniRoyal, Inc., and Numa by American Cyanamid Company.

Consumers like spandex for foundation garments because of its elasticity and comfort. It gives satis-

[12] *Textile Fibers and Their Properties,* Burlington Industries, Inc.

**Figure 14.7.** Typical use of Antron nylon and Lycra spandex in a panty girdle. (*Photograph courtesy of E.I. du Pont de Nemours & Co., Inc.*)

factory control without boning for the small and average figures. With appropriate boning, spandex garments have excellent control. Consumers like spandex because garments are light in weight, cool (the skin can "breathe"), and washable in an automatic washer. Spandex dries quickly. Foundation garments are now being made with spandex by many well-known national manufacturers.

## RUBBER

Rubber is the generic name of man-made fibers in which the fiber-forming substance is comprised of natural or synthetic rubber.

### FIBERS FROM NATURAL RUBBER

The core of fibers is made with natural rubber. (Natural rubber is made of a milky fluid called latex, which is tapped from the bark of the Para rubber tree.) The latex fluid is forced through tiny holes the diameter of the thread desired and is hardened in a solidifying bath. Then the thread is vulcanized, and ammonia is added to preserve it. Round threads retain their elasticity longer than strips cut from sheets, because round threads can have their surface completely vulcanized, whereas strips cut from sheets necessarily have two unvulcanized edges. This latex elastic rubber fiber is covered with cotton, silk, wool, or rayon to form a yarn that can be woven or knitted into cloth for clothing.

Lastex is a trademark for a combination yarn produced by UniRoyal, Inc. The core of the yarn is covered with cotton, silk, wool, rayon, or nylon to make a yarn that can be woven or knitted into cloth or webbing. As webbing, it is used for foundation garments, shoes, garters, suspenders, tops of shorts and briefs, wristlets and anklets, tops of hosiery, shoe laces, and surgical bandages. In cloth, it is used for riding breeches, bathing suits, nets, and laces. Lastex yarns can be used for gathering the tops of blouses, and to stabilize the ribbing of nylon sweaters.

The chief advantage of Lastex is enduring elasticity. Lastex garments shape themselves to the figure of the wearer and hence fit well. The Lastex garment should be laundered frequently with lukewarm suds for best service.

Other pure rubber fibers include Contro (covered yarn) by Firestone and Lactron (uncovered yarn) by Uni-Royal, Inc.

### FIBERS FROM SYNTHETIC RUBBER

A synthetic, manufactured rubber fiber of styrene-butadiene, nitrile, or neoprene is used, covered or uncovered, in knitted and woven goods.

The F.T.C. defines the generic term "metallic" as "a manufactured fiber composed of metal, plastic-coated metal, metal-coated plastic, or a core completely covered by metal."

Real gold and silver are seldom used for textile yarns, but their effect can be duplicated by the use of aluminum in combination with man-made substances. The common types of metallic yarn were discussed in Chapter 3. The three-layer sandwich type is exemplified by Lurex, the trademark for the metallic yarn produced by Dow Badische Company. This yarn is made with aluminum foil in the center and top and bottom layers of polyethylene film.

The chief advantages of metallic yarns are that they are nontarnishable, can be either dry-cleaned or washed, and can be ironed at a low setting. Metallic yarns are frequently used in combination with other yarns for draperies, upholstery, place mats, tablecloths, evening gowns, sweaters, blouses, ribbons, trimmings, fashion fabrics by the yard, and knitting and crocheting yarns.

Some important producers of metallic yarn in the United States include the Dow Badische Company; Metal Film Co., Inc.; Melton Corporation; and Multi-Tex Products Corporation.

## GLASS FIBERS

The generic name "glass" is defined by the F.T.C. as a manufactured fiber in which the fiber-forming substance is glass. The use of glass as a textile yarn began in the 1930's. The process of making glass into fiber was discovered by research engineers of Owens-Illinois Glass Company at Newark, Ohio. The product called Fiberglas was first produced in commercial quantities by Owens-Corning Fiberglas Corporation in 1938. These fibers have had a phenomenal development, and their future looks bright. Other producers of glass fibers are PPG Industries, Inc. (formerly the Pittsburgh Plate Glass Company), Ferro Corporation, Johns-Manville, and others.

Glass marbles five-eighths of an inch in diameter are melted in an electrically heated furnace that has a V-shaped bushing made of a metal with a higher melting point than glass. Molten glass enters the top of the bushing and is drawn downward by gravity. It emerges through orifices at the bottom of the bushing. Each hole make a long continuous filament, and these filaments are combined to make one strand. Then the strands are wound on spools that put in the twist. The winder revolves faster than the molten glass flows, and the resulting tension draws out the filaments. The yarns and cords are then processed on standard textile machinery.

The diameter of the fiber can be controlled by regulating (1) the viscosity of the molten mass through temperature control, (2) the size of the holes through which the glass flows, and (3) the rate of speed at which fibers are drawn.[13]

To make staple fiber, jets of compressed air are used to draw the molten glass. The molten glass flows through orifices at the base of the furnace. The compressed air breaks up the filaments into lengths varying from eight to fifteen inches. The staples so made are drawn upon a revolving drum in the form of a cobwebby ribbon. This web of fibers is gathered into a sliver and wound in such a way that the fibers lie parallel lengthwise. These slivers can be made smaller in diameter and then twisted or plied into yarns by the same type of machinery used to process other long-staple fibers.

Glass fabrics can be permanently crimped without flame at 1200° F. Fabrics produced by this new process have improved resistance to wearing and to crocking and greater tensile and bursting strength.

Glass fibers are fireproof. They are therefore admirably suited for draperies in homes and theater lobbies and for fireproof and waterproof wallpaper. Glass is used for stuffing in beach rolls and backrests, glider cushions, chair pads, and garment linings.

[13] *Textile Fiber Materials for the Textile Industry,* pamphlet by Owens-Corning Fiberglas Corporation, p. 6.

**Figure 14.8.** Hallway entrance to the Metropolitan Opera's executive office area. Window draperies are made of a medium weight, open weave fabric of Fiberglas, "Fresco." (*Photograph courtesy of Owens-Corning Fiberglas Corporation.*)

The tensile strength of glass fibers is considerably greater than that of cotton or rayon. It is quick drying, resists chemicals and soil well, has good colorfastness, has excellent stability to repeated washings, resists sunlight well, and has electrical insulating properties. Its chief drawback is poor abrasion resistance.

Under the microscope, glass fibers resemble translucent rods. The individual fibers do not absorb moisture; therefore, if the surface is wet it will dry off rapidly without affecting the original strength of the yarn. Glass fibers can be easily washed by hand and drip-dried. Cloths of glass fibers should not be ironed. They are not machine washable or dry cleanable. Furthermore, Fiberglas has no odor and is not attacked by microorganisms or insects. Sunlight does not affect the fiber, and it is attacked by hydrofluoric and hot phosphoric acids only. Likewise, Fiberglas is attacked by hot solutions of weak alkalies and cold solutions of strong alkalies. Since it does not shrink, stretch, or sag, accurate measuring for curtains and draperies is possible.

Two general types of finishes are employed on Fiberglas, depending upon its end use (1) as an industrial fiber, or (2) as a decorative fabric. In this book we are concerned with the latter type, with such fabrics as marquisettes and casement cloth, and fabrics that are to be screen-printed. A basic finishing process subjects the fabric to high temperatures to release the stress developed in the yarns during twisting and weaving. This treatment gives fabrics principally a good hand, wrinkle resistance, and durability. Then fabrics are treated to relubricate the filaments. Color can be applied, and a protective agent may be administered to improve abrasion resistance. Coronizing, a finish of Owens-Corning, is a combination of (1) heat setting to relax the fibers, to permanently crimp the yarn, and to set the weave; (2) finishing with resins to produce resistance to abrasion, color retention, water repellency, and launderability. It has been found that a Coronized glass fabric treated with a special chemical solution improves the hand and its dyeability.[14]

Fiberglas can be yarn-dyed, piece-dyed, or printed. Pigmented resins are applied in the same manner as in the pigment printing or dyeing of cottons and rayons.

Fiberglas is admirably suited for nonallergic pillow stuffing, ironing-board covers, and interlinings for women's and men's wear. Fiberglas yarns suitable for wearing apparel are now being developed by Owens-Corning.

Some homemakers who have had trouble sewing glass-fibered fabrics might avoid future difficulties by the following procedures: [15]

1. Using a good-quality, fine cotton mercerized thread

---

[14] *Textile World* (February 1962).
[15] *Of Course You Can Sew Fiberglas,* a pamphlet by the Textile Products Division of Owens-Corning Fiberglas Corporation.

2. Using a longer stitch
3. Using looser-tension top and bottom threads
4. Lightening pressure of the pressure foot
5. Using a sharp needle

Furthermore, the sewing machine should be guided rather than pushed or tugged. Only washable drapery heading should be used with Fiberglas, and Fiberglas fabrics ought not to be lined.

## AZLON

Azlon as defined by the F.T.C. is "a manufactured fiber in which the fiber-forming substance is composed of any regenerated naturally occurring proteins." Azlon, then, includes fibers derived from plant and animal proteins. Natural sources of raw materials (for these fibers are proteins) are milk curd (casein), peanuts, cottonseed, cornmeal (zein), egg white, soybeans, and chicken feathers.

## SUMMARY

Consumers are more aware of fiber content of their garments since the T.F.P.I.A. has required that all fibers be labeled by generic names as specified by the F.T.C. Previous to the enactment of this law, consumers had become familiar with trade names such as Orlon, Dacron, Acrilan, and Dynel. But with the new generic names such as acrylic, modacrylic, and polyester, the consumer not only has to learn what these terms mean but also has to learn the characteristics of each of these new classes of fibers and how to care for them. If informative labels are adequate, learning is relatively easy. Also, if the consumer associates a trade name with the generic class to which it belongs, she will be able to differentiate these new generic names. For example, if she remembers the phrases Orlon acrylic fiber, Acrilan acrylic fiber, Dacron polyester, and Fortrel polyester, she will probably remember the characteristics of each generic classification.

By and large, the man-made fibers with noncellulosic bases have the following plus qualities (unless the structure of the fiber is modified):

1. Dimensional stability (when properly heat-set)
2. Strength and durability (long wear)
3. Ease of care (ease in washing, quick drying, little or no ironing, durable pleats and creases)
4. Resiliency (wrinkle resistance)
5. Elasticity (comfort and fit)
6. Resistance to moths and mildew

Although pilling and static electricity may still exist, ways have been found to overcome or to lessen these objectionable features.

The future of blends seems limitless. Any fiber is a potential contributor to a blended fabric. Testing is going on constantly to find out what the best fiber blends are and what percentages are best adapted to certain uses. The results of tests so far show that no fiber can be ignored as a tool in a blend. But to get the maximum of one quality, such as abrasion resistance, another quality may be sacrificed. If the missing quality is not important in the fabric's use, it will not be missed. All fibers are complementary and supplementary to one another.

None of these man-made fibers is an all-purpose fiber. Technical changes are continually taking place, so that it is not possible to associate for long periods any particular advantages with any particular fiber.

## REVIEW QUESTIONS

1. (*a*) What is the major difference between rayon and the noncellulosics?
   (*b*) What is the major difference between acrylic fibers and nylon?
   (*c*) What is the major difference between polyester fibers and nylon?
2. (*a*) Define polymerization.
   (*b*) Define melt spinning.
   (*c*) Define stretch spinning.
   (*d*) Define curing.
   (*e*) Define pigmentation.
3. (*a*) Name two solvents for nylon.
   (*b*) How can nylon be identified chemically?
4. (*a*) List the important physical properties of nylon.
   (*b*) List the important chemical properties of nylon.
5. (*a*) Give ten specific uses of nylon.
   (*b*) Why do consumers buy nylon?
6. (*a*) Why is Dynel considered a modacrylic fiber?
   (*b*) How does Dynel differ from Orlon chemically?
   (*c*) What specific advantages does Orlon have over Dynel?
7. (*a*) For what purposes is Verel modacrylic suited?
   (*b*) What is an advantage of Orlon acrylic over nylon for a girl's sweater?
8. How does Dacron polyester differ physically and chemically from Orlon acrylic?
9. (*a*) What can be done to overcome static electricity?
   (b) What can be done to prevent pilling?
10. (*a*) Why do consumers like Dacron polyester?
    (*b*) For what uses is Kodel polyester most popular?
    (*c*) What are the advantages and uses of Vycron polyester?
11. (*a*) What is vinyon?
    (*b*) What are its advantages?
    (*c*) For what purposes is vinyon used?
    (*d*) What are its limitations?
12. (*a*) Name the olefin fibers.
    (*b*) In what ways is polyethylene similar to polypropylene?
    (*c*) In what ways are they different?

(d) What are the chief advantages and limitations of saran fibers?
13. (a) What is vinal?
    (b) For what purposes is vinal used?
    (c) What are the advantages of vinal?
14. (a) What is the chemical composition of metallic yarns?
    (b) List the uses of metallic yarns.
    (c) What are the chief advantages of these fibers and yarns?
15. (a) Describe the manufacture of glass fibers.
    (b) What are the chief advantages of glass fibers?
    (c) What are this fiber's limitations?
    (d) For what purposes are glass fibers used?
16. (a) How do azlon fibers differ from nylon polyester and acrylic fibers?
    (b) Name and describe the fibers in the azlon family.
    (c) Where is azlon used?
    (d) What are the advantages and weaknesses of these fibers?
17. (a) Describe the production of natural rubber yarn.
    (b) List the chief uses of natural rubber yarn.
    (c) How does Lastex differ from Helanca yarn?
    (d) What is spandex?
    (e) How does spandex differ from natural rubber fibers?

# EXPERIMENTS

1. *Alkali test:* Take yarns or small pieces of fabric of as many of the newer synthetics as possible. Boil for five minutes in 10 per cent solution of sodium hydroxide. Describe the effect of strong alkali on each fiber.

2. *Acid test:* Place as many of the yarns from the newer synthetics as possible in concentrated sulfuric acid for five or ten minutes. Describe the effect of strong acid on each fiber.

3. *Microscopic test:* Examine the nylon fiber under the microscope. Draw the fiber as you see it. Examine and draw as many of the newer synthetics as possible. Note the similarities between some of these fibers and the difficulty in identifying them by microscope.

4. *Absorbency test:* Cut strips of fabric eight inches by one inch in both warp and filling directions. Brush water-soluble red ink lightly onto the strips to serve as an indicator. Support each strip above the beaker of water (80° F.) so that the edge of the sample is just one inch below the surface of the water. Measure the height to which the water rises at one minute, five minutes, and ten minutes. Rate the fabric as follows at the end of ten minutes:

| | |
|---|---|
| 5 to 6 inches | Excellent |
| 4 to 5 inches | Very good |
| 3 to 4 inches | Good |
| 2 to 3 inches | Fair |
| 1 to 2 inches | Poor |
| 0 to 1 inch | Very poor |

(Weirick Method, Sears Roebuck and Company.)

1. Collect magazine advertisements of five different synthetic fabrics. Obtain a sample of each, and classify it by group origin. Indicate its most appropriate uses (give reasons for your choices). Check veracity of advertisement claims by your own original test or tests.
2. (*a*) What advice would you, as a salesperson, give a consumer on the choice of fabric for automobile seat covers?
   (*b*) How would you advise a consumer to choose fabric for an outdoor American flag?
   (*c*) What could you suggest about choosing draperies for the living room in a new home in Florida?
   (*d*) What kind of wardrobe would you advise for a two-week winter cruise to Puerto Rico and the Virgin Islands, a trip on which there will be limited laundering facilities?

# GLOSSARY

**Acetate.** See Glossary, Chapter 13.

**Acrylic fibers.** The generic name of fibers made from *acrylonitrile*.

**Acrylic resins.** Thermoplastic in nature, of synthetic type. These resins are polymerized from acrylic and methacrylic acid.

**Acrylonitrile.** A chemical compound from which acrylic fiber is made. This chemical compound is made by the reaction of ethylene oxide and hydrocyanic acid.

**Anidex.** A generic name for an elastomeric fiber. See pp. 43, 56.

**Antistatic finish.** A chemical treatment applied to noncellulosic synthetic fibers in order to eliminate static electricity.

**Ardil.** A fiber derived from protein in peanuts; it is made in England.

**Autoclave.** A vessel similar to a pressure cooker in which a chemical solution is heated under pressure.

**Azlon.** A generic name for man-made textile fibers made from protein, such as casein, zein, soybean, and peanut.

**Blend.** See Glossary, Chapter 2.

**Bright yarn.** High-luster yarn.

**Casein.** A protein compound found especially in milk. Synthetic fibers can be derived from this protein.

**Coronizing.** A finish for Fiberglas that heat-sets the fibers, crimps the yarn, sets the weave, and produces abrasion resistance, color retention, water repellency, and launderability.

**Count.** Size of a spun synthetic yarn. See Glossary, Chapter 3.

**Denier.** Size of a nylon or any other synthetic filament yarn. See Glossary, Chapter 3.

**Dimensional stability.** See Glossary, Chapter 13.

**Filament yarn.** See Glossary, Chapter 13.

**Fleece.** Furlike pile fabrics made of Orlon acrylic, nylon, Verel modacrylic, Dynel modacrylic, Dacron polyester, or other synthetic pile.

**Glass fibers.** Very fine flexible fibers of pure glass.

**Heat-set finish.** . The stabilization of synthetic fabrics to ensure no change in size or shape. Methods of setting fabrics of nylon and polyester fibers, for example, include (1) treatment of fabrics at boiling or near boiling temperatures one-half hour to one hour; (2) treatment with saturated steam; (3) application of dry heat. Heat setting also secures maximum dimensional stability of acrylic fibers.

**Hexamethylene-diammonium-adipate.**   A solution of a salt that is polymerized and hardened into a solid and cut into flakes, then melted and extruded into nylon fibers.

**Hydrophobic fiber.**   A nonabsorptive fiber.

**Metallic.**   The generic name of a man-made fiber composed of metal, plastic-coated metal, metal-coated plastic, or a core completely covered by metal.

**Mixture.**   See Glossary, Chapter 2.

**Modacrylic fibers.**   The generic name of man-made fibers composed of less than 85 per cent but at least 35 per cent by weight of acrylonitrile units.

**Monofilament.**   A single filament.

**Multifilament yarn.**   Continuous strands of two or more monofilaments that have been twisted together.

**Nylon.**   A man-made polyamide fiber derived from coal, air, and water.

**Pigmented fibers and yarns.**   Delustered. See Glossary, Chapter 13.

**Pilling.**   Fibers of certain synthetic spun yarns form little balls or pills on the surface of a cloth.

**Polyamide.**   A chemical rearrangement of atoms to form a molecule of greater weight. A resin made by condensation. Nylon is a polyamide.

**Polyester fiber.**   The generic name of a man-made fiber made from a chemical composition of ethylene glycol and terephthalic acid.

**Polymer.**   A large molecule produced by linking together many molecules of a monomeric substance.

**Polymerization.**   The way in which certain small molecules combine into fiber-forming molecules.

**Rayon.**   See Glossary, Chapter 13.

**Rubber.**   The generic name of man-made fibers in which the fiber-forming substance is natural or synthetic rubber.

**Saran.**   The generic name of vinylidene chloride fibers.

**Soybean.**   A small herb of the bean family of India and China; source of protein for certain man-made fibers.

**Spandex.**   The generic name of man-made fibers derived from a chemical substance called segmented polyurethane.

**Spinneret.**   See Glossary, Chapter 13.

**Spun yarn.**   See Glossary, Chapter 13.

**Staple fibers.**   See Glossary, Chapter 13.

**Static electricity.**   Stationary electric charges caused by rubbing an article or exposing it to abrasion. Static electricity attracts small particles to the object.

**Synthetic fiber.**   A man-made fiber produced by chemical synthesis.

**Vinal.**   The generic name of a man-made fiber derived from polyvinyl alcohol.

**Vinyon.**   The generic name of a man-made fiber made from polyvinyl chloride, a derivative of natural salt, water, and petroleum.

**Zein.**   Cornmeal from which protein is derived for synthetic fibers.

# 15

# Care of
# Textile Fabrics

Satisfaction from textile purchases depends not only on selection of an article well suited to its end use but also on the care given the product after selection. For example, a man's suit, properly cared for and cleaned, may be expected to last considerably longer than one that is not cared for properly; and it will also look better all through its period of use. Care includes three elements: storage, refreshening, and cleaning.

## STORAGE

In general, after an outer garment has been worn, it should be brushed lightly and promptly hung on a hanger in such a way that it hangs naturally and is not crushed by other garments on the rack. Good ventilation should be provided to remove dampness, perspiration, and odors. If woolen goods are to be stored for some time, such as through the summer, mothballs should be put in the storage bag, or a similar naphtha preparation should be sprinkled or sprayed on the garments. If the storage space is subject to dampness, goods should be sprayed with a compound to prevent mildew. In the fall, bathing suits should be rinsed in fresh water and thoroughly dried (but not with a hot iron) before packing away.

Knitwear, underclothing, domestics, and draperies should be stored flat in drawers, chests, and closet shelves, preferably in the dark, since light deteriorates some fabrics. Hangers should be particularly avoided for knitwear. Nearby steam radiators and hot-water pipes should be avoided, particularly in the storage of silks, wools, and acetates. The chief requirement is that the merchandise be folded carefully so that it is ready for use without further pressing. A cedar chest or naphtha flakes are recommended for woolens. Fiberglas does not need to be stored, since it is resistant to light, moths, moisture, fire, and fumes. It is best left hanging at the windows.

Some homemakers roll linen in colorfast blue paper before storage to prevent yellowing. It is also desirable to wash new linens before storage, for the starch or dressing plus dampness may promote mildew.

The storing of floor coverings and upholstery will be discussed in Chapters 19 and 20.

## REFRESHENING

Some garments, particularly those of wool fiber, require frequent refreshening in order to maintain freshness and appearance.

Brush wool fabrics at frequent intervals, especially before wearing them. Since wool absorbs oil from the skin, any dirt coming to the fabric mixes with the oil, and a greasy stain is the result. Neckbands, collars, and the portions under the arms of garments should have special brushing. Wool gets dirty slowly, but once it becomes soiled it is more difficult to clean than cotton, linen, or silk. Pile fabrics, however, should not be brushed when wet. When dry, they should be brushed lightly against the pile, and then brushed several times in the direction of the pile.

Blankets, bedspreads, and woolen clothing should also be refreshed by an occasional airing. Hang in the fresh air—in sunlight, if possible.

Fabrics that wrinkle easily often need refreshening long before cleaning is necessary. Pressing between usage is a common practice. In the case of velvets, corduroy, and other pile fabrics, wrinkles are best removed by hanging the garments over a bathtub filled with steaming hot water. In ironing flat goods that require creasing, there should be as few creases made as possible, and folds should be even.

## CLEANING

Cleaning is usually a more technical and more involved process than storage or refreshening. It involves both overall cleaning and spot removal, both of which are considered in this chapter. There are two major overall cleaning methods: washing and dry cleaning. Washing may be either hand washing or machine washing. For either process there are variations in the required water temperature, the nature of the detergent used, the use of bleach, the length of sudsing time, the length of soaking and agitation time, the method of moisture removal, and the method and amount of pressing required.

With the tremendous variety of textile products on the market (made from some twenty-two generic fibers in various mixtures and blends) and the variety of finishes combined into all sorts of garments and domestics, only the expert, backed by laboratory tests, can determine the best way to clean any particular garment. The consumer's best guide is the label or leaflet on care that most manufacturers of branded merchandise attach to the merchandise. Although providing such information is not mandatory, sellers are now recognizing that they have a responsibility to the consumer and that failure to provide correct information on care leads to customer complaint and militates against the attempt to build good will for a brand. Retailers, who at one time used to remove all manufacturers' promotional material, also recognize the necessity of information on care. They are, to an increasing degree, insisting that their suppliers provide the information in readily intelligible form, and they are helping prepare the instructions for care that are attached to goods selling under their own labels.

Reference was made in Chapter 1 to the work of the President's Industry Advisory Committee on Textile Information. The Committee published the Voluntary Labeling Guide—a universal vocabulary of care instructions. It also worked on permanent labels that could be sewn on the garment or printed on existing tab labels. Mills, chain stores, and the Federal Government have promoted the Guide and the use of permanent labels.

Fiber manufacturers have been particularly active in determining best care for the various fibers they produce and in providing labels that may be attached to the finished garments. But such instructions may not be suitable for garments in which a particular fiber, though a major component, is not the only one. Linings, trimming, buttonholes, and sewing thread may have characteristics differing from the characteristic of the basic fabric. Thus the manufacturer of the finished goods has a responsibility not only to use information supplied him but also to adapt it to his particular product.

**CARE INSTRUCTIONS**

Wash by machine or hand using any good soap or detergent. Avoid the use of chlorine bleach. This garment can go through the full washing machine cycle. When home dryers are used, best results will be obtained by using the low temperature setting. If automatic dryer is not used, lay garment flat to dry. If touch-up ironing is desired, use a press cloth and a warm iron (low or synthetic setting). Store garment flat. If dry cleaned, make certain dry cleaner is advised of fiber content.

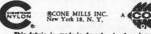 

®CONE MILLS INC. New York 18, N. Y.    A FABRIC

**This fabric is made in America by American craftsmen**

L-1100-19

Figure 15.1. Care instructions appearing on the back of a hang tag to be attached to a fabric of stretch corduroy made of 62½% cotton and 37½% Helanca nylon. (*Reproduced courtesy of Cone Mills, Inc.*)

Where several fibers are present, the consumer is well advised to follow the cleaning instructions for the fiber that requires the greatest care.

In washing woven stretch fabrics, the same rule should be applied as for nonstretch. First, determine the fiber content; secondly, wash the article according to the method required for best results on the most fragile fiber present. Stretch garments can be hung on hangers just like nonstretch articles. It often helps if the stretch garments are allowed to "rest" between wearings in order to restore the fabric to its original dimensions.

Durable press garments are primarily intended for home laundering, but good results can be obtained from the commercial laundry and from dry cleaners. In case the home washer is used, follow any special washing instructions that come with the garment. General instructions follow:

1. Use the wash-and-wear setting.
2. Use cool water for less chance of wrinkling.
3. Use your regular laundry detergent.
4. Don't overcrowd the washer; use several small loads.
5. Tumble-dry and remove from the dryer soon after it stops. If you have no dryer, remove from the washer before the spin cycle, and drip-dry.
6. Hang on nonrusting hangers immediately after drying. Slacks should be hung on spring-clip hangers.
7. If touch-up ironing is desired, a steam iron on a "low" setting is best.
8. Wash durable press garments frequently, since heavy stains are difficult to remove. Use soap or detergent on stains, and cleaning fluid on greasy stains prior to washing.

It is important that care instructions be retained by the consumer rather than thrown away when the merchandise is first used.

### ESSENTIAL CLEANING INFORMATION

There are five major facts that a customer should be able to determine from the label:

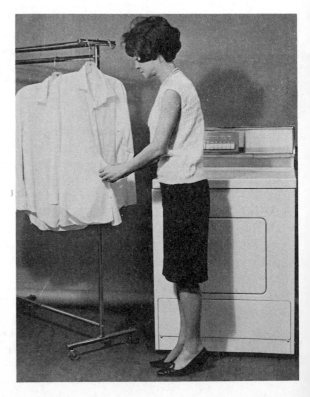

Figure 15.2. To get best performance from durable press shirts, remove them from drier as soon as tumbling stops and hang them up. (*Photo reproduced with permission. Copyright by Consumers Union of U.S., Inc., a nonprofit organization.*)

1. As already indicated, designation of one fiber content is required
by law for most textile products used by the consumer. Although we shall indicate later in this chapter the differences in washing and care recommended for the various fibers, the average consumer and the retail salesperson should depend on the specific care instructions provided with the garment. The fiber information is more likely to be of assistance in determining the suitability of the item than in determining its care.

2. Should the merchandise be (*a*) washed by hand? (*b*) by machine? (*c*) by hand *or* machine? or (*d*) dry cleaned? There are also some fragile textiles, often antiques, that should never be cleaned or should be cleaned only by an expert.

3. If washable, (*a*) Should a mild or an all-purpose detergent be used? (*b*) Should the goods be bleached? (*c*) How hot should the water be? (*d*) Should the sudsing process be long or short? (*e*) Should the soaking and activating process be long or short?

4. How should the goods be dried? (*a*) flat dried? (*b*) hung on line? (*c*) drip dried? (*d*) tumble dried? (*e*) dried rapidly, removing excess moisture between two towels?

5. How should the merchandise be pressed? (*a*) no ironing? (*b*) steam ironing? (*c*) dry ironing (hot, medium, cool)? (*d*) touch-up ironing?

## THE HOME WASHING MACHINE

Most washing today is done by home washing machines, the great majority of which are the automatic type that carry a wash through the following cycles:

1. A filling time, while water flows into the washer.
2. A washing time, which may be preset, while the machine spins and agitates the clothes. There may be soaking time between cycles 1 and 2.
3. A spinning time while the water is forced out by centrifugal force.
4. A rinse effected as the washer continues spinning while fresh water enters.
5. Further spinning.
6. A rinse in the filled tub.
7. Spinning to expel the water until the load is damp dried.

Most modern machines can be adjusted for the following:

1. The capacity claimed by manufacturers of automatic washers ranges from 12 to 18 pounds (a few are larger). According to the Consumers Union, the machine it tested handled 8-pound loads better than 11-pound loads. Clothes should be put in loosely, which makes them weigh less.
2. Temperature, speed, and time are indicated. Modern washing ma-

chines provide a selection of water temperatures: hot, warm, or cold wash; warm or cold rinse; normal or slow wash and spin speeds; controlled long or short wash periods. There is great flexibility in controlling water temperature, speed, and time. A short time cycle should be set for wash-and-wear and for durable press.

3. Water levels can, in most machines, be set for both wash and rinse. Most machines permit a partial wash fill.
4. An automatic safety feature locks the lid automatically during the spin. Or, if the lid is opened during the spin cycle, a switch shuts off the machine.

### CAUTION IN USING AN AUTOMATIC WASHER

1. Turn off the water supply when the machine is not in use, to prevent the hose from rupturing.
2. Remove all articles from the clothing pockets before washing.
3. Keep hands out of the washer when it is in operation.
4. Don't overload the machine. Distribute the loads evenly. Should the machine vibrate or bang, turn it off at once. It is off balance.

### PROCEDURES FOR HOME LAUNDERING

All soiled clothes should be stored in a well-ventilated hamper. If fabrics are badly stained, they should be treated for stain removal as soon as possible, because stains are more easily removed soon after they have been made. Although each homemaker has her own pet ways of doing laundry, a few general rules may prove helpful.

*Sorting.* Separate all colored clothes from the white clothes. Use a table or counter for this purpose to avoid bending over. If there are any colored clothes that have doubtful colorfastness, put them to one side to be washed by themselves. Or try a wash test on an inconspicuous part of each garment before mixing it with other clothes. To make a wash test, place the sample in a jar with detergent and water at the same temperature that will be used in regular washing. Let it stand for a few minutes; then shake the jar. If the water is discolored, or if color is transferred to a white paper or cloth when the fabric is pressed, then it should always be washed separately. Colors in madras shirts are often sold as "bleeding madras." If so, they are expected to bleed and should not be laundered with other clothes.

It is not necessary to make one wash load completely white clothes and another load completely colored clothes. Certain combinations of articles launder and dry well together.

Combination loads that wash and dry well together: [1]

---

[1] *All about Modern Home Laundering,* a pamphlet by Ruud Manufacturing Company, p. 41.

1. White and colorfast sheets, pillowcases, table linen, hand towels, tea towels, men's shirts, white gloves, and pajamas.
2. Heavy bath towels and mats, underwear, light-colored shirts and socks. (Nos. 1 and 2 can be combined if not enough for two loads.)
3. Lightweight colored cottons—dresses, aprons, shirts. Select water temperature by colorfastness.
4. Sheer white and colorfast cottons—organdy, batiste, nainsook, voile, lawn, and dotted swiss. White and colorfast rayons.
5. Acrylics, acetates, nylons, and other man-made fiber fabrics. Silk.
6. Extra-soiled, heavier, and darker cotton pants, overalls, play clothes, socks.
7. Wash separately—shag rugs, pillows, quilts, blankets, slip covers, draperies, curtains.

All torn or frayed fabrics should be put aside to be mended before they are washed. Infants' clothes and those from a sickroom should be washed separately. If garments are stained, put them aside and treat stains before laundering. (See pp. 415 ff. for stain removal.)

*Preparation of the automatic washer.* New automatic washers have accompanying instructions about how many garments or pounds constitute a load. However, it is better to underload than to overload a washer, because clothes get cleaner when they can tumble about freely in the wash water.

The amount of detergent or soap should be carefully measured, and the dial should be set to hot (160°), medium hot (120°), or warm (100°), depending on the fiber content, sheerness, construction, finish, and degree of soil.

A general rule is to wash white and colorfast cottons and linens with proper finish in hot water (160°) for a short time. Lightly soiled lingerie and pastel sheets and other colorfast fabrics can be washed in medium hot water (120°) for four to six minutes.

For the general family wash, consisting largely of sturdy colorfast cottons such as dish towels, sheets, night clothes, blouses, shirts, underwear, and play clothes, hot water (160°) should be used with a synthetic detergent or built soap, and the machine should be run ten to fifteen minutes. (See below for choice of detergents.) Bleach should be diluted and added to the water before articles are immersed. If the articles are badly soiled, they should be prewashed for five minutes at 160° with detergent or built soap.

Sheer cottons, nylon, rayon, acetate, washable silks, and acrylic fibers can be done in an automatic washer with warm water (100° to 120°) with a three-to-five minute washing period. Gentle hand-washing is often preferable. No chlorine should be used in washing garments containing Lycra spandex, since this bleach will discolor the fabric permanently.

Woven and knitted woolens and polyester fibers can be washed in warm water (100°) with mild soap or synthetic detergent for three to five minutes. Unless the woolen has been treated for shrinkage control, it may shrink if agitated too long. Blankets may also be washed in this manner. (See specific instructions for laundering blankets, Chapter 18.)

Cottons and linens used by those who have common illnesses should be laundered for fifteen minutes in water 160° with a synthetic detergent or heavy-duty soap.

For home washing, a reliable supply of hot water at the right temperature and in the right quantity is advisable. Authorities recommend a temperature of 140° to 160° in the automatic washer itself, for white and colorfast cottons, linens and rayons. Such a tub temperature, of course, calls for a higher temperature in the water heater to offset piping and other temperature losses.

The necessary quantity of hot water is determined by the design of the individual automatic washer and varies greatly from one make to another. Modern practice is to provide an automatic water heater with a hot water delivery that will supply the washer on a consecutive, load-after-load basis. Experience has proved that, in most homes with one bathroom, such a water heater will supply not only the washer but bath, kitchen, and all other requirements as well. Quick-heating laundry-rated gas water heaters have proved very popular.

In the late 1960's, detergent producers began to advise consumers to use cold water with a heavy-duty detergent that gets out the worst kind of dirt in cold water. Since a bacteriostat is added to the detergent, it actually germproofs as well as cleans. It is claimed that cold-water washing leaves woolens softer and fluffier than does hot water. Danger of shrinkage is minimized. This treatment is recommended for acrylics, polyesters, and nylon. Even permanent press garments come clean with this treatment. Familiar trade names are Cold Power and Cold Water All.

### DETERGENTS

The home launderer always has the problem of deciding whether she should use a soap detergent or a synthetic detergent. Soap detergent is by far the oldest in use. In fact, synthetic detergents have come into use only since World War II.

Soap is the result from the reaction of caustic soda and a fat. There are pure mild soaps, which are all soap with nothing added, and heavy-duty, all-purpose, built soaps. The heavy-duty soap has special alkalies added to improve cleaning power.[2] Water softeners are usually added.

Synthetic detergents are organic chemicals, the preparation of which is complicated because of the nature of the process involved. There are a number of chemical types of synthetic detergents. A common one consists of fatty alcohol sulfates.

There are several types of synthetic detergents. First, there is the light-

[2] These are enforcing compounds, such as sodium silicate, sodium carbonate, and a variety of sodium phosphates.

duty, mild synthetic detergent for hand washing sheers and nonfast colors; and for machine washing lightly soiled articles and delicate fabrics. Second, there is the heavy-duty synthetic detergent with builder for improved cleaning power plus a suds-making ingredient, intended primarily for badly soiled and greasy articles washed in top-loading automatic washers. Third, there is the heavy-duty, low-sudsing synthetic detergent used in automatic washers, particularly of the revolving drum-front loading type, where an excessive amount of suds decreases the effectiveness of the washing action.

A fourth type is the heavy-duty detergent that not only cleans in cold water but germproofs as well. A fifth type contains enzymes (organic catalysts) that solubilize protein-based soils, such as blood, albumen, body soils, and gravy. Manufacturers of Biz and Axion recommend soaking soiled articles thirty minutes or longer—even as long as overnight—in order to give the enzyme an opportunity to act. Soaking is followed by the usual washing, with the customary detergent. Drive, Gain, and Tide XK are enzyme-containing detergents that are intended for use in the washer in place of a regular laundry detergent. It is claimed that these enzyme products will also remove stubborn stains of fruits, chocolate, beets, lipstick, and grass. The use of an enzyme-containing product will not eliminate the need for an occasional use of bleach. But enzyme and bleach should not be used together. Chlorine will inactivate the enzymes.

In 1971, non-enzyme detergents became popular due to uncertain side effects and unfavorable publicity of enzyme products. However both enzyme and non-enzyme detergents were a public concern when problems of pollution arose. Both types of detergents were high in phosphates (pollutants). Hence some products containing no phosphates, non-enzyme, "non-polluting" ingredients were produced. However, Consumers' Research, Inc. found that these "non-polluting" products do not clean as well as detergents containing phosphates.[3]

The choice of a soap or synthetic detergent will finally be made by the home launderer, as the result of trial and error. Commercial laundries, by and large, favor the use of soap with a softened water. Figures show an increasing amount of synthetic detergents used in the home.

It is frequently recommended to use synthetic detergents in automatic washers when water is hard. Although it doesn't matter whether a soap or a synthetic detergent is used where the colorfastness of a non-wool fabric is questionable, a synthetic detergent is better for colorfastness on wool.

The following table classifies the various laundry aids by type and use. The listing is not complete. There is no endorsement of specific products, nor is there criticism implied of those not mentioned. Some products may be more easily obtained locally than others. The types of products tabu-

[3] *Consumer Bulletin* (March, 1971), p. 13.

lated include cleansing, whitening, disinfecting, and softening agents—
and their brand names and uses.

## SOAPS

| Types | Brands | Uses |
|---|---|---|
| | FLAKES AND GRANULES | |
| Light duty | Ivory Flakes<br>Ivory Snow<br>Lux Flakes | Used for lightly soiled garments and hand laundering of fine fabrics. Also for hand dishwashing. |
| All-purpose | Duz Soap<br>Instant Fels<br>White King Soap | Designed for all-purpose use in family wash, heavy soil, general household use. Can be used for hand laundering and hand dishwashing. |
| Laundry Soap Bars | Fels Naphtha<br>Kirkman's Borax Soap<br>Octagon | Primarily used for hand laundering of heavily soiled garments and for general household use. |

## DETERGENTS

| Types | Brands | Uses |
|---|---|---|
| | A. GRANULES AND POWDERS | |
| Light Duty | Gentle Fels<br>Octagon<br>Trend<br>Vel | Used for lightly soiled hand washables but generally for hand dishwashing. |
| | B. LIQUID | |
| | Ajax<br>Chiffon<br>Dove<br>Gentle Fels<br>Ivory Liquid<br>Joy<br>Lux Liquid<br>Octagon<br>Palmolive<br>Swan<br>Sweetheart<br>Thrill<br>Trend<br>Trend Pink Lotion<br>Rose Lotion Vel<br>White King | |
| | A. GRANULES AND POWDERS * | |
| All-Purpose | Ajax (with enzymes)<br>Bold (with enzymes)<br>Bonus<br>Breeze | General purpose for all types of household wash, from heavily soiled fabrics to delicate fabrics. Also may be used for household cleaning. |

* Since there is some difference of opinion between various manufacturers as to the degree of sudsing, and since no industry-wide standard has been established for one generic description, no specification is given as to whether the products are high, normal, or intermediate sudsing.

| Types | Brands | Uses |
|---|---|---|
| | Cheer | |
| | Cold Power | |
| | Cold Water Surf | |
| | Dreft | |
| | Duz | |
| | Fab (with enzymes) | |
| | Gain (with enzymes) | |
| | Oxydol | |
| | Punch (with enzymes) | |
| | Rinso | |
| | Silver Dust | |
| | Super Suds | |
| | Tide XK (with enzymes) | |
| | White King Detergent | |
| | B. Liquid (See fn p. 404.) | |
| | Cold Power | Good for pretreating clothes. Instantly |
| | Wisk | soluble in all temperatures of water. |
| | A. Granules and Powders | |
| All-Purpose Sudsing | Ad | General purpose for all types of auto- |
| | All (Concentrated) | matic washers, including the front- |
| | All (Fluffy) | loading, tumbler-type. |
| | Cold Water All Powder | |
| | Dash | |
| | Drive (with enzymes) | |
| | B. Liquid | |
| | Cold Water All | Good for pretreating clothes. Instantly soluble in all temperatures of water. |
| | C. Tablets | |
| | Salvo | Offer convenience and premeasurement. |
| | Vim | |
| | A. Granules and Powders | |
| Cold Water All-Purpose | Cheer | Designed for all-purpose use and family |
| | Cold Power | wash in cold water. Certain fabrics |
| | Cold Water All Powder | that tend to wrinkle, shrink, or fade |
| | Cold Water Surf | in hot water need cold water washing. Cold water detergents may also be used for washing in hot water. |
| | B. Liquids | |
| | Cold Power | |
| | Cold Water All | |
| | A. Granules and Powders | |
| Enzyme-Containing All-Purpose | Ajax | Used just like any laundry detergent, |
| | Bold | but add a new dimension in cleaning |
| | Drive | and stain-removal. |
| | Fab | |
| | Gain | |
| | Punch | |
| | Tide XK | |

| Types | Brands | Uses |
|---|---|---|
| | Amaze<br>Axion<br>Biz<br>Brion<br>Sure | These are to be used in soaking prior to washing. Enzymes have the ability to digest complex proteins and, in some cases, carbohydrate soils. The kinds of stain on which they will be particularly effective are body soils, grass, blood, eggs, milk, baby formula, baby food, gravy, chocolate, some vegetables and fruits, and many other food stains. A laundry detergent should be used in the ensuing wash. |

## AMMONIA

| Types | Brands | Uses—never use with chlorine bleach. |
|---|---|---|
| | BoPeep<br>Parson's Ammonia<br>Sea Mist<br>Sparkle X | Cuts grease and, when added to the wash load, helps loosen deeply embedded stains and oily soil. Applied directly, it is also frequently recommended in the treatment of stains such as perspiration, blood, and Mercurochrome. |

## BLEACHES

| Types | Brands | Uses—Bleaches help in soil and stain removal, and in whitening and brightening. |
|---|---|---|
| Chlorine Bleaches | A. DRY<br>Action<br>Hi-Lex Dry<br>Linco<br>Purex | Effective on most white and colorfast fabrics. Should not be used on silk, wool, spandex, nonfast colors, or chlorine-retentive finishes. These bleaches help to disinfect and deodorize. |
| | B. LIQUID<br>Clorox<br>Fleecy White<br>Hi-Lex<br>Linco<br>Purex<br>Roman | |
| Oxygen Bleaches | | Oxygen bleaches are safe for all fabrics and finishes and essentially for all colors. |
| Monopersulfate-based Oxygen Bleaches | Beads-O-Bleach | Effective in all water temperatures. |
| Sodium Perborate-based Oxygen Bleaches | Day-Brite<br>Dexol<br>Lestare<br>Snowy | Totally effective in high-temperature water. |

| Types | Brands | Uses |
|---|---|---|
| Reducing Bleaches | Rit Color Remover<br>Tintex Color Remover | Effective in removing color before re-dyeing. Especially helpful in removing yellow discoloration sometimes caused when chlorine-retentive finishes are bleached with chlorine bleach. |

## BLUINGS AND BRIGHTENERS

| Types | Brands | Uses |
|---|---|---|
| Bluing | Bleachettes (solid)<br>Blu-White (flakes)<br>La France (flakes)<br>Little Boy Blue (liquid) | Imparts a blue cast causing white fabrics to appear whiter. |
| Brighteners | Lightning White<br>Miracle White Super Cleaner<br>Rit Nylon Whitener and<br>    Fabric Brightener | Impart a fluorescence to a fabric, so that yellowness is masked while light reflectance and brightness are increased. |

## DISINFECTANTS

| Types | Brands | Uses—can help prevent spread of disease-causing bacteria. |
|---|---|---|
| Quaternary | Co-Op Sanitizer<br>Roccal | Effective in laundering only if content of "active" ingredient is high. Must be used in rinse water. |
| Phenolic | Al Pine<br>Fast<br>Pine-Sol | Also depend on a high percentage of active ingredients for effectiveness. May be added to wash or rinse water. |
| Pine Oil | Fyne Pyne<br>Fyne Tex<br>King Pine<br>Pine-O-Pine<br>White Cap | Depend on effectiveness as disinfectant when compounded to contain at least 80 per cent pine oil. May be added to wash or rinse water. |

## FABRIC FINISHES AND STARCHES

| Types | Brands | Uses—give body and a smooth finish to fabrics. They also help fabrics stay clean longer. |
|---|---|---|
| Spray Fabric<br>  Finishes or<br>  Sizings | Bab-O-4-in-1<br>Faultless<br>Magic Finish<br>Niagara Fabric Finish<br>Sta-Flo | Offer body to fabrics—particularly synthetics, durable press, and wash-and-wear. They also make ironing easier. |
| Spray Starches | Easy-On<br>Faultless<br>Niagara Spray<br>Pruf<br>Sta-Flo | For use right at the ironing board on dry or damp fabrics. |

## FABRIC FINISHES AND STARCHES (Continued)

| Types | Brands | Uses |
|---|---|---|
| Liquid Starches | Linit Liquid Sta-Flo | Concentrated solutions ready for use when diluted with warm or cold water. |
| Dry Starches | A. HOT WATER TYPE | |
| | Argo Gloss<br>Faultless<br>Linit | Must be mixed with a little cold water to prevent lumping and then combined with boiling water. |
| | B. COLD WATER TYPE | |
| | Niagara | Dry flakes that are readily soluble in cold water. |

## FABRIC SOFTENERS

| Types | Brands | Uses |
|---|---|---|
| | Defend<br>Downy<br>Dri-Soft<br>Final Touch<br>Nu-Soft<br>Petal<br>Soft 'n Fluff<br>Sta-Puf<br>Sweetheart Fabric Softener<br>Vano | Make all washable fabrics feel soft and fluffy to the touch, reduce wrinkling, prevent clinging due to static electricity (especially in synthetic fibers), make ironing easier. |

## WATER SOFTENERS

*Uses—Mechanical softeners: Water may be softened as it passes through a tank-type softener before it reaches a faucet.*
*Packaged softeners: Water is softened by the "sink full" or "post-faucet." Packaged softeners cause a chemical reaction in hard water to make the mineral content inactive. Softeners help to prevent the formation of soap film or scum that tends to leave clothes gray and stiff.*

| Types | Brands | |
|---|---|---|
| Precipitating | Blue Dew<br>Borateem<br>Borax<br>Climalene<br>Melo<br>Rain Drops<br>Sal Soda | Softens water, but the precipitate remains. Use in wash water and rinse out thoroughly. Because of their alkalinity, help to boost cleaning power. |
| Nonprecipitating | Calgon<br>Miracle White<br>Oakite<br>Noctil<br>Spring Rain<br>White King | Combine with hardness minerals and keep them inactive. When used in water with high iron or manganese content, there is less likelihood of staining when chlorine bleach is used. |

The synthetic detergents have the following advantages:

1. They wash satisfactorily in hard, soft, and sea water without leaving deposits on garments or washing utensils.
2. They are effective on woolens.
3. They have excellent grease-removing properties.
4. They have an antistatic effect on the noncellulosic man-made fibers.

Synthetic detergents, called syndets, are produced in various forms: powder, flake, liquid, and cake. The powder form is the most popular for laundering. Although these detergents were first promoted primarily for hard-surface household cleaning, they are now being used for laundering textiles also. In terms of cost for the amount of cleaner needed per gallon of solution, liquids are generally more expensive than heavy-duty soaps or syndets.

Low-sudsing detergents are superior for use in front-loading washers, and they are also less likely to cause drain stoppage and pollution. High-sudsing detergents sometimes pass through the ground from septic tanks and cesspool into wells and other fresh-water supplies, which results in water with a "head" on it. In some areas the problem is already serious, and consumers are advised to use soap or a low-sudsing detergent.

## WATER SOFTENERS

Water softeners, which prevent the formation of soap film or curd that tends to gray the fabric, are necessary only in localities where the water is hard with lime deposits. There are two general types of packaged water softeners—precipitating and nonprecipitating. Both kinds are chemical compounds that are added to the rinse water, or to both the soap and the rinse water if the water is very hard.

1. *The precipitating type* of water softener combines with lime in the water to form solid particles that do not dissolve in the water. If the recommended amount of softener is added to the soapy water, the cleansing action begins immediately, because the alkalinity

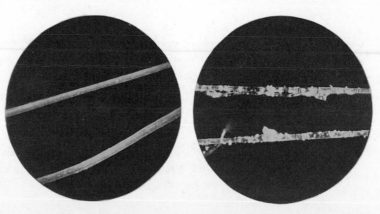

**Figure 15.3.** Photomicrograph of hair showing contrast between uncoated strands and those with flakes of dried soap curds. (*Courtesy of Rohm & Hass Company.*)

helps to remove grease and dirt from the very soiled articles. The directions on the package should tell the amount of softener to use. The instructions should be followed exactly, because if an insufficient amount is used, the soap will combine with the remaining lime that has not combined with the softener to form soap film. Brand names of this type of softener are included in the table on page 406.

2. *The nonprecipitating type* is a conditioner for making the water normally soft. The purpose of this type is to prevent the formation of lime. When the correct amount of softener is added to the water and the soap is put in, suds appear immediately. No soap film appears. If the amount of softener is inadequate, soap film will form; however, the film will dissolve when more softener is added. The advantage of this type of softener is that it is mildly alkaline and does not change the color of the fabric or irritate the skin. However, it is more costly than precipitating softeners. Brand names of this type of softener are included in the table on page 406.

In some homes the cost of water-softening equipment may be considerably less than the cost of soap plus softener for laundering.

### BLEACHES

A fabric that has yellowed with age or has grayed from soap film due to incorrect washing requires bleaching. Occasionally bleaching is advisable for a routine removal of stains. But authorities agree that bleaching is not a substitute for correct washing, because it does not remove soil and its whitening power is limited.

There are liquid (so-called chlorine) bleaches and powder (sodium perborate) bleaches. For brand names see the table on page 404. The liquid or chlorine type, which is most popular, is stronger and quicker but requires more careful adherence to instruction, so that fabrics are not damaged by it.

In Chapter 7 it was stated that optical brighteners (bleaches) can be built into the product and that some may be added to many laundering agents. (See *optical finishes*, Chapter 7.)

### DISINFECTANTS

For antibacterial action in washing of diapers and articles from the sickroom, Borateem is frequently used. Diaper White is intended for diapers.

### BLUING

Bluing, used mostly on cotton and linen and seldom on synthetics, makes clothes look whiter but has no real whitening or cleansing action.

Since most synthetic detergents have a fluorescent dye in them that serves the purpose of bluing, the practice of bluing white clothes is decreasing in importance.

Bluing is often combined with water softeners, starch, detergents, or paraffin and is sold under various brand names. (See the table on page 405.)

## STARCHES

Starches make clothes stiffer, crispier, and shinier. There are two general types of starch: vegetable (made of a white vegetable and corn mixture) and plastic (made of resins). The plastic type is of comparatively recent origin, and is sometimes considered a starch substitute.

The vegetable starches attach themselves to the fabric by covering its pores and by making the surface smooth, which prevents soil from collecting. When soil does collect, it adheres to the starch and is removed easily with the starch in laundering. This type of starch is sold in dry or in liquid forms. Brand names of dry starches are included in the table on page 406.

In contrast to the vegetable starch, the plastic type impregnates the fiber, rather than just covering the surface of the fabric. It is therefore more permanent and will withstand more than one laundering.

Starch in aerosol spray cans is proving very popular, since the housewife can easily spray it on the garment just before ironing rather than having to prepare a solution in which to wet the garment. However, it is relatively expensive. Brands include Salina, Reddi-Starch, Glis, and Easy-on.

## FABRIC SOFTENERS

Advertisements claim that fabric softeners make a wash perceptibly softer and fluffier than an untreated wash; that they make fabrics easier to iron; and that they cause synthetics to lose some of their "fabric cling." The first claim of being perceptibly softer after treatment was judged to be true by a six-woman panel appointed by the Consumers Union for the purpose of evaluating a load of eighteen widely distributed brands of white cotton terry towels. These women found that the softeners did make ironing easier by depositing a waxy, lubricative coating on the fabric. The iron slipped easily over the fabric. The fifth ironing after the use of a softener was easier than preceding ones. It took as much as five launderings for *all* fabrics (Dacron/cotton blends and nylon) to show less cling after treatment.[4] The waxy coating built up on the fabric by the softener tends to repel water, so that softeners tend to decrease fabric absorbency, according to the Consumers Union tests.

[4] *Consumer Reports* (May 1969), p. 254.

The more a fabric softened, the more absorbency decreased. All fabrics were yellowed (from off-white, to cream, to gray) by softeners. One should follow the label in using a softener. A machine half full of clothes takes only half the amount of softener recommended by the manufacturer for a full wash load. Softeners should be added at the beginning of the last rinse cycle. For brands of fabric softeners, see the table on page 406.

### HAND LAUNDERING

Although most of today's fabrics are either machine washable or dry cleanable, hand washing continues to be important, not only for small washes but also for certain materials. In general, silks, sheer fabrics, knitted woolens, and curtains of glass fibers should be washed by hand. Fabrics in which the fastness of color is uncertain should also be washed by hand.

The term "fine fabric" does not necessarily mean that the fabric is of high quality. Fine fabrics usually include such varieties as sheer silks and woolens, crepes, and satins that need special care in cleansing. If they are washable, it is generally advisable to do them by hand. Wool sweaters, nylon stockings, and glass-fibered curtains are also in this category.

For hand laundering, the soap manufacturers advise the following steps:

1. Launder fabrics before they become too soiled.
2. Examine the fabric thoroughly for spots, small tears, or holes.
3. Mend all tears or holes, and mark the spots with thread so that they may be specially treated before or during washing.
4. Remove any accessories that are not washable.
5. If there is any question whether the dye is fast, wash an inconspicuous spot on the fabric first. A small piece of fabric can be clipped from one of the seams. Dry it and compare the washed with the unwashed part. If there is fading or streaking, the cloth should be dry-cleaned.
6. For fine fabrics use a neutral soap with no free alkali, such as Lux, Ivory Snow, or Ivory Flakes.
7. With a cupping of the palms of the hands in lukewarm water and soap, the soap solution should be forced through the fabric. Exceptionally dirty spots must have additional soaping. Several soapy waters may be used—or as many as are needed to cleanse the fabric.
8. Several rinses of water of the same temperature as the soapy water should follow.
9. Roll the fabric in a turkish towel and squeeze out excess moisture. Gently pull the fabric to shape and throw it over a line or chair. Do not use clothespins, especially on knitted goods, for the weight

of the fabric may start a runner. Since rayon is not very elastic, knit goods of rayon should be laid flat on a table or board, pulled to shape, and left to dry. If knit garments are hung, they may dry in longer and narrower proportions than existed before the washing.

## DRYING FABRICS

The old-fashioned method of drying was to remove excess water by hand wringing followed by laying the goods flat in the sun or hanging them on a line. Later, the wringer, consisting of two rubber cylinders, replaced much hand wringing. When operated by electricity, the wringer was very dangerous. In today's machines excess water is removed automatically. Those housewives who do not have combination washers and dryers often have companion dryers that complete the drying operation quickly and easily. Temperature selections in modern dryers may be low (140° F.), medium (158° F.), or high (172° F.). The time control often allows automatic settings up to 120 minutes with a five-minute cooling period at the end of the drying stage. Since such drying equipment uses considerable gas or electricity, the control should not be set for a longer period than is necessary.

Drip-dry fabics, instead of being placed in a machine, should be smoothed out while dripping wet and hung neatly in a place where the drippings will cause no water damage. For best appearance these fabrics usually require light pressing of collars and cuffs.

## PRESSING AND IRONING

Before the advent of durable press, most articles needed some pressing after cleaning to restore them to their original appearance. In those cloths requiring pressing, fibers are affected differently by heat and steam; therefore it is important to know how to iron the goods. The seller's instructions are again the best guide.

In general, cotton and linen can be ironed with a hot iron (400° to 450° F.), but a medium-hot iron (300° to 375° F.) is better for rayon sharkskins and jerseys (which often contain some acetate) and for lightweight satins and crepes. Other man-made fibers that can be subjected to a hot iron (400° F.) are Kodel polyester and triacetate.

A medium-hot iron (300° to 375° F.) is desirable for rayons, acrylics, metallics, acetates, nylons, spandex, and polyesters. A low heat (200° to 275° F.) should be used to iron woolens, silks, the modacrylics, and polypropylene fibers. A very low heat (125° to 175° F.) should be used for polyethylenes, Lastex, saran, and vinyon.

There is no assurance, however, that the foregoing suggested temperatures will always be reliable, since finishing and dyeing processes may increase or decrease the safe ironing temperatures of a fabric. Further-

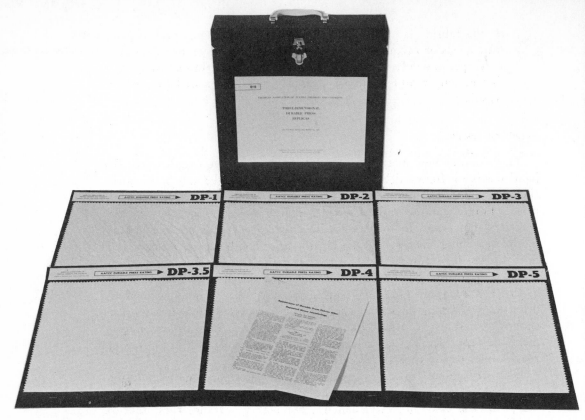

**Figure 15.4.** AATCC 3-D durable press plastic replicas. These replicas are used in evaluation of the retention of the original appearances after laundering of those fabrics intended for use in durable press. Ratings are from DP-1 to DP-5, DP-5 being the smoothest.

more, safe ironing temperatures do not necessarily apply to blended fabrics. For example, a blend of a low-heat-resistant fiber and a high-heat-resistant fiber will assume a resistance to heat that is somewhere between the heat resistance of the two original fibers.[5]

### DRY CLEANING

In general, garments with wool content, crepes, satins, brocades, and pile fabrics in silk or synthetics should be dry cleaned. Again, the safest rule is to follow the instructions on the label. Dry cleaning involves the application of solvents that evaporate quickly. It should not be done at home, because the homemaker does not possess the technical knowledge and equipment necessary to do the job satisfactorily and because there is considerable danger of flammability and poisoning from the fumes. The professional dry cleaner is trained in spot removal and in the appli-

[5] *Textile Fibers and Their Properties*, a pamphlet by Burlington Industries, Inc.

cation of the appropriate dry cleaning solvent to the entire article. After the cleaning, he applies the appropriate pressing and ironing procedures.

Currently available are coin-operated, dry-cleaning machines that clean one to twelve items at a time, about eight pounds. A one-item load might be a slipcover from a large piece of furniture, and a twelve-item load might be lightweight dresses and skirts. The customer loads the machine, inserts six to eight quarters, and the machine goes to work, tumbling the articles for about sixteen minutes in the solvent (perchlorethylene); it then spins fast to remove excess solvent and tumbles the articles for about half hour in warm air. The times given here are approximate, depending on the machine. The cleaned articles come out dry and ready to take home in about fifty minutes. The cost of a load, $2 to $3, compares favorably with the $7 to $9 charge by the professional dry cleaner. But the machine does not wholly replace the professional. He sorts and processes like fabrics together. In the coin-operated machine a load contains varied types and weights of fabrics. It is possible that one fabric may shrink and another may pick up lint if they are all cleaned by the same technique. The machine does not empty pockets, remove trimmings, clean trouser cuffs, and apply special treatment to spots and stains, as the professional dry cleaner does, and it does not press the cleaned merchandise. Also, this process is not suited for the cleaning of garments containing fur, leather, paper, feathers, plastic, rubber, or parts containing these materials. In transporting garments home from a coin-operated dry cleaner, the owner should hang them on enamel wire hangers or unvarnished wooden ones. Plastic varnished hangers may be affected by traces of solvent left in the fabric and may stick to the merchandise at the points of contact.

## SPECIFIC CLEANING AND DRYING REQUIREMENTS OF THE VARIOUS FIBERS

Even though special finishes and mixtures make it dangerous to assume that a knowledge of the fiber reveals the best way to clean it, the following summary may be of some value:

COTTONS. Washable in hot water with a heavy-duty detergent; can be pressed with a hot iron. Unless treated, they wrinkle easily and need frequent pressing.

LINENS. Washable in hot water with a heavy-duty detergent. Heavy starching should be avoided; it tends to break the fibers under heavy ironing. Table linen is best ironed damp on both the right and the wrong sides, moving the iron across the cloth from selvage to selvage. This method brings out luster.

SILKS. Unless labeled "washable," silks should be dry cleaned. If washable, they are best done by hand with lukewarm, mild suds. Remove excess water by rolling the article in a towel, and iron it while damp, on the wrong side. Wrinkles are best removed by placing a damp cotton cloth over the fabric and steaming. Soiled silks should be cleaned at once, since perspiration weakens the fabric.

WOOLS. Washable in warm water, not hot, with a mild neutral soap, mild synthetic detergent, or cold water soap such as Woolite. Use several soapy waters; rinse at the same temperature, but do not remove all the soap, since this prevents felting. Dry slowly away from heat. Knitted fabrics should be pulled into shape while wet and should be dried on a flat surface. It is desirable to measure the original dimensions of the garment before washing and to pull the garment back to these measurements while wet. Liquid or powdered soaps that make suds in cold water are good for hand laundering of wool fabrics. Brand names of cold water soaps are Woolite and Cool Magic. Wools should be ironed, preferably on the wrong side, with a steam iron or damp cloth. To retard shine, two pieces of cheese-cloth may be placed on the right side of the garment when it is pressed on the wrong side. Dry cleaning is often preferable to washing.

RAYONS. Usually washable in hot water with a heavy-duty detergent and may be ironed with a medium-hot iron. Bleaching and bluing are not necessary, since white rayon does not turn yellow. Sheer, dainty rayons should be treated as other fine fabrics—warm water, mild soap, gentle handling, and careful rinsing. Avoid drying in direct sunlight.

ACETATES. Unless the label indicates that the fabric is washable, dry cleaning is recommended. When washed, lukewarm water and mild suds should be used. Drying should not take place near the radiator or a hot stove. The fabric should be ironed at a low temperature on the wrong side while damp, with light pressure.

NYLONS. Require only a minimum cleaning and pressing, since the smooth fibers resist dirt and fiber resiliency minimizes the need for ironing. Since white nylon fabrics may pick up dye from colored clothes, they should be washed with white articles. Also, because white nylons may gray after several washings, they should be bleached frequently with a sodium perborate bleach such as Snowy Bleach. Hand washing is best, but where there is no danger of fraying, machine washing is satisfactory. Squeeze lightly to remove excess moisture; avoid wringing, which may leave creases.

POLYESTERS. Follow general rules, depending upon the sturdiness of the fabric. Rub collars and cuffs with a paste of soap or detergent, or soak in an enzyme product (Axion) before overall washing. Use bleach for white garments. Drip-dry garments should not be put through the spin cycle in the machine. Others should be removed from the dryer immediately to prevent wrinkles.

ACRYLICS AND MODACRYLICS. Sturdy garments of acrylic fibers labeled washable may be washed by machine at a medium temperature. The spin cycle should be eliminated to avoid wrinkles. If pressing is needed, iron at a low temperature. If brushed or napped, brush lightly with a fairly stiff brush. Modacrylics should be ironed at a very low temperature and not steamed.

OLEFINS.   Mostly used for upholstery and may be cleaned with a cloth impregnated with solvent. When used in clothing, olefins are generally combined with other fibers, and the washing instructions that apply to the other fibers should be followed.

GLASS.   Wash by hand in hot, sudsy water; do not scrub. Rinse in clear, warm water; do not wring. Hang over shower rod or clothesline to drip. Rehang damp without ironing. Never machine wash, and avoid dry cleaning.

SARAN.   Does not absorb moisture and is used mostly for upholstery, so it can be wiped clean with a damp cloth. Brushing with soapy water removes stains.

## SPOT AND STAIN REMOVAL

Every consumer is occasionally plagued by getting a spot or stain on a garment or household article. Prompt and proper treatment will save a great deal in dry cleaning bills. Fortunately, some clothing today is treated with a finish that repels stains. A process called Scotchgard, which is indicated on the label of some men's suitings, makes suits resistant to both water and oil stains when they are new and even after a few dry cleanings.

The problem of spot removal is complicated because there are two variables involved: (1) the nature of the foreign agent causing the stain; and (2) the nature of the fabric to which it adheres. The chances of successful spot removal are best with washable fabrics and rough-finished dry-cleanable ones. The first rule is prompt treatment before the stain "sets." Cool water is generally the best treatment for nongreasy stains and particularly for dye stains such as one might get from colored paper napkins. Some fresh grease stains can be removed by absorbent powder such as talcum or cornstarch, or by an absorbent powder mixture. On a dark article, however, this method may lead to the additional problem of removing the white powder. Cleaning fluid will remove grease from colored washables and dry-cleanable fabrics.

If the fabric is washable and colorfast, soaking of a stain in a detergent is helpful in any type of stain re-

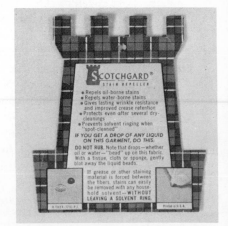

**Figure 15.5.   Label of Scotchgard Stain Repeller. (Reproduced courtesy of Consumers' Research, Inc.)**

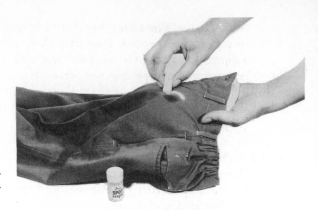

**Figure 15.6.** Removal of fresh grease stain by application of absorbent powder. (*Photograph courtesy of Consumers' Research, Inc.*)

**Figure 15.7.** Removal of fresh grease stain by application of cleaning fluid. (*Photograph courtesy of Consumers' Research, Inc.*)

moval. Soaking in an enzyme product for thirty minutes (or overnight if necessary) will break down or digest by chemical means the various kinds of organic matter, protein, starch, etc., into very small particles. This is a technique of soil release for polyester/cotton blends with durable press finishes. (See Chapter 7, p. 182.)

Rust is often removable with lemon juice and salt. Make each application with a medicine dropper and wash out the lemon juice after each application. If the stain is extensive, the article may be boiled in a cream of tartar and water solution. Commercial rust-removing preparations contain hydrofluoric acid and are too dangerous for home use.

Shoe polish is often removable by sponging with a liquid detergent followed by cleaning fluid. Rubbing alcohol, diluted, is sometimes effective.

Up-to-date information on various specific spot removal problems may be obtained by writing for a publication of the Agricultural Research Service [6] or for a condensation of the same information.[7]

[6] *Removing Stains from Fabrics*, Home and Garden Bulletin 62 (Revised October 1968). Office of Information, U.S. Department of Agriculture, Washington, D.C.

[7] *A Handbook on Fabric Care*, American Institute of Laundries.

Some of the methods that have been found to be particularly effective in removing stains from articles made of the basic fibers are described here. The effect of finishes that change the characteristics of the fibers are not considered.

## COTTON

1. *Blood stains.* These can usually be removed by first soaking in cool water and then washing in lukewarm soapsuds. Cotton is naturally a clean, hygienic fiber, and it can be cleaned easily. That is a reason why cotton is used for sanitary goods, surgical dressings, and nurses' uniforms.

2. *Chewing gum.* Scrape off excess. Rub with ice until remaining gum rolls into a ball; then sponge with dry-cleaning fluid.

3. *Coffee and tea.* The stained portion of the cloth should be placed over a bowl, and boiling water should be poured through it from a height.

4. *Fruit.* Most fresh fruit stains can be removed with boiling water. Peach stains, the exception, may require a bleach such as hydrogen peroxide and ammonia. Follow with a clear water rinse.

5. *Grass stains.* Hydrogen peroxide with ammonia, milk, or alcohol should be applied. Since hydrogen peroxide is a mild bleach, it should not be used on dyed fabrics.

6. *Grease.* A solvent must be used for the fat in the grease—soap and water are not advised. Good solvents are benzine, gasoline, naphtha, carbon tetrachloride, and chloroform. Place a clean blotter under the spot and apply the solvent to the wrong side of the cloth, taking care to rub from the circumference of the

**Figure 15.8.** Durable press sheeting stained for Consumers' Research test of enzyme-active home laundry products. (*Photos and caption courtesy of Consumer Bulletin, Washington, New Jersey.*)

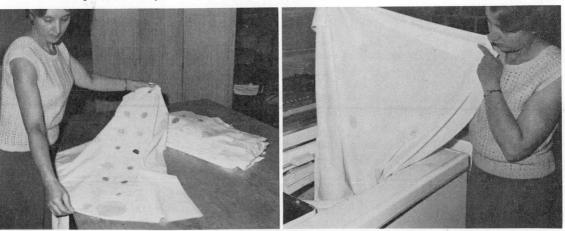

spot inward toward the center. This procedure will prevent a ring from forming around the spot cleaned.

7. *Ink.*   If the cotton goods are white, ink eradicator may be used. Colored fabrics may be soaked in sour milk or salt and lemon juice.
8. *Lipstick and rouge.*   Try rubbing with a piece of bread. Lipstick may then be sponged with dry-cleaning fluid. It may be necessary to apply vaseline to a rouge stain and then sponge with alcohol.
9. *Mildew.*   Strong soap solutions and sunlight are best to remove new stains. A bleaching agent must be used on old stains if the fabric is white. Stains on dyed fabrics should be covered with a paste made from powdered chalk and then exposed to sunlight.
10. *Paint and varnish.*   Turpentine, benzine, or kerosene will usually remove these stains from cotton.
11. *Scorch.*   Sunlight, or rubbing the stain with soft bread crusts, may prove efficacious.

### LINEN

1. *Cream and milk.*   The cloth should be washed at once with cold water.
2. *Grass stain.*   A washing in warm water with naphtha soap usually removes the stain. Ammonia and cold water may be applied before the washing.
3. *Ink.*   Use ink eradicator if the cloth is white; otherwise, soak the fabric in lemon juice, salt, milk, or cultured milk (yogurt).
4. *Meat juice.*   The fabric should be washed first in cold water, then in cold water with soap.
5. *Mildew.*   Soak the mildewed cloth in chloride of lime until the mildew disappears. Follow with a thorough rinsing with clear water.
6. *Paint.*   Turpentine or benzine should be rubbed on the stain from the wrong side.
7. *Scorch.*   Do not wet the fabric, but place it immediately in the sun.
8. *Tea.*   Stretch the stained section of fabric over a bowl and pour glycerine through the cloth. Follow this with boiling water.

In removing stains or in laundering mixed fabrics such as cotton and linen or rayon and linen, the effects of stain removers and soaps should be considered for both kinds of textile materials. A stain remover or soap that is not injurious to either fiber should be chosen.

### SILK

A sponging, with an up-and-down movement (not in a circle) that follows the warp thread, is generally the best cleaner for silks. Stains can be removed as follows:

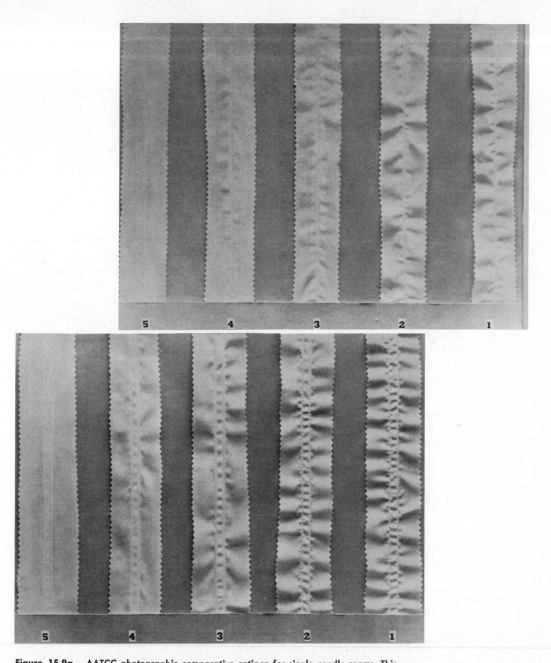

**Figure 15.9a.** AATCC photographic comparative ratings for single needle seams. This test method is designed for evaluation of the appearance of seams in wash-and-wear fabrics. Seamed fabric specimens are subjected to procedures simulating home laundry practices. Evaluation is performed by using the overhead lighting procedure and comparing the appearance of specimen seams with the standard photographs. Five appearance classes are recognized.

**Figure 15.9b.** AATCC photographic comparative ratings for double needle seams. (*Photos reproduced courtesy of the American Association of Textile Chemists and Colorists.*)

1. *Blood.* The stains should be soaked overnight in cold water, then washed in lukewarm water. Old stains may require bleaching. Lemon juice and salt is a good bleach if the fabric is either white or a fast color.

2. *Coffee and chocolate.* These stains are best treated with boiling soft water poured from a height through the stain. The fabric should then be washed in soap and water. Cocoa stains can usually be removed with cold water.

3. *Fruit.* Fruit stains are usually acid in nature and can often be removed by treatment with an alkali, such as ammonia and alcohol mixed in equal proportions. Since ammonia is a weak alkali, it will not be injurious if the dye is fast and if the ammonia is not left too long on the fabric without a rinsing.

4. *Grease and dirt.* Dry-cleaning fluids such as Carbona, naphtha, benzine, gasoline, and Energine usually remove these spots.

5. *Ink.* Aniline inks can be removed with acetic acid (vinegar), because this acid has no detrimental effect on silk. Other fresh inks are best washed or soaked in milk. One of the safest ways to remove ink from colored silks is to soak the fabric overnight in cultured milk (yogurt).

6. *Milk and cream.* Such spots are treated with cold water or with cold water and soap.

7. *Paint.* It is best removed by turpentine or kerosene. On fine fabrics a mixture of turpentine and chloroform is often efficacious.

8. *Perspiration.* Dilute hydrochloric acid will remove stains of perspiration—one part acid to 75 or 100 parts water.

9. *Scorch.* If a silk is slightly scorched, soap and water may remove the spot. If a silk is badly burned, the entire fabric should be dyed.

10. *Water spots.* When they are dry, they can be removed from weighted silks if rubbed with tissue paper, another part of the same fabric, or a shiny nickel coin. The object of the rubbing is to equalize the weighting that has been partially or entirely removed from the watered spot.

## WOOL

1. *Grease.* Sponge lengthwise with warm water and soap. If a ring results, it may be necessary to dry clean.

2. *Ink.* Soak overnight in cultured milk (yogurt). Washable ink stains can be removed with soap and water if action is prompt.

3. *Scorch.* If the scorch is slight, not penetrating to the core of the fiber, sponge with soap and lukewarm water. If badly burned, the cloth may be redyed in a darker color.

4. *Shine from hard-finished worsted.* Steam or sponge with a little hot vinegar or ammonia and water. It is also possible to shrink the

fabric in warm water and then raise a slight nap with a stiff bristle brush. This process may make a difference in the size of the article.

### RAYON

Follow general rules for water solvent and grease stain removal, appearing on page 415 and the special suggestions for cotton stains.

### ACETATE

Follow general rules but avoid cleaners that contain acetone, alcohol, or chloroform, which will dissolve acetate cloth.

### NONCELLULOSIC MAN-MADE FIBERS

Special stain removal treatments for the many new chemical fibers are not yet available. General rules should be applied, and the consumer may experiment with the specific suggestions developed from long experience with the natural fibers.

## SUMMARY

The manufacturer's informative label is the consumer's best guide for the care of fabrics, especially with blends. If, however, there is no label giving instructions for care, then the consumer should clean the blend according to the method required for the fiber that needs the most special care.

Fiber content is one criterion for the kind of care that should be given a fabric to insure proper satisfaction in use. The type of yarn, closeness and firmness of construction, the nature and permanency of finish, and colorfastness are also important factors in determining the proper care for a fabric.

## REVIEW QUESTIONS

1. To insure proper care of textile fabrics, what three elements must be considered? Explain.
2. Explain the following terms: washable, completely washable, fine fabric, cool iron, synthetic detergent, heavy-duty soap, neutral soap, hot water, medium-hot water, warm water, detergent, built soap, soap film, water softener, water conditioner, bluing, starch, dry cleaning, soft water, drip dry, enzyme products.
3. (*a*) How would you recommend that a man's acetate colorfast sport shirt be washed?
   (*b*) How should it be pressed?

4. Describe the procedure for laundering household fabrics such as sheets, pillow cases, and towels.

5. (*a*) Which articles would you wash together: men's colorfast cotton pajamas, women's blue jeans, men's white cotton T-shirts, women's cotton lawn blouses, men's white polyester/cotton shirts, women's nylon slips, tea towels, white nylon gloves, women's colorfast cotton shorts?

(*b*) Describe the method of washing for each lot.

(*c*) Describe how each item should be ironed, if ironing is necessary.

6. (*a*) When should an article be hand washed?

(*b*) What fabrics are best cleaned by hand washing?

7. Describe the method of removing ink stains from (*a*) white cotton, (*b*) colored linen, (*c*) colored silk, (*d*) dark wools.

8. (*a*) What treatment would you recommend for the cleaning of an Orlon acrylic and wool jersey blouse?

(*b*) How would you clean a white nylon taffeta petticoat?

(*c*) How would you clean a 100 per cent acrylic baby blanket with rayon satin binding?

9. A white cotton blouse has become gray from soap film. How would you restore its original whiteness?

10. (*a*) Why is it inadvisable to dry-clean rayons at home?

(*b*) Why is it inadvisable to use acetone or chloroform on acetate?

## EXPERIMENTS

Select as many of the following fabrics as possible for this experiment: white nylon tricot jersey, pure silk shantung, colored dress linen, colored cotton broadcloth, white Dacron polyester and cotton shirting, 100 per cent acetate, or acetate and rayon lingerie crepe.

1. Follow the instructions for either the home automatic washing test or the commercial tests numbered 2, 3, and 4 on p. 194. Analyze the results of each test.

2. Evaluate the results of the test by stating the purpose for which the fabric is best used. Give reasons for your decision. What instructions should the consumer be given for laundering the fabric?

## PROJECT

Write a manual of instructions for the consumer on one of the following topics:

(*a*) Care of men's suits
(*b*) Care of women's street and business dresses
(*c*) Care of men's and women's hosiery
(*d*) Care of household textiles (domestics, draperies, and curtains)
(*e*) Care of men's and women's sweaters
(*f*) Care of men's shirts (dress and sport)

**Bluing.** A liquid, bead, or flake type tint that makes clothes look whiter but has no real whitening or cleansing action; used mostly on cotton or linen.

**Chlorine.** A quick liquid type of bleach.

**Cold water detergent.** An agent that cleans and germproofs in cold water.

**Completely washable fabric.** A fabric washable by machine in water hot enough to clean the fabric efficiently (160° in the tub).

**Detergent.** An agent or solvent used for cleansing fabrics. The term was originally applied to soap, soap savers, and soap softeners. At present the term connotes newer washing products called *synthetic detergents,* which are organic chemicals.

**Dressing.** See *Starch.*

**Drip dry.** A method of drying a fabric without wringing or squeezing it. After a garment has been cleansed and rinsed, it is hung directly on a hanger. Every care is taken not to wrinkle it so that it will drip and dry with no wrinkles, thus reducing ironing to only a touch-up.

**Dry cleaning.** The removal of soil from fabrics by means of a solvent.

**Durable press.** See Glossary, Chapter 3.

**Fabric softeners.** Chemical solutions added to the final rinse to improve the hand of terry cloths and infants' fabrics.

**Fine fabric.** A fabric that usually requires hand washing or dry cleaning.

**Heavy-duty soap.** Pure and mild but has special alkalies added to improve its cleaning power.

**Heavy-duty synthetic detergent.** One that has a builder for improved cleaning power. A suds-making ingredient is added primarily for automatic washers. A low-sudsing detergent is often recommended for the front-loading type of automatic washer.

**Hydrophilic fibers.** Fibers that absorb water readily, take longer to dry, and require more ironing. See *Hydrophobic fiber,* Glossary, Chapter 14.

**Informative label.** Factual information about the goods. See Chapter 1.

**Laundry soap.** A heavy-duty soap with special alkalies added to improve its cleaning power.

**Load.** The number of garments or pounds that can be put into an automatic washer at one time.

**Neutral soap.** A soap that has no free alkali.

**Pure mild soap.** All soap with nothing added. See *Soap.*

**Soap.** A cleansing agent produced by the action of caustic soda and a fat.

**Sodium perborate.** A bleach in the form of powder.

**Soil release.** See Glossary, Chapter 7.

**Sorting.** Separating colored clothes from white clothes so that there will be no danger of colored ones bleeding onto the white ones.

**Starch.** A white, odorless dry or liquid vegetable compound used for stiffening fabrics. Plastic starch is made of resin (plastic) that can permanently stiffen a cloth.

**Syndet.** A synonym for synthetic detergent.

**Unwashable fabric.** A fabric that should not be washed by hand or by machine. Such fabrics are usually labeled "dry clean only."

**Washable fabric.**   A fabric that can be washed. The method of washing (by hand or machine) may not be designated.

**Wash-and-wear.**   See Glossary, Chapter 7.

**Wash-fast fabric.**   One that will not fade or shrink excessively in laundering.

**Wash test.**   A trial washing of an inconspicuous part of a garment to determine if the color is fast to washing.

**Water softener.**   A chemical compound added to the rinse water or to both the soap and the rinse water if the water is very hard. Its purpose is to prevent the formation of soap film that tends to gray the fabric.

**Wet cleaning.**   The professional cleaning of heavily soiled fabrics with soap and water.

# II
# SELECTION OF APPROPRIATE FABRICS

# 16

# Apparel Fabrics
# for Women
# and Children

In the purchase of their apparel most women seek primarily for "look-rightness" and serviceability. For outer apparel, look-rightness is probably the first consideration. It consists in *becomingness* to the individual and *fashion-rightness*, which means acceptance by a sizable social group. Both of these appearance factors depend on the fabric's fiber, yarn, weave, and finish and the garment's color, pattern, design, and accent accessories. In the purchase of underclothing and children's wear, serviceability is commonly the first consideration, although look-rightness is nearly always a factor, too. Serviceability is a combination of suitability of a fabric and the quality of a garment's construction.

It is beyond the scope of this book to discuss color, line, and design. But the contribution of the fabric to both appearance and serviceability will be considered in detail. In fact, fabric is sometimes the major element in fashion.

The silhouette, or outline, of a garment may change from season to season. One season the change may be reflected in the sleeve, the next season in the skirt. But when the silhouette is not radically changed, then fabric (and particularly its texture) plays a more important part in the woman's selection than the silhouette or color. Designers and consumers seem to seek texture changes just for variety. For example, rough, tweedy, and bumpy bouclé textures are often followed the next season by less rough (fleecy) and bumpy (chinchilla) textures, and the following season by the smoother textures, such as soft-finished tweeds, basket weaves, and twist-yarn cord stripes. Dull surfaces, as found in crepes, jersey, cotton lace, and wool flannel, may be followed by the shinier surfaces of satin, wool broadcloth, and metal cloth.

Of course, differences in weight automatically limit some fabrics to particular seasons and uses. In summer the weather calls for thin materials, such as voile, eyelet batiste, sheer crepes, and chiffons; in winter, for heavier materials, such as wool tweeds, homespuns, velveteen, velvet, corduroy, and furlike fabrics. Some stiff fabrics look better when a crisp appearance is required; soft and clinging fabrics are appropriate when a slinky, draped effect is desired; rich and luxurious fabrics look best in the evening; washable fabrics appear to advantage when worn in the house, in the garden, and for sports.

## FABRICS USED IN WOMEN'S AND GIRLS' OUTER APPAREL

The problem of selecting the proper fabric for the particular purpose in view is a formidable one. Fabrics for outerwear may be grouped under the following classification of occasions for which they are worn: (1) sports and casual,[1] (2) street or business, and (3) formal afternoon, dinner, and evening.

To list all fabrics is impossible, because names change and some fabrics are temporarily out of style. Consequently, groups of similar fabrics will be discussed under plain weaves, twill weaves, satins, and the like. This approach should help the reader learn the names of fabrics, their identifying characteristics, and their uses. Staple names rather than brand names will be used. After the study of fabrics is presented, points for selection of garments for women and girls will be considered. A glossary of fabrics for women's apparel is included at the end of this chapter.

### PLAIN WEAVES

*Muslins.* Any plain-weave cotton cloth, ranging from the sheerest batiste to the coarsest sheeting, is called *muslin.* Counts of muslin vary according to fabric names, and these vary by grade. (See the table below.) There is a variety of grades. The better ones have little or no sizing and may be finished in such a way as to be given different names, such as batiste, nainsook, lawn, or voile. Batiste, in the best grades, is generally the finest, most silky of the muslins. Lawn, generally more

---

[1] Casual clothes are garments with easy, fluid, unclinging, flowing lines that express an uncluttered, fresh, crisp, relaxed appearance.

sheer, usually has a higher count than nainsook. Lawn can be sized or not as the use requires. Nainsook may be polished on one side in better grades. When highly polished, the fabric is sold as *polished cotton*. Voile has a lower count than the other cloths mentioned, and it has a "thready" feel, due to the voile twist—ply yarns twisted opposite to the twist of the individual yarns. Cambric is a firmer, more heavily finished cloth than nainsook. For costuming, a lightweight cambric in very low count may be heavily sized and glazed. Percale does not possess the gloss of cambric; the finish is dull and the cloth may be white or printed. Heavy grades are used for sheeting, but the count of percale sheeting is 180, or 200 threads to the inch, whereas shirt and dress percale runs about 80 square, or 160 threads to the inch. Bleached and unbleached muslins, heavy and wide enough for sheeting, are also plain weaves.

**COUNTS OF TYPICAL MUSLINS ***

| Name of Fabric | Low | Medium | High |
|---|---|---|---|
| Batiste | 72 x 68 | 80 x 80 | 108 x 112 |
| Lawn | 70 x 54 (combed) | 80 x 76 | 100 x 96 |
| | 60 x 48 (carded) | | 100 x 96 |
| Nainsook | 80 x 64 | 88 x 80 | 100 x 96 |
| Organdy | 76 x 60 | 84 x 68 | 88 x 76 |
| Dotted swiss (lawn base—see low lawn (counts) | | | |
| Voile (single yarn) | 52 x 52 | 60 x 52 | 76 x 68 |
| Voile (ply yarn) | 60 x 56 | 64 x 64 | 72 x 72 |
| Chambray | 65 x 44 | 84 x 76 | 108 x 92 |
| Gingham | 48 x 44 (carded) | 64 x 56 | 106 x 94 |
| Percale | 64 x 60 | 80 x 80 | 88 x 76 |
| Dimity (stripe) | 96 x 68 | 114 x 64 | 116 x 76 |
| Chintz | 44 x 44 | 64 x 60 | 84 x 76 |
| Costume cambric | 40 x 40 | 60 x 56 | 68 x 60 |

* This table was prepared in the Textile Laboratory at New York University in response to students' requests for grades by counts.

Other muslins include gingham (yarn dyed in plaids, checks, or stripes), madras (white-on-white, woven stripes, cords, end-to-end alternate colored and white yarns in warp and white in the filling), chambray (colored warp, white filling, woven-in designs, iridescent or striped), dotted swiss (organdy or lawn ground with woven clipped spot or swivel designs), and organdy (crisp, sheer, with high count, may be embroidered or frosted designs).[2]

What to look for in buying dress muslins:

1. *Carded or combed yarns.* (About 8 per cent of the cottons are combed.) Good combing is a desirable feature in sheer fabrics like organdy, batiste, and lawn.

[2] Many of these fabrics may be 100 per cent synthetic fibers or synthetic/cotton blends.

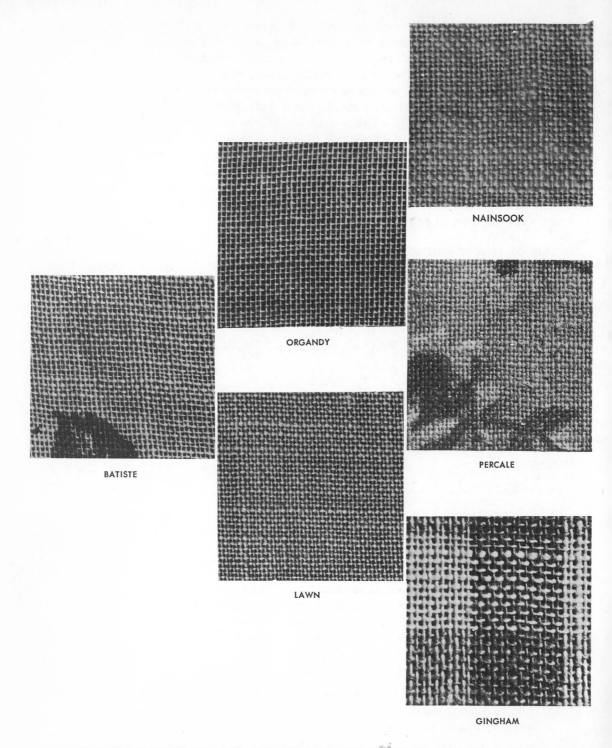

NAINSOOK

ORGANDY

BATISTE

PERCALE

LAWN

GINGHAM

Figure 16.1. Dress fabrics in plain weaves. (*Photo by Jack Pitkin.*)

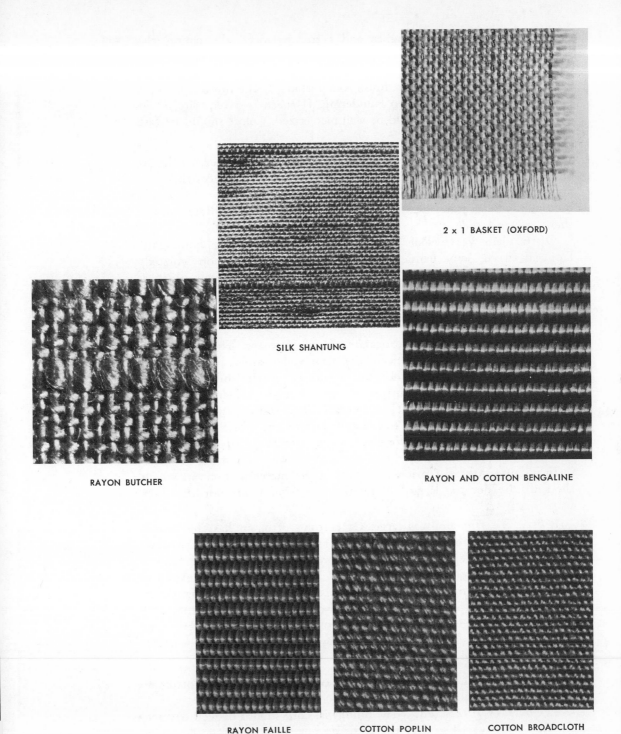

2 x 1 BASKET (OXFORD)

SILK SHANTUNG

RAYON BUTCHER

RAYON AND COTTON BENGALINE

RAYON FAILLE          COTTON POPLIN          COTTON BROADCLOTH

**Figure 16.1.** (*cont.*)  Dress fabrics in plain weaves. The butcher and shantung have slub (uneven) yarns. Others are ribbed except for the oxford. (*Photos by Jack Pitkin.*)

2. *Construction*. The higher and better balanced the count, the better the fabric in its category. A batiste 112 x 108 is better than a 100 x 96.

3. *Finish.* Permanency of finish is important. If the finish is crisp, it should be permanent to laundering. If sheen is a requisite, as in batiste, the fabric should be well mercerized. Colors should be fast to the use intended.

The plain-weave silks, rayons, acetates, nylons, and other synthetics and blends may be studied together, because in many instances the same constructions and names are given to both. Fabrics in plain weave made of silk, rayon, acetate, or synthetics and blends include taffeta, ninon, shantung, and voile.

Of the plain-weave wools, the common woolens are challis, homespun, Donegal tweed, some flannels, and wool crepe; the common worsteds are poplin, tropical worsted, crepe, and shantung. (See *men's suitings*, Chapter 16.)

In linens, plain weaves are found in crashes, dress linen, and handkerchief linen.

3. *Slubs.* The slubbed fabrics are also plain weave. These fabrics— shantung, crash, slub broadcloth, and slub voile—are made with slub yarns in filling only. Sometimes, for novelty effect, the slubs are placed in both warp and filling. Shantung is made either in mixtures or in 100 per cent of silk, rayon, acetate, nylon, acrylic, cotton, or wool. Crash is made in cotton and/or linen. In rayon or acetate, the fabric is frequently called *butcher*, because the original fabric was made of coarse linen, similar to the fabric that the butcher ties around himself while at work.

In judging slubbed fabrics, the best-wearing material is one in which the slubs are not too large and bumpy. Abrasion wears out the slubs first.

*Ribs.* The rib family is large. Of cottons, ottoman has the largest fillingwise ribs, poplin the next largest, and broadcloth the narrowest. Dimity may have spaced warpwise ribs or both a warpwise and filling-wise rib in crossbar design. In silk, rayon, acetate and/or wool, ottoman and bengaline are much more heavily ribbed than poplin, and faille has a flatter rib than poplin.[3] All-nylon, all-cotton, polyester/cotton, and acetate/cotton cords are used for men's summer jackets and men's and women's summer suitings. When selecting a ribbed fabric, the wearing quality will depend upon—

1. *Fiber content.* For instance, if the cord of a bengaline or ottoman is wool, it will drape better than a cotton cord.

2. *Coverage of the cord.* The fillingwise cord should be well covered by warp yarns so that the cords do not show through. Abrasion will cause poorly covered cords to rough.

[3] A rule-of-thumb method for identification: bengaline has twenty-six or fewer ribs to the inch; faille has thirty-six or more ribs to the inch. Stores may call the fabric with twenty-six to thirty-six bengaline faille.

3. *Colorfastness.*   Fastness to light, to dry cleaning, and to laundering (if the fabric is washable) should be considered. The degree
and the factors in colorfastness will depend on the fabric's use.
4. *Finish.*   Permanency of finish for the intended use and dimensional stability in cleaning partially determine wearing quality.

*Crepes.*   The crepe family, a variation of the plain weave, is also
large. Crepes may be arranged according to roughness, ranging from
those with very crinkled sufaces to those with hardly noticeable creping.
A suggested list of silk, rayon, and acetate crepes (roughest to smoothest) follows: matelassé, rough, moss, crepe faille, Romain, georgette,
chiffon, crepe de chine,[4] and flat crepe. In cotton, crepes may be arranged
in order of roughness as follows: seersucker, plissé crepe, and sheer
crinkle crepe (crinkled lightweight organdies and muslins). (See Figure
16.2.)

[4] A very sheer flat crepe of silk or man-made fibers.

**Figure 16.2.**   Crepes. *(Photos by Jack Pitkin.)*

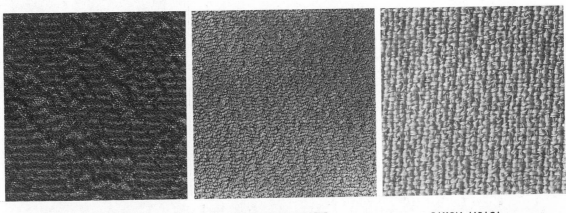

RAYON MATELASSE            RAYON ROUGH CREPE            RAYON ALPACA

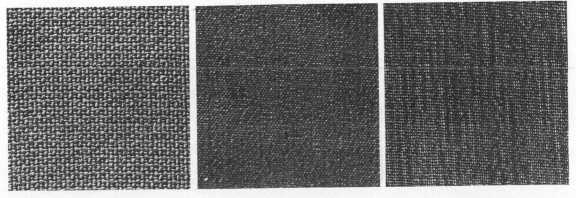

RAYON CREPE ROMAINE            FLAT CREPE            CHIFFON

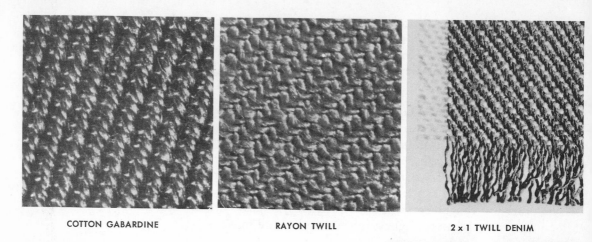

COTTON GABARDINE          RAYON TWILL          2 x 1 TWILL DENIM

**Figure 16.3.** Dress fabrics in twill weaves. *(Photos by Jack Pitkin.)*          RAYON SURAH          WOOL FLANNEL

In judging the wearing quality of crepe fabrics consider:

1. Fiber content for intended use.
2. Slippage. Try the thumb test by putting the tips of the thumbs together on the fabric. Place the index fingers under the fabric so that the fingers touch each other between the first and second joints. Turn the hands inward so that the thumbs press down on the right side of the fabric; turn the fabric over as the pressure continues. This test should show the possibility of seam slippage if warp yarns spread apart with the pressure. It should also reveal weakness of yarns if they break.
3. Permanency of finish and colorfastness for the intended use.

Fabrics in basket weave include the very popular oxford shirting made in cotton or polyester and cotton (2 x 2, 2 x 1, or 3 x 2). Duck, sailcloth, tent cloth, and some tweeds are also basket weaves. Basket weaves are attractive, but they tend to shrink unless controlled for shrinkage. There is more play or give to yarns in this weave than in regular plain weave.

The 2 x 2 weave is better balanced than the 2 x 1 or 3 x 2 and should therefore be less subject to slippage.

## TWILLS AND SATINS

There are comparatively few twill weaves in cotton and silk. Twilling seems to be most common in wool goods. However, a few common cotton clothing fabrics for work, sports, and casual wear are covert, denim, gabardine, jean, serge, and khaki twill. In silk, rayon, acetate, and

RAYON MARQUISETTE       BROCADE (SILK WITH METAL THREADS)

**Figure 16.4.** Dress fabrics in fancy weaves. (*Photos by Jack Pitkin.*)

**Figure 16.5.** Dress fabrics in pile weaves. (*Photos by Jack Pitkin.*)

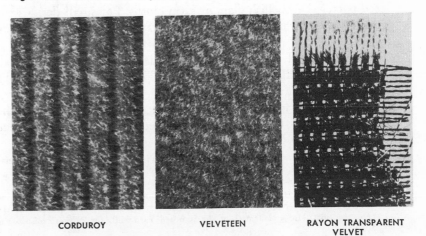

CORDUROY       VELVETEEN       RAYON TRANSPARENT
VELVET

synthetics, there are foulard (a fine twill) and surah (a satin-faced twill in which the top of the wale is flat).[5]

Since spun rayons and synthetics can be made in wool-like textures, the twill is becoming more popular for these fabrics. Some spun rayon and synthetic fabrics in twills include gabardine, flannel, covert, serge, and whipcord.

The most common silk and man-made fabrics in satin weave are highly lustrous, heavy dress satins with long floats; dull, twill-backed slipper satins; and satin crepe, a reversible fabric with satin on one side and crepe on the other. The twill is seldom used for linen dress fabrics.

In woolens and blends with acrylic, polyester, rayon, or acetate the twill is used in some tweeds, flannels, wool cheviots, and wool coverts.[6] Wool cheviot, flannel, and covert are classed as men's suitings, although they may be used satisfactorily for women's and children's coats and suits, generally in a lighter ounce-weight per yard. In worsteds and in blends with man-made fibers, there are covert, cheviot, gabardine, unfinished worsted, serge, whipcord, and others. The satin weave is not satisfactory for wool, because the natural scales on wool fibers do not make a smooth surface—the fibers would curl and rough up if floated. The 100 per cent synthetics can be made in textures resembling natural fibers; therefore the construction would be that of the fibers they are to resemble.

### JACQUARDS AND FANCY WEAVES

Silks, nylons, acetates, rayons, and other man-made fibers lend themselves especially to elaborate weaves. Some of the most common Jacquards in silk, rayon, acetates, and synthetics include brocade, lamé,[7] and damask (similar to brocade but with a reversible, flat design). Metallic yarns are frequently used to give a luxurious appearance. Marquisette is the chief fabric woven on the leno loom. Many embroidered patterns embellish plain or satin cloths. For small designs the dobby method may be used in novelty silks, rayons, acetates, nylons, and mixtures.

The Jacquard weave is used in brocade for cocktail and formal dresses. Although the chief weave for linen clothing fabrics is the plain with variations, Jacquard would be found in novelty linens.

In wool the Jacquard weave is used mainly for brocades, the dobby weave for small designs, and the clipped spot for novelty effects.

[5] Surah has been so highly styled for women's wear that the wales are as fine as the usual foulard.

[6] The word "wool" here means made of *woolen* rather than of *worsted* yarn.

[7] A brocade, damask, or brocatelle in which metallic (laminated) thread or yarns are distributed throughout the fabric, or a cloth in which these yarns are used in the main construction. Also a trademark of the Standard Yarn Mills for its nontarnishable metallic yarn.

When used for clothing, the pile weave is both beautiful and warm. It appears in velvets, velveteens, plushes, and velours.

In cotton the pile weave is used to make corduroy and velveteen. (See pp. 110 ff. for construction of these fabrics.) Terry cloth (turkish toweling with uncut pile) may be used for bathrobes and beach robes. The pile weave is not used for dress linens.

In silk the pile weave makes rich, lustrous fabrics, such as panne, chiffon, and Lyons velvet. Transparent velvet generally has a rayon pile with either a silk or rayon back. In wool there are velvets, plushes, and velours. Some fabrics resembling furs are made in this weave. (See p. 114.) Fleece, or a wool, nylon, or acrylic fabric with a deep soft nap or pile, may be in plain or pile weave or knitted. (For judging the wearing quality of pile fabrics, see Chapter 5.)

## KNITTED CONSTRUCTION

Knitted fabrics have increased in importance for daytime and even for formal wear. The following comments were made at a seminar on fabrics:

> In 1961, according to a reliable statistical source, 9 per cent of the 250 million women's dresses were made of knitted fabric. Today, a well-informed estimate would place the figure at about 35 per cent of the total 350 million units. And the knit share of the market continues to grow. Tricot fabrics have shared in this growth.[8]

Wool jersey is an old, staple favorite that can be worn for casual dresses, blouses, and jackets, and for school, business, and street dresses. Spun rayons, man-made yarns in wool textures, fur fibers, and wool blends are all now adapted to jersey. Some are heavy, others sheer; some are dull, and others have shiny surfaces. Jerseys appear in solid colors, in prints, and in stripes of varied widths. Some finishes are suede-like, some tweedy. Others show diagonal cords or vertical ribs, and still others are creped. A special construction in jersey allows stretch in the width only, so that the fabric should not sag. Some jerseys have a hand-knitted look with mixed grounds, fine honeycomb constructions, and patterns. (See knitted constructions, Chapter 6.)

Knitted woolen fabrics with deep, thick nap are called *fleece*. The groundwork of the fabrics may be cotton with wool nap, which provides good insulating value against cold. This fabric is excellent for women's and children's coats.

Some fabrics of bouclé yarn in various fibers are knitted. The knitted bouclés are excellent for traveling because they do not crease easily. A

[8] From an address by Robert E. Anderson, merchandise manager of women's wear, E. I. du Pont de Nemours & Co., at the Tricot Institute of America's Fourth Executive Seminar, on October 17, 1968, in New York.

tricot knit of rayon, nylon, and triacetate makes an appropriate daytime blouse or dress. The biggest single knitted item of women's apparel is hosiery, but few customers really know the wearing quality of the hosiery they select. Points for selection of hosiery will be discussed later in this chapter.

## POINTS FOR SELECTION OF WOMEN'S OUTER APPAREL

In the previous section, we considered the important factors in judging the wearing quality of fabrics for women's wear. But when these fabrics are used for outer apparel, an additional set of criteria should be applied. Some of the criteria for judging the quality of a woman's dress are the following:[9]

1. Conformance to the standard size [10]
2. Fit as evidenced by the way the garment is cut
3. Workmanship, such as the use of colorfast thread, pinked seams for firm fabrics, overcast seams for pliable fabrics, and seam binding for hem
4. Trimmings—quality and workmanship
5. Seam and hem allowance (wide in better garments)
6. Resistance to seam slippage—pulling apart of warp threads by bending, stretching
7. Standards in dressmaking details, such as reinforcement of a pocket at points of strain, straight and smooth fitted darts, one continuous lengthwise seam as placket closing, bias facings cut on the true bias, front facing turned over the hem.

The consumer who wants maximum serviceability in a garment should look for a label that states that the article conforms to the L22 standard. Ready-made garments manufactured to meet L22 minimum voluntary standard specifications are guaranteed to perform adequately in a given end use. (See Chapter 1 for requirements of the L22 standard.)

## REQUIREMENTS FOR GOOD GARMENT CONSTRUCTION [11]

The home seamstress is more fortunate than she was a generation ago in that patterns today are simpler to follow and construction details are carefully explained and often illustrated.

[9] Clarice L. Scott, "Points to Look for when Buying a Dress," U.S. Department of Agriculture Leaflet No. 105, pp. 456–57.

[10] Voluntary Commercial Standard of the National Bureau of Standards gives standard classifications and corresponding body measurements for dress patterns (CS 13-44). There are no size standards for women's ready-made dresses. (See commercial sizes for men's shirts, Chapter 17.) See the chart on page 444, New Sizing Body Measurement, under Sizes in Women's and Girls' Outer Apparel.

[11] Adapted from Ethel Hoover Brooks, "What the Buyer Should Know about Garment Construction," *Journal of Retailing*, XXII, 2 (April 1946), 50–53.

Whether a garment is made at home or purchased ready-made, the requirements for garment serviceability are similar. The home seamstress or the retail store buyer can check the following points in garment construction for quality:

1. The grain of the cloth should follow the line of dress design. Good fit is insured if the grain of the cloth (the warp) is straight vertically at the center of the bodice. An exception, of course, would be bias-cut blouses or dresses. For straight skirts, the side seams should be cut with the grain of the goods, thus leaving a slightly biased center seam. Since bias-cut skirts tend to sag, an allowance for sagging should be made in the pattern. Some dressmakers find that if the garment is allowed to hang for a few hours before it is completed, the sag can be adjusted.

   Similarly, the lengthwise grain of the cloth (*warp*) should run straight from the shoulder seam to the back of the wristbone. The crosswise grain of the sleeves should then run similar to the crosswise grain of the blouse. The shoulder line will be smooth if the sleeve is eased into the blouse, rather than the blouse into the sleeve. Armholes, to fit well, should not be cut too low.

2. Seam and hem allowances should be adequate and workmanship should be neat.

   Seam and hem allowances:

   (*a*) Side seam—1 inch, especially for drip-dry knits, permanent press, and fabrics with special finishes.
   (*b*) Waist seam—½ inch
   (*c*) Hem—2½ inches deep

   Workmanship:

   (*a*) Colorfast, strong thread darker than the fabric
   (*b*) Pinked seams for firm fabrics
   (*c*) Overcast seams for pliable fabrics
   (*d*) Seam binding for hem

3. Dressmaking details should meet these standards:

   (*a*) Fitted darts should be straight and smooth, inside and outside the garment.
   (*b*) Placket closing should be one continuous, lengthwise seam.
   (*c*) Front facing should be turned over the hem. Bias facings should be cut on the true bias.
   (*d*) Pleats are usually made on the lengthwise grain of the fabric, and the underfold of the pleat should be deep. Pleats should be pressed straight.
   (*e*) Pockets should be sewn onto the garment to appear either functional or decorative. Pockets should be reinforced by tape stitching at points of strain.

The goal of the home sewer in constructing today's new fabrics is to prevent puckered seams, and to have flat open seams, unpuckered zippers, and flat inconspicuous hems.[12] The following directions will help the home sewer:

1. Use fine pins with sharp, smooth points. If fabric pin marks show, use weights to hold the paper pattern during cutting, or pin only in seam allowance. Scotch tape is useful in some situations.
2. Shears and scissors must be sharp. Take long, keen strokes with shears while cutting the garment.
3. Man-made fabrics when cut tend to crawl and ravel. Therefore the fabric needs to be handled as little as possible, and cut edges finished as soon as possible.
4. The cut edges are best finished with the multiple zigzag or serpentine stitch. Use widest zigzag with small stitches (approximately 15 to 18 stitches per inch). Allow the needle to go off the edge of the material on the corner stitch.
5. If a zigzag machine is not available, use small stitches (15 to 18 stitches per inch) for straight stitching, not more than $\frac{1}{8}$ inch from the cut edge.
6. All edge finishes, both zigzag and straight stitching, should be done from wide to narrow bias line. Stitch from hem to waist or hem to underarm.
7. Edge-finish all pieces before beginning to assemble the garment.
8. Garments to be backed with any type of material should have each garment piece pinned to backing not more than $2\frac{1}{2}$ inches apart (pins perpendicular to cut edge).
9. Stitch the backed pieces of the garment (backing on top of garment) as described in step 4 or 5. Plain-stitch center of darts before assembling.

## SUGGESTIONS FOR SEWING WASH-AND-WEAR FABRICS

To avoid seam puckering, wash-and-wear fabrics require slightly different techniques:

1. Fabrics should be sewn no more than fourteen stitches to the inch.
2. Both the upper and lower bobbin threads should be set a little looser than usual.
3. The presser foot should be set so that the fabric will feed through without dragging.
4. A #12 or smaller needle is recommended, and a thread size to fit the needle.

[12] *Home Economics Series #162*, University of Hawaii, Cooperative Extension Service (November 1968).

The popularity of stretch fabrics for women and girls has necessitated that home sewers learn new methods in cutting and sewing these fabrics. A few suggestion:

1. A simple pattern with few seams and a minimum of buttonholes should be selected.
2. The fabric should be placed on a flat surface to "relax" for twenty-four hours before cutting.
3. The pattern should be placed so that the stretch goes crosswise on skirts, bodices, and jackets; either way for pants.
4. Sharp shears should be used to cut the fabric with long, even strokes. The fabric must not be allowed to hang off the cutting table.
5. Seams should preferably be stitched with small zigzag stitches (14 to 16 stitches per inch minimum), with a slightly looser tension than for regular sewing.
6. To check the tension of the machine, two pieces of fabric may be stitched together in the direction of the stretch. The seam should be pulled to see if the thread breaks before the cloth reaches its maximum stretch. Should a break in the thread occur, adjustment of the tension should be made according to the machine's instruction book.
7. Regular interfacing may be used in collars and cuffs, but no rigid underlinings for bodice or skirt. Lightweight stretch or tricot, running with the fabric grain, should be used for a jacket or swimsuit.
8. At raw edges, hems may be turn-stitched or overcast. No seam tape should be used for the hem.

### SUGGESTIONS FOR SEWING BONDED FABRICS [14]

Bonded fabrics are easy for the home sewer to handle provided she follows these suggestions:

1. The pattern should be placed on the right side of the fabric where the grain line shows.
2. The lengthwise grain or rib of the fabric should be followed when cutting.
3. Pins and chalk are better than a tracing wheel for transferring pattern markings to the wrong side of the fabric.
4. Thread suitable for the outer fabric should be selected.

[13] Adapted from *Fiber and Fabric Facts*, Beaunit pamphlet No. 2 of a series by Beaunit Textiles, a Division of Beaunit Corporation.
[14] *Ibid.*, Pamphlet No. 3.

5. Pinking is sufficient for the seam finish, since cut edges of bonded goods do not ravel.
6. No separate underlining is required when a tricot backing is used.
7. Before pressing, a small sample of fabric should be tested. In pressing, the setting of the iron should be suited to the fiber on the side being pressed.

## WOMEN'S SKIRTS

Women's skirts are cut on the straight, the bias, or circularly from the same fabrics that are used for dresses and suits. The fit or, more particularly, the hang of a skirt is important. A skirt should not wrinkle below the waistband and should be even at the hem. The aspects of garment construction mentioned in the list on p. 438 should be checked by the consumer. Sizes for juniors are 5 to 15; misses, 8 to 18; women, 34 to 44. Size may be stated by waist measurement.

The principles for selection of appropriate outer garments for adults are essentially the same for girls. Coats and dresses must be style-right for the occasion. All girls, especially up to ten years, need a roomy garment with large armholes and curved underarms to permit raising the hands above the head without pulling out the seams or distorting the fabric. If there is a belt, it should be especially loose so that there will be no strain on the bodice when the arms are outstretched. Tucks, pleats, and shirring are important because they allow for chest expansion. Fullness of cut means comfort to the wearer and also makes for longer life of the garment.

When garments are skimpily cut, yardage is saved but seams are often too narrow to keep from pulling out. Garments should have reinforcements at points of strain and even, narrow, smooth, pliable seams.

## SIZES IN WOMEN'S AND GIRLS' OUTER APPAREL

It is common to hear a woman say, "I wear a size 12 in a good-quality dress and a size 14 in an inexpensive one." This shopper is implying that the manufacturer of the good-quality dress did not skimp in fullness of cut of the garment, whereas the manufacturer of the inexpensive dress cut the garment slightly smaller to save on material in order to meet his price competition. Again, a woman who wears a size 16 dress may require a size 38 sweater. It would be helpful to her and to salespeople if all the garments a women wears were identified by the same system of size designation. It would be convenient, for instance, if a woman who wears a size 12 dress would be able to buy her coats, blouses, lingerie, sweaters, etc., in size 12. The National Retail Merchants Association has supported this idea as well as other standard sizing programs, and many retail stores have acted independently in backing and cooperating with these programs.

There are five size ranges in women's outer apparel:

1. Misses' sizes—3 lengths: petite, regular, tall ........ 6–22
2. Junior sizes—2 lengths: petite, regular ........ 3–17
3. Women's sizes ........ 36–52
4. Half sizes—2 lengths: short, regular ........ 12½–26½
5. Stout sizes ........ 34½–52½

Until recently, all misses' sizes were in regular length and accounted for the majority of garments sold. These sizes were intended for the "normal" mature figure. But today it is recognized that most women are broader in the shoulders and shorter in the waist than the standards for the regular misses size. Junior sizes are intended for a slightly shorter, more girlish figure, with small bust and waist. Thus, the junior range is basically a size, not an age classification. Women's sizes are fashioned for the tall, mature woman with full hips, bust, and arms. For the shorter woman with relatively fuller hips, half sizes have been created. This half-size range probably fits more women with mature figures than any other. But a stout range is also needed for the very fully developed figure with thick waist, large bust, and broad hips.

These long-established ranges have been found inadequate because of (1) the great variation in body height that in the past made shortening, lengthening, and waist adjustment so often necessary, (2) the increasing customer demand for exact fit without alteration, and (3) the necessity of catering to those with special needs, such as the very tall woman or the teenager.

In response to these consumer demands the wholesale ready-to-wear market has both broadened the size ranges and added new ranges. Whereas misses' sizes used to run 10 to 20, they are now available in sizes 6 to 22; and juniors, once 7 to 15, are now available in sizes 5 to 17. To accommodate the short misses and junior figure, petite misses' sizes and petite junior sizes have been introduced. And for the tall miss, 5 feet 7 inches and over, a special tall size has been created. Similarly, to take care of the woman who is under 5 feet 3 inches, a short half-size has been added. With the regular half-size and the short half-size, it may not be necessary to make regular women's sizes available at all.

Even this wide array of sizes does not wholly solve

Figure 16.6. These figure silhouettes were made from photographs of women, all of whom said they wore a size 34 blouse. Note figure differences that affect the fit of garments and the suitable length for a blouse. (Reproduced courtesy of Consumers' Research, Inc.)

the selection problem. Teenagers who may be fitted with junior petites and regulars want separate styling and a separate department from that catering to older women of similar size. Likewise, subteens, the 10- to 12-year-olds, find petite junior and misses' sizes too large in the bust and hips and too small in the waist. But they are not satisfied with children's styles. Special size ranges are gradually being made available for both groups.

In 1965 the four major pattern companies (Butterick, McCall's, Simplicity, and Vogue) cooperated toward a revision of size standards for patterns. They studied the size standards of the Federal Government and of the popular-priced ready-to-wear and mail-order garment industries. The object was to establish new standard body measurements for the pattern industry, in order to enable the home sewer to buy a dress, coat, suit, or sportswear pattern of the same size as specified for ready-to-wear.

The new standards (see the chart of sizes) took effect in January, 1968. Now the homemaker will actually be buying one size smaller by the new size standard than she did before. Formerly, a size 34 bust (misses) required a size 14 pattern. In the new standard, it calls for a size 12 pattern.

To determine the correct size, the figure type must first be determined. (See Figure 16.7.) The correct pattern size should be based on the measurement of the bust, waist, hips, and back neck-to-waist length.

Figure 16.7. New sizing chart.

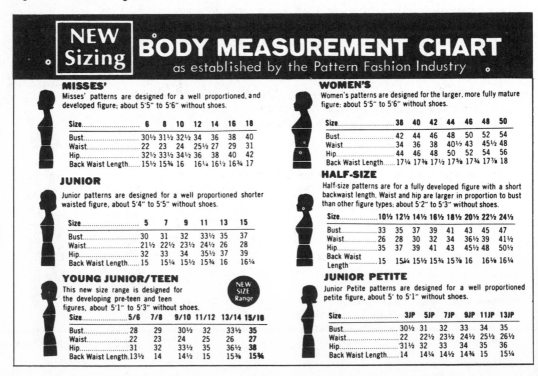

The bust measurement is the primary key to size in all apparel except skirts and slacks, where waist measurement may be used.

One new figure type has been added—a young-junior teen that replaces the former preteen and teen types.

The new range of sizes:

| | |
|---|---|
| Misses' | 6–18 |
| Women's | 38–50 |
| Half-size | 10½–24½ |
| Junior | 5–15 |
| Junior petite | 3–13 |
| Young junior | 5/6–13/14 |

## HOW TO SELECT WOMEN'S SWEATERS

The sweater, a knitted garment for the upper part of the body, has long been a staple for both casual and dressy wear. There are two main or classic types: the pullover or slip-on and the cardigan. Either type may have long or short sleeves, and either type may be in a classic or contemporary style. The classic sweater, not usually bulky, has a round neck without a collar. Contemporary styles are usually bulky and may have cable stitch and cowl necks.

Until the development of the non-cellulosic man-made fibers, wool was the major fiber used for sweaters, with cotton an important fiber for children's wear. But today the acrylics, particularly Orlon and Acrilan, are in first place, with blends second and wool third. The reason for the great popularity of the synthetics is that they can be cleaned in the home laundry machine at the setting for fine fabrics, and they need no reshaping. Wool sweaters, unless labeled "machine washable," have to be hand washed, reshaped, and dried most carefully. Also man-made fibers are usually less expensive than comparable wool products, and are better than wool in resistance to abrasion. The degree of

**Figure 16.8.** Classic styles in women's sweaters. *Left:* Long-sleeved pullover. *Right:* Button front cardigan. (*Photographs courtesy of Montgomery Ward & Co., Inc.*)

softness of sweaters made from man-made fibers depends on the fiber denier (weight and fineness)—the finer the denier, the softer the fabric.

The acrylics provide a wool-like bulkiness by crimping short filaments so that they resemble wool fibers. Thus they provide more warmth than nylon. Nylon, which is crimped also but is less bulky, has a smooth texture and a slightly shiny surface. It is more readily distinguishable from wool than is acrylic fiber.

Acrylic fiber pills more than nylon in laundering and more particularly in rubbing against other garments or furniture. On the other hand, nylon is more easily snagged by sharp objects and fingernails. Sweaters are also made of 100 per cent polyester.

Sweaters are made from many varieties of wool, particularly Shetland; wool and nylon; camel's hair; and mohair blended with wool and polyester. The finest are made of cashmere, noted for its great softness and lightness.

Some suggestions for evaluating sweater construction:

1. For good fit, look for full-fashioning where the panels are individually knit and where the lines of knitting at the seams are turned parallel.
2. Examine seams and buttonholes for finishing; avoid buttons snagged in buttonholes and ribbed neckbands with crooked or uneven seams.
3. Make sure that buttons and buttonhole tabs are securely attached.
4. If possible, try on the garment to note the set of the shoulders.

**Figure 16.9.** Front and back of a puckered sweater waistband. (*Photographs courtesy of Consumers Union, reprinted from Consumer Reports, November, 1961.*)

5. If the sweater is long-sleeved, be sure there is a long-ribbed cuff, well-finished on the reverse side to allow turning up.

6. Where trying on is not possible, buy a size larger than dress size. Women's sweaters run from size 32 to 42; larger sizes, 44 to 48. A woman wearing a size 18 dress would be well advised to buy a size 40 sweater. Children's sizes run 2 to 10, and a 4-year-old would probably wear a size 6.

## BLOUSES

Wash-and-wear blouses are important in any woman's wardrobe. Fabrics that resist wrinkling are those made of the acrylics, polyesters, and cross-linked or specially resin-treated cottons. Blends of polyester and cotton (65/35 per cent), polyester and rayon (55 per cent or more polyester with rayon), 50 per cent or more polyester with acrylic, 80 per cent or more acrylic with cotton, or 55 per cent or more acrylic with wool are likely to give good wash-and-wear performance.[15] One hundred per cent Arnel triacetate, 100 per cent rayon or acetate, and 100 per cent silk are also appropriate fabrics for blouses.

When you select a blouse you should: [16]

1. Try it on to be sure it fits your figure. Make sure of enough fullness at the bust (no diagonal wrinkles below bust), smooth armholes with the seam in upper armhole parallel to center front and center back, sleeves hanging straight without drawing when the arm is raised or stretched, smoothness across shoulders, side seams hanging straight without slanting to front or back.

2. Look at the collar. Be sure it has a smooth, even facing. Make sure stitching is even, with medium to fine stitches.

[15] Recommendation by the American Home Laundry Manufacturers Association.

[16] Adapted from "Blouses for Women," *Consumer Bulletin* (December 1960), 19–21.

**Figure 16.10.** A blouse of Celanese Fortrel Polyester and cotton. (*Courtesy of Celanese Fibers Marketing Company.*)

3. See if seams are adequate in width, are smooth and even, and have no raw edges.
4. Check buttonholes to make sure they are cut on the grain of the goods. Stitching should be close and secure, with no loose, uncut threads. Horizontal buttonholes are preferable for a woman with a full figure.
5. See if buttons are smooth, of uniform thickness, and well fastened.

Sizes in women's blouses are not standardized. Misses' sizes are usually less full through the bust, waist, and hips than women's sizes. Women who wear half sizes, juniors, or talls may have a problem in fit because blouses are not sized to particular figure types.

## COATS AND SUITS FOR WOMEN AND GIRLS

When women buy coats they look for style, color, fabric, fit, comfort, and price. To one woman, color and style may be most important; to another, comfort and price are paramount. And to still another, fabric, color, and fit may be the major considerations.

Because style in coats changes more or less from season to season, it would be inadvisable to stress current styles in this book. But there are styles—basic ones that do not change except for minor details—that are known as staple or classic styles. For example, in dresses we think of the shirtwaist as a classic style, because buyers must always have some in stock to satisfy customer demand.

There are classic styles in coats as well, in both fur and cloth. Since fur is not a textile, cloth coats will be discussed here. The following terms for cloth coats are general categories, whether intended for winter, spring, or fall:

Polo coat—made of beige camel's hair or wool; generally double-breasted with tailored patch pockets and a tailored collar, with or without back belt.

Princess coat—fitted closely through the waist, with darts, and gored skirt that flares at the hem.

Box coat—straight-lined, full-length coat with a collar.

Reefer—a short or long double-breasted box coat.

Balmacaan—a loosely flaring coat with raglan sleeves and small collar. Made of cotton poplin with water-repellent finish or heavy, rough tweed.

Chesterfield—a single-breasted smooth wool coat cut straight or slightly fitted. Usually dark color or black, with a velvet collar.

Officer's, coachman's or guardsman's coat—a heavy, fitted double-breasted coat buttoned up high on the chest. May have wide revers and big collar, a half-belt, and back pleat or flared skirt.

Tuxedo coat—an unfitted coat with a turned-back flat collar that forms a band down the front to the hem. When it has no front fastenings, it may be called a *clutch coat*.

Trench coat—a double-breasted wool, cotton gabardine, or covert, belted all around. It may have a lining.

Sport coats and jackets, though they come in all lengths, are usually short—to the hips or just below. The boxy type is generally water-repellent. The car coat typifies these lines, although it may be belted. Raincoats, which may be either straight or fitted, are waterproof or water-repellent and are sometimes reversible.

In general, suits may be classified as boxy or fitted. The boxy suit hangs straight from the shoulders and is not fitted at the waist. The fitted suit, often called tailored, fits the figure as a man's suit does.

A good fit in a coat or suit means that the style is cut full enough so that the arms can be raised above the head without pulling at the seams. This fit requires large armholes and curved underarms—a feature especially important for girls' wear and for active women. The fabric in the body and sleeves should be cut with the grain of the fabric, and the bottom of the coat or suit should hang evenly. An outer garment should have smooth shoulders that are the right width. Seams should be adequately wide, even, and pliable so that they will not pull out. Reinforcements should be found at points of strain, buttons should be sewn firmly, and buttonholes or loops should be made evenly and strongly sewn.

If the coat has a collar, it should fit the neck snugly. Lapels should be the same width and should roll back smoothly. A belt ought to be stitched firmly at the sides of the coat or be run through slides.

Linings should be cut to fit the outer garment smoothly and should not strain at the armhole when the garment is put on. Seams should be stitched firmly and should not pucker. The linings in coats of good workmanship have loose stitching at the bottom, so that the lining will not show below the exterior of the garment.

### FABRICS FOR COATINGS AND SUITINGS

The weight of outer garments is governed by the season. Spring coats are lighter in weight than fall coats, and winter coats, of course, are of the heaviest fabrics. The following list groups the fabrics suitable for the northern states at different seasons:

#### SPRING AND FALL

Coats—cashmere or cashmere and wool, and wool blends, camel's hair, single and bonded cloths, poplin, faille, worsted sharkskin, wool Shetland (single or bonded).

Jackets—cotton poplin, twills, denim, crash, cotton-backed acrylic/modacrylic flannel, wool flannel and blends, cotton velveteen, corduroy, knitted fabrics.

Coats for evening—ottoman, faille, velvet, taffeta, brocade, satin, furlike fabrics.

Suits and pantsuits—gabardine, whipcord, tweed, faille, covert, serge, corduroy, knitted fabrics.

Raincoats—poplin (all-cotton or polyester/cotton), vinyl backed with cotton, rayon/cotton twill and other blends, acrylic pile liners.

WINTER

Coats—furlike fabrics, wool tweed (single and bonded), cashmere, Ottoman (wool/nylon bonded to cotton and other blends), covert (wool/nylon bonded to acetate tricot), cashmere, melton, wool broadcloth.

Suits and pantsuits—knitted fabric (wool and blends), flannel, tweed, bouclé.

## SPORTSWEAR

Since sportswear is designed for the kind of sport in which the wearer participates, suitability is an important factor in selection. The wearer usually wants a comfortable garment made of a smooth fabric with flat seams that will not irritate skin made sensitive by the sun. Fabrics that are attractive and stylish yet require minimum care are most serviceable. Spot-resistant, crease-resistant, water-repellent finishes and durable press are a great boon to the sportswear business.

Active sportswear can be classified as (1) garments for summer sports and (2) garments for winter sports. Summer garments may include denim dungarees, jeans, culottes, or pants; corduroy, cotton gabardine, cotton madras, sailcloth or crash shorts; knitted or woven shirts; swimming suits of bengaline of acetate, cotton, and rubber or knitted acrylic, nylon, and spandex. The spandex fibers Vyrene and Lycra have advantages in this use over conventional natural rubber fibers because they have more tension or spring and superior fig-

**Figure 16.11.** Classic tailored jumper of gray Hockanum flannel with long-sleeved crepe shirt (from Mary Baine.) *(Photo courtesy of J. P. Stevens & Co., Inc.)*

ure control; they are lightweight, softer, suppler, and cooler; they can be used as stretchable core yarns; and they can be covered with cotton, wool, and other fibers. By the use of spandex yarns, crisp woven cloth can be deftly shaped for swimwear. Sportswear fabrics differ from season to season and vary somewhat by climate. Winter sports fabrics differ similarly, but in moderate and cool climates the ski suit of water-repellent fabrics, such as nylon with polyester fiberfill, cotton poplin, gabardine, or stretch fabric in various fibers, is worn. Outfits of velveteen, corduroy, jersey, or flannel may be worn by enthusiasts.

Golf jackets can be made of nylon, cotton, polyester, acrylics, and blends. The noncellulosic fibers are, by nature, water-repellent, and cotton can be treated for this function. Crease resistance is also a factor in active sportswear. Similar fabrics are used for spectator sportswear.

Young homemakers, and career women when at home, like the fluid, relaxed lines of casual wear to do their housework, cooking, baby tending, shopping, and lounging. A shirt or top of polyester/cotton, double-knit or stretch nylon; a sweater of acrylic or Shetland wool or cashmere, plus pants of rayon/nylon twill, cotton stretch corduroy, wool flannel, or acrylic double-knit would constitute an ensemble for fall and winter casual wear. Culottes or a skirt may be substituted for pants. In summer, shorts, culottes, and pants of sateen, seersucker, corduroy, sailcloth, or denim are appropriate for casual wear.

## SELECTION OF UNDERGARMENTS

Women's undergarments consist of soft, lightweight, attractive, minimum-care articles that are not bulky and that conform to the lines of the outer garment. Undergarments should not stick or cling to the outer garment, nor creep up or twist. Size is also a factor in comfort. A garment should be easy to slip on, should stay in place, should not restrain any movements, should fit smoothly, and should not be irritating. The chief points to notice in judging workmanship of an undergarment are the following:

1. The cut of the garment
2. The finishing of the seams
3. The application of the trimming

In considering the cut, see that the parts of the garment are straight and even and are sewed together so that they coincide properly. Seams should be of equal width, narrow seams being considered more dainty. There should be no puckering, no ragged edges, no lumpy spots or pulled threads. Hand-rolled hems are considered to be better than machine-rolled hems. Trimming, such as lace, embroidery, or appliqué, should be applied with great care, so that it is firmly attached to the garment. Durability includes not only workmanship but also the quality of the fiber, yarns, weave, and finish of the fabric, as well as the quality of the trimming.

Serviceability (the usefulness of the garment in satisfying physical needs), price, appropriateness, brand name, and fashion are minor factors in the choice, although price is often a measure of the other qualities.

## MATERIALS USED FOR UNDERWEAR

Styles in the cut of undergarments vary, as do the types of materials used. A merchandise manual on this subject written in 1920 would stress the importance of the use of cottons for undergarments, whereas one written today would stress rayons, nylons, and spandex.

A few of the garments sold in women's underwear departments are panties, briefs, gowns, pajamas, pettipants, slips (mini- and half-slips), and brassieres. Peignoirs, robes, lounge wear, and bed jackets may also be included here. Panty hose and tights are included under hosiery.

Fabrics commonly used for underwear generally fall into two main classifications: (1) rayon, acetate, nylon, other synthetics, elastic fabrics (rubber and spandex) in mixtures or blends, and (2) any kind of light-weight cotton or blend in plain weave or knitted. Common fabrics used for nylon lingerie include nylon tricot (sometimes called *jersey*), mesh, crepe, and satin. The second classification includes batiste, mesh, and broadcloth.

## CARE OF UNDERWEAR

Cotton is easily laundered by machine or by hand. Since most cotton items are in the minimum-care class, no ironing is needed. In heavier weights, cotton is bulky and does not make so molded a hip line as do the more clinging fabrics of rayon, acetate, or nylon. Although linen launders well, it is expensive in fine grades and crushes badly; therefore linen is seldom used for underwear. In the colder climates wool can be used in knitted union suits and sleeping garments, although shrinkage in laundering may be a problem. Silk, rayon, acetate, nylon, and spandex are very easy to wash in the automatic washer. Nylon should never be dried over hot radiators. If nylon's appearance is improved by ironing, set the temperature control to "nylon" and press the fabric lightly, either damp or dry. If nylon lingerie grays, one or two thorough machine washings may restore the color. White nylon can be bleached with color remover (the home dyestuffs type), or with frequent use of powdered bleach (Snowy). Boiling the nylon fabric in color remover works well, but this may wrinkle the fabric (160° F. is recommended).

Undergarments of part nylon should be cared for as if they were made entirely of the other fiber, which might be rayon, silk, or acetate. Nylon lingerie may fade over a long period of time. Since perspiration may damage the color, nylon lingerie should be washed often and thoroughly. It is recommended not to wring or spin-dry nylon garments; instead, hang them to drip dry after rinsing, and smooth out seams and wrinkles. No ironing is required. The dimensional stability of nylon tricot slips and gowns is now fast to washing because of the heat-setting finish. Pleats are permanent for the same reason.

## SLIPS

Slips are either one-piece dress-length undergarments with shoulder straps or half-slips (garments extending from the waist to slightly above the hemline of the dress). In many instances, slips are trimmed with nylon lace, embroidery, or appliqué. (See *embroidery and lace,* Chapter 18.) The amount, type, and quality of the trimming accounts for some of the differences in the prices of slips.

Slips may be knitted or woven. Knitted constructions predominate because they cost less to produce; they are elastic, porous, resilient, crush-resistant, and easy to launder, and they require no ironing as compared to woven fabrics.

The T.F.P.I.A. requires the fiber identification of fabrics used. But there are other considerations in the selection of a slip besides fiber, yarn, construction, and finish of the fabric. The following points should receive attention:

1. Garment construction. Seams should be overcast to protect the cut edge of the fabric if knitted (pinked if woven).
2. Close, firm stitching. Lace should be attached firmly with close, zigzag stitches, and straps or elastic waistbands should be firmly attached.
3. Residual shrinkage in per cent stated on the label.
4. Garment measurement. The garment should be measured against the customer or tried on in the store to be sure it fits.
5. Laundering instructions. Instructions for laundering should be stated on the label.

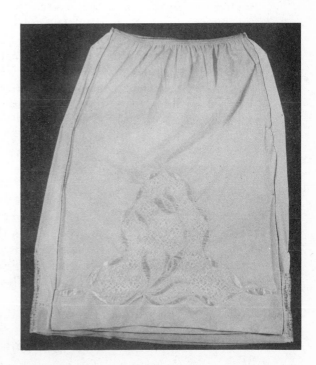

Regular slip sizes run according to bust measure: 32, 34, 36, 38, and so on. Extra sizes are: 46, 48, 50, 52. A person who

Figure 16.12. Both of these slips were marked "Medium." (*Photographs courtesy of Consumers' Research, Inc.*)

wears a size 14 dress should select a size 34 slip; one who wears a size 16 dress, a size 36 slip; and one who wears a size 18 dress, a size 38 slip. The Commodity Standards Division of the U.S. Department of Commerce suggests that half-slips are usually made for younger figures. Therefore misses' standard sizes, 12, 14, 16, 18 are more important than women's sizes 34, 36, 38, and so on.

## SLEEPWEAR

### GOWNS, PAJAMAS, ROBES

Gowns, pajamas, and coat-and-gown or coat-and-pajama sets can be tailored or lace trimmed. The line, design, and colors vary with fashion decree. Some common fabrics used for gowns and pajamas are rayon, acetate, silk or nylon crepe, silk pongee, cotton, plissé, batiste, some chiffons and georgettes, cotton knits, and nylon and rayon tricot.

Dainty gowns may be trimmed with lace, embroidery, appliqué, or contrasting bindings. (See *embroidery and lace*, Chapter 18.)

Sizes of gowns and pajamas are determined by bust measure. The length of these garments depends upon the style.

Garments related to the sleepwear category, and the fabrics in which they are made, are the following:

*Robes and lounge-wear*—wool flannel and blends, all-cotton blanket-type robing, chenille, fleece, quilted fabrics, terry, corduroy, and sateen; also cotton crepe, cotton broadcloth, and poplin (for summer).

*Bed jackets*—knitted wool or acrylic, quilted cotton or synthetic fibers, brushed textured fabrics, and cotton or rayon challis.

*Peignoirs and travel sets* (coat-and-gown or coat-and-pajamas)—spun rayon, acetate or nylon crepe, tricot, all-over lace, trimmings of satin ribbon, lace, fur, metal threads, embroidery, and self-bindings.

## INTIMATE APPAREL

This classification includes bras (short for brassieres), girdles, corsets, panties, and garter belts. There are various styles in each of these articles. (Definitions for these items will be found in the glossary.)

Women are conscious of the lines and fit of their outer apparel, but comparatively few women realize that the fit of a dress can be improved by a perfect-fitting foundation garment. The items of apparel that control and support the figure are specially classed as foundation garments. A girdle of webbing made of spandex or rubber yarns gives a limited amount of support. With additional heavy woven fabric over the abdomen and buttocks, the garment gives improved support and figure control, and with varied amounts and weights of boning, the figure can be well controlled. A professional corsetiere should be consulted in the fitting of a corset. It is advisable to try on girdles, particularly the boned ones, to ensure proper fit and the desired support and control.

Garments that are intended for support are made with at least a portion of webbing of rubber or spandex. Some girdles are made entirely of spandex or power net (nylon, rayon, or acetate and spandex). Girdles with legs may be called *panty girdles*. A girdle with bra attached may be termed *all-in-one*. Fabrics used for foundation garments include nylon and spandex power set, panels of brocade or satin elastic (acetate, cotton, polyester or spandex), trimmings of elasticized lace, and nylon tricot for panel linings and crotches. Abdominal support belts have light boning at the front, sides, and back. They may be made of knitted elastic (cotton, rayon, rubber).

Cotton fabrics for foundation garments are preshrunk by processing with water and steam so that no more than three-quarters of 1 per cent residual shrinkage can be expected in length or width. Even elastic fabrics are washed thoroughly in the finishing process to limit shrinkage.

Bras, styled for various figure types in length, size of bust, and features for control and slimming, are either separate items of apparel or part of a corset. They are made with or without adjustable shoulder straps of corded or satin ribbon of cotton, rayon, or nylon. Bust measurement in inches denotes the size, and cups are designated as A, small; B, medium; and C, large.

The frame and cups may be made of power net, nylon lace, tricot, embroidered nylon, or polyester/cotton. Linings may be cotton or taffeta tricot; padding may be spun polyester or polyurethane.

There are two types of panties: elasticized and nonelasticized. The latter type, with straight or flared legs in varied lengths, is made of acetate or nylon tricot, cotton/polyester blends, and crepe. This type comes in the following sizes:

| *Regular Sizes* | | *Semi-Extra Sizes* | | *Extra Sizes* | |
|---|---|---|---|---|---|
| SIZE | HIP MEASURE | SIZE | HIP MEASURE | SIZE | HIP MEASURE |
| 4 | 32 | 8 | 40 | 10–12 | 44–52 |
| 5 | 34 | 9 | 42 | | |
| 6 | 36 | | | | |
| 7 | 38 | | | | |

Short panties, called *briefs,* may or may not be elasticized. They are made of acetate runproof tricot, cotton and cotton blends, stretch nylon, mesh, and nylon or acetate elasticized tricot. Sizes are small (24–26 waist); medium (26–28); large (29–30); extra-large (31–32).

The elasticized type, sometimes called *panty girdle,* has been discussed under "intimate apparel." Panty girdles come in small, medium, large, and extra-large sizes. A small size would fit a size 12 or under; medium, a size 14; large, a size 16; and extra-large, a size 18.

Garter belts, designed to hold up stockings, may gently firm and control the younger figure (usually under a 29-inch waist). Sizes are small, medium, and large.

## HOSIERY

While cotton hosiery (especially lisle) and wool hosiery are important for sports, children's, and men's wear, the great majority of women today wear nylon most of the time.

Cotton, Orlon acrylic and stretch nylon, cotton and spandex, and 100 per cent stretch nylon are used for women's and girls' socks, and for boys' and men's socks as well.

### STRETCH YARN

To an increasing extent nylon hosiery is being made from stretch textured yarns that are fluffy and have great permanent elasticity (Helanca is the best-known brand). This nylon is made from a continuous-filament fiber and should not be confused with spun nylon made from short lengths of fiber. Because of their stretching property, stretch nylons will adjust themselves to the size of the foot. Thus, three sizes are all a store need carry: small, fits sizes 8 to 9; medium, $9\frac{1}{2}$ to $10\frac{1}{2}$; and large, 11 to 12.

One of the principal advantages of stretch nylon socks for children is that youngsters do not outgrow a pair so fast. Mothers with several small children can buy the same size socks for all and keep the socks together in one drawer. This hosiery has been found to fit snugly and to be fast-drying and comfortable. However, some wearers object to a tight fit at the tip of the toes. In addition, if the sock is too snug, it may develop a hole.

Stretch nylon yarn has been modified to create a leg with elastic-support properties; one such garment is marketed under the name of Supp-hose. The manufacturer claims that these stockings alleviate "leg fatigue," and it is implied that they take the place of surgical rubber stockings used for varicose veins. Although the support stocking probably is not an adequate substitute for the surgical rubber type, many women who are on their feet a great deal feel more comfortable with the tight support provided. These stocking cost $5.95 (or less for un-branded, lighter-weight qualities). Support stockings are now made of Lycra spandex.

### TYPES OF HOSIERY

There are two types of hosiery: full-fashion knit and circular knit. Full fashioned are knitted flat. Stitches are taken off (two stitches are knit as one to decrease the number) so that the fabric is narrowed at the ankle. The two edges of the fabric are sewn together, which provides a real seam from toe to heel and up the back. Two machines may make full-fashioned hosiery: one, called the *legger*, makes the leg; another, called the *footer*, makes the foot. There are also single-unit machines. On either side of the back seam, over the calf, small dots are visible. These dots, really double loops, are the points where stitches are decreased to make the hosiery narrower. They are called *fashion marks*. They are also visible on either side of the seam under the arch of the foot.

Circular-knit hosiery is commonly called *seamless,* because no back seam is present. In this type, the tension of needles is tightened at the time of knitting to shape the stocking below the calf of the leg. Thus, there are the same number of wales at the ankle as farther up the leg. In circular-knit hosiery a seam appears about one inch from the tip of the toe rather than at the toe as it does in full-fashioned hosiery.

## COMPARISON OF THE TWO TYPES

Full-fashioned hosiery, a better-fitting fabric than circular knit, retains its shape better during wear and after washing. For men in particular, the circular-knit hosiery is preferable, because there is no seam over the ball of the foot to irritate tender skin areas. In men's socks the retention of perfect shape during wear is not an important factor. Women's seamless stockings have gained in popularity because they eliminate the problem of crooked seams and because they fit smoothly on the foot.

## PANTY HOSE

Until the advent of the mini skirt, the standard length of women's regular nonstretch knit hosiery was 30 inches from the heel to the top of the garter welt. With the much shorter skirts, longer lengths of hosiery were required. Thus, thigh top and a hip length with opaque panels that hook to an elasticized waistband were made to meet consumer demand. Panty hose (stocking and panty knitted as one garment) have appealed to the consumer. She is assured of a smooth, snug-fitting garment from toe to waist. Furthermore, the stocking section can be patterned in variegated-size mesh, polka dot, point d'esprit, rib, cable, lacy, and crochet-like textures.[17] Also, panty hose can give mild support if the panty is knitted of nylon and spandex. To ensure well-fitting stretch panty hose, a mail-order house provides the following table:

| SIZE | HEIGHT | WEIGHT |
|------|--------|--------|
| A (petite) | 5 ft. to 5 ft. 3 in. | 95 to 115 pounds |
| B (average) | 5 ft. 3 in. to 5 ft. 7 in. | 115 to 135 pounds |
| C (tall) | 5 ft. 7 in. to 5 ft. 9 in. | 135 to 160 pounds |
| D (large) | 5 ft. 7 in to 5 ft. 11 in. | 160 to 180 pounds |

Order next larger size if weight exceeds that shown for height.

[17] See *lace,* Chapter 18.

Tights are also fashionable and practical. They are generally made of a sweater-like knit of 100 per cent stretch nylon for women and children (cotton may be used for girls). The size ranges are as follows:

| Children's | | Women's | |
|---|---|---|---|
| SIZE | UNDERWEAR SIZE | SIZE | HEIGHT |
| Small | 4–6 | A | 5' to 5' 4" |
| Medium | 7–10 | B | 5' 5" to 5' 8" |
| Large | 12–14 | C | 5' 8" to 6' |

### STANDARDS AND SPECIFICATIONS FOR HOSIERY

*Grades.* Hosiery is classified first-quality, irregulars, seconds, and thirds. A stocking may be marked "irregular" if there are irregularities in dimensions, size, color, or knit, without the presence in the hose of any mends, runs, tears, or breaks in the fabric, or any substantial damage to the yarn or fabric itself. Seconds and thirds include hosiery that contains runs, obvious mends, irregularities, substantial imperfections, or defects in material, construction, or finish. Irregulars can be marked seconds or thirds if they have runs, mends, defects and the like, but seconds and thirds cannot be marked irregulars according to government standards.

Because of the two-way stretch of a nylon stocking, the same stocking may measure 32 inches on a slender leg, 30 inches on an average leg, and 28 inches on a full-proportioned leg. To measure the length required, place a yardstick or tape measure at the bottom of the heel and measure straight up the leg to the garter button. Different lengths in foundation garments require different lengths in stockings.

Because of the growing demand for a better fit from the standpoint of length as well as size, stockings can now be purchased in three lengths —short, medium, and long.

*Foot size.* Except for stretch socks, the foot size of hosiery is measured in terms of inches. For instance, a size $9\frac{1}{2}$ stocking should fit an average foot $9\frac{1}{2}$ inches long. If the size is correct, the stocking can be pulled out $\frac{1}{2}$ inch at the heel, at the toe, or at the instep when on the foot. Size is checked on a standard leg form under quality-control standards agreed on by many manufacturers. Flat measurements are inadequate in nylon hosiery because of nylon's two-way stretch.

To facilitate fitting, most salesmen have access to a foot size chart that shows the stocking size needed.

*Gauge.* This term refers to the degree of closeness of knitting. The closer the knitting, the higher the gauge number and the stronger the fabric. Gauge is determined by the number of wales to an inch or the number of stitches to an inch and a half. The number of needles per inch is two-thirds the gauge number. For example, in a 45-gauge knitting machine there are 30 needles to the inch. This 45-gauge machine

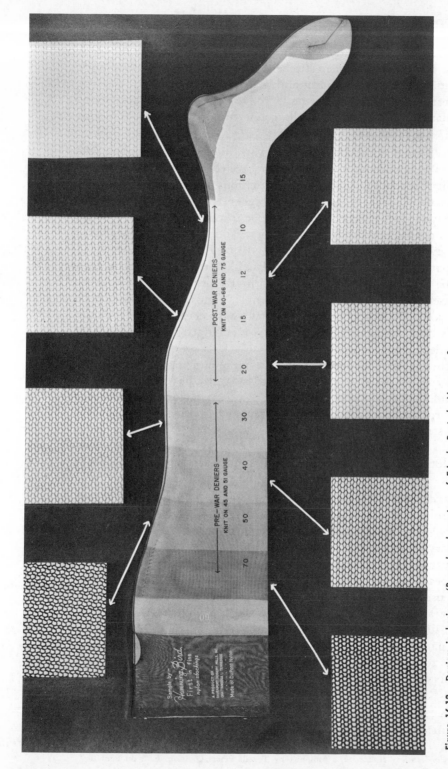

**Figure 16.13.** Deniers in hosiery. (Reproduced courtesy of E.I. du Pont de Nemours & Company, Inc.)

knits a fabric 14 inches wide; so this machine would use 30 x 14, or 420 needles.

Gauge varies from 39 stitches per inch and a half to a high of 66. A high-gauge has more and finer stitches, greater strength because more yarn is used, and better durability and snag resistance.

Gauge refers to full-fashioned hosiery. Needle count refers to seamless (circular knit) stockings. Needle count runs 260 to 434. A needle count of 434 is equivalent to 54 gauge.[18]

*Denier.* Denier means the weight of yarn indicated by number. The term denier is applied to filament rayon, reeled silk and nylon yarn. Nylon hosiery is sold by denier. The designations 30s and 40s marked on hosiery means 30 and 40 denier. The higher the denier number, the coarser, heavier, and stronger the yarn. For instance, 30 denier is twice as heavy and twice as strong as 15 denier. Today the consumer has a choice of several deniers in nylon hosiery: 10 to 50.

While panty hose may be made entirely of sheer 15-denier yarn, they may also be made of two denier sizes—a sheerer denier for the stocking and a coarser one for the panty. For example, regular-knit hose may be 28 denier knitted onto a 40 denier panty; a sheer seamless 21 denier (3 threads of 7 denier twisted together for strength) may be knitted onto a 50 denier opaque panty.

Through the years, hosiery has become more and more sheer. Before World War II, 30 denier was the sheerest; today we have 10, 12, and 15 denier. And then consumers ask: "Why don't my nylons wear the way they used to?" Obviously, since they are much more sheer now, they are not so strong.

When an advertisement refers to nylon stockings as 12/66s, it means that the stockings are made of 12-denier nylon yarn with 66 stitches to 1½ inches of fabric measured around the stocking.

*Reinforcements.* Reinforcements are commonly placed in the toe, heel, and sole in direct proportion to the weight and style of the stocking. Nylon is so sturdy that it will stand a lot of abrasion, so some sheer hosiery styles are not reinforced.

Extra yarns inserted in the knitting machine make the reinforcement, which appears heavier than the rest of the stocking. Frequently nylon yarns are used as reinforcements in wool and cotton socks.

Splicing styles (reinforcements above the heel) change from season to season. One style may call for a short, wide splicing; another may require a narrow, high splicing; another may feature a triangular effect. Whatever form splicing may take, it should be symmetrical for each stocking. Nylon seamless stockings do not necessarily have splicing above the heel.

*Stretch.* The stretch crosswise at the top of the garter welt in women's medium-length hosiery should be 12 to 13 inches when meas-

---

[18] *Nylon Hosiery Handbook,* a pamphlet by Textile Fibers Division, E. I. du Pont de Nemours & Company.

ured flat. Less than 12 inches is not sufficient stretch for comfort. If more than 13 inches, there is danger that the fabric will lose its elasticity and will not spring back to its original width. Such a fabric does not give the trim, snug fit desired.

The stocking should stretch to 7 or 7¼ inches at the instep. To determine this measurement, grip the fabric at the instep and the point opposite on the sole and stretch the cloth. The attempt to make narrow heels may cause some manufacturers to narrow the width of the reinforcement on the sole. Then, when the stocking is worn, too much strain is put on the fabric at the instep. Holes may consequently appear at the point where splicing and sole reinforcement meet.

*Color.* Hosiery is dyed in the yarn before it is knitted or in the piece after it is knitted. Hosiery that is dyed in the yarn is called *ingrain* hosiery, whereas that dyed in the piece is called *dip-dyed* hosiery. The former has a more even, richer, deeper brilliance than the latter.

From the standpoint of economy, the manufacturer prefers to dip-dye his hosiery. He can knit a supply in natural color and dye the fabrics later as the style demand arises. An overstock of ingrain hosiery in an unpopular color may prove difficult to sell to the retailer.

### STYLE

Many women who have worn the patterned mesh hosiery seem to enjoy not only its attractive appearance but also its serviceability.

The mini skirt has caused fashion to focus on hosiery. A variety of fashion colors have appeared, and interesting patterns have been knitted into the stockings. Hosiery has become a fashion item.

Some suggestions for hosiery selection follow:

1. If durability is important, avoid very sheer, low denier, hosiery.
2. If you buy panty hose, be sure to consider your shoe size, your height and weight, and your leg contour. A stocking may fit perfectly, but the panty section may not fit ill-proportioned hips.
3. For children, buy cotton lisle, cotton mixtures, or stretch nylon.
4. Buy wool hosiery a size larger than normal, unless drying forms are used or the label is marked "preshrunk, residual shrinkage less than 3 per cent."
5. For durability, look for a reinforced heel and toe, a special toe guard, a wide garter welt, and a run-stop below the garter welt.
6. Ingrain hosiery is normally to be preferred to dip-dyed; it is likely to retain its color better.

## SELECTION OF CLOTHING ACCESSORIES

In addition to underwear and negligees, which are sometimes classed under accessories, there are many small items of clothing or personal adornment that are made of textiles.

Neckwear may include collars, collar-and-cuff sets, and stoles. Since these pieces, with the exception of stoles (made of wool or acrylic knitted goods and fur-like fabrics), are made of the same materials as dresses, they need no further description. The same is true of scarfs. They are commonly made of silk, rayon, acetate, acrylic, wool, cotton, or mixtures of these materials. Typical fabrics include twills, satins, foulard, crepes, and knitted goods. Scarfs may be square, 23" x 23" or 27" x 27"; oblong, 11" x 36", 15" x 44", or 14" x 64"; or cravat-shaped. The neckwear department often carries small capes and short jackets as well.

### ARTIFICAL FLOWERS

Many artificial flowers are made of nontextiles such as paper, glass, plastic, and wax, but flowers are also made of velvet, velveteen, taffeta, satin, lace, chiffon, and organdy. Very often flowers on coats and dresses are made of the same material as the coat or dress.

### HANDKERCHIEFS

There are different types of women's handkerchiefs for different occasions. Handkerchiefs for everyday wear may be all white, pastel, or printed—with or without monogram, lace, or other ornamentation. These handkerchiefs are made of handkerchief linen, batiste, nainsook, lawn, and washable silk. Frequently, the silk handkerchief is used to tie around the neck to ornament a sweater or jersey blouse. For evening, filmier and larger handkerchiefs are worn. They may be monogrammed, lace-trimmed, or plain with a hand-rolled hem. Chiffon and lace are common materials used for evening.

When buying a handkerchief, consider the following points:

1. General appearance
2. Wearing quality or durability
   (a) Grade of fabric
   (b) Workmanship
   (c) Quality of trimming, embroidery, and design
3. Purpose, or suitability for its use
4. Price

General appearance may include style. If colored borders or printed all-over designs are a style note, they should certainly be considered in the selection.

With respect to durability, the buyer should know that a good grade of linen will outwear the average cotton. White linen will appear fresher and more lustrous after laundering. Thin silks and rayons appear to advantage for evening or occasional wear if frequent laundering is not essential.

Hand-torn handkerchiefs are considered better than the average because their dimensions are more even. Instead of cutting a large number at one time by machinery, the manufacturer tears each handkerchief by following a single thread. Likewise, hems rolled and sewed by hand are considered better than those that are machine-stitched, because they do not pucker and because the stitching, if well done, is not so noticeable. The firmness and quality of the hemstitching or other embroidery are important. If lace or other trimming is used, the sewing that attaches it to the handkerchief should be firm, even, and fine.

The careful buyer selects a handkerchief for a particular occasion. For example, if it is to appear from the pocket of a dress, the color of the dress and the occasion for its use should be considered. Handkerchiefs are made for special occasions, with hearts for Valentine's Day, poinsettia prints for Christmas, and shamrocks for St. Patrick's Day.

Price can be very important. If a woman needs a large stock of handkerchiefs, she will probably select inexpensive ones. If she has a particular fondness for fine linens with real lace trimmings, she must be willing to pay the high prices.

## MILLINERY AND RIBBONS

The common materials used in millinery are straw, felt, leather, and fabrics such as velvet, furlike fabrics, satin, crepe, crash, piqué, plastic-coated fabrics, knitted goods, and ribbons. Leather and fur, since they are nontextiles, will not be discussed here. Some may consider straw and felt nontextiles. Straw is not spun into yarn before it is woven, but since straw products are woven from narrow strips of sisal, baku, and grass, it will be considered as a textile in this discussion. Hat felt is not made of yarn and is not woven; it is made of wool, fur, or synthetic blends, and fibers are massed together by means of a fulling or shrinking process.

When in style, medium-priced felt hats are usually made of wool or wool blend. They are harder to the touch and are duller in appearance than fur felts. (See Chapter 6 for a discussion of felt.)

Velour is a common fur felt that may be identified by a lustrous, heavy nap. Soleil is also a lustrous fur felt, but the nap is sheared shorter than velour. "Suede-finished felt," and "finished felt" are terms used to describe a fur felt sheared short and processed to resemble leather.

The velvet used in millinery may be woven in a narrower width than velvet for dresses. Lyons velvet, with a cotton back, is stiffer than all-silk velvet, and is therefore commonly used in millinery. Velveteen is also used. Transparent velvet (rayon) water-spots badly and needs frequent steaming, but if the fabric is given a water-repellent finish, it will water-spot less easily.

Fabric hats can be made of almost any dress or coat material, though the brims may have to be sized or stiffened. Fabrics for summer hats include gingham, polyester/rayon or cotton sailcloth, linen/rayon/cotton

crash, cotton shantung, crocheted fabrics; for winter, fabrics include
wool jersey, tweed, velveteen, and knitted fabrics. Hoods are made of
furlike fabrics of rayon plush with cotton back, or acrylic pile and
cotton back. Rain hats are often made of polyester poplin and vinyls
Few hats made of washable fabrics are washed satisfactorily at home.
They should be dried and pressed on a block of the right size. Dry cleaning is generally advised.

Hat inner linings are often made of crinoline—a plain-woven cotton
fabric highly sized with glue and starches. A coarse cotton or linen
fabric called *buckram* is also used for this purpose.

Hats are often trimmed with ribbon or knitted bands; artificial
flowers made from textile fabrics, feathers, felt, or leather; and novelty
ornaments such as buckles, stones, and beads. One of the common ribbon
fabrics is grosgrain, a heavy, fillingwise-ribbed rayon, acetate, or silk
material. The ribs may have a cotton core. There is quite a bit of body
to the material and it wears well. Taffeta, moiré, velvet, velveteen, satin
(both single-faced and double-faced), metal cloth, and novelty weaves
are other common ribbon materials. Acetate moiré taffeta has become
popular for ribbons because the fabric can be woven wide and cut into
ribbon width, and the cut edges can be fused by heat. This method
makes the ribbon inexpensive. Velvet ribbons with cut instead of woven
edges can also be used for inexpensive trimmings for millinery. The
velvet with cut edges ravels easily, and hence is not too satisfactory.

In selecting becoming hats, the style, suitability, shape-retaining
quality, colorfastness, and finish are the important factors.

### GLOVES

Although formerly most gloves were made of leather, many are now
made of knitted and woven goods. Fabric gloves may be made of cotton,
wool, silk, rayon, rayon or nylon tricot mesh, crocheted cotton, and
woven goods such as lace and dress fabrics.

### HANDBAGS

Comparatively few handbags are made of textile fabrics. Most of
them are made of leather or a substitute. Faille, bengaline, double-woven
stretch nylon, furlike fabrics, and fabrics to match a coat may be used
for everyday wear. For evening, metallic fabric on acetate backing,
rayon peau de soie, cotton velveteen, satin, and brocade are appropriate.
For summer handbags, the fabrics used include linen crash, homespun,
the fabric of the dress being worn, straw (or a viscose rayon that looks
like straw), straw braid, and nylon that looks like sugarcane. Linings
include rayon-and-silk satin, rayon faille, crepe, and printed cottons.
Large beach bags for bathing suits or for knitting may be made of crash,
homespun, sailcloth, or cotton tapestry. They may be waterproofed.

Most shoes are made of leather, but fabric shoes have become popular for specific occasions: for beach wear, beach sandals made of linen, cotton crash, or cretonne; for street wear, canvas or crash; for evening, brocades, metal cloth, satin, faille, moiré, or taffeta.

The uppers of sneakers are textiles made of polyester/cotton poplin, cotton Army duck, cotton canvas or denim. Slippers for summer can be corduroy, terry, or nylon tricot; for winter, cotton velour with nylon or acrylic lining, rayon plush, quilted cotton, acrylic pile on cotton knit, acrylic and modacrylic blends, cotton knit backed with polyurethane foam.

## INFANTS' WEAR

Certain articles, such as sacques, bootees, dresses, shirts, blankets, diapers, and bonnets, are always essential for infants. The styles in length, type of yoke, and trimming of babies' wearing apparel may change slightly, but the general silhouette does not alter. Infants' clothing is sized according to age: 6, 12, 18, 24 months.

Toddlers' sizes 1 to 4 are designed for tots whose figures still retain the rounded contours of infancy. Coat and dress lengths are short; legs and seats are cut full to accommodate diapers. Height of the child is most important in determining size. For the child who is losing the roundness of infancy, a more fitted style is appropriate (sizes 2 to 6x). Again, height is a most important factor in determining size.

The materials for babies' clothing are, generally speaking, standard. Cotton is used more than any other material, because it washes readily and does not irritate the skin. (See *care of fabrics*, Chapter 15.) The heavier cotton cloths are suitable for winter, and the thin materials for summer. An undershirt with a small percentage of wool may be used in winter if approved by the doctor. The department or specialty store saleswoman can recommend a choice of layette. In some instances, stores have made up suitable lists of layettes at various prices.

Two of the most important items in a layette are diapers and pads. Should the mother decide to use a diaper service or disposable diapers, she may not need to buy any diapers, though a few for emergency are desirable. For traveling, the throw-away nonwoven type are convenient. Diapers are made of gauze, flannelette, knitted and bird's eye in rectangular or fitted types. Gauze, which allows air to circulate, is comfortable and easy to wash and dry. Flannelette is soft but bulky. Pinked edges are more comfortable than hemmed ones. Cotton bibs, pads, and diapers that are double woven allow air to circulate between the layers to dry the material much faster and make it more comfortable.

The double-woven pads are much more absorbent than quilted pads.

As soon as the moisture hits the absorbent pad it spreads out as if it were on a blotter. On the quilted pads the water stays in one spot and then slowly spreads out. Plastic-coated and rubber pads are waterproof but are hotter in summer because they lack porosity.

## SUMMARY

This chapter shows the possibilities that a person faces in choosing clothing fabrics for different uses, and sets forth the distinguishing characteristics of various fabrics. No one becomes expert in judging fabrics until he or she is willing to study their characteristics thoroughly, a pursuit that requires patience, time, and practice.

## PROJECT

1. From the articles of apparel listed here, select one garment for study: Nightgown, robe, shorts, slacks, baby's bonnet, infant's dress, tea apron, head scarf, raincoat, umbrella, sport socks.

   Write up the information in the form of a merchandise manual to include:

   (*a*) Where found in a store
   (*b*) Fabrics of which it is made
   (*c*) Size range
   (*d*) Selling points
   (*e*) Instructions for care
   (*f*) Retail price range

## GLOSSARY [19]

**Alpaca crepe.**  A heavy dull-finished crepe (no alpaca present) in rayon, acetate, or silk made to resemble wool crepe. It is used in fall and winter dresses and blouses.

**Astrakhan cloth.**  A furlike wool fabric of deep pile with curled loops. Inexpensive grades are often knitted.

**Balbriggan.**  Lightweight circular-knitted cotton fabric that often has a napped back; frequently in a tan shade. It is used for underwear.

**Batiste.**  A very sheer, combed, mercerized muslin identified by streaks lengthwise. Better grades are highly mercerized. It is also made in spun rayon, wool, or silk and is used for summer dresses, blouses, lingerie, infants' dresses and bonnets, handkerchiefs.

[19] Since all apparel fabrics cannot be defined in a glossary, for those omitted see *Calloway Textile Dictionary* (Calloway Mills, La Grange, Georgia), *Dan River's Textile Dictionary* (Dan River Mills, New York), or *Fairchild's Dictionary of Textiles,* Fairchild Publications, Inc. (New York).

**Bengaline.** A fillingwise-ribbed fabric similar to faille but heavier, with fewer cords to the inch. It may be silk, wool, or rayon warp with cotton or wool filling; used for dresses, coats, trimmings.

**Bias cut.** A fabric cut diagonally across the warp and filling yarns. A true bias is cut on a 45° angle from the lower left to the upper right of a cloth.

**Bouclé.** See Glossary, Chapter 3.

**Brassiere or bra.** An undergarment that covers the bust and may extend to the waistline.

**Brief.** A short panty. See *Panty.*

**Broadcloth.** A plain-weave cotton fabric, with fillingwise rib finer than poplin. Best grades are made of combed pima or Egyptian cotton. It is used for women's blouses, tailored summer dresses, men's shirts. It can also be made of silk and polyester and cotton blends. See *Wool broadcloth,* Glossary, Chapter 17.

**Brocade.** Fabric with slightly raised Jacquard designs that may have gold or silver threads. It is used for formal dresses, blouses, evening wraps, and bags. See Glossary, Chapter 20.

**Brocatelle.** See Glossary, Chapter 20.

**Butcher.** A coarse rayon or rayon and acetate blend made to resemble the original butcher linen used for the butcher's apron.

**Cambric.** A muslin that is firmer and heavier than nainsook. A lightweight, very low count, heavily sized and glazed cambric is used for costuming.

**Canton crepe.** Thick, slightly ribbed crepe, heavier than crepe de Chine. It may be silk, rayon, or acetate and is used for business and afternoon dresses.

**Challis.** A very lightweight plain-weave wool, spun rayon, or mixed fabric usually printed with small floral designs that is used for dresses, blouses, scarfs, infants' sacques.

**Chambray.** A plain-weave cotton fabric with colored warp and white filling that may have woven-in stripes. It is used for women's and children's summer dresses and blouses and men's shirts.

**Chenile.** A fabric woven from fuzzy caterpillar-like yarns. Usually the filling is the chenille yarn and the warp a regular textile yarn.

**Cheviot.** See Glossary, Chapter 17.

**Chiffon.** A sheer crepe fabric in silk, rayon, or nylon with either soft or stiff finish. It is used for formal dresses, scarfs, and evening handkerchiefs.

**Chinchilla.** Heavy twill-weave coating that may be all wool or mixed with cotton. Little nubs or tufts of nap make the characteristic surface to resemble chinchilla fur. It is used for coats and jackets.

**Corduroy.** Heavy cotton or rayon pile fabric. The cut pile forms wales warpwise. It is used for dresses, coats, sports jackets, slacks, and draperies.

**Corselet.** A type of girdle, with a boned front, that extends from above the bust to below the buttocks. Bras may hook onto girdle.

**Corset.** A heavily boned foundation garment for the torso.

**Coutil.** A cotton or cotton and rayon fabric, closely woven in herringbone construction, used for corsets and bras.

**Covert.** See Glossary, Chapter 17.

**Crash.** A coarse linen, cotton, or rayon fabric with uneven yarns woven in plain weave. It is used for dresses, suitings, table linens, draperies.

**Crepe.** A fabric with a crinkled surface that may be made by several methods.

**Crepe-back satin.** See *Satin-back crepe.*

**Crepe de Chine.** Originally made in silk with the fabric degummed to produce crinkle. As made now, it is a sheer flat crepe in silk or man-made fibers. It is used for lingerie, dresses, and blouses.

**Damask.** A reversible Jacquard fabric. The designs are not raised as in brocade. It is made of almost any fiber or blends. See Glossary, Chapter 20. It is used for afternoon and evening dresses, table covers in linen, draperies and upholsteries in heavier fabrics.

**Dart.** A tapering fold that is stitched in a garment to improve its fit.

**Denim.** A heavy, strong, twill-weave cotton fabric woven with colored warps and white fillings. Originally blue or brown, denims are now also made in stripes and figures. They are used for dungarees, work clothes, overalls, draperies, and bedspreads.

**Dimity.** A sheer cotton with corded stripes or checks—used for children's summer dresses, bedspreads, curtains, and blouses.

**Donegal tweed.** See Glossary, Chapter 17.

**Dotted swiss.** Sheer, crisp, plain-weave cotton fabric with either clipped spot or swivel dots, colored or white. It is used for children's party dresses, women's summer dresses, lingerie, and curtains.

**Dress linen.** See *Crash.*

**Embroidery.** Ornamental needlework done on the fabric itself.

**End use.** Intended use by the consumer.

**Faille.** A flat, crosswise, ribbed fabric with more ribs to the inch than bengaline. It is made of rayon, acetate, cotton, wool, or mixtures and is used for tailored dresses, coats, suits, and draperies. Tissue faille is a lightweight faille.

**Faille crepe.** A silk, rayon, acetate, or other synthetic dress fabric with a decided wavy (crepe) cord fillingwise. It is used for negligees, blouses, daytime and evening dresses, handbags, and trimmings.

**Flannel.** An all-wool fabric of woolen or worsted yarn with a soft napped finish. It may be twill or plain weave and is used for coats, suits, dresses. It is also made in cotton. Viyella flannel is a Williams, Hollins and Company trade name for a cotton and wool flannel made in England.

**Flannelette.** A lightweight cotton flannel napped on one or both sides, which may be printed. It is used for sleeping garments and sports shirts.

**Flat crepe.** A medium weight crepe with creped fillings alternating with two S and two Z twists. The surface is fairly flat. It is used for dresses, negligees, and blouses.

**Fleece.** A fabric with a deep, thick-napped surface that may be of wool, cotton, acrylic, nylon, or other synthetics.

**Foulard.** A lightweight, soft, twill-weave silk, cotton, or rayon fabric that is often printed with small figures on light or dark grounds. It is used for spring and summer dresses, scarfs, robes, and neckties.

**Furlike fabrics.** See Glossary, Chapter 5.

**Gabardine.** A tightly woven, steep twill with rounded wales and a flat back. Made in wool, cotton, rayon, or mixtures. It is used for suits, coats, tailored dresses, and slacks.

**Garter belt.** A fabric belt to which garters are attached.

**Gauze.** A sheer, open, plain-weave cotton fabric used for diapers and surgical dressings. It can also be made of silk or the synthetics for use in curtains.

**Georgette crepe.** A sheer, dull crepe. The texture is obtained by alternating right and left twist yarns in warp and filling. It is used for summer and evening dresses.

**Gingham.** A yarn-dyed plain-weave cotton fabric with woven-in plaids, checks, or stripes. It is used for women's and children's dresses, blouses, men's sport shirts.

**Girdle.** A foundation garment extending from the waist or bust to below the buttocks. It has all-elastic webbing or inserts of webbing and fabric, with or without bones.

**Gros de Londres.** Ribbed or corded fabric. The flat, fillingwise cords alternate wide and narrow. It is used for dresses and millinery.

**Grosgrain.** A heavy ribbed fabric in ribbon width, made in silk or rayon warp with cotton cords. The cords are round and firm. It is really a bengaline in narrow goods and is used for ribbons, neckties, and lapel facings.

**Honan.** A heavy silk pongee, originally the product of wild silkworms of Honan, China. Honan has slub yarns in both warp and filling and may be made with synthetic fibers.

**Jean.** A solid-colored or striped twill-weave cotton fabric, softer and finer than denim. It is used for work shirts, girls' slacks and shorts, and children's overalls.

**Jersey.** See Glossary, Chapter 13.

**Lace.** An openwork fabric made by looping, interlacing, or twisting thread. For kinds of laces, see pp. 516 ff.

**Lamé.** Brocade, damask, or brocatelle in which flat metallic yarns are woven in warp and filling for a luxurious effect. Metallic yarns may be used in the main construction. Also a trademark term for a nontarnishable metallic yarn. It is used for evening dresses, blouses, and trimmings.

**Lawn.** A cotton muslin fabric generally more sheer and with a higher count than nainsook. It may or may not be sized.

**Lingerie crepe.** Formerly called French crepe because it was originally made in France. The creped surface was made by embossing (pressing cloth over a fleece blanket). Since it is no longer pressed, it is not a crepe. It is used for lingerie and spring and summer dresses.

**Marquisette.** See Glossary, Chapter 13.

**Matelassé crepe.** A double cloth with quilted or blistered appearance that is used for afternoon, dinner, and evening dresses and trimmings.

**Melton.** A heavy woolen with clipped surface nap; somewhat felt-like in feeling; lustrous like a dull broadcloth.

**Mesh.** Any woven or knitted fabric with an open mesh texture. It is used for foundation garments and hosiery.

**Moss crepe.** See *Pebble crepe*.

**Muslin.** Any plain-weave cotton cloth ranging in weight from the sheerest batiste to the coarsest sheeting. Muslins include such fabrics as voile, nainsook, lawn, and percale.

**Nainsook.** A cotton muslin fabric heavier and coarser than lawn. In better grades it may be polished on one side. When well-polished, it is sold as polished cotton.

**Negligee.** A loose, robe-type garment, worn in the boudoir, made of sheer fabric and usually lace or fur trimmed.

**Net.** A silk, rayon, nylon, or cotton mesh fabric. The size of the mesh varies as well as the weight of the net. It is used for veils, evening dresses, and trimmings.

**Ninon.** A voile with warp yarns grouped in pairs. It is made of rayon, acetate, silk, or the newer synthetics and is used for dresses and curtains.

**Nun's veiling.** A sheer, worsted, silk or mixed fabric that is dyed black or brown for religious garb and dyed in colors for dresses.

**100-denier crepe.** A 100-denier viscose rayon yarn made in a flat crepe construction.

**Organdy.** A thin, stiff transparent cotton muslin used for summer dresses, neckwear, and trimmings. Permanent starchless finishes do not lose their crispness in laundering.

**Organza.** A thin, stiff, plain-weave silk or rayon fabric used for formal dresses, trimmings, and collars and cuffs. See *Organdy*.

**Ottoman.** A heavily corded silk or rayon fabric. The cords are heavier than bengaline and are widely spaced. The cords usually are cotton or wool.

**Oxford.** A basket-weave cotton fabric (2 x 1, 2 x 2, or 3 x 2), used for sport dresses, blouses, and shirts.

**Pantsuit.** A two-piece garment consisting of jacket and long pants.

**Panty.** A woman's or girl's undergarment, with an elastic waistband, that is bound, scalloped, or lace-trimmed at the bottom. A panty girdle is an elasticized, form-fitting panty.

**Panty girdle.** A foundation garment with legs attached. See *Girdle*.

**Panty hose.** Stockings and panty knitted as one garment.

**Peau de soie.** See Glossary, Chapter 20.

**Pebble crepe.** Usually woven of abraded yarns (rayon and acetate) warp and filling. It is a plain weave with skips of warp over two fillings and two fillings over two warps at intervals, to give pebbled surface. Sometimes called mossy or sand crepe.

**Peignoir.** A loose robe worn in the boudoir or a coat worn over a bathing suit at the beach. It is often made of terry cloth to absorb water after bathing.

**Percale.** A medium-weight muslin similar to cambric but dull in finish. It is generally printed for apparel. Heavy grades in higher counts are used for sheeting. Dress percale runs 80 square or 160 yarns to the inch, whereas percale sheeting is 180 or 200 yarns to the inch.

**Piqué.** A fabric with warpwise wales made in cotton, rayon or other synthetics, or silk. In honeycomb design it is called waffle piqué; in diamond pattern, bird's-eye piqué. It is used for dresses, collars, cuffs, and shirts.

**Placket closing.** A narrow piece of material used to finish an opening made in a fabric to enable the wearer to put on the garment with ease.

**Plissé or crinkle crepe.** A crinkled striped or blistered pattern produced on a cotton, rayon, or acetate fabric by treating parts of the fabric with caustic soda to shrink certain areas.

**Plush.** See Glossary, Chapter 20.

**Pongee.** Fabric originally made in China of tan-colored tussah silk. It is plain or printed for summer dresses and suits and is lighter and less slubby than shantung.

**Poplin.** A crosswise-ribbed cotton fabric similar to cotton broadcloth but with a heavier rib. It may be of rayon, silk, wool, nylon, polyester, or combinations of these fibers. It is used for dresses, coats, jackets, and snowsuits (water-repellent).

**Printcloth.** Term applied to carded, plain-weave cotton fabrics with single yarns with counts 30s and 40s. Finishes may vary to produce cloths like lawn, percale, cambric, and longcloth. For longcloth, see *Muslin sheeting*, Glossary, Chapter 18.

**Rep.** A silk, rayon, cotton, wool, or mixed fabric in rib construction, heavier than poplin. It is used for draperies and men's ties, and in lighter weights for blouses and trimmings.

**Romain crepe.** A semisheer fabric of abraded yarns in warp and filling. It is made of rayon and acetate or wool and is used for street and dressy dresses.

**Rough crepe.** A heavy fabric of rayon, acetate, or mixtures made with alternately twisted fillings, two right and two left (2 x 2).

**Satin-back crepe or crepe-back satin.** A heavy reversible fabric with satin on one side and crepe on the other side. It is used in fall and winter dresses and linings.

**Seersucker.** A cotton, silk, or synthetic fabric made by alternating plain and crinkled stripes. See *Woven seersucker*. It is used for summer dresses, boys' shirts, sunsuits, men's summer suits, and bedspreads.

**Serge.** An even twill-weave worsted fabric with the diagonal wale showing on both sides of the cloth, used for men's and women's suits, coats, and dresses. It is made in cotton or rayon for linings.

**Shantung.** A plain-weave fabric woven with slub filling yarn made in silk, rayon, cotton, the synthetics, or wool. It is used for dresses and suits.

**Silhouette.** The outline of a garment.

**Slipper satin.** A heavy rayon, acetate, or silk satin usually with a cotton back. It is used for bedroom and evening slippers.

**Staple fabrics.** Those cloths which, over a period of years, have a steady sale or demand. Such cloths as muslins, flannels, broadcloth, shantung, and taffeta are staples that have to be kept in stock.

**Staple names.** Name of staple fabrics. See *Staple fabrics*.

**Surah.** A soft twilled fabric made of silk, rayon, or acetate woven in plaids, stripes, solid color, or print. Since the diagonal of the wale has a flat top, it may be described as a satin-faced twill. It is used for dresses, blouses, trimmings, and neckties. Foulard is often sold as surah.

**Taffeta.** Plain-weave, smooth, stiffened fabric in silk, rayon, cotton, or synthetic fibers, solid colored or printed. It is used for dresses, blouses, and ribbons.

**Terry cloth.** See *Terry method*, Chapter 5.

**Texture.** See Glossary, Chapter 3.

**Tights.** Skintight garments closely fitting to the figure and extending from the neck down, or from the waist down.

**Tricot.** See Chapter 6.

**Tweed.** A rough-surfaced woolen, usually yarn-dyed and often made in two or more colors. In women's wear, a tweed may look rough but feels soft or even spongy. It may be nubbed or slubbed. It is all wool unless otherwise indicated. Now cotton, linen, rayon, synthetics, or blends may be made to resemble wool tweed.

**Unbleached muslin.**   Printcloths in grey goods and lightweight sheetings.

**Unfinished worsted.**   See Glossary, Chapter 17.

**Union suit.**   A one-piece knitted undergarment extending from the neck to the knee or longer.

**Velour.**   See Glossary, Chapter 20.

**Velvet.**   Silk, rayon or nylon cut pile fabric made with extra warp yarns. Types of velvet include chiffon, Lyons, transparent, and uncut velvet.

**Velveteen.**   A cotton fabric with a filling pile made to look like velvet. It has a cut pile with plain or twill back and is used for dresses, coats, millinery, and suits.

**Viyella flannel.**   See *Flannel*.

**Voile.**   A low-count, sheer muslin with a thready feel. In better grades, voile is made with ply yarns in counterclockwise twist. It is also made in wool, silk, or rayon and is used for summer dresses and curtains.

**Whipcord.**   A twill-weave wool or cotton fabric resembling gabardine. The wale is more pronounced on the right side. It is used for riding habits.

**White-on-white.**   Fabric with a white dobby or Jacquard design on a white ground, common in madras, broadcloth, or nylon. See *Madras*, Glossary, Chapter 17.

**Wool crepe.**   Made of either woolen or worsted yarns. The crepe texture is produced by keeping the warp yarns slack.

**Woven seersucker.**   A crinkled, striped cotton fabric made by weaving some of the yarns in tighter tension than others. See *Seersucker*.

# 17

# Men's and Boys' Wear

Through the years, certain fabrics have remained classic. One of these is jean. The French used to identify Genoese sailors by their heavy trousers, which they called *gènes* (after the French Gènes for Genoa). The word dungaree (so the story goes) is derived from the Hindustani word dungrī. Sailors wore a garment by the same name. Denim, like jean and dungaree, is related to seafaring. The word denim, a contraction of "de Nîmes," was named after the French city of Nîmes, where the fabric was made for sailcloth.

One of the reasons why jean has been a classic fabric over the years is that it has withstood resistance to wear. It is practically a boyhood uniform. However, not all jeans wear equally well. In all-cotton jeans, the heavier 14-ounce will wear better than the lighter 10- to 11-ounce weight. The same is true of abrasion resistance. Durable press jeans resist abrasion better than untreated fabrics. Tests made by the Consumers Union indicate that a high ratio of synthetic fiber to cotton (11-ounce blend of cotton with about 20 per cent nylon or 50 per cent polyester) will be about as durable as a 14-ounce all-cotton denim.[1]

[1] *Consumer Reports* (May 1968).

## COLOR COORDINATOR FOR MEN'S CLOTHING *

| Color of Suit | Shirt | Tie | Socks | Shoes & Belt | Square or Scarf | Hat | Outercoat | Gloves |
|---|---|---|---|---|---|---|---|---|
| Gray | Blue | Blue | Navy | Black | Blue/White | Medium Gray | Black | Gray |
|  | Yellow | Black/Gold | Black | Black | Black/Gold | Black | Gray | Black |
| Natural | Blue | Black/Blue | Black | Black | Black/Blue | Gray | Navy | Navy |
|  | Yellow | Navy/Gold | Black | Black | Navy/Gold | Gray | Black | Gray |
| Blue-Black | Red/Pink | Red/Blue | Black | Black | Red/Blue | Gray | Gray | Gray |
|  | Gray | Blue/Green | Navy | Cordovan | Blue/Green | Brown | Tan | Brown |
| Green | Tan | Green/Gold | Brown | Brown | Green/Gold | Bronze | Natural | Brown |
|  | Green | Blue/Green | Green | Olive | Blue/Green | Brown | Brown | Brown |
| Brown | Red/Pink | Red/Brown | Brown | Brown | Red/Brown | Brown | Brown | Natural |
|  | Blue | Blue/Brown | Brown | Brown | Blue/Brown | Medium Brown | Camel | Brown |

* Produced by the American Institute of Men's and Boys' Wear.

Therefore, even in classic garments like jeans, the consumer should carefully select items of clothing not only for the end use but also for appropriateness in dress, whether for business, leisure, sports, or the college campus. Accessories, too, should be carefully selected, in order to create a harmonious ensemble.

**475**
Men's and Boys' Wear

## SELECTION OF MEN'S AND BOYS' FURNISHINGS

Men's wear may be classified as (1) men's clothing and (2) men's furnishings. A similar division may be made for boys' wear. Work clothing is often treated as a separate classification.

Men's and boys' furnishings are composed of similar articles, the chief of which are shirts, sleepwear, underwear, hosiery, robes, ties, handkerchiefs, belts, suspenders, garters, mufflers and scarfs, sweaters, and bathing suits. Men's jewelry (nontextiles), such as cuff links, studs, tie clips, and stickpins, are also commonly included in the classification.

Men's clothing includes garments such as suits, topcoats, overcoats, jackets, and slacks. Boys' clothing includes suits, topcoats, overcoats, jackets, and raincoats. With the emergence of fashion as a selling force, there are now more divisions of men's and boys' sections in department and specialty stores. Teen sportswear, and furnishings are becoming individual shops or boutiques—that is, sweater, slacks, swimwear, shirt shops. Furthermore, shops with a certain look—unisex, Edwardian, and Napoleonic —are created to satisfy the youth market, which demands a great variety in fashion merchandise.[2]

### STANDARD SIZES FOR BOYS' CLOTHING

The U.S. Agricultural Research Service has done some research on the sizes of boys' and girls' clothing. Thirty-six measurements of 147,088 boys and girls 4 to 17 years of age were made. From these data, the United States of America Standards Institute has formulated standard sizes of

[2] *Daily News Record*, September 13, 1968. Sec. 2.

Figure 17.1. Boy's three-button traditional gray suit tailored like his father's. Fabric is a light-weight sharkskin blend of Orlon acrylic fiber and wool. (*Photograph courtesy of E.I. du Pont de Nemours & Company, Inc.*)

clothing for boys from kindergarten to junior high school. To arrive at these standard sizes the committee of the Institute chose height and hip measurements. The committee felt that (1) hips are better than the chest as an indicator of the other girth measurements, (2) the hips can be more accurately measured than the chest, and (3) a tape measure is the only equipment needed to make these two measurements.

The following table gives seven standard body sizes as set up by the U.S.A. Standards.

| HEIGHT (inches) | GIRTH (HIPS) (inches) | AVERAGE AGE (years) |
|---|---|---|
| 43 | 22½ | 5½ |
| 45½ | 23 | 6½ |
| 47½ | 24 | 7½ |
| 50 | 25 | 8½ |
| 52 | 26 | 9½ |
| 54½ | 27½ | 10½ |
| 57 | 28½ | 12 |

These standard sizes should make shopping easier for parents, and should lessen the number of return goods. Manufacturers should find them advantageous in making better-fitting children's garments. Mail-order catalogues give measurements of height in inches, and average, slim, and husky chest and waist measurements to facilitate ordering the proper size to fit. (See *infants', toddlers', and tots' sizes*, Chapter 16.)

## SHIRTS

Shirts may be classified according to the occasion for which they are worn: (1) dress (tailored garments worn with a necktie for business, street, and semiformal wear), (2) work, (3) sports, and (4) formal.

Dress shirts are usually all white, solid colored, or striped. For work shirts, khaki, dark blue, or black are common colors. Sports shirts may be white, solid colored, plaids, stripes, or checks.

### SIZES IN DRESS SHIRTS

Men's dress shirt sizes run 14 to 17 (neckband measurement). Men who cannot wear standard sizes should buy custom-made shirts. Sleeve lengths come in sizes 32 to 36. Boys' sizes run 3, 4, 5, 6, and 8, 10, 12, 14, 16, 18, 20. Sleeve lengths are usually identified as long or short.

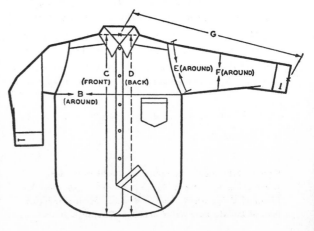

**Figure 17.2.** Commercial standards for men's shirt sizes call for minimum dimensions in five areas that are important for comfort and appearance. (*Reproduced courtesy of Consumers' Research, Inc.*)

Cotton shirtings come under F.T.C. rules for shrinkage. (See p. 165.) That is, if the words "preshrunk" or "full-shrunk" are used, they mean that the fabric will not shrink further. If there is a possibility of residual shrinkage, then the per cent to be expected must be stated. It is advisable to buy a half size larger shirt if the residual shrinkage is over 1 per cent. For shirts marked "Sanforized" this advice is unnecessary.

Standard commercial sizes for men's shirts, as agreed upon by the trade and published by the National Bureau of Standards, are found in the following table:

## STANDARD MINIMUM MEASUREMENTS FOR MEN'S SHIRTS

(ALL MEASUREMENTS ARE IN INCHES)

| | | | | | | | | |
|---|---|---|---|---|---|---|---|---|
| Stamped neckband sizes ............ | (A) | 14 | 14½ | 15 | 15½ | 16 | 16½ | 17 |
| Chest, total circumference .......... | (B) | 42 | 44 | 46 | 48 | 50 | 52 | 54 |
| Front, length of .................. | (C) | 33 | 33 | 33 | 33 | 33 | 33 | 33 |
| Back, length of ................... | (D) | 33 | 33 | 33 | 33 | 33 | 33 | 33 |
| Armholes, length around curve ...... | (E) | 19½ | 20 | 20½ | 21 | 21½ | 22 | 22½ |
| Sleeve, width around ............... | (F) | 14¾ | 15¼ | 15¾ | 16¼ | 16¾ | 17¼ | 17¾ |

### STYLES IN DRESS SHIRTS

Collars in spread, tab, or button-down styles are usually attached to the body of the shirt, Shirts may have a single or a pleated closing that buttons down the front. Cuffs may be single (barrel), French (double), or convertible (buttons in addition to buttonholes for cuff links).

### FABRICS FOR DRESS SHIRTS

All-cotton or polyester and cotton blends are commonly used for broadcloth shirtings. Broadcloth and oxford are staple fabrics for dress shirts. Best-quality domestic broadcloth is made of 2 x 2 combed pima cotton with a count of 144 x 76, mercerized, and shrinkage controlled. Poorer grades may have the following weaknesses: 2 x 1 (two-ply warp and single filling) or single carded yarns in both warp and filling; a count as low as 100 x 56; little or no mercerization; preshrunk fabric with residual shrinkage declared. Oxford shirting is identified by its

**Figure 17.3.** Styles in men's dress shirts. For high fashion sportswear, variations have been made in the length and width of the points and spread of the collar. *(Reproduced courtesy of Montgomery Ward & Co., Inc.)*

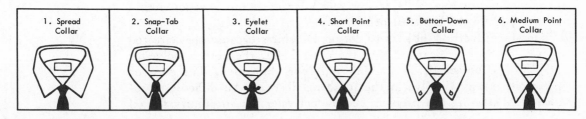

| 1. Spread Collar | 2. Snap–Tab Collar | 3. Eyelet Collar | 4. Short Point Collar | 5. Button–Down Collar | 6. Medium Point Collar |

basket weave in 2 x 2 or 2 x 1. The latter is more common and is less
expensive to construct, but 2 x 2 should wear better and keep its size
and shape better because of its balanced count.

Chambray, a staple yarn-dyed fabric with colored warp and white
filling is also suitable for dress shirts. In better grades are found yarns
single and combed, a balanced count 84 x 76, and shrinkage control.
Tricot, in 100 per cent polyester or 80 per cent polyester/20 per cent
cotton, is quick drying and has minimum-care properties.

## REQUIREMENTS FOR GOOD WORKMANSHIP

To insure good wearing quality, a dress shirt's seams should be stitched
firmly but should not pucker (fourteen to eighteen close, even stitches
to the inch). Buttons (ocean pearl in better grades because they do not
melt as plastic buttons do) should be stitched firmly; buttonholes should
be evenly cut and firmly bound; collar points should be even, sharp, and
neatly sewn. Double needle (two rows of stitching) is stronger than
single needle.

## APPEARANCE AND COMFORT

In addition to size and good workmanship, the careful buyer is
generally interested in the appearance of the shirt, its comfort, durability, launderability, and suitability. The customer looks for style, color,
and cleanness (even the neatness of the cellophane wrapping). A shiny
cotton surface created by mercerization is more attractive and easier to
care for than a dull, fuzzy surface. For comfort, a shirt should be cut
full across the chest. Boys and stout men, especially, need full-cut shirts.
Length of sleeves and size of armholes also affect comfort.

Men are frequently exasperated because shirts do not stay tucked in
after they have been washed; the shirt tail has shrunk. Shrinkage, already
discussed in connection with size, is a major consideration if a garment
is purchased for comfort.

A large proportion of men's dress shirts are durable press (DP). In
fact, all twelve shirts offered by a large mail-order house are durable
press. The 100 per cent cotton DP shirts have an advantage over blends
in that cotton white shirts, being opaque, are whiter; they are also more
comfortable, since they absorb perspiration more readily. However,
cotton DP white shirts are subject to yellowing; they also have reduced
wear qualities owing to the loss of tensile strength and abrasion resistance caused by the DP treatment.

One manufacturer objects to cotton DP shirts because they are too
heavy for his specifications. On the other hand, the cotton/polyester
DP shirt is subject to oil staining and odor absorption. The odor of
perspiration may dissolve in the synthetic fiber and be difficult to remove. Oil staining is a problem because polyester has an affinity for oil

and does not release it readily. The textile industry is attempting three methods to solve these problems: (1) the development of special finishes to prevent staining; (2) the formulation of special finishes to permit easy removal of oily stains; and (3) the development of more effective cleaning agents.[3]

### STYLE AND SUITABILITY TO USE

For young boys, a long shirt that will stay tucked into the pants is appropriate. School-age boys should wear shirts with tails or polo shirts sufficiently long to allow an active child to stoop over easily. Convertible collars and open-neck styles with short sleeves are appropriate for a growing boy.

Boys' shirts sizes 6 to 20 are usually tailored like men's, with tab or pointed collars, tailored fronts, fullness at center back, and barrel-style cuffs. A few details in tailoring may be omitted from these shirts. Suitability of material and style of cut determine the use of a shirt.

Work shirts, for utility wear, are made of sturdy fabrics, such as mercerized cotton twill, polished cotton, a blend of 65 per cent Dacron polyester and 35 per cent pima cotton poplin, blends of 17 per cent nylon and 83 per cent cotton twill, all-cotton chino, 65 per cent Dacron polyester and 35 per cent combed cotton gabardine, all-cotton denim, and all-cotton drill. The emphasis in selecting work shirts should be suitability rather than style. Nowadays the work shirt is not unattractive, because collar styles may be those of the dress shirt or convertible sport shirt with lined collar. The work shirt with the collar style of a dress shirt may be worn with a tie. For comfort, shirts usually have long tails that stay tucked in. Sleeves may be long or short, and sizes are based on the neckband.

Although sport shirts vary in style, a common feature is that they are made to be worn without a tie. They may or may not have a collar and may have either short or long sleeves. Since sport shirts are intended for active sports and for casual wear, a comfortable, easy-to-care-for

[3] *Consumer Bulletin* (September 1967).

**Figure 17.4.** Knitted shirts of Dacron polyester and cotton photographed at the Acropolis, Athens, Greece. Their look is like woven fabrics with the comfort of knitted constructions. (*Courtesy of du Pont Textile Fibers Department.*)

fabric is suitable. In general, sport shirt fabrics are classified as knitted or woven. Knitted constructions include jersey and various types of fancy knits and meshes of cotton, acrylic, nylon, and blends. Woven fabrics may include cotton jean, flannel (wool or cotton and blends with synthetics), cotton cord, chambray, gingham, broadcloth, corduroy, and blends of Dacron polyester and cotton, cotton and rayon, cotton and triacetate, and others. Sizes include small (14- to 14½-inch neck), medium (15 to 15½), large (16 to 16½), and extra large (17 to 17½).

Sweat shirts may be classified as a kind of sport shirt that is pulled on to protect the body from sudden chill. They may be pullover or coat style—of cotton terry cloth, fleece-lined cotton knit, or a smooth cotton print. Cardigan and sweater shirt sets, sweat shirts and jackets, or sweat pants are worn for sports. The terry-cloth-lined jacket or all-cotton printed jacket may constitute a set of jacket and shorts worn on the beach. Trunks of this set, which usually match the jacket, may be made of spandex, nylon stretch yarn, Lastex, cotton gabardine, and all-nylon woven fabric with elastic waist and knit support. (A few words might be appropriate here about comfort in choosing swimming trunks. The garment should not cramp the swimmer's movement, yet should give support; it should dry quickly and have colors that are fast to light, to salt water, and to chlorine in pools. Sizes of trunks are based on waist measurement.)

Shirts for formal wear are usually pleated or plain, with a starched or soft bosom depending on the current mode. Fabrics include piqué, broadcloth, silk or synthetic-fibered crepe, and blends.

### DURABILITY

The durability of a shirt is determined by the grade of fabric (judged according to the quality of the fibers, yarns, weaves, and finishing processes).

Workmanship also affects durability. Stitching and buttons have been discussed under requirements for good workmanship. In addition, the following tips will help the consumer find satisfaction in purchasing shirts:

1. Stripes or patterns in sport shirts should match at seams.
2. A center pleat ensures a good anchorage for buttons.
3. A shirt with six or seven buttons stays tucked in better than one with five.
4. A band inside the collar is highly desirable.
5. Thread should match the predominant color of the shirt.
6. Wide seams and reinforcements increase the length of life of a shirt.
7. Everyday shirts and work shirts for men and boys should be made with a button fastening at the cuff to avoid the inconvenience of cuff links.

8. The lining materials should be shrunk to the same extent as the shirt fabric so that the collar will stay flat after laundering.

## EASE IN LAUNDERING

Ease in laundering is also a factor in durability. Single-cuffed shirts are easier to iron than those with double cuffs, but the latter are usually more durable. For traveling, the white polyester and cotton and the resin-finished or cross-linked finished cotton shirts are popular among men. They can be washed in a lavatory at night, hung to drip dry, and worn without ironing the next morning. (See Chapters 7 and 15.) Since the collars and cuffs of shirts of polyester/cotton blends soil more quickly than the body of the shirt, a small nail brush can be used effectively to apply soap solution to soiled areas. Sometimes a ring around the collar cannot be entirely removed by this method. One needs a soil-release technique with polyester/cotton blends with durable press finishes. As recommended in Chapter 15, soaking the shirt in an enzyme product for thirty minutes or overnight will break down or digest into small particles (by chemical means) the various kinds of organic matter—protein, starch, etc.

## BRAND

Some men prefer to buy a shirt of a familiar nationally known brand. Although there may be a lesser-known brand that is more suited to their needs, some men refuse to switch from a brand to which they have become accustomed. Among the national brands are Arrow, Van Heusen, Manhattan, Marlboro, Truval, National, A.M.C., Towncraft (J. C. Penney), and Pilgrim (Sears).

## PRICE

Price is often a major consideration, in selecting a shirt. In a college class of adults taught by the author,[4] it was found that the men in the class placed the factors of color and collar style first. For the women, however, collar style and *price* were first considerations in buying a man's shirt.

## NECKTIES

There are two main styles in men's ties: the formal and the informal. Formal ties include the bow ties, which may be tied by hand or ready-tied, four-in-hand ties, and Ascots or scarf ties, the ends of which, being tied once, are crossed in front and fastened with a scarf pin. The bow

[4] A class at the New York University School of Continuing Education, titled "Fashion Fabrics in Apparel and Home Furnishings."

tie is worn for formal occasions with dinner jackets and with full dress, and also with business attire. When fashion decrees, ascots are for formal or semiformal morning or afternoon wear with a cutaway or frock coat. Informal ties are usually four-in-hands with pointed or straight ends.

In addition to the style and suitability of a tie, the durability of the material and the workmanship are important. The fibers, yarns, weave, and finishing processes affect the wearing quality.

As for workmanship, the two types of construction are resilient and rigid. The tie with resilient construction is sewn by machine with long, basting-like stitches that allow greater elasticity in tying than do the short, rather tight machine stitches of the rigid construction. The rigid type are inexpensive ties. To determine whether a tie has a resilient construction, grasp it with thumb and forefinger of each hand, pull it gently in opposite directions along the length of the tie, and note whether it gives. Other points to consider in workmanship are the stitching along the edge and the evenness of the hems.

A tie made of a fabric cut on the bias will hold its shape better than one cut on the straight of the material. If the outer fabric is cut on the bias, the lining should be cut on the bias too. Also, a tie that is lined with wool has greater elasticity and therefore holds its shape longer than one that is lined with cotton. A well-made tie has four or five folds at the broad end. A tie with facing at the ends has an improved appearance because no stitching shows.

Ties made from woven goods stay tied better than those made from knitted fabrics. There is less slippage of the knot, especially in the case of rayon knit. Knitted ties wear well and do not wrinkle.

Rayon, acetate, cotton, and weighted silk wrinkle badly, and the wrinkles do not hang out. Wool and pure silk are excellent as tie fabrics, because they are wrinkle-resistant and resilient. Dacron polyester, which is both resilient and spot-resistant, makes a good tie fabric.

## SWEATERS

Many customers are interested in style when they buy a sweater. The two classic styles for men as well as women are the pullover, which pulls over the head and generally has no buttons but may have a short zipper, and the cardigan, which fastens down the front, generally with buttons or a zipper. The pullover with sleeves is more popular than the sleeveless variety, although the latter is often preferred under jackets or coats. Necklines of the pullover may be V-shaped, round, boat, turtle, or crew. Sizes are 36 to 46. The cardigan may be made with or without a shawl collar and two lower pockets.

Sweaters are made in smooth and in bulky, shaggy, hairy, and nubbed textures. The former are more comfortable under a jacket, whereas the latter are particularly suited to sportswear.

Patterns in sweaters are created by variations in the knitted stitch and by color contrast in body, collars, and cuffs. The three classic stitches for sweaters are (1) jumbo, a coarse stitch with large, heavy yarn; (2) gauze, a close stitch with fine, thin yarn; and (3) shaker knit, a weight between jumbo and gauze. Other knitted stitches include interlock, links, cable, waffle, pineapple, fisherman's knit, and bulky rib. Sweaters are made of all wool or all cashmere, all cotton, 100 per cent Orlon or Acrilan acrylic, textured nylon, and blends of 75 per cent wool and 25 per cent mohair. (See *women's sweaters*, Chapter 16.)

## UNDERWEAR

Garments sold in men's and boys' underwear departments include T-shirts, undershirts, drawers, shorts, briefs, and union suits (knitted one-piece garments with sleeves and legs in varied lengths).

The most popular styles in underwear for men and boys are undershirts or T-shirts and shorts or briefs. Although union suits, shirts, and drawers are staple items in the underwear department, they are usually purchased by the older man who lives in a climate of cold winters.

For boys, T-shirts and undershirts come in sizes 2 and 4 and in sizes small (6 to 8), medium (10 to 12), and large (14 to 16). Some size ranges run to 20. T-shirt and undershirt sizes for men are small (34 to 36), medium (38 to 40), large (42 to 44), and extra large (46 to 52).

For underwear, the factor of comfort is very important.[5] Probably the coolest garments for summer are the separate shirt and shorts. Unless the shorts are just the right size at the waist, however, they may slip out of place. A wide Lastex waistband improves posture and keeps the abdomen firm. If the seat is not cut large enough, shorts may be uncomfortable; garments cut especially full at the crotch overcome this objection.

Styles in men's woven shorts are (1) boxer, which has an all-around elastic waist and (2) yoke, which has a snap fastener and elastic inserts in the waist. Sizes, based on waist measurement, run in even numbers 28 to 44. These garments are commonly made of cotton or cotton and polyester blends in broadcloth or percale. Many have wash-and-wear features.

Briefs are knitted articles of underwear of rib-knitted cotton or Dacron polyester and cotton flat knit. A nylonized finish on combed cotton adds strength and wear; a sanitized finish gives hygienic protection. The better qualities are made of cotton yarns like Durene, which is combed, two ply, mercerized for strength and luster, highly absorbent,

[5] American Standard Performance Requirements for Textile Fabrics (L22) include minimum standards for dimensional change and shrinkage of shirtings, pajamas, underwear, neckties, handkerchiefs, beachwear, rainwear, dressing gowns, bathrobes, slacks, woven suiting, woven lining, work clothing, and trouser and jacket fabrics.

and sanitized to check perspiration odor and to arrest growth of bacteria. A durable blend is 80 per cent cotton and 20 per cent nylon.

Support briefs may be made of 94 per cent combed cotton and 6 per cent spandex, with a belt of 64 per cent acetate, 28 per cent rayon, and 8 per cent spandex. A reinforced double crotch and front-panel reinforced seams, nonbinding bound elasticized leg openings, and elastic waistband are considerations in comfort and wear. Sizes in briefs are also by waist measurement.

Probably the most comfortable underwear is made of a knitted fabric, because it gives with movements of the body. It is especially suitable for athletics. Some men prefer a short cap sleeve in knitted undershirts to protect the outer shirt from perspiration. Since cotton absorbs perspiration better than silk, rayon, or nylon, many men prefer cotton for underwear in all climates. Both woolen and worsted yarns can be used in knit underwear. The woolen yarn is soft and pliable and makes a good napped or fleecy surface. Worsted yarn is smooth and lustrous and makes a fine, even, smooth-knitted structure. Wool knitted underwear is very warm.

Knit underwear ventilates the skin. It keeps the body warm in winter and cool in summer; fits the body smoothly without binding; and is easily washed and needs no ironing.

Rayon and nylon yarns, which are often used in combination with another textile to give it luster, may be used alone in lightweight underwear. These yarns, incidentally, are most attractive in white and pastel shades. One hundred per cent nylon knitted underwear, although it is very strong and quick drying, does not absorb perspiration. Nylon thread can be used for sewing seams of underwear because of its great strength. Rayon underwear is inexpensive, is very cool in summer, and, in good grades, washes and wears well. The knitted rayons are apt to drop stitches if they are hung by clothespins to dry. A knitted fabric made of a mixture of cotton (75 per cent) and Merino wool (25 per cent) is comfortable. Since the wool, buried between two layers of cotton,[6] does not touch the skin, the underwear does not cause itching.

In winter, quilted or thermal Raschel knits are often worn for sports. The quilted type may consist of jacket and drawers made with a cotton shell, modacrylic batting, and cotton interlining. This set is being made flame-retardant. The Raschel knits are 100 per cent cotton; or 75 per cent cotton/25 per cent Acrilan acrylic. Heavy stretch thermal knits may be 94 per cent cotton/6 per cent spandex.

Launderability is an important factor in underwear. Both wash-and-wear cotton and the noncellulose synthetics are easy to care for and require little or no pressing. The synthetics have the added advantage of drying quickly, but some men say that their fibers feel clammy because they do not have the absorptive quality of cotton.

---

[6] This fabric is Innerwool by the William Carter Company.

Men want socks to fit well and above all to wear well. A comfortable sock is soft, fits smoothly over the instep, ankle, and heel, does not pinch the toes, does not slip or roll down, and is smooth on the sole of the foot. There are two main styles in men's socks: (1) dress for street wear and (2) socks for sport. Each style comes in lengths that vary from just below the knee to just above the ankle. The sock for street wear, which is more conservative than the sports type, usually comes in solid colors in stockinette or rib knit. Clocks and small patterns often enhance it. Regular knitted men's sock sizes usually run 9, $9\frac{1}{2}$, 10, $10\frac{1}{2}$, 11, $11\frac{1}{2}$, 12, $12\frac{1}{2}$, 13. In stretch hosiery the small size fits $9\frac{1}{2}$, 10, $10\frac{1}{2}$; regular, fits 11, $11\frac{1}{2}$, 12; and large, fits 13 and 14. In boys' socks, sizes in regular styles run, 7, $7\frac{1}{2}$, 8, $8\frac{1}{2}$, 9, $9\frac{1}{2}$, 10, $10\frac{1}{2}$. They also come in stretch type.

Sports socks may be described as (1) crew (bulky rib-knit white fabric with elastic top, or white socks with or without blazer stripes at the top); (2) argyle, with the familiar Jacquard plaid pattern; (3) novelty, with varied designs and colors; and (4) thermal, for winter, made of stretch nylon outside (lined with 50 per cent Herculon olefin/50 per cent cotton), or 80 per cent worsted wool/20 per cent stretch nylon.

For comfort and wear, a sanitized finish inhibits germ growth, which helps feet to stay fresh longer. A nylon-reinforced heel and toe are desirable features. (A blend of heavyweight cotton 90 per cent and 10 per cent nylon, 70 per cent nylon/30 per cent cotton inside for comfort, or 100 per cent stretch nylon wear well.) Support dress hosiery can be made of 93 per cent textured nylon and 7 per cent spandex.

Ingrain-dyed (yarn-dyed) color is a selling point. Bulky Orlon acrylic blends that feel woolly and are shrink-resistant are suitable for sportswear. Also, a 50 per cent lamb's wool and 50 per cent nylon blend and an 80 per cent wool and 20 per cent stretch nylon are appropriate. (See *stretch yarn,* Chapter 3.)

Tops of socks are frequently made of spandex yarn in rib knit. Since these yarns keep the sock from slipping, the wearer need not use garters. Hosiery that gives support is commonly made of Helanca stretch nylon yarn.

## SLEEPWEAR

Just as men seek comfort in underwear, they also want comfort in sleeping garments. If a garment feels smooth and soft, if it is easy to put on and take off, and if it has a full cut and smooth seams, it will generally prove comfortable.

Probably the next most important consideration in sleepwear is durability, which includes launderability. Shrinkage of less than 5 per cent is considered satisfactory. Durable press is a valued selling point. For some men the appearance of the garment is more important than comfort or durability. In such cases, decoration, trimming, or quality of workmanship are noticed.

Pajamas generally include a coat-style or pullover (middy) top and trousers. Small children often wear the same styles as grown-ups, or they may wear one piece, sometimes with feet attached. The separate coat is buttoned down the front, whereas the pullover needs no front closing. The trousers are fastened at the waist with an elastic band or drawstring. For summer, short-length pajama pants and short sleeves are comfortable. For winter, two-piece pajamas made in ski-suit style (with elastic waist and fitted wristlets and anklets) are warm. Other styles include the cossack, with stand-up collar; the tunic, with shaping at the waist and a slight flare at the bottom; and the knee-length sleep coat.

Pajamas are made of the following materials:

| | |
|---|---|
| Balbriggan (See Glossary, Chapter 16) | Knitted jersey |
| Broadcloth | Mesh |
| Chambray | Nylon tricot |
| Cotton crepe (for young boys) | Oxford cloth |
| Flannelette | Percale (printed) |
| Jacquard silk or synthetic | Pongee (silk and man-made fibers) |

The sizes in men's pajamas are indicated by the letters *A, B, C, D.* These sizes are limited because pajamas do not have to be so form-fitting as underwear. Size *A* generally fits a 34 or smaller; *B,* a 34 to 36; *C,* a 38 to 40; and *D,* a 42 to 44. Size *E* is an oversize. In sizes *B, C,* and *D* extra lengths can be procured.

In recent years pajamas have become popular for lounging. The lounging type, generally made of luxurious materials, such as silk, rayon, or the new synthetics, has more ornamentation than the sleeping pajamas. Such fabrics as satin, corduroy, Jacquard, nylon or silk tricot, and crepe are also used.

## LOUNGING ROBES, JACKETS, AND BATHROBES

If a man is interested primarily in appearance as opposed to comfort, he will generally purchase a lounging robe rather than a bathrobe. Both garments serve almost the same purpose. In a lounging robe a man expects a good-looking fabric, the latest style of cut, rich coloring, and excellent workmanship. Lounging robes are usually made of silk, acetate or rayon brocade, or flannel, trimmed with satin or velvet. Jackets, shorter than robes, are made of the same fabrics as lounging robes. Most bathrobes are made of beacon or blanket cloth (a cotton double cloth in blanket colors), flannelette (especially for boys), corduroy, terry cloth, and flannel. The sizes in robes run small, medium, large and extra large.

## HANDKERCHIEFS

Handkerchiefs for men may be classified as monogram, plain white, and fancy (colored handkerchiefs with patterns). High-quality handkerchiefs that are made of pure linen (Belgian or Irish) and have fine line yarns are called *linen lawn* or *handkerchief linen*. The count of cloth is high and well balanced (sometimes as high as 1200). The hems are usually hand-rolled (hand-stitched). A handkerchief may be labeled "pure Irish linen," yet may not be the best quality from the standpoint of yarn, weave, and workmanship. (It may be hemstitched instead of hand-rolled.) Linen (55 per cent) and cotton (45 per cent) in a blend, or 65 per cent polyester/35 per cent cotton, are commonly used for handkerchiefs. If fibers, yarns, construction, and workmanship are good, the article may be higher quality than a poor grade of all linen. The United States imports cotton handkerchiefs from Switzerland that are long-stapled Egyptian cotton, combed yarn, closely woven, and mercerized with hand-rolled edges. They can be sold at the same retail price as pure Irish linen that is not of the best grade. Some handkerchiefs are made of combed domestic cotton yarn that is sent to the Philippines to be woven, finished, cut, and sewn, and then is shipped back to this country. Such merchandise constitutes the low end of the price scale for serviceable goods. Pure Italian silk handkerchiefs are sold for decorative use only. They are more expensive than a good grade of pure linen.

Sizes of handkerchiefs vary from 17-inch squares to 19-inch squares. Bandanas (vivid printed cottons) are generally 18-inch squares, or 24 by 22 inches.

## BELTS

Although most belts are made of leather or a nontextile plastic, some are made of a heavy cotton called *belting*, which is made with very heavy fillingwise ribs or cords. Belting may also have silk or nylon running one way to cover the cords. Fancy belts are made of cord in knitted or crocheted effects. Some belts are made of the same material as the slacks.

Belts differ in the kind of material used and also in length, width, shape (some are curved at the side), color, and design (of buckle as well as material).

## SUSPENDERS AND GARTERS

Suspenders are made of plastic or webbing of very strong yarn, with a core of rubber in the warp yarns. The rubber affords the necessary give. The weave is the rib weave, the ribs running warpwise. A strong webbing is made of lisle yarns (mercerized cotton with a tight twist). Silk, rayon, or nylon may also be used in webbing.

"Invisible suspenders," which are worn under the shirt, are generally made of narrower white webbing.

The older boy may wear men's suspenders. Smaller boys may wear narrow elastic suspenders that clip onto the pants. Suspenders are made in two lengths: the regular (thirty-eight inches long) and the extra-long (forty-two inches).

Garters are also made of webbing, in cotton, silk, rayon, or nylon. There is a very limited demand for garters, even by older men, because most socks now have elastic or spandex ribbing at the tops and because many men feel that garters restrict circulation. However, those who wear garters prefer wide webbing, because it will not slip down the leg as will the narrow webbing. Color may also be a factor to consider. Also, the fastener should be one that will stay fastened; it should be firmly stitched, so that it will not come off. Some garters have double grips. Most present-day garters allow no metal to touch the skin.

### NECKWEAR AND GLOVES

The scarf, thrown around the neck and crossed at the front, is worn under the coat. Scarfs may be long and narrow or square. For formal wear, luxurious fabrics of silk, rayon, acetate, nylon, and polyester are used. Wool flannel, knitted wool, cashmere, and blends are warm for winter wear. Lighter-weight scarfs are made of surah, twills, and crepe in silk or synthetics.

When buying a scarf, a man thinks of warmth and weight, color and design, grade of material, workmanship (including hemming, fringe, and embroidery), size, and use.

Cotton and wool knitted gloves are suitable for sportswear when warmth is important. They come in varied colors, in sizes medium and large. While leather is more popular than fabric gloves, sometimes fabric is combined with leather in gloves used for driving. A wool knit may line a leather glove. Mittens, sized like gloves, are in much less demand in men's wear but are particularly suited for small children.

### HATS

For men who wear hats, fur felt made with wool is the traditionally accepted material for everyday wear. (See *felting*, Chapter 6.) Fur felt is made of Australian rabbit, nutria, and beaver blends. Widths of the brim and bands, the height and width of the hat, and the tapering of the crown vary according to style.

Straw is traditionally worn from May 15 to September 15. While for formal wear, a man may wear a Homburg, bowler, or derby, a top hat is seldom worn except for very formal state occasions. For casual country wear, there has been considerable use of fabric hats of tweed, velour, corduroy, or blend of 90 per cent wool/10 per cent nylon knit. The visored cap of tweed, corduroy, flannel, or twilled cotton is adapted to sightseeing and to sportswear.

Very small boys wear brimmed fabric hats of wool or cotton with or without earlaps. For play in mild weather boys may wear cotton caps with or without visors, and for dress-up they may wear a flannel Eton style. Older boys often go hatless except in cold weather, when they may pull the hood of a parka or jacket over the head or may don a bulky knitted cap.

Men's hat and cap sizes run $6\frac{3}{4}$, $6\frac{7}{8}$, $7$, $7\frac{1}{8}$, $7\frac{1}{4}$, $7\frac{3}{8}$, $7\frac{1}{2}$. To determine a boy's hat size, one should measure straight around the head above the ears.

| If Head Measures | Boy Wears Size |
|---|---|
| $19\frac{1}{8}''$ | $6\frac{1}{8}$ |
| $19\frac{1}{2}''$ | $6\frac{1}{4}$ |
| $19\frac{7}{8}''$ | $6\frac{3}{8}$ |
| $20\frac{1}{4}''$ | $6\frac{1}{2}$ |
| $20\frac{3}{4}''$ | $6\frac{5}{8}$ |
| $21\frac{1}{8}''$ | $6\frac{3}{4}$ |
| $21\frac{1}{2}''$ | $6\frac{7}{8}$ |
| $21\frac{7}{8}''$ | $7$ |
| $22\frac{1}{4}''$ | $7\frac{1}{8}$ |
| $22\frac{5}{8}''$ | $7\frac{1}{4}$ |

## SELECTION OF MEN'S AND BOYS' SUITS

Although men actually buy their suits, women often have much to say when a selection is made. Women do most of the buying of boys' clothing. A surprising fact is that the average woman does not know a tweed from a Shetland.

### TYPES OF SUITINGS

A knowledge of men's suitings can be quickly acquired if one learns the identifying features of 100 per cent wool suitings first, since wool was, until recently the major fiber used for suits. Wool suitings were named according to (1) the geographical source of the raw wool (Shetland, Cheviot, Harris, and Donegal tweed), (2) the original use of a fabric (cavalry twill, covert—to ride to covert, to the hunt), or (3) the finish (mill-finished worsted—slightly napped surface, or hard-finished worsted—no nap). Now that there are blends of polyester and acrylic fibers with wool, the consumer, knowing the name of the all-wool fabric, should have little or no difficulty in identifying the name of a blended fabric, because the names have not changed with the advent of blends.

As mentioned previously, there are two main types of wool fabrics: woolens and worsteds. (See Chapter 12.) Generally speaking, woolens are made of fibers of varied lengths averaging less than two inches. The yarns are carded and are rather rough, and the finishing is customarily done by fulling and then brushing up a nap (it may be sheared). Worsteds are usually made of fibers more than two inches long (all the short fibers have been removed). The yarns are carded and combed, and are even and smooth; the finishing consists of mending, scouring, shearing, and pressing. (See Figures 17.5 and 17.6.) Only unfinished and semifinished worsteds are fulled and slightly napped.

All wool suitings, then, fall into the woolen or the worsted classifications. The main difference between woolens and worsteds lies in the kinds of fibers that are used. For example, coarse fibers make coarse yarn and coarse cloth; fine fibers make fine cloth. Wool from the Australian Merino sheep is usually very fine. Following is a list of the common fabrics for men's and boys' suits, classified as woolens and worsteds. This classification should be memorized:

| WOOLEN SUITINGS | WORSTED SUITINGS |
|---|---|
| Homespun | Hard-finished |
| Tweed | Tropical |
| Wool cheviot | Gabardine |
| Wool covert | Elastique |
| Shetland | Sharkskin |
| Wool flannel | Worsted covert |
| Wool broadcloth | Semifinished |
| | Serge |
| | Worsted cheviot |
| | Unfinished |
| | Worsted flannel |
| | Unfinished worsted |

## WOOLENS

A discussion of the fabrics will reveal their distinguishing characteristics. The woolen materials will be discussed in the order of their weight

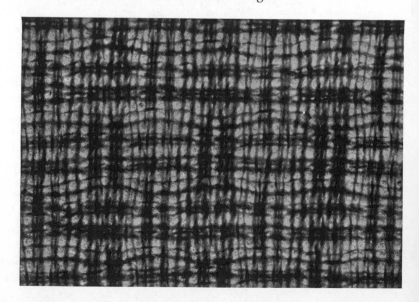

**Figure 17.5. Woolen suiting.**

and coarseness of texture, beginning with homespun. Of course, each of the fabrics is made in different grades, so that one cannot generalize on the wearing quality of one fabric over another unless similar grades of each are compared. For instance, a poor grade of tweed may not wear as well as an excellent grade of Shetland.

1. *Homespun* was originally spun and woven by hand by cottagers in their own homes. Now most of this material is made by machinery in coarse rough textures that resemble the hand-woven goods. Homespun is woven in plain weave (as distinguished from tweed in twill) and is characterized by small bumps, called *knicker-bockers,* in various colors. Homespun is heavier in weight and is coarser than tweed.

2. *Tweeds* are erroneously associated with the Tweed River in Scotland. This large group of wool fabrics was originally known as *twills* or (in Scotland) *tweels.* When used for men's wear, tweeds are characteristically rather wiry but flexible; they are woven in twill construction from heavy, rough yarns of two or more different colors. The first tweeds, made of wool from the Scotch black-faced sheep, were woven by hand. Interesting mixtures are obtained if yarns are dyed in different colors before they are woven. In this way the colors of the brackens and moors of Scotland are reproduced. Wools from the fine breeds of sheep of the Cheviot Hills of England and Scotland may be used for the Bannockburn tweeds, so named after the town of that name in Scotland. These are made of two-ply yarns formed by two single yarns of different colors.

   Harris tweed originated in the Isle of Harris and other islands in the Hebrides group. Hand-woven and dyed with color pigments that were cooked over peat fires by the cottagers, these fabrics had a distinctive odor when the fabric was warm and moist. Today the tweeds from these islands are identifiable by the label "Harris Tweed," which is required as a protective device by the British association of that name.

   For women's wear, tweeds are made in twills, basket, plain, and novelty constructions. If closely woven tweeds are durable but poorly constructed, they are likely to slip at the seams.

3. *Wool cheviot,* made in woolen and worsted, has a name derived from the Cheviot sheep, whose wool provided the yarn of which wool cheviots were originally made. Now most wool cheviots are made of the wool of Cheviot sheep that have been crossbred with fine Australian or New Zealand Merino sheep. Wool cheviots have no appreciable nap and may have interesting woven-in designs in variations of the twill weave. Wool cheviot is made in fine grades, but the lower grades are more common because they furnish interesting patterns at a moderate price.

4. *Wool covert,* made in woolen and worsted, originated in England, where it derived its name from riding to covert in fox hunting. It was an appropriate fabric because its smooth surface did not catch on brambles. When introduced in this country it was first used in topcoats; it has been more recently used in suits and slacks. Covert is generally characterized by a nap finish with a steep twill weave. Worsted covert is semifinished with a very little nap. When it is more heavily napped, it is called *doeskin.* Venetian covert has a smooth finish with the nap practically covering the twill weave.

5. *Shetland cloth* is attractive. The Shetland sheep of the Shetland Islands off Scotland produce the finest wool fiber that we have. In fact, it is so fine that it must be mixed with other wool fibers to give satisfactory wear. Shetland resembles tweed in its general appearance; it is a twill weave but has a softer touch. Tweed is heavier and more closely constructed. Shetland has a great deal of give, which is due to the looseness of the weave. Accordingly, this cloth does not hold its shape very well.

6. *Flannel,* made in woolen and worsted, is one of the most attractive materials for suits. It is generally made from Merino wool; the yarns are loosely spun and loosely woven. The fabric is fulled, or felted, before a heavy nap is raised. The twill weave is almost obliterated by the thick nap. One of the best grades is called *Saxony flannel,* because it originated in Saxony. Very soft, fine, and luxurious, it is generally expensive.

7. *Wool broadcloth,* as described under women's fabrics, is common for men's dinner jackets, and dress suits. It is not very different from flannel, but the nap is silkier (the result of steam lustering) and is usually pressed one way.

## WORSTEDS

Worsted suiting materials may be classified according to whether they have a clear or hard surface, a softer surface, or a smoother, softer-napped surface. Worsteds with clear surfaces are hard-finished worsteds; those with softer surfaces are semifinished or mill-finished worsteds; those with softer-napped surfaces are unfinished worsteds.

1. *Hard-finished worsted,* made of hard-twisted yarns, has no nap. Its surface is so smooth and hard that it becomes shiny rather quickly. Since the twill weave is clearly visible, this cloth is called clear-finished worsted. It wears exceptionally well and is comparatively inexpensive. So-called twists come in this category. Other worsteds in this type include:

   (*a*) *Tropical worsted.* For summer and southern wear, tropical worsted has been popular for many years. It is made of a lightweight, tightly twisted worsted yarn with two-ply warp and single- or two-ply filling. It is woven in a plain weave so that it is porous. Poorer grades are made with cotton warps and worsted fillings. The surface is clear and hard, with no nap.

Summer suits are usually made of an unnapped material loosely woven to let in air and evaporate perspiration. Summer suits may also be made of all-silk shantung, linen crash, cotton seersucker, cotton and polyester blended cords (wash-and-wear), tropical blends of Dacron polyester 55 per cent with 45 per cent rayon (wash-and-wear), 55 per cent Dacron polyester with 45 per cent wool worsted, and 65 per cent wool worsted with 35 per cent mohair.

(*b*) *Gabardine.* Gabardine is characterized by fine rounded wales in twill weave. The wales are clearly visible on the face but not on the back of the fabric. Sometimes gabardine is mixed with cotton or rayon.

(*c*) *Elastique,* sometimes called *cavalry twill,* is a hard-finished, long-wearing worsted in dobby weave. It is characterized by wales in pairs on the right side. At a glance, the fabric seems knitted.

(*d*) Sharkskin is woven in twill or herringbone construction. Yarns in light and dark colors are alternated lengthwise and crosswise to give it its characteristic coloring. Sharkskin is made plain or in stripes or patterns. Nailhead patterns have round, white designs on brown or black grounds. The designs are made in dobby weave. Wool sharkskin wears well and doesn't show shine easily, so it is practical for office workers.

2. *Semifinished or mill-finished worsted.* Although worsteds with softer textures than those of the hard-finished class are not sold to

**Figure 17.6. Worsted suiting.**

the consumer under the name "semifinished," they do not shine quickly and have therefore gained popularity for business suits. This class of worsteds has a slight nap. In fact, some of the fabrics listed as hard-finished may be softened in texture to come in this category. In addition, this group may include:

(*a*) *Serge.*  Serge shows its 45° twill weave clearly, but it is not classed as a hard-finished worsted when it has a slight nap that is sheared short. Serges, usually piece-dyed, appear generally in blue or black. Serge wears and looks well, but at points of friction it soon shows a shine. Some serge is now made with a worsted warp and a woolen filling; this combination lessens the tendency to shine and adds softness. (See *wool worsted, below.*)

(*b*) *Worsted covert.*  This fabric was originally called *pepper-and-salt cloth,* because the white and colored yarns alternating in both warp and filling gave it a speckled appearance. Covert has recently been made without the speckled appearance. It is more common when made of woolen yarns. (See *wool covert,* p. 492.)

(*c*) *Worsted cheviot.*  This fabric has been quite popular for business suits. Almost any substantially constructed worsted suiting with a fairly soft surface might be called a worsted cheviot. It is characterized by interesting patterns in variations of the twill weave, such as herringbone, chevron, and diamond designs. This material may be classified as a semifinished worsted because it has some nap—slightly more than a serge. Woolen cheviots are harsher and coarser than worsted cheviots.

3. *Unfinished worsted.*  This group includes worsteds that have been fulled, lightly napped, and brushed. Actually, these worsteds have more finishing than those in the first two classes, so the term "unfinished" is misleading. Worsted flannel resembles unfinished worsted, but the latter is heavier and is not closely sheared. The fabric called *unfinished worsted,* made in twill weave, is finished with a nap longer than that of any other worsted. The object of this method of manufacturing is to produce a cloth with both the durability of a worsted and the beauty of a woolen. After hard wear the nap usually rubs off; it cannot be a thick nap because the yarns are made of long fibers, carefully combed. Some tailors claim that they can restore the nap when it wears off by brushing the cloth to pull out loose fibers. However, this weakens the cloth. Again, the cloth may be first fulled and then brushed with wire bristles. The latter method does make the cloth look like new and is not so harmful as the other method, for fulling generally strengthens a fabric. But the shrinkage caused by fulling may re-

quire that the suit be a size too large originally so that it will fit after it is fulled.

4. *Wool worsted.*    A very interesting fabric is a wool worsted made of both woolen and worsted stock. In each yarn there is a mixture of woolen and worsted. The cloth has a great deal of tensile strength and a texture that is firm and crisp.

## BLENDS IN SUITINGS

Until 1960 blended fabrics were considered suitable for summer suitings only. But the perfection of a polyester and wool worsted blend in regular weight made blends year-round suiting fabrics. A 55 per cent Dacron polyester and 45 per cent wool worsted came early, to be followed later by such combinations as other polyesters and acrylics (45 to 55 per cent), acrylic and wool (25 to 35 per cent), and, still later, 65/35 per cent wool and Kodel polyester, 65 per cent polyester/ 35 per cent Avril rayon, 70 per cent polyester/30 per cent wool worsted, and others.

**Figure 17.7.** Edwardian influence is shown in this blue and white striped knit sport coat, in 85% Dacron polyester and 15% rayon. (*Courtesy of du Pont Textile Fibers Department.*)

The fall and winter suitings that are worn in climates in the same latitude as the Middle Atlantic States are called *regular suitings*. They weigh about 7 ounces per linear yard (fabric width of 58 to 60 inches).

Fabrics intended only for summer wear weigh about 4 to 5 ounces per linear yard. This summer group has become primarily wash-and-wear and durable press type, whereas the regular suitings feature all wool and synthetic blends.

Men like polyester and wool worsted blends because these blends have inherent wrinkle-resistant properties, durability, and hold their shape well. When acrylic fibers are blended with wool, the acrylic gives strength, crease and shrink resistance, minimum-care properties, and dimensional stability. Nylon when blended with wool for boys' pants gives increased strength and abrasion resistance.

### APPROPRIATENESS OF MEN'S WEAR FABRICS FOR VARIOUS OCCUPATIONS AND FIGURE TYPES

In general, worsteds are more durable and more expensive than woolens.

### WHAT TO WEAR WITH WHAT
#### Your Color Selector for Business Wear

*(This dress-up Selector offers two alternative color schemes. If you elect to use color scheme #1, follow #1 all the way down from top to bottom and the same applies to color scheme #2.)*

| SUIT | GREY | BLUE | BROWN |
|---|---|---|---|
| SHIRT<br>Solid or Stripe | 1. Blue<br>2. Off White/Yellow | 1. Blue<br>2. Off White | 1. Tan<br>2. Off White |
| TIE | 1. Red/Navy<br>2. Black/Gold | 1. Red/Gold<br>2. Blue/Yellow | 1. Brown/Red<br>2. Brown/Yellow |
| SOCKS | 1. Navy or Gray<br>2. Black | 1.⎱ Navy<br>2.⎰ | 1.⎱ Brown<br>2.⎰ |
| SHOES | 1. Cordovan<br>2. Black | 1. Black<br>2. Cordovan | 1.⎱ Brown or<br>2.⎰ Cordovan |
| POCKET SQUARE<br>OR SCARF | 1. Blue<br>2. Black/Gold | 1. Red/Gold<br>2. Yellow | 1. Red<br>2. Yellow |
| HAT | 1. Medium Gray<br>2. Black | 1. Gray<br>2. Brown | 1. Brown<br>2. Green |
| OUTERCOAT | 1. Gray or Black<br>2. Black or Covert | 1. Gray<br>2. Tan | 1.⎱ Brown, Tan or<br>2.⎰ Charcoal |
| GLOVES | 1.⎱ Gray Suede or<br>2.⎰ Black Capeskin | 1.⎱ Gray Fabric or<br>2.⎰ Brown Cape or Mocha | 1. Brown Cape<br>2. Natural Pigskin |
| JEWELRY | 1. Silver Finish<br>2. Gold Finish | 1. Silver Finish<br>2. Gold Finish | 1.⎱ Gold Finish<br>2.⎰ |
| BELT | 1. Cordovan<br>2. Black | 1. Black<br>2. Cordovan | 1.⎱ Brown or<br>2.⎰ Cordovan |

Courtesy of American Institute of Men's and Boys' Wear, Inc.

For a traveling salesman, a doctor, or someone who is especially active, fabrics such as tweeds, unfinished worsteds, worsted cheviot, or gabardine are recommended because they are sturdy and warm and will stand hard wear.

The lawyer, banker, or businessman who must look well dressed all the time and who can afford several suits a year would do well to buy a flannel, a wool covert, or a wool cheviot. They tailor beautifully and look soft and stylish. A young department store salesman, whose sleeves may receive excessive wear in rubbing against the counter, may profitably buy a worsted cheviot, since it does not turn glossy as quickly as does a serge, and it is not very expensive.

In selecting appropriate fabrics for suits, men should try to bring out the good characteristics of their build and try to conceal those parts of the body that are poorly proportioned. The cut of a suit is important in improving the appearance of a figure, but the choice of fabric also has a definite effect on appearance. A short, stout man looks even shorter and stouter in a checked suit of rough fabric. A smooth fabric with narrow stripes or steep twill makes the short stout man seem taller and more slender. On the other hand, stripes make a tall man seem taller, but the tall slender man can wear rough textures with checks, herringbone, or patterned weaves. The tall, stout man, like the short, stout man, should avoid rough-textured fabrics. He should select smooth textures with small, inconspicuous woven designs or stripes. The man of average build can wear almost any texture or pattern he likes.

## POINTS (OTHER THAN FABRICS) FOR JUDGING THE QUALITY OF SUITS

Men want a good-looking, stylish garment of perfect fit, suitable cut, and good wearing quality; they also want comfort, appropriateness for their purpose, and a reliable trade name.

Tailoring is very important to consumer satisfaction. The following points denote good workmanship in a suit:

1. The front of the coat hangs smooth because of a flexible interlining. There is no sagging or buckling at the neck. A firm unbroken line extends from the neck to the shoulder point; no lumpy padding.
2. The collar fits snugly at the neck.
3. The lapels have a smooth roll.
4. The shoulders fit well and are hand-felled for trim lines.
5. The armholes are reinforced with strong tape and shields.
6. The lining is closely woven, firm, and perspiration-proof.
7. The shoulders and chest are padded when style demands padding.
8. The vent at the back hangs straight.
9. Buttonholes are neat on both sides, and hand-worked with silk twist in close, even stitches with a strong bar opposite the eyelet end. Good-grade buttons are sewed on with linen thread.

10. The stitching is done with good-grade thread (silk is preferable), and there are two or three stitchings at points of strain.
11. The seams are wide and finished with hand felling or silk piping. The pattern is matched at center back, coat front closing, pockets, and armholes.
12. The trousers close with a zipper or firmly set buttons. Trousers hang straight; the crease is on straight of goods. No backpull in walking. Comfortable seat fullness, no bagginess. No wrinkles through crotch.
13. The belt loops are well placed and securely sewed.
14. The vest is cut and tailored to fit smoothly.

## SIZES OF MEN'S AND BOYS' SUITS

Sizes of men's suits are based on chest and waist measurements. The usual range of men's sizes is 34 to 46; young men's sizes are 32 to 40. Good-quality suits are made in different models—short, regular, long, extra long, portly, and stout—in each size. The average retail store carries at least short, regular, and long in each size. A man's height and its relation to his chest circumference and to his waist circumference are taken into consideration in making these different models. Then, too, there are the custom-made suits for men who prefer individuality, perfect fit, and excellent tailoring, and can afford to pay the difference in price.

Boys' suits are sized according to age: 2 to 6 for small boys, 7 to 12 for the intermediate age, and 14 to 20 for high school students.

## SPORTSWEAR

Slacks and sports jackets (usually of a material different from slacks) are popular for casual wear and sports. Fabrics used for slacks are cotton chino, flannel (wool and blends), wool hopsacking, stretch nylon, silk and wool plaid, wool or cotton whipcord, gabardine, wool twill stripes, and tropicals.

Shorts in various length are worn with sports shirts, sweaters, or zip-front jackets. Made of the same fabrics as used in slacks, many shorts have wash-and-wear and durable press finishes.

Fashions for men are strongly influenced by the popularity of particular sports as evidenced by the golf jacket, the one-piece coverall of sports car influence, the water-repellent parka with hood, originally worn by boating enthusiasts, and the jumpsuit, worn in the 1950's for the dangerous and expensive sport of parachute jumping.

Fabrics used for other items of sports wear, such as swimming trunks, cabana sets, zip-front jackets, and sport shirts, are discussed in other parts of this chapter.

Boys also wear slacks and sports jackets. Madras, seersucker, and cords are appropriate for summer, whereas flannel and tweed are typical winter materials. The toddler wears overalls of corduroy, cord, denim, or seersucker. For rough play the older boy wears denim dungarees like his father's.

A man's rain suit for sports in bad weather may be made of rubberized rayon or nylon fabric with waterproof mesh back, which keeps out dampness and at the same time gives ventilation.

## WORK CLOTHES [7]

For hard work, men prefer overalls or dungarees (sometimes with jackets to match). Since the prime requisites of these garments are durability and comfort, fabrics such as blue or striped denim, cotton covert, or herringbone cotton are used.

For long wear, the consumer should look for an 8-ounce fabric, Sanforized, with triple-stitched, rip-proof main seams, points of strain reinforced with bar tacks, reinforced big corners, rustproof zipper, snaps, buttons, and buckles, and, on overalls, noncurl, double-thick suspenders. For comfort, overalls should be full cut and have ample pockets. Overalls and dungarees are sold by waist and inseam measurements. Chest measurement is also needed for coveralls. The waist is measured over the trousers without a belt; the inseam is the measurement from the crotch to the desired length. Regular sizes are: waist, 30, 31, 32, 33, 34, 36, 38, 40, 42 inches; inseam, 30, 32, 34, 36 inches.

## SCHOOL CLOTHES

For the schoolboy who gives his clothes very hard wear and the young man who works his way through college, sturdy tweeds, hard-finished sharkskin, or semifinished worsteds (worsted cheviot, worsted covert, or serge in all wool or blends with polyesters and acrylics) are appropriate, for they give him his money's worth in service and comfort. Poplins, cotton twills, and denims are also durable fabrics.

## SELECTION OF OUTERWEAR

### TOPCOATS

A topcoat, which is generally worn in fall and spring, and in warm climates all winter, differs from the overcoat in the weight of the fabric used. The topcoat of 13 to 20 ounces per square yard has virtually re-

[7] See USA Standards Institute, "Standard Performance Requirements for Textile Fabrics, I, Men's and Boys' Woven Coverall, Shop Coat, Overall, and Dungaree Fabrics" (L22).

placed the heavier 23-ounce cloth. With a zip-out lining of 70 per cent acrylic/30 per cent Verel modacrylic, or 50 per cent polyester/35 per cent Avisco rayon, this coat can be worn as an all-weather coat for at least three seasons of the year in a moderate climate. The coat proper is made of water-repellent poplin, gabardine, 100 per cent polyester with acrylic-coated inner surface, 50 per cent polyester/50 per cent cotton, or 80 per cent polyester/20 per cent combed cotton.

### OVERCOATS

An overcoat is usually identified with cold-weather wear. Cashmere (100 per cent) or cashmere and wool, camel and wool, fleece, heavy tweeds, reversible double cloth, worsted covert, and melton are found in men's overcoats. Furlike fabrics may be used as collars and for linings. A three-quarter length coat called a *suburban*, which is suitable for high school, college campus, or suburban wear, may be made of cotton gabardine, wool or cashmere fleece, tweed, hopsacking, or corduroy. The boxy car coat is cut on lines similar to women's box coats and can be made of cotton poplin, gabardine, foam laminated to nylon, fleece, twill blends and corduroy. Some fabrics are water-repellent.

Sizes in men's coats are short, regular, and long lengths in 34 to 48. Boys' coats range from sizes 3 to 10 and 11 to 18.

### OUTER JACKETS

The zip-up jacket continues to be popular for everyday and sportswear. Leather with sheep's-wool lining, water-repellent cotton twill lined with wool fabric or sheepskin, heavy wool fleece, and melton are suitable for winter wear in cold climates. For milder weather, lightweight nylon and cotton blends, rayon, acetate, corduroy, cotton water-repellent twills in 8- to 9-ounce weight (lined or unlined), poplin, and the ever-popular heavy wool plaid shirt worn as a jacket are favorites. Laminated nylon, consisting of a nylon jersey shell laminated to shape-retaining polyurethane foam, makes a rugged jacket that is lightweight. Laminates are also used for the casual short coat. Nylon taffeta or poplin lined with cotton flannel or acetate with wash-and-wear finish makes another lightweight jacket or car coat.

The homemaker usually prefers that the male members of the family wear jackets that are easy to care for. The jackets should be preshrunk (2 per cent residual shrinkage), machine washable, and made of drip-dry fabrics that require little or no ironing and are permanently water-repellent. Colors should be fast to washing, to light, to crocking, and to perspiration. Heavy winter jackets, of course, should be sent to the dry cleaners. (For points to consider in good fit of a coat or jacket, see Chapter 16.)

Linings for suits, topcoats, overcoats, and jackets must be durable, attractive, and easy to slip on. Fabrics in satin weave with short floats or twill constructions in silk, rayon, acetate, or nylon offer attractive appearance and slip on easily. Combed cottons in two-ply mercerized yarns are used in combination with fine-grade rayon yarns. This line includes serges, twills, satins, and fancies. All-silk satins, sateens (cotton), brocades, and twills are common lining materials. Suit pockets are usually lined with a closely woven cotton twill (not heavily sized in good grades). All linings should be preshrunk and colorfast.

Interfacings for suits and coats are, for the most part, shrinkage controlled, and some are automatic wash-and-wear. Better suits have coat fronts lined with a good quality of hair canvas. The shoulders are lined with a fine haircloth covered with flannel or thin felt. Interlinings for collars are made of firm linen. Armholes are taped with thin, strong, preshrunk tape. Fine, soft, flexible padding that does not feel bulky composes the shoulder padding.[8]

Canvas interfacing for sportswear is sheer and may be made of 60 per cent cotton, 40 per cent spun viscose rayon. A nonwoven fabric can be obtained in several weights for this purpose.[9] There are also iron-on interfacings that are both woven [10] and nonwoven.[11]

Since interlinings are intended to give warmth to the garment, an all-wool woven fabric is highly desirable.


## SUMMARY

Men's coatings and suitings are not easily visualized from descriptions alone. A sample of each material should be studied along with the description. Comparisons between similar fabrics should be made. The exercise of patience and determination in learning about these materials will prove gratifying for those who buy for themselves or for their families.


## PROJECTS

1. Plan a complete wardrobe for a boy of ten who is going to a summer camp in New England. Give names and quantities of the articles needed, the fabrics of which each item is made, and approximate retail prices of each.

[8] "A Man's Guide to Good Clothes," a pamphlet by British Woollens. (Printed in the United States.)

[9] An example is Pellon by Pellon Corporation.

[10] An example is Staflex by Staflex Corporation.

[11] An example is Pellomite by Pellon Corporation.

2. Assume you are planning a weekend skiing outing. You will stay at a ski lodge for two nights.

    (*a*) List the articles of apparel in the quantities that you would need to take with you.

    (*b*) Give the names of the fabrics used in each garment and the approximate retail prices.

3. Plan a wardrobe for a male college student who is going to attend a small campus college in Minnesota.

    (*a*) List the article of apparel in the quantities that will be required.

    (*b*) Give the names of the fabrics used in each garment and approximate retail prices.

## GLOSSARY

**Balbriggan.**   An underwear fabric. See Glossary, Chapter 16.

**Balmacaan** (named after an estate near Inverness).   Swagger-style coat with slash pockets and no belt. It has a raglan sleeve and military collar. Fabrics used are cotton gabardine, tweed, and cashmere (in solid colors for dress).

**Barathea.**   A silk, rayon and cotton, or rayon and wool mixed fabric with a pebbly texture in a fine woven design resembling a brick wall. It is used for ties, women's dresses, and trimmings.

**Batiste.**   A very sheer muslin used for men's summer shirts. See Glossary, Chapter 16.

**Beacon robing.**   A heavy cotton fabric napped on both sides, often with large figured or striped designs. It is used for inexpensive men's and boys' robes. See *double-cloth or backed-cloth method*, Chapter 5.

**Belting.**   A heavy cotton, rayon, silk, or mixed fabric with large fillingwise ribs. It may be knitted. See *Webbing*.

**Box coat.**   A single- or double-breasted straight-hanging coat with notch or peak lapels. It generally has a regulation sleeve. Occasionally it is half-belted in back.

**Broadcloth.**   See Glossary, Chapter 16.

**Brocade.**   Used for ties, smoking jackets, vests, and robes. See Glossary, Chapter 16.

**Burlap.**   A coarse, rough fabric often called gunny sacking, made of jute, hemp, or cotton. It is used as interlining in men's suits. This is a poorer fabric than hair canvas for the purpose.

**Canvas.**   A firm, heavy cotton or linen fabric. The unbleached fabric is used for coat fronts, lapels, and linings of men's suits. Hair canvas for interlinings is made of goat hair and wool.

**Cashmere.**   A fabric made of soft fibers of the Indian Cashmere goats that may be combined with sheep's wool. See Chapter 12. It is used for men's sweaters, scarfs, and coats.

**Cassimere.**   A medium-weight twilled woolen made with a soft finish, no nap, used for topcoats and suits. It is not to be confused with cashmere.

**Cavalry twill.**   See *Elastique*.

**Challis.**   Lightweight wool for a tie. See Glossary, Chapter 16.

**Chambray.**   See Glossary, Chapter 16.

**Charvet.** A soft, dull silk or rayon fabric in satin texture identified by shadow stripes warpwise. It may be Jacquard.

**Chesterfield** (adapted from the style worn by Lord Chesterfield). It has a very long skirt; a single- or double-breasted, with or without a velvet collar.

**Cheviot.** A woolen or worsted with a slightly rough texture in a twill weave. It is used for suits and coats.

**Chinchilla.** A men's overcoating. See Glossary, Chapter 16.

**Chino cloth.** A twill-weave cotton originally used for slacks, sport shirts, and summer army uniforms. It is made of two-ply cotton combed yarns, is of vat-dyed khaki color, and is mercerized and Sanforized.

**Corduroy.** A pile fabric with wales warpwise used for jackets, slacks, and sport shirts.

**Covert.** A medium-heavy cotton or wool fabric in twill weave. It originally had a flecked appearance because one of the ply yarns was white and the other one colored; now it is generally made in solid color (in wool or mixtures). Wool covert is used for suits, topcoats, and raincoats; cotton covert is used for work clothes.

**Crochet knit.** Machine-knitted tie fabric made to resemble hand knitting.

**Denim.** See Glossary, Chapter 16.

**Drill.** A heavy, durable twilled cotton suitable for slacks, uniforms, overalls, and work shirts.

**Elastique.** A firmly woven, clear-finished worsted with a steep double twill that is used for riding breeches, army uniforms, and slacks. It is similar to cavalry twill.

**End-to-end.** A colored warp yarn alternating with a white warp yarn; fillings are white. There is end-to-end broadcloth and end-to-end chambray, which is frequently sold as end-to-end madras. It is synonymous with *end on end* or *end-and-end*.

**Faille.** A tie fabric with fillingwise ribs. See Glossary, Chapter 16.

**Flannel.** See Glossary, Chapter 16. Also see *Flannelette*. See *Outing flannel* in this Glossary.

**Foulard.** Soft, lightweight silk, mercerized cotton, or rayon fabric in fine twill weave used for men's ties and women's dresses. It is frequently sold as surah.

**Frieze.** A very heavy woolen overcoating originally woven in Friesland, Holland. It is finished with a fuzzy, rough texture.

**Fuji.** A men's shirting or children's dress fabric with a count of about twice as many warps as fillings. Frequently the warp is acetate and the round, fine fillings are viscose rayon and acetate.

**Gabardine.** Steep-twilled wool, cotton, or rayon mixed or blended fabric, on which the back is flat. It is used for sport shirts, slacks, coats, and suits.

**Grenadine.** An openwork lacelike fabric, made of silk or synthetics. Warps and fillings are joined by looping instead of interweaving.

**Haircloth.** A stiff, wiry cloth of cotton with a mohair or horsehair filling. It is used for interfacing and stiffening.

**Homespun.** A rather loosely woven, rough-textured woolen woven in plain weave that is made to resemble fabric woven by hand in the home. It may be wool, cotton, rayon, mixtures, or blends. It is used for men's coats, suits, and sport jackets and women's coats and suits.

**Jean.** See Glossary, Chapter 16.

**Jersey.** See Glossary, Chapter 13.

**Macclesfield.** Hand-woven silk or rayon fabric with small overall Jacquard patterns. Macclesfield, England, is the town of origin. See *Spitalfields.*

**Mackinaw** (named after Mackinac Island). A short coat used for sports; made of heavy plain coating or of double cloth.

**Madras.** A muslin shirting with a woven-in pattern or stripe in balanced count. The designs may be dobby or Jacquard. White-on-white madras has a white figure on a white ground. India madras has rather subdued colors; usually in plaid design.

**Melton.** See Glossary, Chapter 16.

**Mesh.** Used for summer sport shirts and underwear. See Glossary, Chapter 16.

**Mogadore.** A corded silk or rayon fabric with wide ridges and often with wide stripes that is used for ties.

**Moiré.** Silk or synthetic fabric with watered design made by pressing fabric with heated, engraved rollers. It is used for ties and dresses.

**Moleskin finish.** A cotton fleece-lined with close, soft, thick nap that is used in underwear for cold climates.

**Outing flannel.** A lightweight, soft plain- or twill-weave cotton fabric generally napped on both sides, often with stripes. It is used for pajamas, interlinings, and diapers.

**Oxford.** See Glossary, Chapter 16.

**Pajama check.** A fancy basket-weave cloth of printcloth type. The yarns are grouped to give a checked effect. See *Printcloth,* Glossary, Chapter 16.

**Paletot** (commonly known as an ulster). A very loose overcoat hanging straight from the shoulders.

**Percale.** A muslin used for inexpensive shirts, shorts, and pajamas. See Glossary, Chapter 16.

**Piqué.** Used for shirts. See Glossary, Chapter 16.

**Pongee.** Used for scarfs, sport shirts, and pajamas. See Glossary, Chapter 16.

**Poplin.** Used for shirts, ski jackets, and sports jackets. See Glossary, Chapter 16.

**Raincoat.** A topcoat of a fabric such as covert cloth, poplin, or gabardine—water-repellent to shed the rain; may be rubberized inside.

**Rep.** A heavily ribbed fabric in silk, rayon, cotton, wool, or a mixture. Fabric may be solid or striped. It is used for ties, robes, drapery, and upholstery.

**Sateen.** A cotton fabric in which the fillings float. It is usually mercerized and is used for linings, draperies, comforters.

**Satin.** Silk or synthetic fabric sometimes made with a cotton filling. It has a smooth, lustrous surface, because the warp floats. It is used for linings of coats, jackets, facings, and ties.

**Serge.** Used for men's suits and slacks. See Glossary, Chapter 16.

**Shantung.** See Glossary, Chapter 16.

**Sharkskin.** A worsted fabric originally made in two colors. It is so called because it resembles leather sharkskin in durability. Now made in glen plaids, stripes, bird's-eye, and nailhead patterns; it is used for men's and women's suits, coats, and slacks.

**Shetland.** Wool from Shetland sheep that makes a lightweight, warm, woolen suiting or jacket. It is suitable for women's wear. It is also a type of knitting yarn.

**Silk broadcloth.** A silk shirting fabric in plain weave, often striped.

**Skipdent.** A sheer cotton plain-weave shirting fabric in which warp yarns are omitted at regular intervals to give a striped effect.

**Spitalfields.** An English town, home of Huguenot weavers, now a lace-making center. In this town, the hand-woven Jacquard silk Spitalfields tie originated.

**Trench coat.** The officer's coat worn during World War I. It is double-breasted and belted. It has a high-closing collar and shoulder flaps.

**Tropical.** A plain-weave, lightweight summer suiting in worsted or blends with synthetics; it is also used for women's suits.

**T-shirt.** A knitted cotton undershirt with short sleeves that may be worn also for sports or work without an outer garment.

**Tweed.** A rough-surfaced woolen, usually yarn-dyed. It is generally twill or a variation in men's wear and is used for coats, suits, jackets, and slacks.

**Ulster** (the name originated in Ulster, Ireland). A long, loose, heavy coat made originally of frieze, now made also of other heavy materials.

**Ulsterette.** A more closely fitted, shorter coat than the ulster.

**Unfinished worsted.** A suiting fabric in twill weave, finished with a nap longer than that of other worsteds.

**Webbing.** A strong, tightly woven narrow fabric for straps or belts. With the addition of rubber threads warpwise, this webbing is used for garters and suspenders.

**White-on-white.** A fabric in any fiber mixture or blend that has a white woven-in design on a white ground.

**Wool broadcloth.** A smooth, silky napped woolen in twill weave. Nap obliterates the weave. It is used for men's dinner jackets and formal evening wear—also for women's coats and suits.

**Woolen.** A class of wool fabrics made of short fibers of varied lengths and carded yarns.

**Worsted.** A class of wool fabrics made of long fibers and combed yarns.

**Worsted flannel.** See *Flannel*.

# 18
# Household
# Textiles

Household textiles, also called domestics, are fabrics that serve the home. They dry dishes and hands and cover beds and tables.

In smaller stores, one buyer generally has charge of home furnishings, curtains, and slipcovers plus "linens and domestics." Larger stores have two buyers, one for domestics and household linens and another for blankets, comforters, and bedspreads. Some stores have three departments—linens, domestics, and blankets—but generally one buyer can handle all three lines. A typical merchandise classification follows:

LINEN CLASSIFICATION

1. Towels (bath and beach towels, hand towels, washcloths, dish and glass towels, dishcloths, pot holders, mitts)
2. Shower curtains
3. Bathroom ensembles
4. Table linen (cloths and sets, place mats, doilies, runners, napkins)
   A. Damask
   B. Embroidery
   C. Lace

1. Sheets and pillowcases; also yard goods (sheeting, tubing, ticking)
2. Mattresses and pillows
3. Blankets
4. Comforters and quilts
5. Bedspreads

## LINEN CLASSIFICATION

### TOWELS

Towels, which make up a large category, are an essential part of any linen closet and should be chosen with the same care as sheets, pillow slips, and other household textiles. (Towels will be discussed according to the above linen classification.)

*Bath towels.* Bath towels are made of terry cloth, which is characterized by looped-pile surfaces. This pile construction increases the absorbency; the more loops there are, the more absorbent the towel. (The actual meaning of the term "terry cloth" and its construction are explained in Chapter 5.) The construction, when on the loom, consists of a setup of ground warps in tension, arranged alternately with pile warps that form loops at the proper time as their tension is released. By removing pile warps from a section of the cloth, the group weave is discernible. In a three-pick towel, the filling yarns are grouped in threes, because two fillings are shot through the same shed and one filling is then shot through to interlace with the ground warps. This construction of fillings grouped in threes denotes a three-pick terry cloth. Fewer then three picks gives a minimum of contact between the pile warp and the ground warp. Hence, most towels are three-pick and are of average grade. One- and two-pick towels are poor; towels of more than three picks are better than average. The quality of a terry cloth depends upon the following factors:

1. *Number and length of the pile loops.* The purpose of pile loops is to increase the surface area and thereby increase the absorptive power of the towel. For this purpose loops should be reasonably close together, soft, and not too tightly twisted.

In more expensive towels, pile loops are longer. Long loops in double-thread construction improve absorptive quality, but they catch and pull out easily. (For an explanation of double thread, see *strength of yarns.*) On the other hand, too short loops do not increase the surface area sufficiently. A loop about one-eighth inch deep seems to be generally the best.

So-called "friction towels" are made with all-linen pile or a row of linen pile alternating with a cotton pile.

2. *The tightness of the weave.* Some loops pull out very easily in

·laundering and in use, so that the towel becomes unattractive and weak.
The greater the pickage, the less likely are loops to pull out. A groundwork of twill weave is more durable than a groundwork of plain or
basket weave. A tight weave with balanced count is important.

laundry bill. Also, small or medium-sized towels are easiest for children to manage. Baby's bath towels come in size 36 x 36 inches and wash-cloths in sizes 9 x 9 inches.

The consumer should be warned of possible shrinkage before she considers what size towels to buy. Shrinkage occurs for the most part in the first five launderings; after that, it is negligible. For many towels residual shrinkage is as much as 10 per cent, so that a size that seems adequate when new may be entirely too small after the first five launderings. White towels should be laundered frequently to retain a snowy look. Plenty of warm soapsuds (synthetic or detergent) should be used, followed by two rinses in clear warm water. (A fabric softener put into the last rinse improves the touch of towels.) Towels should be shaken before they are hung out to dry. Terry towels should never be ironed, because fluffy loops absorb moisture better.

*Hand towels.* Terry cloth is also a popular fabric for the smaller hand towels. They appear in sizes 16 x 26 and 18 x 36 inches, and in fingertip size 11 x 18 inches. When made in colors and patterns that match bath towel, washcloth, and bath mat, they compose a useful set. Huck face towels may be made wholly of cotton, wholly of linen, or of cotton warp and linen or rayon filling. Cottons and mixtures are less expensive than linens but are more apt to become linty after several washings.

The huckaback or honeycomb weave is done on the dobby loom. The grade of the fabric is determined by the quality of the fibers used, the quality of the yarns, and the construction. To make a fairly rough and absorbent surface, yarns are selected that are coarse, heavy, and slackly twisted. If the fabric is to be durable, the weave must be close and the count must be balanced; that is, the yarns must be of about the same diameter in warp and filling, and the tensile strength in warp and filling must be proportionate.

Hems should be turned evenly and stitched firmly with fairly short, regular stitches. Hemstitching, although attractive as a finishing for edges, may be ripped like so much perforated paper if care is not exercised in laundering.

Figure 18.1. Huck toweling. (*Photograph courtesy of the Irish Linen Guild.*)

Usual sizes of huck towels are 17 x 32, 18 x 32, 18 x 34 and 18 x 36 inches. Appearance—that is, the attractiveness of the design in the weave and the border—is an important consideration. Absorbency is probably not so important in huck as it is in terry weaves, since huck towels are used mainly for the face.

*Washcloths.* Since the primary purpose of a washcloth is to give friction for the purpose of cleansing the skin, a terry cloth with loops on both sides is better than a knitted back. Knitted washcloths are softer than woven ones, but they are more likely to stretch out of shape, although a locking stitch will prevent this problem. (Knitted washcloths are good for infants.) Durability depends upon a firm, even weave and firm stitching of edges so that corners will not fray or stitching unravel. Washcloths are 12 x 12 or 13 x 13 inches.

*Dish towels.* Regular dish towels may be made of (1) cottonade, a coarse, heavy cotton resembling woolens and worsteds in weave and finish; (2) crash, a rough-textured cotton or linen in plain weave with novelty yarns; (3) damask, a cotton fabric in Jacquard pattern; (4) glass cloth, a cotton fabric with smooth, hard-twisted yarns that do not lint; (5) Osnaburg, a plain, strong cotton fabric with a crashlike appearance, having very coarse yarns in both warp and filling, and made of low-grade, short-staple cotton; (6) linen crash, a rather heavy, plain-weave linen made from tow yarns, and (7) terry cloth. Kitchen towels may be a two-fiber blend of linen and rayon or linen and cotton, or a three-fiber blend of cotton, rayon, and linen in terry cloth.

Crash is excellent for dish and glass towels, for, although it has a hard texture that prevents it from linting, it is still rough enough to be absorbent. Linen crash is preferable to cotton for dish towels because it does not lint so badly, does not seem wet so quickly, and dries faster than cotton. Linen crash towels are generally made of rather poorly hackled tow yarns. These yarns are naturally coarse and bumpy; hence they give the desired texture. Cotton crash is also made of irregular, coarse yarns, which are spun so as to resemble linen. Short fibers are singed in the finishing process to prevent linting as much as possible. Beetling is also used to make cotton resemble linen. An attractively printed linen crash makes an effective "show towel" (one to be seen but seldom, if ever, used).

A fairly high, well-balanced count—comparable to turkish toweling in tensile strength of warp and filling—and workmanship are important for dish towels. Although the designs of crashes are not so intricate as those of terry towel fabrics, almost any color desired can be found to harmonize with a kitchen ensemble. Crash toweling can be purchased by the yard in some stores and by mail order. Ready-made crash dish towels come in sizes 15 x 30, 17 x 32, and 18 x 32 inches.

*Glass towels.* Glass towels are intended for drying glasses and thus should be free of lint. They are lighter in weight than regular dish towels. An all-linen crash makes a satisfactory glass towel. Bar towels also come in this classification. Usual sizes of Irish linen glass towels are 20½ x 21½ and 22½ x 33 inches. Glass toweling is also sold by the yard.

Pot holders of terry cloth and quilted cottons, and quilted mitts for handling hot dishes are usually found in the store near the dish towels.

### SHOWER CURTAINS

Since the fashion of having color in the bathroom has become important, shower curtains have been very prominent and colorful. They can be obtained in solid hues, stripes, or figures. The patterns and designs are nearly as varied as designs in draperies. At present, there is a trend to coordinate shower curtains with towels. In so doing, care should be taken not to create a busy, unesthetic effect. Some fabrics of which shower curtains are made are taffeta, satin (in acetate, rayon, nylon, silk), moiré taffeta, and novelties such as a polyester schiffli-embroidered marquisette curtain over a plastic liner.

Fabrics for shower curtains may be either water-resistant (water-repellent) or waterproof. All-plastic sheet curtains (nontextile), plastic-coated fabrics, and cloths with plastic liners are waterproof. A more expensive process and a durable one is the *oiled silk* method. The silk fabric is treated with a solution of rubber and oil that so impregnates the fibers that the waterproofing substance becomes a part of the fabric itself. The fabric remains waterproof as long as it lasts.

Shower curtains in regular sizes are 68 x 72 inches and 72 inches square.

### BATHROOM ENSEMBLES

Face and bath towels, washcloths, tank toppers, lid covers, window and shower curtains, and bath mats are sold separately or in sets. A smaller set may include bath and face towels, washcloths, and a bath mat. Bath mats are made of terry cloth (pure cotton or cotton with rayon pile), chenille, modacrylic, or rubber. When sold in a set the mat is usually terry cloth, as is the tank topper and lid cover. Window and shower curtains are the same color and pattern in a different fabric. Bath rugs are made of nylon in solid colors with etched or carved patterns. A dense plush nylon pile is locked with rubber coating to a cotton duck back to hold the pile tufts in place and to make the rug skid-resistant. Wall-to-wall nylon carpeting is gaining in popularity for bathroom floor covering.

### TABLE LINEN

People often speak of their "table linen" and their "bed linen," although actually much of it is cotton or mixtures of rayon. Yet linen is used extensively for dining tablecloths because (1) it looks clean; (2) it is somewhat lustrous; (3) stains can be removed from it easily; and (4) it wears and washes well, retaining its luster and beauty after many washings.

*Cloths for dining tables.* Cloths for dining tables include dinner cloths, banquet cloths, luncheon cloths, dinette and tea sets, place mats, napkins, table pads (made of felt or baize—a loose, plain-weave, napped fabric in imitation of felt—or a quilted material similar to that used for mattress covers), and hot spots (heavy, novelty mesh or doily material placed over pads of cork or silver).

The chief selling points for the cloths and sets mentioned here are appearance, suitability, serviceability, durability, minimum care, and size. For example, if a customer wants a cloth for a dinette where small children have their meals, the salesperson might show her a screen-printed, cotton woven cloth covered with a coat of vinyl plastic that can be wiped off, or a 65 per cent polyester/35 per cent cotton that is machine washable and durable press. In some instances, a soil-release finish lets stains wash out quickly and thoroughly. A small square cloth, 54 x 54 or even 45 x 45 inches, might suffice. A vinyl-faced laminated cloth would be equally suitable. Place mats of plastic-coated fabric might also be suggested. (One hundred per cent plastic mats are also appropriate, but they are nontextiles.)

Place mats have become varied and imaginative in design. For a patio or barbecue pit, the homemaker might want a light, bright, gay, carefree touch. For indoor dining, she might prefer a richer, more elegant, quieter mat. Juvenile place mats should have a design that appeals to the child.

Table covers for outdoor dining are frequently made of laminated rayon, cotton terry, flannel-backed polished cotton in solid color, gay prints, checkerboards, and stripes. For informal dining indoors, a solid or printed cotton, rayon and cotton, all-linen crash cloth, or Fiberglas Beta (no-iron, soil-release), with or without napkins, are appropriate. Sizes are 54 x 54, 54 x 72, or 63 x 80 inches.

Luncheon and bridge sets, doilies, runners, and napkins are often made of linen crash. The consumer should look for the following points when buying a linen crash cloth:

1. Smooth yarns of even diameter.
2. Count and balance: excellent grade, 80 yarns per square inch; medium grade, 64 yarns per square inch; poor grade, 55 yarns per square inch.
3. Dyes fast to sunlight and to washing.
4. Hems evenly turned and firmly stitched.
5. The amount of sizing. Although good-quality linens are not heavily sized, a little starch may be added in the finish to give the leathery stiffness common to new linens. Flimsy cotton crash is

often heavily sized to resemble heavy linen. The friction test will reveal the presence of excessive sizing.

6. Amount of bleaching. Although snow-white linens are beautiful, it is often advisable to buy linen cloth that is not fully bleached when it is purchased. Each time a full-bleached linen is laundered, the chemical bleaches used by the laundry overbleach the cloth, thereby tendering it. To ensure long service, linen cloths should be oyster-bleached (slightly bleached) or silver-bleached (deep cream color) when purchased.

7. Minimum-care finishes, such as durable press and soil release.

For cocktails, small napkins about 5 x 8 inches or 7 inches square are used. These may be of linen or cotton crash or handkerchief linen. The corners or edges may be embroidered.

**Figure 18.2.** Lace cloths of 100 per cent Dacron polyester for oblong, oval, and round tables. (*Photograph courtesy of the Quaker Lace Company.*)

*Textiles used for table linen.* With the advent of improved minimum-care finishes, the tablecloth has become more popular for informal as well as formal dining.[1]

For formal dining, a lace cloth of cotton, Dacron polyester, or nylon, or a cloth of embroidered linen or linen damask is appropriate. Machine-made lace cloths in ivory, ecru, white in venetian motifs, filet and novelty patterns can be used. A discussion of laces of various types is to be found at the end of this section.

*Damask.* Damask tablecloths come in standard sizes, and the choice of size depends on the number of people to be seated at the table. A damask cloth 72 x 90 inches comfortably seats eight people, and a cloth 72 x 108 inches seats twelve. Banquet cloths are 60 x 116, 72 x 126, or 72 x 144 inches. Dinner napkins generally match the tablecloth and may be 18 or 22 inches square.

Table damasks are pure linen, pure cotton, or mixtures of these fibers. Sometimes rayon is included to make the design more prominent and lustrous. Damasks are made in Jacquard weave with a warp satin design and a filling sateen ground, or the reverse. The twill weave is sometimes used for the design and the satin weave for the ground.

From the standpoint of construction there are two types of damask: simple or single, and compound or double. Both types are woven single; the name applies to the type of weave. Single damask has a four-float

[1] Crava-Lin, by the Cravenette Co., can be applied to 100 per cent Belgian linen tablecloths. It is said to dry without a wrinkle. Soil-release finishes for 100 per cent Belgian linen have been developed by Leacock & Co., and by Northern Drying Co.

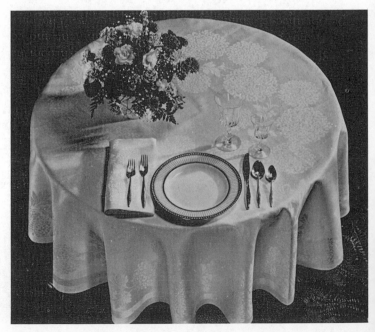

**Figure 18.3.** Linen damask tablecloth. (Photograph courtesy of the Irish Linen Guild.)

construction, whereas double damask has a seven-float construction. The count of cloth of double damask is higher than that of single damask (some authorities say double damask should have a count of 180 with at least 50 per cent floating yarn).

*Quality of damask.* To judge the wearing quality of a damask, the following factors should be considered:

1. *The length of the fibers.* Since damasks are woven in a satin construction necessitating floats, long fibers do not pull out and fuzz as quickly as short ones; and, since linen fibers are generally longer than cotton fibers, they are more adaptable to satin weaves.
2. *The evenness of yarns.* If yarns are unevenly spun, then the cloth will be thick and thin in spots. Such a cloth presents a poor appearance and also gives poorer service.
3. *The closeness of the weave.* A loose weave is a weakness in a damask because it allows yarns to slip and thereby wear out the float. A close, firm weave is necessary if a damask is to be durable.
4. *The length of the floats.* Floats in this construction may pass over four to twenty yarns. A float that passes over four yarns is considered short. Although they will wear well, short floats do not give a lustrous surface. The longer the float, the greater the light reflection and the more beautiful the cloth. For elaborate leaf and floral designs, a long float (eighteen or twenty yarns) is necessary. Long floats allow a great amount of yarn to be exposed to friction on the surface. Consequently, long floats are not durable.

*Embroidery and lace.* Not only are laces and embroideries used for apparel, but they are also used for the table covers, doilies, scarfs, and trimming of household textiles.

1. *Embroidery.* Embroidery is ornamental needlework done on the fabric itself, whereas lace is a fabric created by looping, interlacing, braiding, or twisting threads. Embroidery can be done by machine or by hand. The latter method, if the work is well done, is preferable but generally more expensive than the machine product. Machine embroidery is often rather coarse, and the wrong side may not be well finished. A few common types of embroidery follow:

1. Japanese hand embroidery—large designs
2. Philippine embroidery—very small designs
3. Mexican drawnwork—lacy, spiderweb effects
4. French embroidery—silky looking with small designs
5. Madeira—floral patterns with punchwork

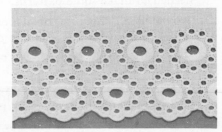

**Figure 18.4.** Embroidery. *(Photograph courtesy of Max Mandel Laces, Inc.)*

Much of the eyelet all-over embroidery and edges for trimmings on tablecloths, curtains, spreads, dresses, lingerie, and blouses is embroidered by a machine called the Schiffli. This machine can embroider almost any design on either woven cloth or net. The machine itself is a double-decker about fifteen yards long. It is equipped with boat-shaped shuttles ("schiffli" means little boat) and needles, and it operates somewhat like a sewing machine. The design is controlled by punched Jacquard cards. Eyelets are punched by a separate operation.

Cotton batiste, lawn, organdy, nylon sheers, cotton piqués, edgings, and flouncings are but a few of the fabrics that may be schiffli embroidered. Since schiffli designs are more intricate than swivel, clip spot, or lappet, they are also more expensive.

*2. Lace.*[2] This is an important trimming, for it is used for tablecloths, curtains, handkerchiefs, dresses, and underwear. Lace consists of two elements: (1) the pattern, flower, or group, which forms the closer-worked and more solid portion, and (2) the ground or filling, which serves to hold the pattern together. The two main types of laces are "real," or handmade, and machine made. Linen thread is usually used for real lace, but cotton, rayon, nylon, or silk may be used for machine lace. The former is softer, more irregular in mesh and pattern, and more expensive. There are five kinds of real laces: (1) needlepoint, (2) bobbin (pillow), (3) darned, (4) crocheted, and (5) knotted. All of these patterns are also made or imitated by machine.

*Needlepoint lace.* The design for needlepoint is drawn on parchment stitched to a backing of stout linen, and the lace is made by filling in the pattern with buttonhole stitches. When the lace is completed, the parchment is removed. Two of the most common needlepoint laces are Venetian and Alençon. See the illustrations.

*Bobbin lace.* Sometimes called pillow lace, the lace design is drawn either on a pillow or on a paper that is placed over the pillow. Small pegs or pins are stuck into the pillow along the design, and a large number of small bobbins of thread are manipulated around the pegs or pins to produce the lace. As the lace is completed, the pins are pulled out and the lace is removed from the pillow. Making pillow lace requires great skill and dexterity, for as many as three hundred bobbins may be needed to make some patterns.

*Duchesse.* Because of its exquisite large, clothy design, duchesse is the queen of the bobbin laces. Other bobbin laces are Binche, Val, Chantilly, Torchon, and Cluny. (See the illustrations and accompanying descriptions.)

*Darned lace.* When made by hand, the design of darned lace is sewn with thread and needle passed in and out of a square mesh net.

[2] See "Lace," *Fairchild's Dictionary of Textiles,* Fairchild Publications, Inc. (New York, 1967).

Carrickmacross, an Irish appliquéd lace with a floral design. The pattern of handmade Carrickmacross is cut from fine cambric and appliquéd to the ground by point stitches. The pattern and ground of machine-made Carrickmacross are made at 'he same time.

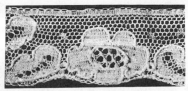

Alençon, a needlepoint lace. Fine loops of thread form the background and produce a double-thread. Natural floral patterns are outlined by heavy threads.

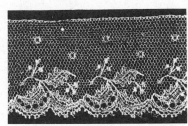

Chantilly, a bobbin lace made of silk. The pattern is usually a rather simple branch design, but sometimes Chantilly has vine or spray motifs. It usually comes in white or black. This lace has long been a favorite trimming for bridal veils.

Breton (embroidered net). The design is made of heavy thread embroidered on net. This lace is used for trimming women's underwear.

Binche, a bobbin lace. Real Binche is made by appliquéing the flat spriglike design to a rather coarse net ground, the mesh of which resembles a cane chair seat. The design and background of machine-made Binche are made at the same time.

Cluny, a rather geometric bobbin lace. The design is so open that the finished product is light and pleasing. Cluny is used to trim dresses, luncheon sets, and so forth.

**Figure 18.5. Types of laces.**

*Duchesse,* an exquisite bobbin lace. The design is large and clothy. Brides, or threads, join the various parts of the design. The lace is usually made in wide widths.

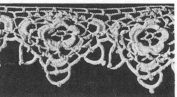

*Irish,* a fine crocheted lace with rose or clover-leaf patterns that stand out from the background. It is a heavy lace that is comparatively inexpensive. Irish crochet lace is easily made by hand.

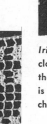

*Filet,* a darned lace with a square mesh. It is made by darning the thread in and out of the meshes. The pattern and background of machine-made filet are made in the same operation. Filet comes in narrow widths for trimming, and is also made in large pieces such as table covers, runners, and bedspreads.

*Tatting,* a knotted lace. The knots are made by passing a shuttle in and out of loops in the thread.

**Figure 18.5.** *(cont.)* Types of laces.

*Venetian point*, a needlepoint lace that is sometimes known as *raised point* because the design is thrown into relief by a sort of embroidery or buttonhole stitching. The pattern, in the form of flowers, is rather large, and is united by brides, or bars. When the pattern is in the form of a rose, the lace is called *rose point*. Venetian point is usually wide and quite heavy. In all-over patterns it makes very attractive blouses.

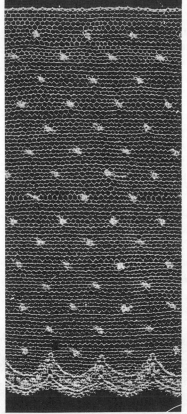

*Point d'esprit,* an embroidered tulle or net used to trim evening gowns. The dots or small squares are closely set at regular intervals.

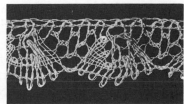

*Val* (Valenciennes), a flat bobbin lace with a diamond or lozenge-shaped mesh ground. The lace is worked in one piece, and just one kind of thread is used for the outline of the design and every part of the fabric. The pattern is usually sprig-like or floral. Val comes in narrow widths for trimming babies' garments.

*Torchon* (beggar's lace), a coarse pillow lace made with a loosely twisted thread. A shell pattern is a common design. It is an inexpensive, common lace—hence the name "beggar's lace." Machine-made cotton torchon laces are quite durable, and they wash well.

**Figure 18.5.** *(cont.)* Types of laces.

*Crocheted lace.* When real, this is made with a crochet hook, working usually with specially twisted cotton thread. It is a comparatively inexpensive heavy lace. Irish crocheted lace (not necessarily made in Ireland) is typified by a rose or shamrock design that stands out from the background.

*Filet lace.* Characterized by a flat, geometrical design, this lace may be either crocheted or darned. It is very common for household use, particularly for doilies, runners, antimacassar sets, and tablecloths. It may also be used for dress trimming.

*Knotted lace.* This is made by twisting and knotting thread by means of a shuttle. When made by passing a shuttle in and out of loops in a thread, it is called *tatting*. It is identified by a circle-like motif and picots around the edge of the motif.

*Machine-made laces.* Nearly all the laces classified as "real laces" can be duplicated by machine with slight variations and simplifications.

Machinery for making looped net was invented about 1764. But the forerunner of the present lace machine, the bobbinet machine, was patented by John Heathcote in the early 1800's and was later modified by several other inventors, one of whom was John Levers, whose name has come down to us via the Levers machine we now use.

*Bobbinet.* The design is embroidered on a plain hexagonal mesh cotton or rayon net. The embroidery is done primarily by the Levers machine, but the Schiffli machine may be used for certain types, and the net is sometimes embroidered by hand. Bobbinet, which comes in wide widths like dress goods, is often imported from France. Bobbinet is sold by the hole count. To compute hole count count the actual number of holes to an inch in a straight line, then repeat the count of the last hole and count the holes on the diagonal to an inch. Multiply the first figure by the second figure. (See Figure 18.6.) The greater the hole count, the finer the quality. Bobbinet, when stiffened, is used for veiling, evening gowns, and dress linings. Nylon bobbinet has recently become popular.

*Tulle.* This is similar to bobbinet but is made in silk, rayon, or nylon and has a higher hole count. Tulle is stiffened. The nylon tulle, very sheer and rip-resistant, can be made fireproof, permanently crisp, and resistant to steam or rain.

*Point d'esprit.* Point d'esprit is an embroidered tulle or net. When made by hand, the dots or squares are embroidered into

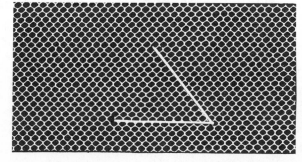

**Figure 18.6.** In bobbinet, there are thirteen holes to the inch horizontally and sixteen holes to the inch (counting the corner hole twice) on the diagonal. Therefore 13 x 16 = 208 hole count.

the net with point stitches. Point d'esprit (machine-made) is usually higher priced than bobbinet of the same grade.

*Breton.* A heavy thread is used for the design of this embroidered net. When embroidered by hand, the net is sold as *hand run*. This net is used for trimming slips and nightgowns.

*Princess.* Although real princess lace can be made by bobbins, it is usually an embroidered net made on the Schiffli machine. As an embroidered net, it can be used for bridal gowns and veils, and is comparatively inexpensive.

Some of the most common laces, both machine- and hand-made, are illustrated on the preceding pages.

*Uses of laces.* Laces are made in different widths for different uses. For example, a narrow lace with a scalloped edge is used for trimming a baby's dress; a lace with slits or eyelets is so made that ribbon may be run through it. There are seven uses of laces: [3]

1. *All-over laces.* An all-over lace is a fabric up to 36 inches wide with the pattern repeated over the entire surface. The fabric is cut and sold from the bolt like woven dress goods. The dressmaker cuts it to pattern and makes it up into formal evening, dinner, and cocktail dresses and blouses.
2. *Flouncing.* Flouncing applies to laces 18 to 36 inchs wide with a plain edge at the top and a scalloped edge at the bottom of the fabric. It is used for wide ruffles or flounces. Often these flounces are arranged in tiers to form a skirt.
3. *Galloon.* A galloon is a lace up to 18 inches wide with a scalloped edge at top and bottom. It may be used as an insertion between two cut edges of fabric, or it may be appliquéd to a fabric in bands or as a border.
4. *Insertion.* Insertion is a band of lace sewn between two pieces of fabric or on a fabric at the straight top or bottom edges. A variety of insertion is footing, which has a straight edge at top and bottom but no pattern. Footing is often used at the bodice or at the bottom hem of a slip.
5. *Beading.* Beading has slots through which ribbon may be run. These slots may be found in edgings or galloons but are much more common in insertions.
6. *Edging.* An edging is a lace never more than 18 inches wide that is straight at the top and scalloped at the bottom. It is sewn to the edge of a dress, gown, blouse, or handkerchief.
7. *Medallion.* A medallion is a lace in a single design that can be appliquéd to a fabric ground for ornamentation. It is sometimes used in the corners of napkins or as an ornament for a dress.

[3] The first six classifications and their descriptions are adapted from *Lace*, pamphlet by Max Mandel Laces, Inc.

ALL-OVER LACE

FLOUNCING

GALLOON                                    INSERTION

**Figure 18.7.** Uses of laces. (*Photographs courtesy of Max Mandel Laces, Inc.*)

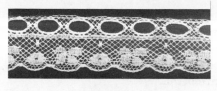

BEADING

EDGING

MEDALLION

Figure 18.7. (cont.) Uses of laces.

## DOMESTIC CLASSIFICATION

### SHEETS AND PILLOWCASES

The word "muslin," as we have noted, is derived from the French word *mousseline,* which in turn originated with the city of Mosul in Mesopotamia. We often hear of *mousseline de soie* (silk muslin), which is a very thin, crisp silk organdy. Muslin is the name commonly applied to various cotton cloths in plain weave ranging in weight from thin batiste and nainsook to heavy sheetings, such as longcloth and percale. (See p. 429 for a description of dress percale.) The lightweight muslins have been discussed in Chapter 16 under fabrics for women's apparel; the heavier, sheeting-weight muslins will be discussed here.

Although we speak of "bed linen," it would be difficult to find a home using real linen sheets or pillow slips. Most sheetings sold are cotton muslins or blends. There are also nonwoven (disposable) and rubber sheetings, often with a cotton back, for babies and the sickroom; acetate satin; and cotton fleece sheets (used for cold climates and for light summer blankets). Nylon sheets, which appeared in retail stores in the early 1950's, are bought by consumers who like their lightweight silky appearance, their machine washability, and their quick-drying and no-ironing properties. Nylon tricot fitted sheets are now on retail shelves, and rayon satin sheets have a wide range of colors that give them gift appeal. Pillowcases with nylon face and slip-resistance back of no-iron Dacron polyester, nylon, and cotton reduce the hair-do problem.

There are two kinds of cotton sheets—muslin and percale. *Percale* is the better grade and has the higher count. Actually, the term muslin should include percale, because percale is a kind of muslin. But by *muslin* the salesperson really means *longcloth,* although she seldom knows it by that name. The poorer grades of sheets, then, are longcloth, and the better grades percale. When a blend of 65 per cent polyester/35 per cent

523

cotton is used, there has been some difference of opinion in the trade as to whether blends should be called "muslin" or "percale," since these terms have always signified all-cotton. At present, when the word "percale" is used in advertising, the phraseology seems to be "all-cotton percale" or "percale of 65 per cent polyester and 35 per cent cotton."

Probably the average housewife buys her sheets and pillow slips without direct consideration of durability. A no-iron finish, size, price, brand, and general appearance are considered, however. In fact, many women know very little about sheets—younger customers especially. For example, few women are aware that the standard twin-bed sheet is usually 72 x 104 or 72 x 108 inches. When 5- to 6-inch hems are made (3 inches at the top, and 2 at the bottom) the finished size of the 72 x 104 is 72 x 98. Some mills are now packaging their sheets with the finished size marked rather than the "torn" (unfinished) size.

Nowadays sheets are sold primarily on the basis of the no-iron feature rather than durability.[4] The consumer dislikes the drudgery of ironing sheets. She wants a sheet that is smooth and nonwrinkled after washing and drying. She also wants a colored sheet fast to repeated washings. Consumers' Research (CR) believes that the wise customer would do well to take into consideration the construction and probable life of a sheet.

How long will a sheet last? On the basis of a home-use test, CR estimates an all-cotton Type 140 (the figure refers to the total thread count) fitted-bottom sheet lasted for five years, representing 125 weeks' use with 125 launderings. The life of a sheet is related to its breaking strength.[5] The USA Standard L22.30.8 calls for a minimum breaking strength of 55 pounds for the 180 (B-grade) and 200 (A-grade) percales. This standard for new sheets has been lowered from 60 pounds minimum breaking strength to 55 pounds. There is some question whether this standard is too low, if consumers are interested in durable sheets. However, it should be noted that CR found, in some cases, that a sheet can increase in breaking strength as much as 15 per cent after 20 launderings. In other cases, a sheet may lose as much as 10 per cent in one direction. But in the CR test of thirteen brands of polyester/cotton blends that originally met the standard of 55 pounds minimum for new sheets, no sheet fell below the standard.

*Wearing quality of sheets.* Two sheets of different brands may be purchased at the same time and be given the same number of washings; yet one sheet may outwear the other. A study of the fibers, yarns, weave, and finish will reveal the reason.

1. Cotton fibers should be of good quality and as long as possible if they are to be spun into regular, even, strong yarn. The best sheets contain cotton fibers at least one inch in length. An even yarn will

---

4 "Permanent-Press Sheets," *Consumer Bulletin* (July 1968), p. 21.
5 *Ibid.*

stand washing better than one with thick and thin places in it. A bumpy yarn may protrude on the surface, and, besides making an unsightly appearance, will be subjected to more friction and wear than would an unprotruding yarn. Yarns with thin places in them are apt to break in laundering and so make a hole in the cloth.

2. Yarns to be durable should be spun tightly. Since most sheets contain cottons whose fibers are comparatively short, a tight twist will keep the fibers from pulling out with wear. The tensile strength of tightly spun yarns is greater than that of loosely spun yarns.

3. To be considered "first" or "standard" quality, a sheet should be free from imperfections in the weave, such as thick and thin spots due to uneven yarns. *Run-of-the-mill* means that the defects are due either to imperceptible uneven threads or to little oil spots that occurred in the manufacturing process. These defects do not affect the wearing quality of the sheet. Sheets are marked "seconds" if there are some defects in weave or imperfections in the yarns. Each manufacturer has his own rule of what constitutes a second. If a manufacturer's standards are high, then slight flaws will not seriously affect the durability. Some imperfections merely affect the appearance of the sheet. Such a second, sold at a lower price than first quality, may be an economical purchase.

4. The count is also important. The number of warp and filling yarns to the inch determines the count of the cloth; the proportion of warps to fillings indicates the balance. A high-count cloth with a good balance will generally outwear a low-count cloth with poor balance. To illustrate: a high-count sheet of good balance would be 108 x 104; a low-count sheet with poorer balance would be 76 x 60. In each case the warp yarns are expressed first. Counts may vary from 54 x 47 for a sleazy sheet to 109 x 97 for a very fine one; the average count is 73 x 62.

USA Standard specifications for bleached bed sheets and pillow-cases (L22.30.8) appear on the following page.[6]

| | Type 200 [7] Combed Yarn | Type 180 Combed or Carded Yarn | Type 140 Carded Yarn | Type 128 Carded Yarn |
|---|---|---|---|---|
| Combined thread count warp and filling (per inch square) | 200 | 180 | 140 | 128 |
| Warp breaking strength (pounds) | 60 | 60 | 70 | 55 |
| Filling breaking strength (pounds) | 60 | 60 | 70 | 55 |
| Maximum added sizing (per cent) | 1 | 2 | 4 | 6 |
| Weight (ounces per square yard) | 3.6 | 3.6 | 4.6 | 4.0 |

[6] All standards are minimum specifications, with the exception of sizing, which is maximum.

[7] "200" and other numbers represent types or grades (by counts) of the U.S. Bureau of Standards and L22:

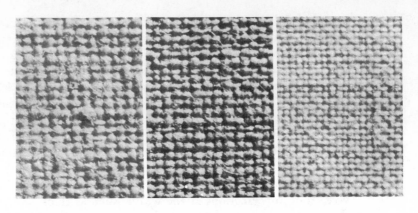

Figure 18.8. Sheetings.

TYPE 128          TYPE 140          TYPE 200

| MUSLIN | PERCALE |
|---|---|
| 112—C grade | 180—B grade |
| 128—B grade | 200—A grade |
| 140—A grade | |

5. Tensile or breaking strength is an important factor in durability. The number of pounds required to break a strip of cloth an inch wide is called the *tensile strength* of that cloth. Since the warp is usually stronger than the filling, it has a slightly higher breaking strength. If in one sheet warps break at 62 pounds and fillings at 56 pounds, that sheet will wear better than one whose breaking strength is 47 pounds for warp and 34 pounds for filling. Furthermore, a sheet may have a well-balanced count and still have a low breaking strength. The two factors, count and tensile strength, must be considered separately. In general, sheets with satisfactory thread counts have been found to have good tensile strength, and vice versa.

6. When sheets were made primarily of cotton, they often had a great deal of sizing. Sizing in the form of starch or China clay was commonly used for finishing poor-quality sheets. Sizing makes the finish appear smooth; seems to give weight to the cloth; and covers up imperfections in construction. However, after a heavily sized sheet has been washed, it looks flimsy and fuzzy. With the polyester/cotton blends, sizing is not present in appreciable amounts. In all thirteen brands tested by CR, sizing amounted to less than 4 per cent, the maximum sizing permitted by the L22 Standard. The chemicals applied in durable press treatments do not wash out because they become a part of the fabric.

Sheets vary in weight. According to the L22.30.8 Standard, a Type 180 percale sheet should weigh a minimum of 3.6 ounces per square yard. The Type 140 muslin weighs 4.6 ounces per square yard. Most all-cotton sheets shrink somewhat in laundering.

Loosely woven sheets shrink more than closely woven ones. Unless shrinkage-controlled, an allowance of $4\frac{1}{2}$ to 5 per cent should be made for shrinkage. There was no appreciable shrinkage (1.5 per cent) in the CR tests cited.

Consumers have now discovered the comfort of smooth durable press sheets. These sheets make a more tailored-looking bed, and they dry wrinkle-free with no ironing needed.

*Determining quality.*  To be sure, a consumer cannot use a tensile tester or a counting glass, but laboratory tests can be made by any testing bureau for the benefit of the store's buyer.

Most national and private brands of sheets now bear informative labels that specify size, thread count, tensile strength, weight, and per cent of shrinkage. But what does a thread count of 128 mean to the consumer? She must be able to interpret that figure to know whether it specifies a grade A or a grade B muslin.

The appearance and feeling of the sheeting can be noted easily by the consumer. She can detect bumpy yarns at a glance. By holding the cloth to the light, she may notice any streaked effect. If there is a predominance of warp, there will be a heavy, warpwise streaking. She may also notice the closeness of weave. The closer the weave, the higher the count and, other factors being equal, the stronger the cloth.

If the sheet is hemmed, the stitching should be noticed. A fairly short, even, machine stitch is preferable to a long or an uneven stitch. A minimum of fourteen even stitches per inch is recommended.

Strong thread should be used, and the ends of threads should be fastened securely. Evenness of hems is ensured if the sheeting used has been torn and not cut into lengths. Furthermore, if hems are to be even, they should be folded on the thread of the material. Hems with closed ends are to be preferred.

The selvage should be examined carefully, because it may be the first place to show wear. The edge should be firm, with all the yarns caught in securely. The taped selvage is recommended for added wear.

*Size influences serviceability and comfort.*  The choice of size is really dependent on individual preference. But, largely through ignorance, many customers buy their flat sheets too short. If a bed is about 6 feet long, the customer is apt to think that a 90-inch sheet allows ample coverage. A standard mattress is 74 inches long and 5 inches thick. Therefore 10 inches should be allowed to cover the mattress at head and foot. In addition, tests show that the average all-cotton sheet shrinks $4\frac{1}{2}$ per cent after seventy-five washings.[8] If shrinkage-controlled, the sheet will shrink 2 per cent or less. A 108-inch sheet, then, would shrink about 5 inches. This shrinkage should be considered in deciding size. Hems are generally 3 inches at the top and 2 inches at the bottom. Also,

---

[8] Tests of forty-five sheets of different brands were made in a laundry under methods approved by the Laundry Owners' National Association.

some allowance should be made for tucking in at top and bottom—about 7 inches. Accordingly, 74 inches (mattress) plus 5 inches plus 5 inches (thickness of mattress at both ends) plus 5 inches (allowance for shrinkage) plus 5 inches (for hems) plus 7 inches plus 7 inches (tuck-in allowance for both ends) equals 108 inches. The sheet required here is the 108-inch length (108 inches is the torn length before the sheet is hemmed). Since a polyester/cotton blend's shrinkage is negligible, the 104-inch length would be adequate.

To make flat sheets wear evenly, some buyers prefer hems of the same width at top and bottom; either end may be used as the top. Others prefer a wider hem at one end to distinguish top from bottom.

The lower and top sheets are the same size. The lower sheet should be long enough to tuck in at the head and foot and thus cover the whole mattress. The top sheet should tuck in 6 or 7 inches at the end and should fold back over the blanket about half a yard.[9] The following sizes of flat sheets are sold in most stores:

| TYPE OF BED | SIZE OF SHEET (inches) |
|---|---|
| Crib | 42 x 72 |
| Youth bed | 63 x 108 |
| Twin bed or three-quarter bed | 72 x 108 |
| Double bed | 81 x 108 |
| Extra-wide double bed | 90 x 108 |
| Queen size | 90 x 113; 90 x 120 |
| King size or Hollywood size | 108 x 122½ |

Fitted or contour sheets make bed-making easier. West Point–Pepperell, Inc., lists the following selling points of their fitted sheets: (1) they will not wrinkle; (2) they do not toss and turn with you; (3) beds need no remaking; (4) a perfect fit is assured by the Sanforized label; (5) easy, fast, corners slip on quickly; (6) they need no ironing; (7) mattress lifting is eliminated; (8) they hold mattress pad in place; (9) they require less space in washer; (10) they come in hard-to-find sizes; (11) an exclusive seaming process makes fitted sheets one-third stronger at the corners.

Bottom-fitted sheets are often preferred over top-fitted ones. Bottom-fitted sheets come in the following mattress sizes:

| TYPE OF BED | SIZE OF SHEET (inches) |
|---|---|
| Cot | 30 x 72 |
| Youth | 33 x 66 |
| Single | 36 x 76 |
| ¾ Bed | 48 x 76 |
| Day bed | 33 x 74 |
| XL Twin | 39 x 80 |

[9] *The Art of Bed Making,* a pamphlet by the National Cotton Council of America (formerly the Cotton Textile Institute).

| Type of Bed | Size of Sheet (inches) |
|---|---|
| XL Full | 54 x 80 |
| Queen | 60 x 80 |
| King | 72 x 84 |
| Super | 78 x 76 |
| XL Super | 78 x 80 |

Top-fitted styles have two slip-on corners with "kick-room" allowance. Usual sizes are twin and full (double).

An improvement over the fitted sheet is the one with stretch around the corners and across the entire end of the sheet. It gives the consumer ease of bed-making without reducing the strength of the corners of the sheet.

*Color.* Solid colors and prints have brought fashion to an otherwise uninteresting staple bed sheet. In addition to the bleached white staple, there are basic pastel colors—blue, yellow, and pink—that can be matched by printed "companion" sheets. These are stripes and florals and combinations of these designs. There are also embroidered sheets and pillowcases; they come separately or in sets.

*Brands.* Some customers say, "I know what brands are good, so I buy one of them. If I can afford to pay more, I select X brand; if I cannot, I buy Y brand." These buyers are doubtless buying satisfactory goods. The best standard brands are backed by years of reliable service and sustained high standards of quality. Probably many customers do better if they buy by brand than by quality, because many of them do not know the factors determining wearing quality.

Some of the large department stores have their private brands that they wish to sell in preference to the nationally advertised brands; and many of the reliable stores do have a product as good as those nationally advertised and possibly cheaper. If the customer is able to judge quality, she may get a bargain in the private brand.

The intelligent consumer should learn how to judge quality and other factors making for value in use and thus choose the brand, style, or line number that best suits the combination of personal requirements.

*Sheeting by the yard.* Sheeting can be bought by the yarn unbleached or bleached, and sheets can be made any desired length. Unbleached sheeting usually wears better than the bleached, but better qualities of bleached sheeting wear almost as well, owing to present-day careful control of the bleaching process. Most customers prefer made-up sheets, so the sale of sheeting by the yard is negligible. Pillow tubing and ticking is also sold by the yard.

*Linen sheets and sheeting.* Although there is almost no demand for linen sheets, there are some distinct advantages in buying them. Linen sheets of good grade outwear cotton of good grade, but the cost of linen is considerably higher. After a linen sheet has served its life as a sheet, it may be cut up into doilies, hand towels, and dress trimmings. Even if linen is old, it has a rich brilliance that an old cotton does not have.

The wearing quality of linen sheeting is determined by the grades of fiber, yarn, weave, and finish. A sheeting should wear well if it has long, even fibers of good tensile strength; well-hackled, even yarns; a close, firm weave; and a smooth beetle finish—and if it is not overbleached. Hems should be even and hemstitching of good quality. Finished sizes are 72 x 108 for twin and 90 x 108 for double beds.

*Pillowcases.*   Some pillowcases are made to match the sheet; the two may be bought in sets attractively packaged. These make desirable gift items. Bolster pillows, when in style, lead to sales of pillow protectors and bolster pillowcases.

Pillowcases should be about 10 inches longer than the pillow and about 2 inches larger around. The following chart shows the size of the pillow and the appropriate size for a pillowcase. The length is the torn length before hemming.

| SIZE OF PILLOW (inches) | SIZE OF PILLOWCASE (inches) |
|---|---|
| 20 x 26 | 42 x 36 or 42 x 38½ |
| 20 x 28 | 42 x 38½ |
| 22 x 28 (standard size) | 45 x 36 or 45 x 38½ |
| 22 x 30 | 45 x 40½ |

The same points to be considered in judging the wearing quality of sheets should be applied to the selection of pillowcases and bolster cases. The hems should be 3 inches wide, straight and even. Seams should be firmly and evenly stitched (14 stitches to the inch) and finished to prevent raveling.

Disposable pillowcases and sheets are now made of Kaycel, a fabric that looks like cloth but has strong yarns bonded between layers of cellulose wadding. For hygienic utility in hospitals, sickrooms, and clinics, these pillowcases have proved acceptable. They can also be used as laundry and shoe bags and as wastebasket liners. They come in white and a few colors.

*Obtaining longer wear from sheets.*   Many times customers complain that sheets in service only three or four months show signs of wear. The customer blames her laundry, and the laundry claims the fault lies in the poor quality of the sheet. It is difficult to determine which is at fault. Accordingly, salespeople should give customers a few hints that will help to get longer wear from sheets.

1. Sheets wear out where shoulders rub. Experiments made in hotels show that most sheets wear out first at this point. If the sheets have hems of the same width at both ends, head and foot can be reversed to equalize wear. If hems are wider at the top, the lower sheet may be turned head to foot.
2. A sheet that is the right size for the bed will wear longer than

one that is too short or too narrow. Sheets too small for a bed are subjected to unnecessary strain.

3. Bedsprings, splinters, and nails on the bed may snag a sheet. A loose nail may work its way through the covering of a box spring; a projecting sliver of wood may catch a sheet when it is pulled off; the threads may become weakened and a hole may consequently appear. In short, a bed may be giving a sheet harder wear than the laundry.

4. Mattress pads or covers prolong the life of both the sheet and the mattress.

5. Sheets will wear longer if all holes and tears are mended before they are laundered.

6. Whether sheets are laundered at home or by a commercial laundry, strong bleaches should not be used because they weaken the cloth.

7. Folds of sheets and pillowcases should not be ironed. It weakens the fabric. No-iron sheets obviate this problem.

8. The bed should be made with a light touch rather than with force.

9. Laundries may wear out sheets by putting them through the ironer too fast. As a result the selvage may roll or fold. Continued mangling in this manner may wear the sheet out along these folds in the selvage before the body of the sheet shows wear. Shrinkage is minimized if sheets are mangled at home. Shrinkage may also be cut down somewhat by varying the method of mangling. If the flat sheet is inserted in the mangle from selvage to selvage, it grows shorter and wider. The shrinkage takes place in the length. If the sheet is run through the mangle in the other direction, the shrinkage in length may be lessened.

10. Discarded sheets should be replaced immediately. By so doing, the homemaker will get better wear than to continue to use a smaller and smaller number of sheets until they are all worn out.

## MATTRESSES AND PILLOWS

*Mattresses.* Although most housewives buy mattresses only a few times in their lives, when they do buy they want a mattress that is comfortable and durable. Probably comfort in some minds is associated with softness. Certainly in the days of feather beds softness and warmth were considerations. But there is much to be said for the firm, level mattress that does not let the sleeper sink down deeply into it and that provides good support for the body. This type will buoy up the small of the back and will be apt to keep the spine in a straight line rather than a sagging one. Beds that are too soft often restrict the normal body movements of a sleeper; beds that are too hard do not permit perfect relaxation and often restrict circulation.

Health experts say that a mattress should be adjustable; that is, the mattress should adjust itself to various degrees of pressure from different parts of the body. The body should not be required to adjust itself to an unyielding mattress.

The filling is largely responsible for comfort and durability. Probably the inner-spring mattress retains its resiliency longest (with the exception of the foam rubber). In the inner-spring or polyurethane plastic foam mattress there are approximately 200 to 850 coil springs mounted in a steel-wire frame. This spring unit is contained between two layers of padding (generally cotton) and insulating materials consisting usually of fiber pads. All these units are encased in a ticking. The durability of the inner-spring mattress depends, in a large measure, on the quality of steel used in the springs. A large number of springs is not necessarily a measure of good performance. A smaller number of well-designed springs, suitably tied and combined with padding and insulation, should give comfort, firmness, and good performance.

The majority of these mattresses have their coil springs tied with twine, wire, or metal clips in a manner to permit individual springs to move independently up and down. This movement helps the mattress to conform to and support the human body. The most popular bedsprings are box springs, in which the springs are stapled to wooden slats that are tied together at the top and fastened to an outer frame. In good-grade mattresses the springs are wrapped in muslin to prevent the wear of friction and also to eliminate creaking.

Mattresses without inner springs are filled with horsehair, kapok, felted cotton, loose cotton, or foam rubber. South American horsehair is the most durable, most resilient, and most expensive. Cattle hair is considered next best to horsehair. Kapok is less resilient than horsehair but is well suited to damp climates, because it throws off moisture and dries quickly. Felt fillings of combed cotton felted into strips and laid in layers are slightly less resilient than kapok. Loose cotton, which is often used for inexpensive mattresses, becomes lumpy in time.

Ever since the 1940's, foam rubber mattresses have been used in homes and hospitals. They are simpler in construction than inner-spring mattresses—just a rectangular slab of foam encased in ticking. A foam rubber mattress conforms to the contour of the body and supports it at all points, even the small of the back. These mattresses are about half as heavy as inner springs and never should be turned. They are expensive, but they have the advantage of being nonallergenic and not unduly hot in summer or cold in winter. They do not mildew or harbor insects; there are no buttons or tufting. Since foam rubber tears easily, any moving of the mattress should be done by its cover, the ticking. Foam rubber should never be soaked to clean it. Removing the ticking and washing the rubber with a dampened cloth is sufficient. The mattress should not be exposed to the sun, because the ultraviolet light deteriorates it.

The plastic polyurethane foam mattress, which is light and less expensive than foam rubber, assures firm, healthful support. It is very light (only 15 pounds) compared with foam rubber or inner-spring mattresses. The homemaker can easily lift it.

The mattress covering or bag that holds the filling is called *ticking*. It comes in twill weave, with variations of herringbone and Jacquard, and less frequently in sateen and satin weaves.

The color of the covering may sell the mattress to the woman who must have a harmonious color scheme in her bedroom. Drill—a stout, medium-weight twilled cotton—and cotton and rayon mixed fabrics are used. A slightly undersized ticking is preferable with the foam rubber filler in order to keep the filler from spreading.

*Tufting,* a brushlike button of clipped cotton yarn, appears at regular intervals on mattresses. These buttons, or tufts, are the ends of yarns that are drawn straight through the mattress to prevent the filling from slipping or becoming lumpy. In a good mattress, tufts are directly opposite each other on either side and are about twelve inches apart. Deep indentations at the point of tufting are noticeable. Tufts that are merely sewed on the surface of the ticking are found in the poorer grades of mattresses. Handles on either side of a mattress facilitate easy turning.

Air mattresses for station wagons and for camping are made of double-coated, rubberized woven nylon or cotton, often with built-in pillows. Also, they may be made of embossed vinyl plastic (nontextile), water-repellent poplin, or vinyl-plastic-coated cotton sheeting. Liners are cotton broadcloth, cotton flannel, or oxford. Sleeping bags may be filled with layers of polyester or goose down for insulation.

Another requisite of a good mattress is a firm edge that will hold its shape. Felted cotton used as the core of a cord stitched around the edge of the mattress insures firmness. Better grades may also have the sidewalls reinforced with filling and cloth stitched together. A selling point of the inner-spring variety is the small, screened, hole ventilator. The air drawn into the mattress every time weight is removed keeps it sanitary and prolongs its life. A cloth tape is frequently bonded to the foam rubber edges to add strength. A zipper or chain-stitched seam permits removal of ticking for cleaning.

A cover protects the mattress and also keeps sheets and blankets from soiling if the mattress is dusty. Mattress covers come in standard sizes. They are made of muslin (unbleached, printed, or in pastel shades), taffetized 100 per cent vinyl plastic, cotton muslin bonded to foam rubber, and bleached white cotton quilted pads. The plastic-foam-filled quilted mattress pad is easy to care for, nonallergenic, mildewproof, and fire- and liquid-resistant, and it will not sag because it has a strong, elasticized tuck-under to prevent slipping.

Although mattress covers should not be used primarily to cover a dirty mattress, they can often be used to cover an old, faded one. Covers should be removed and laundered at regular intervals. At this time a thorough vacuum cleaning will help keep the mattress completely dry and will prolong its life. Vacuum cleaning is even more essential when covers are not used.

*Pillows.* The factors of comfort and durability considered in buying a mattress are also considered in purchasing pillows. Some people prefer loosely filled pillows in which the head sinks deeply; others feel smothered by a soft pillow and prefer a thin, hard one. But most people seem to prefer a soft, plump one that is very resilient and light in weight.

The kind of filling used determines the comfort, wearing quality, and price. Fillings may be graded in order of excellence, beginning with the best: (1) down from the breasts of geese or ducks, (2) goose feathers, (3) duck feathers, (4) kapok, (5) fine chicken and turkey feathers, (6) mixed feathers, (7) acrylic or polyester staple fibers, and (8) foam rubber.

Of the feathers, white ones are considered best because they are apt to be finer, softer, and lighter in weight than dark ones. Down from the breasts of geese or ducks is very light, soft, spineless, and resilient. A pillow plumply stuffed with crushed goose down is a real sleep inducer. It is most expensive, however. Goose or duck feathers with quills are heavier and less resilient than down. They can be felt through the pillow casing if it is not of close construction. Turkey and hen feathers are about twice as heavy as down and are stiffer, less soft, and less buoyant. Different kinds of feathers may be mixed in the same pillow. Hen feathers are comparatively inexpensive but, like goose and duck feathers, they may come through the casing if it is not sufficiently close in weave.

Kapok and foam rubber are real boons to sufferers from asthma or hay fever. Feathers often irritate people with these diseases, whereas kapok (a vegetable fiber) or foam rubber does not. Kapok is also suitable for pillows used at the seashore, since it does not feel damp quickly, and, if it becomes wet, it dries in a short time. Cushions for canoes, cruisers, and yachts are satisfactory when stuffed with kapok, because if they fall into the water they float. Kapok-filled pillows are inexpensive, but they mat or become lumpy in time.

Synthetic staple fiber fill is nonallergenic, buoyant, odorless, and moth- and mildewproof. Better qualities of bed pillows are covered with tightly woven ticking in floral, stripes, or all-over printed patterns. Medium and poorer covers are made of percale. Any cover should be closely woven and seamed, so that stuffing does not come through. Corded edges make for durability. Separate zippered pillow protectors can be purchased to protect covers.

Foam latex pillows are springy and durable, cool for the summer months, and nonallergenic. Urethane foam is a synthetic material available in one piece or chopped form.

The following list should serve as a guide in buying pillows: [10]

---

[10] Anne Sterling, *Buying and Care of Pillows.* The author of this pamphlet is Director of Consumer Education, American Institute of Laundering, Joliet, Ill. Merchandise bearing the seal of this organization has passed extensive tests for washability and wear.

1. Balance the pillow on the hands. The lighter pillow is the better choice.
2. Press both hands into the center of the pillow. When the hands are lifted, the pillow should spring back.
3. Hold one end of the pillow and shake it vigorously. Filling should not shift easily and pack at one end.[11]
4. Pound the pillow with the fist to see if dust emerges or lumps appear. These are undesirable features.
5. Sniff the pillow for odor. If there is odor, do not buy it.
6. Notice whether the cover is closely woven and seams are welted for durability.

A few suggestions for the care of pillows follow: [12]
1. All rips and tears in a pillow ticking should be repaired immediately to prevent loss of filling.
2. All pillows should be cleaned after an illness.
3. Should a pillow sag when placed over one's arm, it needs cleaning and professional renovation.
4. Soiled tickings soil pillowcases. The use of a washable, zippered pillow cover is suggested.

## BLANKETS

Blankets, like sheets, are an essential item of bed covering. Although blankets are purchased less frequently than sheets, the consumer is just as anxious to get her money's worth when she does buy.

Blankets may be made of 100 per cent wool, cotton, rayon, acrylic and polyester fibers, or blends of these with other synthetics. Wool and cotton, longtime blanket fabrics, are now meeting competition from the newer synthetic fibers and blends. In 1967 an all-Dacron polyester un-napped Fiberwoven blanket appeared in Chatham Manufacturing Company's line.[13]

A polyester blend or 100 per cent Sanforized cotton in flat or fitted styles is commonly used for the dual-purpose sheet blanket.

The following points will guide the consumer in buying a blanket:

*Warmth.* The weight of a blanket is not a true indication of its

---

[11] According to Cameron A. Baker (research director of Better Fabrics Testing Bureau, New York), pillows properly selected don't need to be punched and tucked under for individual comfort. He has developed a device to measure filling materials, which enables a manufacturer to standardize production methods with the result that gives consumers the degree of firmness or resiliency they prefer. It is possible that performance evaluation will appear on a tag or label. The best fillers, according to Mr. Baker, are Polish goose down and Taiwan duck down (both expensive). Other fillers include chicken and turkey feathers, solid and shredded foams and rubber, man-made fibers, cotton batting, and kapok. From *Consumer Bulletin* (January 1969).

[12] Anne Sterling, *op. cit.*

[13] Fiberwoven is the registered trade name of a process that converts fiber into fabric, thus eliminating yarn-making and weaving.

warmth. Blankets average three to five pounds in weight, but very light-weight wool blankets may be just as warm as, or warmer than, heavy, tightly woven felted ones. The lighter the blanket, the more comfortable it is as a bed covering. The warmth of a blanket is determined largely by its thickness and nap, not by weight and fiber content. Since a closely napped cloth traps more still air than an unnapped cloth, it should be warmer. Pockets of still air act as insulation against cold air.

Loosely twisted filling yarns can be more successfully napped than tightly twisted yarns. The amount of twist in the filling yarns is a factor in warmth. To improve the napping of a cloth without jeoparding dura-bility, the core of the filling yarn may be tightly spun and the fibers then twisted loosely about the core. Since cotton is a vegetable fiber, cotton blankets may feel damper and therefore colder than wool if they are used in damp climates, especially at the seashore. Cotton holds mois-ture on the surface and therefore feels damp more quickly than wool, which can absorb much moisture before it begins to feel wet.

After several washings cotton blankets may shrink or felt to such an extent that they feel heavy, but they are no warmer than they were at first. To restore fluffiness or loft and air-retaining ability, cotton blankets should be renapped after laundering. A "pouf-like" finish can be applied to blankets of 100 per cent Acrilan acrylic, rayon, and blends in order to keep them from shedding, pilling, and matting. It is claimed that soft-ness and loft are retained after repeated washings.[14]

If one is looking for a very lightweight, durable, lint-free covering, then a thermal-weave blanket should be considered. Many of these blankets are full of holes and look like the afghans of Grandma's day.

In winter, a cover is placed on top of the blanket so that air warmed by body heat is trapped between the yarns. In summer, the cover is omitted and body heat is permitted to escape through tiny "air cells." Consumers' Research tests revealed that the thermal weave blankets with a cover were not as warm as a heavy wool blanket ($4\frac{1}{2}$ pounds). All the thermal-weave blankets tested with a cover were as warm as, or warmer than, a lightweight ($2\frac{1}{2}$ pounds) acrylic blanket.[15] Further-more, all the thermal-weave blankets without a cover were cooler than the woven wool blanket, but only five of the nine brands tested were cooler than the woven acrylic blanket. In this CR study, the napped blankets lost lint in laundering, but not enough to affect their original weight. Blankets were rated good to fair after three launderings. Some of these thermal weaves are known to withstand two hundred launder-ings.[16]

*Attractiveness.*   Color, design, and the finishing of the edges make for attractiveness. Blankets are made in solid colors, plain white, plaid,

[14] This protective finish is Nap-Guard, by West Point–Pepperell, Inc.
[15] *Consumer Bulletin* (December 1965).
[16] *Ibid.*

checks, novelty color combinations, and with colored borders. If a blanket is to be used as an extra "throw" (folded on the bed during the day), the color selected should harmonize with the furnishings in the room. Even if blankets are covered by a bedspread, the color-conscious consumer will want the colors in blankets to be harmonious. The edges of blankets may be whipped (a kind of scalloped machine embroidery), or bound with cotton, acetate, or nylon bindings.

Blankets with a soft texture are usually the most attractive. If wool fibers are fine, of sufficiently long staple, and smooth, the blanket is sure to be soft. Acrylic fibers have an almost cashmere-like softness.

*Durability.* Whether a blanket is wool, cotton, acrylic, rayon, or a blend, certain factors are important in judging the wearing quality:

1. *Length of the fibers.* Long fibers do not pull out or slip so readily as short fibers. If fibers are too short, they often pull out in the napping process, thereby weakening the yarn. The quality of the fibers is also important.

2. *Tensile strength of the fibers.* If fibers in a yarn are weak, the yarn is correspondingly weak. Therefore the first requisites for a long-wearing blanket are good-quality fibers sufficiently long and strong to make strong yarns.

3. *Tensile strength of yarns.* It is particularly important that warps have sufficient strength to withstand the tension in the loom and also to bear the weight of water in washing. Fillings are generally spun more loosely than the warps in order that fibers may be brushed up for the nap. Some manufacturers, however, sacrifice durability for appearance by spinning fillings too loosely and by making too thick a nap. Ply yarns usually have greater tensile strength than single yarns and so are often used for warp.

4. *Construction.* This factor depends upon the balanced strength of warp and filling—that is, a balanced count together with firm, even weaving. In considering the proportionate strength of warp to filling, it should be understood that the warp must be stronger than the filling in order to withstand the friction and tension of the loom. But if fillings are spun too loosely, they may be proportionately so much weaker than the warps that the blanket may split or shred when it is washed. This shredding occurs when strong cotton warps are used with short-staple filling fibers made of slack-twisted yarn. A well-balanced count ensures an even distribution of warps and fillings, and longer wear. Most blankets for home use are twill or a variation of the twill. This construction throws more filling to the surface for the purpose of napping.

One of the best ways to test the uniformity of the weave is to hold the blanket to a strong light. Thick and thin spots indicate poor construction. If there is a border, the weave should be the same in the border as in the rest of the blanket. A difference in closeness of the weave in the border may result in ripples or puckers after laundering.

When the blanket is held toward the light, one can see whether it has been cut straight. The ends of the blanket should run parallel to the filling yarns.

A process of tufting blankets has been developed that may, in time, compete costwise with woven blankets. (See *tufted bed-spreads and tufted rugs.*)

Nonwoven constructions are the latest innovations in blankets. One process, called Fiberwoven, converts fiber directly into fabric. Invented by Dr. Alexander Smith, a former professor at the Massachusetts Institute of Technology, the process is conducted by interlocking of many loops of fibers, shaped or entangled by fast-moving rows of barbed needles. Blankets so constructed are claimed to be warm and strong, to shrink less, and to last longer than commercially woven blankets.

The newest nonwoven blanket is produced by West Point–Pepperell, Inc., under a patented process called "Vellux." The blanket is built around an inner core of synthetic foam that has special thermal qualities that trap warmth despite the lightness of the fabric. Nylon fiber is electrostatically bonded permanently to to both sides of the core. The fabric is claimed to be soft, warm, lightweight, velvety, and luxurious. It will not shrink when laundered and is very durable; it is moth-resistant; it comes in solid colors and prints; and it can be reversed. Carved dimensional effects are available in a luxury blanket.

5. *Amount of nap raised.* As has been stated, a heavy nap of short fibers pulled out from loosely twisted yarn decreases durability. If filling yarns have sufficient tensile strength and fibers are long, a moderate nap makes a blanket attractive and warm and does not affect durability. To determine the durability of the nap, rub the surface of the blanket. If little balls of fiber roll up, the nap is made of too-short fibers, and the blanket will lose its warmth. Nap should be uniform in thickness and in coverage of the surface. Another way to test the durability of the nap is to take a pinch of it between the thumb and forefinger and lift the blanket slightly. If the nap does not pull out, the fibers are long and well anchored in the yarn.

6. *Bindings and finishes of the ends.* These should be neat and strong. Bindings should be eased onto the edge of a blanket and should be firmly stitched with two or three rows of parallel stitching or with close featherstitching. Some blanket corners fit closely like fitted sheets. Nylon makes a durable binding. Rayon and acetate are very attractive but have to be replaced sooner than nylon. Cotton sateen is inexpensive and usually wears well.

*Size.* The size of the blanket may also affect the wearing quality. A blanket too small to be tucked in sufficiently at the foot or sides, aside from giving insufficient protection to the sleeper, may wear out quickly from being pulled here and there to tuck in or to protect the shoulders of the sleeper.

In selecting blankets, as in selecting sheets, allowance for ample tuck-in should be made.

A good rule to follow is to buy a blanket as long as the length of the mattress plus the thickness of the mattress with a minimum allowance of six inches for tucking in. To determine the proper width, one should add the width of the mattress to twice the thickness plus tucking-in allowance. Blankets are made for cribs (35 x 50), single beds (60 x 80), twin beds (66 x 90), double (72 x 90), and king-size beds (80 x 90).

Blankets bear labels showing size, and must, according to the T.F.P.I.A., show fiber content. Some manufacturers also state the weight in ounces per square yard, residual shrinkage, and how to care for the blanket.

*Care of blankets.* The proper care of blankets adds to their wearing quality.

Both the wool and acrylics may be dry-cleaned satisfactorily, but this method of cleaning causes wool blankets to exhibit greater pilling, surface distortion, and change in hand than do the acrylics. Nevertheless, dry cleaning seems to be the better method for maintaining wool blankets, since it eliminates the high shrinkage from laundering.

When blankets are put away for the summer, they should be thoroughly cleaned. Cottons and synthetics are not affected by moths, but wool blankets are vulnerable, especially when dirty. Wools may be protected in mothproof cases or drawers, or paradichlorobenzene crystals may be left in a closed closet. When blankets are packed, plenty of space should be allowed for them, for, if they are pressed down tightly, they become hard and the meshes that retain air are closed up.

If the blanket has a stitched-on label giving its fiber content, it should be left on to aid the laundry in washing the blanket.

Many people who like great warmth without the weight of heavy wool prefer the electric blanket. The synthetic fibered types are completely washable, mothproof, mildewproof, and nonallergenic. They come in attractive colors, with nylon bindings. Some automatic blankets have snap bottoms so they may be converted in seconds from flat to fitted, twin, full, and king sizes.

To secure long service from electric blankets, one should not fold them, sit on them, or lie on them, since these actions may cause the fine wiring to pull out or break. Purchasers of these blankets should look for the longest guarantee and buy a well-known brand. A UL symbol (Underwriters' Laboratories) indicates that the design and safety of the blanket has been checked.

Until recently, few innovations have appeared in electric blankets. They looked and performed like an electrical appliance. But a blanket manufactured by J. P. Stevens & Co. is new in internal design: there are no more wires; it is regulated by body temperature; there are no moving parts so it is virtually unbreakable; it doesn't "go on and off"; and the control box can be eliminated because sensitive thermisters (heat sensors) are imbedded in the blanket at the chest and feet levels and because of solid-state electronic circuitry. These thermisters are said to regulate the heat within one degree of the desired setting.[17] This is possible because the solid-state circuitry has the power to modulate the amount of electrical energy entering the blanket to produce the desired heat. (The old system just turned the electrical energy on when it got too cold and off when it got too hot.) The electrical control is encased in a candy-bar-sized shell at the foot of the blanket. The control switch, the size of a coin, is placed in the blanket's upper binding.[18]

There are also electric sheets, made to be used between the regular sheet and the top bed cover. These are more easily washed than the blankets and are considerably cheaper but not so warm.

### COMFORTERS

Comforters are stuffed or quilted bed coverings. In parts of New England, a soft, lightweight, very resilient comforter is called a *puff*.

A consumer may be attracted to a beautiful brocaded satin comforter; the covering is all that she knows or cares about. It will look attractive in her room; her friends will admire it; so she buys it. But, although the covering is an important consideration, this customer has neglected a vital factor from the standpoint of comfort and wear—the filling. Just as in mattresses and pillows, the filling can make the comforter light or heavy, soft or hard, resilient or not. No one wants to be weighed down with heavy bed coverings that are hard and possibly lumpy. Heaviness does not necessarily make the comforter warm, for a resilient comforter, like a blanket, enmeshes air to retain warmth.

To test the amount of resiliency or buoyancy of a comforter, put one hand on the top and the other hand on the bottom of the comforter and press them together. Note how much it can be compressed and how fast it returns to its original shape. If it does not spring back to shape, there is a good chance of its becoming bunchy and misshapen in a comparatively short time when in use. If two comforters of the same thickness are compared, one may compress greatly and spring back quickly, whereas the other may compress very little and return to shape slowly. The former is usually the lighter in weight and will retain its resilience longer while in use.

[17] *New Idea in Electric Blankets,* a pamphlet by Linens and Domestics, Inc., 153 West 3rd Street, New Richmond, Wis. (November 1968).

[18] Sears Roebuck's automatic blanket, with solid-state control, is guaranteed for five years.

*Fillings.* Fillings for comforters can be made of cotton, acetate and cotton, wool, down, feathers, acrylic, and polyester fibers. Long-staple cotton of good grade is resilient, wears well, and is inexpensive. Short-staple cotton, a coarser and poorer grade than the long-staple, is the second-best type of cotton filling. Short fibers, because they do not cling together as well as long ones, lump or bunch more readily. Cotton linters are poor because they do not have sufficient resiliency. Excellent grades of cotton are superior to poor grades of wool.

Fine, long-staple Australian wool makes a soft filling. The first shearing from the lamb is particularly fine and soft. The better-grade fillings are made of carefully scoured and carded wool. Poorer grades are grayish in color, poorly scoured, poorly carded, and less soft. Often poor scouring leaves burrs and foreign substances in the filling, which in time may work their way through the covering of the comforter. Short ends removed from the sliver in the carding of wool are often used for poor-grade fillings. These short fibers are wool waste and are often coarse. Reused wool may also be used. As with cotton, long, well-carded fibers are necessary if a filling is to cling together and not lump.

Down and feathers are also used for filling. The former is the softest, lightest, most expensive filling. It is very resilient and warm. Down from the breast of the goose or duck is good, but down from a large sea duck, the eider, is even better. As a substitute for down, chopped chicken feathers are often used. But despite careful chopping, the quills can usually be felt if the comforter is pressed from above and below. Quills may work their way through a covering and shorten the life of the comforter. To prevent this, a covering should be closely woven, or two thicknesses of covering should be used. Man-made fibers are being used in comforters to replace down. The synthetic fiber fills of acrylics or polyesters are moderately priced, allergy-free, snow white, mildewproof, odorless. Their resiliency has been greatly improved.

*Coverings.* Comforter coverings should be soft and pliable, with good draping qualities; that is, they should cling to the other coverings on the bed and not look too bulky. A stiff, harsh material makes a cover that is hard to quilt—that is, to sew in a pattern or design. Corners may also appear bulky if the covering is too stiff.

Some fabrics slip easily, and no matter how well they are tucked in they do not seem to adhere to the bed. Rayons made in long-float satin weave have this undesirable characteristic. In fact, any satin of silk, acetate, or rayon will slip more than a fabric with a ribbed or dull surface. A closely woven nylon taffeta is both attractive and durable, but it too may slip. A fabric made of tightly twisted yarns in a firm weave is best. Brocaded satins are luxurious in appearance and adhere better than plain satins. Sateen and polished cotton are both practical and inexpensive. Cotton corduroy and percale can also be used for less expensive coverings. A wrinkle-resistant fabric is desirable for a covering. If washable, a durable press fabric is desirable.

Coverings should be made with finishes permanent enough to dry
clean or launder. A homemaker should save and follow instructions for
care given on the attached label.

*Quilts.* Quilts are thinner and less expensive than comforters.
Antique patchwork quilts, pieced by hand, in some instances are works
of art. Artistic, well-made ones are collectors' items and, if in good condition, are expensive. Favorite designs were the star, wedding ring, or
conventionalized florals. Frequently the maker made her own designs. She
cut her own pieces, sewed them together in blocks or motifs, and sewed
the blocks together to form the top covering of the quilt. Generally
these covers were bright-colored solid or printed cottons, occasionally
silk. When the covering was finished, a fabric the exact size for the back
was cut and made ready for the next step, quilting. Cotton batting was
placed between the covering and the backing. Then great-grandma was
ready for her quilting party. Friends came in for the afternoon to help
her sew the three layers (cover, batting, and back) together. Geometric
or floral patterns were made with fine quilting stitches. Quilting was
done on a frame to keep the fabrics smooth and in shape. The edges of
the fabric were bound with bias-cut strips of cloth.

There are no standard sizes for antique patchwork quilts. Size was
governed by the size of the bed to be covered and by the pieces of fabric
available for the purpose.

Designs of modern patchwork quilts are frequently copies of old designs. Modern quilts may not have the sentiment connected with the old
quilts, but their colors are faster. The machine stitching makes them
firm, yet gives the homemade effect. Some so-called patchwork quilts
have covers made of one piece of cloth printed to resemble small pieces
sewed together. They are quilted or tufted. This type of quilt is quite
inexpensive. Filling may be cotton or polyester.

Modern cotton patchwork quilts can be laundered at home or can be
sent to the laundry. Antique quilts should be dry cleaned, because there
is no assurance of the fastness of the colors. Furthermore, the fabric may
have tendered with age.

### BEDSPREADS

One who is beginning to furnish a new home decides what type each
room is to be—formal or informal—and what period or periods are most
appropriate to each room. She usually buys large pieces of furniture first.
The accessories, such as bedding, curtains, and pillows, come next.
Although the average consumer may not think of style or appearance
first when she buys pillows or a mattress for a bed, appearance is the
first consideration in purchasing a bedspread. The intelligent buyer tries
to visualize the bedspread in its intended setting. She asks herself, "Will
it harmonize with my curtains, rugs, and upholstered chairs?" Fortunate
is the woman who has this power of visualization.

*Principles of Selection.* A few simple principles will guide the consumer in the selection of bedspreads:

1. Materials should be of a texture that will not wrinkle or crush easily. This is particularly important when beds are to be used as seats during the day.
2. Materials should be cleanable by automatic washing or dry cleaning. Preshrunk fabrics that require no ironing are desirable.
3. The spread should be large enough for the bed. If pillows are to be covered so that they give the effect of a bolster, the length should be 105 or 108 inches. The sizes (without flounce ruffles) stocked in stores are as follows:

| Type of Bed | Size of Spread (inches) |
|---|---|
| Bunk | 63 x 100 |
| Twin | 76 x 105, 79 x 108 |
| Double | 88 x 105, 96 x 108 |
| Queen size | 102 x 120 |
| King size | 120 x 120 |

4. The spread should be cut and sewed so that it has a trim appearance, whether tailored or boxlike. Flat spreads often have rounded corners. A spread of heavy material generally fits better if the corners are cut out for a fourposter bed. It is not so important to cut out corners if the material is light. Split corners and corner inserts help to give a good fit.
5. In tailored spreads, double interlocked seams and cord welt edges ensure serviceability. Matching the bedspread with draperies, upholstered chairs, or cushions makes a pleasing effect, provided the

**Figure 18.9.** Quilted bedspread. (Courtesy of the Lawtex Corporation.)

colors do not become monotonous. The modern homemaker considers the design as well as the utility of bedroom and bathroom, and she chooses her draperies, curtains, bedspread, blankets, sheets, towels, and accessories accordingly. Cooperation of manufacturers in ensembling their related products makes shopping quick and easy.

Some of the quilted spreads are filled with polyester or acetate fibers.

Flounce ruffles, pillow shams, and draperies may be made of the same fabric as the spreads. These items can be purchased separately as well as in ensembles.

The following fabrics are used for bedspreads:

| | |
|---|---|
| Washable corduroy | Cotton sailcloth * |
| Loop woven cotton Jacquards with knotted fringe | Quilted rayon, acetate, nylon |
| | Textured cotton and blends |
| Candlewick (cotton) | Tufted cotton (see Glossary) |
| Broadcloth (cotton) * | Embossed cotton * |
| Chenille (cotton, rayon) | Crocheted lace |
| Embroidered fabrics | Taffeta (rayon, acetate, nylon) |
| Polished cotton * | Elaborate Jacquards (Old World look) |

* Particularly well suited for children's spreads.

## SUMMARY

Bed coverings, towels, and table coverings are a very important part of home furnishings. Now that dyes are fast, printing more attractive, and woven designs more varied, style has really entered the domestic field. Some department stores feature ensembles for the bathroom in a special department, or bath shop. In short, a consumer should give as much consideration to the assembling of bed and table coverings and towels as she does to the buying of ready-to-wear clothes and accessories. Care in selection and proper care in use ensure the durability and long life of domestics.

## PROJECTS

1. Plan a color-coordinated ensemble for a bathroom that has one window, beige tile walls, pink fixtures and red wall-to-wall carpeting.
   (a) List all the household textiles you will need in this room for a family of two adults and two children (aged four and six).
   (b) Include the names of each fabric, its size, color, and design.
   (c) In a few paragraphs, give the reasons for your choices.
2. Plan the household textiles of either a college girl's or a college boy's bedroom.
   (a) Accurately describe or draw a floor plan of the room.
   (b) Accurately describe fabric or include swatches of fabric that you would suggest for bedspread, curtains or draperies, and accessories.

(*c*) Draw or accurately describe the style and size of each item.

(*d*) In a few short paragraphs, give the reasons for your choices.

3. Plan a table setting for a Sunday dinner for a family of two adults and four children of high school and college age.

   (*a*) Describe the table covering and napkins with regard to fabric name, texture, size, color, and price.

   (*b*) List and describe the household textiles used for the occasion.

4. (*a*) Make a count of colors, sizes, and prices of terry cloth bath towels sold in three retail stores.

   (*b*) Tabulate the results of your findings.

   (*c*) Analyze your data, and come to some conclusions as to how well these stores are meeting customer demand in the community.

## GLOSSARY

**Bar towels.**  A variety of glass towel. See *Glass towels*.

**Bath rug.**  Usually a comparatively small rug with cotton, rayon, or nylon pile suitable for a bathroom.

**Bed linen.**  Any cotton, linen, or nylon sheeting for use on a bed.

**Blanketing.**  A heavily napped fabric of wool, cotton, or synthetics in blends or mixtures, woven 60 or 80 inches or more in size in plain or twill weave.

**Bolster.**  A long, rectangular pillow the width of the bed.

**Candlewick.**  See *Tufted fabric*.

**Cheesecloth.**  A sheer, very low count, slackly twisted, carded cotton fabric.

**Chenille.**  See *Tufted fabric*.

**Chintz.**  See Chapter 20.

**Comfortable.**  Synonym for *comforter*.

**Comforter.**  A quilted bed covering made with a layer of stuffing between two fabrics of taffeta, brocaded satin, sateen, or printed muslin.

**Contour sheets.**  See *fitted sheets*.

**Crash.**  A linen, cotton, or mixture suitable for dish, glass, and kitchen towels. Better grades may be used for luncheon sets, doilies, and bureau scarfs. See Glossary, Chapter 16.

**Cretonne.**  See Glossary, Chapter 20.

**Crocheted lace.**  For bedspread or table cover. See *Lace*.

**Damask.**  A fabric for table cloth and napkins in Jacquard weave. The pattern is reversible. Linen, cotton, rayon, or a combination of fibers are made in double or single damask.

**Dimity.**  See Glossary, Chapter 16.

**Domestics.**  A classification of textile merchandise that includes towels, table covers, and all bed coverings.

**Embroidery.**  Ornamental needlework done on the fabric itself.

**Felt.**  Used for table covers. See Chapter 12.

**Fitted sheets.**  Those whose corners are made to fit the mattress. Both bottom and top fitted sheets are available.

**Gingham.**  Used for bedspreads. See Glossary, Chapter 16.

**Glass towels.**  Towels made of linen crash, cotton, or mixtures suitable for drying glasses because they are lint free.

**Guest towels or finger-tip towels.** Lightweight and smaller than hand towels. They are made of lightweight linen crash, huck, damask, terry, in white, solids, and designs.

**Huck towels.** Cotton, linen, or mixtures, occasionally with rayon in honeycomb dobby weave. They may have Jacquard borders. Face or hand towels in white or colors are made.

**Lace.** A fabric created by looping, interlacing, braiding, or twisting threads.

**Longcloth.** Synonym for *muslin sheeting*.

**Muslin.** See Glossary, Chapter 16.

**Muslin sheeting.** A carded muslin for bed sheets in white or colors made in types 140 (A grade), 128 (B grade), and 112 (C grade).

**Patchwork quilts.** Made of small pieces of cotton or silk fabric cut in various shapes and sewn together to form patterns. They are quilted on a frame when done by hand. See *Quilt*. Modern patchwork quilts may be printed to resemble the hand-sewn.

**Percale sheeting.** A combed muslin (may be carded in poorer grade) for bed sheets, in white or colors, made in type 200 (A grade) and 180 (B grade). See *Percale* for dresses, Glossary, Chapter 16.

**Pickage.** The number of fillings that pass between two rows of pile yarns plus the number of fillings under the pile loops. Two fillings shot through the same pile shed and one filling shot through to interlace with the ground warps $(2 + 1)$ equals 3 picks.

**Plastic-coated fabric.** Used for shower curtains and dress covers. It is a plastic film supported by fabric or coating covering a textile fabric. See Chapter 6.

**Puff.** Synonym for a resilient comforter.

**Quilt.** A bed covering, usually thinner and less resilient than a comforter, made of two thicknesses of printed cotton muslin with cotton, wool, or batting between. Fabrics and batting are sewn together with fine quilting (running) stitches.

**Seersucker.** Used for bedspreads. See Glossary, Chapter 16.

**Silence cloth.** A padding placed under the tablecloth on a dining table.

**Table linen.** Any fabric, regardless of fiber content, that is suitable for a table covering.

**Taffeta.** Used for bedspreads. See Glossary, Chapter 16.

**Tapestry.** Used for table covers. See Glossary, Chapter 20.

**Terry cloth.** A cotton pile fabric commonly made with uncut loops usually on both sides of the fabric. It may have linen pile in a "friction" towel. It is used for bath and face towels, face cloths, and beach robes. See Chapter 10.

**Thermal woven.** A porous cloth so constructed that air warmed by the body is trapped between the yarns. First used in underwear, now also used for blankets and the reverse sides of comforters.

**Thread.** In towels (double or single). In double thread, each loop is made of two parallel threads not twisted together, and these threads come out of the same space between two fillings. Single thread is made of a single yarn and is less durable and absorbent.

**Ticking.** A heavy, tightly woven carded cotton fabric in alternate stripes of white and colors, suitable for pillow and mattress covers. It is usually twill but may be sateen weave.

**Tufted fabric.**   A fabric ornamented with soft, fluffy, slackly twisted ply yarns (usually cotton). Most tufts are inserted by needles into a woven fabric like unbleached muslin, textured cotton, and rayon plain-weave cloth. When tufts are spaced (as coin dots), the bedspread is called *candle-wick;* when placed in close rows, the fabric is chenille. "Loom tufted" means tufts woven in as the cloth is woven. See *Rugs,* Chapter 19. Tufted fabrics are used for bedspreads, mats, and robes.

**Tufting.**   A brush-like button of clipped cotton yarn that appears at regular intervals on mattresses.

**Turkish towel.**   A bath towel, face towel, or washcloth made of terry cloth

**Unbleached muslin.**   A cotton plain-weave fabric used for ironing board covers, dust covers, and dustcloths. See Glossary, Chapter 16.

# 19

# Period Styles
# in Home Furnishings
# and in Rugs

If a room is to be newly furnished, decide what sort of atmosphere you wish to create—formal or informal. This decision depends partially on the use for which the room is intended. (The following suggestions are generalizations and are not put forth as hard-and-fast rules.) For example, the living room is just what its name implies—a place to live. It should be intimate, comfortable, colorful, and hospitable. It forms an appropriate background for a gracious hostess; therefore cold formality would not be suitable. A drawing room, however, may be more severe or elaborate or formal. A library is best described as quiet and dignified. Rooms that are used less frequently may be a little more bold and vigorous. Foyers, halls, and dining rooms come under this description. A bedroom should be restful, charming, and restrained; a nursery, restful and quiet but bright; a dinette, inviting and cheerful; a sunroom, brilliant and gay. The purpose of decorating is usually not to carry out to the letter exact reproductions of the furniture and furnishings of the period decided upon, but rather to convey the spirit of the period and still make the room appropriate to its particular purpose. Sometimes two or more similar types of period furniture are most effectively used together, and the monotony of one type is thus avoided. The chief principle in combining periods is not to mix massive styles with graceful, feminine types. The styles combined must have some similarity. Although furniture is not a textile and so does not rightfully come within the scope of this book, it is important to know the most common styles in order to select the appropriate fabrics for draperies, upholsteries, and rugs.

## PERIOD FURNITURE AND DESIGN

There are seven outstanding styles in furniture and home furnishings that are in use today: Italian, Spanish, French, English, American, Modern, and Contemporary. If all decorators do not agree to such a general classification, each style group may be subdivided into periods named for the king, queen, or cabinetmaker whose style in furnishings typified those times.

### ITALIAN STYLE

Large, massive furniture ornately carved—with gorgeous, vivid, striking designs in upholstery, hangings, and draperies—is characteristic of the Italian style in general. Luxury and magnificence controlled the furnishings and the fabric decorations in the days of Italy's grandeur. The Italian Renaissance (1400–1643) marked the revival of the classic arts.

Oak, willow, lime, sycamore, chestnut, ebony, and walnut were the woods used for the furniture. The designs in fabrics were large and impressive, consisting of flowers in vases or baskets, or the fluorescent artichoke or pineapple motifs, and clusters of round dots. Brocades, damasks, brocatelles, velvets, and velours are all suited to the Italian style.

This style requires large, preferably formal rooms. An upholstered sofa and a Jacobean chair or television cabinet would harmonize with the Italian style, for all these pieces have a quality of massiveness.

### SPANISH STYLE

For the Spanish bungalow or large Spanish home, the Spanish style (1451–1504) is, of course, the most appropriate.

The days of Queen Isabella, Columbus, and the Invincible Armada are reproduced in the Spanish decoration of today. Designs are large, bold in outline, often a combination of the Moorish and the Italian. Like the Italian, Spanish interiors should be spacious, since furniture and designs tend to be large, striking, and imposing. Ship designs reminiscent of the Armada and of Columbus are favorites. Scrolls and motifs similar to the Italian types are found. Fabrics suitable for a formal Spanish room include damasks, brocatelles, and velvets. For an informal room, particularly a Spanish bungalow, printed linens or coarse cottons in colorful stripes or Spanish motifs are suitable.

### FRENCH STYLES

The accepted periods of decoration are the following: Louis Quatorze (1643–1715), Louis Quinze (1723–1774), Louis Seize (1774–1793), Directoire (1795–1799), and Empire (1804–1825).

During the reign of Louis XIV, renewed interest was taken in the arts and fabric weaving. The silk industry at Lyons flourished under the patronage of the king, and France again became a producer of fine fabrics. French brocades and damasks were known for their fine quality throughout Europe. Probably the artistic interest of Louis XIV was fired by the woman whom he was courting, Louise de la Vallière, the woman who had called his hunting lodge crude and bare. In reply to this jibe, Louis built the palace of Versailles.

Louis himself loved brilliance and so was often called *le roi soleil*—the Sun King. He preferred very large designs, such as flowers in baskets, immense fleurs de lis, feather and flower motifs. Rich colors borrowed from Italy—dark red, blue, dark green, and old gold—were his favorites. But a woman's choice again influenced color preference, and new, delicate colors such as yellowish pink (called aurora), plum, yellow, and flame appeared.

So far as the cultivation of the arts is concerned, The Grand Monarch, Louis XIV, is the most important of the French kings.

French furniture of this period is thoroughly French, whereas that of the French Renaissance showed a marked Italian influence. Flat, box-like lines of the sixteenth century were replaced by framework with rounded contours, characterized by much ornamentation, such as elaborate scrolls, engraved white metal ornaments, inlays of tortoise shell, and mountings in bronze. André Charles Boulle was the outstanding furniture maker of the period.

In the reign of Louis XV, the king's favorites, Mmes Du Barry and Pompadour, were responsible for the ornamentation characteristic of all decorating of this period. Gilded wood continued to be used a great deal, and the Chinese influence began to show itself in imitations of Chinese lacquer for commodes, bookcases, and cabinets. Many more pieces of furniture were used in this period, and fabric decoration favored realistic flowers, scrolls, and chinoiseries. Beauvais tapestry was fequently used for upholstering fine sofas and chairs. The two famous furniture makers of this period, who continued to be famous during the reign of Louis XVI, were Riesener and Roentgen.

The reign of Louis XVI is marked by less ornate design, of more delicate and refined treatment. Designs of this period were copied from furniture and murals excavated at Pompeii and Herculaneum. The lines of the Louis XV period are curved and twisted, whereas Louis XVI furniture and design are straight-lined and right-angled. Chair legs are usually straight and fluted longitudinally like columns, with the smallest part at the base.

Marie Antoinette, wife of Louis XVI, was interested in a rural life. Pastoral scenes, interlocked rings, musical instruments, turtle doves, bowknots, and gardeners' tools were popular motifs for upholstery and hangings. Bows of ribbon often surmounted furniture panels and chair backs. Brocade, satin, damask, and *toile de Jouy* prints were common upholstery coverings and draperies. More background and less design is shown in this period. The Jouy prints were the first roller prints (made by direct printing) and became so much the vogue that they rivaled the brocades of Lyons.

The Directoire period (1795–1799) was a transition in design from Louis XVI to Empire. Napoleon emerged as the central figure after the French Revolution ended the monarchy. He admired Rome and so had

Figure 19.1.    A drawing room. (*Courtesy of Owens-Corning Fiberglas Corporation.*)

palaces redecorated in formal styles. The bee and the butterfly were his symbols. Designs were rich in color and perfectly balanced. Motifs were classical, probably taken from works of art excavated at Pompeii. Stripes, medallions, cornucopias, circles, and squares were typical designs. Napoleon preferred golden yellow, red, and green; his wife, Josephine, liked pale blue, white, yellow, mauve, and gray. Woods commonly used in furniture were ebony, mahogany, and satinwood. For upholstery, heavy brocades, silks, and satins were used.

Then followed the Empire period of decoration (1804–1825). Furniture became more solid and heavy, and was frequently ornamented with brass or bronze mountings. Mahogany, ebony, and rosewood, often inlaid with ivory, were used for furniture. Chair legs were fluted in front, somewhat like the Louis XVI type, but they were heavier. The back legs were curved in the classic mode. Some legs were made in the form of bundles of arrows, or fasces. Upholstery was heavy, consisting of damasks, velvets, and prints. Jacob was the leading cabinetmaker of the period. A simplified Empire style suited to the less pretentious life of the provinces is called Biedermeier in Germany.

*French provincial.* For rustic simplicity, the style of the furniture and furnishings of the French nobility who created it in the provinces is reproduced for use in American homes. This style makes an interior informal, gay, and inviting. The furniture is made of hardy woods, usually maple, and can be combined very well with Early American styles. Chairs are comfortable with their wide seats and padded backs, and tables are spacious. Floral or pastoral designs in chintz, cretonne, linen crash, and rough-textured peasant linens are in good taste.

## ENGLISH STYLES

The periods of English decoration may be divided into three main classifications: Early English, Georgian, and Victorian.

*Early English* styles may be subdivided into Jacobean (1603–1688), William and Mary (1689–1702), and Queen Anne (1702–1714).

During the Tudor days, when Henry VIII reigned, portable furniture and decorative refinements were rare. Cushions and fragments of cloth were used for decoration, if any cloth was used. But when Elizabeth became queen in 1558, she encouraged all forms of needlecraft and weaving. Velvets and tapestries were imported. She had walnut trees planted abundantly so that succeeding generations might profit and not be dependent upon oak for furniture. So, although the Jacobean style of decoration did not begin until 1603, the foundation was laid in Elizabeth's time; her interest in window, bed, and wall hangings spurred textile imports and encouraged weaving and needlework at home.

Elizabeth's successor, James I, furthered the new movement by interesting himself in embroideries and tapestries; the result was that handsome designs prevailed in Jacobean hangings and upholsteries. The

Jacobean floral is the characteristic design of the period. It is a rather large pattern full of gorgeous colors that emphasize movement and rhythm. English traders were bringing home from the Far East, especially India, fabrics which English designers copied. The Indian tree design and crewel embroidery were introduced into England in this manner. Heraldic insignia were important patterns for wall hangings.

Lines in furniture were straight or coldly curving, with vigorous scroll work and trimmings; pieces were consequently sturdy and heavy and often massive. Oak and some walnut were used. Embroideries, printed fabrics, needlepoint, brocade, velvet, and leather comprise the leading upholstery fabrics.

The next important period in Early English styles is that of William and Mary (1689–1702).[1] The ruggedness of Jacobean styles was modified by a Dutch influence that lent a more homelike and cheerful effect. Straight lines changed to sweeping curves; proportions were a bit finer. Walnut was the principal wood used in furniture. Needlework, chintz, damask, and leather were the common upholstery fabrics.

The period called Queen Anne (1702–1714) was not influenced much by Queen Anne herself, for history records that she possessed little originality or taste. It was a time of great commercial activity—a get-rich-quick era when gambling, dueling, and drinking were pastimes. It forms a period of transition from the massive furniture of the Early English style to the more delicate Georgian type.

Rooms of that time were spacious, sometimes with ornamented ceilings. The furniture does show a marked tendency toward comfort. The "easy chair" came into use; one type is the wing chair. These chairs were upholstered and often overstuffed. Love seats also came in. Common upholstery fabrics were petit point, needlepoint, and gros point. The period marked the popularity of the highboy (made in two sections for convenience in moving), the kneehole desk with hidden drawers, writing tables, and secretaries. For hangings, Chinese embroideries and India prints were popular, and chintz in oriental designs was used for window draperies. Some authorities credit Queen Anne with originating the fashion of covering furniture entirely with fabric. At any rate, the idea was a good one. A customer who wishes to cover a Queen Anne chair for the living room should consider fabrics having sturdy textures and well-defined yet small patterns in appropriate colorings that harmonize with other furnishings.

*The Georgian period of decoration* (1710–1806) was marked by the expert craftsmanship of a new group of cabinetmakers: Chippendale, Hepplewhite, Sheraton, and the Adam Brothers. During this period, as was true in France at the time of Louis XV, rooms became smaller, less like Roman temples, and pieces of furniture became more numerous. This was an era of chairs. Whereas chests, benches, and stools were suffi-

---

[1] Some authorities place the elegant, gay Carolean style between the Jacobean and the William and Mary.

cient as seats for lesser members of a household in earlier days, chairs now became essential for all. This demand for chairs afforded Chippendale an opportunity to express his ability. Mahogany supplanted walnut and oak. Much of Chippendale's furniture stressed the Chinese influence, but the Adam Brothers emphasized the classical; even Chippendale, toward the end of his career, showed the new classic influence in his work.

One of the four Adam Brothers (all architects) became interested in travel and studied Roman ruins extensively. He introduced the classical feeling later expressed in their work. He also created the interest in exquisitely decorated painted furniture and popularized the use (in England) of satinwood and inlay. The Adam Brothers are particularly well known for artistic chairs and sofas. French brocades and moirés were favorite upholsteries.

Hepplewhite and Sheraton were contemporaries of the Adam Brothers. Furniture became more delicate in proportion, more slender and refined. Mahogany, satinwood, and rosewood inlay were used. Fabrics for the Hepplewhite period took on a French appearance. The French satin stripe became popular, together with silks and satins and designs of festoons, tassels, and ribbons. The designs that Sheraton approved were more conservative and classical than Hepplewhite's. Lightweight silks, damasks, and printed linens in designs of urns, musical instruments, and medallions were favored by Sheraton.

*Victorian period.* Queen Victoria of Great Britain had the longest reign in English history. The Victorian era (1837–1901) was the day of the horsehair sofa, the very high architectural headboard on beds, wax flowers covered with glass, the parlor with its mantelpiece and whatnot covered with bric-a-brac, red plush seats in chairs and railroad coaches, and the marble-top table. In short, there was much gingerbread work. Black walnut, oak, and mahogany were commonly used woods. Some of the architecture and furniture of the period borders on the hideous, it is true, but revivals of Victorian styles take the most attractive elements and eliminate the gewgaws. Victorian pink was revived in dress and home furnishings. Many of the old horsehair sofas and chairs still sell at a premium.

### AMERICAN STYLES

American styles begin with Early American (1607–1725), the period of early colonization, and continue through the period 1725–1790, often called Colonial. These two periods before the colonies became states will be discussed together.

Much of the early furniture and furnishings used in America were essentially English styles: Jacobean, Queen Anne, Chippendale, Hepplewhite, and Sheraton. Some furniture was brought from England, and the rest was made here in reproduction of the styles with which the

Figure 19.2. The Green Room of the White House. This room is furnished as a classical room of the early nineteenth century. (*Photograph of the White House.*)

Figure 19.3. One of a pair of early nineteenth-century mahogany and satinwood settees covered in authentic embroidered cotton of the period. (*Photograph courtesy of the White House.*)

colonists were familiar. English oak and walnut were used, as were also woods from native forests, such as maple, pine, cedar, cherry, ash, and hickory. The fact that the colonists were lacking in tools for making elaborate styles in furniture, and the great necessity for thrift, brought forth a style that is plain and sometimes crude, yet individual.

The first fabrics used in this country were imported from England, Italy, and France; it was not until the colonists had become fairly securely established that they began to make their own. In the first efforts of the colonial craftsman, present-day interior decorators find their models of Early American interiors. Homespun, damask, chintz in small designs, and quilted cottons were made. In the latter part of the eighteenth century more fabrics were imported from England and the Continent, with the result that homes became more elaborate, with silk damasks, brocatelles, Genoese velvets, and Chinese brocades. In general, Colonial styles were Georgian, Chippendale, Hepplewhite, and Sheraton.

Then came the Federal period, following the signing of the Constitution, made memorable with respect to furniture by our own great cabinet-maker Duncan Phyfe (fl. 1795–1847). He was often called "the American Sheraton." His mastery of carving and his skill in making curved lines did much to establish the Sheraton influence in America. Furniture became slender and graceful. Mahogany and walnut were the favorite woods. Striped brocades, satins, damasks, and haircloth were common upholstery fabrics.

Many of Duncan Phyfe's styles are reproduced in fine furniture of today. Some of the most common are the sectional dining table, each part of which, when not in use for dining, can be used as a separate table tilted back against the wall; and the lyre-back side chairs and sofas. The furnishings of the White House are typical of the early Federal period. (See Figures 19.2 and 19.3.)

## MODERN STYLE (1928–1948)

So-called "modern" styles appeared as early as 1911. They were a direct contrast to the work of previous periods of overabundant ornamentation. The keynote was simplicity—the elimination of all unnecessary detail. Furniture became angular and followed architectural designs. Straight lines replaced curves. Bright and dull metals, metallic wood, and inlaid wood were used in furniture. Chairs, beds, and divans were slung close to the floor, and very little ornamentation was used. During the later years, designers of modern furniture depended largely on unique construction for effect.

Although the first examples of modern furniture may not be considered entirely livable, many later modifications are good styles that will probably have a permanent place with the classic period styles. From 1928 on, the modified modern pieces gained in popularity because buyers appreciated their comfort, simplicity, and utility. The value of modern furniture lies in its functionality. If a customer wants a nightstand, she can buy one that has drawers for everything needed by the bedside and conveniently reached from the bed. Modern designers did not primarily attempt to make a nightstand look like the conventional stand; they concerned themselves first with the articles it is to hold and their ease in use, and they let the exterior take shape and size later.

Improved indirect lighting did much to change the glow in a room. Lights could be regulated to give a tone of misty gray, a beam of moonlight, or a sunny, warm gold. A gauze window curtain or draperies in silver or neutral shades could lend themselves to artistic lighting effects.

Motifs in fabrics tended toward simple geometric patterns or mechanical symbols. Casement cloth in modern designs, armure, modern tapestry, corded cloth, chenille in modern motifs, monk's cloth, modern tapestry, and rough linen-weave hangings help interpret the modern feeling.

### CONTEMPORARY STYLE (1948–     )

Contemporary style is concentrated vitality; it is fundamentally twentieth century. This clear, uninhibited expression of decorative arts and crafts is considered essential in our present and future living.

Materials have become an integral part of design for function, and there has been a lightening of structural parts. Beautifully grained plywoods have replaced all kinds of dust-catching moldings and carvings. Materials such as glass brick and unbreakable sheet glass have put dark corners in the past and have brought a view of the outdoors and gardens into the furnishing of a room.

Interiors are planned for functional efficiency with a sophisticated simplicity and mobility that is as arresting as it is livable. The use of plastics in furniture and accessories has been tested and accepted, and the use of mirror and glass for walls and interior divisions has given a new dimension to our rooms.

Fabrics with texture and with geometric designs are becoming increasingly important. Fabrics are being used lavishly from ceiling to floor and from wall to wall. The use of the traverse rod allows fabrics to be drawn across an entire wall with a simple pull on a cord.

Designs that were originally offered to a comparative few have been brought to the majority of consumers through the application of a photographic process to fabrics and wallpaper. Many textures and designs can be simulated by this method at much less cost than the original.

Contemporary is designed for today and tomorrow. It is adaptable to the pretentious as well as the unpretentious; to the public building as well as the private dwelling. Furthermore, the rare old family pieces of several generations will look as well in this contemporary setting with its color, lighting, and intrinsic beauty of materials, as a rare old gem in a new setting.

The use of the room has been considered in the light of the kind of atmosphere the owner wishes to create: formal or informal, elaborate or simple. An elementary knowledge of period design should help a homeowner to come to a decision about the type of furniture he or she wishes. There are a few other points to be considered, however.

Massive furniture makes a small room seem smaller, whereas a few pieces of small furniture and small designs make a small room seem more spacious than it really is. In short, furniture and designs should be in proportion to the size of the room. (See Chapter 20, pp. 599 ff. for other factors in creating a harmonious ensemble.)

## SELECTION OF FLOOR COVERINGS

Textile floor coverings are broadly classified as rugs and carpets, although in common parlance the two words are used synonymously.

Rugs are soft floor coverings laid on the floor but not fastened to it. A rug does not usually cover the entire floor. Scatter rugs are small rugs, about 2 x 3 and 4 x 6 feet, which can be placed in front of doors, couches, and stairs. Usual sizes of rugs are $2\frac{1}{4}$ x $4\frac{1}{2}$, 9 x 6, 9 x $10\frac{1}{2}$, 9 x 12, 9 x $13\frac{1}{2}$, 9 x 15, 9 x 18, 12 x 12, 12 x $13\frac{1}{2}$, 12 x 15, 12 x 18, and 12x 21.

A carpet is a soft covering fastened to the entire floor. Wall-to-wall, stair, and hall carpets are examples.

A broadloom is a seamless carpeting of any weave or style, six to eighteen (or more) feet wide. Most production today is in the form of roll goods that can be bought as wall-to-wall carpeting. Broadloom is also cut into rugs of all sizes and shapes.

Broadlooms are popular because there are no seams to break the attractive pile surface. A solid-color broadloom or one that has a two-tone effect will blend nicely with any period of furnishings.

A rug has often been called the heart of a room. If this is true, unusual care should be taken in its selection. Although today's homemakers tend to change their room decorations more frequently than the homemakers of a generation ago, a floor covering still usually represents an investment, and every consumer wants to get her money's worth in wear as well as satisfaction from her purchase.

There are several decisions a consumer has to make when a floor covering is selected—decisions as to color, design or pattern, suitability, quality, and price.

### COLOR

Although the consumer often turns to the salesman for advice, choosing colors is really a personal problem. In general, it may be said that

# PERIOD STYLES WITH APPROPRIATE WOODS, RUGS, AND UPHOLSTERY AND DRAPERY FABRICS

| Period * | Type of Furniture | | | Rugs | Upholstery and Drapery Fabrics |
|---|---|---|---|---|---|
| | Lines | Proportions | Woods | | |
| **ITALIAN** | | | | | |
| Renaissance 1400–1643 | curved and straight | massive | chestnut ebony lime oak sycamore walnut willow | oriental designs rich in coloring, with ruby red dominant | brocade, brocatelle, damask, satin, tapestry, velour, velvet; large expanse of background in fairly rich colors |
| **SPANISH** | | | | | |
| 1451–1504 | | similar to Italian | | similar to Italian | brocade, brocatelle, cottons (coarse), damask, linen (printed), velvet |
| **FRENCH** 1643–1825 | | | | | |
| 1. Louis XIV 1643–1715 | straight, also rounded | massive | chestnut ebony oak walnut | plain carpeting and designs of the period; also Chinese and some Near-East oriental designs | brocade, damask, satin, tapestry, velvet |
| 2. Louis XV 1723–1774 | curves | small and graceful | mahogany oak rosewood walnut | plain carpeting and designs of the period; some oriental designs | brocade, damask, cretonnes, moiré, needlepoint, prints, satin, taffeta, tapestry, toile de Jouy, velvet; pastel grounds, ribbons and flowers, swags, bouquets, medallions, vases; naturalistic flower designs important |
| 3. Louis XVI 1774–1793 | straight, a few curves | small, dainty, and light | mahogany rosewood satinwood walnut | same as Louis XV | similar to above; classic influence beginning to be felt; stripes |

* The dates are approximate, referring to periods of greatest influence.

559

| Period | Lines | Type of Furniture Proportions | Woods | Rugs | Upholstery and Drapery Fabrics |
|---|---|---|---|---|---|
| 4. Directoire 1795–1799 | transition from straight to straight with ovals, classic influence | small and graceful | ebony mahogany satinwood | plain carpeting and designs of the period; fairly strong colors; Near Eastern oriental and Chinese designs not suitable | materials same as Louis XIV; fabric designs classic; also stripes and small floral motifs |
| 5. Empire 1804–1825 | straight with ovals | heavy and massive | ebony mahogany satinwood | plain carpeting or Empire designs in strong, full colors | damask, brocade, moiré, satin, taffeta; medallions, swags, tassels, vase motifs, wreaths, arrow motifs, vertical stripes, scenic chintz, Indian printed cottons |
| 6. French Provincial | straight, some curves | simple and sturdy | beech fruit woods maple walnut | hooked, fiber, and rag rugs | crash (linen), cretonnes, homespuns; small wild flowers, gay plaids |
| ENGLISH | | | | | |
| 1. Jacobean 1603–1688 | straight | strong and sturdy | oak walnut | oriental patterns with distinct, vigorously drawn motifs, reds predominating | brocade, chenille, corded fabrics, leather upholstery, needlepoint, velour, velvet |
| 2. William and Mary 1689–1702 | straight, changing to curves | lighter | walnut | Chinese designs with blue and old-gold grounds; oriental designs in softened colors and small motifs | chintz, cretonne, damask, leather upholstery, needlepoint |
| 3. Queen Anne 1702–1714 | curved, little carving | light and graceful | walnut, some mahogany | similar to William and Mary | brocade, Chinese embroidery, chintz, gros point, needlepoint, petit point, India prints |
| 4. Georgian 1710–1806 (a) Chippendale 1750–1775 | straight with flowing lines, more carving | light and graceful | mahogany | oriental designs, small patterns; with Chinese Chippendale, Chinese designs with blue grounds | brocade, damask, leather upholstery, needlepoint, satin, tapestry, velour, velvet |
| (b) Hepplewhite 1765–1795 | curved, except chair legs | small, slender, and sturdy | mahogany rosewood inlay satinwood | plain carpeting or contemporary French designs; oriental designs light in coloring with fine patterns and texture | Damask, haircloth, striped and figured moiré and satin, trimmings of ribbons and tassel; classic designs |

| Period | Line | Character | Woods | Floor coverings | Fabrics |
|---|---|---|---|---|---|
| (c) Sheraton 1757–1806 | straight, a few curves | delicate, slender, narrow, and refined | mahogany rosewood inlay satinwood | similar to Hepplewhite | brocade, damask, haircloth, linens (printed), silks (lightweight); floral motifs on small scale |
| (d) Adam Brothers 1760–1792 | straight, rectangular | graceful | mahogany maple pine satinwood | carpeting matching walls in darker tones; no orientals | brocade, moiré, silks (lightweight) |
| 5. Victorian 1837–1901 | curved | fairly large with much ornamentation | black walnut mahogany oak | Brussels carpeting, tapestry rugs, Wiltons; in floral designs | brocade, damask, horsehair upholstery, plush, velour, velvet |
| **AMERICAN** | | | | | |
| 1. Early American 1607–1725 | straight | simple and sturdy | ash cherry maple oak pine | hooked rug designs, rag rugs, plaid carpeting | chintz, crash, cretonne, denim, dotted swiss, homespun, marquisette (dotted), monk's cloth, novelty cottons, organdy, rep |
| 2. Colonial 1725–1790 | curved and straight | solid and substantial | black walnut mahogany | as above; also oriental rugs in close, quiet patterns | same as Early American; also brocades and velvets being introduced |
| 3. Federal 1795–1847 | curved and straight | graceful and slender | mahogany walnut | plain carpeting or designs of the period; oriental patterns with well-colored designs | similar to Georgian |
| Modern 1928–1948 | straight, angular, and sharp pointed | solid, substantial, and simple | metal metallic-painted woods inlaid woods | plain carpeting in light and soft colors; modern designs | armure, casement cloth, chenille, corded fabrics, gauze, modern tapestry, mohair, monk's cloth, rough linens and cottons; large sweeping and block designs, exaggerated in size but simplified in line |
| Contemporary 1948– | sophisticated simplicity | sturdy, mobile, functional | grained plywoods, glass brick, unbreakable sheet glass plastics | carved and textured; geometric designs; cotton, wool, and synthetic blends | antique satin, bouclé, hand-woven effects, textured cottons, linens, gauze for curtains |

colors harmonize if they have something in common. For instance, they may belong to the same hue or color family. Colors, like people, have personalities. Some colors are gay, light, and airy, whereas others are heavy and ponderous. It would therefore be inadvisable to introduce a delicate rose into a room with massive Italian period furniture and luxurious draperies in somber colors. A decorator might advise a middle-value green or rust to relieve this somber atmosphere. It should also be remembered that the extent to which colors are used and the way of using them are additional considerations. In some combinations, one color dominates but does not overpower the color scheme, because balance is emphasized by visualizing where the colors are to be used and the relative size of ceiling, floor, upholstery, draperies, and accents. Furthermore, there is a tendency today to stress those colors that emphasize informality and easy living. Home and women's magazines, furnishing displays in retail stores, home pages of newspapers, and salesmen's advice will help the homemaker answer her color questions.

### DESIGN OR PATTERN AND TEXTURE

Floor coverings are solid-colored, two-toned, or varicolored, and are frequently called *sculptured* or *carved*. The carved rug is made in Jacquard design with different heights of pile; for example, the design might be deeper pile than the ground. Carved rugs have become very popular in contemporary styles. The choice of design in a rug is contingent upon other factors, such as use and size of room, style of decoration, and colors and designs already present in draperies and upholstery. Generally speaking, solid-colored floor coverings show footfalls more than the two-toned or varicolored types.

Sometimes a pattern in a carpet is really not obvious, yet there may be a semblance of a pattern. Three of these types of carpets and rugs for contemporary décor have emerged: the shag, the plush, and the random-tip shear. The smart "shag look" is executed in nylon, acrylic, wool, or a polyester pile. The pile is relatively long and loose, intended to provide a random-pile appearance. Shags are resilient. They come in tweed tones and high-fashion colors. Plush carpets have one level of cut pile made of soft twist yarn; they do not show any yarn texture. Random-tip shears have a high pile sheared at random.

Wool Rya rugs come from Denmark. They are made of blended wools from New Zealand and Scotland in patterns suited to contemporary décor. The pile is thick and strong for luxury and wear. The designs are woven through to the back, achieving the effect of hand craftsmanship. Rya rugs are advertised as colorfast and mothproof.

### SUITABILITY

A salesman may ask his customer, "Do you live in the room or just walk through it?" If there is heavy traffic, as in an entrance hall, a durable floor covering that will not show soil should be selected. The salesman may show the customer a *twist*, a broadloom made with uncut pile, in which yarns of different colors may be twisted together to form the pile loops. The resultant blending of colors is attractive, and the carpet doesn't show footmarks so quickly. For a bedroom, where there is little traffic, a cotton rug or a hooked rug may be appropriate.

Carpets make suitable floor coverings because they virtually eliminate floor noises such as scraping of chairs and clicking of heels. They also absorb airborne noises and reduce incidence of slips and slides. Furthermore, carpeting is comfortable—it is soft, warm, and easy to stand on.

For institutional use, a careful selection should be made, since once installed the carpet may remain in use for years. The following table compares the wear-life and other factors of five carpeting fibers: [2]

## COMPARATIVE BEHAVIOR OF CARPET-TYPE FIBERS

| FACTOR | WOOL | NYLON | ACRYLIC | MODACRYLIC | POLYPROPYLENE |
|---|---|---|---|---|---|
| Wear-life | High | Extra High | High | High | Extra High |
| Texture retention | High | Medium | Medium | Medium | Low-Medium |
| Compression resistance | Medium | Medium | Medium | Medium | Low |
| Resilience | High | Medium | High | Medium | Medium |
| Soil resistance | High | Medium | High | High | High |
| Stain resistance | Medium | High | High | High | High |
| Wet cleanability | High | High | High | High | High |
| Static generation | Medium | High | Medium | Medium | Low |
| Cost | Medium | Medium | Medium | Medium | Medium |

Indoor-outdoor carpets are floor coverings that are suitable both inside the house and outdoors—for example, carpets for boats, patios, terraces, miniature golf courses, kitchens and bathrooms. They are made in tufted construction, in 100 per cent olefin in dense pile plush-type or in a grasslike carpet of saran and 50/50 saran/polyethylene blend. They are also being made of acrylics and blends.

Consumers' Research (CR) cites an article in the *Fire Journal* of the National Fire Protection Association that describes a fire on one floor of an eleven-story fire-resistive apartment building.[3] The fire spread rapidly a distance of 84 feet down a hall corridor. Several occupants of apartments along the corridor were hospitalized because of smoke inhalation. One death occurred. The polyethylene-fibered carpeting with burlap backing laid over a foam rubber pad about an eighth of an inch thick was responsible for the fire. Consequently CR advised that this type of carpeting be used only outdoors.

[2] Courtesy of the American Carpet Institute.
[3] *Consumer Bulletin* (March 1969), published by Consumers' Research, Inc.

The Consumers Union (CU) tested fourteen brands of 100 per cent acrylic fibers for flammability when used as carpeting.[4] Ten of the fourteen were found to be flammable. Tests were also made on acrylic blended with at least 20 per cent modacrylic fibers; one out of fourteen brands proved flammable. The Textile Fiber Products Identification Act requires that carpet fiber content be disclosed in percentages. More than ordinary fire precautions should be taken by the home user of acrylic carpeting.

One hundred per cent cotton does not wear so well as wool; it is less resilient and therefore harder to walk on. It is inexpensive and can be found in interesting colors and varied textures. Preshrunk, colorfast, small-sized rugs with rubberized backing can be washed by machine. With the increasing use of man-made fibers, cotton as a pile surface for rugs has declined appreciably. Cotton yarns may be used for chain warps —those that bind the front and back of the rug together—and for filling in rugs. The price of silk makes it almost prohibitive for use in moderately priced rugs. Silk pile is exquisite in orientals but is not so durable as wool.

Fiber rugs are really made of tightly twisted strips of paper, often vinyl-coated to resist friction and moisture. They are quite inexpensive and are especially adaptable to use in summer cabins, sun porches, and so forth. Rugs of straw, sisal (often sold as hemp), and grass are suitable for the same purposes as fiber rugs.

The man-made fibers used in floor coverings were especially developed for the carpet industry and are not substitutes but permanent additions to carpet raw materials. Carpet rayon, acetate, nylon, and acrylic fibers

## APPROXIMATE DISTRIBUTION OF NUMBER OF OPEN LINES BY FIBER TYPE
(Per cent of Total)

|  | 1965 | 1966 | 1967 (R) | 1968 |
|---|---|---|---|---|
| Nylon & nylon blends | 51.6% | 53.7% | 48.4% | 45.7% |
| Acrylics & acrylic blends | 15.7 | 18.0 | 23.7 | 23.8 |
| Wool & wool blends | 27.4 | 22.9 | 18.4 | 15.9 |
| Polypropylene | 1.9 | 3.4 | 5.2 | 5.4 |
| Polyester | * | 0.5 | 3.4 | 8.7 |
| Cotton & rayon | 3.4 | 1.5 | 0.9 | 0.5 |
|  | 100.0% | 100.0% | 100.0% | 100.0% |

\* None reported.
(R) Revised.

Source: Estimates compiled from *Annual Floor Coverings Directory, Home Furnishings Daily*, February 23, 1968.

[4] *Consumer Reports* (July 1968), published by the Consumers Union of U.S., Inc. No flammability standard has been set for carpets. They did not come under the Flammable Fabrics Act until 1967, when amendments to the act authorized the Secretary of Commerce to start proceedings for the public's protection against flammability of carpeting. The Secretary has been notified of the CU's findings. Fiber companies have their own quality standards, which may require a "built-in" flame-retardant additive.

are the result of long years of research, and they are an answer to the limited world carpet wool supply.

Eighty-five per cent of all face fibers used in floor coverings produced in 1968 were synthetics.[5] These plastics will certainly help to keep our products within the consumer's budget as labor and overhead costs continue to rise. (Plastics are also making vast inroads in the furniture and hardware industries.) No data are available on carpet yardage sold by type of fiber, but there are data for 1965–68 on the percentage of distribution of various lines of carpeting fiber types, as shown in the accompanying table.

### WEARING QUALITY

Wearing quality of domestic floor coverings is based on (1) kind of fibers used, (2) quality of the yarns, (3) closeness of weave, (4) height of pile, and (5) construction of the back. (See *classification of rugs,* pp. 569 ff.)

Fibers for floor coverings should have resilience, luster, length, and strength. Wool, because it has all of these properties and also absorbs noise, was once used for almost all floor coverings.

Some rugs are made of wool; some are made of cotton, silk, paper, jute, straw, acetate, rayon, noncellulosic fibers, and blends.

The wool produced in this country is too fine and soft for use in textile floor covering. Carpet yarns are made instead from coarse, wiry, tough fleeces of low-grade wool. New Zealand and Argentina continue

[5] *Home Furnishings Daily* (March 25, 1969).

**Figure 19.4.** Enkaloft continuous filament nylon. In this enlarged picture comparing strands of Enkaloft on the left with strands of another yarn on the right, note that the crimps in the Enkaloft yarn sample are orderly; they are in waves, and this gives clearer pattern definition. The other yarn has a random crimp—its curls are irregular. (*Reproduced courtesy of American Enka Corporation.*)

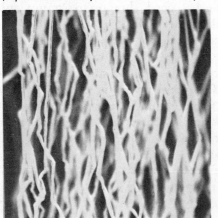
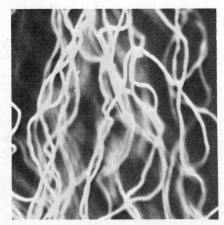

| MANUFACTURER | FIBER TYPE | REG TRADE NAME |
|---|---|---|
| Allied Chemical Corp. | *Continuous filament nylon* | Caprolan<br>A.C.E. Nylon |
| American Cyanamid Co. | *Acrylic staple* | Creslan |
| American Enka Corp. | *Continuous filament nylon*<br>*Nylon staple* | Enkaloft |
| American Viscose Corp. | *Rayon staple*<br>*Rayon filament* | Avisco<br>Avicron |
| The Chemstrand Corp. | *Acrylic staple*<br>*Continuous filament nylon* | Acrilan<br>Cumuloft |
| Courtaulds (Alabama) Inc. | *Rayon staple*<br>*Rayon staple (solution dyed)*<br>*Cross-linked rayon staple*<br>*Cross-linked rayon staple* | Coloray<br>Corval<br>Topel |
| Dow Chemical Co. | *Acrylic staple* | Zefran |
| E. I. du Pont de Nemours & Co. | *Acrylic staple*<br>*Continuous filament nylon*<br>*Nylon staple* | Orlon<br>Nylon 501<br>Antron |
| Eastman Chemical Products, Inc. | *Modacrylic staple* | Verel |
| Firestone Synthetic Fibers Co. | *Continuous filament nylon* | Nyloft |
| Hercules Powder Co. | *Continuous filament olefin*<br>*Olefin staple* | Herculon |
| National Plastics Products Co. | *Continuous filament olefin* | Vectra |
| Union Carbibe Corp. | *Modacrylic staple* | Dynel |
| U.S. Rubber Co. | *Continuous filament olefin* | Polycrest |

to be the major sources of our carpet wool imports. We also import carpet wool from the United Kingdom, Pakistan, Ireland, Iran, Italy, Iraq, India, and other countries.

Early in 1962 polypropylene fibers appeared in the pile of carpets. It is claimed that polypropylene has good abrasion resistance and resilience, is easy to clean, and makes a dense pile.

Olefin fibers are being used in indoor-outdoor "needle-punched carpets." (See definition in the Glossary.) The surface fibers are 100 percent Herculon olefin; they are interlocked and supported by a woven monofilament backing fabric. This construction is said to increase the depth of the wear surface by 50 per cent; it makes a durable, stable carpet that lies flat and does not curl. Olefin is also being used in automobiles. Yarns are bulked continuous filament, with no loose ends to cause fuzzing, pilling, or shedding.

Polyesters were introduced in 1966. They are made in sculptured designs, plushes, shags, and random-tip shears.

[6] Courtesy of the American Carpet Institute.

For the backs of carpets, cotton, jute, flax, kraftcord (a tough yarn made from wood pulp), woven and nonwoven man-made fibers, and foams are used.

Jute dominates backings in the United States, for it constitutes over 75 per cent of our primary backings market. Over 70 per cent of all carpets have secondary backs made with jute. But man-mades are increasing. The more than 20 per cent share of man-mades in the primary backings market may become 50 per cent by 1972, many in the carpet industry believe. Since there is a shortage of jute, man-made backings have come to fill the demand.[7]

The first synthetic primary carpet backing was Poly Bac (Patchogue-Plymouth), a woven fabric of polypropylene ribbon yarn.[8] Then came Loktuft (Phillips Fibers Corp.), a nonwoven polypropylene-fibered web reinforced with cotton scrim. Vinyls have also come on the market. They are durable, nontoxic, and impermeable to moisture, and they have low maintenance cost. They are used for secondary backings. Another nonwoven polypropylene fabric is Typar, by du Pont. Latex (styrene butadiene [SB] types) and polyurethane high-density foams make durable, nonskidding backings and underlays. Natural latex is still being used in contract carpeting, underlay mats, and scatter rugs. Urethane foams are important as underlay materials in contract carpeting; these foams are entering the market as a secondary backing for the needle-punched construction.[9]

A double-faced reversible rug is made out of old carpets, rags, and clothing. These materials are supplied by the prospective purchaser or by the rug manufacturer on a pound rate. For the most part, the durability of the rug will depend on the grade of fibers used.

Quality of yarns is an important factor in considering wearing quality. Wool rugs are made from either woolen or worsted yarns. The woolen fibers for rugs average three inches in length (for clothing, less than two inches). Wool fibers are purposely intertwined or interlocked in the carding process and are made into two-ply yarns. Approximately thirty more mill operations are needed for worsted than for woolen manufacture. Worsted fibers are about five times as long as woolens and are coarse and resilient. In the combing, all fibers under three-quarters inch in length are extracted. Worsted yarns have little twist and are smaller in diameter, more glossy, more wiry, and stronger than woolen yarns. The worsted yarns range from the two-ply to the six-ply variety. In wool rugs, the yarn weight (number of yarns per ounce) affects the density of the pile. Since density is a factor in wearing quality, weight of yarn is important.

Cotton yarns for rugs are made from one-inch staple and are used

[7] *Textile World* (November 1968), p. 58.
[8] "Backing Materials for Carpets," *American Dyestuff Reporter* (August 28, 1967), p. 75.
[9] *Textile World, op. cit.*

for the entire rug or for the base of the weave and to combine the surface yarns with cheaper jute yarns at the back.

Carpet yarns are made single-ply, two-ply, three-ply, and four-ply. Probably the major production is in two-ply and three-ply yarns. However, as far as wearing quality is concerned, a rug manufacturer claims that it makes no difference whether the yarn is two- or three-ply. For striated effects, three-or four-ply are used, and for very heavy fabrics three- and four-ply are necessary. Since most wear is on the pile yarn, these yarns must be of the right size and diameter, full, and lofty. They should be single or ply to give the best coverage to the surface, good appearance, and adequate tensile strength.

New bicomponent acrylic-fibered yarns, the texturized and bulky synthetic yarns, have afforded new possibilities for styling in floor coverings.[10] Multiple random colors are possible with space-dyed yarns. (See Chapter 3 for description of space dyeing.)

### CONSTRUCTION

Closeness of weave is another factor in judging wearing quality. Although density of the pile is affected by the weight of the yarn, there are two more factors figuring in density: the pitch and the rows of pile per inch. Pitch is the number of pile warp yarns to the 27-inch width. The standard of 27 inches is used because the original carpeting was woven 27 inches wide. The greater the number of rows, the closer the pile. In chenille and Axminster construction, the term *rows to the inch*, referring to yarn tufts in the lengthwise direction, is used to express closeness of the pile surface yarn. The more rows to the inch, the denser the pile and the greater the durability, provided the size of the yarn is correct. One could not expect a dense pile even though the pitch was good if the pile yarn were thread size. If any white lines show crosswise, the rug is called a "grinning" rug and is not a good quality.

Height of pile is still another factor in construction. Closely woven worsted rugs require a low pile, whereas some Axminsters call for very high pile. The manufacturer decides what length to use. But in general, high-pile rugs flatten and show footfalls more quickly than those with low pile (depending somewhat on the resiliency of the fibers). High piles are usually more difficult to keep clean.

A strong backing supports the pile and forms the foundation of the carpet. A close, firmly woven back gives this support.

Long wear, however, is not as important as it used to be in the selection of a floor covering, for modern homemakers are making more frequent changes in their furnishings than was done formerly. Lower-priced rugs fit into this picture.

---

[10] See Chapter 2 for definition of bicomponent fiber.

Many factors have made possible a general decrease in the prices of rugs. A new process of construction, called *tufting*, has speeded up carpet construction and has brought prices down. Wool and man-made fibers alone or in blends in a wide range of colors and textures make tufted rugs popular. Also, cotton rugs, which can be purchased in variety stores, have an average price that is much lower than all-wool or mixtures. (All-cotton rugs sell on the average slightly higher than fiber.) A mixture of rayon or acetate with wool is lower in price than all wool. Then, too, the olefin fibers and polyesters have entered the market.

### CLASSIFICATION OF RUGS

Rugs may be broadly classified as domestic and imported. Or they may be divided into handmade and machine-made groups.

Handmade rugs include hand-tied orientals and hand-hooked, hand-braided, and hand-crocheted rugs. Domestic and European oriental, Wilton, Axminster, chenille, tapestry, and grass rugs are made by machine. Hooked and rag rugs made by machine also come under the latter grouping.

## DOMESTIC RUGS AND CARPETS (MACHINE-MADE)

### MAKING THE DESIGN

The choice of the weave to be used after the yarns are spun depends upon the design required. If the design is Jacquard, it is worked out

Figure 19.5. Tufted domestic carpet: 100 per cent SPECTRODYE nylon, six producer dyed, continuous filament pile yarns; double jute backing; random, multicolor pattern. (Courtesy of American Enka Corporation.)

in point-paper pattern first, with the warp pile indicated. The design is then sketched in miniature; the master design is laid out and painted (preliminary sketching is done with charcoal, then temporary colors are applied); Jacquard cards are cut to control the weaving processes; and these cards are stamped. For a 9 x 12 rug, it takes five to six weeks to prepare the cards that control the loom and about three hours to weave the rug.

In present-day advertising, probably much more emphasis is placed on the fiber content and brand name of a rug or carpet than on the weave or construction. In former years rugs were sold on the basis of construction alone. Knowledge of the construction should be a great help to a consumer in getting her money's worth in wearing quality and in selecting an appropriate construction for a specific use.

Despite the wide variety of patterns and textures in modern carpeting, about 98 per cent of all carpeting sold in the United States is made in woven, knitted, or tufted types.

### WOVEN

A single fabric is created by simultaneously interweaving the surface pile and backing. Until recently, this was the common method of making machine-made rugs. Woven carpets include Wilton, Axminster, velvet, chenille, fiber, and grass. These carpets will be discussed fully. Many handmade rugs, such as hand-tied orientals, are woven.

### KNITTED

Like woven carpeting, the knitted type is made in one operation. But unlike the woven, the knitting process loops together the backing yarn, the stitching yarn, and the pile yarn with three sets of needles in much the same way as in hand knitting. Knitted carpeting is usually made with uncut loops, both single and multilevel. For cut pile, modifications must be made in the knitting machine. To give additional body to a carpet, a coat of latex is applied to the back. Frequently, a second backing is added.

### TUFTED

In the tufting process, pile yarns are sewn to a broad fabric backing of jute, of kraftcord, or cotton canvas by wide-multiple-needled machines. To lend additional "hand" and dimensional stability a second backing may be added. A coating of latex on the back of the carpet holds ends of yarn in place. Tufted rugs come in 9-, 12-, and 15-foot widths. Originally tufted constructions were solid-colored because dyeing follows construction. Owing to new developments and variations in tufting construction, the tufted pile can be multilevel, cut, or uncut.

Carved and striated effects are made. Looped or plush textures are among those available. Twenty years ago, there was no tufted carpet industry. Now 90 per cent of the square yardage produced is tufted.[11]

[11] *Textile World* (April 1968), p. 277.

**Figure 19.6.** The tufted process. (*Reproduced courtesy of the American Carpet Institute Inc.*)

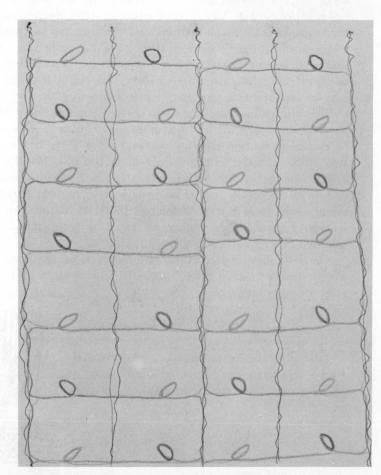

**Figure 19.7.** Trendtex, a tufted rug. The loop is angled in different directions so that the pile will not mat in one direction. (*Reproduced courtesy of Mohawk Carpet Mills Inc. Drawing by Richard Fleming.*)

### WILTON

As early as 1740 some weavers were imported from France to England, and a carpet factory was established at Wilton, England. In 1825, the Jacquard loom was adapted to Wilton carpeting. There are two types of Wilton rugs: wool Wiltons and worsted Wiltons, the name depending on the type of yarn used.

Yarns for Wiltons are skein-dyed; consequently the dye penetrates to the core of the yarn. Since the rugs are woven on a Jacquard loom, intricate patterns are possible. One color at a time is drawn up as pile, and the other colors are buried beneath the surface. For this reason the number of colors in a Wilton is limited. Buried yarn gives body, strength, and resilience to the carpet. The flat wires used to form the pile loops have knives on the ends that cut the top of each loop as the wires are withdrawn. The pile of a Wilton is therefore erect and cut. The depth of the wire regulates the depth of the pile. If a round wire is used instead of a flat wire, the pile is uncut and the construction is called *round-wire carpet*. To explain further: cotton warp yarns are set up in the loom first. Cotton is used because the fiber can be twisted into a yarn stiffer and stronger than any that could be made from other fibers of similar diameter. These cotton warps are so placed that there are 256 to every 27 inches, a standard width. This count is called the *pitch* of a rug. In a poor-grade rug the pitch is as low as 120.

The fillings in Wiltons are also cotton, but the pile yarns forming the pattern are wool (woolen or worsted), cotton, or blends with synthetics. In this construction there are either two or three filling yarns between two rows of warp loops holding down the pile. Such a filling yarn is called *pickage* in terry cloth, but it is called *shot* in rugs. Each row of pile, or tufts, on the surface of a rug is called a *wire*. A rug with thirteen wires to the inch represents the best grade of Wilton; an eight-wire rug is a poor grade. The number of wires, or rows of pile, can be easily counted on the back of the fabric.

Good-quality Wilton rugs are long-wearing, luxurious carpets. With a wide range of solid colors, patterns, and textures, Wilton carpets and rugs are very desirable.

### AXMINSTER

Although the Axminster loom was invented by an American, the name comes from a town in England. The special mechanism of this

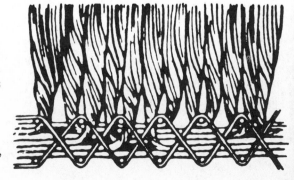

Figure 19.8. Wilton carpet. (Reproduced courtesy of the American Carpet Institute Inc.)

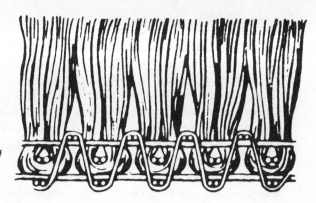

loom permits carpets of an unlimited number of colors and designs to be constructed on it. The pile yarns, all on the surface, are not concealed (buried) inside the rug as in the Wilton. These yarns are made of wool, man-made fibers, or blends; they are inserted in the fabric and held by binder yarns. When pulled out, pile yarns are V-shaped. The back of an Axminster is usually jute, is heavily ribbed, and cannot be rolled crosswise—only lengthwise.

More time is expended in preparing the yarns for weaving the Axminster than in the actual weaving operation. Different colors are carefully designated, and each color needed is wound on 6-inch spools.

Each pile yarn in the row running across the fabric is provided with its own spool of yarn in the exact color required. Then these yarns are rewound on larger spools, the number of spools for each row of pile depending on the number of rows to be woven before the pattern is repeated (as many as 1,600 may be required). Each spool carries the right amount of yardage. The spools are arranged in order by numbers and are then hung end to end on a chain. A row of spools is lifted by a frame to bring the ends of the yarn on the spools down into the upper chain warp. The wool thus brought down is caught between the warps and bound tightly by a weft shot; the ends are turned up and cut off by knives; and the spools are pulled back to their original position. The frame that brings the spools down to the warp seems almost like a human arm in its operation. The Axminster has a greater similarity to the hand-knotted oriental than any of the other machine-made fabrics, because of the way in which the pile yarns are fastened.

To estimate the durability of an Axminster, look at the back. If there are $10\frac{1}{2}$ rows to the inch, the rug is of fine quality; 8 rows indicate a medium grade, and 5 rows a poor grade. Another requisite is that the rug have 3 shots and 2-ply filling. A good standard pitch is 189 warps to 27 inches. Axminster as a construction is not as durable as the Wilton.

## CHENILLE

Although chenille rugs are of more recent origin in this country than the others, the chenille process was patented in Glasgow, Scotland, in

1839. Chenille rugs are aristocrats. They are often custom woven. *Chenille* is the French word for caterpillar. Like the caterpillar, chenille rugs are soft and have beautiful colorings. They have the deepest pile of any rug, any number of colors or designs may be woven into them, and they may be any shape or size. Two looms are needed in making this type of rug. The first one weaves the chenille fur, or *blanket*. Cotton warps are set up in the loom, and large woolen yarns are woven in as fillings. The fabric so made, the chenille blanket, is later cut into narrow strips, lengthwise of the fabric, by revolving knives. The strips are pressed into steam-heated V-shaped grooves, uniting with the cotton yarns at the point of the V. This is the fur or yarn that resembles a caterpillar. It is used as a filling in the weaving of the rug on a second loom. The chain warps and stuffer warps may be cotton or jute. Extra filling yarns for backing may be of wool. After the weaving, the pile is sheared to the desired depth.

To make certain of durability, the consumer should buy chenille rugs made by a reliable manufacturer. Chenilles are the highest priced machine-made rugs. There are inexpensive chenilles, but it is not economical to buy them, because their durability is questionable. Poor chenilles have a weakness: if a binder yarn breaks, an entire strip of pile may be loosened.

Chenille rugs, because of their soft pile, luxurious appearance, and flexibility in size and design, are particularly suited to living and dining rooms, hotel and theater lobbies, and stairs.

A variation is known as the *round chenille*. The strips of fur are round rather than V- shaped, and form a reversible rug with pile and pattern alike on both sides. Another variation combines characteristics of the Wilton and the Axminster; there is a heavy wool back, yet the manufacturing process allows an almost unlimited number of colors and a high pile to be used, as in the Axminster. Chenilles are sheared by revolving shear knives. Plain chenilles are often carved by hand in floral patterns or scrolls. Figured chenilles may also be carved.

### VELVET

The word "velvet" sounds rich and luxurious when applied to floor coverings, and the colors, range, and texture of these rugs are all that the word implies. A plush effect results when the pile is erect and is cut. Uncut looped pile gives a pebbly surface or may appear in distinct rows like friezé. Pile can be woven in different heights to form a pat-

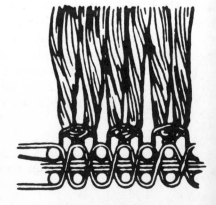

**Figure 19.10.** Chenille carpet. (*Reproduced courtesy of the American Carpet Institute Inc.*)

Figure 19.11. Velvet carpet. (Reproduced courtesy of the American Carpet Institute Inc.)

tern or hit-and-miss effects. When a combination of cut and uncut pile is used, a still different effect is created. These varied surface textures do not require a Jacquard loom but can be created by a regular velvet loom —the simplest of all carpet weaves. For this reason, and because less pile yarn is required for velvet than for Wilton, velvet construction is inexpensive. When it is closely woven, velvet carpeting is durable and rich-looking.

### "AMERICAN ORIENTALS"

"American orientals" and "domestic orientals" are really misnomers. They are machine-made domestic rugs with oriental designs and colors that are carefully blended to resemble hand-tied oriental rugs. They can be made by Wilton, Axminster, or velvet construction. Washing or brushing in a chemical solution adds luster. Some of these rugs have the ordinary type of back found in domestics; others have the pattern woven through to the back, as genuine orientals have.

Good grades of domestic orientals will stand hard wear. They are moderately priced but average higher than the Axminsters. Their sheen makes them most suitable for living and dining rooms. These rugs have been a great boon to those who appreciate oriental designs and colorings but cannot afford the genuine articles.[12] The durability of the construction is determined by the number of wires to the inch; eight wires indicate a good grade.

### FIBER RUGS

The paper for fiber rugs, made from fir or spruce pulp, is cut into strips, twisted into yarn, and woven in plain, twill, and herringbone weaves on a flat loom. The strength of the rug depends partly on the tightness of the twist. A vinyl coating improves its wearing quality appreciably. The color for the rug is introduced into the paper pulp. The standard sizes of fiber rugs are 27 x 54 inches and 6 x 9, 6 x 12, 8 x 10, and 9 x 12 feet.

---

[12] Familiar brand names are Karastan, Karagheusian, and Gulistan.

A competitor of the fiber rug is made of cured grass from prairie marshes in Wisconsin, Minnesota, and the territory near Winnipeg, Canada. The straws are usually light yellow or greenish yellow and are too brittle to be twisted. They are bound together with cotton strands into uniform "ropes" or grass twine. These ropes are woven together by a cotton yarn running both vertically and diagonally to the rug. A pattern may be stenciled on the rug after it is finished, or the rug may be painted.

Another competitor of the fiber rug is the rush rug, which comes in the same sizes and has the same use. It is sometimes woven in 1-foot squares, which can be pieced together into any desired shape. Rush rugs are made of tough reeds that grow in sluggish waters of Europe and the Far East. Japan is the chief producer. They are also made in Belgium, Holland, and Germany.

Sisal (often sold as hemp) is a fiber produced from the leaf of a plant grown in Central America, Kenya, and the West Indies. Sisal rugs will stand moisture far better than fiber rugs, but they are more expensive.

Still another type of fiber rug is the Belgian Mourzouk of twisted coconut fibers. These tough rugs, particularly suited to porches, are too coarse in texture for indoor use. The coconut fibers are dyed first and then handwoven, often in designs that are modernistic and bright in color. The rugs are made in standard sizes.

### BATH MATS AND RUGS

Bath rugs are often made of cotton or rayon chenille, rag, or very heavy terry cloth. (The chenille bath rug is not made in the same construction as the chenille carpet described earlier in this chapter.) For bath mats the chenille fur, which may be cotton, rayon, or nylon, is usually stitched onto a backing of duck, which is latex-coated to prevent skidding. Sculptured nylon pile may be locked to a nonskid, resilient foam-rubber or polyurethane back. There are also acrylic and polyester mats of furlike softness. Wall-to-wall carpeting is also appropriate for modern bathrooms, as was mentioned in Chapter 18.

### NONWOVEN FLOOR COVERINGS

Nonwoven carpets have tufts that are usually punched through a burlap backing. Although this construction is quite inexpensive, its service life is limited. (See *Needle-punched carpeting* in the Glossary.)

### RUG CUSHIONS

Rug cushions, sometimes called *underlay,* are made of sponge rubber or hair felt. The latter comes in different weights. The former comes in different thicknesses and styles.

Rug cushions, or underlays, are made of sponge rubber, jute, or hair. The sponge rubber may have a cotton scrim or web reinforced top, or a rubber coating on both sides. It comes in different thicknesses and styles. Widths are 3, 9, 12, and 15 feet. The jute and hair types have waffle or other designs and come in different weights. Sponge rubber, which is more expensive, is serviceable for hard wear in halls or on stairs, but it does become stiffened with age and finally disintegrates. Unless floors have been waterproofed, rubber padding should not be used on concrete floors below ground level. Moisture may seep upwards through the floor. The alkaline salts picked up in the passage of moisture through the concrete deteriorate the rubber. Above ground level, rubber padding may be used. Hair felt tends to flatten in use and may be damaged by carpet beetles and moths. Jute is weakened by dampness. (See *Jute*, Chapter 10.)

The purpose of rug cushions is to provide a luxuriously soft feel and to increase the life of the carpet. According to a study by the National Bureau of Standards, the increased service of the rug depends on the kind of cushion and carpet as well as the conditions of use. A cushion is more effective when used under carpets with short pile than under those with high pile.

Patent-back broadloom carpeting locks each tuft of pile in place by a mixture of latex or pyroxylin; the carpet may be cut in any direction and will not ravel. This construction makes possible a vast range of designs and color combinations, since pieces of differently colored carpeting can be inserted, as in a mosaic, without the patching being visible. Damaged portions can be readily removed and new sections inserted. No separate rug cushions are needed.

A more recent development bonds the loop pile to foam-rubber padding, which prevents skidding and carpet slippage. A cushioned carpeting of this sort comes at budget prices.

## RELATIVE IMPORTANCE OF THE VARIOUS CONSTRUCTIONS

Most carpeting today is *broadloom*—that is, it is of the Wilton, velvet, Axminster, chenille, knitted, or tufted types made on a loom or machine six feet wide or wider. The length of most woven carpets today is twelve or more feet.

Of total domestic carpet and rug shipments of manufacturers to distributors and retailers, measured by yardage, 90 per cent are tufted, with woven and knitted accounting for the rest. Chenille rugs are mostly custom-made. Until the early nineteen-fifties Axminster was the leading type, and the volume of tufted broadloom was negligible. But the ease and speed of construction and the various interesting effects that can be created have made the tufted carpet a most attractive and inexpensive product.

1. Look at the back of the rug. If the back is made of very stiff fibers, it is probably jute rather than wool, cotton, or man-made fibers. Although there is nothing wrong with rugs that have jute backings, they do not give as long wear as rugs made with other fibers. The presence of sizing in the backing usually indicates a loose weave that has to be strengthened in some manner. If, when the back of the rug is held about a foot from the eyes, the horizontal and vertical ridges can be readily counted, the wire and pitch are low. Consequently the rug is loosely woven and not of good quality.

2. Lay the rug face down and roll back an edge. Look at the depth, stiffness of the pile, and the coverage of the surface by the pile. (See p. 568 for discussion of density.) A chenille rug should have a deep pile. It should stand up like bristles in a brush but should not separate and show foundation yarns. Look also for the number of shots of filling between the rows of pile; a three-shot rug is considered better than a two-shot or a one-shot.

3. Walk on the rug and notice the softness. Then look at the rug closely to see if any white lines show through. A "grinning" rug is not a good buy. If a consumer cannot make a decision in the store, she may find that the merchant will come to her home with samples. In-the-home selling is on the increase because displaying the carpet in the room where it is to be used results in greater customer satisfaction.


## HANDWOVEN RUGS

The most exciting of all handwoven rugs are the orientals. They are discussed on pp. 580-584 according to place of origin, uses, design, color, prices, and selection.


### HOOKED RUGS AND RAG RUGS

In the early years of American colonization, hooked and rag rugs were made by hand. They were popular as scatter rugs in New England and Nova Scotia.

For the very old handmade hooked rugs, a backing of linen was used; later burlap became common. The pile made of yarn or strips of cloth is pulled through the back by means of a hook. The resulting pile is sometimes cut.

Patterns in hooked rugs may be geometric or floral; animals, ships, and domestic scenes are depicted. The hooked rug made in New England in the early days is considered more valuable than the Nova Scotia rug.

because of its more intricate designs and more beautiful colorings. Many modern Nova Scotian rugs have geometric designs copied from modern linoleum patterns. Japan is a source of many inexpensive hand-hooked rugs. Certainly many hand-hooked rug patterns are not beautiful and are even crude, but their very amateurish look is attractive to many people.

Most modern hooked rugs can be cleaned by shampooing, because the modern textiles from which they are made have generally fast dyes. Old hooked rugs should be sent to a reliable cleaner, for the burlap foundation may be weak and may fall apart when wet.

Hooked rugs are best suited to bedrooms and Early American interiors. They may be purchased in room size as well as scatter size. Old hooked rugs vary in size and shape, but large machine types are more or less standard.

Rag rugs are made of strips of twisted rags braided, crocheted, or bound together by cotton thread. Handmade rag rugs are less plentiful than handmade hooked rugs, even though they require less skill in the making and sell at lower prices. There are no particular patterns. Braided rugs are usually oval or round. Hit-or-miss rugs, made of many-colored twisted rags bound together, are generally oblong.

Machine-made rag rugs are woven with a cotton warp and a rag filling. Machine-made braided rugs are often made of mildew-resistant core

**Figure 19.12.  Two hooked rugs.**

yarns covered with tubular braids electronically fused together. They may also be made of tubular braided outer surface yarns of polypropylene olefin or 80 per cent acrylic and 20 per cent modacrylic fibers. These covered yarns are spot- and stain-resistant.

### NAVAJO RUGS AND MATS

The Navajo Indian in the western part of the United States originally made blankets and mats for his own use, but now these are made commercially. The Navajo loom consists of warp yarns suspended between two horizontals sticks. The filling is passed over and under the warp yarns by means of a pointed stick on which the yarn is wound. At points where the design is to appear, another color is introduced. Designs are geometric, and favorite colors are bright red on a white or gray ground, or white on a red ground. Originally, the Navajos obtained wool for rugs and blankets from their own flocks, which were carefully tended. Now their fine blankets are made of Germantown wool yarn made ready for weaving.

Weaving by this method is slow. When weavers were more skilled than they are today, it took an expert weaver about a month to make a blanket 5½ x 6¾ feet.

### ORIENTAL HAND-TIED RUGS

Hand-tied orientals are of three kinds: Near Eastern, Indian, and Chinese. Although some hand-tied rugs are made in Europe, most of them come from Persia, Asia Minor, and the Caucasus region.

Oriental rugs are made on a vertical loom. The wool or silk yarns that form the pile are tied by hand and cut with a knife at the depth desired. Two kinds of knots are used: the Ghiordes (Turkish) and the Senna (Persian). In the Ghiordes the tufts of pile yarn come in pairs between two warp yarns; in the Senna the tufts pass singly between two warp yarns. (See Figure 19.13.) In both cases the pile does not stand vertically on the ground but rather leans toward the end of the rug first woven.

Dates on the origin of handwoven rugs cannot be stated exactly, but probably oriental rugs are as old as civilization and date back to 5000 B.C. Until we have further evidence, the date of origin must begin with the old Egyptian civilization. Later on,

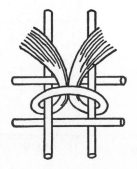

**Figure 19.13.** *Left:* The Ghiordes knot. *Right:* The Senna knot.

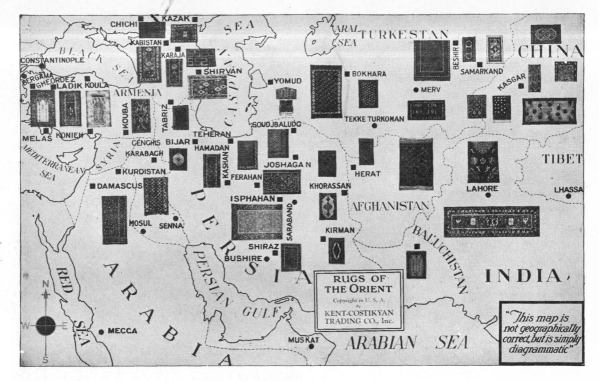

**Figure 19.14.** A rug map of the Orient. *(Photograph courtesy of Kent-Costikyan, Inc.)*

Assyria and Chaldea became the home of oriental rugs. The Persians, who were the master weavers, probably learned the art from the Babylonians. Some historians believe that the origin of the oriental rug antedates the early Egyptian times.

Oriental rugs may be classified according to their geographical origin and also as to use. (See Figure 19.14.)

### PERSIAN

Persian rugs are perhaps the most sought after of the orientals because of their artistic, intricate designs and fineness of construction. It is said that the Italianesque touch in the design of some Persian rugs is traceable to the time of Shah Abbas, a Turkish ruler of the sixteenth century. He sent some young men to Italy to study art under Raphael, and it is through them that rugs reached their zenith of development. Designs of Persians are usually predominantly floral with now and then a depiction of animals or human figures. Straight fringes, which are the actual continuation of warp yarns, appear at both ends. Sometimes fringes are braided or knotted.

The names of the rugs are derived from the towns where particular designs were first made. Some of the most common contemporary Persian rugs are Kashan, Hamadan, Kirman, Shiraz, Teheran, Khorassan, Bijar,

Saraband, Ispahan, and Sarouk. Nain and Ghum rugs are extremely fine knotted constructions and sell at high prices. In Iran the chief rug markets are at Teheran, Sultanabad, and Tabriz, with less important ones at Hamadan, Meched, and Kirman. The popular Sarouk rugs are not produced in one town but in a district south of Teheran.

## TURKISH

The patterns of Turkish rugs are less intricate than the Persian, and they tend to be more geometric in design. The pile is longer than the Persian, and the rugs are somewhat coarser in construction. Some of the most common types are Bergama, Ladik, Ghiordes, Kulah, and Milas. Turkish rugs are marketed through Istanbul (Constantinople) and Ismir (Smyrna).

## CAUCASIAN

These rugs come from Caucasia and Transcaucasia on the Black Sea and the Caspian. Characteristics of these rugs are their geometric patterns with sharp outlines. Blues, yellows, and reds are favorite colors. These rugs seldom come in large sizes. Kabistan, Shirvan, Kazak, and Karaja are common Caucasian rugs. It is said that Kazak originated from the word *Cossack*, the name of a nomadic people. The designs in this type of rug are more geometric and cruder than those made by more civilized groups.

## TURKOMAN

Rugs from Turkestan, which is north

**Figure 19.15.** Persian animal rug, Kurdistan; eighteenth century. Animals and birds against a background design of trees and flowers, a type of composition derived from Persian court carpets of the classic period. Colors: field, red; animals, white, rose, light and dark blue; background pattern, white, cream, rose, reds, and blues; border, red and light blue on dark blue. Size: 13' 3" x 6' 7". (Collection of Mr. and Mrs. Arthur M. Brilant. Photograph courtesy of The Asia Society and Antiques Magazine.)

**Figure 19.16.** Turkish prayer rug, Anatolia, Ghiordes; first half of the eighteenth century. A floral decoration takes the place of the mosque lamp in the mihrab, or niche; the stylized flowers in the border are derived from Turkish court rugs. Colors: niche, red; spandrels, light blue with yellow; border, dark blue with pattern in white, tan, green, red, and black. (*The Metropolitan Museum of Art, Gift of James F. Ballard, 1922. Photograph courtesy of The Metropolitan Museum of Art, The Asia Society, and Antiques Magazine.*)

**Figure 19.17.** Caucasian floral rug, Kazak; first half of the nineteenth century. Modified cross in lobed floral medallion. Colors: field, red; border and background of medallion, white; pattern, yellow, rose, light and dark blue, black. Size: 7' 2" x 4' 10". (*The Metropolitan Museum of Art, The Wilkinson Collection. Photograph courtesy of The Metropolitan Museum of Art, The Asia Society, and Antiques Magazine.*)

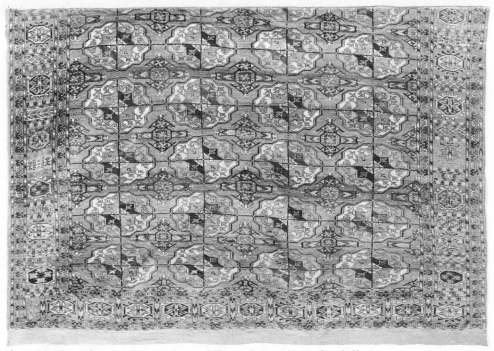

Figure 19.18. Turkoman geometrical rug, Tekke (called Bukhara); first half of the nineteenth century. All-over pattern of roughly octagonal guls, or medallions. Colors: field, red brown; pattern, white, orange, dark blue, red. Size: 9' x 6'. (*The Metropolitan Museum of Art, Gift of James F. Ballard, 1922. Photograph courtesy of The Metropolitan Museum of Art, The Asia Society, and Antiques Magazine.*)

of Iran and east of the Caspian Sea, are usually characterized by wide webbing at the ends. The designs in the center field are rows of octagonal medallions. Red, white, brown, and green are the principal colors found. The most common Turkoman rugs are the Bokhara, Beshir, Tekke Turkoman, and Samarkand. Pakistan is now making many Bokharas.

### BALUCHISTAN

Baluchistan is a section extending between Kirman on the west and India on the east, from Afghanistan on the north to the Arabian Sea on the south. Rugs from Baluchistan, often called *Baluch*, have wide-webbed ends and are similar to the Turkoman. Vivid reds and browns predominate.

### INDIAN

Indian rugs can be classified into three groups: hand-tied rugs, numdahs, and druggets. The hand-tied rugs come from the district around

Lahore in the province of Punjab, India. The numdahs come from India (Punjab) and Tibet. The druggets are made throughout India from the fleece of wire-haired sheep.

The numdahs come in different grades. They are made of felted goat's hair, not woven hair. Designs are embroidered by hand, the patterns being generally floral or vinelike. The *tree of life* design appears frequently. The usual dimensions of numdahs are 2 x 3, 3 x 4, and 4 x 6 feet. These rugs are comparatively inexpensive.

Druggets also come in different grades. The better ones are all wool; the poorer ones have a pile made of wool mixed with cow's hair. The groundwork of these rugs is jute. Patterns are usually very colorful and quite simple. Druggets are used on sun porches and in summer cottages.

India rugs should be dry.cleaned, not washed.

### CHINESE

The pile is deep and rich. Blue and tan are common colors. Dragons and flowers in circles are characteristic motifs, although when modern furniture came into vogue, Chinese rug manufacturers had their designers create patterns to meet the style. Then, when there was a demand for plain colors, they made them in plain colors. However, these rugs are not so durable as Persian and Turkish, and they require much care. Harder to keep clean, they show footprints easily. The political situation between the United States and China has limited the supply of these rugs to those few used rugs that are selling at auction and to stores selling old rugs.

### ORIGINAL USES OF ORIENTAL RUGS

The artistic and poetic temperament of oriental peoples expresses itself in the beautiful pictures on their rugs. These designs have been copied by occidental peoples, but the latter have never really been able to duplicate the works of art handed down through the centuries.

Although our present-day rugs are used chiefly as floor coverings or hangings, the old oriental rugs were created for other purposes as well.

1. *Prayer rugs* are characterized by a design in the form of a niche at the center. (See Figure 19.16.) These rugs were originally carried by Mohammedans and spread down on the ground to kneel on at the time of prayer. They placed the arch of the niche in the direction of Mecca and faced that way themselves. Prayer rugs were used in mosques as well.
2. *Hearth rugs* are usually about 3½ x 5 or 7 feet in dimension. They are generally characterized by two niches, one at either end. They were once used for family prayers.
3. *Grave rugs* were used to cover the dead before interment and to cover the grave after burial. A typical design is the cypress tree, symbol of mourning.

4. *Dowry* or *wedding rugs* were considered part of a girl's dowry. Girls began to weave these rugs at an early age. In early times, some localities estimated a man's wealth by the number and size of the rugs he owned. When his daughter married, he would give, as her dowry, rugs, camels, and donkeys.

5. *Mosque* or *Mecca rugs* are the finest examples of rugmaking. They were taken to Mecca by the rulers as a gift to the mosque. A good many valuable rugs stolen from mosques find their way into rug markets, where they have frequently brought fabulous prices.

6. *Saddle bags* are made in the form of two pouches joined together by webbing. Each pouch can be laced up to keep the contents from spilling. These saddle bags may be thrown over the camel's back to transport merchandise. Many of the saddle bags now extant have been cut apart and used as pillows for couches. *Saddle covers* were made to fit the back of the camel.

7. *Runners* are long strips of rug fabric that the orientals laid on couches. We now use these runners for halls and foyers.

8. *Hangings* are either silk rugs or kilims (ghileems). They have no pile. A dyed filling thread is bound around the warp threads by means of a shuttle or needle. This process makes the fabric alike on both sides, and the construction resembles that found in tapestry. The orientals used kilims for rugs as well as for portières, couch covers, and tablespreads. In the modern home, kilims are not very satisfactory as floor coverings because they are thin and they slip on hardwood floors unless they have a cushion of felt or rubber. The orientals did not walk on their rugs with spiked heels. They removed their shoes and wore slippers in the house. This practice preserves the rugs, and the wool pile is polished by slippered feet.

9. *Pillowcases* used by the orientals are generally small Anatolian mats. We can use these mats on tables, in front of doors, and as pillows.

10. *Bath rugs* are approximately three square feet. In olden times they were given to the bride by her parents on her wedding day.

11. *Sample corners* are pieces about two feet square that were used to show the quality of weaving to wealthy rulers who might purchase the rugs represented by the samples. These pieces are very rare.

12. *Floor coverings.* Nearly all the rugs mentioned, with the exception of the kilims, valuable antiques, or silk rugs, may be used as modern floor coverings. There are room-size rugs, scatter rugs, and mats. Antique orientals were not made in standard sizes, but the commercially produced modern orientals do come in standard sizes (dimensions in feet): 1½ x 3, 2 x 3, 3 x 4, 3 x 5, 4 x 6, 4 x 7, 5 x 7, 4 x 8, 6 x 9, 8 x 10, 9 x 12, and 10 x 16, and larger. The colors in Turkish, Persian, and Caucasian rugs now most in

demand are rose, blue, gold, and burgundy. The most popular designs fall under two headings: (1) floral with allover patterns or medallions; (2) geometric with allover patterns or medallions.

Although it is romantic to think of the original uses of oriental rugs, it should be remembered that in our modern civilization the old uses have in many cases disappeared. In the selling or buying of rugs, then, the salesman or customer should try to visualize a rug in use in a home— not in a mosque in Turkey. Salesmen should remember that modern orientals are made solely "for the trade" and are not intended to be used in mosques, in Mohammedan homes, or for transporting merchandise.

### DESIGN OF ORIENTAL RUGS

The geometric designs are the most primitive. Although they are not so complicated as the floral types, their simplicity makes them popular. Authorities on designs in rugs feel that geometric patterns originated with the rug itself. It must be remembered that the whole family used to weave rugs. The mother would tend the baby while weaving, and, to keep the child amused, would often weave into her rug some figures or symbols specially for the child. Possibly some of the irregularities in antique rugs are due to interruptions of the weaver, although the story is that no faithful Mohammedan would wish to make a rug perfect in symmetry of design and weaving because he might offend Allah, who alone is the symbol of perfection. Furthermore, the representation of human figures, birds, or beasts was forbidden in strict observance of Mohammedan laws. Consequently the original geometric designs were perpetuated.

Floral patterns are now identified with Persian rugs, but the oldest floral patterns were not developed in Persia. Greece and neighboring countries borrowed simple geometric designs from Egypt and Assyria and developed beautiful, complicated floral designs. Persia received this art centuries later.

The present designs in our modern oriental rugs are copies of old pieces. The symbolism attached to designs in antique rugs no longer exists. Swastikas for happiness, latch-hooks for good luck, a geometric figure supposed to represent a dog who preceded Mohammed when he first entered Mecca, are all symbols of the early rugmakers, who also wove their life histories into their rugs. The same designs are present today, but no symbolic meaning is intended by the weaver.

### COLOR IN ORIENTAL RUGS

The original oriental colors are brilliant red, blue, yellow, and white. If the colors are too vivid, they can be toned down by a treatment with a solution of chlorine or acetic acid after the rugs reach this country. This process is called *washing*. A rug so treated is termed a *washed rug*. The rug may also be treated with glycerin to develop sheen. If the chemical treatment is carefully done, it does not materially weaken the fiber.

The dyestuffs used for antique oriental rugs can be compared with the embalming fluids used by the Egyptians. The secret of making these dyes was held by different families. They are dyes made from natural products, vegetable in content. Certain families held the secret for making the blue dye, others the secret for red, and so forth. These colors were bright, were not affected by dirt, and always kept a peculiar gloss. Industrial chemists have tried to analyze these dyes and to develop color substances with the same characteristics. As a result, rugmakers now have aniline dyes made from coal tar that are fast in the present sense of the word; that is, rugs so dyed can be shampooed, can be vacuum-cleaned, do not fade in sunlight, and do not shed pile with friction. We do not expect our rugs to last for centuries. Many customers are contented with ten years' wear from a rug. They tire of it by then and want another. Surely the rug business would slump appreciably if consumers bought rugs only once in a lifetime.

### ANTIQUE VERSUS MODERN ORIENTALS

A rug, to be considered antique, should be at least a hundred years old. Sometimes rugs about twenty-five years old are called semiantiques. The colors of antique orientals have been softened and subdued by constant wear and by dirt, and the pile is worn down in places, with the result that there is an effect of light and shadow on the surface. These mellow colors are quite different from the garish brilliance of recently loomed orientals. Antique orientals also have a natural sheen; they were never chemically treated to produce luster. If one examines the pile, he will see the same color at the end of the pile as he does near the knot. Some of our poorer aniline dyes show fading at the end of the pile, or, even worse, may change color. Poorly dyed rugs have been known to fade in two years from a deep red to a rust.

To acquire a thorough knowledge of rugs would require a lifetime. Reading one book or a few chapters here and there will not suffice. There is still misrepresentation in wholesale markets and auctions. Some of it is ignorance and some is pure shrewdness. It is therefore advisable for a customer to go to a department store or a reliable importer who knows his merchandise and is willing to stand back of it. A guarantee of an unethical merchant or auctioneer is meaningless. Some so-called antiques are really modern rugs; very often they are not even treated with chemicals but are filled with dirt and dust to make them appear old.

### COMPARATIVE PRICES OF ORIENTAL RUGS

The most popular types of the modern washed orientals are the Sarouks, the Kashans, and the Kirmans. Their silky sheen is particularly in demand by some customers. The older unwashed orientals are more typical, however, of the traditional in the art of rugmaking. As a class, the Persian rugs sell at a higher price per square foot than the other kinds, with the exception of the fine qualities of Chinese rugs, which, when available, compete with Persians. There are grades of each class, however.

### FACTORS TO CONSIDER IN THE SELECTION OF AN ORIENTAL RUG

In buying an oriental rug, first consider the interior in which it is to be used. For example, oriental rugs fit into nearly every type of living room except possibly one with Colonial, French Provincial, or Directoire furniture. Bedrooms look best with hooked or rag rugs, or solid-color carpets. Floors in dining rooms, halls, and libraries are usually appropriately covered with machine-made or real orientals. In decorating a room, remember that the rug usually covers the largest or second largest area. Accordingly, if one already has chairs upholstered in vivid, patterned fabrics, and draperies in patterned materials, it would be wise and in good taste to select a plain-color rug, possibly a domestic.

If a consumer decides to buy an oriental rug, he should consider these points:

1. *The size best suited to the space.* If the room is large, a rug at least 9 x 12 feet in size would be advisable, because too many small scatter rugs seem to cut up the floor space. One large rug with smaller ones in front of doors, the fireplace, or stairs is a better arrangement, because the large rug forms a center for the room. Some people prefer a room-size carpet in a neutral shade over which they throw small scatter-size orientals. With this plan, the small rugs do not slip on hardwood floors, whereas small rugs alone require a felt or rubber mat under them. However, small orientals may slip when placed on a long-piled acrylic broadloom.

2. *The design.* If one has no furniture or draperies as yet, any appealing designs or colors may be used. But if there are other furnishings, their color and type must be considered to make a harmonious ensemble. The outline of the design should be distinct, and whites should be clear.

3. *The closeness of construction and evenness of weave.* Turn the rug over on the back and notice the closeness of the weave. The more knots to the inch, the stronger the rug. An evenly woven rug will be flat on the floor and will not pucker at the ends. The thickness of the rug and the depth of the pile have no definite bearing on durability; some of the thinnest orientals with short pile wear longest, because they are very closely woven of Grade A wool. A new rug should have even pile, and the color should be the same on the surface as it is at the knot. The average consumer cannot hope to be expert in judging the wearing quality of an oriental rug. He or she must rely upon the retailer, who must be ethical if he wants patronage. Consumers as well as dealers may

buy at public auction. But it is advisable for the average customer who knows comparatively little about rugs to buy from a reliable retailer. A great deal can be learned at exhibitions held by auction rooms prior to their sales. The catalogues often give detailed descriptions of each rug, and the better auction establishments have appraisers who price the rugs according to what they believe they will bring at auction. These appraisals may be had for the asking prior to the sale. By attending the sale one can compare the purchase prices with the appraisals.

## CARE OF RUGS

If they are to give long service, all rugs should have proper care. When a domestic rug is new, a certain amount of woolly fluff may brush out of it. This is to be expected, for in the process of shearing, particles of wool often fall back into the pile. The regular vacuuming will, in time, remove all fluff.

If the surface of the pile is not even, however, any long ends, tufts, or knots projecting above the surface should be cut off. Pulling out long ends may injure the construction.

Sometimes a solid-color rug seems to have dark and light spots in it. These marks are called *shading* and are common in chenilles. Shading is due to a crushing of the pile in spots—often caused by someone walking or moving furniture on the rug. The crushing of the pile may be somewhat reduced if the rug is turned around occasionally; the wear is thus distributed evenly. Running the sweeper or vacuum cleaner in the direction of the pile will decrease shading. Professional cleaning may prove a cure.

By going over soft floor coverings with a carpet sweeper once a day or every two days or with a vacuum cleaner once or twice a week, one can keep a rug comparatively clean. A stiff broom may injure the pile of the rug and so should be used lightly. The sweeping should be in the direction of the pile, not against it. New rugs should be vacuumed as often as old rugs. Hand-hooked rugs should not be shaken or cleaned with a vacuum, as the pile may be loosened by the suction; the old-fashioned carpet sweeper or broom is the best cleaner. If ends of pile or warp of any rug appear above the surface, they should be clipped off level and not pulled out.

Rugs are best kept free of moths by hard use. Rugs used for hangings should be examined frequently to see that moths are not in them. A weekly spraying with an insecticide will generally keep rugs free of moths during the summer months, and vacuum cleaning is also helpful. In the South, where the woodworm sometimes eats the jute back of rugs, naphthalene can be used as a preventative.

Soap, water, or chemicals may injure wool domestic rugs unless one knows how to use them. Soil embedded in carpets and rugs can best be thoroughly cleaned by commercial cleaning services. Domestic and oriental rugs and carpets that can be removed from the floor may be sent to a rug-cleaning plant for most thorough and efficient cleaning. Wall-to-wall coverings can be done professionally in the home. Care in selection of a commercial rug cleaning establishment is important.[13] Cleaning a carpet or oriental rug on the floor by hand is hard work, but a shampooing device that holds and distributes a special detergent as it is run over the rug does a satisfactory job. Unless a rug is made of fibers that soil easily, shampooing is not required very often. Prompt and careful treatment of stains is important for good serviceability in any carpet or rug.

For removing spots from acrylic and nylon pile carpets, use a dull-edged spoon to dislodge as much of the soil as possible. With tissues or white cloth, blot up all you can of the soil. Apply a detergent or cleaner sparingly. To avoid spreading the stain, work from the edge to the center. Rinse with water and blot with tissues after each application of

---

[13] National Institute of Rug Cleaning, 7355 Wisconsin Ave., Bethesda 14, Maryland, will supply names of member cleaning plants in a given area.

**Figure 19.19.** This young housewife is demonstrating the use of a spray foam rug cleaner. The foam is worked into the rug and then left to dry. After two to four hours, the loosened dirt is ready for vacuuming. "Glory" is said to be a rug cleaner that does not require a special applicator or mixing of ingredients. (*Courtesy of S. C. Johnson & Son, Inc.*)

cleaner. Then put a half-inch stock of tissues, weighted down with a heavy object, on the cleaned area and leave it on overnight. Remove the tissues, which have absorbed moisture in the carpet. Brush up the carpet pile lightly. The spot should have disappeared.

## CLEANING SOLUTIONS TO USE AT HOME [14]

1. Detergent solution, a dry powder household detergent. (Tide, Cheer, Fab, etc.): mix one tablespoon to a pint of lukewarm water. Do not use liquid detergents.
2. Dry-cleaning solvent. Any approved consumer brand. Do read the label carefully. Take notice of safety precautions.
3. Alcohol—denatured or isopropyl.
4. Amyl acetate—a common drugstore brand; or nail polish remover without lanolin, or lacquer thinner.
5. Bleach solution, nine parts water, one part of chlorine bleach.
6. Sour solution, one part white vinegar, one part water.

   A word of caution: Rings on the surface of a carpet may be caused by excessive soaking. Follow the instructions of the solvent maker, because water alone can cause a brown or yellow stain. Therefore, don't overwet the carpet. Use a towel or tissue to soak up excess water.

## SUMMARY

The decoration of an interior should grow out of the use to which the rooms are put and the personal preferences of the occupants; but a knowledge of period styles in furniture and furnishings is useful and necessary.

Since the rug takes up a large area in a room, it is a very important consideration in decoration. A rug usually proves to be a good buy if it is carefully selected and properly cared for. In modern domestic rugs, colors and patterns can be found that fit with any decorative scheme. If one can afford to possess an oriental, there are innumerable designs from which to choose. Again, care in selection repays the buyer many times over.

## PROJECTS

1. Draw the layout of a department that sells soft floor coverings in a large retail store.

[14] "How to Care for Your Carpet of Acrilan, Acrylic Pile" and "How to Care for Your Carpet of Cumuloft Nylon Pile," pamphlets by Monsanto Textiles Division, Monsanto Company, New York.

(*a*) Classify carpets and rugs sold in each section; give their names, sizes, colors, approximate prices.

(*b*) Constructively criticize the layout and stock assortment.

2. Clip advertisements for rugs in your local newspaper.

(*a*) Classify carpets and rugs offered by various stores.

(*b*) Tabulate fiber contents, sizes, colors, and prices of each article.

(*c*) Analyze your data to determine which floor covering is the best value for the price. Which is the poorest value? Rate articles in order from best to poorest.

(*d*) Support your conclusions.

Alternate: If advertisements of soft floor coverings cannot be obtained, visit a large department or specialty store that carries carpets and rugs. Follow steps *a, b, c, d* above.

## GLOSSARY

**Antique oriental rug.**  A hand-tied oriental rug at least one hundred years old.

**Axminster rug.**  A tufted rug (usually of woolen or worsted yarn) of solid color or Jacquard.

**Baluchistan rug.**  A hand-tied oriental rug from Baluchistan, commonly called *Baluch*

**Bath mat.**  A floor covering often made of tufted chenille. See Chapter 18.

**Broadloom.**  A seamless woven carpet six to eighteen feet or more in width.

**Carpet rayon.**  A specially constructed fiber and yarn for carpets that has greater tensile strength and is coarser than rayon for clothing.

**Carpeting.**  A soft floor covering that can be made of a variety of different fibers. It is sold by the yard and can be cut to any size.

**Carved rug.**  See *Sculptured rug*.

**Caucasian rug.**  Hand-tied oriental from Caucasia and Transcaucasia on the Black and Caspian Seas. Names include Kabistan, Shirvan, Kazak, and Karaja.

**Chain warp.**  A warp that joins or binds together the upper and lower surfaces of a rug.

**Chenille blanket.**  A loosely woven fabric (often cotton warps and large woolen fillings) cut into narrow strips that are pressed V-shaped.

**Chenille rug.**  A floor covering made with chenille (caterpillar) yarn used as a filling. It may be carved. See *Chenille blanket*.

**Chinese rug.**  A hand-tied oriental rug made in China, often characterized by dragons and flowers in circles.

**Contemporary style.**  A present style in home furnishings that emphasizes the mobile and functional in furniture.

**Contract carpeting.**  Floor covering in considerable yardage contracted for by motels, bowling alleys, schools, and institutions.

**Domestic rugs.**  Floor coverings manufactured in the United States.

**Drugget.**  A rug of all wool or wool and cow's hair mixed pile with a ground of jute. It is used for sun porches and summer cottages.

**Embossed type rug.**  See *Sculptured rug*.

**Fiber rug.** A floor covering made of tightly twisted strips of paper, finished to repel friction and moisture.

**Frame.** Denotes the number of colors possible in a Wilton rug; for example, five frames means five colors are possible, one frame for each color yarn. Frame holds spools of colored pile yarn in Axminster construction.

**Ghiordes.** Type of knot used to make pile in Turkish hand-tied rugs.

**Grass rug.** Made of cured prairie grass.

**Hearth rug.** A hand-tied oriental rug characterized by designs in the form of niches, one at either end.

**Hit-or-miss rug.** A floor covering made of many colored twisted rags bound together.

**Hooked rug.** Handmade by using a large hooked needle to pull yarn or bias-cut strips of fabric through a coarse burlap fabric. Some types are made on the Jacquard loom in round wire construction, to imitate the hand-hooked type.

**India rug.** Hand-tied rugs made in India in the province of Lahore, numdahs, and druggets.

**Indoor-outdoor carpeting.** Floor coverings suitable for both inside the house and outdoors.

**Ingrain carpet.** A reversible floor covering made with two-ply or three-ply yarn dyed before the fabric is woven. It is usually made with cotton or wool warp and wool filling.

**Kilim (Ghileem).** Near Eastern oriental woven with a shuttle or needle, with no pile. Kilims are used by the orientals as portières, couch covers, and table covers.

**Luster rugs.** Rugs that are chemically washed to give them sheen. They may be Wilton, Axminster, or velvet construction and are frequently referred to as "American" or "domestic" orientals.

**Modern style.** A style in home furnishings that emphasized simplicity, angularity, and straight lines in furniture.

**Mohair rug.** Floor covering with mohair pile and jute back.

**Needle-punched carpeting** (needle loom). A nonwoven nonpile carpeting with a felt-like surface. A lap, web, or batt of loose fibers is applied to a base of cotton fabric, burlap, plastic, rubber, etc. Needles having downward-facing barbs are forced into the base, thus causing the tufts of fiber to adhere to the base.

**Nonwoven floor coverings.** Carpets having tufts that are usually punched through a burlap backing.

**Numdah rug.** A rug from India, made of felted goat's hair. Designs are embroidered on the rug by hand.

**Oriental rug.** Hand-tied rug made in the Near East, India, or China.

**Patent back.** Carpeting that has its tufts locked in place by a mixture of latex or pyroxylin.

**Persian rug.** A hand-tied oriental rug made in Iran. Names of Persian rugs include Kirman, Kashan, Shiraz, Teheran, Saraband, Ispahan, Sarouk, Hamadan, Meched, Tabriz, Nain, and Ghum.

**Pile warp.** The warp yarn in a carpet that forms the looped pile.

**Pitch.** The number of pile yarns to the 27-inch width.

**Plush carpet.** Floor covering with one level of cut pile made of soft twisted yarns that do not show any yarn texture.

**Prayer rug.**   A hand-tied Near Eastern oriental rug characterized by a design in the form of a niche.

**Rag rug.**   Floor covering made of strips of twisted rags braided, crocheted, or bound together by cotton thread or cord.

**Random-tip shears.**   Carpets and rugs with a high pile sheared at random.

**Round-wire carpet.**   A Wilton construction in which a round wire is used instead of a flat wire to make the pile. Pile is therefore uncut.

**Rows to the inch.**   Rows of yarn tufts to the inch lengthwise.

**Rug.**   A thick, heavy fabric that can be made of a variety of different fibers and textures. Term is often used synonymously with carpet. Rugs are made with ends finished with binding or fringe.

**Rug cushion.**   A fabric of sponge rubber or hair felt placed under the rug to prevent the rug from slipping and to make the rug more soft and cushiony.

**Saxony carpet.**   A floor covering made in a variation of the Wilton construction with soft cut pile—a poor-quality Wilton.

**Sculptured rug.**   A floor covering with a Jacquard design made with different heights of pile.

**Senna knot.**   Type of knot used to make pile in Persian hand-tied rugs.

**Shading.**   Crushing of the pile of a rug so that it seems to have light and dark spots in it.

**Shag.**   A floor covering with relatively long, loose wool or man-made fibered pile.

**Stuffer warp.**   A warp that passes straight through the carpet to form a stuffing.

**Toile de Jouy.**   Used for draperies. See Glossary, Chapter 20.

**Tufted carpet.**   Made by needling pile yarns into a previously woven backing of jute or cotton.

**Turkish rug.**   A hand-tied oriental rug made in Turkey. Names of Turkish rugs include Bergama, Ladik, Ghiordes, Kulah, and Milas.

**Turkoman rug.**   A hand-tied oriental rug from Turkestan. Names include Bokhara, Beshir, Tekke Turkoman, and Samarkand.

**Tweed.**   Heavy wool, cotton, or mixed fabric made in handwoven effects, used for draperies and upholstery.

**Twist.**   A carpet made with uncut pile. Yarns of different colors may be twisted together to form pile loops.

**Underlay.**   See *Rug cushion*.

**Velvet rug.**   A floor covering woven on a plain harness loom with cut pile. It has solid-color or printed or stamped pile.

**Wall-to-wall carpeting.**   A carpet of any fiber or fibers and in any construction that covers the entire floor.

**Wilton.**   A floor covering (usually woolen or worsted) with buried pile, cut or uncut. It is often made with carved designs in plain color or multicolored.

**Wire.**   Each row of pile or tufts on the surface of a rug. See *Rows to the inch*.

# 20

## Draperies, Curtains, and Upholstery

No harmonious decorative scheme comes into being without thought. A carefully considered plan must be worked out before a satisfactory living area or an efficient working space can be created. Each individual reacts in a different way to the design of a space where he will live or work. Consequently, each person involved in using these areas should be considered by the decorator.

### WHAT IS DESIGN?

Design, to most people, means the choice and arrangement of certain shapes or forms to produce a decorative effect. Design must include both color and form, for without color, there is no form.

Structure is the composition and foundation of creative decoration. Everything depends upon the structural idea—the relationships between the construction of the room and the shapes or forms of the furnishings in the room. In designing a room, it is important to see the whole rather than only the parts—the furniture, colors, and decorations. For instance, if one has only a floor plan without wall elevations, one cannot determine the height of the ceiling, door opening, windows, and the like. Design is a functional factor of every single object in the decorating and furnishing scheme.

**598**
Draperies, Curtains, and Upholstery

### THE CREATION OF STRUCTURAL DESIGNS IN FABRICS

Home furnishing fabrics, like apparel fabrics, are made with structural or printed designs. A structural design is a woven-in pattern as opposed to a printed one. (See *types of printed designs,* Chapter 8.) An intricate structural design, made in Jacquard or dobby weave, is first worked out on point paper. Then cards or narrow wooden strips are made to govern the loom operation. (See Chapter 5.) Structural designs may also be called *visual designs,* when the design shows up in the effect done in the weave. For instance, if one pure color is used in the warp and another pure color is used in the filling, the effect is an iridescent one or even a brand-new shade. This combination of colors in a weave may create a sheen; or a black warp and a gold filling may give a metallic gold appearance. Visual designs are popular in contemporary styles because of their textural interest.

Any natural or synthetic yarn or blend may be used for a visual design. The designer tries, on her handloom, the fiber and the color in the warp that will give the effect she desires. This trial-and-error method is called *direct designing:* no point-paper patterns are drawn because the weave is usually a basic one. There are unexpected hazards, however, in such an approach to designing. For example, a designer working with spun saran found that its static electricity caused it to pick up pieces of varicolored lint around the plant. As a result, the woven cloth appeared multicolored instead of the two colors she had planned.

Figure 20.1. Visual design. (*Photo by Jack Pitkin.*)

Some visual designers who are novices in weaving may sacrifice certain basic qualities in a cloth just for the visual effect. A company lost $50,000 on an upholstery fabric with a cotton warp and jute filling because there were too few ends to the inch to withstand abrasion in use.

When a designer for a fabric house is satisfied with the design she has created on the handloom, she has the design approved by the chief designer. Then the design is checked by the testing laboratory to see if it is adequate for its intended uses. If it qualifies it is sent to a mill to be power-woven on a commercial basis.

In addition to designs created by its own staff, a fabric house may buy designs from free-lance designers. There seems to be no sure way of patenting or trademarking a structural or visual design. For by merely changing the count of the cloth, the fiber content, or the color of the yarn, the design can be proved not to be a copy. It is disheartening to a fabric house to find another manufacturer adding one insignificant metallic yarn to a borrowed design so that it is different from the original.

## A HARMONIOUS ENSEMBLE

To create a harmonious decorative scheme, there are four essential points to be kept in mind: (1) style of the furniture, (2) size of the room, (3) use of the room, and (4) size and shape of the windows.

Two interior decorating terms require clarification. Some homemakers make a distinction between curtains and draperies; draperies, they believe, are heavier fabrics and curtains, lighter fabrics. A professional decorator, however, calls all fabrics that hang over windows *curtains* no matter what their weight. *Draperies,* on the other hand, is the decorator's term for fabrics that frame a window.

Style of drapery treatment is a first consideration. Draperies and curtains should be used to emphasize and beautify the structural opening with which they are associated. Is the room to become dignified, dramatic, cottage-like, theatrical, or masculine? These factors naturally have more bearing on the choice of hangings than on the grade of the fabric. Draperies, an intrinsic part of home furnishings, help to build up the character and mood of each room, whether it is a room in a home, office, theater, hotel, or restaurant. Depending on the choice of fabric for draperies, one can make a room formal or informal. A formal room would require a fine fabric: velvet, damask, silk taffeta, satin, or antique satin. Choice of color can depend on exposure of the room or personal likes or dislikes of the homemaker. A scheme may be built up around a fine oriental rug or an antique Aubusson rug that the homemaker owns or wishes to purchase.

Curtains and draperies are usually not the first decision. Rather, they are a background for the style of furniture, the rug or carpet, and the upholstery to be used. The exception would be a room where a fine French or English blocked chintz or linen is proper. The colors in the drapery would be a guide for the carpet, wall color, and upholstery.

### STYLE OF THE FURNITURE

In Chapter 19 the different period styles in furniture were discussed. To select suitable draperies, one needs to know the fabric with the exact design and texture that best typifies the spirit of the period represented by one's furniture. (The table in Chapter 19 gives the fabrics appropriate to different periods.)

### SIZE OF THE ROOM

The size of the room is an important consideration in the selection of appropriate furniture and also in the selection of a drapery design. Ordinarily small designs are best for a small room and large designs for a large room. A striped pattern hung horizontally normally makes a room appear lower and broader. Mirrors on one side of the room with draperies on the opposite side tend to make the room seem larger and more luxuriously draped.

### USE OF THE ROOM

Some rooms are used much more than others. Much-used rooms include living rooms, nurseries, and bedrooms; those used less frequently include foyers, dining rooms, and guest rooms. Appropriate color schemes are based on the use for which the room is intended. In general, rooms lived in most of the time should be decorated in muted tones.

The color scheme for a house or an apartment should be thought of as a whole, not room by room. A feeling of shock is experienced by the visitor who walks from a red hall into a lavender living room or into a rose or blue dining room. It is like looking at a display of model rooms in a department store.

Style trends of the moment might influence the young bride or homemaker to choose stark black and white décor, bubble plastic inflated furniture, parsons tables, and chrome frames for chairs, all of which may be fleeting fads. A designer or decorator should offer suggestions on items of major expense, such as carpeting, chandeliers and draw curtains. The fad items will eventually have lost their glamour, and then the articles of better taste suggested by the decorator will create a good background. When the young homemaker's taste has matured, she will be ready to purchase the traditional articles for more permanent family living.

It is important for the skilled and trained decorator as well as for the homemaker to exercise great control in combining colors. There are very real personal psychological reactions to color, and one cannot presume to dictate taste in color to another person. It is too subtle and too personal a matter for mathematical formulas.

## SIZE AND SHAPE OF THE WINDOWS

There are various sizes and shapes of windows that have to be draped, curtained, or both. Some windows are tall and narrow, some are short and wide, and some are arranged in groups. Each shape is a problem in decoration.

In general, a high, narrow window looks wider if the drapery extends beyond the window on the wall at either side. The amount of widening would depend on the architectural features of the wall space; for example, the draperies might be brought out six to ten inches on either

**Figure 20.2.** Optical effect of drapery lines. (*Drawings suggested by Mrs. J. Orton Buck.*)

STRAIGHT FABRIC
COVERED CORNICE

SWAG AND JABOTS

DOUBLE HUNG OR
CAFE CURTAINS

COVERED CORNICE IN
FRENCH PROVINCIAL DESIGN

TREATMENT FOR
A DORMER WINDOW

side of the window frame for balance. However, there is no set rule. One might want to cover as much as three or more feet of wall to balance the room. In fact, it is fashionable today to drape a whole wall, whether it contains one or more windows. This treatment usually consists of one pair of curtains with French pleating and heading installed on a traverse rod. The curtains have 150 per cent fullness allowed for heavy fabrics such as damasks, brocades, and raw silk organzas, and 300 per cent for tissues (lightweight fabrics) such as silk gauze, voile, and net.

A valance—a decorative fabric or board installed across the top of a window—is usually made of buckram or wall board, padded slightly and covered in the same fabric as the draperies. The bottom of the valance is often shaped to carry out the period style of the room. A shirred valance is used most often when the fabric is sheer and unlined.

Curtains for French doors or inswinging casements are held firmly down at the top and bottom of the door or window by small brass rods. If the doors open into another room, the upper panes may be left bare, but if they open to the outdoors, the curtain should cover the entire door.

French doors may be treated with draperies to ensure privacy and add color to the room. They may be made so that they can be drawn and treated as a window.

Another window treatment is the use of two long panel draperies that hang at either side of a window or at either end of a group treatment for side decoration.

If there are sufficiently wide strips of woodwork between windows, drapery panels may be hung between the windows. In another treatment, mirrors are used to cover or even to black out an unsightly window.

Sometimes a wide valance is hung across the top of several windows in a group to make them seem like one.

## CLASSIFICATION OF DRAPERIES AND CURTAINS

The types of draperies and curtains that may be used are classified on the following pages. (See also Figure 20.5.)

### DRAPERIES OR OVERHANGINGS

These are decorative fabrics that are hung at the sides of the windows or doors for artistic effects. They may soften the line of the doors and windows or screen a doorway. They also add a note of color and interest. Draperies may be made of cotton, linen, rayon, silk, wool, synthetic fibers, or mixtures of these fibers. (See the Glossary for the names of fabrics commonly used for draperies.) In the choice of draperies, as in that of upholsteries, the fabric should correspond with furnishings in the room. Textures in a formal room should be woven in silk, silk-like textures, or raw silk. The cotton textures may be used in informal rooms. Cotton draperies are comparatively inexpensive, simple, homelike, practical, and generally informal. Linens are more formal, durable, serviceable, and vigorous. Silks are formal, suggesting regalness, luxury. Rayons, acetates, nylons, polyesters, acrylics, and glass fibers are used in the same weaves and textures as silks.

Most synthetic fibers can be dry cleaned. Wools are especially appropriate for masculine decoration, such as in hunting lodges, libraries, and dens. Wools are also adaptable for transportation fabrics (fabrics used as curtains and seat covers in vehicles of transportation) and hotel lobbies, and rooms; and in clubs. Wool, a heavy fabric, drapes beautifully but requires care insofar as it attracts moths unless treated. Wools are informal, suggesting warmth, orderliness, and masculinity.

### INNER CURTAINS

These are hung next to the window frame or glass. They may be divided into four groups:

*Sheer curtains* are made of very thin materials and are hung on a rod by hooks or casings. They average two and one-quarter to three yards in length and usually hang loosely to the sill. A casement curtain is a type of glass curtain hung from an inside rod, the outside rod holding the overdraperies. Casement curtains are usually made of casement cloth of polyester, acetate, nylon, or silk gauze. Fiberglas, heavy lace, filet net, cotton lawn, and cotton voile are particularly well suited to windows of the outswinging leaded type where neighbors are close.

*Tambour curtains* are made in imported Swiss, heavily embroidered batistes, lawns, or net in elaborate and exquisite designs (white on

**Figure 20.3.** Swiss tambour muslin curtain. (*Photograph courtesy of E. C. Carter & Son, Inc.*)

white). These curtains can take the place of glass curtains or draperies, and they may be formal or informal. The net style is often used for ecclesiastical purposes.

*Draw curtains* are used as window shades to ensure privacy or to shut out bright light. Equipped with a draw cord or traverse rod, they usually hang from an outside rod to the sill, to the bottom of the apron, or to the floor. They are made of opaque fabrics and are generally lined.

*Sash* or *café* curtains are hung on a rod attached to the lower window sash or to the lower half of the window casing. Bathroom or kitchen windows can be curtained in this way so that curtains do not hinder the raising or lowering of the windows. Windows that are opened frequently are best treated in this manner so that curtains do not soil or tear by blowing out of the window. French doors may be curtained with a sheer fabric such as marquisette or voile held taut at top and bottom by small brass rods.

Café curtains (orginally styled in France) consist of one, two, or three tiers of fabric that can be installed with (1) plain heading with brass rings sewn on, (2) clips, (3) shirred headings, or (4) fabric loops. The length of the tiers depends on the number of tiers desired; usually tiers overlap each other three inches. Headings and hems of the café curtains may be cut in scallops or squares or left straight. These curtains can be made of any informal fabric.

### HOMEMADE CURTAINS

Although curtains and draperies can be purchased ready-made, many homemakers prefer to make their own in order to achieve greater individuality at lower cost.

The first thing to do is to estimate correctly the amount of material needed. This estimate requires careful measuring of the window with a ruler or yardstick. (A string or tape stretches and is therefore likely to be inaccurate.) In estimating, add 9 inches to each curtain length: 6 inches for a bottom hem, and 3 inches for a top hem. Sheer materials look best when the hem is turned over three times. A 5-inch hem is customary for the top and bottom of unlined curtains.

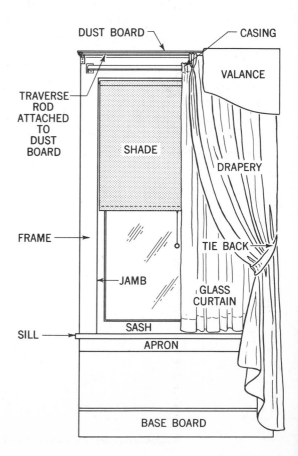

**Figure 20.4.** The parts of a window. Drapery should be pleated at top and hung on track that is on dust board. Draperies can be either stationary or draw. (*Adapted from illustration provided by Singer Sewing Machine Company.*)

Sheer inner curtains usually just clear the sill or hang to the bottom of the apron. A graceful drapery reaches to the bottom of the apron or to the floor. Very formal draperies spread out on the floor.

When sheer materials are shirred on rods, a fullness of three times the width of the window should be allowed. Curtains or draperies may also be pleated at the top. A Flemish or a French pleat is a box pleat with three loops caught together about 3 inches from the top and hung by a hook or ring. Seven pleats are generally made in 50-inch materials, which leaves a panel 25 inches wide. Five pleats in a 36-inch fabric leave an 18-inch panel. When using a 36-inch width, allow one third again as much fabric as you need for a 50-inch material, whether for draperies, upholstery, or slip covers. If you are using a patterned fabric, allow for repeat of the pattern.

The valance or decoration of ornamental material hung at the top of the window may be of these types:

1. Shirred on an outside rod (not on same rod as the side draperies)
2. Flat (pulled straight, no fullness)
3. French-pleated (three small pleats pinched together at intervals)
4. Box pleated (pleats spread flat and pressed, sewed at even intervals)
5. Side pleated (pleats basted at even intervals and pressed in one direction)
6. Dutch (valance shirred on same rod and placed between the side draperies)
7. Cornice board (a piece of wood carved or cut to serve as a valance and painted in the color scheme of the room)
8. Swag and jabots (top, or swag, hangs in draped curves between two or more points). Side panels are jabots. See Figure 20.2

Figure 20.5. Types of valences.

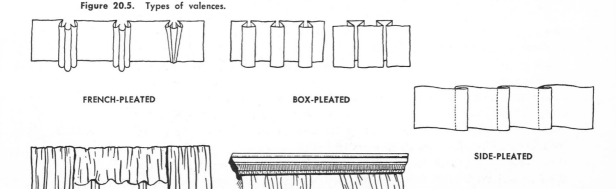

FRENCH-PLEATED          BOX-PLEATED

SIDE-PLEATED

KITCHEN          CORNICE BOARD WITH WOOD MOULDINGS

Nearly every type of glass curtain or casement curtain is now available ready made. Curtains are hemmed or trimmed at the bottom but left unhemmed at the top so that the length can be adjusted to fit the window. Ready-made draperies and glass curtains can also be purchased. The most common types of ready-made glass curtains are these:

1. Ruffled (with tie-backs, with or without valance; well suited to informal rooms, bedrooms, nurseries, and so forth)
2. Crisscross (two panels cross each other at the top and are tied back; appropriate for Colonial rooms)
3. Sash curtains (cover the bottom sash of the window; appropriate for kitchens and bathrooms)
4. Plain pairs of curtains (sold in pairs; narrow hems down the sides and wider hems across the bottom; may or may not have fringes)
5. Panels (single curtains; one panel is made to cover the entire window)
6. Café (consist of one, two, or three tiers of fabric that usually overlap about three inches.

## SELECTION OF MATERIALS FOR DRAPERIES

There are so many types of drapery fabrics that at first it may seem difficult to make an appropriate selection. But if three important factors are considered, *color, texture*, and *design*, the task should be easier. Color having been determined, texture can next be settled. Texture means the roughness or smoothness of the surface of a fabric. The one rule that governs texture combination is that textures should be neither too much alike nor too dissimilar. For example, silk velvet should not be combined with rough linen-like textures, or taffeta with monk's cloth. On the other hand, there should be enough textural contrast to create interest. In a room in which the draperies are of silk damask and the glass curtains are of silk gauze, the upholstery may be of silk brocade, silk striped taffeta, plain taffeta, or velvet. For an informal room a pleasant combination might be achieved by combining a toile de Jouy for draperies and bedspread with a solid-color antique satin for a wing chair and a small bench. (See Glossary at the end of this chapter for names and identifying features of drapery fabrics.)

In selecting appropriate designs, remember that too much pattern in a room is tiresome and should be avoided. The same principle that applies to color applies to one's selection of design.

In choosing drapery materials, a practical consideration is the effect of sunlight on the different fibers. Nearly all fabrics are weakened somewhat by sunlight. Rayon is about as resistant to sunlight as cotton, and acetate is more resistant than cotton. Sunlight decreases the strength of

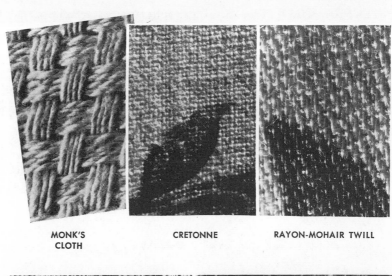

MONK'S          CRETONNE          RAYON-MOHAIR TWILL
CLOTH

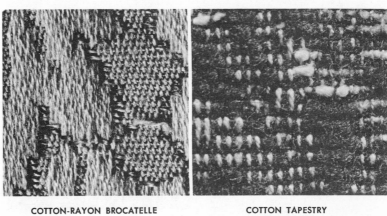

COTTON-RAYON BROCATELLE          COTTON TAPESTRY
(RIGHT SIDE)

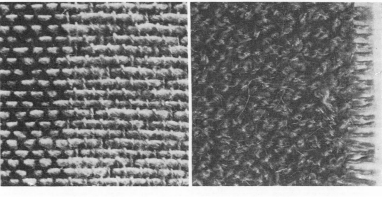

COTTON TAPESTRY          MOHAIR-
(WRONG SIDE)          COTTON FRIEZÉ

**Figure 20.6.** Some fabrics used for draperies. (*Photos by Jack Pitkin.*)

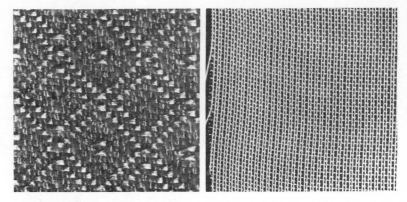

CASEMENT CLOTH          RAYON NINON

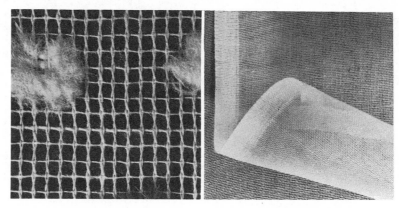

FIGURED MARQUISETTE          ORGANDY

**Figure 20.7.** Some fabrics used for curtains. (*Photos by Jack Pitkin.*)

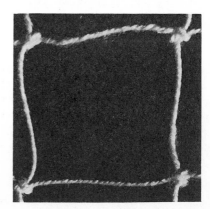

**Figure 20.8.** Linen fish net.

**Figure 20.9.** Toile de Jouy. *(Photo by Jack Pitkin.)*

pure silk. Strong sunlight also injures nylons. It is recommended that all types of curtains except gauze be lined for protection. Linings serve as filters for sunlight, soot, and dust.

## CARE OF DRAPERIES AND CURTAINS

If instructions for care of draperies and curtains appear on a label attached to the merchandise when purchased, that label should be saved for reference when the curtains must be cleaned.

Most cottons, particularly those blended with polyesters, can be washed in an automatic washer. They may or may not be pressed, depending on their appearance after laundering. Some all-cotton curtains require starching to give them a crisp finish. If the label indicates that they are permanent starchless finish, then starching is unnecessary. Curtains that require minimum care usually should be thrown over a line or hung at the window (with paper underneath to catch the water) to drip dry. Little if any ironing is generally needed. All-cotton velveteen, velour, and tapestry should be dry cleaned.

Should the label indicate that the article is hand washable, a neutral soap solution of lukewarm water should be used. The soap solution should be squeezed through the fabric many times until the fabric is clean. Water should be extracted gently. The water for rinsing should be lukewarm to cool. Cotton fabrics containing rayon should be dried flat or hung over a line with the edges straight, away from heat or sun. The strain of drying should come on the cotton (the warp), not on the rayon. Since clothespins cause threads to bulge or break, they should never be used. Fabrics containing synthetic fibers should be pressed with a warm not a hot iron.

Linen draperies are usually washable provided the dyes are fast. They are usually fairly heavy, sturdy cloths and so do not require special treatment in laundering. If ironing is required to remove wrinkles, it is advisable to do so while the fabric is still damp.

The average silk fabric is better dry cleaned than laundered. A few of the lightweight fabrics, such as gauze, lace, marquisette, shantung, and voile, may be washed if they are treated as fine fabrics. Use neutral flake soap and warm water; squeeze suds through the fabric; rinse it in clear water of the same temperature as suds; roll it in a towel to remove excess moisture; throw it over a line to dry; press with a warm iron.

Sheer fabrics made of nylon, polyester, and acrylic fibers should be treated like sheer silks. Glass-fibered curtains are machine washable if the machine has a "modern fabrics" setting. They should be removed before the damp-dry cycle and hung at the window to drip dry. When washed by hand, such sheer curtains should be dipped in a soap solution, rinsed, and hung to dry. No ironing is needed. Since glass fibers do not absorb moisture, fabrics should be cleaned and dried quickly, without wrinkling, shrinking, or losing their shape. When used in sheer curtains, glass fibers are smooth and may slip in laundering unless care is taken. Hems may need hand smoothing after washing to prevent puckering.

Wool fabrics and blends should be dry cleaned. They are generally too heavy to be managed in laundering. To keep moths from attacking the wool in upholsteries and draperies, vacuum-clean and treat for moth prevention. A thorough cleaning of wool fabrics at regular intervals will rid them of odors, dirt, and moths.

Before curtains or draperies of any fabric are stored for a season they should be laundered or cleaned. Dirt and grit tend to rot cotton fabrics. Soiled silks and rayons look much better when they have been dry cleaned, for then their natural luster returns.

## UPHOLSTERY

Fabrics used for covering upholstered furniture and cushions and for slipcovers are classed as upholstery fabrics. Upholstery fabrics may be classified as follows:

1. Textured—a surface that is woven with a nubby yarn in the construction; may be made in any fiber
2. Velvets—cut loops; thick, dense pile
3. Damasks (reversible) and brocades (nonreversible)—woven in elaborate Jacquard designs including brocades, brocatelles, and damasks

4. Rib weaves—including tapestries (having large pictorial designs) and reps (having solid colors with crosswise ribs)

Any textile fiber can be used for upholstery provided the cloth is sturdy enough to resist friction, sunlight, dry cleaning, and, in some cases, laundering. Silk, wool, cotton, and nylon are probably the most satisfactory for upholstery. Silks, being luxury fabrics, should be used with discretion. The synthetics, rayon and acetate, are less expensive and are easier to care for. Plastic-coated fabrics have their place and are suggested where durability is paramount. Rayons and acetates are decorative and are best used in homes where there are no young children who may soil or tear fine fabrics. Nylon is strong, resists abrasion, and is easily cleaned.

If upholstery is to have hard usage, inconspicuous patterns and colors that will not show soil should be chosen. A few silk, rayon, or metal threads shot through a cotton or wool upholstery fabric give it luster and additional beauty. For durability, yarns should be tightly twisted and the weave close.

Upholstery fabric retains its freshness longer if it is covered during the summer months. Linen and cotton fibers are excellent for summer use as slipcovers; they make a chair or divan upholstered in wool seem cooler. Bright, cheerful designs in chintz or cretonne can change a formal room into an informal one. If upholstery is somewhat shabby, new slip-covers will freshen it. Some of the fabrics commonly used for slip-covers are chintz, cretonne, linen crash, cotton rep, nylon and cotton blends, rayon and cotton blends, cotton broadcloth, denim, and knitted stretch fabrics.

Some of the most commonly used fabrics for covering upholstered furniture and cushions are textures (in wool or cotton), brocade, damask, brocatelle, plush, velvet, velour, mohair, leather and its sub-stitutes, tapestry, needlepoint, and laminated fabrics. (A description of the fabrics listed here appears in the Glossary.)

The relation between the style, size, and use of the piece of furniture to be covered and the selection of fabrics is the same as that between the room and the draperies and curtains.

### CARE OF UPHOLSTERY

Upholstery should be brushed and vacuum-cleaned frequently, not only to remove dirt but to prevent attacks by moths on wool.

To guard against moths, when a new piece of furniture is bought, make sure the upholstery fabric is treated chemically to make it moth-proof. A muslin covering inside the upholstery fabric will keep moths from the inside of the furniture.

If moths do get into an upholstered chair, spread paradichlorobenzene crystals (two to three pounds) over it. Then carefully wrap the chair in paper to confine the odor.

Spots should be removed when they first appear, with either soap and water (if the fabric is washable) or a dry-cleaning fluid. A white fabric often can be cleaned at home. Sprinkle dry powdered magnesia on it, rub the magnesia in, and then brush it off. If upholstery is badly soiled, take it to a reliable upholsterer for cleaning.

## TAPESTRY

Tapestry is an ornamental textile with a long service record. It is basically a hand-woven fabric made with a bobbin worked from the wrong side on a warp stretched vertically or horizontally. The bobbin is carried only to the edge of the pattern and not from selvage to selvage. The surface consists entirely of filling threads. If the warp is stretched vertically, the loom is called *high warp*; if horizontally, *low warp*. In the high-warp loom the outline is designed in ink on the warp; in the low-warp loom the weaver places a cartoon (sketch of the design) under and close up to the warp, making inking unnecessary.

The warp yarns may be of wool, linen, or cotton. The warp of wool is elastic and is likely to produce a cloth with a crooked shape; warp of linen or cotton is stiffer. The filling yarn is generally wool, except in Chinese tapestry. Although silk is attractive in satin and brocade, it is

**Figure 20.10.** An Aubusson tapestry.

flat and uninteresting in the interpretation of large pictures. The texture and vibrant character of tapestry is caused by three factors: the ribs formed by the covered warps, which form the highlights; the hatchings, the fine filling threads in vertical series, which form the middle lights; and last, the slits (holes grouped in diagonal series), which form the shadows.

Handmade tapestries are still produced, and machine-made reproductions are woven on Jacquard looms. Two sets of warp and filling yarns are used. The wrong side is smoother than that of a handmade tapestry.

Tapestries are distinguished according to period and origin as follows:

1. Primitive—from Egypt; woven as early as 1500 B.C.
2. Gothic—from France; about the fourteenth century
3. Renaissance—from France; wide borders; composition clear and picturesque; texture inferior to Gothic
4. Gobelin (early)—from France; seventeenth century; Gobelins originally a family of dyers who added a tapestry factory; Louis XIV in 1662 made the factory a state institution; early Gobelin tapestries characterized by solemnity, conformity, and dignity; inspired by paintings of Rubens and LeBrun
5. Gobelin (later)—brightness, individuality, and grace replaced earlier characteristics; inspired by Watteau and Boucher
6. Beauvais—from a famous factory north of Paris; private but backed by Louis XIV; coarser and less expensive than Gobelin tapestries; mostly landscapes
7. Aubusson—from the city of Aubusson, 207 miles south of Paris; less expensive than Beauvais; depict especially groups of personages; coarse, loose texture (See Figure 20.11.)
8. Tapestries produced outside France—German, Swiss, English, Spanish, Russian, Turkish, and Chinese

Tapestries were used in the Middle Ages as a protection against draughts and as wall decorations. Although in modern homes we do not need them as protection against draughts, we still use tapestries for hangings, either as a background or as pictures. Modern tapestries woven on the Jacquard loom are suitable for fire-screen covers, covers for benches or stools, reupholstering of furniture, knitting or shopping bags, and handbags.

## SUMMARY

One who prefers individuality in home furnishing may follow that preference by using his or her own taste in choosing fabrics for draperies and curtains. Those who favor period styles may follow that inclination in decoration provided appropriate fabrics are coordinated with the furniture and rugs. The most important thought to bear in mind is that harmony of design, color, and the texture of the fabrics must be maintained. In addition, the style of furniture, the size of the room, the use of the room, and the size and shape of the windows are important considerations.

## PROJECTS

1. Plan the fabric decorations for a master bedroom (18 x 13 feet) of a suburban home. Two windows face north, and walls are painted in a grayish, pale, warm beige. Furniture is Early American. If possible, include swatches of actual fabric together with prices for ready-made articles or for fabric by the yard.
2. Plan the décor for a living room (20 x 18) of a city apartment. Casement windows open onto an unsightly, dark court. Walls are painted a light gray. Furniture is contemporary with an oriental influence. Wherever possible, the prices of fabric by the yard or the ready-made article should be included.
3. Plan the fabric decorations for a teenage boy's or a teenage girl's sunny bedroom in a small ranch-type home of five rooms. The wallpaper in the boy's room is patterned with large motifs of sailing vessels. The wallpaper in the girl's room has a spaced design of varicolored nosegays. The rooms each have a square, medium-sized window with louvers of clear glass. Furniture is contemporary.

## GLOSSARY

**Antique satin.**  A fabric made to resemble a silk satin of an earlier century. Has a slub face and a satin back.

**Antique taffeta.**  A pure silk fabric with a nubby texture.

**Bouclé.**  A fabric made of novelty yarn that is characterized by tight loops projecting from the body of the yarn at fairly regular intervals.

**Brocade.**  A drapery or upholstery fabric in Jacquard weave with raised designs. It has contrasting surfaces or colors that emphasize the pattern. Metallic threads may be shot through the fabric.

**Brocaded satin.**  A satin fabric with raised designs in Jacquard weave.

**Brocatelle.**  A drapery and upholstery fabric made in double-cloth construction with a silk- or rayon-fibered face. Best grades have linen back. The design stands in relief from the ground, giving a padded effect.

**Burlap.**  A coarse, stiff fabric in plain weave. It is made of jute, hemp, or cotton and is used for draperies.

**Café curtains.**  Consist of one, two, or three tiers of fabric that usually overlap about three inches.

**Casement cloth.**  Any medium-sheer drapery fabric suitable for casement windows.

**Chenille.**  Fabric of silk, wool, cotton, or synthetic fibers, made with chenille yarns or tufts, used for draperies and bedspreads. See Chapter 18.

**Chintz.**  Glazed cotton fabric, often printed in gay colors, used for draperies, slipcovers, and upholstery.

**Contemporary style.** See Glossary, Chapter 19.

**Corduroy.** In cotton or wool for draperies. See Glossary, Chapter 16.

**Cretonne.** A plain-weave carded cotton fabric, usually printed with large designs. Cretonne is unglazed and is used for draperies and slipcovers.

**Damask.** A drapery or upholstery fabric of silk, rayon, and cotton, or other combinations of fibers, woven in Jacquard weave with reversible flat designs.

**Denim.** Twilled cotton fabric made of single hard-twisted yarns. Staple type has colored warp and white filling. Woven-in stripes and plaids are popular for draperies, upholstery and bedspreads.

**Design.** The choice and arrangement of shapes or forms and color to produce a decorative effect.

**Direct designing.** A trial-and-error method in the use of yarns of different fibers and blends to create a visual design. It is done directly on a hand-loom with no point-paper pattern.

**Faille.** Used for draperies. See Glossary, Chapter 16.

**Fiberglas.** See Glossaries, Chapters 2 and 14.

**Fishnet.** Large novelty mesh fabric of cotton or linen made to resemble fishing nets in white or colors. It is used for curtains.

**Friezé.** Heavy pile fabric with rows of uncut loops. It is made of mohair, wool, cotton, or synthetics and is used for draperies and upholsteries.

**Fringes.** Thread or cords of any fibers grouped or bound together and loose at one end, used for trimming draperies and upholstery.

**Gauze.** Sheer, loosely woven plain-weave fabric suitable for curtains. It is made in wool, silk, or synthetic fibers.

**Gingham.** Used for curtains. See Glossary, Chapter 16.

**Homespun.** A very coarse, rough linen, wool, cotton, or synthetic mixture or blend in varied colors; generally in plain weave resembling wool homespun. It is used for draperies and upholstery.

**Hopsacking.** A coarse, loosely woven fabric in basket or novelty weave. The original hopsacking was used for sacking hops. Now made to resemble the original of linen, spun rayon, or cotton, and used in blends. Also used for dresses and coats.

**Lace.** See *laces*, Chapter 18.

**Louver.** A fitted window frame with slatted panels.

**Marquisette.** A sheer curtaining material of silk, rayon, nylon, polyester, or acrylic fibers woven in leno weave.

**Matelassé.** A heavy Jacquard double cloth with quilted appearance that is used for draperies and upholstery. See *matelassé* for dresses, Glossary, Chapter 16.

**Moiré.** A design having a watered appearance, usually on a ribbed textile fabric. When the fabric is sufficiently heavy, it may be used for draperies.

**Monk's cloth.** A heavy cotton fabric in basket weave (4 x 4 or 8 x 8). It comes in natural color, solid, or stripes, and is used for draperies and couch covers.

**Monochromatic scheme.** The use of a combination of different shades of one color.

**Needlepoint.** An upholstery fabric. Designs are usually floral, embroidered with yarn on coarse canvas.

**Net.** See Glossary, Chapter 18.

**Ninon.** A sheer plain-weave glass curtaining made in rayon, acetate, nylon, or other synthetic fibers. The warp yarns are arranged in pairs.

**Organdy.** Sheer, crisp, cotton curtaining in plain weave. See Glossary, Chapter 16.

**Percale.** Plain-weave, closely woven muslin fabric in dull finish that may be dyed or printed. It is used for curtains.

**Plastics.** Fabrics made of plastic-impregnated or plastic-coated yarns (core of yarn made of cotton, rayon, linen, silk, glass, nylon), plastic-finished fabrics, and all-plastic extruded fibers and yarns suitable for webbing and woven fabrics for porch and beach furniture. (See *saran*, Chapter 14.)

**Plush.** A heavy-pile fabric with deeper pile than velvet or velour. It may be mohair, silk, or rayon and is used for upholstery.

**Pongee.** Used for draperies and casement curtains. See Glossary, Chapter 16.

**Poplin.** See Glossary, Chapter 16.

**Rep or repp.** Heavy fillingwise corded fabric, heavier than poplin. It may be silk, rayon or other synthetics, wool, or cotton. It is used for draperies and upholstery.

**Sailcloth.** A generic name for fabrics used for sails. May be made of cotton, linen, jute, nylon, or polyester. Cotton sailcloth is also used for draperies, upholstery, and sportswear.

**Sateen.** A mercerized cotton fabric in sateen weave used for lining draperies. It may be printed for draperies.

**Satin.** Silk, silk and cotton, acetate and cotton, or other fiber combinations woven in satin weave. It is used for draperies and upholsteries.

**Satin antique.** See *Antique satin*.

**Seersucker.** See Glossary, Chapter 16.

**Shantung.** Used for draperies. See Glossary, Chapter 16.

**Sheer curtains.** Thin cotton fabrics that hang next to the window glass.

**Shiki (shiki rep).** Heavy rayon, acetate, and cotton or other mixtures identified by wavy fillingwise cords. It is used for draperies.

**Structural design.** A woven-in pattern as opposed to a printed one.

**Swiss (dotted or figured).** Used for curtains. See *Dotted swiss*, Glossary, Chapter 16.

**Synthetic fibers.** See Chapter 14.

**Taffeta.** A plain-weave, stiff-finished fabric in silk or the synthetics used for draperies. See *Antique taffeta*.

**Tambour curtains.** Imported Swiss, heavily embroidered batiste or lawn curtains.

**Tapestry.** A Jacquard woven fabric in cotton, wool, or other fibers. The design is woven in by means of colored filling yarns. On the back, shaded stripes identify this fabric. It is used for draperies and upholstery.

**Textured.** A surface that is woven with a nubby yarn construction. May be made in any fiber.

**Toile de Jouy.** Cotton fabric printed in pictorial designs. The original toile was printed by Oberkampf in 1759 at Jouy, France. It is used for draperies.

**Tweed-textured.** An exaggerated chevron or tweedlike structural design with accentuated nubs.

**Valance.** A decorative fabric or board that is installed across the top of a window.

**Velour.** A smooth, closely woven pile fabric usually of cotton or wool. The fabric is heavier than velvet and is used for draperies and upholstery.

**Velvet.** Silk, rayon, or nylon cut pile fabric. When used for draperies and upholstery it is somewhat heavier than dress velvet.

**Velveteen.** An all-cotton pile fabric for draperies and upholstery that is heavier than dress velveteen. See Glossary, Chapter 16.

**Visual design.** When the design shows up in the effect done in the weave.

**Voile.** A sheer plain-weave curtain fabric of cotton, rayon, or synthetic fibers made of hard-twisted two-ply yarns.

**Whipcord.** Hard-woven worsted fabric with fine diagonal cords on the face that is used for draperies and upholstery.

# Bibliography

Birrell, Vera L., *A Handbook of Fabric Structure and Design Processes* (New York: Harper & Row, 1959).

Bowers, Mabel Goode, *Decorate Your Way* (New York: Charles Scribner's Sons, 1968).

*Calloway's Textile Dictionary* (La Grange, Ga.: Calloway Mills, n.d.).

Chambers, Bernice G., *Color and Design* (Englewood Cliffs, N.J.: Prentice-Hall, 1951).

Chambers, Helen G., and Verna Moulton, *Clothing Selection* (Philadelphia: J. B. Lippincott Co., 1969).

Cook, J. Gordon, *Handbook of Textile Fibers,* vols. 1 and 2, 4th ed. (Merrow Publishing Co., 276 Hempstead Road, Watford, Herts, England).

Crawford, M. D. C., *One World of Fashion,* 3rd ed., Josephine E. Watkins and Bernice Zelin, eds. (New York: Fairchild Publications, 1967).

*Dictionary of Textile Terms,* 8th ed., George E. Linton, ed. (Danville, Va.: Dan River Mills, 1967).

*Fairchild's Dictionary of Textiles,* 5th ed., Isabel B. Wingate, ed. (New York: Fairchild Publications, 1967).

Garrett, Pauline G., *You Are a Consumer of Clothing* (Waltham, Mass.: Ginn & Co., 1967).

Jacobsen, Charles W., *Oriental Rugs: A Complete Guide* (Syracuse, N.Y.: Published by the author, n.d.).

Joseph, Marjory L., *Introductory Textile Science* (New York: Holt, Rinehart & Winston, 1966).

Klapper, Marvin, *Fabric Almanac* (New York: Fairchild Publications, 1967).

Kopp, Ernestine, Vittorina Rolfo, and Beatrice Zehn, *Apparel Through the Flat Pattern* (New York: Fairchild Publications, 1966).

McJimsey, Harriett, *Art in Clothing Selection* (New York: Harper & Row, 1963).

Merrill, Gilbert R., and D. S. Hanby, *American Cotton Handbook* (New York: Interscience Publishers, vol. 1, 1965; vol. 2, 1966).

Pollard, L. Bess, *Experiences With Clothing* (Boston: Ginn & Co., 1968).

Reichman, Charles, J. D. Lancashire, and K. D. Darlington, *Knitted Fabric Primer* (New York: National Knitted Outerwear Assn., 1967).

Schlosser, Ignaz, *The Book of Rugs: Oriental and European* (New York: Crown Publishers, 1963).

Stout, Evelyn, *Introduction to Textiles* (New York: John Wiley & Sons, 1965).

Tate, Mildred T., and Oris Glisson, *Family Clothing* (New York: John Wiley & Sons, 1961).

United States of America Standards Institute, *USA Standard Performance Requirements for Textile Fabrics,* vols. I–II (New York: USA Standards Institute, 1968).

Vanderhoff, Margil, *Clothes, Part of Your World* (Waltham, Mass.: Ginn & Co., 1968).

Von Bergen, Werner, and Herbert R. Mauersberger, *American Wool Handbook,* Part I, 3rd ed., 1969; Part II, 3rd ed., n.d. (New York: Interscience Publishers).

## FILMS [1]

### I. Clothing

#### A. READY-TO-WEAR

Coronet Films, Coronet Building, Chicago, Ill. 60601. "Clothes and You: Line and Proportion," 16 mm sound. 11 min.

Coronet Films, Coronet Building, Chicago, Ill. 60601. "Clothing for Children," 16 mm sound color film. 11 min.

Du Pont de Nemours & Co., Motion Pictures, Advertising Dept., Wilmington, Del. 19898. "It Figures," 16 mm color film on foundation garments elasticized with Lycra spandex fiber. 15 min.

#### B. HOSIERY

Deering Milliken & Co., 1045 Avenue of the Americas, New York, N.Y. 10008. "Agilon Film." 16 mm sound. 10 min.

Modern Talking Pictures Service, Inc., 1212 Avenue of the Americas, New York, N.Y. 10022. "A Stocking Yarn," 16 mm sound, color film by Cameo Stockings and Monsanto. 18 min.

[1] All films are on free loan.

## II. Home Furnishings

### A. CARPETS

American Carpet Institute, Inc., 350 Fifth Ave., New York, N.Y. 10001. "Choosing Your Carpets and Rugs." Color film strip with sound.

American Cyanamid, 111 West 40th St., New York, N.Y. 10016. "Cindy and Bill's New Carpet." 35 mm color silent filmstrip. 10 min.

Du Pont de Nemours & Co., Motion Pictures, Advertising Dept., Wilmington, Del. 19898. "Step Out on Color." 16 mm color sound film. 17 min.

Sterling Movies U.S.A., Inc., 43 West 61st St., New York, N.Y. 10023. "The Magnificent Needle" (production of tufted carpets, bedspreads, and novelty items). 16 mm sound color. 15 min.

### B. HOME DECORATION

Colorizer Association, Colorizer Associates, P.O. Box 1322, Salt Lake City, Utah. "Good Taste in Decorating." 16 mm sound color. 25 min.

National Cotton Council, 350 Fifth Ave., New York, N.Y. 10001. "Why Cotton in Home Furnishings." 16 mm sound color film. 9 min.

Modern Talking Picture Service, Inc., 1212 Avenue of the Americas, New York, N.Y. 10022. "Accent Décor," by Scott Paper Co. 16 mm sound color. 10 min.

Owens-Corning Fiberglas Co., Decorative Department of Home Furnishings Division, 717 Fifth Ave., New York, N.Y. 10022. "The Magic Marble." 16 mm sound color. 12 min.

### C. DRAPERIES

Modern Talking Picture Service, Inc., 1212 Avenue of the Americas, New York, N.Y. 10022. "From Fiber to Fabric," by Pittsburgh Plate Glass Co. 16 mm color film. 30 min.

## III. Fibers and Fabrics

### A. FIBERS

American Viscose, Division of FMC Corporation, 350 Fifth Ave., New York, N.Y. 10001. "FMC Fibers and Films." 16 mm sound color motion picture. Released 1965. 20 min.

E. I. du Pont de Nemours & Co., Motion Pictures, Advertising Dept., Wilmington, Del. 19898. "The Wonderful World of Nylon" (also covers spandex, Orlon and Dacron). 16 mm sound color film. 26 min.

Association Films, Inc., 600 Madison Ave., New York, N.Y. 10017. "Bedtime for Janie" (cotton picking and processing) 16 mm sound color film by Hanes Knitting Mills. 26 min. "Iphansis: The Art of Weaving," by Burlington Industries. 16 mm sound color film. 10 min.

Irish Linen Guild, 1271 Avenue of the Americas, New York, N.Y. 10020. "Linen Wonderland." 35 mm. color film & 33⅓ record with microgroove needle. 20 min.

Man-made Fiber Producers Assn., 350 Fifth Ave., New York, N.Y. 10001. Filmstrip book giving each frame of filmstrip "Man-made Fibers."

Modern Talking Pictures Service, Inc., 1212 Avenue of the Americas, New York, N.Y. 10022. "The Belgian Art of Linen." 16 mm sound color film. 14 min. "Only Silk is Silk." 16 mm sound color film 17½ min.

Association Films, Inc., 600 Madison Ave., New York, N.Y. 10017. "Touch of Wool." 16 mm color film. Produced 1966. 13½ min.

## B. FABRICS

Du Pont de Nemours & Co., Motion Pictures Advertising Dept., Wilmington, Del. 19898. "Heat's On" (durable press). Color filmstrip and record. 12 min. "Ze Pel." 16 mm sound color film. 11 min.

Celanese Fibers Marketing Co., Consumer Relations Dept., 522 Fifth Ave., New York, N.Y. 10036. "Look for the Label Arnel." 16 mm sound color film. 17 min.

Owens-Corning Fiberglas Co., Decorative Department of Home Furnishings Division, 717 Fifth Ave., New York, N.Y. 10022. "A Fine Thing." (Fiberglas beta piece goods information.) 5 min.

National Association of Bedding Manufacturers, 724 Ninth St., N.W., Washington, D.C. "Invest in Rest" (buying the best bedding). 35 mm sound color slide with 33⅓ rpm record. 12½ min.

Bradford Dyeing Assn. (U.S.A.), Inc., Attention Mr. R. Leibowitz, 111 West 40th St., New York, N.Y. 10018. "The Wonderful World of Bradford." 16 mm sound color film. 14 min.

### NONWOVEN FABRICS

Disposables Inc., 151-51 Seventh Ave., Whitestone, N.Y. 11357. Information on Abanda Disposable clothing of nonwoven nylon reinforced cellulose fiber for industrial, medical, dental, and food processing fields. Swatches.

E. I. du Pont de Nemours & Co., Tyvek Marketing, Center Road Building Wilmington, Del. 19898. Pamphlet on Tyvek, a spun bonded olefin sheet product for commercial garments.

### LAUNDERING AND FABRIC CARE

Johnson Wax Company, Consumer Education Dept., Racine, Wis. 53403. Handy Hint Bulletins: "How to Clean Rugs and Carpets the Easy Way with Glory" and "How to Treat Carpet Problems, Spots and Stains."

### MISCELLANEOUS

Nelson Doubleday, Inc., Garden City, N.Y. Handbook, "25 Decorating Ideas Under $100," by Carolyn Bishop.

## SUGGESTED SOURCES FOR INFORMATION ABOUT TEXTILE FIBERS AND FABRICS

For those seeking specific information about textile fibers and fabrics, the organizations listed below have expressed a willingness to provide information and, in some instances, materials. While some of the booklets and materials listed may not be available to the individual inquirer, they can probably be obtained for group instructional purposes. The person writing for the information should mention the fiber or fabric in which he is especially interested, since some companies have mills and departments specializing in different materials.

## COTTON

National Cotton Council, P.O. Box 12285, Memphis, Tenn. 38112. Information on how cotton is grown, processed, marketed, and manufactured; care of cottons; catalogue of educational materials.

## LINEN

Irish Linen Guild, 1271 Avenue of the Americas, New York, N.Y. 10018. Booklet, "The Story of Irish Linen." Other pamphlets, and "Teacher's Educational Kit on Irish Linen," including twenty swatches and six wall charts.

Hamilton Adams Imports, Ltd., 24 West 40th Street, New York, N.Y. "Moygashel," a pamphlet describing how Moygashel linen is made and specific qualities of linen.

*Linens and Domestics,* a monthly trade publication, 155 West 3rd St., New Richmond, Wis. 54017.

## SILK

International Silk Association, U.S.A., Inc., Educational Department, 185 Madison Ave., New York, N.Y. 10016. Sample kit consisting of "Teacher's Guide" and "Student Guide," and price list.

Japan Silk Association, Public Relations Department, 385 Fifth Ave., New York, N.Y. 10016. "Silk and Japan" (silk processing and care); "Silk: Japan's Cultural Symbol" (silk in Japanese traditional costumes), and a box of cocoons.

## WOOL

American Wool Council and the Wool Bureau, Inc., Wool Education Center, 520 Railway Exchange Building, Denver, Colo. 80202. "The Story of Wool."

Lemon, Hugo, "How to Find Out About the Wool Textile Industry," Title No. 3925, Titles on the Textile Industry, Fairview Park, Elmsford, N.Y., Pergamon Press, Inc.

*World Wool Digest,* a trade periodical, gives a fortnightly review of the wool trade in the United States and wool markets of the world. Published by the International Wool Secretariat, Wool House, Carlton Gardens, London S.W. 1, England, and Wool Bureau, Inc., 360 Lexington Ave., New York, N.Y.

## MAN-MADE FIBERS

American Cyanamid, Fibers Division, Public Relations Department, 111 West 40th Street, New York, N.Y. 10018. Information on Creslan in blankets, carpets, home decoration, and apparel; sewing and stain-removal guides.

American Enka Corporation, 530 Fifth Ave., New York, N.Y. 10036. Bulletins containing technical information about their products.

Beaunit Corporation, 261 Madison Ave., New York, N.Y. 10016. Series of pamphlets: "Fiber and Fabric Facts" (about polyester, stretch, tricot, durable press, and soil release).

Celanese Fibers Company, 522 Fifth Ave., N.Y., N.Y. 10003. "Textile Topics (a technical quarterly for teachers only). Booklets: "Up-to-Date Guide to Permanent Press." "New Dimensions in Bonding," "Textiles Today and Tomorrow."

Dow Badische Company, Textile Fibers Department, Williamsburg, Va. Information on Zefkrome, Type 200 acrylic fiber.

E. I. du Pont de Nemours & Co., Inc., Product Information Department. Information on nylon, Orlon acrylic, Dacron polyester, Lycra spandex. Information on care and sewing. Pamphlets: "Du Pont Fiber Facts," Facts About Fabrics," "Home Cleaning Guide."

Eastman Chemical Products, Inc., Fibers Division, 1133 Ave of the Americas, New York, N.Y. 10036. Information on Kodel polyester, Chromspun acetate, Estron acetate, and Verel modacrylic.

Man-Made Fiber Association, 350 Fifth Ave., New York, N.Y. 10001. Filmstrip book giving each frame of filmstrip, "Man-Made Fibers."

Monsanto Company, Textiles Division, 350 Fifth Ave., New York, N.Y. 10001. Pamphlets covering their "Actionwear" program including how their fibers are made, several manuals on carpets and their care.

Owens-Corning Fiberglas Corporation, Toledo, Ohio, 43601. A booklet on "Textile Fiber Materials for Industry." Includes properties of Fiberglas textile fibers, how fibers are made; how to select Fiberglas fabrics and tapes.

United Piece Dye Works, 111 West 40th Street, New York, N.Y. 10018. "Guide Book to Man-Made Textile Fibers and Textured Yarns of the World." Reference book for sources of fibers, New York, N.Y. 10001. "A Voluntary Industry Guide for Improved and Permanent Care Labeling of Consumer Textile Products" (adopted March 1967).

## MISCELLANEOUS INFORMATION

American Carpet Institute, Inc., 350 Fifth Ave., New York, N.Y. 10001. "Choosing Your Carpets and Rugs"; "Basic Facts" (statistical annual); "Sound Conditioning"; "Cutting Costs with Carpets"; "It's Easy to Care for Your Carpets and Rugs"; "Excellence in Economy" (institutional economy).

American Home Economics Association, 1600 20th St., N.W., Washington, D.C. 20009. "Home Economics Has a Career for You in Textiles and Clothing." Booklet describes major duties, employment opportunities, and work conditions for a variety of textile and clothing careers.

American Textile Manufacturers Institute, Inc., 1501 Johnston Building, Charlotte, North Carolina 28202. Teaching Kit; booklet on "Your Career in Textiles"; filmstrip, "Textiles for Everyone"; classroom map showing textile production and distribution of employment in textile and apparel industries.

Coats and Clark, Inc., Educational Bureau, 430 Park Ave., New York, N.Y. 10022. Folders and pamphlets on sewing techniques, knitting, and crochet patterns; thread charts.

Good Housekeeping Institute, 939 Eighth Ave., New York, N.Y. 10019. Pamphlets on durable press, buying mattresses and bedding, stretch fabrics and carpets.

Home Economics Extension Leaflet 37, Stone Hall, Cornell University, Ithaca, N.Y. 14850. "Stretch in the Wardrobe" gives pointers for selection of stretch garments and other information about stretch fabric clothing construction.

Household Finance Corporation, Prudential Plaza, Chicago, Ill. 60601. "Money Management, Your Clothing Dollars" (1967).

Kirsch Company, Sturgis, Mich. A manual, "How to Make Your Windows Beautiful," outlines a complete step-by-step path to new décor through creative window treatments within the most limited budgets. Available free to home economics teachers.

J. C. Penney Company, 1301 Avenue of the Americas, New York, N.Y. 10019. Booklet, "Understanding Today's Textiles." Leaflets on "Fabrics"; "Fashions and Fabrics" (biannual).

Rosenthal, S. Howard, 5 Heller Road, Metuchen, N.J. 08840. Manuals: "On Selling Ties" and "Men's Neckwear and Fact Book."

The Sanforized Company, 530 Fifth Ave., New York, N.Y. 10001. Information on wash-and-wear, comfort stretch, Sanforized-Plus-2. Booklet, "The Curious Mr. Cluett."

Sears Roebuck and Company, Consumer Information Services, Dept. 703 Public Relations, 7401 Skokie Boulevard, Skokie, Ill. 60076. "Hidden Value Series"; "Silhouettes of Fashion"; "Color in Home Furnishings"; "Young Fashion Forecast"; filmstrip and study guide.

## GOVERNMENT BULLETINS

Federal Trade Commission; Washington, D.C. 20580. Commercial Standard no. 19153 on Flammability.

U.S. Department of Agriculture, Office of Information, Washington, D.C. 20250. Catalogue of government bulletins on textiles.

U.S. Government Printing Office, Superintendent of Documents, Washington, D.C. 20402. Catalogue of government bulletins on fibers, fabrics, and sewing aids.

Rules and regulations under the Fur Products Labeling Act as amended January 10, 1969.

Rules and regulations under the Wool Products Labeling Act, effective 1939; amended November 20, 1965.

Rules and regulations under the Flammable Fabrics Act, effective July 1, 1954; amended May 4, 1967.

Rules and regulations under the Textile Fiber Products Identification Act, effective March 3, 1960; amended March 13, 1966.

Questions and Answers: Relating to the Fur Products Labeling Act; the Wool Products Labeling Act; and the Textile Fiber Products Identification Act.

## GENERAL TEXTILE TRADE

*Textile Chemist and Colorist.* Journal of the American Association of Textile Chemists and Colorists, P.O. Box 12215, Research Triangle Park, North Carolina 17709.

*American Fabrics,* 24 East 38th St., New York, N.Y. 10016.

*A.S.T.M. Standards on Textile Materials,* American Society for Testing Materials, 1916 Race St., Philadelphia, Pa.

*Ciba Review,* Ciba Limited, Basel, Switzerland.

*Daily News Record,* 7 East 12th St., New York, N.Y. 10003.

*Department Store Economist,* 100 East 42nd St., New York, N.Y. 10017.

*Journal of the Textile Institute,* 16 St. Mary's Parsonage, Manchester 3, England.

*Papers of the A.A.T.T.,* American Association of Textile Technologists, 7 East 12th St., New York, N.Y. 10003.

*Stores Magazine,* The National Retail Merchants Association, 100 West 31st St., New York, N.Y. 10001.

*Testing League Bulletin,* United States Testing Company, Inc., 1415 Park Avenue, Hoboken, N.J. 07030.

*Textile Age,* 22 West Putnam Avenue, Greenwich, Conn. 06830.

*Textile Organon,* 10 East 40th St., New York, N.Y. 10016.

*Textile World,* 330 West 42nd St., New York, N.Y. 10036.

*Women's Wear Daily,* 7 East 12th St., New York, N.Y. 10003.

## FASHION APPAREL AND HOME FURNISHINGS

*American Home Magazine,* 641 Lexington Avenue, New York, N.Y. 10022.

*Glamour Magazine,* 420 Lexington Avenue, New York, N.Y. 10017.

*Good Housekeeping Magazine,* Eighth Avenue at 57th St., New York, N.Y. 10019.

*Harper's Bazaar,* 572 Madison Avenue, New York, N.Y. 10022.

*House and Garden Magazine,* 420 Lexington Avenue, New York, N.Y. 10017.

*House Beautiful,* 572 Madison Avenue, New York, N.Y. 10022.

*Ladies' Home Journal,* 641 Lexington Avenue, New York, N.Y. 10017.

*McCall's Magazine,* 230 Park Avenue, New York, N.Y. 10017.

*Mademoiselle Magazine,* 420 Lexington Avenue, New York, N.Y. 10017.

*Seventeen,* 320 Park Avenue, New York, N.Y. 10022.

*Vogue,* 420 Lexington Avenue, New York, N.Y. 10017.

## TRADE JOURNALS

(a) Clothing Accessories

*Corset and Underwear Review,* 111 Fourth Avenue, New York, N.Y. 10003.

*Knitted Outerwear Times,* 51 Madison Avenue, New York, N.Y. 10016.

*Millinery Weekly, Inc.,* 56 West 39th St., New York, N.Y. 10018.

(b) Women's and Children's Outer Ready-to-Wear

*Clothing Trade Journal,* 300 Speedwell Avenue, Morris Plains, N.J. 07950.

*Infants' and Children's Review,* Earnshaw Publications, 101 West 31st St., New York, N.Y. 10001.

*Parents' Magazine,* 52 Vanderbilt Avenue, New York, N.Y. 10017.

*Sportswear on Parade,* 393 Fifth Avenue, New York, N.Y. 10016.

(c) Men's and Boys' Wear

*The Boys' Outfitter,* 71 West 35th St., New York, N.Y. 10010.

*Esquire Magazine,* 488 Madison Avenue, New York, N.Y. 10022.

*Men's Wear,* 7 East 12th St., New York, N.Y. 10003.

(d) Home Furnishings

*Curtain and Drapery Department Magazine,* 70 Hudson St., Hoboken, N.J. 07030.

*Linens, Domestics and Bath Products,* Target Communications Inc., 373 Fifth Avenue, New York, New York 10016.

*News from West Point–Pepperell,* 111 West 40th St., P.O. Box 55, Midtown Station, New York, N.Y. 10018.


## SOURCES OF INFORMATION FOR CONSUMERS AND SALESPEOPLE

*The Boys' Outfitter,* 71 West 35th Street, New York, N.Y. 10001. Pamphlet, "How Boys' Apparel Is Made."

*Consumer Bulletin,* Consumers' Research, Washington, N.J. 07882.

*Consumer's Guide,* U.S. Department of Agriculture, Washington, D.C. 20250.

*Consumer Reports,* Consumers Union of U.S., Inc., 56 Washington St., Mount Vernon, N.Y. 10553.

# Appendix

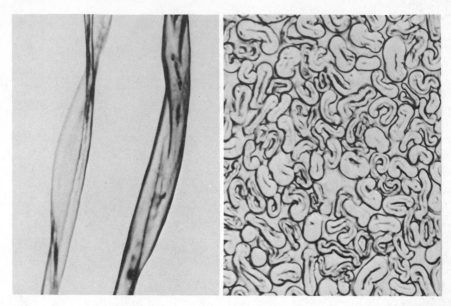

**Figure A.1.** Unmercerized native cotton: longitudinal and cross-sectional views. (*Photomicrographs courtesy of the Southern Regional Research Laboratory of the U.S. Department of Agriculture.*)

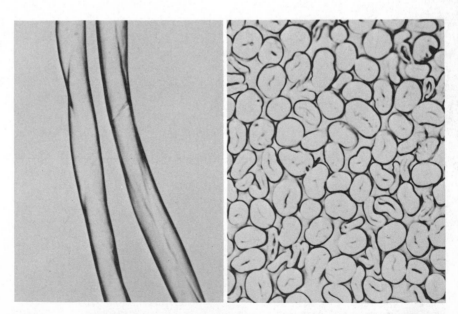

**Figure A.2.** Mercerized cotton: longitudinal and cross-sectional views. (*Photomicrographs courtesy of the Southern Regional Research Laboratory of the U.S. Department of Agriculture.*)

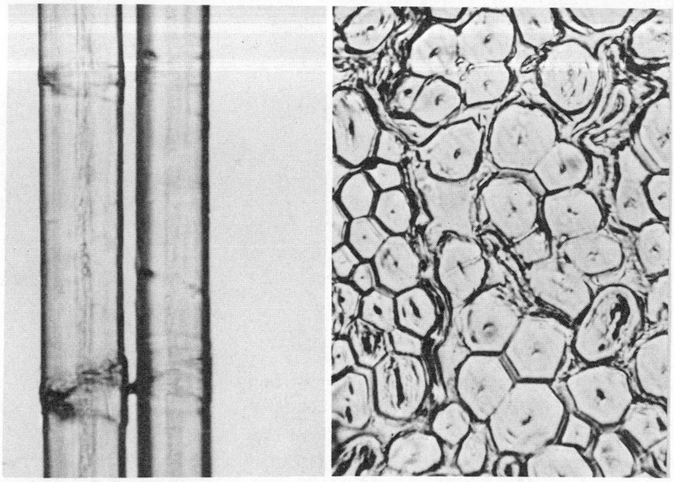

**Figure A.3.** Flax fibers: longitudinal and cross-sectional views magnified 500 times. (*Photomicrographs courtesy of the Southern Regional Research Laboratory of the U.S. Department of Agriculture.*)

**Figure A.4.** Ramie fibers: longitudinal and cross-sectional views magnified 500 times. (*Photomicrographs courtesy of the Southern Regional Research Laboratory of the U.S. Department of Agriculture.*)

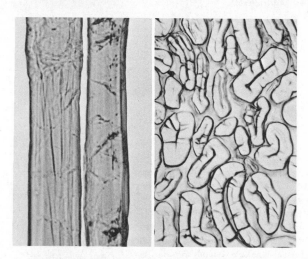

**Figure A.5.** Jute fibers: longitudinal and cross-sectional views magnified 500 times. (*Photomicrographs courtesy of the Southern Regional Research Laboratory of the U.S. Department of Agriculture.*)

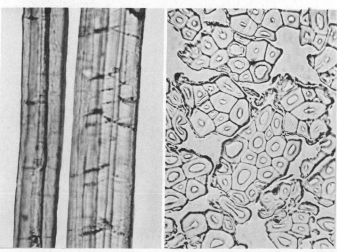

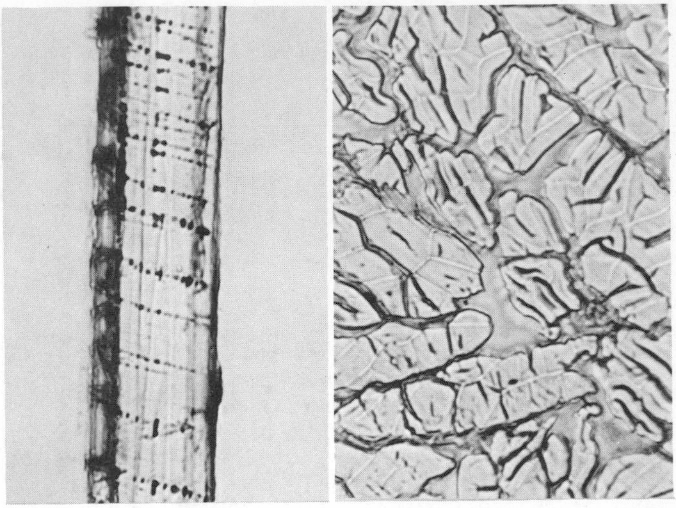

**Figure A.6.** Hemp fibers: longitudinal and cross-sectional views magnified 500 times. (*Photomicrographs courtesy of the Southern Regional Research Laboratory of the U.S. Department of Agriculture.*)

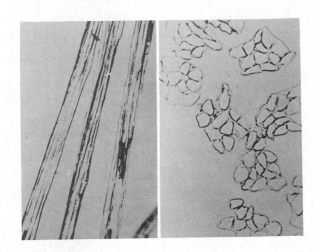

**Figure A.7.** Cultivated raw silk. *Left:* Longitudinal view of silk fibers, showing the sericin, which forms an outer layer around the fibroin, or main core, of the fiber. *Right:* Cross sections of raw silk threads reeled from six cocoons. Since each thread is doubled, there are actually twelve filaments bound together by the natural gum, or sericin.

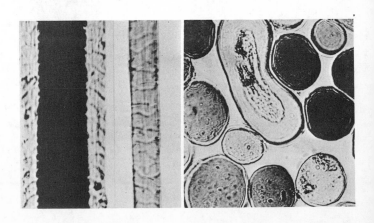

**Figure A.8.** Mohair: longitudinal and cross-sectional views. (*Photomicrographs courtesy of the Forstmann Woolen Company.*)

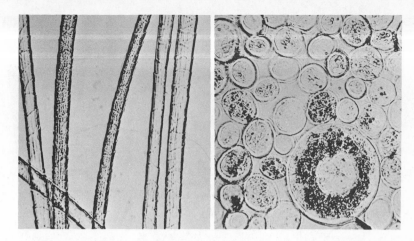

**Figure A.9.** Cashmere: longitudinal and cross-sectional views. (*Photomicrographs courtesy of the Forstmann Woolen Company.*)

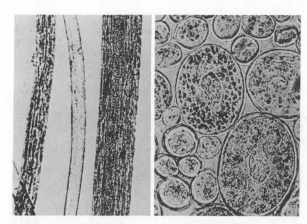

**Figure A.10.** Camel's hair: longitudinal and cross-sectional views. (*Photomicrographs courtesy of the Forstmann Woolen Company.*)

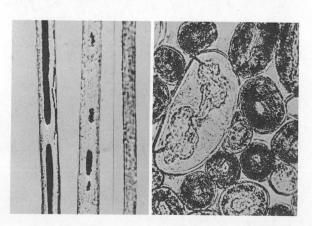

**Figure A.11.** Alpaca: longitudinal and cross-sectional views. (*Photomicrographs courtesy of the Forstmann Woolen Company.*)

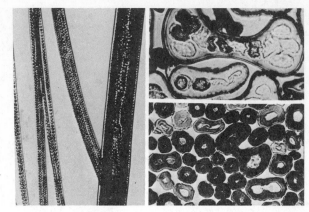

Figure A.12. Rabbit's hair: longitudinal and cross-sectional views. (*Photomicrographs courtesy of the Forstmann Woolen Company.*)

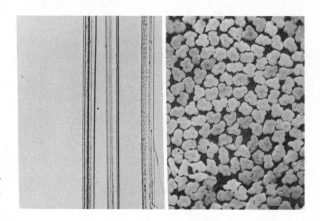

Figure A.13. Fortisan rayon: longitudinal and cross-sectional views. (*Photomicrographs courtesy of Celanese Corporation of America.*)

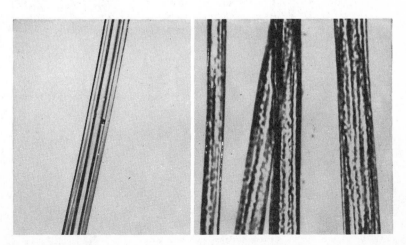

Figure A.14. Viscose rayon. *Left:* Bright. *Right:* Delustered. (*Photomicrographs courtesy of the United States Testing Company, Inc.*)

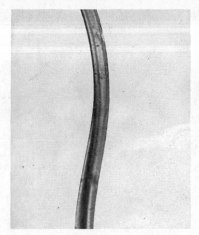
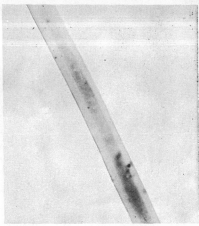

**Figure A.15.** *Left:* Cuprammonium rayon (bright). *Right:* Acetate (bright). (*Photomicrographs courtesy of the United States Testing Company, Inc.*)

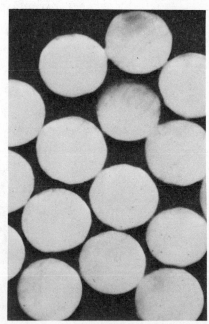

**Figure A.16.** Nylon: cross-sectional view magnified 660 times. The seventeen filaments are almost perfectly round and very smooth. This is a thread used in sheer stockings and fine knit goods. (*Photomicrograph courtesy of E.I. du Pont de Nemours & Company, Inc.*)

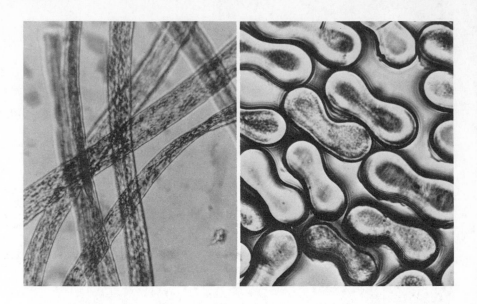

**Figure A.17.** Orlon acrylic. *Left:* Longitudinal view of continuous filament yarn shows the striated surface of the fiber. *Right:* Cross-sectional view of staple yarn magnified 500 times. (*Photomicrographs courtesy of E.I. du Pont de Nemours & Company, Inc.*)

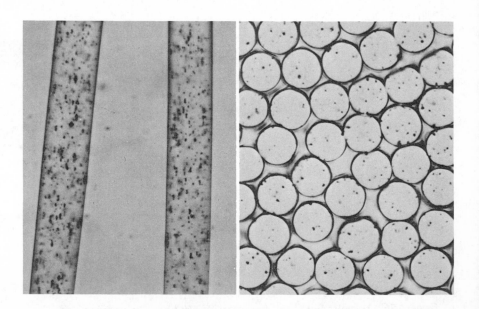

**Figure A.18.** Dacron polyester: longitudinal and cross-sectional views magnified 1000 times. (*Photomicrographs courtesy of E.I. du Pont de Nemours & Company, Inc.*)

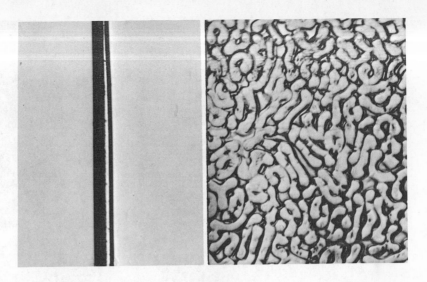

**Figure A.19.** Dynel modacrylic: longitudinal and cross-sectional views. (*Photomicrographs courtesy of Carbide and Carbon Chemicals Company.*)

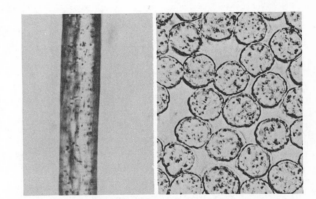

**Figure A.20.** Acrilan acrylic: longitudinal and cross-sectional views. (*Photomicrographs courtesy of The Chemstrand Corporation.*)

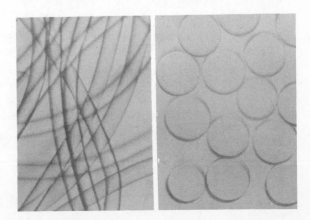

**Figure A.21.** Saran: longitudinal and cross-sectional views. (*Photomicrographs courtesy of the National Plastic Products Company.*)

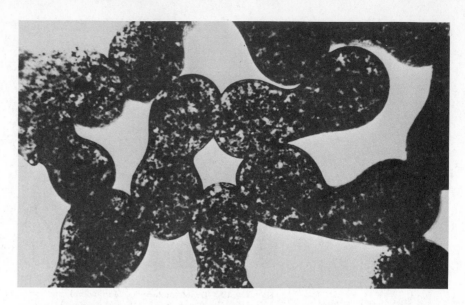

**Figure A.22.** Lycra spandex: cross-sectional view magnified 500 times. (*Photomicrograph courtesy of E.I. du Pont de Nemours & Company, Inc.*)

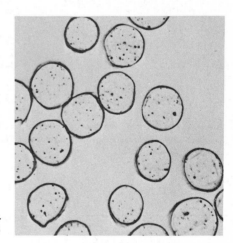

**Figure A.23.** Polypropylene olefin: cross-sectional view magnified 500 times. (*Photomicrograph courtesy of E.I. du Pont de Nemours & Company, Inc.*)

# Index

Bridget
Gail
Vaughan